*The exceptional
individual*

Third Edition

The exceptional individual

Charles W. Telford
San Jose State University

James M. Sawrey
Austin Peay State University

Prentice-Hall, Inc., Englewood Cliffs, New Jersey 07632

Library of Congress Cataloging in Publication Data

TELFORD, CHARLES WITT.
  The exceptional individual.

  Includes bibliographies and indexes.
  1. Exceptional children—Education.   I. Sawrey,
James M., joint author.   II. Title.
LC4031.T4 1977   371.9   76-44470
ISBN   0-13-293837-5

Prentice-Hall International, Inc., *London*
Prentice-Hall of Australia Pty. Limited, *Sydney*
Prentice-Hall of Canada, Ltd., *Toronto*
Prentice-Hall of India Private Limited, *New Delhi*
Prentice-Hall of Japan, Inc., *Tokyo*
Prentice-Hall of Southeast Asia Pte. Ltd., *Singapore*

Contents

Preface, *vii*

Preface

Like most other textbooks written in one's teaching area, this book initially grew out of a conviction that a different conceptual framework, selection and organization of material, and manner of presentation would be superior to the ones then current. While our claims to originality in these respects are limited, this third edition continues to have some unique features:

- the inclusion in a single text of the highly creative, the bicultural, and the intellectually borderline as categories of exceptional people;
- the consideration of persons beyond childhood and adolescence, including the aged;
- the consistent use of a cultural frame of reference in defining exceptionality and in identifying and dealing with the problems of exceptional people and their families;
- the handling of the problems of exceptional people as essentially the magnified problems of individual differences among people in general;
- the emphasis on the generality of most of the problems of exceptionality

All classifications of exceptional people are arbitrary and useful only with reference to the times and purposes they serve. Our inclusion of the highly creative, the bicultural, and the intellectually borderline reflects current interest in these categories of people.

Our extension of the age range to include adults and older persons, and our use of the terms *exceptionality* and *exceptional people* rather than *exceptional children,* reflect our conviction that exceptionality is often more the problem of the entire family and culture—the tone of which is set by the adults—than it is the property of a unique individual. Moreover, there are more adults than children in many categories of exceptionality.

The acceptance of a dominantly cultural frame of reference in dealing with exceptional people results in an emphasis on the relative nature of the deviations and a recognition of the extent to which the problems of exceptionality cut across categories. For this reason the early chapters of the book deal with those problems common to exceptional people in general, irrespective of the nature or origin of their exceptionalities.

The third edition of this book contains a significantly expanded section on deviance and stigma. The chapter on care and education of exceptional people is enlarged and emphasizes the developing programs for exceptional individuals. The chapter on the bicultural individual has undergone extensive revision. The decreasing emphasis on the specific categories of exceptionality, the diminishing importance of etiological classifications in social and educational remedial programs, and the increasingly humanistic point of view in dealing with the socially devalued classes of deviant people are reflected in this edition.

This book is intended for use at the upper division or graduate level as an introduction to the problems of exceptional people. It is intended as a survey for people who will specialize in one of the specific areas of exceptionality and for the prospective or current teacher, principal, supervisor, superintendent, occupational therapist, physical therapist, nurse, or physician who will work with a wide variety of deviant individuals but who will not become a specialist in the field.

Every book has many hidden contributors. Our wives, Una Mae Sawrey and Aldene E. Telford, have contributed through their encouragement, their tolerance of our neglect of family responsibilities, and their critical reading of the manuscript. Ms. Emi Nobuhiro typed most of the manuscript and helped in many other ways during its development. Instructors, colleagues, students, and clients too numerous to mention have, over many years, contributed to the writers' knowledge of exceptional people while they were students; teachers on the elementary, secondary, and college levels; clinicians; school psychologists; and consultants.

1

Introduction to exceptionality

Photo by Mimi Forsyth, Monkmeyer Press Photo Service

Chapter 1

Some basic psychological and social considerations

To be exceptional is to be rare or unusual. The unusual, the bizarre, and the unexpected have always attracted attention and have often aroused awe and wonder. A change from the accustomed order of things arouses people's curiosity. Science has originated largely from their attempts to explain the unexpected. The commonplace, on the other hand, poses no problems for the uninitiated: It takes some sophistication to see problems in the obvious.

When the regular movements of the sun, moon, and stars were taken for granted and seemed to require no explanation, comets, meteors, and eclipses still attracted attention and led to an interest in astronomy. Errors of astronomical observation led to investigation of the sources of these errors, which resulted in a long series of reaction-time experiments in psychology. The discovery that the sources of variations in reaction time could be identified led to the investigation of the more complex psychological processes. Speculation concerning the origins of more obvious errors of observation and belief, such as illusions and delusions, led John Locke to consider the origins of knowledge in general and the nature of ordinary perceptual experience. The irrational and bizarre behavior of the mentally ill (the psychotic) and the mentally retarded (the feebleminded) attracted attention and seemed to require explanation, while the behavior of the normal person apparently went on by itself and seemed self-explanatory. The occurrence of sporadic dwarfism and gigantism helped to focus attention on the problems of physical growth in general. Instances of precocious puberty (*pubertas praecox*), which have resulted in girls eight and nine years of age bearing children, as well as female virilism characterized by excessive hairiness, loss of the feminine body configuration, and amenorrhea, have stimulated interest in the problems of sex determination and the sexual development of normal people.

Regular, everyday occurrences not only seem to require no explanation; they also cause society relatively little trouble. It is possible to anticipate the regularly recurring events of life, and to profit by them, avoid them, or endure them. On the other hand, unpredictable catastrophes, such as cyclones, floods, and droughts; unusual events, such as eclipses of the sun or moon, and comets; irrational behavior, such as of the psychotic, the epileptic, and the mentally retarded; deviant developmental patterns, such as of the midget and the acromegalic, precocious sexual development of children, and adult feminization of males and masculinization of females—all these not only attract attention, they also become matters of personal and public concern. They threaten the personal security and social status of the afflicted persons and create trouble for their families, for other individuals, and for society. The occurrence of unusual events and circumstances stimulates individual efforts and social movements concerned with the understanding, care, prevention, and control of these conditions and events.

While it may be going too far to claim that most of the significant developments in science in general, and in psychology in particular, have arisen from the curiosity aroused by the unusual events in life and the social needs resulting from them, nevertheless many socially significant lines of investigation and matters of public concern have so originated. A healthy, normal state of affairs seldom draws attention to itself. We have already mentioned Locke's investigation of the origins and nature of cognitive experiences. Sigmund Freud's conception of the nature of motivation, his interpretations of dreams, and his beliefs concerning the psychodynamics of everyday behavior grew out of his studies of the mentally ill. The first intelligence tests were developed and initially used for the identification and classification of intellectually exceptional individuals—first the mentally retarded, and later the gifted. The existence of blind and deaf people focused attention on the problems of normal vision and audition and the role of these senses in ordinary life. The personal, family, and social problems resulting from blindness and deafness have stimulated research efforts, educational movements, and social welfare programs concerned with the prevention and amelioration of these conditions.

WHEN THE OTHER PERSON SURPRISES US

In terms of a rough set of norms, people build a large set of expectancies concerning others. We expect most people to be "normal," and when our expectancies are not realized we develop additional categories to fit deviations from the normal. Deviant persons and activities become categorized as "abnormal." We develop different expectancies for the abnormal in general as well as for specific types of abnormalities. These categories and related expectancies provide a certain degree of predictability in social interactions. People are disconcerted when their expectations are not realized; social forces are exerted to bring norm violators into line with those expectancies, which have become crystallized. Norm violators are unpredictable, and this unpredictability increases the costs of social interactions (Kiesler, 1973).

Particularly troublesome is the person with status incongruities, such as a physically deformed person who is highly intelligent. This condition may manifest itself in the deviant member of a dominant in-group (such as a white drug addict) being more strongly condemned and socially rejected than a comparably deviant member of a minority out-group (such as a black drug addict). This phenomenon has been demonstrated experimentally (Seidman & Koulack, 1973). Such status incongruity seems to have widespread effects. For example, S. V. Kasl and S. Cobb (1967) found that even reasonably "normal" people with incongruent status indices display a disproportionate number of psychosomatic symptoms of stress, such as rheumatoid arthritis. These people also rank low in mutual trust, social intimacy, and congeniality. There is a pervasive tendency to equate the deviant with the pathological and to expect an overall pathology from persons perceived as significantly deviant. Not only are there generalized attitudes toward the handicapped, there are also attitudes and expectancies that are specific to each category. This means that we expect people to act appropriately for their perceived status—neither too deviant nor too "normal" and in keeping with the nature of their disability (Comer & Piliavin, 1972).

Behavior high in appropriateness for both the person and the situation is taken for granted and does not seem to require any special explanation. However, behavior highly inappropriate to the situation and the person (low in predictability) seems to demand unique interpretations (Price & Bouffard, 1974). Historically these explanations have taken various forms.

PRESCIENTIFIC CONCEPTIONS OF DEVIANT PEOPLE

Although the existence of deviant human behavior and development aroused curiosity and focused interest on normal behavior and development, mystical and supernaturalistic interpretations of deviations persisted long after naturalistic explanations of the more ordinary behavioral events and developmental sequences had been generally accepted. It seems that belief in evil or benign spirits as the cause of deviant behavior has been evident from the beginning of recorded history. The substitution of naturalistic for supernatural explanations of the unusual in human behavior and development has been a slow process and is not complete even today. The tremendous popularity of the book *The*

Exorcist and the movie by the same name indicates that a large segment of the general population still either believe in or are intrigued by demonological interpretations of deviant human behavior.

QUALITATIVE VERSUS QUANTITATIVE CONCEPTIONS OF THE DIFFERENCES BETWEEN EXCEPTIONAL AND NORMAL PEOPLE

The substitution of a naturalistic for a supernatural explanation of the origins and nature of the deviant characteristics of an individual did not solve the problem of the nature of the exceptional person. In some respects, the demonological conception of the exceptional person was a qualitative as contrasted with a quantitative one.

A qualitative conception of exceptional individuals is that they constitute separate and, in many ways, distinct categories or classes of people. As separate categories of people, they are considered to have traits and characteristics which make them fundamentally different from the general run of humanity. The titles of certain books and courses—the "psychology of" the gifted, the mentally retarded, the blind, the deaf, women, blacks, or chicanos—suggest that there is a separate kind or brand or category of psychology which "explains" these categories of people and that such explanations are fundamentally different from the "psychology of" normal people. Such a view implies that a separate and unique set of conceptual categories or ways of thinking is required to understand and deal with exceptional individuals. They are supposed to learn, perceive, think, and adjust in ways which are unique to them; therefore they cannot be understood in terms of those principles of learning, thinking, perceiving, and adjusting which have been derived from and are applicable to normal people. The trend of thinking over the last hundred years has been away from qualitative conceptions, and toward a quantitative frame of reference (Bogdan & Taylor, 1976).

The quantitative conception of exceptionality holds that the differences between the deviant groups, on the one hand, and the normal, on the other, are differences only of degree and not of kind. Thus the perceptual, conceptual, learning, and ideational processes of all people—whether normal or deviant—are fundamentally the same. We all learn, retain, recall, perceive, think, and make personal and social adjustments according to the same general principles and patterns, but some of us do these things faster, better, more accurately, or more appropriately than others. In its extreme form, the quantitative conception of the mentally retarded is that they are intellectually inferior to the normal by designated amounts, as roughly indicated by test performances, school achievement, and social competence, and that they are essentially normal in ways unrelated to intellectual competence. Except as a consequence of their intellectual deficiencies, their personalities, characters, physical characteristics, and social characteristics are normal—or, at least, their deviations from the normal in these respects are not necessarily or inherently a part of their intellectual deficiencies. The author of a recent study of the physical and motor development of the mentally retarded concludes that, while the retarded are consistently found to be markedly inferior to the nonretarded in physical development and in both gross and fine motor abilities, the structure and organization of motor abilities in the retarded are essentially the same as those in the nonretarded (Bruininks, 1974). Similarly, most researchers believe that although disability increases the likelihood of certain classes of experiences such as conflicts and frustrations, these are in no way unique to the handicapped. The disabled are simply likely to experience them more often than their nondisabled peers. The reactions and "styles of life" found in deviant individuals are as varied as those found in nondisabled individuals, and are of essentially the same types (TeBeest & Dickie, 1976).

The evidence that there is a basic continuity between the handicapped and the nonhandicapped, between deviants and nondeviants, is impressive. For example, A. H. Chapman and E. B. Cooper (1973), studying the nature of stuttering, found that the stuttering behavior of the mentally retarded was basically similar to nonretardates with respect to onset, adaptation effects, consistency, and expectancy phenomena. N. J. Anastasiow and N. G. Stayrook (1973), as well as H. Helmreich and O. Bloodstein (1973), found that the language errors and grammatical functions of mental retardates were similar to those of nonretardates of lower chronological ages (Stephens, 1972; Suppes, 1974; Bartel, Bryen, & Seehn, 1973). These authors as well as others believe that mentally retarded children proceed developmentally through the same cognitive and linguistic states as do nonretardates but at a slower rate. The notion that the cognitive and linguistic development and functioning of the handicapped are qualitatively similar to those of the nonhandicapped but may be at a slower rate and/or level of development is accepted by most but not all researchers in the field (Suppes, 1974; Friedman & Pasnak, 1973; Rogow, 1973).

F. C. Shontz (1971), and C. P. Baldwin and A. L. Baldwin (1974), have reviewed the extensive literature relevant to the assumptions that specific types of disabilities are associated with or produce certain behavioral and personality characteristics, or that disability in itself constitutes sufficient cause for psychological maladjustment. They conclude that there is no evidence that particular personality characteristics are associated with deviant physiques or that severity and/or type of disability are causally related to level of psychological adjustment. These authors claim that the problems faced by the different categories of handicapped and their reactions to these problems are not related to the nature of the handicap. Thus physical handicaps, emotional disturbances, and normal adjustments are seen merging imperceptibly into one another, while each child is viewed as an individual coping with his individual problem (Baldwin & Baldwin, 1974).

E. C. Thomas and K. Yamamoto (1972) studied the feelings and attitudes of four groups of exceptional middle-school and high-school children. The four groups consisted of 175 educable mentally retarded, 200 seriously emotionally disturbed children, 200 blind students, and 200 deaf children. Comparisons were made with a group of 400 normal children. The data concerning attitudes and feelings were obtained via the semantic differential—a technique widely used for this purpose. Semantic differential scores were obtained for four people-related concepts ("classmates," "parents," "teacher," and "myself") and for four curricular concepts ("social studies," "language," "science," and "mathematics"). The data thus obtained were factor-analyzed to disclose the "semantic structure" of the attitudes of these groups of exceptional children. The authors conclude that the semantic structures of the groups of deviant children are essentially similar to that of nonexceptional or "normal" children. They conclude, "The semantic space of the attitudes of these groups of children [is] not structured in a different manner from that of normal children of the same age."

In the next chapter we shall document that individuals who are significantly deviant in physique, intellect, behavior, or beliefs are subject to a variety of internal and external stresses as well as socially- and self-imposed restrictions which make them more vulnerable and more likely than normals to develop over-defensive, aggressive, or withdrawal patterns of behavior. These behavior patterns, however, are found among every segment of the population, and are not peculiar to the deviants.

R. I. Williams (1974), a black psychologist, seems to argue for qualitative ethnic differences when he says, "It is my contention, further, that there is a white psyche and a Black psyche, a white life style and a Black life style." [Consequently] "the white professional . . . has no business treating the Black mind" (pp. 17–18). However, W. H. Grier and P. M. Cobbs (1968), two black psychiatrists, say,

There is nothing reported in the literature or in the experience of any clinician known to the authors that suggests black people function differently psychologically from anyone else. Black men's mental functioning is governed by the same rules as that of any other group of men. Psychological principles understood first in the study of white men are true no matter what the man's color. . . . The clinician may find it difficult to avoid placing the black patient in a class which has in his own mind certain "givens" that apply to all its members. "Lower-class laborer" may mean one thing and "lower-class Negro laborer" may mean something else again, and neither set of images may have any relation to the unique life of the man who sits across the desk (pp. 129, 131).

Quantitative studies of different ethnic groups have indicated that differences are largely quantitative rather than qualitative in nature. Analysis of the test performances of white, black, and Mexican-American children on both culturally loaded and culture-reduced tests shows that while there are fairly large and consistent group differences, these differences can be matched both quantitatively and qualitatively when children of the same races but separated by two years in age (younger whites or older blacks and Mexican-Americans) are compared. The test items which differentiate most or least among the three racial groups also discriminate similarly among individuals *within* each group. This indicates that the differences among these racial groups are similar in nature to the differences within the groups (Jensen, 1974).

If disproving the qualitative conception of the difference between the disabled and the normal is difficult, eradicating the widespread acceptance of the idea will be even harder. When a disabled person achieves commensurately with a normal person despite the handicap, he or she is perceived as overcompensating. The overdependency of a similarly disabled person is also seen as a direct expression of the defect. Much of what the deviant individual does is seen as a manifestation of the deviancy. When a blind, deaf, crippled, or mentally retarded individual gets into trouble or has an accident, the difficulty is readily ascribed to the defect. The same experiences of normal people are seen either as situation-evoked or as ordinary events in a normal life requiring no explanation.

Few people can accept that a handicapped person's under- or over-achievements can arise from ordinary motives and serve the identical functions in his life as they do in the lives of ordinary people. The belief that the achievements of the handicapped require some unique explanation is so widespread that such people are expected and required to develop a special rationale to explain their "normal" behavior, a special philosophy to account for their achievements. The handicapped are expected to have a unique philosophy to explain why they want the same things as the nonhandicapped and work for them in similar ways. Handicapped individuals respond to these expectancies by stating their philosophies, which are largely reflections of the prevalent stereotypes concerning their particular disability. When the behavior of deviant persons violates our expectations, we often "de-normalize" them by imbuing them with special powers to account for their unexpected acts. The blind are said to have a sixth sense; the person deprived of any sense is believed to have a compensatory hyperacuity of the other senses. The notion that deviants—particularly psychotics and the blind—have access to realities that are closed to other people is old and persistent (Brown, 1973; Wright, 1974).

CURRENT CONCEPTIONS OF EXCEPTIONALITY

What is normal and what is abnormal in human behavior and development? What determines whether an individual is usual or unusual, normal or exceptional? Exceptionality and abnormality are popular concepts with variable meanings. Except as they are defined operationally for certain administrative or research purposes, they will always have to be understood in the particular social context in which they are used.

Statistical definitions of exceptionality

Many operational definitions of exceptionality are statistical and quantitative in nature. The mentally retarded can be defined operationally as persons who are significantly below normal in adaptive behavior and have IQ's below 70 as measured by the Stanford-Binet Intelligence Scale or comparable tests and a comparably low score on a measure of adaptive behavior. They can alternatively be defined as the intellectually lowest 2 or 3 percent of the population as indicated by test scores or some other criteria. The intellectually gifted can similarly be defined in terms of test scores or of demonstrated performance, or as the upper 1 or 2 percent of the general population as measured by some designated intelligence and/or achievement test. The hard-of-hearing and the deaf can be identified in terms of hearing loss as measured in decibels by a standard audiometer. Blindness is typically defined legally as visual acuity of 20/200 or less in the better eye after maximum correction or as possession of a visual field limited to 20° or less. There are no conventional quantitative indices of most other types of deviant individuals, such as the orthopedically handicapped, the socially maladjusted, the emotionally disturbed, the epileptic, and the individual with speech defects. In most of these conditions the diagnostic judgment of trained specialists replaces quantitative measurement. However, it is at least theoretically possible to devise statistical criteria of exceptionality in these areas also.

Pragmatic, social definitions of exceptionality

While it is often legally and administratively necessary to use independent quantitative criteria for the identification of exceptional individuals, the final test of the validity of these criteria is that of social usefulness. If deficiencies in adaptive behavior and ; 1 IQ of below 70 are accepted as the arbitrary criteria of mental retarda ion for placement in special classes, but it is found that many children v ith IQ's of 75 can profit equally by placement in such classes, the 70 limit loses much of its usefulness as a criterion. It then becomes necessary either to change the limit or to expand the criterion so as also to take into consideration demonstrated school achievement and physical and social maturity. The audiometric criterion for deafness or partial deafness and the visual acuity criterion for blindness or partial sightedness are meaningful and valid only insofar as experience proves that individuals thus designated are correspondingly handicapped educationally, socially, and vocationally. The judgments of specialists as to the degree of exceptionality represented by the orthopedically handicapped, the speech defective, and the socially and emotionally maladjusted are validated to the degree that individuals so identified do require, and are found to profit by, special education and treatment specifically designed for them. Because of the priority given to the pragmatic social criteria, the term *exceptional individual* usually refers to those people who differ from the average to such an extent that they are perceived by society as requiring special educational, social, or vocational treatment. True, such criteria lack specificity and vary from culture to culture and from one generation to another, but they seem to be the most meaningful yet suggested. Such a relative, social conception of the exceptional individual finds quantitative criteria to be useful only insofar as they correlate with the social. If it is found that all or most of the test-identified exceptional children also meet the educational and social criteria, test performance can be used for identification purposes. But when educational methods and requirements change, when social demands vary, and when occupational opportunities are modified, the tests' usefulness will also change.

Critics find considerable fault with a definition of the exceptional individual as that person who deviates from the norm in physical, mental, emotional, or social characteristics to such a degree that he requires special social and educational services to develop his maximum capacity. In actual practice, a combination of traditional practice, cultural values, social needs, and even political pressures determines what dimensions and degrees of individual differences are sufficiently significant for something to be done about them.

The variable nature of social criteria of exceptionality   In a primitive culture, where survival and effectiveness depend upon one's skill in hunting, physical handicaps are serious defects, whereas the inability to learn to read, write, calculate, and handle abstract concepts is much less significant. Where individual and tribal survival and prestige are determined by sensory acuity and by physical agility, strength, and endurance, physically defective infants may be abandoned even though they may be intellectually superior. In an agricultural community which is sparsely settled and unmechanized, a psychotic, mentally retarded, or socially inadequate individual may be a problem to his immediate family without becoming a matter of general social concern. The rural boy who fails to learn in school can still do useful work under the supervision of his parents and siblings and can become a contributing member of the family.

Variations among people are universal, but society determines which deviations will be considered disabilities or assets, impairments or enhancements of personal worth. Assets and disabilities are dictated as much by the tasks a culture demands or expects of its members and by the meanings it attaches to deviations from the norm as by the objective facts of exceptionality.

Today's increasing social concern for the extreme intellectual deviates (the mentally retarded, the intellectually gifted, and the creative) is, in part, a reflection of our cultural expectancies and values. A discussion of the reasons for the increasing social problems of mental retardation and the current interest in the gifted and the creative will point up the cultural frame of reference within which all categories of exceptional children are perceived.

In present-day America, the need for unskilled and semiskilled workers is rapidly declining, while the demand for professional, managerial, scientific, and technically trained workers is increasing. The bulk of the work requiring good hands and a strong back is being automated, and we are experiencing the substitution of knowledge for strength. Inventiveness, creativity, and intellectual activity are becoming the real human assets. An advanced industrial culture requires a well-educated, creative, and adaptable labor force. Today's young students can expect to see a complete technological revolution during the course of their lifetimes. The jobs they might hold today will probably not exist when they are fifty. As adults they may well be working with processes not yet developed and using machines still to be designed. In such a highly automated and rapidly changing industrial society, the need is for people to invent, design, install, monitor, and service equipment. Someone who offers manual dexterity, brute strength, and endurance is no longer truly productive. Adaptability rather than a specific skill, creativity rather than rote information, the capacity for change rather than a given fund of information in one limited area are the assets valued by such a culture. The concept of a position or industrial occupation as a specialized activity is being replaced by an emphasis on the more general and abstract occupational and professional aptitudes. The greater plasticity and adaptability characteristic of higher intelligence are becoming imperative.

One result of these cultural changes is that mentally and/or educationally retarded individuals, for example, are increasingly becoming a social liability. Even the farm is changing. The demands of scientific farming, the rational use of complicated modern farm machinery, the pressures of mechanized, large-scale, efficient production have forced the marginal farmer and farm worker out of the market. The reduction in the absolute number of farm laborers, as well as the even greater decrease in their relative number, have driven hordes of marginal farm workers, tenants, and owners to the cities, where they gravitate to the slums and swell the rank of the urban culturally disadvantaged.

In the urban centers, persons with marginal intelligence come to the attention of the educational, public health, police, and public welfare agencies designed to help them, their intellectual limitations become obvious, and public concern is aroused. With increasing numbers of people becoming labeled as intellectually marginal and inadequate in terms of the social and occupational demands of the culture, the need for special assistance increases tremendously (Grossman, 1973). Handicaps are always relative to the social context.

AREA OR MODE OF DEVIATION

The first classification of exceptional individuals is the *area* or *mode* of primary deviation. This is a qualitative type of classification. The modes or areas selected for consideration reflect the current cultural values of the society. We have selected six general areas or modes of deviation for primary consideration.

Intellectual and academic deviance   We shall deal with intellectual deviations in both directions from the mean. On the lower end of the scale of intelligence and scholastic aptitude are the mentally retarded, the borderline, the dull, and those with more specific learning disabilities. At the high end of the intellectual scale are the gifted. Creative and potentially creative persons, although they probably do not possess the same kind of exceptionality as the intellectually gifted, the normal, and the retarded, are probably a subgroup of the gifted, but they will be considered separately because of the current interest in them. A certain minimum of intellectual capacity is necessary to be creative, but creativity seems to correlate only moderately with general intelligence. Therefore we will deal with the creative and the intellectually gifted as two overlapping, but not identical, categories.

Sensory deviance   The sensorially exceptional—the hard-of-hearing and the deaf, the partially sighted and the blind—constitute a second area of exceptionality. There are, of course, people who have no sense of pain (analgesia), who lack all sensitivity in local skin areas (cutaneous anesthesia or anaphia), and who have no sense of smell (anosmia). There may also be people without a sense of taste, or gustatory sensitivity, and without motor sensitivity, or kinesthesis, although the authors have never heard of them. Such conditions are exceptional in a statistical sense and often constitute medical and psychological curiosities, but they do not pose social problems and therefore are not typically considered in discussions of exceptionality.

Motor deviance   The third mode of exceptionality is in the motor area. In this group we shall consider the crippled, or orthopedically handicapped, and the speech defectives. While no one will question that the first subgroup are principally motor deviants, many will insist that most speech disorders are functional rather than organic in nature. However, speech defects have their motor aspects, and we shall subsume them under the motor deviants rather than placing them in a class by themselves.

Behavioral and personality deviance   The fourth area or mode of exceptionality is the general behavioral and personality category. This mode resists definition and delimitation even more than the intellectual, sensory, and motor modes of deviation. We can, of course, conceive of a theoretically normal range of emotional and personality adjustment. This normal range of adjustment grades imperceptibly into the minor personality maladjustments, which in turn pass into the more serious disturbances—the neuroses and the psychoses. The simplest view of the fundamental nature of the personality maladjustments is a quantitative, social-learning conception. Its proponents consider personality deviations to be the end results of the process of social learning. Psychosis and neurosis are thought to be understandable in terms of excessive anxiety, frustrations, conflict, and repression, which are basic processes common to all people. The personally distressing and socially handicapping neurotic and psychotic manifestations are considered to be the end results of the many defensive mechanisms which develop as a consequence of the individual's attempts to handle life's stresses (Sawrey & Telford, 1975). There are, of course, other ways of viewing personality maladjustments. The 1960s and '70s have witnessed an increasing public concern with problems of mental health and mental illness.

Social deviance   The social deviant has traditionally been the primary concern of law enforcement agencies. Juvenile delinquents and adult criminals are, by definition, social deviants. However, society has become increasingly aware of the existence of subcultural groups—ethnic minorities and the economically disadvantaged—who, for a variety of reasons, deviate so far from the dominant social norm that they constitute educational and social problems. The bulk of these people live in poverty, and when cross-cultural studies are made of such people the world over, they seem to possess sufficient common characteristics to cause one to wonder if there does not exist a worldwide "culture of poverty."

Partly for historical reasons and partly because of the need to focus attention on certain critical areas, juvenile delinquents and the culturally deprived will be discussed as two categories of exceptional people. They constitute the two subdivisions of our fifth area of exceptionality.

Problems of the aged   Selecting a particular age range as a sixth category for special consideration is arbitrary. All five modes of deviation are found among the aged and many of these are discussed under the appropriate categories. However, some more general problems of adjustment are unique to this age range. These problems are only beginning to receive the attention they deserve. Since we have committed ourselves to consider exceptionality throughout the entire age range, we feel it is appropriate to include a separate discussion of the problems of elderly persons.

The overlapping of areas or modes

The enumeration of discrete categories of exceptional individuals oversimplifies the facts of life. Many, or even most, exceptional people are exceptional in more than one area. Everyone knows of people who are both blind and deaf; in 1973, 5,300 people were so identified in the United States (Csapo & Clarke, 1974). Most individuals with cerebral palsy have speech, sensory, or intellectual defects in addition to their motor handicaps, and it is very difficult for an extremely physically, sensorially, or mentally handicapped individual not to become, to some degree, a social or personality deviant. It is also true that people who are handicapped in one way may excel in another. The cripple may be a genius or an artist.

It is obvious than an almost infinite number of possible combinations of abilities and disabilities will be found in a typical population. One of the primary tasks of this book is to indicate the relationships commonly found among the many modes of socially significant deviations. We shall attempt to unravel some of the genetic, organic, social determinants, and relationships among these deviations.

Why only these areas of deviations?

It is obvious that there is no consistency in our selection of the particular areas and direction of deviation for consideration. We deal with both the exceptionally bright and the exceptionally dull, but we limit ourselves to the negative deviants, the handicapped, in all the other areas.

Why are we not just as concerned with the child who has *superior* sensory or motor capacities as we are with the child who has a motor or sensory handicap? There are several partial answers to this question. One is that the physically superior people do not constitute social problems; they do not cause trouble. We also are not aware of any possible public costs or social losses resulting from our failure to develop and capitalize on the supernormal abilities of these individuals. Perhaps our society is such that it cannot profit significantly from the superior sensory and motor capacities of its citizens. The telescope and the microscope have so extended the limits of human vision that the difference between the average person and the person with the most acute vision is relatively unimportant. It may be that artificial devices—amplifiers of sensory capacities—and the natural adaptability of the sense organs can bring the sensory aptitude of all but a small percentage of people above a certain minimum, and that differences above this level are not socially and economically critical.

In a way, we do recognize and reward motor facility, even though the physically and athletically superior are not usually considered in texts on exceptional children. In college, and to a lesser degree in high school, we hire and pay large salaries to people who follow the athletic records of prospective students, scout their games, and actively recruit, train, and coach them. We award the selected students scholarships purely on the basis of athletic aptitude; we provide special housing, "training tables," tutoring services, and special medical care, to ensure that they will remain in school and will either maintain or increase their athletic prowess. Their uniforms, equipment, and accessories are given to them. Athletic teams are provided with special transportation over great distances, so that they can compete with other, similarly subsidized teams. Special post-season games are held in exotic places to provide the teams with vacation trips at public expense. Star performers receive special awards, testimonial dinners, and public acclaim. And the termination of the athlete's collegiate program may be the beginning of a professional career with similar monetary and social rewards.

Without labeling it as such, we do provide very special programs for the physically superior. But such programs are seldom rationalized, like the programs for the intellectually talented, in terms of the "development and utilization of human resources." Intercollegiate athletic programs are considered part of the physical education program, but the principal justifications for such programs are monetary reward, personal and institutional prestige, and entertainment.

Some interest in individuals who are above average in terms of personality integration and social adjustment has recently developed. Mental health is still largely conceived of as an absence of mental illness, but there have been several attempts to define superior social and personal adjustment. There have also been some studies of the antecedents of superior mental health (Sawrey & Telford, 1975). However, we do not yet have enough relevant information to justify the inclusion of individuals with superior social ability and personality in our discussions of exceptional people. Similarly, we consider the problems of the culturally disadvantaged without giving comparable attention to the culturally advantaged.

THE TREND TOWARD NONCATEGORIZING

Three large-scale movements, now in progress, minimize traditional categories of deviants. One is the deinstitutionalization movement—the transfer of a large percentage of the psychiatric population from institutions to the local community. Another is "mainstreaming"—the return of many school children from their special classes to the regular classrooms. The third movement, which is also involved in the other two, consists of widespread attempts to reduce the deleterious effects of categorizing and labeling deviants. The net effect of these three trends has been a proposal to deal with all deviants noncategorically. While we are in sympathy with this general trend, it does have limitations. We have stressed that all the handicapped, and to a degree all deviants, have much in common. However, there are some treatment, educational, social, and vocational problems unique to several of the conventional categories.

Blind persons have unique problems learning to read and becoming independently mobile. The deaf have special problems in learning to speak via the visual, cutaneous, and kinesthetic senses. The limited motor potential of the orthopedically handicapped and the deviant speech of the stutterer pose problems requiring unique approaches.

There are many service needs that are category-related. This means that categorical specialists are still needed to design, administer, and monitor special instructional, training, and care programs for these persons. Certainly, groupings should be on the basis of the individual's care, training, and educational requirements rather than the conventional medical, psychological, social welfare, and legal categories.

DEGREE OR INTENSITY OF EXCEPTIONALITY

Exceptional people differ in the *degree* of their deviation as well as in the mode of their exceptionality. Deviation has intensity as well as direction. We have already made incidental reference to this factor. It is obvious that people range intellectually from the extremely gifted (IQ's of 200 have been reported) to low-grade, totally dependent individuals with IQ's near zero. It is obvious that the extent of deviation required for designation as exceptional will always be relative to one's purpose. The current practice is to designate as intellectually gifted those indi-viduals who score above a designated point, usually somewhere between 120 and 140, and who meet certain other criteria. The intellectually inferior are usually divided into several subgroups for most purposes. At the lowest end of the scale (formerly called the "idiot" level) are the most severely retarded individuals—the "total-care," or "custodial," or "institutional" cases whose IQ's are below 20 or 30. The next-higher group, previously the "imbecile" category, are now called the "trainable," the "moderately retarded," or in some classifications the "severely retarded," whose IQ's are typically between 30 and 50. These are followed by the "mildly mentally retarded" (formerly the "moron" group) or "educable mentally retarded," whose IQ's range from 50 to 70. There is less agreement as to the most appropriate names and IQ ranges for the higher categories, but those with IQ's of 70 to 90 are often called "slow learners." This range includes the groups previously labeled "dull" or "dull normal" (IQ's of 80 to 90) and "borderline" (IQ's of 70 to 80). There is considerable variation in terminology, but it is usually clear from either the general context or the data presented which categories are under consideration.

It is clear that the degree, or intensity, of mental retardation may be as important as the fact of retardation. The *degree* of mental retardation is the primary difference between the slow learner, who will be a grade or two retarded in school, but who may eventually finish high school, learn a trade, marry, raise a family, and live a reasonably normal, independent existence, and the total-care case, who will require supervision and nursing care comparable to that of an infant for his entire lifetime. The *fact* of retardation may be less significant than its intensity.

The intensity of exceptionality is just as important in the physical as in the intellectual area. Educationally, minor auditory and visual deficiencies seem to be relatively unimportant. Even the hard-of-hearing (audiometrically defined) and the partially sighted can be educated and can live essentially like children with normal sight and hearing, whereas those whose visual or auditory acuity is below a certain critical point (usually the legally blind and deaf) require special techniques and facilities for their education and vocational training.

It is harder to indicate objectively intensity or degree of deviation in the remaining types of exceptional individuals. However, it is important to know the extent and location of motor involvement. Designations such as monoplegia, diplegia, triplegia, and quadraplegia indicate the number of limbs involved in cases of paralysis. It is just as important to know the degree of functional impairment of locomotion and manipulation resulting from the motor disability.

Specialists in speech pathology have made considerable progress in indicating the severity of speech defects. Speech defects can range all the way from articulatory deviations that are hardly noticeable to the unintelligible vocalizations of the extremely impaired cerebral-palsied or aphasic individual.

The intensity of deviation present in epilepsy is related to the form that it takes (*grand* or *petit mal*), the frequency and severity of the seizures, and their relative responsiveness to medication. Epilepsy can range all the way from a minor inconvenience, when it is of the mild *petit mal* form which may be entirely controlled by appropriate medication, to an incapacitating disorder, when the individual suffers from frequent uncontrollable *grand mal* convulsions.

We have already indicated that the degree or intensity of personality maladjustment can be conceptualized as minor personality disturbances, neuroses, and psychoses. These terms indicate differences in intensity as well as possible qualitative differences.

The social deviant is placed in the broad general diagnostic categories of the delinquent or the culturally deprived, but some indication of the adequacy of his personal and social competence is equally helpful. Conceivably, the degree of social delinquency can be roughly indicated by the types of crime (major or minor) and the number of delinquencies. The extent of cultural deprivation can be inferred from the person's cultural background, which can be roughly quantified by the use of rating scales, or from his behavior. The latter is judged largely by subjective evaluation, although "social maturity" scales might conceivably be useful.

It is obvious that intensity refers to the *degree of individual differences,* not only between the groups of people designated as exceptional and the normal, but also within the deviant groups. The uninformed always overestimate the homogeneity of the identified groups of exceptional people. That the individuals making up a designated category of exceptional people have a narrowed range of aptitudes in one respect does not necessarily make them any more alike in other ways than the general run of people.

EXTENSITY OR BREADTH OF EXCEPTIONALITY

Extensity, a third way in which exceptionality may be characterized, is used here to refer to the degree of specificity or generality of the handicap or asset in terms of which the individual is exceptional. Extensity is indicated by the degree to which the primary deviation affects other aspects of one's personality and behavior. As we suggested earlier, the average person probably overestimates the breadth or spread of exceptionality. The belief in a broad syndrome of behavior traits characteristic of the various classes of exceptional individuals has been widely held. These popular beliefs are typified by the conception of the intellectually gifted child as a socially inadequate and physically weak individual who is predisposed to physical and mental illness and likely to "burn out" and die at an early age. The mentally retarded individual is likewise stereotyped as a big, dumb brute, likely to be oversexed and criminally inclined. The deaf child is thought to be withdrawn, unsocial, morose, suspicious, and unhappy. Epileptics are alleged to display a characteristic personality syndrome, the "epileptic personality." The orthopedically handicapped individual is typically considered to be a mental as well as physical cripple. The failure of the blind to see and of the deaf to hear is widened into a general syndrome of disability. So we shout at the blind, expect others to speak for them, and attempt to lift them into streetcars as if they are crippled. These beliefs assume that there is an inherent relationship between deviation in one area and corresponding behavioral and personality deviations in other areas (Wright, 1974).

Research studies have provided little support for these social stereotypes. Where relationships between the conventional categories of physical deviations and personality traits or other behavioral characteristics have been found, the evidence does not support the belief in an inherent *causal relationship* between the two. There are some exceptions, and the topic will be discussed in more detail in connection with each class of exceptional individuals, but the following broad generalizations are probably justified.

Research studies regularly find a greater incidence of social withdrawal, overaggressiveness, personal unhappiness, and all types of defensive behavior patterns among people who deviate from the norm in ways culturally defined as undesirable than among those individuals who are either closer to the group norm or who deviate in socially approved directions. Consistent, but low, correlations are found between many physical handicaps and various measures of personal and social adjustment. However, in most cases, the assumption of a direct causal relationship between the two variables is questionable. The relationship between the physical variable and the behavioral trait is usually the result of intervening social variables (Shontz, 1971). While there are important relationships between physical deviations on the one hand and social values and personal adjustment on the other, there is no one-to-one relationship between form of deviation and type of personal adjustment. Few psychological experiences and problems are peculiar to exceptional people. The personality and behavioral problems of exceptional people —even those who are completely blind or deaf or crippled—arise from such matters as actual or threatened social isolation, personal dependency, and the denial or acceptance of personal limitations, experiences which all people have.

TERMINOLOGY

There is relatively little standardization of terminology in the field of exceptionality. Only recently terms such as *insane, blind, deaf, crippled,* and *criminal,* as well as the term *feebleminded* and its subdivisions— *moron, imbecile,* and *idiot*—were used to refer to various categories of exceptional individuals. The present tendency is to substitute less stigmatizing, gentler, and less emotionally toned terms for the older ones which have acquired connotations of helplessness and hopelessness.

Mental deficiency was first substituted for *feeblemindedness;* still more recently, *mental retardation* has become the term approved by the American Association on Mental Deficiency (Grossman, 1973). It is recommended that degrees of retardation be indicated by the terms *borderline, mild, moderate, severe,* and *profound.* However, in educational contexts, the term *educable* refers to the level called *mildly retarded* by the American Association, and the educators' *trainable* group roughly approximates the *moderately retarded* as defined by the Association. The matter is further complicated because the educators often refer to the educable and the trainable as "mildly" and "severely" retarded, respectively, thus departing from the Association's recommendations.

The terminology used for the other categories of the exceptional is not quite so involved. However, it is considered better to speak of the "orthopedically handicapped" than of the "crippled." Although it is more awkward, the blind are often called the "sightless" or the "visually impaired." The deaf or the partially deaf have become the "aurally handicapped." The older terms *lunatic* and *insane* have been replaced by *psychotic* and *personality deviants,* which cover a broad, indefinite spectrum of deviant behavior in the same general area.

Originally, these categories of deviant people were all referred to as *disabled* or *handicapped.* However, when the intellectually superior were included along with the intellectually and physically handicapped, the term *exceptional* was adopted to refer to the entire group. This non-specific designation, having no connotations of inferiority or inadequacy, is now used to refer to any or all of the deviant categories, although the general public often objects to this usage because the term is often understood in terms of its common dictionary definition as "uncommon; hence, superior." Occasionally, we find the terms *unusual child* or *special child* used in place of *exceptional child.*

While the renaming of old categories partly reflects changing conceptions and greater precision in definition and classification, it is more a reflection of our cultural emphasis on the democratic belief that all people are created equal and of our attempt to avoid the connotations of inherent inferiority which eventually accrue to the terms applied to groups of people perceived as handicapped. Although labels are necessary for certain purposes, there is a tendency to use them as little as possible because of the stigmas attached to many of them. This is discussed more fully in the following chapter. It is paradoxical that the more we learn about exceptional people, the less confident we become about our ability to usefully classify them (Grossman, 1973; Bogdan & Taylor, 1976).

SUMMARY

The study of deviant people is really a study of all humankind. The problem of exceptional people is a part of the larger problem of individual differences in general. Prescientific conceptions of the origins and nature of the more extreme forms of development deviation and behavioral aberration tended to be supernatural and mystical. Later, the handicapped were regarded as separate categories of human beings. Deviants were considered basically different from other people, and their behavior was explained by special theories and concepts distinct from those used to understand the behavior of "normal" people. The current conceptions are quantitative, holding that the differences between the normal and the exceptional are of degree only. The emphasis today is on the large core of normality found in every deviant individual. Understanding handicapped children means first understanding them as children, and only then understanding the ways in which their deviations may influence their development and behavior.

The basic social, psychological, and educational needs of exceptional children are identical with the needs of all children and can be met in much the same general ways. Only the specifics differ. There are probably few psychological experiences peculiar to exceptional people. The basic motivations for affection, acceptance, and approval exist whether the IQ is 50 or 150, whether the body is beautiful or a caricature, whether the movements are graceful or made awkward and incoordinate by crippling disease or accident, whether speech is melodious or guttural. These exceptional children, like any others, can be comfortable and secure when they feel that they are accepted, appreciated, and liked. They will be equally uneasy and insecure when they are rejected and depreciated. Disability increases the probability of occurrence of certain frustrations and conflicts for the disabled, but these experiences are not unique to disabled persons. They simply experience them more often than do their nondisabled peers.

Strengths and weaknesses are found in varying degrees in all categories of people, the advantaged as well as the disadvantaged, the normal and the abnormal, the deviant and the nondeviant, and in all ethnic groups.

Deviations are conceived of as having several aspects: area (sensory, motor, intellectual, emotional, social); intensity (degree of the deviation, from mild to severe); and extensity (the range of behavior that is affected). The visibility or obviousness of a deviation also influences its personal and social significance.

REFERENCES

ANASTASIOW, N. J., & N. G. STAYROOK, "Miscue Language Patterns of Mildly Retarded and Nonretarded Children," *American Journal of Mental Deficiency*, 1973, 77, 431–34.

BALDWIN, C. P., & A. L. BALDWIN, "Personality and Social Development of Handicapped Children," in J. A. Swets & L. L. Elliott, eds., *Psychology and the Handicapped Child* (Washington, D.C.: U.S. Department of Health, Education and Welfare, 1974).

BARTEL, N. R., I. BRYEN, & S. SEEHN, "Language Comprehension in the Moderately Retarded Child," *Exceptional Children*, 1973, 39, 375–82.

BOGDAN, R., & S. TAYLOR, "The Judged, Not the Judges: The Insider's View of Mental Retardation," *American Psychologist*, 1976, 31, 47–52.

BROWN, R., "Schizophrenia, Language, and Reality," *American Psychologist*, 1973, 28, 395–403.

CHAPMAN, A. H., & E. B. COOPER, "The Nature of Stuttering in a Mentally

Retarded Population," *American Journal of Mental Deficiency*, 1973, *87*, 153–57.

COMER, R. J., & J. A. PILIAVIN, "The Effects of Physical Deviance upon Face-to-face Interaction," *Journal of Personality and Social Psychology*, 1972, *23*, 33–39.

CSAPO, M., & B. R. CLARKE, "Blind-deaf Children in Canada," *The New Outlook for the Blind*, 1974, *68*, 315–19.

FRIEDMAN, J., & R. PASNAK, "Attainment of Classification and Seriation Concepts by Blind and Sighted Children," *Education of the Visually Handicapped*, 1973, *50*, 55–62.

GRIER, W. H., & P. M. COBBS, *Black Rage* (New York: Basic Books, 1968).

GROSSMAN, H. J., ed., *Manual on Terminology and Classification in Mental Retardation* (Washington, D.C.: American Association on Mental Deficiency, Special Publication Series #2, 1973).

HELMREICH, H., & O. BLOODSTEIN, "The Grammatical Factor in Childhood Disfluency in Relation to the Continuity Hypothesis," *Journal of Speech and Hearing Research*, 1973, *16*, 731–38.

JENSEN, A. R., "How Biased Are Culture-loaded Tests?" *Genetic Psychology Monographs*, 1974, *90*, 185–244.

KASL, S. V., & S. COBB, "Effects of Parental Status in Congruence and Discrepancy on Physical and Mental Health of Adult Offspring," *Journal of Personality and Social Psychology Monograph*, October 1967, 7 (2) Whole No. 642.

KIESLER, S. B., "Preference for Predictability or Impredictability as a Mediator of Reactions to Norm Violation," *Journal of Personality and Social Psychology*, 1973, *27*, 354–59.

PRICE, R. H., & D. L. BOUFFARD, "Behavioral Appropriateness and Situational Constraint as Dimensions of Social Behavior," *Journal of Personality and Social Psychology*, 1974, *30*, 579–86.

ROGOW, S. M., "Speech Development and the Blind Multi-Impaired Child," *Education of the Visually Handicapped*, 1973, *5*, 105–109.

SAWREY, J. M., & C. W. TELFORD, *Adjustment and Personality*, 4th ed. (Boston: Allyn & Bacon, 1975).

SEIDMAN, E., & D. KOULACK, "Race, Adjustment, and Rejection," *Journal of Counseling and Clinical Psychology*, 1973, *40*, 298–303.

SHONTZ, F. C., "Physical Disability and Personality," in W. S. Neff, ed., *Rehabilitation Psychology* (Washington, D.C.: American Psychological Association, 1971).

STEPHENS, W. E., "Equivalence Formation by Retarded and Nonretarded Children at Different Mental Ages," *American Journal of Mental Deficiency*, 1972, *77*, 311–23.

SUPPES, P., "Cognition: A Survey," in J. A. Swets & L. L. Elliot, eds., *Psychology and the Handicapped Child* (Washington, D.C.: U.S. Department of Health, Education and Welfare, 1974).

TEBEEST, D. L., & J. R. DICKIE, "Responses to Frustrations: Comparisons of Institutionalized and Noninstitutionalized Retarded Adolescents and Nonretarded Children and Adolescents," *American Journal of Mental Deficiency*, 1976, *80*, 407–13.

THOMAS, E. C., & K. YAMAMOTO, "A Note on the Semantic Structures of the School-related Attitudes in Exceptional Children," *Journal of Psychology*, 1972, *81*, 225–34.

WILLIAMS, R. I., "Black Pride, Academic Relevance, and Individual Achievement," in R. W. Tyler & R. M. Wolf, eds., *Crucial Issues in Testing* (Berkeley, Ca.: McCutchan Publishing Corp., 1974).

WRIGHT, B. A., "An Analysis of Attitudes: Dynamics and Effects," *The New Outlook for the Blind*, 1974, *68*, 108–18.

Chapter 2

Conceptual models of deviancy

Social attitudes concerning the education, care, and rehabilitation of deviant individuals, and public provision for them, are largely a reflection of a set of more general, culture-wide beliefs and attitudes concerning the obligations of society as a whole to its individual citizens. Ever since the 1930s, the trend in the United States has shifted toward increasing responsibility of society to provide environmental circumstances conducive to the development of good physical and mental health, to make it possible for every adult to become gainfully employed, and to provide maximum opportunities for the development of one's potential. The assumptions basic to the providing of universal opportunities for educational advancement, vocational outlets, and self-actualization for the "normal" have been expanded to include all people simply because as human beings they are worthy of respect and consideration and are deserving of the entire range of opportunities previously afforded to only a part of the population.

Despite some claims to the contrary, the failure of society to provide facilities and opportunities for deviant individuals as appropriate to their needs as those made available to the normals probably has not been the result of conspiracies to deprive certain segments of the population of their rights. Failures to provide educational and vocational programs and opportunities appropriate to the capacities and needs of the deviant minorities resulted incidentally from the efforts of reasonable, well-meaning people directed at other socially useful purposes.

The promise of universal educational opportunities has usually meant, in practice, one educational program available to all those able and willing to profit by it. The inability of deviant individuals, and groups of individuals, to take advantage of the programs provided because of sensory, motor, emotional, or intellectual limitations was explained in terms of demoniacal possession, retribution for parental sins, inborn perversity, punishment for individual delinquencies, inherent moral weaknesses, defective genes, or the inevitable accidents of normal life, according to the prevailing beliefs of the times—not as a result of society's failure to provide programs and opportunities appropriate to the special needs of these people. In the apportioning of blame for the social failures of deviant citizens, the responsibility was predominantly that of the deviant himself. In a less moralistic framework, the question was, "Why isn't this person able to take advantage of the opportunities which his society provides?" rather than, "Why doesn't society provide educational, rehabilitative, and vocational facilities and programs appropriate to this individual's needs?"

The climate of the times that progressively has provided more adequately for the blind, the deaf, the orthopedically handicapped, the mentally deficient, and the emotionally disturbed has expanded to a similar concern for the culturally disadvantaged (Afro-Americans, American Indians, Mexican-Americans, Puerto Ricans, many rural whites, and ghetto dwellers of all colors and ethnic origins). Studies of the culturally disadvantaged have disclosed that large segments of the population were born into and reared under circumstances which inevitably imposed handicaps upon them. Furthermore, it is now evident that these handicapping circumstances were created and perpetuated by the practices arising from the basic assumptions and beliefs of the larger society.

Society increasingly has assumed the obligation of providing help for all individuals and groups who for whatever reason require assistance. It has also become concerned with changing those conditions, practices, and erroneous beliefs contributing to the handicaps of these people.

The emergence of a widespread concern for handicapped and disadvantaged people has resulted in the state's assuming increasing responsibility for extending the rights and privileges of full citizenship to all people. This extension of responsibility has manifested itself in the civil rights movement, the war on poverty, Head Start and many related programs, and judicial decisions extending the rights, privileges, and immunities once available only to the affluent or knowledgeable to all citizens. Many Supreme Court decisions that have been widely criticized as coddling or protecting the criminal are really designed to extend to the poor, the ignorant, and the disadvantaged the same legal protections and rights previously available only to the more advantaged segments of the population. When the Court insists that every person taken into custody as a criminal suspect must be informed of his rights concerning self-incrimination and legal counsel, it is simply making available to the lowliest citizen of the nation the same protections and privileges previously enjoyed only by the more advantaged segments of the population. The well-informed, the better educated, and the more affluent criminals, with legal counsel prompting them at each critical point, know that they need not give self-incriminating testimony and are able to obtain legal counsel and advice. The ignorant bowery wino, the poorly informed first offender, and the disadvantaged delinquent are not aware of their legal rights and privileges and consequently may be convicted and punished, not because they are guilty but because they are ignorant, ill-informed, or poor.

The recent redefinition of mental illness as failure in social living, and the development of a communitywide public health approach to those problems of personal and social maladjustment previously viewed as purely personal afflictions, have accompanied increasing public concern for deviant and, particularly, disadvantaged people. There is increasing professional and public recognition of the existence of a complicated and thorny set of interrelationships among poverty, unemployment, crime, physical illness, emotional disturbance, personality disorganization, mental deficiency, and educational retardation.

One manifestation of the changing climate is the increase in public espousal of humanistic as well as humanitarian values. Historically, special programs for the handicapped—the blind, the deaf, the orthopedically handicapped, the mentally deficient, and the emotionally disturbed—were designed to reduce the level of dependency of the disabled, on the one hand, and to express humanitarian concern for people less fortunate than ourselves, on the other. Rehabilitative and educational procedures were designed to increase the productive efficiency of disabled individuals and thus make them less of a financial and personal burden on society.

Programs for the intellectually gifted and the potentially highly creative were conceptualized as maximizing the superior individual's contributions to society. The aptitudes and capacities of superior people were conceived as community assets to be used to the fullest possible extent so as to maximize their value to the state. In the 1960s a surge of interest in the intellectually superior and the creative individual was motivated, at least in part, by the "space race" and the belief that it was necessary to use the intellectual potential of these people to the maximum if we were to make the scientific and technological advances necessary to attain or maintain national superiority.

To a degree, people were seen as a national commodity to be managed for maximum productivity. The intellectual capacities of citizens constituted tools for the realization of personal—but more importantly—social and nationalistic goals. Education has always served a dual function. It contributes to self-actualization on the one hand and to socialization and increased public worth on the other. Recently, the goal of education has been conceptualized more in terms of self-realization and less in terms of productive efficiency. The failure of any individual to realize his potential is seen more as a personal disappointment than as a social loss.

SOME VALUE CONSIDERATIONS

How a society handles the problems posed by the presence of handicapped and disadvantaged minorities reflects its fundamental conception of the nature and worth of the individual and its basic assumptions concerning its communal obligations to him. Americans have traditionally seen themselves as devoid of social class bias and their society as uniquely open and fluid. For the most part, they have taken the oft repeated statement that all people are born free and equal as factual. They have assumed that making free public education available to all citizens provided equality of educational opportunity to all people.

Over the last generation Americans have become acutely aware of the discrepancy between their philosophical commitments and preachments on the one hand and their practices on the other. They are discovering that uniformity of opportunity is not necessarily equality of opportunity. Supplying unlimited numbers of free books to all children does not provide educational opportunity equally to blind, trainable mentally retarded, and sighted children of normal mentalities. Educational opportunities equivalent to those provided to normal children by ordinary educational procedures require that alternatives be provided to deviant individuals that are as appropriate to their special characteristics as the ordinary school curriculum and methods are to the average child. The freedom and equality to which all people are entitled are those of equity in law, and equal rights to life and self-realization. The ideal of maximum opportunities for each person in terms of his unique constellation of traits and characteristics is replacing that of uniformity of opportunities. Each person has equal rights to dignity, courtesy, respect, and the maximum possible provision for him to develop whatever potential he has, not because these will make him a more productive being and a more socially acceptable person, but because these are his birthright as a human being. The notion of maximum opportunity for self-realization for all requires the use of all resources available to capitalize on the assets and minimize the deficits of each individual. Optimum human development rather than maximum productivity becomes the primary goal of educational and rehabilitative efforts. Of course, it is only on the level of concrete goals and specific programs and procedures that such an abstract tenet can be realized.

In chapter 1 we indicated that the assets and liabilities of deviant individuals are determined as much by the tasks and demands of society as by the objective fact of the type and degree of exceptionality. However, the relative degree of fit between a given person's aptitudes and the requirements of his culture is only part of the story. In addition to the social and vocational utility of a person's aptitudes, values also accrue to many essentially nonrelevant personal characteristics.

Despite the democratic contention that physique is a superficial characteristic which has little influence on our judgments of others, incidental observation, as well as a long series of research studies, have demonstrated that physical appearance is an important determiner of social acceptance and success. The existence of a multi-billion-dollar cosmetic industry, plastic surgery, and the fashion industry is evidence of a widespread concern with physical appearance. Physical beauty, as a social stereotype, shows remarkable uniformity across age, sex, intellectual level, and socio-economic status (Willey & McCandless, 1973; Cavior & Dohechi, 1973). Even in nursery school, more attractive children, as judged by adults, are more popular with their peers and are perceived as having more socially desirable personal characteristics, better academic potential, and better social relationships than their less attractive counterparts (Landy & Sigall, 1974; Krebs & Adinolfi, 1975; Dion, 1973, 1974). Attractive people are seen as more deserving of reward and more readily elicit voluntary help from others than otherwise comparable but less attractive people (Mirns, Hartnett, & Nay, 1975). In simulated court situations, attractive or high-status victims or defendants receive more favorable treatment than do comparable less attractive or low-status persons (Landy & Aronson, 1975). It seems clear that we all form impressions and make judgments about others on the basis of their physical attractiveness, and that we make more favorable attributions to good-looking than to unattractive people. An actor simulating a hippie is much more likely to be reported for shoplifting by other shoppers than is the same actor simulating a "straight" person (Steffensmeier & Terry, 1973). Attractiveness operates to evoke positive responses from others, and those who evoke more positive responses also emit more (Clifford & Walster, 1973).

Thus, physically attractive persons attract others, who then engage is a benign escalation cycle where each overpays the other in a series of reciprocal exchanges (Stapleton, Nacci, & Tedechi, 1973). This is one form of the self-fulfilling prophecy. It has also been shown that individuals are evaluated more favorably when they simply associate with physically attractive persons (Sigall & Landy, 1973). It seems clear that, while most underlying traits bear no necessary relationship to physical beauty, people make inferences and display expectancies which result in advantages to those blessed with a "whole" body and physical attractiveness; conversely, an increment of social disadvantage accrues to those persons who are physically deviant in ways perceived as unattractive.

Those persons who both give and receive more socially positive responses, develop greater potential for satisfactory adjustment (Barocas & Vance, 1974). Thus a cultural value—body wholeness and physical beauty—becomes an important determiner of personal-social worth (Mathes & Kahn, 1975).

Marred physical beauty, such as facial disfigurement, without physical limitations, carries with it a social stigma and is generalized to indicate personal and social inadequacy much more than is an invisible defect, such as surgically uncorrectable congenital heart disease, a progressive disability resulting in a shortened life span and restricted educational, vocational, and recreational activities. The cultural ideal of physical wholeness and physical attractiveness means that visible disabilities generally produce more negative reactions and social discrimination than more disabling invisible disabilities (Goldberg, 1974). Other social values are also intertwined with basic aptitudes in determining the total assets or disabilities of a person. Social stereotypes also function as value-laden norms in the intellectual and behavior realm. The ideal of "a sound mind in a sound body" is still a norm in most societies. With widespread literacy and technological developments, physical strength and agility become less important, while intellectual ability and academic skills are more highly valued. As society places greater value on superior intellect, it necessarily stigmatizes and rejects those who do not have it. A person with low intellect becomes one with an "unsound mind." If intellectual ability were valued on a par with artistic skill, manual dexterity, or athletic prowess, it would be a good thing to have, but individuals would not be particularly stigmatized or ostracized when they lack it. However, so long as "brainpower" is an important personal measure, efforts by parents and teachers of the less endowed to devalue it will be largely futile. Ego-deflating personal comparison in terms of intellectual capacities is an inevitable part of contemporary society. A child can hardly see himself as an adequate individual simply because his parents and/or teachers tell him that he is, when the rest of society is continually telling that he is not. In the larger social context, his very identity often revolves around the thing which he lacks. Of course, parents can improve the situation by putting less emphasis on academic grades, by underplaying intellectual prowess and academic achievements. They can insist that other achievements are equally valid measures of personal worth and success. However, when the child asks, "Why can't I read?" or "Why do the other kids call me a dummy?" it doesn't help much to say, "I love you anyway." Mental soundness and superiority along with physical soundness and attractiveness are important cultural values which influence the status and treatment accorded deviants.

Another cultural value, which overlaps the supremacy of intellectual aptitudes, is that characterized as the middle-class Protestant ethic, even though it is found in its purest form in some societies and persons who are poor, non-Christian, and who have never heard of Calvin or Knox (Nair, 1970). In essence this value makes productivity the measure of personal worth. It idealizes the virtues of independence, self-reliance, diligence, and hard work. In terms of this value, the individuals who, because of physical or mental defect or weakness of character are non-productive and dependent upon others for their livelihood or care, are devalued as persons.

The problems of devalued deviants are as much matters of philosophical values and consequent social practices as they are of the objectively defined deficits of the individuals. Attitudes, values, and expectations are as important as physical restraints and internal limitations in determining the total handicap of a person with a disability.

CONCEPTUAL MODELS OF THE ORIGINS OF DEVIANT BEHAVIOR

While many models of the nature and primary causes of deviancy have been proposed, we will differentiate only the two more extreme ones.[1] The first model is the organically-oriented, "person-centered" one. The other is the social-psychological or social-learning model—a "situation-centered" model (Hersch, 1972; Ekehammar, 1974).

The person-centered theorists believe that organic lesions, developmental defects, and biophysical, biochemical, and glandular derangements are the *primary causes* of handicapping deviancy. Observing that infections, intoxications, metabolic disturbances, glandular malfunctions, and genetic factors can manifest themselves in muscular weakness and paralysis, maldevelopment, blindness, deafness, psychosis, and mental retardation, they extend the model and claim that similar organic, genetic, and biochemical causes will be found eventually for most or all intellectual defects, abnormal behaviors, and maladaptive social behavior. Persons of this orientation see the primary causes of handicaps as residing within individuals. The limitations are theirs and efforts at remediation must center on changing the individuals.

The situation-centered (social-learning) theorists, conversely, find the principal causes of handicapping deviancy in the environment. The observation that mental illness, mental retardation, and social maladjustment are related to socio-economic and other environmental variables has been extrapolated to support the proposition that most, if not all, handicapping deficiencies are caused and sustained by the social-psy-

[1] See Siegler & Osmond, 1975, for a discussion of several alternative models.

chological circumstances of the individual's life. The social-learning interpretation of mental and behavioral deviancy is that the manifestations of these conditions are acquired, maintained, and altered in precisely the same way as are those processes considered "normal." According to these theorists, if people could be provided with appropriate physical, social, and psychological environments, mental illness, mental retardation, and social handicapping deviancies would be eliminated. The social-learning theorists emphasize the paramount importance of the effects of categorizing, labeling, segregating, criminalizing, and treating deviants as second-class citizens.

The more extreme situation-oriented theorists—the "conspiratorialists" —have focused on mental illness and mental retardation and claim that these terms are labels attached to abrasive, deviant beings to justify segregating and isolating them from the rest of society (Leifer, 1969; Szasz, 1963, 1974; Sarbin & Mancuso, 1972; Currie & Reid, 1973; Braginsky & Braginsky, 1973, 1974; Mercer, 1973). B. M. Braginsky and D. D. Braginsky (1974) claim that mental retardation is a myth society uses to justify the institutionalization and segregation of this category of troublesome citizens. When it has already been decided that a child must be removed from the regular class, school, or family, the label "mental retardation" is applied to him to justify the act. Braginsky and Braginsky insist that professionals should concentrate on the real source of the child's problem—the home, the school, the social system—rather than defending the delusion that the condition is something within the individual.

In the same vein, R. J. Currie and W. R. Reid (1973) state that special education is an administrative device for relieving institutional guilt. Their principal thesis is that "deviance is a function of the degree to which behavior or sets of behavior are abrasive to the dominant culture." Deviants constitute those persons who, as the result of our socialization failures, are abrasive to the dominant majority. The WASP cultural values of mastery and future-orientation are harmful to nonachievers because they hold that individuals derive their worth according to their ability to be independent and productive. The members of the dominant culture "wreak their revenge" on those who deviate. "The special educator is expected to socialize these children, i.e., to grind them down." The situation can be remedied only by "a significant reordering of national priorities."

According to R. Leifer (1969), N. Hurvitz (1973), and T. S. Szasz (1974), the "mentally ill" person is marked off from others not by his hidden "pathological" mental processes, but by the fact that authorities wish to stigmatize him and control his conduct. To disguise this motive, psychiatrists and others postulate special mental illnesses or defects which they claim to "treat" or "correct." The term *mental illness* disguises our social failures, shields us from the embarrassing facts of coercive and manipulative techniques used under the guise of medical treatment and educational procedures, and legitimizes the use of social power to alter an individual's thoughts, feelings, and actions.

These more extreme situation-oriented theories, for obvious reasons, have been called conspiratorial (Eysenck, 1973). Such theories hardly seem appropriate. The members of the helping professions—psychiatrists, psychologists, counselors, social workers, and teachers—are reasonably conscientious, dedicated, and competent individuals doing the jobs defined for them by society. Their value systems, attitudes, and expectancies are somewhere near the norms of their cultures. If there are any conspirators, they are the social mores and institutional arrangements which nurture the very handicapping conditions which the procedures of the helping professions are designed to remedy. For example, correctional institutions may provide the delinquents instruction in crime; institutions and classes for the mentally retarded may limit opportunities to learn; hospitals for the mentally ill may encourage and perpetuate aberrant behavior. However, these are the unanticipated and largely unrecognized side effects of activities designed to improve the conditions of the clients. While finding and eliminating the "conspirators" or appropriately assigning blame for the ills of society may help define the problems, they are probably not the most fruitful approach to the complex problems of the handicapped.

An evaluation of the person-centered and the situation-centered points of view

Most scholars today probably agree that neither of the extreme positions presented above is warranted. The fundamental but infinitely complex task for the student of human behavior—both normal and deviant—is to unravel and understand the *interactive outcomes* of environmental (situational) circumstances, on the one hand, and the conditions and capacities of the individual (person), on the other. No human characteristic or behavior is solely the result of either one or the other.

However, one's perception of the *relative importance* of "person" and "situation" in the determination of human traits and acts has practical as well as theoretical significance. What is done about a problem depends to a large extent on how it is perceived and defined. When deviancy is perceived as an abnormality which is a part of, or inside, the person, remediation will take the form of changing the person so that the condition is improved and its consequences minimized: "If the shoe doesn't fit, there is something wrong with your foot." Person-centered problem-definitions place the blame on the deviant population. When the person-centered stigmatized population accepts its complete blame-worthiness, its self-definition induces further deviance and alienation from the norm group. A feeling of psychological distance between a person and a significant reference group (normals) is anxiety-arousing. When anxiety mounts and the stresses of life exceed critical limits, various defenses function to maintain a tolerable equilibrium, and often a lowered self-definition justifying a lower level of aspiration makes its possible for the individual to live with a minimum of discomfort. This is one behaviorally limiting outcome of the acceptance of the extreme person-oriented concept.

The extreme dogmatic situation-centered (social-blame) orientation provides the handicapped individual with a ready rationalization for avoiding responsibility and a legitimate excuse for his failures. It pictures the stigmatized deviant as a blameless, helpless individual with no control over his fate. If insanity is perceived as a category manufactured by society to justify confining "abrasive" individuals, if the real defect of the lower-class citizen is simply a failure to incorporate the Protestant ethic which the dominant majority would impose upon him, and if the problem of the schools is that culturally biased test scores have excluded children of divergent cultures from participating in the important institutions of American society, as has been claimed (Braginsky & Braginsky, 1973, 1974), the fault is in the environment and not the individual (Williams, 1974; Currie & Reid, 1973).

The extreme situation-centered person will focus attention not on the deviant individual but on the damaging environment. Social engineering by others, not individual effort, must be the concern of the person who sees the problems of the handicapped as social rather than personal. This may serve as a good excuse for not trying to improve overall.

THE INTERACTIONISTIC CONCEPT OF THE HANDICAPPED

The interactionist insists that the question of whether deviancy resides principally in individuals or in their environments cannot be answered in the abstract. All behavior—normal or abnormal, conventional or deviant, socially valued or stigmatized—is the result of the dynamic interaction of both dispositional and environmental factors. The interactionist conceives of a gradient of environmental (situation) factors and a continuum of inherent-organic (person) factors which interact to produce varying degrees of competence and disability. This is a difficult concept to translate into prevention-remediation programs. The person-oriented gradient includes the combined effects of such things as genetic potentials (single gene, chromosomal abnormalities, multigenic factors), hormonal and biochemical deficiencies and imbalances, and maldevelopments and organic impairments. The environmental continuum includes dietary and disease contingencies, child-rearing practices, and a wide variety of socio-economic factors which may operate cross-culturally. In addition, a number of culture-specific factors such as attitudes, values, social demands, and expectancies, as well as cultural mores and legal restrictions, influence or determine the relevance and values of the particular patterns of personal traits and characteristics of the individual. (See figure 2-1.) A multitude of person and situation variables combine in complex ways to produce a continuum of competencies and disabilities. (See figure 2-2.)

According to Ekehammar (1974), the statistical analysis of the interaction relationship has shown that person–situation interaction is more important than either individual (person) differences or situational differences by themselves in accounting for behavioral variance. Despite the current emphasis on situationism, the available evidence supports the interactionist position. A restatement of the current alternative interaction position, as we have interpreted it, follows:

1. Some mental deviations arise and are sustained *primarily* by organic defects, others arise from pathological personal-social experiences, and still others are sustained by their official and unofficial stigmatization and criminalization.
2. In the etiology of some *disorders,* the social-personal, or the organic, or the stigmatization components outweigh the others in importance, but the others also make significant contributions.
3. All mental disorders involve, to some degree, the interaction of organic vulnerability; environmental circumstances including social inequities, inappropriate socialization, familial inadequacies, and individual experiences; and consequences of being formally and informally categorized and labeled in socially devalued ways.

The programmatic implications of the interaction position

For the short term, the positive program of the interactionist will focus dominantly on people in trouble and on their immediate situation. If people are to be helped, it is usually necessary to change the individuals and their immediate environments for the better in the here-and-now. As a long-term program, the interactionist will engage in eugenic as well as in group-oriented social-action programs designed to change

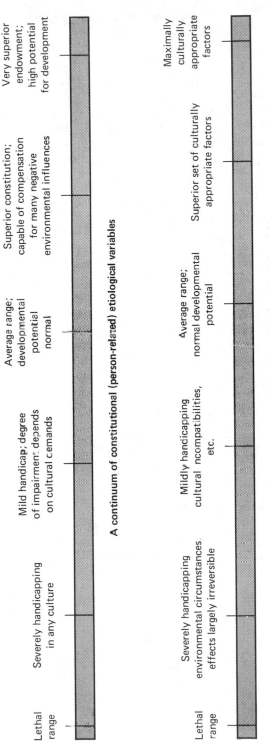

Very superior
endowment;
high potential
for development

Superior constitution;
capable of compensation
for many negative
environmental influences

Average range;
developmental
potential
normal

Mild handicap; degree
of impairment depends
on cultural demands

Severely handicapping
in any culture

Lethal
range

A continuum of constitutional (person-related) etiological variables

Maximally
culturally
appropriate
factors

Superior set of culturally
appropriate factors

Average range;
normal developmental
potential

Mildly handicapping
cultural incompatibilities,
etc.

Severely handicapping
environmental circumstances:
effects largely irreversible

Lethal
range

A continuum of environmental (situation-related) etiological variables

Figure 2-1

those environmental components perceived as deleterious and to promote those environmental inputs believed to promote positive growth and well-being for future generations. Social reform will be directed at such humanitarian concerns as poverty, racism, family planning, and social and economic injustices, as well as at the broader social and economic arrangements and value systems which underlie them. Even the most humanitarian individual recognizes that these broad social-action programs will produce significant changes only within years, decades, or even generations; these effects are too remote to help the individual in need of immediate assistance.

When the extreme situation-oriented counselor tells the juvenile delinquent, or the educationally handicapped child, or the person suffering profound emotional distress, that he is really not to blame for his conditions—that it is the evil and corrupt society that has made him what he is—it is not likely to be helpful. This reification of the environment as the malignant causal agent responsible for their condition provides the handicapped with a ready rationalization for completely avoiding responsibility, a legitimate excuse for all their failures, and a justification for their refusal to exert themselves in their behalf. If the individual's difficulties are all imposed upon him by a malevolent society, he is completely justified in responding in kind, either by striking back at it aggressively or by passively waiting for the crippling society to change. Neither of these strategies is likely to change either the person or the situation for the better.

A large body of research shows that the perception of threatening or handicapping events as subject to control or amelioration by the individual reduces their handicapping potential. Behavior change and its maintenance are facilitated by one's belief that such change can be brought about by the individual himself, rather than that handicapping events are caused by uncontrollable external forces, powerful individuals, or purely chance factors (Kopel & Arkowitz, 1975). The acceptance of an extreme situation-centered orientation may result in individuals succumbing as victims in situations when they need not be.

At the other extreme is the largely "person-centered" orientation. Certainly there are self-punitive individuals whose feelings of personal inadequacy and guilt prevent them from focusing on their problems realistically and coping with them to the extent that they are able. Such persons need to be reassured and desensitized with reference to their feelings of shame and guilt. Providing insight into the social origins of their difficulties may be an essential part of this process. Shedding a major portion of their self-imposed burden of responsibility and feelings of guilt may be necessary for self-improvement. The historical person-blaming concepts of sinfulness, weak will, laziness, stubbornness, and orneriness as explanations of deviancy are not helpful. However, there is an intermediate range of situation vs. person orientation which is probably most conducive to most effective coping with life's situations.

One prerequisite, on the personal side, is a reasonably satisfactory self-image tempered with a bit of "divine discontent" which motivates the individual to strive to decrease the discrepancy between what he is—his self-concept—and what he would like to be—his ideal self-concept. Also required is an element of trust—a belief that what one does can make a difference and a realization that this difference is often neither obvious nor immediate.

If person-initiated improvements are to take place, modifications of the environmental input may also be necessary. Depending upon the individual's age and the degree and nature of his disability, these changes may include changes in attitudes and treatment for other family members; foster-care placement; short- or long-term residential or hospital care; educational changes such as home training, tutoring, special resource teachers, special class or special school placement, and vocational training and/or placement; and providing appropriate social and recreational opportunities and programs. Chapter 3 and portions of each succeeding chapter will deal with these in more detail. J. Rappaport et al. (1975) provide a good discussion of alternatives to the blaming-the-victim versus blaming-the-environment dichotomy.

A continuum of interactive factors

If we consider the consequences of deviancy as moving accumulatively along a continuum, at the lower end of the continuum are those behavioral deviancies dictated by the inherent nature of the differentness, and added to this component are the many official and unofficial social evaluations and restrictions imposed by society's value and/or legal systems. Sensing that they are different in a way that is socially devalued, socially devalued deviants internalize lowered self-concepts, which move them one step farther along the continuum of handicapping. The definition of the behavior as criminal moves the deviating individual to the extreme end of the continuum of negative effects. The criminals are not only deviant in ways that are socially devalued; they also sense and acknowledge their differentness, and also become lawbreakers—criminals. This is shown diagramatically in figure 2-2.

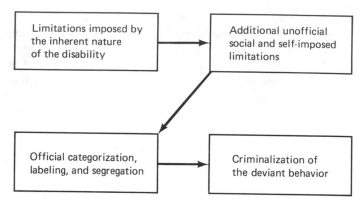

Figure 2-2   An accumulative handicapping sequence.

FIRST- AND SECOND-ORDER EFFECTS
IN THE CARE AND TREATMENT OF DEVIANTS

A. M. Graziano and R. S. Fink (1973), F. J. Scheidt (1974), and N. Hobbs (1975) have suggested a useful distinction between the more immediate and intended effects of care-treatment-educational procedures—the primary or first-order effects—on the one hand, and the unintended and incidental effects of such things as categorizing and labeling—the second-order effects—on the other. Hospital, institutionalization, and educational procedures are carried out under the assumption that they will change the individual for the better. These are the intended first-order effects. It is assumed that the beneficial first-order effects more than counterbalance any possible negative second-order influences. Although these authors do not make the point, it is clear that some immediate and first-order effects may also be quite different from those intended. Two dramatic examples from the area of general medicine illustrate such negative primary effects.

One of these is the disorder known as retrolental fibroplasia, at one time a major cause of blindness in the United States. After extensive study this disorder was finally discovered to be the result of high levels of oxygen administered to prematurely born infants to reduce their high mortality rate. However, before its cause was discovered, several thousand children were blinded as the result of this medical procedure assumed to have only beneficial effects. This will be discussed more fully in the chapter on visual defects.

The second example from medical practice was the birth of several thousand infants with defective hearing and missing or misshapen limbs, results of a tranquilizing drug taken by their mothers early in pregnancy. A tranquilizer containing thalidomide, called contergan, was placed on the market by a West German pharmaceutical firm in 1957. It was said to be the ideal tranquilizer—"the safest thing since water." One person attempting suicide swallowed 144 contergan pills and survived with no apparent aftereffects. Fed to children in liquid form, it was said to produce "normal sleep" and became known as West Germany's number one "baby sitter." In 1961, Karl-Hermann Schulte-Hillen, a lawyer from Menden, West Germany, became concerned when his son was born malformed. He started an investigation which disclosed the existence of an epidemic of births of similarly physically defective children in West Germany. Schulte-Hillen enlisted the assistance of a Hamburg pediatrician and together, through a series of detective-medical investigations, they finally determined that the hearing defects, misshapen limbs, and other irremediable deformities were caused by the thalidomide ingredient of the tranquilizer, contergan, taken by the mothers early in pregnancy. The drug was withdrawn from the market. The chemical firm was brought to trial, convicted of criminal negligence, and required to pay several million dollars to the families of the victims (Mellin & Katzenstein, 1962). Off the market for about fifteen years, thalidomide is now being used successfully in the treatment of Hansen's disease (leprosy).

The unintended second-order effects of educational and mental-health practices are largely beyond the control of the persons or agencies initiating the procedures designed to produce positive primary effects. Are the deleterious second-order effects more than counterbalancing the positive first-order effects of programs for mental and physical deviants? In some situations many people say, "Yes, the outcome of diagnosing, categorizing, and labeling of many categories of deviant individuals conveys social and self-stigmatization, the effects of which are more destructive than beneficial."

Such claims have been made most vigorously with reference to the mental and social deviates—the mentally ill, the mentally retarded, and certain categories of social deviates such as homosexuals and drug addicts. Those persons most actively supporting these claims either explicitly or implicitly subscribe to the conspiratorial conceptual model of the causes of stigmatized deviancy. Despite the social derogation which disability entails, there are secondary gains available which if capitalized on may also add to the handicap. The disability may serve as a socially and personally acceptable excuse for all of one's inadequacies, procrastinations, and disappointments. It can be used as an escape from threatening competition and as a way of avoiding social responsibility. Even the promise of limited success may be threatening. There is always the thought: "If I succeed I may then have to compete on equal terms for previously renounced goals. By succeeding I may be giving up a good excuse for not achieving."

The correction of a defect may pose problems for the deviant person who has enjoyed many of the secondary gains of disability. The correction of a disability deprives the individual of many of the protections and immunities previously enjoyed (Shontz, 1971). The surgical repair of the cleft lip, the operation that straightens the misshapen nose, the repair of the damaged middle ear which restores hearing, or the obtaining of a functionally adequate prosthesis may set the individual adrift from his previous anchorages and defenses. Much to his surprise and discomfort, the rehabilitated individual finds that life does not become conflict-free and success-laden when he becomes "normal." Deprived of previous defenses, he may develop a set of more subtle, but functionally similar, psychosomatic or psychoneurotic symptoms.

CATEGORIES AND STEREOTYPES

Just as feelings of deviancy have important general effects on people's behavior and self-evaluations, so the categorizing and stereotyping of people are also universal features of social interaction. Stereotypes have generally been considered as evils to be eradicated and are usually portrayed as incorrect "pictures in the mind" that distort perception and nurture distorted social relations between people. Social categories and stereotypes can hinder the perceiving and knowing of others as unique individuals to be judged on their merits, as typified by the self-fulfilling prophecy.

The self-fulfilling prophecy

Perceiving individuals in terms of categories always contains the germs of the self-fulfilling prophecy, the basic idea of which is that our perception of a situation may change the situation to fit our perception. One of the most blatant examples of this mechanism is the situation of blacks in America. In perspective, it is clear that as the result of unique historical conditions, slavery in America took the form of chattel slavery and assigned blacks to an inferior category of humanity. Although official slavery has been abolished, the assumptions and attitudes that it nurtured, and the prejudices, expectations, and discriminatory practices that it produced, have persisted. For example, since blacks "are" intellectually inferior and poorly motivated, it is a waste of money to try to educate them like whites. So blacks were provided with less financial support for their schools and poorly trained teachers who shared the low expectations of the culture. Sure enough, blacks' achievements proved to be below those of whites. The belief resulted in the condition, and the condition perpetuated the belief.

The primary message of the women's liberation movement in America is that women, like blacks, have been the victims of culturewide stereotyping which has functioned as a self-fulfilling prophecy. The historical origins of the current cultural stereotypes of "woman's role" and "masculine behavior" are not so well-known as the sources of our attitudes toward blacks. Perhaps they are so remote in time, so diffuse and varied in their sources, and so pervasive in the culture that the recognition of their existence and the identification of their roots become very difficult.

It seems clear that American society, which places a high value on competence and achievement, provides greater rewards for the "male" characteristics of independence and mastery than it does for the "female" characteristics of dependency and submissiveness. Consequently, females can receive positive social reinforcement either by adopting male characteristics, such as competence and independence, or by fitting into the more stereotyped role that society has structured for women. For the male, only the conventional male role provides consistent positive reinforcement.

The culturally perpetuated expectancy concerning the sexes is internalized in early childhood, becomes a component of one's self-concept, and powerfully conditions each individual's aspirations and expectations. To accept both the black–white and the male–female stereotypes, one must be reared in a society in which the differences postulated by these stereotypes are components of a self-evident system of beliefs.

The self-fulfilling prophecy (expectancy effect) has been invoked to explain the disappointing performances of children in special compensatory education programs and the limited success of many other special education programs. It has been used by frustrated spokesmen for the socially disadvantaged because it shifted the blame from the handicapped individual and the social planner to the teacher, the schools, and society.

However, it remained for the widespread publicity given to R. Rosenthal and L. Jacobsen's *Pygmalion in the Classroom* (1968) to bring the concept of the self-fulfilling prophecy out of the realm of academics and into real life. As a result of this study, most research on the topic has focused on learning in the classroom. Rosenthal and Jacobsen claimed that providing teachers with fictitious information that purported to indicate which of their students had much greater potential than they were using, which would probably be late bloomers, and which would show considerable improvement during the school year, produced the reality. The results of the study were alleged to show that the high expectations and supposedly different treatment provided designated students resulted in their making significantly greater improvement than comparable children not so designated. This study has been widely quoted and all sorts of inferences drawn from it, many of which, containing some elements of truth, resulted in some far-reaching but unwarranted conclusions.

One result of this study was to overemphasize the behavioral effects of official labeling and stigmatization. The study seemed to say that children in general do poorly because teachers expect them to do so. The mentally retarded function as they do because test scores reinforce the teachers' expectations of low achievement and help rationalize the minimal efforts exerted in their behalf. The children succumb to these expectations, cease trying, and thus close the circle to make the expectation become the reality. If we would stop testing, assigning low IQ's to, stigmatizing, and then segregating these children into special classes, and would instead anticipate high achievement from them, they would respond to these high expectations.

Many who were convinced of the reality of the self-fulfilling prophecy in a larger social context felt the Rosenthal and Jacobsen results were too good to be true. They did not believe that teachers' and students' levels of expectation and self-images are as easily modified as the study seemed to indicate. Teachers have many sources of information concerning students other than real or alleged test scores. Many teachers entertain a healthy skepticism toward test scores and evaluation by counselors and/or psychologists. Students, although sensitive to observed and inferred statements from teachers concerning their status as students, also have many additional sources of information concerning their academic selves. Outside the schools, parents and other significant persons in their world convey to the children much about themselves. Many children have already established, unconsciously, a fairly definite and stable self-concept. A teacher's evaluation of the child, as mediated by different treatment over a few months, is not likely to change the child's self-concept significantly, just as the minor amount of information provided by intelligence test scores is not likely to produce a radical change in the teacher's expectations concerning the child. Although neither teacher nor student says so out loud, each in effect says, "How can I hear what you say when so many other past and present voices, both without and within, are telling me something else?"

A wide variety of studies has demonstrated that acquiring a skill, performing a task well, or receiving favorable evaluations by others in a research context can produce significant temporary changes in self-evaluation in the related areas (Jones & Tagar, 1972). However, persistent and general changes in self-image occur only when the changes in performance and social evaluations are consistent and persistent over time and when they are reinforced by a larger input of relevant information.

Because of the great significance of Rosenthal and Jacobsen's results, were they to prove genuine and amenable to generalization, there were repeated attempts to replicate the study, largely without success. Interested readers will find in E. S. Fleming and R. G. Anttonen (1971) a good review of many of these attempts at duplication as well as of their own extensive study, which also failed to support the claims of Rosenthal and Jacobsen. These authors also showed how repeated critical re-evaluations of the Rosenthal and Jacobsen data indicate that the original data did not warrant the claims and generalizations that were made.

The Fleming and Anttonen study, as well as others (for example, Finn, 1972), show that the self-fulfilling prophecy in education does not operate as Rosenthal and Jacobsen claim. Most teachers are able to identify children with inappropriately assigned, inflated test scores and high predictions of probable achievement. Living with these children day to day, with constant evaluative input, they receive information that completely overshadows the results of a faulty test-derived evaluation. The external imposition of an expectation is readily canceled when it is dissonant with the continual flow of information relative to the student's potential and achievement. J. B. Dusek (1975) made a comprehensive survey of the published studies in which teachers either were told that certain identified students should do well and significantly improve academically, or were given specific false test scores or trait assignments, to determine the degree to which this information would bias teachers' judgments and/or influence the students' performances. After a critical examination of the available evidence, Dusek concluded that the research evidence offers little or no support for these propositions.

However, a good deal of evidence indicates that teachers, like all others, do categorize and stereotype children on the basis of culturewide attitudes and expectations. Some of these category-related attitudes and expectations involve such variables as sex, social class, race, and ethnic group. Culturewide stereotypes and social expectations can become self-fulfilling prophecies, particularly when they are inculcated early in life and receive widespread support from society. Studies of the various factors operative in assigning children to special-education classes have brought to light several of these stereotyping expectations (Finn, 1972).

Not all teacher-student expectations constitute handicapping stereotypes. Dusek (1975) surveyed the relevant literature and found that teachers' self-generated expectations are positively related to student achievement. On further inquiry, he found that teachers' expectations often resulted in different treatment of students, reflecting the teachers' perception of the most effective ways of teaching children with differing aptitudes and needs, rather than prejudicial stereotyping. Teacher expectations may be beneficial when they lead to different treatment designed to meet the child's individual needs and characteristics.

Children placed in special or homogeneous classes are presumably segregated for their own good. These specialized, high-cost programs are designed to provide for the unique educational needs of deviant children so as to reduce the extent of their handicap and make it possible for them more nearly to realize their potential. Most of the people concerned with selecting children and certifying their eligibility for placement in special facilities, programs, and sections are reasonably competent, well-intentioned people, sincerely interested in providing deviant children with the best possible education. In practice, however, many informal and unacknowledged selective factors operate in the actual placement of children in special-education classes. Children certified as eligible by committees who screen candidates for special-class or special-school placement are almost universally initially referred by teachers. Children referred as possibly mentally retarded, educationally handicapped, neurologically impaired, or emotionally disturbed are so nominated for a variety of reasons. For example, a child technically within one of these categories has an increased probability of being referred for possible removal from the regular class if, in addition to his primary disability, he is also male rather than female, lower- rather than middle- or upper-class, black rather than white, and hyperactive or delinquent rather than docile and well-behaved. Practically every school system has more equally handicapped children in regular classes, with no special provision for their education, than in special classes and/or schools. The likelihood of a child's being transferred back into a regular class from the special class or school decreases as the child has an increasing number of these socially devalued characteristics.

It will be unfortunate if the discrediting of the data and claims of the Rosenthal and Jacobsen study leads to the wholesale discarding of a concept that has considerable validity and usefulness in a broader social context. Experimental evidence, as well as general observation, indicate that one barrier to achievement is lack of motivation, and one component of achievement motivation is expectation of success. A person does not try if he does not believe that he has a reasonable prospect of success. Teachers must have confidence in their students. Certainly teachers who believe that their students cannot learn, do not wish to learn, and have parents who are unconcerned are poor teachers. Similarly, the child who, for whatever reason, is convinced that he cannot learn or that it is not worthwhile to try must somehow have these expectations modified as a necessary prerequisite for learning.

Some studies have attacked the problem of teacher influence on learner expectations of achievement by bypassing the teacher as mediator and providing the student directly with information allegedly indicating whether he has superior or inferior aptitudes for the assigned learning tasks. The difference between these studies and the Rosenthal and Jacobsen type will be clearer if we indicate the different mechanisms assumed to be operating in the two experimental designs. In the Rosenthal-Jacobsen design, the following processes are postulated:

1. Teachers form different expectations for students' achievements in accordance with the information provided them.
2. The teachers then treat students differently because of their different expectations.
3. The students, in turn, respond differently to their different treatment by the teachers.
4. The students' behavior tends to complement the teachers' expectations, which in turn reinforces the teachers' expectations and perpetuates their different treatment.
5. The students' achievements are enhanced or depressed in the direction of the teachers' expectations.

In the studies that bypass the teacher, the students are told that, according to their past achievements and scores on tests, they have either an exceptionally high or low aptitude for achievement in the assigned learning tasks. In one subgroup, which available evidence indicates has high potential, half are told they have high aptitude, whereas the other half are told that they have low potential. Two subgroups of students with low indices of achievement are similarly treated. Studies of this type have shown fairly consistently that there is an interaction between achievement and the type of evaluative information provided. Students with high potential perform better with negative information, whereas students with less actual potential perform better with positive information (Means & Means, 1971).

The interpretation of the different effects produced by expectations, which are themselves presumably induced by the information provided, is not clear. Perhaps the "good" students react to the prediction of lesser success than they are accustomed to as a challenge and attack the problem with greater energy because of the implied threat. The "poor" students, more accustomed to failure, may see the prediction of increased probability of success in the forthcoming learning task as an added incentive to acquire some of that scarce commodity.

In a related study by M. M. Rappaport and H. Rappaport (1975), information designed to induce positive expectations concerning student achievement was given (a) to the teachers, or (b) to the students, or (c) to both. This study found that inducing positive expectations in the pupils was more effective than doing the same for the teachers, and the pupil-alone situation was just as effective as when the information was supplied to both pupils and teachers. R. K. Yoshida and C. E. Meyers (1975) tried to determine to what extent labeling a child as mentally retarded initiated and sustained a self-fulfilling prophecy in teachers. In their study, experienced teachers were shown the videotaped performances of a black child said to be either in a regular sixth grade or in an EMR special classroom. The learning task videotaped was a concept formation task presumably covering a considerable period of time. The teachers observed a child responding to four sets of concept formation tasks defined as tests. The teachers were provided with a description of the child doing the learning. In all cases the descriptions were identical except, in some cases, the child was described as in a regular sixth grade and in other cases in an EMR class. Following each of the four presentations, the teachers were asked questions designed to measure their expectations concerning the child's probable future performance on the concept formation tasks. They were also asked to predict how many of the next set of ten items the child would answer correctly. In this study the EMR label did not elicit lower mean expectancy scores. For both labeling conditions the teachers showed progressively higher expectancy scores following each of the four tests. It seems that the teachers' personal evaluations of the student's demonstrated performance determined their expectancies, rather than the educational-diagnostic label.

Recent concern over attitudinal barriers to the occupational aspirations of women has highlighted the fact that groups such as women and the lower social classes, not usually classed as handicapped, share some of the characteristics of the latter. For example, girls have a more negative self-image than boys, and girls from lower socio-economic backgrounds are even less certain about their self-worth than are comparable girls from middle-class backgrounds (O'Leary, 1974). Sex and social class stereotypes induce social discrimination, negative self-images, and low levels of aspiration which constitute formidable barriers to achievement, even among the inherently non-disabled.

One study of seventy-six physically disabled college students found significant positive relationships among (a) acceptance of disability, (b) satisfaction with personal relationships, and (c) self-esteem. Measures of self-esteem and acceptance of disability correlated +.52; acceptance of disability and satisfaction with social relationships correlated +.54 with each other. Thus, the manner in which these people view their disabilities is related to how they view themselves in general as well as to their perception of their relationships with others (Linkowski & Dunn, 1974).

LABELING THE DEVIANT

There is abundant evidence that assigning a person to a category and giving him a label create sets and expectations that powerfully influence perception and behavior. We previously indicated that an individual categorized as beautiful or physically attractive is evaluated and treated in more positive ways than an equally competent ugly or less attractive person (Dion, 1972, 1973). Even such minor things as having a name which is perceived as popular and attractive results in one's products being judged as superior in quality to the same products ascribed to a person whose name is judged unpopular and unattractive (Harari & McDavid, 1973).

In one study, clinicians rated interviewees labeled as "patients" as significantly more disturbed than when they were labeled "job applicants" (Langer & Abelson, 1974). In another research study, 180 teachers were asked to indicate the probable degree of incapacity of four cases when the individuals were identified (a) by diagnostic labels only (mentally retarded, neurotic, or schizophrenic); (b) by behavioral descriptions only; and (c) by behavioral descriptions with diagnostic labels. The two conditions in which labels were assigned yielded significantly higher estimations of incapacity than did the behavioral description alone (Herson, 1974). It has been shown that persons with fictitious information indicating that a reasonably normal individual has a history of mental illness (a) prefer to work alone rather than with the ex-mental patient, (b) perceive them as less adequate workers, and (c) blame their mental condition for their failures to cooperate (Farina & Ring, 1965). Even the best-intentioned persons are in conflict when in contact with a person whom they know or believe to be an ex-mental patient. They find their presence slightly disturbing and yet feel that they should support and help them (Farina et al., 1974; Farina & Felner, 1973). Individuals exhibiting identical behavior are increasingly shunned or rejected by others as they are perceived as having (1) not sought help, or as having sought help from (2) a clergyman, (3) a physician, (4) a psychiatrist, or (5) a mental hospital (Phillips, 1975).

Unofficial labeling and stigmatization

As we have stated, the development of perceptual and conceptual categories of people is inevitable. Concomitant with this is the attachment of evaluative judgments and feelings to these categories. Words used to describe, identify, categorize, and label a person inevitably carry evaluative connotations as well as denotative meanings. Relatively affectively neutral words such as *unemployed, poor,* and *obese,* while primarily descriptive of a person's condition, also have value connotation (good or bad, desirable or undesirable) (Gifford, 1975). It is impossible to avoid the stigmatization of socially devalued individuals and/or acts. The facts of socially devalued deviancy are apparent to all sharing these underlying values and are not dependent upon official labeling. Three incidents in the life of one of the authors (C. W. T.) are pertinent to this observation.

The "village idiots" were well known to all the residents of the small community (population 500) where he was reared. Three members of one family were generally recognized as belonging to this category. This was not because of the low status of the entire family, for the parents and two other siblings were recognized as quite normal. The three mentally deficient children were never officially identified or labeled in any way, but this did not prevent their unofficial labeling. Another individual in the same community, less severely deficient, was also the victim of unofficial labeling. On one occasion, several young men were considering some venture and the village wag started to count the members present: 1, 2, 3, 3-1/2—the 1/2 was the village "half-wit," a mildly mentally retarded individual. Everyone laughed at the characterization, which was funny, but also very cruel! The fact of the boy's stigmatized deviancy was apparent to all in the community.

The third incident occurred when the writer was taking a course in mental testing during the early years of the testing movement. One course requirement was the administration of twenty-five individual Binets and one group test. Rewarding the first child five cents for taking the Binet resulted in an ample supply of volunteers for the individual test. However, gaining access to an appropriate group was not so easy. After several turn-downs, the principal of the local high school said that he would allow a group to be tested. On reporting to his office, the writer was referred to an unoccupied classroom where individuals to be tested would assemble. The hour proved to be the general convocation period, and the principal was sending designated children to the room one at a time. As they strolled in, they looked around inquiringly and asked why they had been sent. They were told to take seats and when they were all there, an explanation would be given. The early comers kept up an active conversation as to what it all meant. Finally, when about half the group was assembled, one of the first boys to enter the room said, "Oh, I know, we are all the dumbbells!" He was right and the others agreed. The principal had picked out the "slow learners" to be tested. None had been given mental tests and they were not segregated or otherwise officially designated or labeled. However, they were self-labeled, and also categorized by their peers.

Unofficial labeling precedes the corresponding official process and mediates many of the same effects. Judging from the available evidence, recent attempts to eliminate the stigma of special-class placement in school have not been particularly successful. Almost without exception, the studies that originated with G. O. Johnson in 1950 and have continued down to the present (Goodman, Gottlieb, & Harrison, 1972; Jones, 1972; Gottlieb & Budoff, 1973; Iano et al., 1974) have shown: (1) that intelligence-test-defined mentally retarded children in regular classes are uniformly informally labeled and sociometrically either isolated or actively rejected by their peers; (2) that the physically integrated mentally retarded school children are not more socially accepted by their peers than are comparable segregated mental retardates; and (3) that retarded children in the new "open" ungraded classroom situation are rejected as often, and in one study (Gottlieb & Budoff, 1973) more often, than are comparable children in an integrated regular "walled-in" single-grade classroom. J. Gottlieb and M. Budoff found that the mentally retarded children in both these integrated-classroom situations were more rejected by peers than were segregated mildly mentally retarded children.

The research evidence of the pre-psychotic or prelabeled status of the mentally ill is less satisfactory than is that concerning the mentally retarded. However, available evidence indicates that mentally ill persons are not solely the prisoners of the stereotype and the social policies and practices resulting from their being labeled, as some people have contended. The "myth" of mental illness has often been presented as a modern invention. However, the conditions encompassed by this term have apparently been found in every society known to us. The major categories of mental illness are known in all cultures, although the terms applied to them, and the theories concerning them, differ sharply from our own. Western psychiatrists, native healers, and medicine men alike identify a person with overt psychotic symptoms as abnormal. Mental disorders are identified even when the language has no distinctive label for the category. The signs and symptoms of mental deterioration and derangement are recognized in practically all societies (Eisenberg, 1973).

The absence of formal diagnosis and labeling does not abolish the behavior or category. What does differ cross-culturally is conceptions concerning etiology and differences in social management.

In many societies, the patient's immediate or extended family or the local community of neighbors assumes the responsibility for the affected individual's care and protection. J. W. Eaton and R. J. Weil (1955) lived in and studied the incidence of mental illness and mental retardation in a relatively isolated and closely knit community of Hutterites. It was believed that mental conditions were practically nonexistent in such communities. However, Eaton and Weil found people displaying all the symptoms of mental disorders and mental retardation. What did differ from the larger surrounding culture was that such individuals were encouraged to participate in the normal life of the hutterite community as much as possible, and the entire community assumed responsibility for their care and protection. The deviant individuals were known by all the people in the community, and their limitations were accepted without their being labeled or rejected. Only rarely did they become residents of a state hospital and consequently a statistic. The favorable mental-health record of the hutterites was not the result of the absence of potential "patients," but rather reflected the unique communitywide attitudes and ways of handling the problem.

The cultural content of labeling

The social scientists who view mental illness as purely a matter of cultural relativism point out that behavior considered abnormal in one society is valued and considered admirable in another. Only within limits does this seem to be true. At times the blind have been considered as specially blessed and have been revered as seers and prophets. Sometimes they were believed to possess an inner sight denied to those with normal vision. In other times, the babblings of the psychotic have been interpreted as messages in a foreign tongue that required a special interpreter. Certainly what is taken for reality or for fantasy is relative to the times and social context. If we regard as mad any person who believes in the devil and in demoniacal possession, then for centuries entire populations, diverse civilizations, and certain contemporary subgroups have been composed only of the mad. For a member of a werewolf cult or an untutored Jamaican to claim powers of witchcraft or to claim to be bewitched is not indicative of any mental disorder. However, for a Harvard professor seriously to make these same claims is to bring his mental stability into question. That many symptoms of mental disorder are subject to cultural relativism complicates the problem but does not mean that delusions and hallucinations are myths fabricated by society and purely matters of arbitrary labeling. Whatever the cause of a mental disorder—organic, psychogenic, social, or a mixture of all three—the form of the accompanying delusions, hallucinations, obsessions, phobias, and compulsions is molded by the individual's cultural background and his unique repertoire of information and beliefs. In the expression of these disorders he will use the language he knows best and employ the imagery and beliefs of his culture. The person with delusions of grandeur will fancy himself Jesus in one society, Mohammed in another, Buddha in a third, and a talented medicine man in a fourth. This obviously means that the identifications involved and the metaphors used for the expression of delusions are social in origin, but it tells us nothing about the origins of the underlying autistic processes.

Official statistics show tremendous cross-cultural and urban-versus-rural differences in the relative number of *identified* mentally ill. However, this is largely the result of the complex social processes involved in transforming a troubled person into a statistical "patient." This social process involves the socio-educational-economic level of the family, the state of available medical and psychological information, and the availability of diagnostic-treatment facilities. Proximity to treatment facilities, knowledge concerning and belief in the efficacy of treatment, and ease of access to treatment facilities with low-stigmatizing designations all facilitate high admission rates. These factors have nothing to do with the actual prevalence of people in trouble, but do influence the number of cases officially tabulated. These facts make the determination of the impact of population densities, ways of living, and other cultural variables exceedingly difficult.

We have stated that available evidence indicates that the major categories of mental deviants are found in every society. Studies of the probability that a person will be diagnosed as schizophrenic seem to vary only slightly from country to country at comparable levels of development. In countries as diverse as Switzerland, Iceland, and Japan, the rates vary from .73 to 1.23 percent. The modal figure for all the nations reporting is 1.0 percent (Eisenberg, 1973). J. M. Murphy (1976) estimates the rates of nonhospitalized schizophrenia in Swedish, Canadian, Eskimo, and Yoruba (West African) populations to be 5.7, 5.6, 4.4, and 6.8 per 1,000 population respectively. Murphy says the symptoms of mental illness are manifestations of a type of affliction shared by virtually all peoples. Some social-learning theorists have argued that the frantic pace of life (the rat race) and high population densities in the industrialized nations have increased the incidence of mental disorders. However, using all the available evidence, H. Goldhamer and A. W. Marshall (1949) estimated that the incidence rates in the state of Massachusetts did not change substantially in the years from 1840 to 1940. Surveys indicate that the rate of psychotic illness in Berlevaag—a relatively isolated community in northern Norway—were practically the same in 1973 as in 1944 (Bjarnar et al., 1975). This does not mean that social factors are not involved in the etiology of mental disorders, but it does indicate that these factors are probably more constant cross-culturally and over time than the proponents of a purely cultural relativism would imply.

Although the available evidence is less extensive than for the mentally retarded, it indicates that teachers and peers alike recognize as significantly different from others those children who later become psychotic. Their unofficial labeling as "queer" or "nuts" long precedes their official categorization (Bower, Shellhamer, & Dailey, 1960; Robins, 1966; Westman, Rice, & Berman, 1967; Cowen et al., 1973).

WHEN DEVIANCY IS CRIMINALIZED

Becoming criminals further alters people's self-image and also drives them into additional ways of acting that create new problems of deviancy for themselves and society. Some of these incremental deviancies are the focusing of their life more and more around their deviancy, their entering into deviant subcultures, and their engaging in additional types of secondary crime, such as robbery, prostitution, pimping, and trafficking in drugs, partly as a consequence of the official criminalization of the original deviant acts.

One of the primary effects intended to result from the enactment and enforcement of criminal laws is the prevention of certain acts from occurring. However, the criminalization of specific acts also has widespread secondary effects, many of which may aggravate the situation that the laws were intended to improve. These secondary effects are most obvious when legal sanctions are used to control behavioral deviancies that are on the borderline of criminality, morality, mental health, and social mores. Pornography, sexual deviancy, and drug addiction are examples of such deviancies.

Although the bulk of the behavioral deviations conventionally labeled "mental health problems" have not been officially criminalized historically and even today, persons judged to be mentally ill and mentally retarded have been treated in ways very similar to convicted criminals. The "careers" of the convicted criminal and the institutionalized mental patient both begin with deviant behavior judged sufficiently serious for someone to initiate action. Both begin with a complainant—someone who initiates the action that ultimately leads to institutionalization.

The official view is that inmates of facilities for mental deviates are there because they are suffering from mental defects, and prisoners are incarcerated because they have broken the law. However, at any given time, the number of undiagnosed and unsegregated mentally defective individuals, as well as the number of undetected and/or unconvicted lawbreakers, far exceeds the number convicted, or diagnosed and institutionalized. This means that, in both cases, contingencies other than the official "cause" of their incarceration are involved in their institutionalization.

The admitting procedures for both mental deviates and convicts are remarkably similar. Historically both have been deprived of most of their liberties and civil rights. The physician and the jailer are given legal mandates over the treatment and fate of the inmate. The lives of both are regulated and ordered according to an authoritarian disciplinary system. Quiet and obedient behavior leads to "promotion" and early release. Obstreperous and unruly behavior is indicative of continued pathology or criminality and leads to detention and further restriction of one's activities or withdrawal of privileges. Prisoners and mental deviates alike learn that it is to their advantage to play the institutional game well. Both are stigmatized and largely deserted by society. The secondary effects of a diagnosis of major mental defect and the conviction of a crime and institutionalization are very similar. E. Goffman (1963), Szasz (1974), Warren (1974) and Hobbs (1975) have treated this topic in much more detail.

DENIAL VERSUS ACCEPTANCE OF A DISABILITY

The person with a disability, and those who work with the disabled, have problems in two related areas. One problem involves capacities and aptitudes, abilities and disabilities. The second has to do with levels of motivation and the setting of realistic levels of aspiration. The problem of abilities and disabilities, as previously indicated, can be attacked with tests and other measuring devices. Medical, psychological, educational, and sociological testing instruments and rating devices make it possible to indicate roughly the extent of organic, educational, psychological, and social impairment.

However, the problem of establishing realistic levels of aspiration in the social, personal adjustment, educational, and occupational areas is much more complex. It not only involves the individual himself, particularly his self-concept, but also his family, school, and community—indeed, his whole society. The point of crucial impact of all of these social influences is the individual's self-concept, which is largely a distillation of other people's evaluations of him. Each person comes to conceive of himself as adequate or inadequate as he sees himself reflected in the evaluations of others.

Because so many disabled people's lives tend to revolve about their disabilities rather than their abilities, their self-concepts are often unrealistically low. Consequently, their self-expectations, levels of aspiration, and general motivational levels are unnecessarily diminished. Recognizing this, many people are motivated and encouraged by others to *deny* the fact of their disability. When an entire culture puts a high premium on a given ideal state, there is a great deal of reinforcement of behavior which conceals, minimizes, or denies the existence of deviations from that ideal. To associate with the normal on their terms, to act normal, to compete with the normal, then becomes the ideal pattern of one's life. The person with a disability observes that the rewards in this world go, not to the person who accepts those limitations which are seemingly dictated by his condition, but to the individual who either refuses to accept the disability as a handicap or who strives for the cultural ideal despite his condition.

Because of the advantages of being considered normal, almost every person who is able to do so will "pass" on certain occasions. People with epilepsy under control, the hard-of-hearing person, and the partially blind can and often do pass for normal. Homosexuals, drug addicts, and prostitutes, as social deviants, conceal their identities (pass) with the general public, and particularly with the police, but in various ways disclose their identities to special classes of people—clients, connections, pushers, and fellow-members. One solution to the problem of denial versus acknowledgement of a deviancy is to divide one's world into an in-group who "know" and a larger group within which the handicapped individual passes. Nonperceptible handicaps may be known only to one's doctor and immediate family. Those in the know protect the handicapped in his passing. Those sharing a common stigma often provide mutual aid in passing. Homosexual overtures are made in ways nonhomosexuals will not recognize. Ex-prisoners and ex-mental patients assist each other in concealing their previous status to people on the "outside" (Schur, 1965).

However, there are certain genuine limitations which are not to be denied. The blind person cannot enjoy the beauties of the landscape. The use of auditory cues is denied to the deaf. The trainable child cannot master calculus. To expect these people to strive for such goals is asking them to try for the impossible. To deny completely the existence of a disability requires that the person act as if the condition did not exist. And to do this, the individual, as well as those about him, must pretend that he is something or someone other than himself. He must become an actor, and acting twenty-four hours a day is hard work. Concealment indicates shame and involves strain. Despite eternal vigilance and constant work, the person with a disability often cannot get away from his disability. The individual who either verbally or by his actions says, "Treat me just like a nondisabled person, no matter what!" often finds himself in impossible situations.

For example, the blind host who elects to deny his blindness may be faced with the problem of pouring cocktails for his guests. None of the alternatives open to him permit him to act like a seeing person. The usual way for a blind person to fill a glass is to hook one finger over its edge and then pour until the liquid reaches the finger. In this way the glasses can be uniformly and properly filled. However, this method is not available to the person who is acting like a sighted individual; besides, some people object to having another person's fingers in their cocktails. Another method of pouring, which follows the pattern of the sighted, is to pour the liquid from a sufficient height so that it makes a noise as it flows into the glass. The fullness of the glass can be estimated from the change in sound and the weight of the glass as it fills. But this method is not very accurate; it is hazardous to pour from a distance without visual guidance and difficult to judge when the glass is properly filled. There is no practical way for a blind person to fill glasses as do the sighted.

Again, a person who is hard of hearing may try to act as if his hearing were normal. Such a person tries to listen hard. He must never say "What?" He tries to watch other people's faces and gestures for cues. In dimly lit rooms he pretends to be in reverie or asleep. He develops ways to get people to repeat without actually asking them to. He invents humorous stories to account for mistakes which result from his failure to hear accurately. He fakes daydreaming, absentmindedness, boredom, and indifference. In situations where hearing is difficult, he talks all the time. Frances Warfield (1948) gives a vivid autobiographical account of these and other defensive maneuvers of the partially deaf individual who tries to deny his disability. A post-polio adolescent who denied his orthopedic handicap was Raymond Goldman (1947), who would swim early in the morning to prevent others from seeing his legs. When girls were present, he would not walk. When his braces were first fitted, he hated them and refused to wear them. When he was in the fifth grade he took his cue from a telephone repair man and referred to his braces as "tree-climbers."

One solution to the problems posed by socially devalued deviancy is to accept the reality of the deviancy but to deny the stigma, diminish the stigmatizing effect by pointing out the greater defects in "normals," or insist that the deviant individuals really possess special positive values. The Garveyites, the Black Muslims, and other black separatists have propounded a militant segregationist or secessionist ideology for the blacks of America. The black separatist emphasizes the special values, distinguishing characteristics, and unique contributions of his kind. He flaunts the stereotypical attributes such as color (black is beautiful), distinctive dress ("native" costumes and "natural" hair style), and articles of diet ("soul food"). The orthopedically handicapped sometimes develop the concept of the greater defects in supposedly "normal" people. The outwardly healthy and robust body hides an inwardly crippled and corrupt mind. The blind sees the normally sighted as having eyes but failing to see. They are blind to the real meanings and significances of the things they experience. People with normal ears are deaf to the pleas of other people. The socially devalued deviant may convert the stigmatized component of his self into a symbol of superiority. This effect can be facilitated by a derogation of the "normal" referent group.

The price of passing is high and the effort is often futile. When a person must constantly be vigilant to deny his disability, it becomes the central focus of his life. He may resort to partial social isolation to help conceal his defect and thus fend off possible discovery.

If denial is not feasible, what about accepting one's disability? Mental hygienists insist upon the virtues of acceptance of oneself as a prerequisite of mental health. But acceptance of one's disability involves a lowering of one's level of aspiration and a renunciation of many of the goals of the nondisabled. In a culture which places a high value on either the normal or the ideal, the acceptance of one's disability often carries with it an acceptance of a generally inferior status—a devaluation of the disabled individual as a person.

Acceptance of one's handicap includes the acknowledgment of the contaminated aspects of his social identity. The acknowledgment of the handicap implies acceptance that some of his attributes warrant his social derogation. If the person accepts all the implications of his disability, he may so succumb to his condition that he becomes just as unrealistic as the person who elects to deny his disability. When the disabled person concludes, because of his condition, that "it is not worthwhile to live," when he tries "to go into hiding and never show his face for the rest of his life," when he feels so sorry for himself that he expects others to do for him many things that he can well learn to do for himself, he is succumbing to his disability.

Goffman (1963) points out the paradox that when handicapped individuals are urged to accept themselves and either explicitly or implicitly are told that as members of the genus they are entitled to full acceptance and respect from others as whole people, they are also told that they are different and that it is foolish to either deny or ignore this difference. The normal's acceptance of the handicapped is always conditional. Satisfactory social relationships between normals and deviants are dependent upon the latter voluntarily refraining from "cashing in" on the claim of acceptance beyond the point that normals find comfortable. Positive relationships are dependent upon the implied promise that the extended credit of complete acceptance will never be fully used.

Goffman also shows that a previously stigmatized person does not attain complete acceptance as a whole human being following remediation or repair of his defect. The full restoration of function does not typically result in his acquisition of fully normal status. The change of status is from that of one with a defect to someone with a history of having corrected a defect, but the stigma of having been defective persists. The "reformed" alcoholic and the "cured" drug addict are still perceived as more vulnerable and less complete human beings than are individuals with no such histories of deviancy.

Any show of anger by an ex-convict or an ex-psychotic is seen as a direct expression of his basic criminal or psychotic nature. A sarcastic remark to a companion, a heated argument with a spouse, or a sudden change in mood is perceived as a manifestation of his defectiveness. These same responses by a nonstigmatized person are seen as the normal reactions of ordinary people, signifying nothing in particular.

In this connection it may be helpful to make clearer certain distinctions which have long been implicit and are now becoming explicit in our thinking concerning the disabled. Just as we found the distinctions between the concepts of disability and handicap to be useful, similar distinctions between *denying* one's disability and *coping* with it, on the one hand, and between *accepting* one's limitations and *succumbing* to them, on the other, may be equally helpful.

Accepting a disability without succumbing to it

How to accept one's limitations without succumbing to them is the problem. To accept one's disability and oneself as a person with a disability requires a clarification of what one can and cannot do. When this is achieved, the individual renounces the goals that are closed to him and devotes himself to the achievement of the possible. When a person is able to say to himself and to others, "This is my limitation; these things I cannot do," he eliminates much uncertainty and ambiguity from his life. He is now free to study the requirements of new or different situations realistically and objectively in terms of his abilities and disabilities. Acceptance does not require that the status quo be rationalized in a Pollyannaish way as the most desirable, nor does it require a flight into apathy, egocentricity, or hypochondria. The disability can be perceived as inconvenient and limiting without being debasing, and the person can strive to improve his condition in a realistic way. Beatrice Wright (1960, 1974) has developed the concept of the "acceptance of loss" very well. Interested readers will find her book very helpful.

One difficulty with those charitable agencies and individuals who are dominantly sentimentally helpful in their approach to people with disabilities is that they may unwittingly reinforce a tendency toward succumbing. Pity and charity, as approaches to rehabilitation, often do not focus on acceptance and coping. The more helpless and dependent the individual, the more he is worthy of sympathy, compassion, pity, and charity—but these may operate to reinforce his dependent behavior.

COPING WITH A DISABILITY WITHOUT DENYING IT

The difficulties which arise from denying the existence of a disability have already been indicated. Concealing the disability does not eradicate it. The too strenuous striving for acceptance by others negates itself. Denial grows out of the individual's inability to accept himself, and acceptance of one's limitations is a prerequisite to coping with them. Having accepted a disability without succumbing to it, the individual no longer needs to deny the limitations; he is free to cope with life to the best of his abilities. Coping involves making the most of what one has, and arranging one's life according to one's abilities. The person deprived of vision copes by learning to read and write in Braille; learning to type; and learning to use a cane or a seeing-eye dog. He acquires those skills which are open to him. He investigates and makes use of all of the educational and social facilities that are available, he does not disregard his difficulties (that would be denial), nor is he overwhelmed by them (that would be succumbing). But *how* to cope with one's disability without denying its existence and *how* to accept an infirmity without succumbing to it are two major problems of the disabled.

When the disabled person cannot get away from his disability, the question becomes how he can best get along with it. Overcompensating in the area of one's disability, even when possible, may drive the individual to outward success, but not to personal adjustment. It is only when a person feels guilty about his disability that he has something to disprove or make up for. It is only when one feels especially bad in one respect that he must be especially good in another to counterbalance it and thus disprove that he is unworthy. The successful person copes with the problems of status by engaging in activities in which the prospects of satisfactory achievement and personal satisfaction are greatest, rather than by feeling compelled to do better in the area of his disability (in order to deny his handicap) or in a closely related area (in order to make up for his deficiency). For the person with serious disabilities to insist on competing and winning over the nonhandicapped may mean that the individual has not adjusted to the infirmity and is over-motivated to achieve in this particular area just to prove the extent to which it does matter—the extent to which it is overvalued.

Wright (1974) has dichotomized a series of attitudes and practices which encourage either coping or succumbing behavior on the part of the handicapped. These are summarized and paraphrased below:

Encouragements to coping	*Encouragements to succumbing*
1. Emphasizing what the individual can do	1. Emphasizing the individual's limitations rather than his assets
2. Perceiving the person's basic self as worthwhile	2. So overvaluing the defective components of the self that the person has an unrealistically low social and self-image
3. Seeing the handicapped individual as playing an active role in planning and living his life	3. Seeing the handicapped person as passively directed and helped by others
4. Valuing even minor accomplishments in themselves, not because they attain or exceed a norm	4. Evaluating accomplishments in terms of external norms
5. Perceiving the limiting and negative components of the self as manageable	5. Seeing the person's limitations as overwhelming
6. Managing limitations by ameliorating them to the degree practical and then living on satisfactory terms with the inherent limitations	6. Giving up in the face of difficulties

Ideally, the handicapped person sees himself as a full human being, one who at worst happens to be excluded from a limited area of social or occupational life. He is not a type or category but a unique human being, in the same way as the nonhandicapped. He should fulfill the obligations of the nonhandicapped as fully as he can, stopping short only when the effort required to overcome or deny his defectiveness increases its obviousness.

SUMMARY

Every person and every social group develops a set of expectations concerning other people and groups, a set of criteria for discriminating among them, and a set of values for judging these people and their acts.

Historically more attention has been focused on the deviating individuals than on the social origin and consequences of the deviancies and the effects of these unofficial expectations and official definitions of the deviants and their acts. Recently the social factors contributing to deviancy have been emphasized. It does not require official identification and/or labeling to identify most individuals who deviate in socially devalued ways. The general public identifies and, in many ways, segregates, rejects, and makes life difficult for stigmatized deviants. Official identification and labeling add to the unofficial stigmatization but are often necessary to provide legal, financial, and educational assistance to those who require it.

What is done about a personal-social problem is powerfully influenced by how it is defined and perceived. When a problem is defined or perceived as "person-centered" (something inherently within the individual), solutions will be sought by changing the person. When the same problem is perceived as "situation-centered," remediation will be directed at changing the socio-economic-educational system. However, neither the extreme "person-centered" position nor the solely "situation-centered" position seems tenable. All human traits and behaviors are the result of the interactive outcomes of environmental circumstances and the nature of the individual.

Deviances can be conceptualized as forming a continuum in terms of their inherent-organic and social-environmental determiners. At one extreme are those organic deviants who are so disabled as to be incapable of independent existence and/or functioning in any conceivable society. In the intermediate positions are those categories of disabilities in which the total handicap has both significant inherent-organic and social-environmental contributions. At the other extreme are those disabilities in which the major portion of the handicap is imposed by social attitudes and restrictions as well as legal constraints.

Denial of a disability (acting as if it does not exist) is distinguished from *coping* with a disability (developing the most adequate substitute alternatives). *Accepting* a disability (learning to live with it) is differentiated from *succumbing* to it (being overwhelmed by the threat).

REFERENCES

BAROCAS, R., & F. L. VANCE, "Physical Appearance and Personal Adjustment Counseling," *Journal of Counseling Psychology*, 1974, *21*, 96–100.

BJARNAR, E.; R. MELSOM; H. REPPERGAARD; & C. ASTRUP, "A Social Psychiatric Investigation of a Rural District in Northern Norway: A Preliminary Communication," *Acta Psychiatrica Scandinavia*, 1975, *51*, 19–24.

BOWER, E. M., T. A. SHELLHAMER, & J. DAILEY, "School Characteristics of Male Adolescents Who Later Became Schizophrenics," *American Journal of Orthopsychiatry,* 1960, *30,* 712–29.

BRAGINSKY, B. M., & D. D. BRAGINSKY, "Mental Hospitals as Resorts," *Psychology Today,* March 1973, *6,* 22–23.

BRAGINSKY, B., & D. D. BRAGINSKY, "The Mentally Retarded: Society's Hansels and Gretels," *Psychology Today,* 1974, 7 (10), 18–30.

CAVIOR, N., & P. R. DOHECHI, "Physical Attractiveness, Perceived Attitude Similarity, and Academic Achievement as Contributors to Interpersonal Attraction among Adolescents," *Developmental Psychology,* 1973, *9,* 44–54.

CLIFFORD, M., & E. WALSTER, "The Effect of Physical Attractiveness on Teachers' Expectations," *Sociology of Education,* 1973, *46,* 248–50.

COWEN, E. L.; A. PEDERSON; H. BABEGIAN; L. D. IZZO; & M. A. FROST, "Long-term Follow-up of Early Detected Vulnerable Children," *Journal of Consulting and Clinical Psychology,* 1973, *39,* 1–5.

CURRIE, R. J., & W. R. REID, "Abrasion: Synonym for Trouble," *Journal of Special Education,* 1973, *7,* 365–71.

DION, K. K., "Physical Attractiveness and Evaluation of Children's Transgressions," *Journal of Personality and Social Psychology,* 1972, *24,* 207–13.

DION, K. K., "Young Childrens' Stereotyping of Facial Attractiveness," *Developmental Psychology,* 1973, *9,* 183–88.

DION, K. K., "Children's Physical Attractiveness and Sex as Determinants of Adult Punitiveness," *Developmental Psychology,* 1974, *10,* 772–78.

DION, K. L., "Cohesiveness as a Determiner of Ingroup-Outgroup Bias," *Journal of Personality and Social Psychology,* 1973, *28,* 163–71.

DUSEK, J. B., "Do Teachers Bias Children's Learning?" *Review of Educational Research,* 1975, *45,* 661–84.

EATON, J. W., & R. J. WEIL, *Culture and Mental Disorders* (New York: Free Press, 1955).

EISENBERG, L., "Psychiatric Intervention," *Scientific American,* Sept. 1973, *229* (3), 116–27.

EKEHAMMAR, B., "Interactionism in Personality from a Historical Perspective," *Psychological Bulletin,* 1974, *81,* 1026–48.

EYSENCK, H. J., ed., *Handbook of Abnormal Psychology* (San Diego, Ca.: Robert R. Knapp, 1973).

FARINA, A., & R. D. FELNER, "Employer Interviewer Reactions to Former Mental Patients," *Journal of Abnormal Psychology,* 1973, *82,* 268–72.

FARINA, A., & K. RING, "The Influence of Perceived Mental Illness on Interpersonal Relations," *Journal of Abnormal Psychology,* 1965, *70,* 47–51.

FARINA, A.; J. THAW; J. D. LOVERN; & D. MARGANE, "People's Reactions to a Former Mental Patient Moving to Their Neighborhood," *Journal of Community Psychology,* 1974, *2,* 108–12.

FINN, J. D., "Expectations and the Educational Environment," *Review of Educational Research,* 1972, *42,* 387–410.

FLEMING, E. S., & R. G. ANTTONEN, "Teacher Expectancy or My Fair Lady," *American Education Research Journal,* 1971, *8,* 241–52.

GIFFORD, R. K., "Information Properties of Descriptive Words," *Journal of Personality and Social Psychology*, 1975, *31*, 727–34.

GOFFMAN, E., *Stigma: Notes on the Management of Spoiled Identity* (Englewood Cliffs, N.J.: Prentice-Hall, 1963).

GOLDBERG, R. T., "Adjustment of Children with Invisible and Visible Handicaps: Congenital Heart Disease and Facial Burns," *Journal of Counseling Psychology*, 1974, *21*, 428–32.

GOLDHAMER, H., & A. W. MARSHALL, *Psychoses and Civilization* (New York: Free Press, 1949).

GOLDMAN, R., *Even the Night* (New York: Macmillan, 1947).

GOODMAN, H., J. GOTTLIEB, & R. H. HARRISON, "Social Acceptance of EMR's Integrated into a Nongraded Elementary School," *American Journal of Mental Deficiency*, 1972, *76*, 412–17.

GOTTLIEB, J., & M. BUDOFF, "Social Acceptability of Retarded Children in Non-graded Schools Differing in Architecture," *American Journal of Mental Deficiency*, 1973, *78*, 15–19.

GRAZIANO, A. M., & R. S. FINK, "Second-order Effects on Mental Health Treatment," *Journal of Consulting and Clinical Psychology*, 1973, *40*, 356–64.

HARARI, H., & J. W. McDAVID, "Name Stereotypes and Teacher Expectations," *Journal of Educational Psychology*, 1973, *65*, 272.

HERSCH, C., "Social History, Mental Health, and Community Control," *American Psychologist*, 1972, *27*, 749–54.

HERSON, P. F., "Biasing Effects of Diagnostic Labels and Sex of Pupil on Teachers' Views of Pupil's Mental Health," *Journal of Educational Psychology*, 1974, *66*, 117–22.

HOBBS, N., *The Futures of Children* (San Francisco: Jossey-Bass, 1975).

HURVITZ, N., "Psychotherapy as a Means of Social Control," *Journal of Consulting and Clinical Psychology*, 1973, *40*, 232–39.

IANO, R. P.; D. AYERS; H. B. HELLER; J. F. McGETTIGAN; & V. S. WALKER, "Sociometric Status of Retarded Children in an Integrative Program," *Exceptional Children*, 1974, *40*, 267–71.

JOHNSON, G. O., "A Study of the Social Position of Handicapped Children in the Regular Grade," *American Journal of Mental Deficiency*, 1950, *55*, 60–86.

JONES, R. L., "Labels and Stigma in Special Education," *Exceptional Children*, 1972, *38*, 353–64.

JONES, S. C., & R. TAGAR, "Exposure to Others, Need for Social Approval, and Reactions to Agreement and Disagreement from Others," *Journal of Social Psychology*, 1972, *86*, 111–30.

KOPEL, S., & H. ARKOWITZ, "The Role of Attribution and Self-perception in Behavior Change: Implications for Behavior Change," *Genetic Psychology Monographs*, 1975, *92*, 175–212.

KREBS, D., & A. A. ADINOLFI, "Physical Attractiveness, Social Relations, and Personality Style," *Journal of Personality and Social Psychology*, 1975, *31*, 245–53.

LANDY, D., & E. ARONSON, "The Influence of the Character of the Criminal and his Victim on the Decisions of Simulated Jurors," in D. J. Steffensmeier & R. M. Terry, eds., *Examining Deviance Experimentally* (Port Washington, N.Y.: Alfred, 1975).

LANDY, D., & H. SIGALL, "Beauty Is Talent: Test Evaluation as a Function of the Performer's Physical Attractiveness," *Journal of Personality and Social Psychology*, 1974, *29*, 299–304.

LANGER, E. J., & R. P. ABELSON, "A Patient by Any Other Name . . . : Clinician Group Differences in Labeling Bias," *Journal of Consulting and Clinical Psychology*, 1974, *42*, 4–9.

LEIFER, R., *In the Name of Mental Health* (New York: Science House, 1969).

LINKOWSKI, D. C., & M. A. DUNN, "Self-concept and Acceptance of Disability," *Rehabilitation Counseling Bulletin*, 1974, *18* (1), 28–32.

MATHES, E. W., & A. KAHN, "Physical Attractiveness, Happiness, Neuroticism, and Self-esteem," *Journal of Psychology*, 1975, *90*, 27–31.

MEANS, R. S., & G. H. MEANS, "Achievement as a Function of the Presence of Prior Information Concerning Aptitudes," *Journal of Educational Psychology*, 1971, *62*, 185–87.

MELLIN, G. W., & M. KATZENSTEIN, "The Saga of Thalidomide," *New England Journal of Medicine*, 1962, *267*, 1184–93, 1238–64.

MERCUM, J. R., *Labeling the Mentally Retarded* (Berkeley: University of California Press, 1973).

MIRNS, P. R., J. J. HARTNETT, & W. R. NAY, "Interpersonal Attraction and Help Volunteering as a Function of Physical Attractiveness," *Journal of Psychology*, 1975, *89*, 125–31.

MURPHY, J. M., "Psychiatric Labeling in Cross-Cultural Perspective," *Science*, 1976, *191*, 1019–28.

NAIR, K., *The Lonely Furrow: Farming in the United States, Japan, and India* (Ann Arbor: University of Michigan Press, 1970).

O'LEARY, V. E., "Some Attitudinal Barriers to Occupational Aspirations in Women," *Psychological Bulletin*, 1974, *81*, 809–26.

PHILLIPS, D. L., "Rejection: A Possible Consequence of Seeking Help for Mental Disorders," in D. J. Steffensmeier & R. M. Terry, eds., *Examining Deviancy Experimentally* (Port Washington, N.Y.: Alfred, 1975).

RAPPAPORT, J.; W. S. DAVIDSON; M. N. WILSON; & A. MITCHELL, "Alternatives to Blaming the Victim or the Environment," *American Psychologist*, 1975, *30*, 525–28.

RAPPAPORT, M. M., & H. RAPPAPORT, "The Other Half of the Expectancy Equation: Pygmalion," *Journal of Educational Psychology*, 1975, *67*, 531–36.

ROBINS, L. N., *Deviant Children Grow Up* (Baltimore, Md.: Williams & Wilkins, 1966).

ROSENTHAL, R., & L. JACOBSEN, *Pygmalion in the Classroom* (New York: Holt, Rinehart and Winston, 1968).

SARBIN, T. R., & J. C. MANCUSO, "Paradigms and Moral Judgments: Improper Conduct Is Not Disease," *Journal of Consulting and Clinical Psychology*, 1972, *39*, 6–8.

SCHEIDT, F. J., "Deviance, Power, and the Occult: A Field Study," *The Journal of Psychology*, 1974, *87*, 21–28.

SCHUR, E. M., *Crimes Without Victims* (Englewood Cliffs, N.J.: Prentice-Hall, 1965).

SHONTZ, F. C., "Physical Disability and Personality," in W. S. Neff, ed., *Rehabilitation Psychology* (Washington, D.C.: American Psychological Association, 1971).

SIEGLER, M., & H. OSMOND, *Models of Madness, Models of Medicine* (New York: Macmillan, 1975).

SIGALL, H., & D. LANDY, "Radiating Beauty: Effects of Having a Physically Attractive Partner and Person Perception," *Journal of Personality and Social Psychology*, 1973, *28*, 218–24.

STAPLETON, R. E., P. NACCI, & J. T. TEDECHI, "Interpersonal Attraction and the Reciprocation of Benefits," *Journal of Personality and Social Psychology*, 1973, *28*, 199–205.

STEFFENSMEIER, D. J., & R. M. TERRY, "Deviance and Respectability: An Observational Study of Reactions to Shoplifting," *Social Forces*, 1973, *51*, 417–26.

SZASZ, T. S., *Law, Liberty, and Psychiatry* (New York: Macmillan, 1963).

SZASZ, T. S., "Our Despotic Laws Destroy the Right to Self-control," *Psychology Today*, 1974, *8* (7), 19–24, 29, 127.

WARFIELD, F., *Cotton in My Ears* (New York: Viking Press, 1948).

WARREN, C. A., *Identity and Community in the Gay World* (New York: John Wiley & Sons, 1974).

WESTMAN, J. C., D. L. RICE, & E. BERMAN, "Nursery School Behavior and Later School Adjustment," *American Journal of Orthopsychiatry*, 1967, *37*, 725–31.

WILLEY, N. R., & B. R. McCANDLESS, "Social Stereotypes for Normal, Educable Mentally Retarded, and Orthopedically Handicapped Children," *Journal of Special Education*, 1973, *7*, 283–88.

WILLIAMS, R. L., "Scientific Racism and IQ: The Silent Mugging of the Black Community," *Psychology Today*, 1974, *7* (12), 32–41, 110.

WRIGHT, B. A., *Physical Disability: A Psychological Approach* (New York: Harper & Row, 1960).

WRIGHT, B. A., "An Analysis of Attitudes: Dynamics and Effects," *The New Outlook for the Blind*, 1974, *68*, 108–18.

YOSHIDA, R. K., & C. E. MEYERS, "Effects of Labeling as Educable Mentally Retarded on Teachers' Expectancies for Change in a Student's Performance," *Journal of Educational Psychology*, 1975, *67*, 521–27.

Chapter 3

Deviance and stigma

In this book we are principally concerned with the individual who is sufficiently different from his peers to warrant special consideration of some type. However, we consider the minor differences found among "normals" and the deviations of "exceptional" individuals to constitute a continuum. As previously indicated, we believe that the reactions of people along this continuum to their differentness can be understood and handled within a single conceptual framework. The individual differences of ordinary people, people whose deviancies are borderline, the officially labeled deviants, and those individuals whose behavioral deviancies are designated as either exceptionally meritorious or criminal are matters of degree. Furthermore, there is considerable evidence that all degrees and kinds of deviancies have something in common.

REACTIONS TO DEVIANCY

J. L. Freedman and A. N. Doob (1968), T. Moriarty (1974), and C. Maslach (1974) in an interesting series of experiments, have studied the effects of deviancy per se, without regard to the particular deviant characteristic, and have demonstrated that deviancy or feelings of deviancy have marked effects on an individual's behavior. The research was carried out in controlled laboratory situations with "normal" subjects. The studies were deliberately designed to study deviancy more or less in a vacuum without the confounding effects of particular types of deviancy. Using this general research design, they were able to induce feelings of deviancy in their subjects which were similar to the feelings of people who were really deviant in a statistical sense. The subjects receiving deviant feedback rated themselves as more deviant than did comparable subjects who had received nondeviant scores under the same circumstances. The subjects made to feel deviant preferred associating with other deviants more than did nondeviants. The preference of deviants for other deviants held true even for deviants who were unlike themselves. Persons made to feel deviant but whose deviancy was un-

known to others minimized social contacts and avoided being conspicuous in situations where their deviancy might become obvious. Deviants
were found to be treated better by similar deviants than they were by
nondeviants. Deviancy was found to be an important determinant of
how a person is treated. In experimental situations where subjects were
given free choice of subjects upon whom to bestow rewards or punishments, nondeviants chose known deviants more often for punishment
than for reward, while deviants chose other deviants more often for reward than for punishment. The findings indicate that the deviant subject is strongly concerned about minimizing his deviancy and behaves
in ways that will produce this effect. In studies of social influence, these
same researchers found that the deviant is excessively concerned about
possible mistreatment and is therefore reluctant to expose his differentness publicly. The more intimate and threatening the situation, the
greater this reluctance becomes.

   These studies represent the laboratory counterparts of the formation
of clubs, social groups, and subcultures by various deviant groups such
as the blind, deaf, homosexuals, and drug addicts as well as by many
minority ethnic, religious, and political groups. Some of these will be
described and discussed in later chapters.

   The experimental evidence, as well as anecdotal evidence and self-
observation, all indicate that individuals who are markedly deviant in
physique, behavior, or beliefs are subject to a variety of internal and
external pressures to reduce the extent or perceptibility of their differentness (Asch, 1952). Feelings of deviancy have important effects on the
individual's behavior independent of the dimension of his deviancy or
the social evaluation of the differentness. Everyone who feels deviant
is to some extent affected in similar ways and is motivated to behave in
similar ways. Although most people prefer not to be exactly the same as
the norm of their reference groups, they also prefer not to be too different. Exactly where individuality turns into anxiety-arousing deviancy
varies tremendously for different people, circumstances, and dimensions.
However, at some point most people begin to be concerned about their
deviancy.

   In addition to deviancy as such, each dimension or category of deviancy carries with it an assortment of social and personal meanings and
values. While each category and degree of differentness can be considered
to be either positive or negative in value, it seems necessary to assume
that, on balance, deviation is dominantly considered negative. This seems
to follow from the experimental findings, already reported, in which
statistically "normal" subjects who were fed information which made
them believe that they were deviant, with no specification of the personal

or social significance of their differentness, behaved in the same way as do people who are deviant in personally and socially devalued ways. Thus it seems from anecdotal evidence, research studies, and introspection that deviancy itself causes people to be concerned about possible diminished social acceptance, personal devaluation, or actual mistreatment because of their deviancy.

Except in the controlled conditions of the laboratory, significant deviancy involves social evaluations and consequences of a negative or positive sort, self-judgments of a similar type, and sometimes institution-alized and legalized sanctions, prohibitions, and punishments.

It is clear that extreme deviancy is a matter of concern both to the deviant and to others. There seems to be a common core of attitudes and expectancies with reference to the handicapped as a group that cut across all categories of the disabled (Jones, 1974a). Factor analysis of people's expressed attitudes toward the blind, partially sighted, chronically ill, crippled, deaf, hard-of-hearing, delinquent, speech handicapped, mildly mentally retarded, severely mentally retarded, intellectually gifted, and normal has disclosed the existence of a hierarchical order of attitudes toward these specific exceptionalities. A general factor was found—atti-tude toward the disabled. The gifted and normals were differentiated from this common core and did not show any of this general attitude toward the disabled.

Unique components were also associated with attitudes toward specific exceptionalities and groups of exceptionalities. The group factors were differentiated into attitudes toward (a) the physically handicapped (blind, partially sighted, deaf, hard-of-hearing, chronologically ill, speech handi-capped, and crippled), (b) the psychologically-socially handicapped (de-linquent, emotionally disturbed, and severely mentally retarded), and (c) the gifted, who do not share any of the general attitudes toward the disabled. The mildly mentally retarded share to some degree in the general attitude toward the psychologically handicapped, but they also share in the same configuration of attitudes as are held toward the non-exceptional. Attitudes toward the unqualified "mentally retarded" are usually negative, apparently because the image evoked by the term is that of the severely retarded. However, when the two categories are differenti-ated, the mildly mentally retarded share the attitudinal domain of the nonexceptional, as opposed to that of the psychologically and physically disabled (Jones, 1974; Gottlieb & Siperstein, 1976). The negative atti-tudes (stigmas) toward the physically disabled are less extreme than are those toward the psychologically handicapped (Panda & Bartel, 1972).

It is probably this status hierarchy of disabilities which makes people prefer one label to another. For example, sophisticated parents may seek centers or diagnosticians more likely to give a preferred diagnosis or label. Of course, in addition to preferring a "higher status" diagnosis, parents may find one diagnosis or label more acceptable than another because it implies hope of improvement or because it suggests that they are not to blame. Thus, a diagnosis of "minimal brain injury incurred at birth" is preferable to "mental retardation of unknown etiology" because the former is physical rather than mental, it relieves the parent of blame, and it provides an apparently simple explanation of the child's behavioral deficiencies.

Since all the categories of exceptional people considered in this book, except the gifted and the creative, are handicapped and hence negatively valued, the rest of this chapter will be devoted to the psychological and behavioral consequences of stigmatizing exceptionality.

VARIABLES CONTRIBUTING TO TOTAL DEVIANCE

It is possible to distinguish three factors that account for the total effects of organic or behavioral deviance. First, there are first-order effects, limits imposed by the inherent nature of the deviation. Midgets, the orthopedically handicapped, the blind, the deaf, and the albino are organic deviants who have certain limitations imposed by the very nature of their deviance. Their behavioral repertoires remain limited in certain ways, irrespective of social attitudes and expectations or their self-evaluations. The second factor (a second-order effect that influences the deviant's behavior) is society's evaluations of and expectations for such individuals and the extent to which society has devised and made available to such people alternative ways of behaving to compensate for the means closed to them by the nature of their deviance. The individual's total handicap may be diminished or increased by these social factors. The third factor (another second-order effect contributing to the deviant person's total handicap) is his self-evaluation and expectations. If, as many people believe, people's self-concepts are formed largely from a distillation of other people's evaluations of them, the second and third factors are intimately related. Evidence indicates that mental patients are as negative in their opinions concerning the category to which they belong as in the general public. Their beliefs concerning the nature of mental illness and the proper management of mental patients resemble those of nonpatients with similar social and educational backgrounds (Rabkin, 1972). These findings are consistent with the belief in the social origin of the self-concept. Another tremendously important second-order effect is the designation of deviant behavior as criminal.

DRUG ADDICTS AS DEVIANTS

The secondary effects of the criminalization of deviant behavior are most obvious in drug addicts. The repeatedly documented consequences of treating drug addiction as a legal offense are the emergence of illegal traffic in drugs, the development and crystallization of the addict role, and the development of a specific drug subculture.

H. Finestone (1957) has graphically portrayed these effects in his description of a subculture of young male black addicts in Chicago. These addicts develop a way of life including a particular jargon, a limited set of associates who are "in the know," knowledge of the gathering places for addicts and suppliers, the development and constant tuning in of the grapevine of current information concerning the availability and nature of drugs, the presence of informers or agent-decoys, and the best means of obtaining money to support their habits. Like all stigmatized minorities, drug addicts develop a justifying ideology to bolster their morale and reduce their stigmatization. The addict jargon and gestural habits aid in the identification of in-members as well as offer morale-enhancement. Members of the drug subculture are joined together as a stigmatized and persecuted fraternity with unique rituals and passwords.

The immersion of drug addicts into a separate world is inextricably related to their being cast out of respectable society, to their stigmatization, and to the criminalization of their lives. Some people have claimed that drug use is really a part of a general pattern of criminality and that drug addicts were involved in crime before their addiction. Because illegal drug trafficking is concentrated largely in areas in which crime and delinquency in general are high, there is some truth to the claim. However, if allowance is made for delinquency-rate variations due to social class and regional differences, the preaddiction crime rates of drug users and otherwise comparable nonusers are not significantly different. The persistent involvement of drug users in theft and prostitution to support the drug habit is an almost inevitable secondary consequence of the criminalization of their activities. There is no evidence that their criminal behavior is the direct effect of the drugs themselves (Goffman, 1963; DuPont & Greene, 1973; Brecker, 1972; Walsh, 1973; Jacobs, 1974; Regush, 1971). H. M. Bahr (1973) has described how a vicious circle of negative encounters binds the skid row inhabitant to his environment, lowers his self-esteem, and reinforces his sense of hopelessness.

Drug use without stigma

Tangential evidence indicates that the *primary effects* of addiction to narcotics do not account for addiction as a way of life. Those who become addicts but have professional access to medical supplies move in an entirely different world from that of the ordinary addict of limited financial resources, who must obtain his drugs through illegal sources— the pusher and the underworld traffic. Physicians, pharmacists, and nurses who become addicts almost never associate with other addicts, and do not use and may not even know the rituals, jargon, and passwords of the drug subculture. Many of them are able to conceal their addiction and keep their drug intake under sufficient control to live reasonably normal lives (Savada, 1975). In Great Britain, where the availability of drugs through legal sources largely eliminates the need for addicts to become involved in the illegal underworld of drug processing and distribution, a distinct addict subculture has not developed (Wakefield, 1963; Schur, 1965). D. J. Pittman and D. G. Gillespie (1967), in a study of addicts in London, found that many had never resorted to criminal activity to support their addiction.

PROVIDING ASSISTANCE TO THE DISABLED
WITHOUT DEMEANING THEM

The perennial dilemma faced by those who would help the disabled or the disadvantaged is how to render assistance without generating dependencies. When a normal, socially advantaged, emotionally sensitive individual has intimate contact with an organically impaired or socially disadvantaged person, his reactions are likely to be a mixture of sympathetic concern, compassionate involvement, and social guilt, which he is motivated to reduce. Emotionally motivated and sustained nurturant assistance is likely to reinforce dependency and perpetuate a self-derogating role which the proffering of assistance implies. Self-humiliation and condescension are not constructive components of a helping relationship. The helping hand and the forgiving attitude may imply, "We must be tolerant and understanding with these inadequate people. We, unlike them, must be patient, accepting, and forgiving." Such attitudes only reinforce the acceptance of inferiority. On the other hand, making impossible demands and expecting normal or superior performance from a truly handicapped person makes failure and disappointment inevitable.

The attempts of whites in America to help blacks have been caught up in this dilemma. When whites display attitudes of tolerance, understanding, and acceptance of the blacks, when they overlook or excuse defects and delinquencies in blacks that they condemn in whites, it carries inevitable overtones of condescension. The whites seem to be saying, "These blacks are children. They have to go through this stage in growing to maturity, and so we have to overlook their deficiencies." This kind of talking down to blacks often results in needed help being rejected because its acceptance demeans the recipients. (Note that even "tolerance" has overtones of magnanimous condescension. We never speak of being tolerant of people we think of as superior to ourselves.)

THE ANXIETY LEVEL OF THE DEVIANT INDIVIDUAL

In addition to inducing unrealistic self-concepts and levels of aspiration, being disabled may, by inducing excessive anxiety about status, lower one's ability to achieve. The answers supplied by the important individuals and social groups in a person's life to the questions "Who am I?" and "What am I?" are never unequivocal. The exceptional child is likely to receive more conflicting answers to these questions than the more normal individual. What he learns about himself from his father may not be the same as what he learns from his mother. What he learns about himself in the home he may unlearn on the playground. What his teachers say about him may contradict what his playmates say about him. When a person experiences many confusing and contradictory evaluations of himself, his anticipations become ambivalent and his level of aspiration vacillates. His failure to find a firm and reasonably consistent answer to the question "What kind of a person am I?" produces inner weakness. He lacks self-confidence and becomes anxiously concerned about his exceptionality.

Thus the deviant individual is more vulnerable to anxiety than the average person. He is more threatened by the ordinary demands of his culture. High levels of anxiety resulting from such threats reduce his ability to cope realistically with his environment, and he tends to react impulsively, compulsively, rigidly, constrictedly, and fragmentarily. Such reactions result in a high incidence of socially inappropriate, self-defeating, and blind-alley solutions to many of life's problems. The individual develops defenses which unnecessarily restrict his activity, maintain his aspirations at a low level, and induce a minimal self-definition. The defense mechanisms minimize the threat of failure and reduce anxiety. An experience of differentness and a feeling of psychological distance between a person and his significant reference group is anxiety-arousing.

The stigmatized individual sometimes tries to "pass" as normal, sometimes he withdraws from competition, and sometimes he becomes either defensive or aggressive concerning his stigmatizing characteristic. All of these reaction patterns are likely to be accompanied by status anxiety.

THE MORE LIMITED RANGE OF EXPERIENCE OF THE DISABLED

Several categories of exceptional people are defined in terms of their limited range of experience or activities. Blind children have one avenue of learning closed to them, the deaf have another, crippled children's powers of locomotion are restricted, and the capacity of the mentally retarded for profiting by experience is reduced. While these limitations can be compensated for, to a degree, the average disabled child does not have the variety of experiences of the nondisabled. And the more limited experience, combined with higher levels of anxiety, often results in a decreased flexibility of behavior and ideation and a less coherent approach to life situations. The person with a disability is more likely to engage in fewer and simpler activities and to function in a more limited area. Again, this restriction is dictated partially by the nature of the disability, but it is also partially the result of social attitudes and cultural expectancies. When children have many things done for them, when they do not have to use their initiative, and when their social relations are limited and stereotyped, they have less opportunity and motivation for free and adventuresome ideation and activity. When any child, disabled or not, finds more simplified and easier approaches to life's problems to be adequate, he is not motivated to master the complexities of a more expanded world.

The limitation of experiences imposed by a disability is, to a great extent, an index of the degree to which society has devised and provided compensatory educational, vocational, and social experiences for these people. There is considerable evidence that the social and personal compensatory and restitutive mechanisms available to the disabled child are often either underestimated or neglected (Wenar, 1953). The result is that the secondary handicaps become greater than the basic disability requires. Children who could learn to feed themselves are often spoon-fed, both literally and figuratively, for many unnecessary years. Socially engendered fearfulness and self-pity encourage a dependence upon others. Devoted but unwise care may similarly nurture helplessness and dependency beyond that dictated by the primary disability.

VISIBILITY OF A DISABILITY AS A HANDICAPPING VARIABLE

Blindness and orthopedic disabilities have high visibility. Consequently these conditions have practically always been matters of individual and social concern. Deafness and intellectual deviations, being less obvious deviations from the normal, elicit less sympathy and understanding from the general public. Deafness, particularly if only partial, and mental retardation, when not extreme, are often equated with inattention and lack of interest or apathy. It is assumed that the partially deaf and the mildly mentally retarded could be normal if they would only try hard enough. The low visibility of their deficiencies delays identification and hampers the development of an understanding of their conditions.

While high visibility may help to focus public attention on a problem, it may also be a source of feelings of aversion. Social acceptance, particularly initial acceptance, is related to visibility. The different significance of a scar or mark, for example, may depend on its location. A scar on the trunk is much to be preferred to one on the legs, and the latter is better than a comparable blemish on the face. A scar on a girl's leg is more of a burden than the same defect on a boy's leg. Facial scars assume great significance both because of high visibility and because tradition has long regarded the face as the mirror of the personality. Consequently, the facially disfigured are often regarded as deviant in personality as well as in looks (Goldberg, 1974).

Much effort is directed toward decreasing the visibility of deviations considered undesirable. The resistance occasionally encountered to the use of canes, crutches, eyeglasses, and hearing aids often arises because these devices proclaim the presence of a disability even though they diminish the accompanying functional impairment. Contact lenses and disguised hearing aids owe part of their appeal to their decreased visibility. Many individuals attempt to decrease the obviousness of a deformity by special clothing, gestures, or postures. For example, one mother put a large cap on her child even in the hottest weather, to hide his ear defect. Another parent had an artificial ear constructed and required his child, who lacked a pinna, to wear it. A person may try to show only one side of his face, to hide the defect on the other.

Among amputees, the cosmetic problem is often critical. Amputation changes one's appearance, both in the victim's eyes and in the eyes of others. The visibility of the defect is greater when an upper limb is amputated, and the amputation of a lower limb is more visible in the female than the male. Most amputees profit both functionally and psychologically from a prosthesis. A part of the psychological profit from prosthetic devices derives from the decrease in visibility of the loss of limbs, although some people feel that the prosthetic device *increases* the visibility of their defect (Fishman, 1962).

The visibility of a defect is often an important consideration in making educational plans for an exceptional child. In the eyes of the parents, attendance in a regular classroom decreases the social identifiability of the deviant child.

REDUCING THE STIGMA

Since the stigmatization effect seems to be most amenable to social control, many recent developments in the area of mental health, special education, and rehabilitation have been designed to minimize stigmatization. The increasing tendency to eliminate or reduce the segregation of deviants into institutions and special classes is an effort to reduce their stigmatization. The constant renaming of negatively valued conditions and behavioral categories is sustained partly by this motive. Renaming deviancies in the personality realm as "mental illness," "maladjustment," and "inadequacies in personal-social living" is partly a reflection of different ways of conceptualizing the conditions, but it is also an attempt to divorce these disorders from the negative connotations of "lunacy," "insanity," and "psychosis." We previously indicated that "mild," "moderate," and "severe mental retardation" have replaced "feebleminded," "moron," "imbecile," and "idiot" for similar reasons. However, these efforts are only partly successful, and the reason for their limited success is fairly clear.

Although cultures differ considerably in the dimensions of behavior considered of major significance, the existence of a scale of prestigious and shameful differentness is a universal feature of social life. In any group of people who share a set of values in terms of which they develop social norms, those who do not adhere to these norms are deviants and become socially stigmatized. When the deviancies are sufficiently extreme and social reactions to the deviancies exceed critical limits, the deviants become segregated from the normals. The deviancies become stabilized and take on added significance when the affected individuals are labeled and given formal status.

Official labeling serves a number of useful primary purposes but also has many unintended secondary consequences. Descriptive and classificatory systems are used as designations of specific clusters of symptoms (behavioral syndromes). They are economical of time and energy in summarizing, giving meaning to, and communicating with others about symptoms, etiologies, and processes. The primary reason for assigning people to professionally defined categories is to facilitate the generation of relevant hypotheses concerning the treatment of the persons concerned. Labeling a behavior syndrome as indicative of mental illness, mental retardation, epilepsy, orthopedic handicaps, legal blindness, deafness, or learning disorders has a series of consequences designed to benefit the individual by giving him the right to appropriate treatment. The only legitimate justification for official labeling and categorizing is that it leads to more effective treatment. The questions raised by many workers in the field of mental health are: Can more effective treatment be provided without categorizing and labeling? If not, then how can we retain the benefits derived from categorizing the handicapped while diminishing the negative consequences of categorizing?

Arguments against official labeling

Official labeling attaches a disability label to the handicapped individual which results in a generalized devaluation and a restructuring of the individual's opportunities as well as his social and self-expectations. The individual becomes a prisoner of his own reputation. Categorizing people emphasizes their differentness, and because we see an individual as different in one negatively valued way, our perception of the many ways in which he is like the unimpaired is blurred. People in trouble and in need of assistance can be given such help without artificial, arbitrary categorization. The "help" provided under the guise of treatment and hospitalization often does more harm than good.

Specifically defined and delimited categories discriminate against people who do not fall within the categories but who are equally in need of help. Every human being in need of assistance should be entitled to such help, whether or not he falls within the prescribed categorical limits. Providing special assistance only to special categories of the disabled results in the multiplication of such categories and the assigning of people to these groups, rather than focusing on the social circumstances and processes that cause the disabilities. It concentrates on the rehabilitative treatment aspects of mental health rather than on the prevention and life-enhancing potential of mental-health practices and policies. The persistence of medically-oriented categories and labels has perpetuated the person-problem orientation that militates against making needed social changes in dealing with stigmatized deviants.

Arguments for official labeling

Unofficial categorizing and labeling are inevitable, precede the corresponding official processes, and mediate many of the effects ascribed to the official labels. Official categorization and labeling are necessary or helpful in identifying clusters of symptoms characterizing clinical entities. They provide a shorthand professional descriptive nomenclature which is useful in conceptualizing and transmitting information about patients and processes. Descriptive categories and labels are also necessary for setting administratively and legally as well as professionally— or personally—dictated requirements for admission to "patient" status. Legal and administratively authorized financial and care benefits are limited to those who "fit the category." For example, special financial aid and educational assistance are provided people who are legally blind, deaf, orthopedically handicapped, mentally retarded, or mentally ill. Failure to be officially certified precludes an individual's obtaining such help. Defining behavioral disorders as "mental illness" or some equivalent term may be necessary before people with such conditions can be covered by medical and hospital insurance benefits. A categorical label may open doors for those in need of assistance.

Conventional labels serve as rallying points for mobilizing people and resources. Practically all voluntary organizations—golfers, antique car buffs, societies for crippled children, or the Epilepsy Foundation of America—are organized in terms of categorical interests. Even though such groups prefer less stigmatizing labels for their categories, the terms have emotional appeal vital in mobilizing constituencies, initiating movements, promoting legislation, and planning programs. Decategorizing the handicapped may decrease the commitment and involvement of these groups.

LEGAL DECISIONS AND LEGISLATION
AFFECTING THE SOCIAL CLIMATE

Laws not only reflect changing social attitudes and beliefs, they also facilitate changes. Just as the law was long instrumental in sustaining segregation and other discriminatory practices toward minority groups, the Supreme Court school-desegregation decision of 1954 and the flood of civil rights legislation and court decisions that followed have greatly facilitated the reduction of these discriminatory practices. The effects of these laws and court decisions concerning the treatment of disadvantaged ethnic minorities have expanded to include and encourage movements directed at reducing and/or eliminating comparable discrimination toward a wide variety of categories of deviant individuals, including the mentally disordered.

In general, the legal conception of mental handicaps has changed from one of irreversibility requiring segregation to one of a curable condition meriting appropriate treatment. The legal status of the mentally handicapped person is also changing, from that of an individual who is incompetent, unable to make judgments affecting his welfare, and deprived of most of his civil and personal rights, to that of a person not necessarily unable to exercise these rights. The redefinition of mental illness, the reorientation of mental-health programs toward the community, the decreasing use of residential institutions as the primary place of treatment, and the increasing use of voluntary rather than involuntary institutionalization, have all resulted in a narrowing of the differences in social and legal status and rights of the mentally deviant and the mentally normal (Stone, 1971).

In a flood of judicial decisions, the courts have ruled that the handicapped have:

1. A right to treatment and to refuse treatment
2. A right to effective treatment and/or education (the principle of "zero rejects")
3. A right to a humane physical and psychological environment and treatment
4. A right to privacy
5. A right to be subjected to proper standards and criteria for class assignment and/or institutionalization
6. A right to public assistance
7. A right to due process (the person and/or his parents have a right to receive a statement of reasons for assignment, placement, or treatment and a chance to be heard and to be represented by counsel)
8. The obligation of professionals to assert the rights, claims, and needs of their clients
9. The right to a fair wage for nontherapeutic work performed during institutionalization
10. The right to sue for damages for malpractice and negligence in the treatment of mental illness or incapacity according to the principles applicable to physical ailments
11. A "right to liberty" (nondangerous mental patients cannot be confined against their will if they can safely reside outside an institution)[1]
12. The right to receive education, care, and treatment in the "least restrictive situation"

[1] For a more complete discussion of the cases involving these principles, see Casey, 1973; Schwitzebel, 1973; Marker & Friedman, 1973; Kuriloff et al., 1974; Goldberg & Lippman, 1974; Turnbull, 1975.

THE MINORITY STATUS OF EXCEPTIONAL INDIVIDUALS

Several people have likened the status of exceptional individuals to that of the disadvantaged minority ethnic and religious groups (Barker, 1948; Tenny, 1953; Wright, 1974). While there are many ways in which exceptional people, particularly those with disabilities, resemble certain underprivileged racial minority groups, there are also some significant differences.

The nondisabled majority tend to maintain a certain social distance, often treating the disabled as outsiders. Many normal people feel uncomfortable in the presence of a disabled individual. They find it very difficult to accept and mingle with the disabled as they do with other people, and since they have the greater prestige and power, they can restrict the opportunities of the handicapped. Nearly two-thirds of a sampling of college students stated that they would not marry an amputee (one leg), and half would not date such a person. Nearly three-fourths would not date a deaf person (Rusk & Taylor, 1946). The handicapped are thus often forced either to associate with each other or to become socially isolated. They are frequently segregated—physically, psychologically, and socially. Disabled persons sensing social discrimination gravitate to their own kind who can accept them without reservations. And, like members of a minority racial group, they resent their group identification, even though they feel more comfortable there. Noreen Linduska indicates in her autobiography, *My Polio Past,* that she first resisted new group identifications by refusing to answer letters from her readers who had disabilities, but gradually came to realize that she had slipped into a different category of society (that of the disabled) even though she did not like it.

There are some advantages to identification with a group of similarly disabled people. Within such a group the individual is, to a degree, protected from the frustration, conflict, anxiety, and disappointment which might result from trying to compete with and gain acceptance from the more able majority. Within the world of the disabled one may find understanding and acceptance, friendship and love, respect and status in a way which is impossible while remaining a marginal person in the culture of the more able majority. The disabled are no longer motivated to act "normal."

In the larger urban centers there are many organizations and clubs for particular types of exceptional people, particularly the blind and the deaf. In New York City, for example, the Union League of the Deaf rents an entire building for its use. The deaf publish journals and newspapers, own an insurance company, and periodically hold a World Conference of the Deaf and a World Deaf Olympics. They have a church and largely take care of their social work. They have even lobbied *against* additional income tax exemptions for the deaf similar to those allowed the blind. In this respect the deaf are behaving like many minority racial groups.

Some social and behavioral deviants develop subcultures that, like the ethnic and racial ghettos, constitute havens where the individuals can live openly and with mutual support and insist that they are just as good as anyone else. Ethnocentrism (the tendency to enhance the status of one's in-group) is found among the disadvantaged just as it is in the more favored groups. Members of a particular deviant group generally hold more favorable attitudes toward members of their group than toward members of a different, equally handicapped group (Nelson, Thornton, & Pasework, 1973). Typically, individuals are altruistic toward co-members and glorify their in-group, whereas they tend to derogate and may even exploit members of out-groups (Dion, 1973). People ascribe more benign or prestige-enhancing motives to members of their group than they do to out-group members performing the same deviant acts. For example, J. F. Mann and D. M. Taylor (1974) have shown that an out-group member behaving in a racially biased way is perceived as internally motivated (manifesting a prejudice—a less worthy motive), whereas an in-group member performing the same act is perceived as coerced by external factors (a more socially acceptable explanation). S. Worchel and V. A. Andreoli (1974) found that the obligation to reciprocate either a favor or punishment is enhanced if the other person's behavior is perceived as internally motivated (intentional) rather than elicited by the situation. Thus, acts by members of an in-group elicit more reciprocation than acts by comparable out-group persons.

Social deviates such as homosexuals and drug addicts may congregate in enclaves or live in small communities and take the line that they are not only just as good as, but actually better than "normals," and that the lives they lead are superior to those led by the majority. The socially stigmatized individual, by entering a subculture, accepts his alienation from the larger society, and by identifying with like souls claims to be a full-fledged normal or even a superior human being; it is "the others" who are not truly human. The members of the deviant minority are superior, and the only problem is the unjust outside world which unfairly labels and stigmatizes them. This type of adjustment is more available to ethnic minorities such as Jews, Amish, and black separatists, and to stigmatized social deviants such as hippies, drug addicts, and homosexuals, than it is to the blind, the deaf, and the orthopedically handicapped. The socially devalued deviants who are able to pass present this fact as evidence of the absurd and contradictory claims of the normals who stigmatize them. That the deviants are able to pass proves that all claims concerning stigmatizing differentness are mere fabrications. Goffman (1963) points out that the deviant "passer" may delight in arranging conversations with normals so that the latter will make statements concerning such deviants which the presence of the unrecognized passer completely disproves.

The disabled, like disadvantaged ethnic groups, experience vocational discrimination. While it is true that the vocational outlets for the disabled may be realistically circumscribed, the restrictions are often extended to areas where the limitations are not inherently confining. Failure to graduate from high school, for example, may prevent a person from even being considered for a job requiring only manual labor; the absence of significant physical defects may be a prerequisite for employment in a company which has jobs in which many disabilities would not be at all handicapping. Unrealistic requirements close the doors of employment to many of the disabled.

And, as we have already mentioned, the disabled are subject to the consequences of group stereotyping. Like minority racial and ethnic groups, the persons with disabilities are often discriminated against on a wholesale basis.

Disabled people are supposed to feel and act inferior, and other people expect them to act accordingly. People see in others what they expect to see and resist modifications of these expectancies. People also tend to respond to others according to how they expect these others to respond to them (Baron, 1974). The person with a disability who acts in a normal or superior manner is considered to be compensating or overcompensating for his inferiority. Each individual is perceived in terms of the presumed characteristics of the group to which he is assigned. H. Chevigny, in his autobiography (1946), indicates that when he became blind, people expected him to act like a tragic figure. They are disconcerted and disbelieving when a blind person insists that he is not a tragic figure. In the same way, people are disturbed when disadvantaged ethnic groups fail to act inferior and even indicate that they feel as worthy as any other group. People are expected to keep their places and play the roles dictated by cultural stereotypes! When reality violates our expectations, we try to normalize reality by fitting it into our most appropriate perceptual categories (Wright, 1974; Korten, 1973).

Unlike certain ethnic minorities, the disabled do not constitute organized threats to companies, organizations, and groups which discriminate against them. They seldom walk picket lines or create dramatic social crises. However, in some instances the handicapped are organizing and becoming more militant in their behalf. For example, deaf students in Saskatoon, Canada, staged a week-long walkout in protest over being denied instruction in sign language and over the inability of certain staff members to communicate with them. In Louisiana, deaf people marched on the state capitol to protest the appointment of a new superintendent whose background was in music—not in preparation to teach deaf children. Similar protests have been launched by the orthopedically handicapped and the blind (McCay, 1974). The disabled typically do not have the group support of others like them, as do the members of other minority groups. Except within the organizations found in large cities, the individual with an infirmity is often a single isolated individual among the more able majority, and unable to acquire the ready-made and shared reactions to prejudice and discrimination which are available to members of the minority racial groups.

Much of the avoidance of the disabled by the nondisabled results from anxiety as well as from realistic evaluations of the consequences of association with the deviant individual. When people have been repeatedly punished for being different, they will respond with anxiety at the mere sight of other people's deviant behavior. When being significantly different from other people regularly brings personal discomfort, the perception of differentness either in oneself or in others eventually arouses anxiety and a person may then avoid contact with exceptional people because of his anxieties. The negative discrimination reduces identification and hence the anxiety aroused as a consequence of one's social history. A person may intellectually perceive disability as a condition for which the individual is not responsible, recognize that the person is neither bad nor inferior, and yet be disturbed by that person's presence or behavior. The physically normal and the physically handicapped both often feel uncertain and uncomfortable when interacting with each other (Comer & Piliavin, 1972).

A woman may prefer not to date an orthopedically disabled man because she loves to dance. She is no more prejudiced against the orthopedically handicapped than she is against the nondisabled man who either does not know how to dance or who will not dance because of religious beliefs. A realistic appraisal of the situation may dictate a negative choice which is not necessarily a prejudiced one.

There are also other unprejudiced bases for discrimination against the disabled. The average person has considerable uncertainty about how to behave toward the disabled. For many people, associating with a handicapped person is an ambiguous, even threatening, experience. The nondisabled often consult each other to learn how to act with the disabled. Whether to help, how much to help, and when to offer help are recurring problems to the inexperienced. Children sometimes tease the deviant individual because they do not know how else to deal with his disturbing differentness. When situations are vague and uncertain, contacts may become stilted and formal. The awkwardness and uncertainty of social relationships with the disabled can be reduced by avoiding them or by keeping them at arm's length in formalized situations. One can also contribute funds to organizations devoted to the care of the handicapped (Wright, 1974).

Of course, this difference between prejudice as displayed toward all members of certain minority racial and ethnic groups and negative discrimination with reference to people with a disability is a relative one. They both have emotional overtones and both may be rationalized in a defensive way, but the social avoidance of disabled people is more likely to result from individual, first-hand experience and to be less the result of a culturally transmitted stereotype than is racial or religious prejudice.

Activities designed to help the handicapped, but which may require their segregation, are socially sanctioned, whereas segregation arising from prejudice is generally condemned (Jordan, 1963). Where the isolation of ethnic groups is socially sanctioned, efforts to help these disadvantaged minorities are discouraged; whereas efforts to help minority handicapped groups, and thus reduce their segregation, are socially approved. Handicapped groups are seldom used as scapegoats by the nondisabled, while the disadvantaged ethnic groups are often so used. The disabled are infrequently manipulated economically, socially, and politically for the benefit of the more able majority, whereas minority ethnic groups are often used in this way.

On the other hand, the disabled are in a better position than are the ethnically, religiously, or socially disadvantaged groups to manipulate government, educational, and welfare agencies, as well as sympathetic private individuals, for their own advantage. The handicapped are also more able to avoid responsibility, to fail to achieve in accordance with their abilities, and to obtain other secondary gains because of their disabilities than are the minority ethnic groups.

In certain situations a handicapped person may be perceived in a more *favorable* way than a comparable nonhandicapped individual. For example, a counselor seated in a wheelchair and perceived by counselees as physically handicapped was rated as "more aware of one's situation," as "more actively reaching out to the client," as "holding the client in more positive regard," and as being "more genuinely understanding of the counselee" than was the same counselor sitting in an ordinary chair and consequently viewed as not disabled (Bradham & Thoreson, 1973; Mitchell & Allen, 1975). Apparently the counselor perceived as disabled was held in higher esteem because "he had made it despite his disability" and "because of his experiences, he had become the real expert."

RAMIFICATIONS OF THE PROBLEMS OF EXCEPTIONALITY

If, in addition to the exceptional individuals themselves, we include the families and professional personnel involved, the problems of exceptionality affect a sizable fraction of the total population. If we include within the category of exceptional people those individuals who become dependent upon others for special assistance, care, treatment, or education at any time in their lives, they will number in the millions and include most of the population. Such a broad interpretation of exceptionality would cover children who are born "too soon," people who live "too long," and those in between who, because of either hereditary factors or environmental influences, deviate in socially significant ways from the norm.

As advances in medicine and nutrition reduce the percentage of the handicapped who are either stillborn or die in infancy, on the one hand, and who increase their longevity, on the other, the problems of exceptional people, and particularly of the handicapped, will increase. There are probably few people whose lives are not touched, directly or indirectly, either by physical, intellectual, emotional, or personality disability or by the challenge of the exceptionally able.

When the problems of exceptionality are viewed in terms of people's self-concepts and in a social-psychological context, they become even more extensive. This is a social world, and people's destinies are probably determined as much by what others think of them and what they, in turn, think of themselves as by the characteristics which they "truly" possess. Many of the problems of exceptional people are also the lot of those who, for reasons which may be invalid, *perceive themselves as handicapped or otherwise exceptional.*

It was noted earlier that many people who are statistically within the normal range perceive themselves as handicapped in view of their levels of aspirations and the groups with which they compare themselves. In addition to these, a large percentage of people who are statistically normal have, at some time, experienced feelings of inferiority about their physiques (Frazier & Lisanbee, 1950; Wright, 1974). To the extent that the adjustment problems of the handicapped stem from their feelings of inadequacy or inferiority, they are universal problems.

The child with sexually inappropriate physical characteristics has many of the experiences of the more extreme physical deviates. The late-maturing boy who is considerably below the norm of his age group in size, strength, and general manliness often suffers from feelings of inferiority (Jones & Bayley, 1950). Similarly, the early-maturing girl who is not only the biggest and tallest girl in her group, but actually larger than most boys her age, experiences the consequences of a sexually inappropriate physique. The late-maturing girl may deviate just as far as does her physically precocious classmate, but she can still be perceived as cute and feminine, for it is sexually "appropriate" for girls to be small, and to be petite is to deviate in the direction of femininity. Conversely, the boy who matures early may be statistically as deviant as his late-maturing peer, but his precocity is in a sexually "appropriate" direction for males. He is perceived as muscular, athletic, masculine, and more attractive than the average male of the same age (Jones & Bayley, 1950; Sawrey & Telford, 1973). Whatever the context, the problems and challenges of exceptionality are of concern to everyone. Any discussion of exceptional children should be addressed to everyone.

SUMMARY

Deviance has both positively and negatively valued components. Individuals want to be different in certain ways and resist efforts to deny them their individuality. However, when deviance becomes extreme, it is generally perceived negatively, induces anxiety, and initiates activities designed to reduce the person's differentness.

Research studies, as well as general observation, indicate that people who feel deviant in negatively valued ways (1) prefer to associate with other deviants rather than with nondeviants, (2) minimize their social contacts with nondeviants, (3) avoid being conspicuous in situations where their deviancies may be obvious, (4) treat other deviants better than they do nondeviants, and (5) minimize the negative consequences of their deviancy by passing as nondeviant when possible, and by indicating the essential normalness or desirability of their deviancy.

There is a common core of attitudes and expectancies toward all categories of the handicapped. There are also some group components differentiating the physically handicapped from the psychologically-socially handicapped. The negative attitudes displayed toward the physically disabled are less extreme than are those held toward the psychologically-socially handicapped. The total behavioral consequences of negatively valued deviance include those emanating from (1) the inherent limitation imposed by the disability, (2) social attitudes and expectations as well as the compensations available to the deviant, and (3) the deviant's self-image, aspirations, and self-expectations. The deviant's coping behavior may also be limited by excessive anxieties, his more limited range of experiences, and the criminalization of his deviant acts.

Programs designed to reduce the stigma of deviancy must deal with social values and attitudes, official and unofficial labeling, as well as legislative and court actions. Devalued deviants, like disadvantaged ethnic minorities, experience social and vocational discrimination, develop and withdraw into separate subcultures, and are excessively stereotyped. The problems of deviancy are the problems of all humanity. People are not helped if their deviancies are ignored when these deviancies are relevant to treatment, training, or educational procedures, on the one hand, or when they are classified, labeled, and treated in terms of medical or psychological categories irrelevant to education and treatment, on the other.

REFERENCES

ASCH, S., *Social Psychology* (Englewood Cliffs, N.J.: Prentice-Hall, 1952).

BAHR, H. M., *Skid Row: An Introduction to Disaffiliation* (New York: Oxford University Press, 1973).

BARKER, R. G., "The Social Psychology of Physical Disability," *Journal of Social Issues*, 1948, *4*, 28–38.

BARON, P. H., "Self-esteem, Ingratiation, and Evaluation of Unknown Others," *Journal of Personality and Social Psychology*, 1974, *30*, 104–9.

BRADHAM, R. E., & R. W. THORESON, "Relationship of Client Preferences and Counselor's Physical Disability," *Journal of Counseling Psychology*, 1973, *20*, 10–14.

BRECKER, E. M., *Licit and Illicit Drugs* (Boston: Little, Brown, 1972).

CASEY, P. J., "The Supreme Court and the Suspect Class," *Exceptional Children*, 1973, *40*, 119–25.

CHEVIGNY, H., *My Eyes Have a Cold Nose* (New Haven, Conn.: Yale University Press, 1946).

COMER, R. J., & J. A. PILIAVIN, "The Effects of Physical Deviance on Face-to-face Interaction," *Journal of Personality and Social Psychology*, 1972, *23*, 33–39.

DION, K. K., "Young Children's Stereotyping of Facial Attractiveness," *Developmental Psychology*, 1973, *9*, 183–88.

DUPONT, R. L., & M. H. GREENE, "The Dynamics of a Heroin Addiction Epidemic," *Science*, 1973, *181*, 716–22.

FINESTONE, H., "Cats, Kids, and Color," *Social Problems,* July 1957, *5* (7), 3–13.

FISHMAN, S., "Amputation," in J. F. Garrett & E. S. Levine, eds., *Psychological Practices with the Physically Disabled* (New York: Columbia University Press, 1962).

FRAZIER, A., & L. K. LISANBEE, "Adolescent Concerns with Physique," *School Review*, 1950, *38*, 397–405.

FREEDMAN, J. L., & A. N. DOOB, *Deviancy: The Psychology of Being Different* (New York: Academic Press, 1968).

GOFFMAN, E., *Stigma: Notes on the Management of Spoiled Identity* (Englewood Cliffs, N.J.: Prentice-Hall, 1963).

GOLDBERG, I., & L. LIPPMAN, "Plato Had a Word for It," *Exceptional Children,* 1974, *40,* 325–35.

GOLDBERG, R. T., "Adjustment of Children with Invisible and Visible Handicaps: Congenital Heart Disease and Facial Burns," *Journal of Counseling Psychology,* 1974, *21,* 428–32.

GOTTLIEB, J., & G. N. SIPERSTEIN, "Attitudes Toward Mentally Retarded Persons: Effects of Attitude Referent Specificity," *American Journal of Mental Deficiency,* 1976, *80,* 376–81.

JACOBS, J., *Deviance: Field Studies and Self-disclosures* (Palo Alto, Ca.: National Press, 1974).

JONES, M. C., & N. BAYLEY, "Physical Maturing Among Boys as Related to Behavior," *Journal of Educational Psychology* 1950, *41,* 129–48.

JONES, R. L., "The Hierarchical Structure of Attitudes Toward the Exceptional," *Exceptional Children,* 1974, *40,* 430–35.

JORDAN, S., "The Disadvantaged Group: A Concept Applicable to the Handicapped," *Journal of Psychology,* 1963, *55,* 313–22.

KORTEN, F. F., "The Stereotype as a Cognitive Construct," *Journal of Social Psychology,* 1973, *90,* 29–39.

KURILOFF, P.; R. TRUE; D. KIEP; & W. BUSS, "Legal Reform and Educational Change: The Pennsylvania Case," *Exceptional Children,* 1974, *41,* 35–42.

LINDUSKA, N., *My Polio Past* (Chicago: Pellegrini & Cudahy, 1947).

McCAY, V., "Deaf Militancy," *American Annals of the Deaf,* 1974, *119,* 15.

MANN, J. F., & D. M. TAYLOR, "Attribution of Causality: Role of Ethnicity and Social Class," *Journal of Social Psychology,* 1974, *94,* 3–13.

MARKER, G., & P. R. FRIEDMAN, "Rethinking Children's Rights," *Children Today,* 1973, *2* (6), 8–11.

MASLACH, C., "Social and Personal Bases of Individuation," *Journal of Personality and Social Psychology,* 1974, *29,* 411–25.

MITCHELL, J., & H. ALLEN, "Perception of a Physically Disabled Counselor in a Counseling Session," *Journal of Counseling Psychology,* 1975, *22,* 70–73.

MORIARTY, T., "Role of Stigma in the Experience of Deviance," *Journal of Personality and Social Psychology,* 1974, *27,* 849–57.

NELSON, M. B., L. W. THORNTON, & R. A. PASEWORK, "Group Membership and Attitudes Toward Offenders and Mental Patients," *Journal of Community Psychology,* 1973, *1,* 425–26.

PANDA, K. C., & N. R. BARTEL, "Teacher Perception of Exceptional Children," *Journal of Special Education,* 1972, *6,* 261–66.

PITTMAN, D. J., & D. G. GILLESPIE, "Social Policy as Reinforcement," in D. J. Pittman, ed., *Alcoholism* (New York: Harper & Row, 1967).

RABKIN, J. G., "Opinions about Mental Health," *Psychological Bulletin,* 1972, *77,* 153–71.

REGUSH, N. M., *The Drug Addiction Business: A Denunciation of the Dehumanizing Politics and Practices of the So-Called Experts* (New York: Dial Press, 1971).

RUSK, H. A., & E. J. TAYLOR, *New Hope for the Handicapped* (New York: Harper & Row, 1946).

SAVADA, S. W., "Research Approaches in Illicit Drug Use: A Critical Review," *Genetic Psychology Monographs*, 1975, *91*, 3–60.

SAWREY, J. M., & C. W. TELFORD, *Educational Psychology*, 4th ed. (Boston: Allyn & Bacon, 1973).

SCHUR, E. M., *Crimes Without Victims* (Englewood Cliffs, N.J.: Prentice-Hall, 1965).

SCHWITZEBEL, R. K., "Right to Treatment for the Mentally Disabled," *Harvard Civil Rights–Civil Liberties Law Review*, 1973, *8*, 513–35.

STONE, A. A., "Psychiatry and the Law," *Psychiatric Annals*, 1971, *1* (2), 19–43.

TENNY, J. W., "The Minority Status of the Handicapped," *Exceptional Children*, 1953, *18*, 260–64.

TURNBULL, III, H. R., "Accountability: An Overview of the Impact of Litigation on Professionals," *Exceptional Children*, 1975, *41*, 427–33.

WAKEFIELD, D., ed., *The Addict* (Greenwich, Conn.: Fawcett, 1963).

WALSH, J., "Lexington Narcotics Hospital: A Special Sort of Alma Mater," *Science*, 1973, *182*, 1004–8.

WENAR, C., "The Effects of a Motor Handicap on Personality: I. The Effects on Levels of Aspiration," *Child Development*, 1953, *24*, 123–30.

WORCHEL, S., & V. A. ANDREOLI, "Attribution of Causality as a Means of Restoring Behavioral Freedom," *Journal of Personality and Social Psychology*, 1974, *29*, 237–45.

WRIGHT, B. A., "An Analysis of Attitudes: Dynamics and Effects," *The New Outlook for the Blind*, 1974, *68*, 108–18.

Chapter 4

The care and education
of the exceptional individual

Almost all of eighty-five leaders in special education who were asked recently to identify the most important problems in special education indicated that *mainstreaming* continued to be the major issue. These leaders were concerned that the problem had been poorly handled (Dailey, 1974; Zneimer, 1975). Mounting concern with special education in general is one of the major educational events of the 1970s. Between 1966 and 1972, money spent on public school programs for handicapped children tripled, reaching the level of $2,000,000,000 in 1972. In that year, eight hundred bills with special provisions for handicapped children were introduced into state legislatures. Two hundred fifty of these were enacted into law (Gallagher, 1974). From 1963 to 1973 the membership of the Council for Exceptional Children, one of the major professional organizations for people concerned with the exceptional, increased from 16,000 to 48,000. Since 1948 the number of handicapped children receiving special education services has increased sixfold (Brenton, 1974). American society in the 1970s has spoken through its legislative and judicial systems in strong support of appropriate education for all.

SEGREGATION VERSUS MAINSTREAMING

In the 1800s, residential schools were established in the United States for several categories of handicapped children—the deaf, the blind, and the mentally retarded. Before 1850 the handicapped depended upon local charities for subsidy and were sent to jails or almshouses when they became serious problems (McCarver & Craig, 1974). The primary goal of these early institutions and schools was to cure or rehabilitate the handicapped and return them to the community as acceptable citizens. Since that time segregated facilities—residential institutions, special schools, or special classes—have become the most popular sites for the care and education of the handicapped. However, during the past decade, increasing discontent with segregated facilities has fostered the development of a variety of alternative systems. This discontent had several origins and has manifested itself in several ways.

The development of mainstreaming can be seen most clearly in the case of the mentally retarded and the mentally ill. The modern era in the understanding and treatment of the mentally retarded dates from the work of J. M. G. Itard and his successor, E. Seguin. In 1798 a party of hunters came upon a boy about twelve years old in the woods of Caune, Aveyron, France. The boy was running naked through the woods like a wild animal, apparently feeding upon acorns and nuts. The hunters caught the boy, who was eventually placed in the custody of Dr. Jean Itard, chief medical officer of the National Institution for the Deaf and Dumb.

Itard was an extreme sensationalist or associationist who accepted John Locke's conception that the mind at birth is a "tabula rasa"—a blank tablet—upon which experience writes. Locke claimed that all human experiences and knowledge are derived from experience; there are no innate ideas, as was claimed by the opposing school of thought, the nativists. Individual differences in knowledge and intellect are largely, if not entirely, the result of differences in experience. On the basis of this assumption, Itard believed that if he could compensate for the prior experiential deprivation of his "wild boy" by providing an ordered set of enriched experiences, he could turn him into a normal human being.

After five years of intensive labor, Itard admitted his failure, and the first recorded educational project to rehabilitate a mentally deficient individual ended. However, others did not share Itard's pessimism. He had not turned his "wild boy" into a completely normal human being, but he had brought him a long way from where he had found him. Itard had demonstrated that the mentally retarded *were* capable of learning. This inspired his pupil, Edouard Seguin, to continue the work. Seguin recognized the significance of Itard's work and became the first great teacher and leader in the field of mental deficiency. Like Itard, he believed that mental deficiency was not an inherent, irremediable defect but a remediable defect. Seguin founded the first successful school for the education of the mentally deficient in Paris in 1837. His work was the inspiration for the establishment of similar schools in the United States in the 1840s and '50s.

All of these early schools were organized for the purpose of largely overcoming, if not curing, mental retardation, so that these unfortunate individuals could be returned to the community capable of independent living. However, this early promise was never realized. It soon became apparent that only a small proportion of the pupils admitted to these schools could return to their communities, even after many years of training. With many students remaining in the institutions for prolonged periods, the schools soon became filled with the more severely retarded, who required custodial care for their entire lives. Thus the concept of the institutions as schools was largely abandoned, and their roles as custodial facilities for the prolonged and often lifetime care of the retarded became dominant.

About the same time that the first schools for the mentally retarded were being established with such optimism, a comparable movement was taking place in the area of mental illness. This movement was initiated by Philippe Pinel, another French physician. The son of a physician, Pinel, like Itard, was strongly influenced by the writings of John Locke, the associationalist. Pinel was alive during the French Revolution and knew and was influenced by many of the leading liberal thinkers and politicians of that turbulent era. In addition to being influenced by the prevailing spirit of rational inquiry, Pinel subscribed to another movement characteristic of the Enlightenment—a zeal for social reform and moral uplift. He was convinced that people could shape their destiny by social action based on the scientific study of social phenomena. When Pinel took over the administration of the Bicêtre, an institution in Paris that housed "madmen," he himself was considered mad by his contemporaries for releasing the patients from the chains that shackled them, feeding them with nourishing food, and insisting that they were ill and entitled to be treated with kindness. Two years later (1795), when he was placed in charge of the Salpêtrière, where "madwomen" were similarly chained, he reformed that institution in the same way.

Pinel believed that mental illness was a natural phenomenon to be studied and treated, like physical illness. He referred to his therapy as "moral treatment," asserting that it was impossible to determine whether the behavioral deviations of patients resulted from basic mental illness or from the effects of the chains and the treatment they had received. His humane approach to the mentally deranged, his principles of institutional management, and his claims about the effects of institutionalization are still essentially valid. Pinel's primary contributions were his insistence that the mentally ill were sick people deserving and requiring medical treatment, and his claim that "moral treatment" was appropriate treatment for mental illness (Alexander & Selesnick, 1966).

Jean Jacques Rousseau's contention that "man is born free, yet everywhere he is in chains" was taken seriously by Pinel, as well as by others of his time. In England at about this time, there was considerable agitation for improved treatment of the prisoners in English jails. Sir John Pringle, an Edinburgh physician, organized a group to work for fairer treatment of prisoners of war. (This group was the forerunner of the Red Cross.) Christopher W. Hufeland, an English public health crusader, claimed that mental health was a community problem. J. H. Pestalozzi, the Swiss educational reformer, insisted that the miserable plight of the insane should be drastically changed (Alexander & Selesnick, 1966).

The contributions of these men can be conceptualized as an outcome of the philosophy of the Enlightenment, which incorporated the doctrines of equality, natural goodness, and the limitless perfectability of humankind. The individual's inherently good nature is subverted by bad environment, wrong upbringing, and corrupt political and social institutions. Change these environmental circumstances in accordance with reason, and his inborn goodness will reassert itself. The French Revolution and later the Bolshevik Revolution were designed to offer the requisite opportunities.

The decline of moral treatment and the education of the mentally retarded were the result of several factors. First and most important was the growth of the institutions. Since institutionalization was the only regular treatment provided for the mental deviates, the hospitals rapidly filled to capacity and became overcrowded. Hospital size was doubled and redoubled without adequate provision for increases in professional personnel. The doctor–patient ratio steadily declined. As the hospitals expanded in size, patients grew farther and farther removed from those responsible for their care. Hospital doctors became administrators who had little contact with the problems of the patients in their charge.

J. S. Bockoven (1963) claims that the work of Dorothea Dix (1802–87) inadvertently contributed to the replacement of moral treatment by institutional and custodial care. In 1841 Dix, a New England schoolteacher, learned that large numbers of mentally ill persons in her state of Massachusetts were suffering terrible abuse in the jails and almshouses. She visited and observed the humane (moral) treatment provided patients in some of the small mental hospitals in Massachusetts and then set out on a crusade to see that every "insane" person was placed in a mental hospital instead of a jail or almshouse. By persistent effort and singleness of purpose, she persuaded the state legislature to construct many new hospitals and expand the old ones. Although she was a broad humanitarian who undoubtedly bettered the condition of the mentally ill who had previously resided in jails and almshouses, she inadvertently contributed to the decline of moral treatment of the "insane." It was simply impossible to provide the kind of intimate personal care for the hoards of patients removed from the jails, almshouses, cellars, and attics that Dorothea Dix had observed in the small institutions.

Dix, as a self-appointed inspector and critic of the new hospitals, unintentionally had another deleterious influence. Her imperious attitude, critical evaluations, and sometimes petty fault-finding, combined with the considerable political influence that she had obtained, placed hospital administrators on the defensive. The protection of patients against any and all physical hazards as an institutional need led to tighter and tighter regulation of institutional life and stagnation of the hospitals. The careful, accident-avoiding, restrictive, watchful, criticism-sensitive custodian replaced the more open, optimistic, enthusiastic moral therapist. Interest in control, protection of the public, and questions of legal responsibility replaced interest in the treatment of the individual patient.

Concomitant with the development of the large, impersonal hospitals was a resurgence of the organic point of view. Dr. John P. Gray, who assumed editorship of the *American Journal of Insanity* in 1855, insisted that insanity was always due to physical lesions. He introduced the microscope into the laboratories of American mental hospitals and recommended the study of postmortem material for the understanding of mental illness. He encouraged mental-hospital personnel to treat mentally ill patients as physically ill. Patients with emotional and behavior problems were cast in the same role as patients with demonstrable organic illnesses—a role that required a passive and submissive individual. Effective treatment must wait on the discovery of basic causes. When etiology was unknown, appropriate treatment could not be devised—so none was given.

With the increase in the ratio of patients to professional staff, the attendant, rather than the physician or other professional person, became the individual most intimately associated with the patient. The unskilled and poorly paid psychiatric aide or ward attendent became responsible for the care of a large ward of patients. His primary task was to keep the patients reasonably clean and quiet, rather than to help them improve so they could leave the institution. The "better" patients were often placed "on detail" to assist the aide in ward routines and patient control, and the aides often hoarded these good patients because they lightened their burden. The ward personnel reinforced those activities which facilitated the smooth, efficient, and economical running of the institution; this often increased the likelihood of passive, conforming, submissive behavior and prolonged institutionalization.

The popularity of the philosophy of *social Darwinism* also contributed to the decline of the more idealistic and humanistically-oriented moral treatment of the mentally ill and education of the mentally retarded. The advocates of social Darwinism contended that the evolution of social order and social institutions is determined by inherent laws of nature, analogous to those documented by Charles Darwin for biological evolution. Mental illness and retardation are forms of unfitness, and the unfit do not survive or prosper. Helping the unfit to survive shifts the responsibility for their support to future generations. The rediscovery of Gregor Mendel's work on heredity in 1900 and the extrapolation of his thoughts to the inheritance of mental defects in humans contributed both to the belief in the organic etiology of mental defects and to the contentions of social Darwinism.

If mental defectiveness was largely genetic, as the extreme hereditarians of the time contended, and was essentially incurable, as the institutional statistics seemed to indicate, the only solution to the problem was custodial care for the unfortunates and the prevention of their reproduction by segregation and/or sterilization. Although such extreme views were not universal from the 1920s to the 1950s, they were fairly typical and tended to dominate during this period.

RESIDENTIAL INSTITUTIONS

The first facilities for the handicapped either were or soon became residential hospitals or asylums. Typically, they were built in relatively rural areas and often became segregated, isolated, sheltered asylums with little community contact. Today most countries, and all the states of the United States, provide residential institutions for various types of handicapped children and adults—the mentally retarded, the mentally ill, the blind, the deaf, the delinquent, and in some cases the epileptic and the orthopedically handicapped. These residential institutions are both publicly and privately supported and administered, at the national, state, regional, county, or municipal level. They range all the way from schools which provide relatively short-term care, rehabilitation, education, and training for mildly handicapped individuals to facilities which provide lifelong custodial care for the totally dependent. Sometimes the entire range of care is given within one institution.

The total residential population of the handicapped in the United States increased regularly from the inception of residential institutions until the middle 1950s. Since that time the residential population has declined precipitously. For example, the patient population in public mental hospitals declined by half (from 500,000 to 250,000) between 1955 and 1973, despite a 40 percent increase in the general population of the United States. However, in 1975, in addition to the quarter-million people (mostly adults) in mental hospitals, there were nearly twice this many children and young people living in twenty-four-hour residential institutions (Gula, 1974). During this period many people were calling for the total abolition of segregated facilities—institutional, special school, and special class—for the handicapped. They believed that all the handicapped should be integrated into the community and/or regular school classes (Smith & Arkans, 1974; Hobbs, 1975).

Exposés of segregated social institutions (prisons, mental hospitals, and residential schools), which have regularly disclosed patterns of isolation, rejection, neglect, and the ultimate dehumanization of individuals as the result of practices supposedly designed for the good of those segregated, have been partially responsible for a swinging of the pendulum to the opposite extreme. The deinstitutionalization movement is also consistent with the current national policy for human services which emphasizes broad developmental and preventive programs from birth and before, rather than crisis intervention, correction, and repair after the damage is done (Perrucci, 1974).

A national policy seeking equal access for all children to opportunities essential to the fullest realization of their potential began to manifest itself in the early 1960s. To some, it seems that American society in the 1970s had reached a new plateau of maturity in this respect (Hobbs, 1975), reflected in the wealth of legislation enacted in the interest of the disadvantaged. This legislation started with the establishment of the President's Panel on Mental Retardation in 1961 and the subsequent building and staffing of twelve Mental Retardation Research Centers and twenty university-affiliated facilities to provide professional teaching and clinical personnel to work with the mentally retarded. This development was followed by important programs and facilities such as Head Start, Home Start, Health Start, the Center for Child Abuse, Comprehensive Emergency Services, Action for Foster Children, Parent-Child Centers, Education for Parenting, Child Development Associates, and the Developmental Disabilities Program. We have already discussed court rulings requiring equal access to educational opportunities, better procedures for identifying and classifying the handicapped, humane treatment of the institutionalized, and the extention of civil rights and legal protection to the handicapped and disadvantaged. The humanists, concerned with the dehumanizing effects of segregated institutions, have been joined by those responsible for the financing of these facilities. Our public institutions—whether reformatories and prisons or state schools for the handicapped and mental hospitals—have uniformly been inadequately financed, overcrowded, and understaffed. Despite increasing appropriations, the funds available were never able to meet the increasing costs. For example, the cost per patient per year for residents in state and county mental hospitals in the United States increased from $1,116.59 in 1955 to $9,207.90 in 1973. The direct cost of community care is less than that of institutional care. For example, the average yearly cost for maintaining a child in the California Youth Authority institution in

1971 was $5,800, as contrasted to $2,300 required for the Community Treatment Program (Palmer, 1971; Hobbs, 1975). State legislators and governors often saw deinstitutionalization as a way of decreasing the tremendous costs of caring for the special needs of the handicapped. Consequently, they joined the cry for the elimination of large residential institutions. However, the real savings effected by well-designed, adequately staffed, and properly executed community-based programs should be their demonstrated superior performance in preparing people to live more normal, productive, and self-fulfilled lives, rather than the immediate savings in money.

By the mid-1970s many people were having second thoughts about the entire desegregation movement (Martin, 1974; Dailey, 1974; Balla, Butterfield, & Zigler, 1974; Wilkins, 1974). They were concerned partly because the wholesale elimination of existing programs was not accompanied by the provision of better or even equivalent alternatives. For ___ individuals the movement from the mental hospital, residential ___ special class into the group home, the board-and-care facility, ___ar school or class may be a step forward, but for others it is ___ J. F. Winschel and E. A. Lawrence (1975) state, "So far, ___ been an adventure for which none of us—children, ___essionals—has been adequately prepared and which ___ continued miseducation of retarded children." K. ___ (1976) similarly comments that "deinstitutionalization has all too often meant the unceremonious dumping of former patients into hostile communities, where they roam the streets aimlessly or live in the degradation of welfare hotels or flophouses—with no semblance of follow-up care or treatment."

The original awesome growth of large custodial residential institutions for dependent, delinquent, retarded, and mentally ill individuals occurred largely because local community services for these individuals were not available. The turnabout (deinstitutionalization) can be a disaster if equivalent or better conditions and services are not provided in the local community. These conditions include not only an operational community service system but acceptance and support of the services by local legislative, executive, and legal bodies, and even more important, a willingness of the general citizenry to accept and help these deviant individuals (Gula, 1974; Hobbs, 1975). Resistance to deinstitutionalization is also inevitable because of tradition, job protection (the California State Employees Association vigorously opposed the closing of some state hospitals in that state), anxiety when large numbers of released patients are relocated within a small area (a square mile surrounding San Jose State University in San Jose, California, houses some 2,000 of the patients released from the Agnews State Mental Hospital located on the outskirts of the city), and the fear that the welfare of both the handicapped and the general public is being jeopardized. It is interesting to note that despite much local criticism of and opposition to deinstitutionalization, A. Brandt (1975) considers the San Jose program one of the two in the entire country that are doing any real good.

The old solution was to make the "problem" disappear by putting it out of sight in an institution. When the festering sore of the institution was repeatedly exposed to view, we believed that the institution was the problem, which would disappear when the unfortunates were returned to the community. However, we forget that the institutionalized deviants were "problems" in the eyes of the community before their institutionalization; their return to the community, in itself, solves nothing.

Not only have we failed to provide better care and treatment facilities in the communities, we have also failed to anticipate and deal with community resistance (prejudices) to the everyday presence of other human beings who are deviant. The community grapevine still i̶ that "these people are scary," "these people are dangerous," "t̶ our neighborhood," "their presence decreases property val̶ people are better off in a place of their own" (Klein, 19̶ tion of problems and our proposed solutions are ̶ limited by current social attitudes. When and only ̶ ception of mental, physical, and social deviates is ̶ normalization and mainstreaming of the̶e people beco̶ possib̶ is a basic prerequisite to the committing of the always limited resources to the problems of these individuals.

F. N. Arnhoff (1975) points out that one of the reservations concerning the movement to desegregate mental deviants has arisen from the recognition that, although many of these people *can* be treated and maintained in the community, there remain a large number of individuals who are unable to exist outside an institutional setting or its equivalent. Arnhoff also insists that conventional comparisons of community, family, or small-group care with institutional monetary costs overlook a large segment of the cost of the former—using the term *cost* in its broadest sense. Cost-benefit comparisons must consider the increased psychological and social disruption in integrated situations. Sometimes hospitalization is avoided by keeping the mentally retarded or psychotic person in the family. In such situations, the cost to the other family members from exposure to a psychotic parent or sibling in varying states of medicinally-controlled remission must also be considered. The disruption of normal family functioning, the psychological stresses, and the labor costs are often tremendous, and must be considered along with the monetary savings to the taxpayer. The presumed, or demonstrated, benefits to the patient and the possible reduced direct monetary costs to the state must be weighed against the broadly-defined psychological and social costs to all involved.

In the opinion of some people, the abuses and neglect of patients have simply been transferred from the large institution to the nursing and board-and-care facilities in the community. Investigating committees are now compiling recommendations for upgrading conditions in the small community-based facilities, including more professional care, better-educated staff, more recreational and social opportunities for the residents, and more meaningful activities and purposeful occupations (Hobbs, 1975). These have the familiar ring of the recommendations made over the years by innumerable commissions which have investigated large residential institutions. It is possible that considering the total social costs, the precipitous closing of large institutions, without providing better facilities in the community or preparing the citizenry to accept those released, will defeat a potentially fruitful reform (Thurman & Thiele, 1973).

It seems unrealistic to expect that *all* handicapped can be returned to their homes, foster homes, group homes, or other open, community-based programs. There will still be a need for institutional care for the severely disabled, particularly the multiple-handicapped. Some individuals will require intensive care in closed facilities and some may require lifelong institutional care (Wilkins, 1974; Zneimer, 1973, 1975).

SOME ALTERNATIVES TO THE INSTITUTION

The deinstitutionalization movement is not new (Gula, 1974). As early as 1916 a Jewish orphanage in New York established an auxiliary group home to help prepare orphaned adolescent girls for normal home and community living. During the 1930s social legislation was passed in the United States to provide financial aid to families with dependent children, child welfare services, public adoption agencies, and foster home care as alternatives to orphanage care for neglected and dependent children. As a result, the number of children in orphanages was reduced by half in the next two decades. However, the number of institutionalized delinquents, mental deficients, and mentally ill continued to increase (Gula, 1974).

In the late 1950s and early '60s a major drive began for the development of group homes and similar community facilities as alternatives to custodial institutions. The 1970s have seen the beginning of comprehensive community-based human-services systems for social-service and health delivery. While these broad human service systems are still in the conceptualization and planning stage, they are perceived as an alternative to the proliferation and fragmentation of human service facilities which still prevail in the United States. This fragmentation of services is largely the result of the funding of services according to categories of disabilities by federal, state, and local appropriating and governing bodies.

The movement to blanket the conventional categorical service facilities (mental illness, mental retardation, blindness, deafness, delinquency, and so on) into a broad coordinated service system may be facilitated by several concurrent developments. Among these are class action law suits establishing constitutional rights to effective services for all the handicapped, and the concern with the effects of labeling and stigmatizing individuals (one of the secondary consequences of providing services by categories). The advocacy groups working for specific categories such as minority ethnics, homosexuals, prisoners, females, and the more conventional categories of the handicapped are discovering that they have much in common; they may eventually combine their efforts in favor of broad service systems. In the meantime, less comprehensive national, state, and local efforts at establishing the more conventional community services as alternatives to institutionalization continue.

Our discussion of the deinstitutionalization and mainstreaming movements has focused on the mentally retarded and the emotionally disturbed because these groups have been the focus of recent concern. However, most of the components of the models proposed for attaining these ends for mental deviates have long been part of the programs available to the physically handicapped. While there has been considerable discussion of the relative merits of the residential versus the special class for the blind, the deaf, and the orthopedically handicapped, the questions have centered around the types and categories of children who could be most effectively educated in these respective settings. Institutionalization was never the norm. Long before the current deinstitutionalization movement got under way, residential schools for children in these categories were decreasing in importance, and special classes in day schools were increasing. The deinstitutionalization of the bulk of these handicapped children began long ago.

Most of the special educational classes for these categories of handicapped were also partially integrated. Most frequently, a special teacher had the major responsibility for the handicapped, but integrated the children into regular classes to the extent that it was feasible. Partial integration was also the most common administrative arrangement for the educable mentally retarded at the high school level. Completely self-contained classes for the mentally retarded were largely confined to the elementary grades. In the compartmentalized high school, the mentally retarded typically studied industrial arts, home economics, music, art, and physical education along with the "normal" students. They were segregated only in their home rooms and in more academically demanding courses. Thus, many components of the current normalization or mainstreaming movement have long been part of most conventional special education programs. Among the facilities that have functioned as alternatives to the residential institution are day hospitals, day care centers, foster and adoptive homes, halfway houses, boarding homes, and sheltered workshops.

Day hospitals or day treatment centers

Day hospitals have been used principally for psychiatric patients who need intensive treatment and who are able to spend their nights elsewhere—usually in their homes. Day hospitals are less expensive than the usual residential facility, and they keep the patient related to home and community rather than separated and isolated from them. The first such hospital was established in Moscow in 1932. Since that time similar facilities have been established in many countries. In 1960, 5,000 patients a year were receiving care in twenty-six American day hospitals (Winich, 1960); California has established several such centers (MacMillan & Aase, 1964).

The day hospital reduces the likelihood that the patient will become over-dependent on institutional life. Many individuals adapt to institutional life too readily. They feel secure in the hospital and become fearful of a return to their homes and community. The day hospital reduces this "hospitalization effect." Experience indicates that some patients respond to treatment more readily in a day hospital than they do in a residential setting which offers total care.

The day hospital also seems to incur less stigma than does the regular psychiatric facility, partly because the patients continue to live at home and partly because legal commitment is avoided. Day hospitals must be in or near larger population centers and have adequate public transportation.

In addition to physical therapy, pharmacotherapy, and individual and group psychotherapy, there is usually provision for occupational therapy, school classes, libraries, and recreation. Occupational training or retraining is also offered in almost all day centers. Patients may be transferred to outpatient departments, halfway houses, day care centers, or other facilities upon completion of treatment, or, when they do not respond or are judged to be too ill for the day hospital, they may be transferred to a custodial institution. The day hospital has been used more for adults than for children. One study reports that only 10 percent of the patients were below the age of twenty. Day hospitals have also been used primarily for the more seriously emotionally disturbed patients—the neurotics and psychotics (Kramer, 1960).

Day care centers for the handicapped

The disabled child who is either too young or too severely handicapped to take advantage of the special education and other training programs of the community often places a tremendous strain on the personal and financial resources of his family. When such children remain isolated at home, they also lack the social contacts and experiences which are necessary for maximum development. To lessen the burden on the family and to provide some social contacts for these children, day care centers have been established in most larger communities. Private day care centers have been operating for many years, and publicly supported agencies have recently been established (Jew, 1974).

The original day care programs provided physical care alone, but more recently self-help and socialization training have been added. Several states have established nursery school programs for preschool mental retardates.

The advantages of day care centers for the handicapped are: (1) the parents are relieved of the twenty-four-hour task of caring for the handicapped child; (2) nonhandicapped siblings will not be neglected because the excessive demands of the handicapped child will be diminished; (3) the rest of the family can live a more normal social life because the emotional strain is diminished and a more wholesome family atmosphere facilitated; (4) the parents may be able and willing to keep the child at home instead of placing him in an institution or boarding home; and (5) the training received in such centers may raise the child's level of functioning to the point where he can attend special classes, become partially self-supporting, or at least be less of a burden to others. Day care centers for many types of the handicapped stand midway between the traditional outpatient clinic and inpatient hospital services. The day care facility provides more constant and intensive supervision, care, and treatment than does an outpatient service. It combines care, treatment, and rehabilitation. In some cases, a single administrative organization may operate an inservice unit, a day care program, an outpatient department, and, either on its own or in cooperation with other agencies, vocational rehabilitation services (Wolins, 1974).

Outpatient clinics

Another community-based facility serving the disabled which is expanding rapidly is the outpatient clinic. Individuals no longer requiring the supervision and intensive treatment of the residential facility or the day care center may report to an outpatient clinic daily or weekly, as required, for treatment or counseling. The community outpatient clinic may serve as a diagnostic center, as a limited treatment facility, and as a referral agency.

The future will probably witness still more significant changes in the development of comprehensive community-based services for exceptional people. Many such centers, to provide for all the needs of the handicapped, including preventive, diagnostic, and rehabilitative care and consultative and educational needs, are now in operation, and still more are being planned.

Foster home or family care facilities

Most states provide some type of family care for handicapped children (Zeller, 1974). Appropriate public agencies normally approve or license and supervise the homes and children involved. Children so placed can take advantage of community education and training programs, to the extent of their ability to profit from them, and foster homes or families provide a more normal and stimulating life than the average residential institution. This type of placement is particularly advantageous for the child who cannot live in his own home but who has the potential for living an at least semi-independent life in the community. Families providing homes for such children are usually paid by the state or county. Some families accept several handicapped children of a given type and operate what is, in effect, a boarding home for small groups of children.

The demand for foster homes far exceeds the supply, and handicapped children rank low among the categories considered favourable for foster home placement. The parents of the handicapped are often the most willing to accept other handicapped children into their homes as foster children. Two handicapped children in the same home can often provide companionship for each other and relieve the nonhandicapped siblings of the responsibility of being a "playmate by default" to the handicapped sibling (O'Regan, 1974).

Adoption services for the handicapped

At one time moderately or severely handicapped children were considered unadoptable. However, most of these children are now referred to as hard-to-place children, and many are being adopted (Nash, 1974). Many such adoptions are facilitated by the Adoption Resource Exchange of North America (ARENA), a clearinghouse organized and operated by the Child Welfare League of America to help agencies find homes for their hard-to-place children. Any licensed adoption agency may register—without charge—children for whom they are unable to find homes, and approved families who are willing to accept a hard-to-place child can do likewise. From this information, families and children are tentatively matched and referred to local agencies for further consideration and action.

While many agencies are phasing out their adoption services because of the shortage of infants, others are accepting for placement more of the hard-to-place children—minority ethnic group children, older children, and the handicapped. Handicapped children whose adoption has been facilitated through ARENA include those with dwarfism, mental retardation, blindness, deafness, cardiac disorders, epilepsy, emotional disturbances, speech defects, hyperactivity, and albinism (Nash, 1974). Many children previously "lost" in foster homes and institutions are now being "found" and placed for adoption. Some agencies see the current imbalance between available infants and adoptive applicants as an opportunity to extend their services to those children and families who have been largely overlooked in the past. Today's definition of an adoptable child as "any child in need of a permanent family who can benefit by family life" (Gallagher, 1972) makes this feasible.

One development which has enlarged the categories of adoptable children and adoptive families is that of subsidized adoptions (Gallagher, 1972). Financial reimbursement makes possible the adoption of handicapped children by otherwise acceptable parents who cannot afford to assume the financial responsibilities involved. By the mid-1970s, thirty-nine states and the District of Columbia had passed subsidized adoption legislation to provide a subsidy for children who are handicapped (Kravik, 1975). Such financial assistance often enables a family to adopt a child requiring special medical, nursing, or psychiatric care, or educational-rehabilitation programs. Organizations are becoming increasingly active in promoting the interests of children who are awaiting adoption and in providing post-adoptive services to adopted children and their adoptive families (Gallagher, 1972; Neilson, 1972).

Halfway houses

Sometimes the boarding home is used much like a dormitory in a residential institution. The halfway house provides a facility for older adolescents and adults, in which handicapped persons may live for varying periods of time preparatory to going out into the community entirely on their own. People residing in such facilities may be working in a sheltered workshop or on competitive jobs; they may be receiving vocational rehabilitation or simply seeking employment. The halfway home is typically an intermediate step for individuals who will soon return to the community following a period of institutionalization; but, like family care and the boarding home, it can serve as an alternative to institutionalization.

The halfway house, as an aftercare facility which has been used primarily for discharged patients, is designed to assist the patient's transition from hospital to community life. It is used for alcoholics, criminals, the mentally ill, and juvenile delinquents. It facilitates the movement of the individual from his dependent existence in an institution in which he received total care to the free community, by providing an intermediate situation—a more independent, but still relatively simple life in a supervised residential facility. Vermont has established a network of such houses as a transitional facility between the state mental hospital and a rehabilitation agency (Wechsler, 1960b). The halfway house provides a sheltered social environment in which new roles and behaviors can be tried and developed. Most provide professional counseling and supervision (Wechsler, 1960a). The period of residence is typically limited to from three months to a year.

Similar facilities in rural settings are sometimes known as "work camp houses." In such settings, jobs are available on the grounds and the residents are usually there twenty-four hours a day (Wechsler, 1960a, 1961).

Group homes

While halfway houses in the past were primarily pre- or post-institutional facilities, many group homes today are part of the broad deinstitutionalization movement. Group homes are operated for the emotionally disturbed, the mentally retarded, actual or potential delinquents, alcoholics and ex-alcoholics, and drug addicts and ex-addicts, detached from earlier pre- or post-institutional connections. Group homes, like halfway houses, provide residential care, supervision, counseling, and/or therapy for a broad class of deviant individuals (Jewett, 1973).

Group homes have been established in large family dwellings, apartments, high-rises, and public housing units. Their quality varies greatly, and many have been criticized for several reasons. Some programs lack dedicated leadership, sufficient funds, and public support. One fear is that such community facilities place potentially dangerous mental defectives and delinquents free on the streets. As we mentioned earlier, in some cases deinstitutionalization has meant precipitously moving the mentally ill and mentally deficient from "back wards" to "back alleys" without needed resources and services.

A recent court ruling focuses on this problem. A 1970 National Institute of Mental Health study reported that 56 percent of the 3,600 patients in the St. Elizabeth Hospital in Washington, D.C.—once regarded as the finest mental institution in the United States—did not belong in the hospital and would be better off in alternative care facilities. In 1974 a class action suit was filed in the U.S. District Court. Judge Aubrey Robinson ruled in *Dixon* v. *Weinberger* that the federal government must provide alternative care facilities such as nursing homes, foster homes, and halfway houses for St. Elizabeth's inpatient population capable of living in such community-based settings. Judge Robinson stated that a full range of treatment must be made available to those placed in these residential facilities (Schaar, 1976).

VOCATIONAL REHABILITATION PROGRAMS

All the states of the United States provide vocational rehabilitation programs for disabled adults. The public program of vocational rehabilitation had its beginnings in World War I, was started officially in 1920, and has expanded tremendously since World War II. Many state rehabilitation programs have recently been expanded to include mentally retarded and psychiatrically disabled adults, as well as the physically handicapped. Rehabilitation personnel are also cooperating with the schools. They take those individuals who either finish the school program or exceed the age limits for school attendance and provide them with additional vocational training, counseling, and supervision.

To be eligible for the services of the Vocational Rehabilitation Agency, the person must be substantially handicapped as a result of a physical or mental disability; he must be of employable age by the time the rehabilitation services are completed; and he must show promise of becoming employable or of attaining a higher level of vocational adequacy as a consequence of the service. These requirements limit the program to older adolescents and to those with milder handicaps.

The vocational rehabilitation agencies have no training facilities of their own, but purchase such services from existing resources. The financial help provided by this service has facilitated the development of training centers, sheltered workshops, and on-the-job training programs for the handicapped. Anyone can refer a handicapped person to a local vocational rehabilitation office. The vocational rehabilitation program includes evaluation (medical, psychological, and vocational), training (school, sheltered workshop, or on-the-job), and eventual job placement. All these services are provided at no direct cost to the client (Borrelli, 1972).

SHELTERED WORKSHOPS

As the name indicates, a sheltered workshop is a facility providing training or employment geared to the capacities and need of people who cannot satisfactorily be trained or employed in normal competitive job situations because of special disabilities. Such workshops are found in public and private residential institutions and as independent endeavors in the community. Like the vocational rehabilitation programs, they are primarily for adults.

Individuals working at sheltered employment may, at the lowest level, spend their days in the workshop, keeping busy. Even with maximum assistance and supervision, these people produce little of economic importance, although they act like ordinary employed adults. The workshop serves somewhat the same function for these people that the day care center does for younger children. The work done by individuals with greater aptitude—the "sheltered employable" group of persons—can contribute significantly to their support. People functioning on this level may be partially self-supporting in the workshop, but they can probably never compete in an ordinary environment. Individuals with greater potential—the "deferred employable" group—use the sheltered workshop purely for training, preparatory to their placement in ordinary employment. On this level, the sheltered shop mediates between idleness and regular employment. The workshop is primarily a means of controlling the stress on the workers and of assisting handicapped people to increase their self-sufficiency. The shop often provides training in skills which can be used in other jobs; in addition, it may inculcate general work habits, attitudes, and self-confidence which, it is hoped, will carry over to future employment even in different jobs. It is assumed that the disabled person in a sheltered workshop can develop a "work personality" consisting of punctuality, cooperative work habits, and desirable ways of relating to authority, as well as favorable attitudes toward a job, a boss, fellow workers, and earnings (Borrelli, 1972).

People in sheltered workshops may make new things for sale, repair or recondition used articles for resale, or contract or subcontract work from private industry. Such workshops have long provided employment and training for the auditory, visually, and orthopedically handicapped; more recently, some workshops have also accepted the mentally retarded and the mentally ill. Many separate workshops have also been established solely for the mentally retarded or emotionally disturbed (Borrelli, 1972; Walthall & Love, 1974). In 1960 there were more than 600 sheltered workshops in the United States. Over 100 of these were operated by one organization, Goodwill Industries (Olshansky, 1960).

SOCIAL AND RECREATIONAL PROGRAMS

The handicapped child, like every other child, needs a social life and recreation. The overprotection provided in some homes, the failure of ordinary groups and organizations to accept the handicapped, and the inherent limitations of the uniquely disabled necessitate special provision for the social and recreational needs of the handicapped. In communities where special educational programs, training facilities, vocational programs, and occupational outlets for the disabled are either not available or are very limited, recreational and social programs may provide the handicapped with their sole opportunities for social contacts.

While many handicapped individuals can participate in the regular social and recreational programs of the community, many others cannot. Recreational programs for the handicapped may not differ markedly from those provided for the general public, but it often necessary to provide some special equipment, training, and supervision. In addition to regular, supervised playground activities and group games, these programs may include conducted field trips, day and summer camps, social groups, and clubs. The programs are often provided or sponsored by city or school recreational departments, voluntary groups and agencies, churches, the YWCA and YMCA, the Boy Scouts and the Girl Scouts, and similar organizations.

One type of cooperative self-help organization contributing to the recreational and social life of some types of handicapped adults is the expatient club. Such clubs were first started in England in 1940. By 1959 an estimated seventy clubs were operating in the United States, the largest concentration of such clubs being in California (Olshansky, 1960).

RESPITE CARE

A Respite Home Program has been developed by the Hartford Regional Center (an agency of the Connecticut Department of Health, Office of Mental Retardation) to provide temporary care to enable families with handicapped children to take vacations, to cope with emergencies, or just to find temporary relief from the constant stress of caring for a handicapped individual. The respite program is a community-based, family-centered alternative to institutional care. Temporary care (not exceeding thirty days) is provided a handicapped child in the home of another family—a "respite family." Social workers screen prospective respite families, match natural and respite families, and provide back-up and emergency services when needed. Emergency medical services are also available. When such a placement seems desirable, the social worker arranges a preplacement visit in the home of the respite family; the natural parents, the child, and the coordinator himself are present. If both families are agreeable, the contract for the period of care is signed. The fees ($10 a day for the first two days and $5 a day thereafter) are paid by the natural parents to the respite family. Funds are available for the care of children whose parents cannot afford the cost (Case, Fitzgerald, & Ficarro, 1975).

When the California state residential facilities for the mentally retarded operated school programs, many of the children enrolled in these schools spent their summer vacations at home with their families. Since this left space available in the institutions, other mentally retarded children were accepted for temporary placement to permit their families to be free for vacations and other activities, just as the Hartford Respite Home Program currently does.

PROGRAMS OF HOME TRAINING AND COUNSELING

Most parents of handicapped children lack the knowledge and skills needed to train them effectively. Yet home training services, although they are an essential part of a comprehensive program for the disabled, are available in few communities. The John Tracy clinic in Los Angeles provides information concerning home training techniques for the parents of deaf children; it conducts a nursery school for deaf children and special training classes for parents; and it has hundreds of parents enrolled in its correspondence course. Similar services are provided by the Chicago Hearing Society and Clinic. The Volta Bureau in Washington, another good source of information for parents, also teaches special educational techniques to parents of deaf children. Similar sources of information and training are available to the families of the blind. The National Association for Retarded Children, which has its headquarters in New York and has many state and local affiliates, serves as a clearinghouse for information about the mentally retarded. The United Cerebral Palsy Association, Inc., and its local affiliates perform a similar function for victims of cerebral palsy. The United States Children's Bureau in Washington, D.C., is a good source of information on all types of exceptional children.

The counseling facilities available to the parents of the mentally retarded and most of the other categories are still quite inadequate. Clinic staffs, private physicians, city and county health officials, social workers, nurses, and school personnel all provide some counseling and information for parents of exceptional children, but this is usually sporadic and not followed up. Most parents need and welcome assistance in understanding the significance of their child's condition and would benefit from more information and counseling about handling and training the child.

One agency, whose historical exclusive function has been the placement of children who needed separation from their parents, has recently developed a program of home services designed to keep such children at home (Goldstein, 1973). This agency accepts the fact that long-term treatment is inevitable in most such cases. Treatment includes not only conventional casework, counseling, and sometimes psychotherapy, but also the development of personal-social, home-making, child-care, and vocational skills. The social work job becomes that of "parenting" both children and parents. Social workers share in planning and carrying out many ordinary daily tasks and activities, providing many direct, concrete supportive services. Fewer than 5 percent of the children served by this program have required separation from their parents. The program involves long-term treatment—children have received treatment for as long as five and a half years at a cost of approximately $1,000 per year per child.

The exceptional person himself needs special counseling and guidance. Achieving self-understanding, establishing goals consistent with one's abilities and disabilities, and making realistic life plans are major problems in everyone's life, but they are especially critical and difficult for the exceptional individual. While there seems to be nothing distinctive and unique about the personalities of exceptional people, the handicapped do have more severe problems of adjustment and are thus in greater need of counseling. The evaluation of the aptitudes of exceptional children is difficult, and their educational programs are often different. Their vocational opportunities are unique, and the need for specially trained counselors is great.

EDUCATION OF THE GENERAL PUBLIC
CONCERNING EXCEPTIONAL CHILDREN

One of the greatest needs of exceptional people is increased public awareness, acceptance, and understanding of exceptionality—particularly of disabling exceptionality. In the first place, unless a substantial part of the public recognizes the needs of the handicapped, the disabled will not be provided with the necessary facilities, programs, and opportunities. Second, unless the general public understands the nature of the difficulties and the needs of the various types of disabled persons, even the available resources and opportunities may be denied them.

The handicapped person does not need sympathy and pity. He needs understanding and acceptance as a person with certain limitations. There is little use in training a handicapped child to become socially adept and aware if fearful and anxious neighbors will not let their children play with him. It is not helpful to teach him to play games, or to sing and dance, if he remains socially unacceptable. Occupational and vocational training programs are wasted if employers will not give the handicapped an opportunity to demonstrate their competence. Many a business person will send a handicapped child to summer camp but not employ him when he grows up. There has been a significant increase in public awareness and understanding of the disabled, but there is still much to be done and too few agencies to do it.

FROM SPECIAL CLASSES TO MAINSTREAMING

In the century since the first special classes were established in the United States, segregated special classrooms or schools have been the most popular administrative arrangements for educating the handicapped. However, during the last two decades two movements have changed the nature of special education in America. One of these has been the "right to education" or "zero reject" trend. Until recently, large numbers of children were excluded from school programs because they were "too something-or-other"—too mentally deficient, too emotionally disturbed, too crippled, or too unmanageable. However, since recent legal decisions have enunciated the legal right to education, many children previously excluded from school have been provided with special programs.

Changing social attitudes have also facilitated this trend. The inclusion of more and more of the mentally retarded in the school program is fairly typical. In most states, provision for the mentally retarded has followed a common course over the past thirty years. First, additional funds (usually in the form of special state aid) were made available to school districts which elected to provide special programs for the mildly mentally retarded (the educable mentally retarded). Next, it was made mandatory for school districts to provide such programs. A decade later, the same sequence of events—first permissive and then mandatory programs—resulted in the establishment of similar provisions for the moderately retarded (the trainable mentally retarded). Still more recently in some states, special programs for the severely mentally retarded have been provided under educational auspices.

Recent legal decisions and legislation have both reflected and accelerated the movement to require that all children, regardless of handicap or

level of functioning, have access to appropriate education and/or training. The courts have said, in effect, that none of the conventional reasons
for exclusion from school—no money, no room, no facilities, no teachers,
or low aptitude for learning—could be used to justify the withholding of
education from certain categories of children. If communities do not have
at their disposal the additional money necessary to provide teachers,
space, equipment, and transportation for these new students, they must
reallocate the available resources currently assigned exclusively to other
categories of children.

Another movement that is changing the nature of special education
in America was mentioned earlier: providing services on a noncategorical
basis and retaining the deviant child in the regular classroom with supplementary instructional assistance and support provided by specialized
personnel—popularly referred to as mainstreaming. The current emphasis
on noncategorical treatment and mainstreaming was brought about by
a series of events including:

1. The failure of research studies to establish the effectiveness of special
   classes for the handicapped.
2. A realization of the inadequacy of medically and psychologically defined
   diagnostic categories for educational purposes.
3. Studies indicating that many educationally and aptitude-irrelevant factors,
   such as race, social class, personality characteristics, and manageability,
   were operative in special class placement (Rubin, Krus, & Balow, 1973).
4. A realization of the deleterious effects of officially categorizing and
   labeling, a traditional prerequisite for providing needed educational
   assistance.
5. Court judgments and legislation of the type already mentioned (Chaffin,
   1974).

Some philosophical assumptions

One of the most basic assumptions underlying the current trends is
that every human being—handicapped or not—is entitled to the fullest
measure of the available educational resources. Society, via its educational system, has the obligation to devise programs and provide treatment tailored to meet the deviant child's individual needs, rather than
simply sorting them according to the degree that they fit existing programs and techniques and excluding those who do not fit. It is also
assumed that mainstreaming will foster the valuing rather than the
stigmatization of human differences.

Labeling and segregating the deviants increases their distinct categorization and stigmatization. Consequently, keeping them in the regular classroom will increase the mutual understanding and acceptance of
normal and deviant. Public policies and educational practices should
encourage not mere tolerance, but a positive valuing of differences. They

should encourage respect for individuality and an appreciation of the differing talents of persons who are different physically, mentally, linguistically, and culturally. Current classification systems (institutional, special class, or special school placement) have fostered stigmatization and have discriminated against the poor and certain minority ethnic groups.

It is also assumed that mainstreaming the handicapped will result in the improvement of instruction for all children.

SOME PROPOSED PROGRAM CHANGES

Specific programs for exceptional children can best be understood as a part of larger programs and movements. We have indicated that community services for troubled and handicapped children in the United States have always been inadequate. The rapid growth of large custodial residential institutions for dependent, delinquent, retarded, and emotionally disturbed children occurred largely because no alternatives were available. The multi-billion-dollar expenditures for these institutions, which increased each year, diverted funds from potentially more effective community resources. Beginning in the early 1960s and gathering momentum in the 1970s, a concerted movement arose to develop nationwide community services as alternatives to custodial and other segregated facilities (Gula, 1974; Hobbs, 1975).

The fragmentation of services

Commissions which have surveyed the services available for exceptional individuals have uniformly been appalled by the disarray. The dispersion of responsibility among dozens of overlapping and sometimes competing agencies, the fragmentation of services, and the frequency with which persons in need of services become lost in the system have been documented repeatedly. The confusion is equally dismaying when seen from the inside by the families involved, as well as by the handicapped themselves. It is often difficult for families or individuals to learn what services are available. The handicapped may be referred endlessly from agency to agency, never receiving comprehensive evaluation or assistance. All agree that the old system—or lack of it—is costly, ineffective, and sometimes does more harm than good.

Integrated human service systems

In the 1970s several events indicated that the movement to establish a set of nationwide comprehensive community-based service systems was taking root. Already established systems which involve this concept are the community mental health centers and the regional mental retardation centers; there are proposals for new social service and health delivery systems. Each of these combine traditional service systems to establish more comprehensive community-based services. Several ambitious programs of this type have already been launched (Gula, 1974; Rosen, 1974). A number of states (thirty in 1974) have established coordinating offices for human resources (Hobbs, 1975). These offices usually include all, or several, of the following conventional departments: welfare, corrections, mental health, mental retardation, and physical health. We currently seem to be moving toward programs providing a wide range of coordinated human services systems including instruction, counseling and support for parents in their homes, medical and legal services, day care services, emergency shelters and temporary facilities, foster homes, hostels, group and halfway houses, rehabilitation services, sheltered workshops, day hospitals, night hospitals, hospitals for intensive care, convalescent and nursing homes, outpatient care, categorical and noncategorical self-contained special classes, partially and completely integrated school classes, and short- and long-term custodial institutions. Such an array of integrated services should enable the parents of a child with special needs to register the child at birth; the system would then assume lifetime responsibility for providing the services needed in assisting or replacing the family in caring for the child. Registration should occur as soon as the handicapping condition is suspected.

A genuinely comprehensive public services program requires that society accept responsibility for the total welfare of all its citizens. Although such programs will be involved in preventing personal waste and human misery and increasing personal competence, they are also concerned with those experiences, conditions, and institutions that promote, nurture, and perpetuate self-realization and social effectiveness.

When intervention in the form of support or treatment becomes necessary, the usual objective is to maintain the deviant individual as close to his intimates in the family and community as possible. When an individual becomes unable to mantain himself without additional help, a spectrum of services is used; a series of increasingly supportive levels of intervention which will ordinarily be kept at a minimum, oriented toward gradually decreasing levels of support leading to the client's return to his home and/or community.

The first level of sustaining support is the client's primary group, usually his family. The goal of the first level of intervention is to maintain the individual in his home or, if necessary, to remove him from this setting and then return him as soon as possible. The person's intimates need to be involved in the treatment process from beginning to end.

The second level of support involves the more active participation of a caseworker or paraprofessional. This person assists the members of the family in providing the additional support necessary, determines if, and when, additional treatment is necessary, and then follows through on these needs.

When a higher level of intervention seems necessary, outpatient care by higher-level professionals may be provided. When sustaining on an outpatient level is deemed insufficient, a still higher level of intervention involving semiprotective or total-care institutionalization may be necessary. The overriding principle involved is that the most appropriate treatment should be provided in the least restrictive alternative situation (Jew, 1974).

One of the most important recent pieces of legislation concerning the handicapped is the Education for All Handicapped Children Act of 1975, signed by President Gerald Ford on December 2, 1975. This act commits the federal government to contribute significantly to the education of every handicapped child in the nation. To qualify for federal assistance under the new law, states are required to adopt policies and plans for assuring all handicapped children a free, appropriate public education. Such programs must provide individualized instruction for each child and must involve the parents in planning programs and in bolstering the educational process at home (Williams, 1975). The act requires that priority be given to handicapped children not in school and to the most severely handicapped. It also mandates that treatment and/or education of these individuals take place in the least restrictive environment consistent with their maximum development.

SOME CHARACTERISTICS OF CURRENT EDUCATIONAL PROGRAMS

Even a cursory survey of the current literature indicates that a large number of mainstreaming programs are in operation. While these programs vary widely in administrative organization and variety of services provided, they have enough common features to warrant some generalizations (Deno, 1973; Birch, 1974; Chaffin, 1974; Guerin & Szatlocky, 1974).

A hierarchy of auxiliary services

Special education under mainstreaming becomes a set of services facilitating the tailoring and monitoring of educational programs to meet individual needs, rather than a device for sorting children according to the degree that they fit existing programs. Deno (1973) calls this array of special education services a "cascade of services"; others have simply referred to it as a "service hierarchy" (Chaffin, 1974).

The minimal service provided within such a hierarchy consists of observing the child referred for special consideration, surveying existing records, conferring with the regular classroom teacher, and suggesting the use of procedures and resources already available. At a slightly higher level, it will be necessary to provide a new program specifically for the child with learning problems. At this level, observation of the child is supplemented by formal and informal testing. The auxiliary personnel (school psychologist, resource teacher, speech therapist, or the like) assist the regular teacher in academic diagnosis, program planning, and supply any needed additional instructional resources. At this level, the child stays in the regular classroom but receives supplementary, diagnostic, and instructional services.

At a somewhat higher level of special services intervention, the child leaves the regular class for special assistance, either to receive tutoring or to spend small portions of each day with a resource teacher. Very often, the tutoring or other special assistance is provided in a resource room or center. *Consulting room, floating room, headquarters room,* and *learning center* are alternative terms sometimes used for these service areas (Birch, 1974). When the learning problems are more acute, part-time assignment to a special class may occur. At this level, the major responsibility for the child may be with either the regular or the resource teacher, depending upon the amount of auxiliary instruction provided. The regular and resource teachers both instruct the child and are jointly responsible for the child's progress.

When the child's needs are considered to be so unique or extreme that the combined regular teacher–resource teacher efforts are insufficient, either part-time or full-time special-class placement may be required. Despite the best auxiliary services, the mainstreaming of all children is not possible. Some extreme deviants will always need separate and markedly different educational facilities, even closed residential institutions.

Under a system of special services intervention, the individuation of instruction is emphasized. School psychologists and other auxiliary special education personnel participate in assessing each child's assets and limitations, devising individualized programs which will capitalize on the assets and maximize the student's learning and personal-social development. Tests are used not so much to make comparisons with other children or with a norm as to set up realistic specific educational objectives and subsequently to determine the degree to which these objectives have been attained in preparation for the next steps. Such tests used to monitor progress are known as "criterion-referenced" as contrasted with the more conventional "norm-referenced" tests (Hambleton, 1974). Representative samples of the educational tasks selected from the relevant instructional areas are organized into a criterion-referenced test. Test information is then used to evaluate the child's progress toward instructional objectives and to locate him so as to appropriately select or design his next instructional tasks.

SOME SECOND THOUGHTS CONCERNING MAINSTREAMING

Many leaders in the field of special education believe that mainstreaming is being poorly handled (Dailey, 1974). While there is general agreement that the movement is a healthy one, the following observations and criticisms are common:

1. Too often the special programs have been dropped and students simply re-placed in the same situations from which they came. Under pressure from militant activists who are armed with evidence of the equivocal results of the effectiveness of special classes for the mentally retarded, and with support for the claim that culturally biased tests often result in false diagnosis and inappropriate placement of minority group children in special classes for the retarded, the movement toward the elimination of all special classes for the handicapped in many cases becomes precipitate.

Too often, in our legitimate concern over biased selection procedures, inappropriate placements, stigmatization, and de facto segregation, we forget the overriding fact that these children have overwhelming learning problems. Although race, social class, sex, and general behavioral deviance are often involved, the primary cause of placement in special classes is the failure of the child to learn in the "mainstream." Children referred for possible placement in classes for the mentally retarded, learning disabled, slow learners, or educationally disadvantaged are seldom identified before they enter school. Their differences become apparent as they fail to make the expected progress in kindergarten and first grade. Depending on school policy, they are either retained or socially promoted. Even though the educational-learning deficit is noted from the beginning, it is usually followed by three or four years of schooling in the regular classes. During this time, the children fall further and further behind their peers in school, learn to dislike academic activities, and in many cases develop emotional and behavior problems which interfere with classroom activities. It is typically only after several years of progressively greater educational failure that educationally handicapped children are referred for possible placement in special classes (Hobbs, 1975).

At the point of teacher referral and subsequent consideration for special class placement, secondary factors such as sex, social class, and race become biasing determinants in the disposition of the case. In only the most flagrant cases will a child who is successful educationally be referred and inappropriately placed in a special class. The overriding fact of educational retardation must be present for such placement to occur. A blind faith in the efficacy of "mainstreaming" which places children back into the situation from which they came, expecting that they will somehow "catch up," is paradoxical. As has been suggested, throwing an educationally handicapped child back into a pool of normal learners where he must either sink or swim should never be permitted until the regular teachers have been trained as competent lifesavers (Chaffin, 1974). It would seem axiomatic that the handicapped should not be returned to the regular class until the regular teachers are trained and prepared to teach them and willing to have them.

2. Massive efforts will be required to train more teachers in the requisite skills. Even greater efforts will be required to deal with the prejudicial attitudes of other students, school personnel, parents, and the general public. Without sympathetic and understanding acceptance of the deviants, we may subject many children to even more painful and frustrating educational experiences in the name of progress.

3. Mainstreaming will fail if it means abandoning all assessing, sorting, and classifying and pretending that everyone is educationally equal. Within the mainstream, there will be smaller streams and eddies. Unless, and until, completely individualized diagnostic-prescriptive education is available for all children, groupings and subgroupings will be made along aptitude-educational-competence lines.

4. To be successful, mainstreaming of the handicapped must include provision for a wealth of auxiliary staff people and materials to support and supplement the efforts of the regular teachers. We indicated earlier that the lack of supportive services in the home and community accounted for much unnecessary institutionalization of the handicapped. The continuing absence of these same services is currently threatening the success of the deinstitutionalization movement. The same can be said of the movement to eliminate special classes and "normalize" the children previously enrolled in these classes.

If the return of exceptional children to the regular classes is truly "normalizing," resource teachers, itinerant teachers, master teachers, guidance people, and school psychologists will all have to be intimately involved in developing and effectively executing small-group and individualized programs for the wider range of individual differences in the classroom.

J. R. Lent (1975) points out that mainstreaming of the mentally retarded has been going on for years. For example, of over 11,000 school-age children identified as mentally retarded in New Jersey in 1953, 41 percent were in special education classes, while 49 percent were in regular classes, and 10 percent were not attending school. Thus, the majority of the mentally retarded in New Jersey were mainstreamed in the regular classes. Lent is skeptical that keeping or re-placing the retarded in the regular classes will help them since, in his opinion, these schools are not doing a good job with a sizable percentage of the "normals." He insists that before regular class placement is going to help the retarded, the schools will have to become more effective in teaching the large numbers of nonretarded whom they are now failing.

5. Too often, the administrative problems associated with mainstreaming have not been anticipated and dealt with. The logistic problem of having children with special educational needs meet with itinerant or resource teachers or attend "learning centers" for limited periods of each day or week must be considered. Adequate administrative models must be developed for regular teachers, resource teachers, itinerant teachers, master teachers, and school psychologists sharing responsibilities and duties in identifying and teaching deviant students.

6. Eliminating all special classes may be as big a mistake as eliminating all institutions for the mentally deviant. We may still need some special classes. Experience in mainstreaming indicates that we probably need a continuum of services and facilities. At some point, and under some circumstances, deviancy is so extreme or unique that special class placement, special school attendance, or total care including institutionalization is required. The question that will eventually be asked is not, Should all special classes be eliminated? but rather, What is the range of individual differences and types of deviancy that can most effectively be accommodated in the regular classes? Some auxiliary self-contained special classes, both categorical and noncategorical, may still be necessary.

THE INDIVIDUATION OF INSTRUCTION

Practically all mainstreaming programs emphasize the importance of individualizing instruction. However, the idea of developing individualized programs to meet individual student needs is not new; for over half a century there have been periodic efforts to move in this direction. In the 1920s several continuous (nongraded) individualized programs were developed and had limited acceptance (Washburne, 1922; Hambleton, 1974). However, only in the last decade have such programs been implemented on a large scale. This movement has been accelerated by right-to-education legal decisions and various research studies indicating that conventional schools provide adequately for less than half of their students (Hambleton, 1974; Flanagan, 1973).

One reason the individualized instructional programs of the 1920s did not flourish was the tremendous amount of work involved in developing and executing such a program. However, the technology of the 1970s is sufficient to sustain successful programs of this type. Automated individualized instructional programs have been used successfully in innumerable school systems in various countries. The estimate that 100,000 students have used these programs successfully is probably very conservative (Hambleton, 1974; Gronlund, 1974). The extent to which automation can be used to meet the specialized educational needs of the auditorially and visually impaired has not been explored. However, with the mentally retarded, the slow learner, and children with learning disabilities, whose educational problems are only quantitatively different from the "normal," the conventional automated programs are quite appropriate. At any rate, a wide variety of diagnostic-prescriptive programs for exceptional children are in use (Ysseldyke & Salvia, 1974) and the need for individualized instruction remains an article of faith for most special educators.

DECATEGORIZING AND DELABELING

The new, comprehensive programs which have accompanied the deinstitutionalization and mainstreaming movements have been designed to reduce the stigmatizing effects of labeling those persons who need specialized services and to eliminate rigid categorical classifications which group individuals by handicap rather than by service needs. We have already dealt at length with the problem of stigmatization. Simply renaming and reclassifying these individuals will probably have limited beneficial effects. Grouping them together and designating them as "individuals with exceptional needs" instead of as "handicapped" or "disabled" may help. Subdividing these needs for certain purposes into the categories of communicative (deaf, hard-of-hearing, and linguistically disordered), physical (visually impaired, orthopedically handicapped, other health impaired), and learning (learning disabilities, behavior disorders, mentally retarded) only temporarily substitutes more euphonious terms for the old ones (California State Board of Education, 1974). Labels and terms initially devoid of negative connotations acquire them, in time, and become pejorative and stigmatizing. There is evidence that mainstreaming, to be effective, must retain the positive components of individualized specialized instruction and smaller classes, and at the same time reduce the stigmatizing effects of segregating and labeling.

It seems that in many cases, the attitudes of mentally retarded children (for whom the effects of categorizing and labeling are most extreme) are negative with reference to special class placement and labeling, while their attitudes toward school, peers, and teachers are predominantly positive. For example, one study of the attitudes of nearly 350 junior high school mentally retarded children, attending twelve different schools, had results which verified this hypothesis (Jones, 1974). When the responses of these segregated mentally retarded children to a series of questions were compared with those of their nonretarded peers attending the same schools, more retarded than nonretarded were found to endorse such statements as:

1. This school has helped me develop hobbies, skills, and interests I didn't have before.
2. Our school assignments are fair and reasonable.
3. The community really supports our school.
4. The older children at this school are very friendly toward the younger ones.
5. Most teachers here help me to feel more comfortable and at ease in class.
6. Students here pretty much get the grades they deserve.
7. I would not change a single thing about my school even if I could.
8. I am lucky to get to attend this particular school.
9. Each morning I look forward to coming to school.

On the other hand, less than 2 percent of these children indicated that special classes were their preferred educational placement. These children were aware of the official and unofficial derogating labels attached to their classes and were ashamed of being in such classes, but perceived overall educational experiences favorably.

All efforts to reduce the negative attitudes associated with deviance should be encouraged. Alternatives to special classes may reduce the official stigmatization effects, but if these programs do not have the supportive services required to induce and perpetuate positive attitudes such as those expressed above toward specific educational experiences, the overall handicap may be as great as those imposed by the older segregated classes.

SUMMARY

Ever since the first residential institutions and special classes were established for the handicapped, such segregated environments have been the most popular setting for caring for, treating, and educating such persons. However, during the last two decades, increasing discontent with these segregated facilities has emerged and many alternative arrangements have been proposed and implemented. The deinstitutionalization movement came about partially as the result of widespread recognition that, in many cases, the segregated institutions were doing more harm than good. Innumerable investigations over a century disclosed that such institutions, created for the good of their residents, had repeatedly become classic patterns of neglect, isolation, and dehumanization. The ever-increasing cost of such facilities together with their chronic overcrowding, understaffing, and insufficient funding led to a search for less expensive alternatives.

The alternatives to large mental hospitals have been community mental health centers, small local facilities, placing of previously institutionalized patients in group homes, and maintaining the handicapped in their own homes. Alternative educational programs for the handicapped retain the deviant child in the regular classroom and provide supplemental support to the regular classroom teacher. This practice is usually referred to as *mainstreaming*.

The current emphasis on mainstreaming has been brought about partly as the result of:

1. The equivocal results of research reports dealing with the effectiveness of the segregated programs.
2. A realization that categorizing and official labeling may add appreciably to the diagnosed handicap.
3. The increased awareness of the biasing effects of race, social class, sex, and educationally irrelevant behavioral characteristics, which have resulted in inappropriate placement of many individuals in segregated facilities.
4. Court judgments concerning institutional and special class assignments and the rights of patients and exceptional children to appropriate psychiatric and/or educational treatment.

Many people believe that the swinging of the pendulum toward the elimination of all such segregated facilities may be subjecting many of the handicapped to even more painful and frustrating experiences in the name of "normalization." Today the question is not "to segregate or not to segregate" but rather, "What is the least restrictive and most normalizing setting in which this individual's personal and educational needs can be met?" It seems clear that this will require a continuum of services with many program alternatives, including noncategorical resource rooms, learning centers, categorical rooms and/or teachers, special classes, and segregated residential facilities. It is not yet clear what extent and nature of handicapping conditions can be effectively accommodated in the mainstream of the school, community, and family, even with the support of resource or itinerant teachers, learning centers, and community mental health resources.

REFERENCES

ALEXANDER, F. G., & S. T. SELESNICK, *The History of Psychiatry* (New York: Harper & Row, 1966).

ARNHOFF, F. N., "Social Consequences of Policy Toward Mental Illness," *Science*, 1975, *188*, 1277–81.

BALLA, D. A., E. C. BUTTERFIELD, & E. ZIGLER, "Effects of Institutionalization on Retarded Children: A Longitudinal Cross-institutional Investigation," *American Journal of Mental Deficiency*, 1974, *78*, 530–49.

BIRCH, J. W., *Mainstreaming: Educable Mentally Retarded Children in Regular Classes* (Reston, Va.: Council for Exceptional Children, 1974).

BOCKOVEN, J. S., *Moral Treatment in American Psychiatry* (New York: Springer, 1963).

BORRELLI, A., "Occupational Training for Retarded Persons," *Mental Retardation*, 1972, *10* (5), 15–17.

BRANDT, A., *Reality Police: The Experience of Insanity in America* (New York: Morrow, 1975).

BRENTON, M., "Mainstreaming the Handicapped," *Today's Education*, March–April 1974, *64*, 20–25.

CALIFORNIA STATE BOARD OF EDUCATION, *California State Master Plan for Special Education* (Sacramento: California Bureau of Publications, 1974).

CASE, R., A. S. FITZGERALD, & J. M. FICARRO, "Respite Care," *Exceptional Parent*, 1975, *5* (1), 7–11.

CHAFFIN, J. D. "Will the Real 'Mainstreaming' Program Please Stand Up?" *Focus on Exceptional Children*, 1974, *6* (5), 1–18.

DAILEY, R. F., "Dimensions and Issues in '74: Tapping into the Special Education Grapevine," *Exceptional Children*, 1974, *40*, 503–6.

DENO, E. N., ed., *Instructional Alternatives for Exceptional Children* (Reston, Va.: Council for Exceptional Children, 1973).

FLANAGAN, J. C., "Education: How and For What?" *American Psychologist*, 1973, *28*, 551–56.

GALLAGHER, J. J., "Phenomenal Growth and New Problems Characterize Special Education," *Phi Delta Kappan*, 1974, *60*, 516–20.

GALLAGHER, U. M., "Adoption in a Changing Society," *Children Today*, 1972, *1* (5), 2–6.

GOLDSTEIN, H., "Providing Services to Children in Their Own Homes," *Children Today*, 1973, *2* (4), 2–7.

GRONLUND, N. E., *Individualizing Classroom Instruction* (New York: Macmillan, 1974).

GUERIN, C. R., & K. SZATLOCKY, "Integration Programs for the Mildly Retarded," *Exceptional Children*, 1974, *41*, 173–79.

GULA, M., "Community Services and Residential Institutions for Children," *Children Today*, 1974, *3* (6), 15–17.

HAMBLETON, R. K., "Testing and Decision-making Procedures for Selecting Individualized Instructional Programs," *Review of Educational Research*, 1974, *44*, 371–400.

HOBBS, N., *The Futures of Children* (San Francisco: Jossey-Bass, 1975).

ITARD, J. M. G., *The Wild Boy of Aveyron,* trans. G. Humphrey and M. Humphrey (New York: Appleton-Century-Crofts, 1932; originally published in 1894).

JEW, W., "Helping Handicapped Infants and Their Families," *Children Today,* 1974, *3* (3), 7–10.

JEWETT, D. R., "The Group Home: A Neighborhood-based Treatment Facility," *Children Today,* 1973, 2 (3), 16–20.

JONES, R. L., "Student Views of Special Placement and Their Own Classes: A Clarification," *Exceptional Children,* 1974, *41,* 22–29.

KLEIN, S. D., "Disappearing in the Community," *Exceptional Parent,* 1974, *4* (4), 34.

KRAMER, B. M., "The Day Hospital: A Case Study," *Journal of Social Issues,* 1960, *16,* 14–19.

KRAVIK, P. J., "Adopting a Retarded Child: One Family's Experience," *Children Today,* September–October 1975, *4,* (5), 17–21.

LENT, J. R., "The Severely Retarded: Are We Really Programming for Their Future?" *Focus on Exceptional Children,* 1975, 7 (1), 7–11.

McCARVER, R. B., & E. M. CRAIG, "Placement of the Retarded in the Community," in N. R. Ellis, ed., *International Review of Research in Mental Retardation,* vol. 7 (New York: Academic Press, 1974).

MacMILLAN, T. M., & B. H. AASE, "Analysis of the First 500 Patients at the San Diego Day Treatment Center," *California Mental Health Research Digest,* 1964, *2,* 11.

MARTIN, E. W., "Some Thoughts on Mainstreaming," *Exceptional Children,* 1974, *41,* 150–54.

NASH, A. L., "Reflections on Interstate Adoptions," *Children Today,* 1974, *3* (4), 7–11.

NEILSON, J., "Placing Older Children in Adoptive Homes," *Children Today,* 1972, *1* (6), 7–13.

OLSHANSKY, S., "The Transitional Workshop: A Survey," *Journal of Social Issues,* 1960, *16,* 33–39.

O'REGAN, G. W., "Foster Family Care for Children with Mental Retardation," *Children Today,* 1974, *3* (1), 20–21.

PALMER, T. B., "California's Community Treatment Program for Delinquent Adolescents," *Journal of Research in Crime and Delinquency,* 1971, *8,* 74–92.

PERRUCCI, R., *Circle of Madness: On Being Insane and Institutionalized in America* (Englewood Cliffs, N.J.: Prentice-Hall, 1974).

PINEL, P., *A Treatise on Insanity,* trans. D. D. Davis (New York: Hafner, 1962; originally published in 1806).

ROSEN, D., "Observations of an Era in Transition," *Mental Retardation,* 1974, *12* (5), 61–67.

RUBIN, R. A., P. KRUS, & B. BALOW, "Factors in Special Class Placement," *Exceptional Children,* 1973, *39,* 525–32.

SCHAAR, K., "Community Care Ordered for D.C. Mental Patients," *APA Monitor,* February 1976, 7 (2), 1.

SEGUIN, E., *Idiocy and Its Treatment by the Physiological Method* (New York: W. Wood, 1866).

SMITH, J. O., & J. R. ARKANS, "Now More Than Ever: A Case for the Special Class," *Exceptional Children*, 1974, *40*, 497–502.

THURMAN, S. K., & R. L. THIELE, "A Viable Role for Retardation Institutions: The Road to Self-destruction," *Mental Retardation*, 1973, *11* (2), 21–22.

WALTHALL, J. E., & H. D. LOVE, *Habilitation of the Mentally Retarded Individual* (Springfield, Ill.: Charles C Thomas, 1974).

WASHBURNE, C. W., "Educational Measurement as a Key to Individualizing Instruction and Promotions, *Journal of Educational Research*, 1922, *5*, 195–206.

WECHSLER, H., "Halfway Houses for Former Mental Patients: A Survey," *Journal of Social Issues*, 1960a, *16*, 20–26.

WECHSLER, H., "The Expatient Organization: A Survey," *Journal of Social Issues*, 1960b, *16*, 47–53.

WECHSLER, H., "Transitional Residences for Former Mental Patients: A Survey of Halfway Houses and Related Rehabilitation Facilities," *Mental Hygiene*, 1961, *45*, 65–76.

WILKINS, P. K., "Disappearing in the Community," *Exceptional Parent*, 1974, *4* (4), 30–31.

WILLIAMS, H. A., JR., "New Era of Hope," *Exceptional Parent*, 1975, *5* (6), 12–13.

WINICH, C., "Psychiatric Day Hospitals: A Survey," *Journal of Social Issues*, 1960, *16*, 8–13.

WINSCHEL, J. F., & E. A. LAWRENCE, "Short-term Memory: Curricular Implications for the Mentally Retarded," *The Journal of Special Education*, 1975, *9*, 395–408.

WOLINS, M., ed., *Successful Group Care: Explorations in the Powerful Environment* (Chicago: Aldine, 1974).

YSSELDYKE, J. E., & J. SALVIA, "Diagnostic-prescriptive Teaching: Two Models," *Exceptional Children*, 1974, *41*, 181–87.

ZELLER, V. M., "Developing a Statewide Program for Foster Children," *Children Today*, 1974, *3* (5), 10–15.

ZNEIMER, L., "The Private Residential Program as an Alternate to State Institutions," *Exceptional Children*, 1973, *39*, 329–33.

ZNEIMER, L., "Magic Words," *Exceptional Parent*, 1975, *5* (6), 30–32.

Chapter 5

Family and personal problems
of exceptional people

THE DYNAMICS OF FAMILY RELATIONS

Just as people with different stigmas must face similar problems and adjust to them in similar ways, the problem of a family with a mentally retarded, blind, deaf, orthopedically handicapped, or epileptic child is an instance of a universal experience—how the family copes with unexpected disappointment and trauma. Family crises, frustrated ambition, and occasional high levels of stress are experiences common to most families. Likewise, the basic problem faced by the families of exceptional individuals is essentially that of all families—how to cope with the problems of living in ways that will enhance rather than hinder family members' growth and development. The behavior of the deviant is shaped by the actions and attitudes of others, and the adjustments of the family of an exceptional child can either limit and distort or encourage and facilitate the child's potential for growth.

When working with the handicapped, it is easy to focus attention so completely on the defective individual that we forget he is a member of a family and that the family may be as much a casualty as is the handicapped member. The family, in turn, is a part of a still larger social context. As we have indicated in earlier chapters, the dominant cultural patterns of society, the subculture in which the individual has membership, and the local community where one resides all have their impact on the handicapped individual. However, the individual family is the primary mediating agent through which these larger social units exert their influence on the individual. This is particularly true of the young child and of the person with a disability.

While the family's impact on the exceptional child has been stated repeatedly, there has been less recognition of the effect of the child on the family. The family is a small, interdependent social system containing still smaller subsystems. The number of subsystems found in any family will depend upon its size and its unique alignment of members and role relationships (Heisler, 1972; Kogan & Tyler, 1973; Kantor & Lehr, 1975). The smallest of these subsystems is a social dyad—a two-person inter-

126

action. In this context, the mother-child pair is typically the focal subsystem embedded in the larger family system. Whatever happens to a family member affects the subsystems of which he is a part, and anything that affects the subsystem is reflected in the system as a whole. Conversely, any stress on the family will have repercussions on the subsystems and on the individual. There are interacting and reciprocal effects throughout the family, and beyond it. This means that when we discuss the exceptional child and his relationships with his parents or siblings, we are artificially isolating the individual or subgroup for purposes of discussion.

What the individual child is, and what he does, affect all the members of the family; their behavior, in turn, affects the child. When the child acts the mother reacts, and the child in turn reacts to the mother in a circular fashion. The father, in turn, reacts to his perception of the child-mother interaction, and thus the father-mother-child subsystem reverberates to both the child's behavior and to the mother-child interaction (Hayden, 1974).

Families, like most other social groups, develop internal patterns of alignment and relationships. Because the mother has historically been the central figure in the family, she is typically considered to be the focus of the most significant family alignments. When it becomes necessary to extend investigations of a problem child beyond the child himself, the focus of attention in child counseling and psychotherapy usually shifts to the mother-child relationship. Indeed, many counselors and psychotherapists refuse to work with a problem child unless the mother will undergo concurrent therapy or counseling. This has been a long-standing rule for many clinics and individual clinicians, although in some clinics concurrent parent-child psychotherapy is being replaced by entire family therapy.

The widespread belief that the family—particularly the mother-child relationship—is in large part responsible for the mental health of the child is a compelling one. However, it is difficult to substantiate this belief with research findings. The evidence of a significant relationship between *specific* maternal child-rearing practices and personality characteristics in the children is meagre and contradictory (Caldwell, 1964; Behrens, 1954; Johnson & Medinnus, 1975). It is becoming increasingly clear that individual acts and practices become significant only as part of a larger social context. For example, while Marjorie Behrens found no correlation between the personality of children and *specific* child-rearing practices in feeding, weaning, and toilet training, she obtained highly significant correlations between the child's adjustment and indices of the "total mother" as seen in the mother-family relationship. Specific child-rearing practices and parent-child relationships became significant only when viewed in the context of a larger pattern.

These data support C. R. Rogers's (1939) claim, made over thirty-five years ago, that if we were predicting the outcome of the treatment of a problem child and had to base our predictions on a single factor, we would do best to disregard the child entirely and base our forecast on the "emotional climate" of the home as indicated by the way the parents accept their children and the way they act toward them. A minor study of the same period (Witmer, 1933) also indicated that the factor showing the closest relationship to success in working professionally with "problem children" is the "emotional tone" of the home and the parents' attitude toward the child. When the parents are well-adjusted themselves, when the home atmosphere is reasonably calm, and when the parents have normal affection for the children, the probability that the problem child will ultimately make a satisfactory adjustment is very good.

The same attitude is reflected by V. Heisler (1972), who insists that it is the kind of person the parent is, and the relationship between parent and child, rather than the specific things the parent does that influence the child's growth and development. The parent can make mistakes because of inadequate skill or information and still be an adequate parent with an overall positive effect on the children, if the home atmosphere is wholesome and demonstrates parental affection. Heisler and others believe that children have a high level of resilience and tolerance so long as they feel accepted and loved by their parents.

The emphasis on the importance of such broad global factors as "emotional tone" and "emotional climate" of the home, as contrasted with specific child-rearing practices, is supported by several studies. R. R. Sears, G. E. Maccoby, and H. Levin (1957) found that the mother's personality and the general atmosphere of the interaction were more important to the child's development than any specific practice associated with feeding and toilet training. These same authors, as well as M. J. Radke (1946), found child behavior to be most significantly related to the broad permissiveness–restriction and autocratic–democratic rating scales for parental behavior. E. S. Schaefer (1959) found that two major characteristics of parental behavior could be derived from the results of a large number of studies of parent-child relationships and arranged meaningfully on an autonomy (freedom)–control (passive) and a hostility (rejecting)–love (accepting) scale. Later, Schaefer (1961) presented some support for the relation of these very general maternal characteristics to significant categories of children's behavior.

Still more recently, M. Wulbert et al. (1975), in a study of significantly language-delayed children, found that the most significant difference in the homes of these children as compared with those of "normal" children was in maternal involvement with the child. The mothers of the normal children referred to their children in positive terms, caressed them often, and spoke to them in warm and accepting ways. These mothers seemed to enjoy their children, actively encouraged their social interactions, and took pride in their accomplishments. On the other hand, the mothers of the language-delayed children referred to their children in critical ways and seldom praised or caressed them. These mothers and children lived together in parallel fashion with a minimum of social interaction. The evidence indicates that none of these speech-delayed children were perceived as retarded or abnormal until language was noticeably delayed in development. The characteristic patterns of mother-child interaction were well established *before* any deviancy was noticed or diagnosed. However, by the time formal diagnosis was made, the poor interaction was definitely reciprocal in nature.

Because of these findings, attention has shifted from the mother-child relationship to the entire family constellation (Jackson, 1970; Reiter & Kilmann, 1975). The unique family pattern, rather than either the individual child or the parent-child relationship, has become the primary focus of concern. Consequently, we find individuals and agencies recommending that counseling and psychotherapy should involve the whole family as a group (Keith, 1974; Kantor & Lehr, 1975). Changes in the complex interrelationships among family members and subgroups within the family inevitably arise as the result of effective counseling, psychotherapy, or the removal of a member of the family by death or institutionalization. No matter how disturbing the deviant behavior of a family member, if the behavior pattern has persisted for a time and the family constellation has remained intact, some stability has been established. Even conflict-laden equilibrium and stability have their rewards. The removal of the deviant individual from the home, or a marked change in the individual's behavior resulting from counseling, psychotherapy, or more active intervention from without, disrupts the existing relationships. Sometimes these changes operate to the detriment of other family members; more often they are beneficial. E. Smith, B. M. Ricketts, and H. Smith (1962) have provided some dramatic illustrations of the possible consequences of institutional placement of a handicapped sibling. In one case cited, Mary, a mentally retarded, deaf, brain-damaged ten-year-old, was institutionalized. No attention was paid to Mary's jealousy of her sister or to the statement of this sister that the mother was institutionalizing Mary to get rid of her. The family's life had centered around Mary's condition. Her hyperactivity and temper tantrums had kept the family in a perpetual turmoil. A follow-up interview a year later indicated relief and satisfaction with the move by all family members, except the older sister. The sister had become obsessed with the belief that the placement of Mary was cruel and that she was being mistreated in the institution. The sister's depressed agitation, apparently based on her feelings toward Mary, was sufficiently severe for her to require psychiatric treatment.

Modifications in the family constellations are most disturbing when such changes are rapid. For example, the death or institutionalization of a child may require modification of the patterns of separateness and connectedness which underlie every family relationship. Mother and child, or father, mother, and handicapped child, may have constituted a somewhat independent subgroup from which the other siblings have either withdrawn or been excluded. When the deviant child leaves the family, or when, as the result of counseling, the parents try to establish new relationships with the other children and with each other, a reorganization of all interrelationships ensues. The existence of reasonably stable family alignments and clearly defined roles reduces the amount of constant decision-making concerning family relationships. Each person in a well-structured family knows the part he or she is to play and how to behave. Any marked change in family constellation necessitates a realignment of individuals and a redefinition of their roles. A lot of additional decision-making is required before the family is restructured. For example, where child and mother, or child, mother, and father, have constituted a somewhat independent dyad or triad with the handicapped child as the principal focus of this subgroup, the removal of the child from the home or a decision to break up the cohesive subgroup may be a disturbing factor to the normal siblings as well as to the handicapped child. With one or both parents dominantly concerned with the exceptional child, the siblings may have been free to take care of themselves and act independently. When the focus of the parents' life shifts from the dependent child and they then insist upon exerting more direction and supervision of the other children, a major reorganization of the family life becomes necessary. If the family is large, the older children may have assumed the major responsibility for the care and supervision of the younger normal siblings while the parents were preoccupied with the disabled family member. When the parents suddenly elect to reassert their authority and control over all family members, considerable conflict may follow while new lines of authority and control are being established.

The authors have been impressed with the parents' exclusive concern with the handicapped child's probable reaction to prospective foster-home or institutional placement. Many times the adjustment of the parents and siblings is much more difficult than that of the institutionalized child. The separation is more traumatic to them and requires more of a readjustment of their lives. This is particularly true when the care of a severely handicapped child has been a major family concern. Family members are seldom aware of the extent to which mutual dependencies and reciprocal relationships have dominated their lives. The removal of the child from the home requires many of the other family members to make other commitments and establish new roles for themselves. Sometimes the entire family is the casualty, as in the following case.

Family problems—a case study

Jerry, eight years old, has cerebral palsy. His parents have filed for a divorce. How did it come about? To go back to the beginning: According to Jerry's mother, she didn't really want a baby. "I knew something was wrong during my pregnancy. Sometimes I think this is God's punishment, although I really know that is crazy," she reported. When the initial state of shock wore off, the mother took over. She never asked anyone what she should do; she just plunged in to work with her son. She read everything she could find on cerebral palsy and became an authority on the topic. Initially the husband approved and was proud of her.

Slowly but surely the entire family life became organized around Jerry and his special needs. This did not bother the husband until he noticed that their daughter was badly in need of new clothes. When he asked his wife to buy their daughter some new clothes, she gave him a blank stare but said and did nothing. The husband finally asked his sister to help his daughter buy some new clothes. The wife became angry and complained to her sister-in-law about her spoiling the girl and how useless the husband was around the house.

For a while after his son's birth, the husband tried doing things for the handicapped child. However, he decided it would be better if Jerry tried to do more for himself, and began doing less for him. The wife took up the slack by doing more and more for her son. The husband felt that the only way he could be useful to his family was to earn more money. Consequently, he began working longer hours, and weekends as well. After a few years he gradually came to the realization that their marriage had come to an end. They no longer did anything together—never went out or visited friends; and no longer had any sex life. Half the time the wife slept in Jerry's room. At other times, husband or wife or both were too tired.

The wife was at her son's call twenty-four hours a day. At his slightest sign of distress she would rush to his side. When Jerry was seven the family moved to a house in the suburbs, nearer the hospital. The husband did not complain, even though it increased his commuting time from twenty minutes to an hour. A year later, he came home one evening, told his wife it was all over, and asked for a divorce.

The divorce came as a surprise to everyone. There had been no fighting, quarreling, or bickering. The wife was too preoccupied and tired to be involved with her husband, and the husband had ceased bothering her. Although the request for a divorce came as a shock to the wife, in some ways she was relieved by it. For a long time the husband had been just one more mouth to feed and one more person to work for and clean up after. Their divorce settlement was amicable; very little explanation was given to other people.

About a year later, the former husband married again and took his daughter to live with him and his new wife. The former wife offered no objections to this arrangement. She was still completely wrapped up in Jerry, and had little time or energy to spend with her daughter.

This case is an extreme example of the problems common to families with severely handicapped children. It is very difficult to provide the handicapped child with the extra care and money required and at the same time not to deprive the other family members of their rightful share of attention, time, and affection. Another mother admitted, "My own divorce did not result from my son's deafness, but rather from my response to his deafness. I jumped so headlong into my son's problems and the problems of the deaf that I completely neglected my family and marital obligations, which led to the break-up of our marriage."

Patterns of parental reaction to a defective child

While there are almost as many different patterns of reaction to evidence of inadequacy in one's offspring as there are parents with such children, certain types of reactions are sufficiently common to warrant description. Some of the more common reactive patterns to the advent of a defective child into a family are realistic coping with the problem; denial of the reality of the handicap; self-pity; ambivalence toward or rejection of the child; projection of the difficulty as the cause of the disability; feelings of guilt, shame and depression; and patterns of mutual dependency.

None of these reactions is peculiar to parents in general or to the parents of defective children; they are the common reactions of normal people to frustration and conflict. The average parent will, in the course of his lifetime, display or experience these reactions to his nondisabled children as a part of normal life processes, and it is helpful to the parents of handicapped children to be aware of the universality of their reactions. Many parents of deviant children not only experience feelings of guilt and shame but feel guilty and ashamed of themselves for doing so. That is, in addition to feeling guilty, they feel guilty about feeling guilty. Such guilt is a secondary source of emotional disturbance to parents who are already overladen emotionally. The presence of a handicapped child in the family constitutes an additional stress, and defensive reactions are likely to occur more often and to a greater degree in such families than in families all of whose members are reasonably normal (Kogan & Tyler, 1973).

One source of conflict is that the presence of a severely handicapped child in a family arrests certain components of the family cycle. The severely disabled child may permanently occupy the social position of the youngest child in the family. He does not develop the independence and autonomy of adulthood. This is often the situation in the family with a severely mentally retarded child. There the parental role is fairly constant regardless of the child's birth-order position; the severely mentally retarded individual is the permanent infant and never emerges from his infantile or childish status. One sibling of such a child had the following to say:

> I came to be aware of my sister's condition only gradually. As I grew older I realized that she was decidedly different. She developed very slowly, so even though I was two years older than her, I was soon much larger and more mature in every way. She has been almost a perpetual infant. We have always referred to her as "the baby." My sister's condition never really was explained to me. I can recall my mother telling me that my sister was sick and that she would probably never be really well. Not until I was nearly grown did I learn that she was severely retarded as the result of a rubella infection contracted before she was born. Her mental capacity is less than one year. Presently, she is institutionalized in a state hospital. My parents see her about once a week. I see her once every month or two. For some reason, I find the visits becoming more and more difficult. My sister is very happy where she is and it really makes no difference to anyone, except my parents, whether I see her or not.

Coping realistically with the problems of the exceptional child   Because of our concern with the problem parent as well as the problem child, we can easily overlook that many parents are able to cope in a healthy and constructive way with the problems presented by the presence of a defective child. Many people meet the initial decisions and the additional stresses in a realistic, well-integrated way, just as they meet the other crises and stresses in their lives.

For example, a twenty-two-year-old congenital quadruple amputee with prostheses describes his family's treatment of him as follows:

> In my estimation my treatment by my family couldn't have been better. I have two sisters, both older than myself. My parents agreed completely on how I was to be treated. However, it seems that my father took the lead in setting the general tone concerning my treatment. As long as I can remember, he insisted that I do everything that I could do—and no funny business!

Very early he explained my handicap to me. He told me that there were certain things I probably could not do, but that I *could* do most things. He always insisted that I try practically everything. I was always given specific duties around the house. I performed all the normal duties—helping set the table, carrying out the garbage, and running errands.

My sisters, taking their cue from my parents, never let me get away with anything. They were certainly aware of my handicap, but hardly ever referred to it. They assumed that I was essentially normal and that I would do everything until it was positively demonstrated that I could not. When I finally told them that I couldn't do something, they usually accepted it as a fact. In school, there were no special classes or teachers. However, my father explained to my teachers how I was treated at home and told them to do likewise. My teachers accepted that I could not write at the blackboard. My first grade teacher immediately informed me that I was going to learn to write. I was sure that I would never be able to. However, she taped a piece of paper to my desk, placed a pencil in my clamp, and said, "Now write." I eventually learned to write and to type. This was just a normal school with an understanding teacher.

When I came home from school and asked my father why people stared at me, he simply told me, "It's because you have clamps for hands and artificial legs which make you limp."

I liked sports and played as much as possible. Of course I was a miserable player. When I was nine or ten I told my father that I was going to be a professional athlete. He sat me down and told me that someday I would realize that I would never be a professional athlete. He said that I would have to learn to use my head more than my arms and legs.

I never recall blaming anyone else for my disability. I was told that it was really no one's fault—it had just happened. Of course I used to fantasize and dream that I had normal arms and legs. I never saw my wheelchair in a dream. I was a great athlete and won games—but all in my dreams. I have never been sensitive about my disability. When a child asks me about my hands and his parents try to shut him up, I usually tell them to let him ask. Then I answer the questions and explain it to both the child and his parents.

Denial of the child's disability   Except for the most obvious disabilities, most parents react with some denial to evidence of their child's inadequacy. Powerful social and personal forces motivate a parent to do so. Many of these factors were discussed in earlier chapters. The cultural stereotype of the ideal child, the parents' expectation that their offspring will successfully play the roles that society and his parents assign to him, the parents' hopes that their child will attain or surpass their accomplishments all contribute to their "it just can't be so" reaction when the child is apparently defective. Because parents identify with their children, participate in their successes and failures, bask in their reflected glory, and are belittled by their shortcomings, they inevitably experience a loss of self-esteem when one of their offspring is less than expected. A defect in the child is seen as partly that of the parent.

When the initial realization of an infant's defectiveness comes suddenly and traumatically, the more unconscious defensive reactions may occur. One mother actually believed that she had *only imagined* that she had held her physically deformed, day-old child in her arms when the nurse took the infant back to the nursery. Later she was unable to recall the first six weeks at home with her defective child. One father reports that when asked how many children he had, he would say "two." He actually had three but the third was a badly deformed thalidomide child. One father of a thalidomide infant was unable to take a second look at his deformed infant for three days. Another parent says, "I stumbled in darkness for three years searching for . . . I do not know what. It was so painful to carry this secret dread that something was wrong with my son, wanting to know, yet fearing to hear the actual words spoken. I felt I was living somewhere alone on an island. For a long time I was unable to read anything about mental retardation. I started to read Pearl Buck's book about her own mentally retarded daughter but quickly put it aside—something in me would not let me read or think about it" (Gregory, 1972). Acceptance is seldom a one-time act of faith; it is not that simple. Acceptance often starts as a fleeting thing, a continuous, ever-changing process which fluctuates at different levels at different times and in different contexts.

One mother said, "The time immediately after the birth of my child with multiple congenital defects was the loneliest time of my life. I felt that neither encouraging family and friends nor competent and sympathetic doctors could really help, for none of these had ever given birth to such a child" (Ouellet, 1972).

Another parent has suggested that "adapting and coping are more realistic goals than acceptance. Anger, resentment, and guilt at having a disabled child and distress concerning the situation are to be expected and may continue indefinitely. Parents can adapt to the situation and cope with the problems of a handicapped child without becoming resigned to it and happy with the circumstances" (Eisenpreis, 1974).

One mother says, "As we moved along with Kathryn there were many episodes which stand out as if they were still frames in a motion picture. Each episode marked a new idea or a confirmation of a suspicion, producing what some call the 'Aha!' response. Each one moved me along a road now paved with convictions" (Bennett, 1974).

The parents of a physically disabled child seem to identify more completely with their child's physique than do the parents of the non-handicapped. It is not surprising that perceptual distortion, misinterpretation of evidence, and all the defenses in one's repertoire will be used to deny evidence of inferiority in one's offspring. Sometimes this denial takes the form of a prolonged trek from doctor to doctor and clinic to clinic, in search of a more favorable diagnosis. Failing this, the parents claim that the specialists are all wrong. Any parent knows his child better than all the professionals!

Sympathetic friends, relatives, and even professional people often unwittingly support the parents' denial of their child's inadequacy. They stress the child's assets and minimize his limitations. They emphasize the difficulties of diagnosis, the uncertainties of developmental trends, and the limitations of our knowledge. There are no certainties in this world! Telling a parent bluntly and with certainty that he has a defective child is a hard task for any counselor and is often postponed, or temporized, or modified in the hope that it will be easier on the parents and in the certainty that it is easier on the counselor (Michaels, 1974).

Many parents never progress beyond the stage of partial acceptance. They may accept the diagnosis but reject its prognostic implications. How about the miracle drugs, a new operation, a novel form of psychotherapy, a radically new diet, or unlimited amounts of parental love? Parenthetically we might mention that the most recent evaluation of the many drug and dietary treatments of mental retardation for which positive claims have been made concludes that, despite great enthusiasm on the part of their proponents, no such programs have been demonstrated effective (Share, 1976).

Self-pity   Except when the parents are able to assume and maintain a realistic and objective attitude toward their child's disability, some feelings of self-pity are likely to be experienced: "What a terrible thing to happen to me," "Why did this happen in my family?" "What have I done to deserve this?" The threat to the parents' and the family's prestige represented by the presence of a defective child looms large in most middle- or upper-class households.

When the emotional reaction is extreme, the devout religionist may question his fundamental religious beliefs. "How could a benign Diety permit such a thing to happen? Why did He do this to me?" As the result of such questioning and doubt, the parent may become embittered and atheistic. Other people find solace in their religious beliefs. Although the evidence is conflicting, some studies find Catholic mothers, who are generally more religious than Protestants, to be more accepting of their defective children than are comparable non-Catholics (Zuk, 1962; Boles, 1959).

One mother describes her mixed emotions as follows:

> I am sure that it is only after we have lived through our anger, grief, doubts, and self-torture, and recognized these reactions for what they are, that

we can really go on to positive action. For years I thought I was the only one who felt guilty and ashamed of my thinly disguised hostile feelings and death wishes. Not until I met with other parents and heard them compile their reactions—alarm, anger, anxiety, anguish, bewilderment, bitterness, denial, depression, disbelief, despair, and even impulses to destroy the child—did I realize that these were universal experiences. I then became unashamed to admit that I had experienced every one of them and was finally able to transform them into positive action. I have finally attained the place where I am able to discuss my emotions frankly with other people.

Ambivalent feelings toward the handicapped   Even the best parents feel ambivalent toward their normal children. Parental attitudes, while dominantly positive, always have overtones of resentment and rejection. The restriction of activities, the additional responsibilities, the minor disappointments of parenthood, the anxieties, and the irritations which are a normal part of the bearing and rearing of offspring inevitably produce ambivalent parental reactions. Parents accept and love, but they also reject and dislike their children.

It is inevitable that the negative components of this ambivalence will be accentuated when the child is handicapped. These negative reactions vary all the way from the conscious and overt wish that the child would die or had never been born to repressed, unacknowledged, veiled, and symbolic hostility and rejection. In any case, ambivalent feelings give rise to guilt reactions, which in turn often result in overprotection, over-solicitousness, and a parental life of martyrdom—an attempt to deny or compensate for the hostile feelings of which the person is ashamed.

One parent says, "After a period of mourning and denial, a state of relative acceptance occurred. However, while feeling proud of my mature acceptance of my child's limitations, I now see the school band marching and it suddenly strikes me that my child will never do that and I cry. In church, all the other children march in on Children's Day and her father carries in my child. I curse silently at the unfairness and cry again."

Parental ambivalences are often involved in the *treatment* of disabled offspring. Trying to find and tread that narrow path between withholding the realistically necessary care and assistance, on the one hand, and doing too much and nurturing helplessness and overdependency, on the other, is always difficult. In trying to find this path, many parents are more demanding and less tolerant of excuses from their disabled child than they are of their normal offspring. When the disabled child asks the parent to do something for him, the parent hesitates and asks himself, "Can he do it for himself?" He often does not do for the disabled child many things that he does immediately and without question for

Parental pathology

his more able offspring because he is less aware of the dangers of instilling overdependencies in the latter.

   Projection   Projection is a common defense against feelings of anxiety. Anxiety concerning personal guilt, or unacceptable feelings of resentment and hostility, can be diminished by blaming someone other than oneself for the threatening situation. Parents made anxious by the conditions arising from the handicapped child will often project the causes of the child's deficiencies onto convenient scapegoats. Resentment and hostility may be directed at the other children, the spouse, the doctor, the teacher, the counselor, or society in general. Professional people working with such parents can expect to serve as the innocent victims of this process. Unprovoked attacks against others often represent displaced hostility resulting from the chronic frustrations engendered by the defective child. One mother who has had such experiences reports:

> When I discovered that because of our child's condition we were labeled and stigmatized as a family, I experienced a deep resentment against society, doctors, psychologists, teachers, and people in general. This resentment was directed principally toward those who were closest to me—my husband, mother, father, and my other children. My escape from the hurt, confusion, and resentment was to become involved in programs of positive action. I joined our local Mental Health Association and became active in getting a special school program established for emotionally disturbed (autistic) children. I started to "reach out" and look at all handicapped children and adults. Only then was I able to do something other than blame and blame and blame. Yes, we need laws, but you cannot legislate informed concern and love, and that is what it takes. We need to stir ourselves, to stir our friends and neighbors, our schools and our government in these terms. Please hold my hand, lest I forget!

   Guilt, shame, and depression   Guilt and shame are components of several of the reaction patterns already discussed. However, they are sufficiently important in themselves to warrant further discussion. Shame, as used here, refers to the "What will other people think and say?" reaction, whereas guilt refers to the individual's feelings of self-reproach or self-condemnation. Shame is more other-people oriented; guilt, more self-directed. Shame involves the expectation of ridicule or criticism from others, while guilt involves self-blame, personal regret, and a feeling of decreased personal worth. Shame and guilt both involve anxiety, and popular usage does not differentiate them. Empirical studies indicate that guilt and anxiety, as indicated by self-report, are highly correlated (Laxer, 1964). Feelings of guilt, or self-blame, with their accompanying anxiety and lowered self-concept, result in depression. Shame and its accompanying anxiety, on the other hand, may protect the self-concept by directing hostility outward.

Some feelings of guilt or shame are common experiences of the parents of handicapped children. When the parental reaction is dominantly that of shame, the threat to one's personal prestige and the family's social status looms, often realistically, like an ever-present shadow. *Actual* social rejection of the child with a disability ranges all the way from a slight uneasiness on the part of the neighbors when they are in the presence of the disabled individual to thinking of the handicapped person as subhuman and dangerous. The parents of disabled children are aware of many beliefs centering around the sins of the parents and "bad blood," as well as such notions as that neglect or carelessness of the parents are possible causes of many disabilities, particularly when the etiology is either obscure or unknown.

The anticipation of social rejection, ridicule, and loss of prestige, when extreme, may result in an immediate and drastic solution to the problem. To avoid social rebuffs, some parents try to withdraw from social participation. Other parents assume the role of martyr to allay any suspicion of lack of parental concern or inadequacy of parental role as a possible cause of the child's defect. By devoting one's entire life to the child, the parent says to the world, "See what a dedicated and devoted parent I am! How can anyone suggest that the child's difficulties arise from my carelessness or inadequacy?"

Attempts at immediate foster-home or institutional placement of the defective child may be the parental reaction to the threat of social ostracism. Less drastic attempts to keep the child from public exposure are a common reaction. The defective child, in either case, becomes the traditional skeleton in the closet, the forgotten child. The fear of social disclosure may force parents to prefer private to public institutional placement even when they can ill afford the additional expense.

Some of the complications involved in institutional placement are suggested by the parent who said, "I was relieved when we finally placed our son in a residential home—then I felt guilty for feeling relieved."

Every institution housing the severely disabled—particularly the psychotic and the severely mentally retarded—contains a sizable group of children who are never visited by their parents or other relatives. The writers have been impressed by the large number of severely handicapped children in the higher-priced private institutions whose families reside in distant parts of the country. Many of the children in private institutions in California, for example, come from outside the state, some from New York, Pennsylvania, and Florida. The only contact many of these families have with their children is to send a Christmas present, possibly a birthday present, and mail a monthly check to the institution. The implication is that these children are the forgotten ones and that excessive distance from home is an advantage to the family. Private institutions with ambiguous names, such as Pleasant Hill Manor, The Pines, Yorktown Hall, or The Hudson Country School, are often preferred to public institutions whose names are indicative of the types of children enrolled.

Feelings of guilt and self-accusation, like shame, may result in a parental life of martyrdom. However, the martyrdom resulting from shame is an attempt to prove to other people that the parent is competent and adequate, while the same behavior motivated by guilt is directed at defending the parental *self-concept*. The guilt-motivated parent is trying to deny or compensate for his feelings of hostility and rejection. Overconcern, oversolicitousness, excessive care, and protection are ways in which parents may reassure themselves that they are good parents. Showering the child with presents, clothes, and other material things, sacrificing to send the child to expensive schools and to provide care beyond the child's needs may be motivated by the parent's need to prove to himself what a good and devoted parent he is. Some parents find solace in the rewards of martyrdom.

The guilt-ridden parent is always in danger of giving the child more protection than the realities of the situation demands. Of course, the handicapped child *realistically* requires more protection than does a normal child. The parent with little, if any, prior experience with the disabled does not know how much extra care and protection the child requires. It is therefore easy for the parent to rationalize the expenditure of enormous amounts of time, energy, and money, and the bestowal of excessive affection and care, which really represent compensations for feelings of rejection (Kogan & Tyler, 1973).

Feelings of depression are frequent experiences of either shame- or guilt-laden people. Grief reactions typical of the loss of a loved one are to be expected. Whenever anxiety mounts and the stresses of life seem overwhelming, despondency and depression are likely to ensue.

Patterns of mutual dependency   An earlier section mentioned the interaction and circularity of effects in family relationships. Parent and child, most often mother and disabled child, develop self-perpetuating patterns of mutual dependency. We have indicated the ways in which the parent—particularly the overanxious parent—can foster overdependency in the handicapped child. It is less obvious that the parent can become almost equally dependent on the disabled child. Whenever a parent invests a large part of himself, both materially and emotionally, in the care of a handicapped child, a condition of circular dependency can easily develop. Such children, either through their real needs or their parents' exaggeration of their needs, become dependent on the parents. The parents, in turn, need the excessive care and dependency of the children to prove their adequacy as parents. At times the excessive supervision, protection, and care provided by the oversolicitous parent increases and perpetuates the child's dependency. These reciprocal needs may be perpetuated indefinitely. By devoting so much of their time and energy to the handicapped child, parents invest so much of themselves in the project that their entire lives become centered in the child. When this occurs, parents may actually resist efforts to relieve them of the burden because of the void it would leave in their lives. Sometimes the handicapped child's lack of motivation is the result of an adult-fostered dependency and immaturity which is sustained by the neurotic satisfaction the parent derives from the child's dependency. The child, in turn, feels secure within the protecting parental arm. There is evidence that when such a neurotically sustained relationship involving a severely handicapped child has persisted for several years, it is very difficult to reverse.

Neurotic dependency can also develop in the disabled member of a dyad. This is particularly true when a predisposed adult develops a disability. A paralyzing stroke may accentuate or crystallize processes of surrender, dependency, and resignation already in progress. The neurotically inclined adult can exaggerate his incapacities, relinquish activities he is capable of doing, become more demanding of others, and institute a cycle of functional dependency. A chronically "hurt" child can learn to use his hurt as a weapon. The cycle is self-perpetuating in more than one way. The failure to use one's remaining physical capacities results in their atrophy, which in turn increases the organic disability and the real dependency. There is a dynamic interplay of physiological, psychological, and social factors in all aspects of exceptionality.

Siblings' reactions to the exceptional child

Evidence indicates that the siblings largely adopt the parents' attitudes toward the disabled child (Klein, 1972). When the parents view the defective child with shame or hostility, the siblings do likewise. When the family has been helped by counseling, the presence of a young mentally retarded child need not have an adverse effect on teen-age siblings. The family may be so concerned with an obviously handicapped child, however, that a less obviously deviant sibling who is more seriously emotionally disturbed and more in need of help than the more visibly disabled child may be overlooked (Love, 1973).

When the nonhandicapped siblings are required to supervise, care for, defend, and protect the handicapped child, resentment often develops. When the defective child receives excessive attention and affection, when the additional expense incurred by the deviant child deprives the others of educational and recreational opportunities, the resentment is aggravated. The overprotection of the handicapped is often accompanied by varying degrees of neglect of the other children. The siblings and their possessions may suffer directly at the hands of a demanding, hyperactive, and destructive handicapped child. Some sibling problems are illustrated in the following comments, adapted from S. D. Klein (1972).

> As a kid, I did not realize that there was anything really wrong with my brother. I found his crutches and wheelchair fun to play with. It was only when other kids made fun of him that I began to realize that he was handicapped. My parents strove very hard to make him seem normal. They asked me to help him but they never suggested that he was sick or abnormal. Then all of a sudden, we started taking him to the hospital. Once a week my mother and I would sit in the hospital waiting room for hours and hours. I saw other children and marveled that they were so different.
>
> Then, one time, several doctors went with my brother into an adjoining room and it suddenly dawned on me that they were all concerned about his condition. One of the doctors brought my mother an X ray photograph of his short leg. I looked at it with her and said, "Mama, that is someone's foot, only a part of it goes down like this, and this part is missing." At that moment it dawned on me—that was really my brother and he was defective.
>
> I think we all feel like protecting and defending our handicapped siblings. My brother went to a special school so I was never in school with him. However, when I was in the seventh grade some guy who did not know me was talking in the back of the bus about how dumb my brother was. He said you could make him do anything and all that kind of stuff. I walked back to the kid and slugged him in the face. I was really mad but he, of course, could not understand what was happening. From then on, I was always protecting my brother from something—from teasing, from fights, and from other kids trying to take advantage of him. I knew that many things I did were foolish but you can't help getting emotionally involved. One day, one of my friends told about some other kids who had picked on my brother and how sorry he felt. Then he turned to me and asked, "What did happen to your brother to make him that way?" "Don't ask me that, and the next person who asks that will get punched in the face," I retorted. Even when I said that, I knew that it was foolish, but it had made me mad. I felt strange about the whole thing and now wonder if my reactions were not the result of my own lack of understanding.

Practically every systematic study of exceptional people and their families stresses the need for more and better counseling. In their fervent search for solutions to their dilemma, the parents of exceptional children are perpetually looking for counsel (Hobbs, 1975; Kroth, 1975).

The goals of parental counseling

The goals of counseling are essentially the same irrespective of who is being counseled. The nature of the information imparted, the ways in which the person is informed, and the methods used may vary, but the purposes of counseling remain constant. Counseling goals are intellectual, emotional, and behavioral in nature.

In the intellectual realm, the parents of exceptional children need information concerning the nature and extent of the child's exceptionality—diagnostic information. They want to know the probable cause of their child's condition—etiological information. They require information concerning facilities and services available for the care, treatment, and education of these children—information concerning remediation. They should be informed of what the future may hold for the handicapped child, as well as of the specific programs most appropriate to the needs and capacities of their child—prognosis.

However, the imparting of information is seldom enough. The purely intellectual or factual approach to problems involving emotionally-laden relationships is notoriously insufficient in itself. The feelings of people often carry more weight than do their intellects. Therefore, it is just as important to help parents with their attitudes and feelings as it is to provide them with adequate information. Counselors must concern themselves with the parents' fears and anxieties and their feelings of guilt and shame. They should attempt to reduce the emotional vulnerability of the family members. While the strains and tensions suffered by the family of the exceptional child cannot be eliminated, it is often possible to increase their ability to tolerate tension. Adequate counseling will also result in modified behavior by parents. Every counseling program should involve specific plans for the family and the handicapped child.

The goals of counseling for the parents of exceptional children are considerably more modest than are those of psychotherapy. Counseling is not intended to change the personality of the counselee. It is intended to help reasonably well-integrated people understand and deal more adequately with the problems growing out of the presence of the deviant child in the family. Work with the families of handicapped children is closer to social work than to psychotherapy. It is more concerned with environmental manipulation and the handling of practical problems than with the personalities of the family members (Tavormina, 1975).

Parental dissatisfactions with counseling

Attending meetings of parents of the handicapped, one has the impression that dissatisfaction with their experiences with professional people is almost universal. One mother characterized her conferences with professionals as "a masterful combination of dishonesty, condescension, misinformation, and bad manners" (Bennett, 1974). Hardly anyone seems pleased with the way he found out about his child's handicap and what could be done about it. Clients and professionals alike blame each other for this dissatisfaction. On the one hand, professionals point out that people blame the bearer of bad news, that what parents hear and what professionals say are often distinctly different, that purely descriptive diagnostic information is perceived by parents as "blaming the parent," and that parents often expect the impossible, as indicated by statements such as "If he would only tell me what my child's condition *really is*, I'm sure I could deal with it" and "I felt there was some sort of key and if he would just give it to me, it would reveal the secret of her recovery."

Parents, in turn, claim that most doctors know very little about many categories of exceptionality, that they are more pontifical than helpful, and that they avoid telling the parents what they know or believe by temporizing or giving vague hints and irrelevant observations which only distract and confuse. Parents also complain that doctors provide diagnostic information either in highly technical jargon or in purely pejorative terms, and that too often the parents are either told nothing beyond "You have a big problem there!" or are pressured to accept premature simple solutions—"Institutionalize the child" (Anderson & Garner, 1973).

There is nothing to be gained by attempting to apportion blame for this state of affairs. Certainly, some parents are not informed and others are tactlessly informed of their child's disability. Professionals can be insensitive to parents' feelings and unresponsive to their needs. They can either under- or overestimate the parents' capacity and readiness to understand and accept the child's disability and the realities of the situation.

Parents furious at the treatment they have received at the hands of some professionals tell other parents, and they all learn to distrust professionals. Parental hostilities, in turn, repel the professionals and reinforce their beliefs concerning parents. Professionals are human, too, and often respond to hostility with counter-hostility. Thus these two groups, who need each other's cooperation, are driven apart. What parents tell other parents is important. One parent with a bad experience tells others about it, leading them to expect similar experiences.

Some elementary principles of parental counseling

Interested readers and prospective professional counselors should consult the professional literature on family counseling. We shall present only a list of suggestions for the nonprofessional counselor who either elects to or must counsel the parents of exceptional children. Many different professional people counsel the parents of the handicapped—physicians, psychologists, social workers, school administrators, teachers, speech and occupational therapists, and physical therapists—and few of these people are professionally trained counselors.

The importance of listening   Most counselors, particularly teachers, talk too much. They have faith in the efficacy of instruction and exhortation, and they commonly assume that beliefs and actions derive directly from information and that people behave inappropriately simply because they don't know any better. To be effective, however, counseling must be appropriate to the feelings, attitudes, and personality of the counselee, as well as to his intellectual and informational level. The only way to determine the counseling needs of a given person is to let him tell you, and the best way for him to tell you is in his own way.

In the initial interview the counselees should be permitted to lead. They should do most of the talking and dominate the interview. If both parents are present—as they should be—much can be learned by permitting and encouraging them to talk about their problem child, the nature of the problems with which they want help, what has been done for the child, the plans they have made, and their expectations.

Permitting the counselees to tell these stories in their own ways provides clues to the stage of thinking they have attained in their concern for their children. It will indicate whether they are still concerned about diagnosis or the acceptance of diagnosis. The terms they use and their general vocabulary may indicate the level of sophistication and understanding they have attained. A listener can usually form some idea of the feelings and attitudes of the speaker. He can deduce something concerning the degrees of guilt, conflict, and confusion the counselees are experiencing.

The problem of terminology Most parents of exceptional children are lay people who do not understand professional jargon. Communication must be in terms of the counselee. If the parents talk first, the counselor learns their vocabulary and the terms that they find acceptable. Laymen often perceive professional terminology, even when they understand it, as stigmatizing and threatening. If parents refer to their child as a "slow developer" or as "nervous" or "handicapped," the counselor can adopt and use these terms in discussing the child. Their meaning will become clearer as the exact nature of the child's condition becomes clearer. Terms such as "crippled," "moron," "psychotic," "feebleminded," or even "mentally retarded" and "orthopedically handicapped" may well be set aside in an attempt to determine specifically the child's developmental status—what he can and cannot do. As we pointed out earlier, the fact that a disability exists—whether it be a language deficiency, an orthopedic handicap, a disorganization of personality, or mental retardation—may be less significant than the degree of the disability and the extent to which the person is handicapped by the deficiency.

Professionals will improve their relationships with parents by treating each handicapped person as an individual rather than as a "case," no matter how unusual and interesting. Referring to a child by name, or at least as "your daughter" or "your son," makes the person something more than a statistic. If the patient is an infant, holding it in a respectful and caring way during the discussion conveys to the parents the fact that the professional considers the baby human and worthy of concern and acceptance. In this context, one parent said, "Although it is now nineteen years since my child with Down's Syndrome was born, it is still painful for me to recall the coldness, the brutality and the inhumanity of the manner in which my doctor held my daughter by the nape of her neck, like a plucked chicken, and pointed to her typical mongoloid features" (Pender, 1975). The counselor should be interested in learning about the abilities and disabilities and the unique characteristics of the individual under study, rather than in simply classifying, categorizing, and labeling him.

The problem of acceptance   The counselor will remember that while his primary concern is for the exceptional child, the parents are also emotionally disturbed. They are in conflict. They have feelings of shame and guilt. They are subject to terrific social pressures and are vulnerable to criticism. Many parents have developed self-defeating and blind-alley resolutions of their conflicts. Their attitudes and practices may actually be aggravating their child's condition.

Merely to judge, disapprove of, or condemn parental attitudes and practices does not help, however. Overt or implied criticism of parental practices only adds to the emotional load of people who are already overwhelmed by their problems. Criticism from the counselor therefore is often met with hostility; the parents become defensive and invite counter-hostility. Understanding, acceptance, and empathy are a fundamental requirement of a helpful counseling relationship. Unconditional acceptance of the family as worthy and deserving of regard and assistance—the parents as well as the exceptional child—is a requisite of a helping relationship.

To be warm and sympathetic, to be understanding and helpful without fostering overdependence, is one of the challenges of counseling. To help parents to a better understanding of themselves, their child, and their relationships, yet not take over by providing too much advice and assistance, is a critical task. If the counselor is to be most effective, the parents must see that it is primarily their problem and that no one else can solve it for them.

A nonjudgmental, noncondemning, accepting, and understanding attitude toward people does not imply uncritical endorsement and support for whatever is done or proposed. The ultimate goal is to formulate and carry through plans which will most benefit the exceptional child, and with which the family can live at peace. The consequences of current or proposed practices can be suggested, alternatives can be proposed, and appropriate plans can be sanctioned. Additional information can be supplied in such a way as to reinforce certain behavior and discourage others without rejecting or disapproving the individuals involved.

The importance of counseling the entire family   Some reasons for counseling the entire family have already been listed. Another important reason is that it facilitates communication among members of the family. It is very difficult for a mother—for it is usually the mother who is counseled—to go home and restate, explain, interpret, and answer questions concerning a long and involved counseling session, the nature of which she may only partially understand. Selective perception and memory distortion preclude accurate reporting. Emotional tension may be making communication between family members difficult. Effective communication between family members may even have broken down.

The advent of a child belonging to one of the familiar disability syndromes such as Down's Syndrome (mongolism), whose condition is usually recognized at birth, poses special counseling problems. Recognizing that the parents have the right to know, professionals usually give diagnostic information as soon as possible after the delivery. If a couple is left to learn about their infant's condition from someone other than their physician, their relationship with the doctor, as well as with other professionals with whom they might consult, is jeopardized. Whatever their race, religion, or socio-economic status, learning that their newborn infant is seriously defective is a traumatic experience. Parents need all the support and assistance they can be given. Therefore, the initial diagnostic information should be presented to both parents. Some counselors prefer to discuss the child's condition with the father before they go in together to talk with the mother. They also try to arrange to have a close friend or relative present when the initial diagnostic information is conveyed, if the father is not available. It is felt that the vulnerable new mother should not be alone at this time (Golden & Davis, 1974).

Conferences involving the entire family may reopen avenues of communication and help unite the members in the interest of making plans for the exceptional person's welfare. The emotional isolation in which each suffers in silence, is afraid to express his fears, and is reluctant to precipitate the issue is too often a part of the burden imposed on the nondisabled family members.

Effective planning and execution involve the whole family. When all the concerned family members participate in counseling, conflicting beliefs and attitudes come to light, and differences of opinion can be ventilated and possibly reconciled. Family members are more likely to share responsibility and cooperate for a common goal if all are involved in the discussion and planning. Unfortunately, counseling of the entire family is not yet the general practice.

The importance of feelings and attitudes   Feelings are often strong than admonitions and logical decisions. Self-pity, anxiety, guilt, and shame are primarily feeling states. While some parents act inappropriately because they do not know how to act any other way, far more act less adequately than their information dictates because of anxieties, hostilities, and guilt feelings. It is therefore essential that counseling be as concerned with feelings and attitudes as with giving information and making formal plans. Parents need help in clarifying their feelings. They need assistance in wandering through their emotional mazes. When deepseated emotional disturbances and emotional disorientation are present, however, the problems may be beyond the reach of the ordinary teacher, counselor, physician, or school psychologist, and long-term psychotherapy may be necessary.

Feelings and attitudes must often be dealt with before the parents can progress to the point of planning rationally for their child. Confused, frightened, and grieving parents should neither be offered stereotyped solutions nor be pressed for lifetime decisions. Frightened and bewildered by the diagnosis, they may welcome an opportunity to escape the problem when a solution such as foster-home or institutional placement is suggested. However, if it is acted upon, they soon discover that the initial placement of the child does not solve the problem. They begin to wonder whether the child would not have done better if he had stayed at home, they experience guilt over their apparent rejection of their infant, and they feel betrayed by the doctor who suggested placement. The feelings and conflicts which are aroused at the birth of a defective child are not resolved when the doors of the institution or foster home close behind the baby. Rather than making any major decisions, the more immediate problem is to help the family deal with the acute grief and chronic sorrow they are experiencing. This cannot be done in one or two short discussions.

When the diagnostic information has been imparted, the parents' comments and questions should be solicited. The counselor should be willing and able to accept critical questions and expressions of doubt, as well as a wide variety of emotional reactions. The parents should be encouraged to discuss the matter between themselves and return to continue the discussion. If they are in need of immediate assistance in caring for the child, they can be told how to contact a public health nurse or social worker. Some parents go through a long period of denial and mourning before acceptance reaches the point where they can mobilize their resources and begin serious, long-range planning.

The place of interpretation in counseling   Interpretation can occur at several different levels. At one level, it may be largely a matter of providing information. All parents need information. However, information often requires interpretation; as we indicated earlier, the meaning of the facts of a disability is more important than the presence of the condition.

Some people need self-understanding more than an understanding of the handicapping condition of their child. Some parents need help but do not realize it; others realize they need assistance but cannot ask for or accept it; some seek advice but are unable to follow it. Many parents agree to plans they are unable to carry out. Parents, like all other people, often contradict what they say by what they do. All such people can profit by a greater understanding of themselves and their needs. They need to be interpreted to themselves.

Interview questions may point up gross inconsistencies. Questions of concern may be discussed without parental defenses being probed too deeply. Interpretation in depth is hardly practical in counseling which stops short of psychotherapy. Defense mechanisms have value for the individual. To probe deeply and deprive an individual of his defenses without carrying through and helping him to substitute a more adequate adjustment may do more harm than good.

The interpretations of the average counselor will provide information which is as complete and accurate as possible. They will dispel misconceptions. However, even the latter may be carried too far. When the actual causes of the handicapped child's condition are unknown, parents often develop very positive beliefs about its etiology. These beliefs have considerable value for the parents, for the parents can discuss their child's condition frankly and openly when they are able to present the alleged causes as the real ones. In such cases, so long as the belief does not result in inappropriate treatment for the child, the belief may represent a useful fiction which is just as well left undisturbed.

Imparting diagnostic information   One function of counseling is to help parents realize the nature and extent of their problem as early as possible. Many valuable years are often lost because of failures either in diagnosis or in parental acceptance of the factors or implications of diagnostic information. The parents of exceptional children often say, "Why didn't someone tell us?" or "If we had only known sooner!" In many cases these parents had been told in various ways, but their ears were not open. Parental attitudes have to develop to a certain level before there is receptivity to the facts and implications of threatening diagnostic information. Understanding and acceptance of diagnosis cannot be forced. Time is required, and counselors can only present the available data as completely and as honestly as possible and hope for its eventual acceptance.

Test data and general impressions must be stated in the counselee's terms. Exact test scores are seldom disclosed. Intellectual status and achievement are usually most meaningful when they are stated in terms of approximate mental age or school grade equivalents. Asking the parents to indicate their estimates of the child's level is often helpful. When the parents' estimate is in approximate agreement with intelligence test scores and other evidence of achievement, a simple confirmation of the parental judgment may be sufficient. When the data are discrepant, additional information may be needed. When parents are reluctant to accept diagnostic information no matter how complete, the counselor may supply the names of several other specialists or agencies from which the parents may select those with whom they wish to consult. One diagnosis or one statement of a diagnosis is seldom enough. It is normal for most parents to want to shop around. Many parents need to nurse their doubt and maintain their defenses until they are able to dispense with them. The initial rejection of many diagnoses and their implications is to be expected. Only the parents can make the critical decisions. Counselors can only assist in the process.

It will facilitate acceptance and action if the parents can be involved every step of the way. If the parents are involved in the diagnosis and in planning educational or treatment procedures, the question of the parents' "right to know" will never arise. Providing parents with copies of diagnostic reports and decisions made concerning their child will give them an opportunity to discuss and better understand the information. Today, parents have the legal right of access to such information.

Acceptance of a realistic diagnosis is furthered by accenting positive assets rather than the liabilities of the exceptional individual. The handicapped person is typically under special study because of his disability, and his limitation tends to be the overshadowing fact of his life. But every person has some positive attributes, and diagnosis should be as concerned with what the person *can* do as with what he cannot do. Plans which are built around what the child is able to do and formulated to take maximum advantage of his abilities may be more palatable to the parents than plans which are dominated by the child's disabilities.

The importance of plans   Specific plans for the exceptional child should be considered as early as possible. Sometimes an early shift in emphasis from diagnosis to what can best be done for the child immediately will indirectly bring acceptance of an implied status while resistance to an explicit statement is still great. Parents are often able to accept the facts of the child's present level of functioning while rejecting their implications for the child's future attainments.

When the parents have not sufficiently accepted the realities of the child's status to be able to make long-range plans, they may still be receptive to suggestions for dealing with the problems of living on a day-to-day basis. Plans which make use of the family and community resources to meet the child's immediate needs may then gradually be extended to the more remote ones.

The typical starting point for planning is the parents' conception of their child's future. A plan which they have considered, together with alternatives suggested by the counselor, is the beginning. Planning for the future is a continuing process and is never complete. Plans are realized one step at a time and need constant revision in the light of the individual's progress. If the parents leave a conference with nothing more than a commitment to attend a meeting of parents with similar problems and exchange information and plans with these parents, they have taken an important first step. Reading suggested literature on their child's condition may be an additional small step toward making long-range plans for their child.

Group counseling   Group counseling ranges all the way from an informal exchange of information and experiences among a group of parents with common problems to formal counseling by a trained and experienced leader. Group counseling directed by a leader can range from lecture, lecture and discussion, directed discussion, or free discussion to directive or nondirective psychotherapy.

Group guidance, counseling, and psychotherapy were originally used and justified because they saved the time of the counselors and psychotherapists who are in such short supply. However, experience indicates that working with groups may have some unique advantages over individual counseling or psychotherapy. Recently there has been a tremendous growth in group approaches to many training, guidance, counseling, and psychotherapeutic problems (Heisler, 1972).

The parents of mentally retarded children, often under considerable environmental stress, are confronted with day-to-day problem behavior. One study evaluated the relative effectiveness of behaviorally oriented and reflective group counseling. The members of the behaviorally-oriented counseling group were taught the principles and applications of techniques for dealing with specific child-rearing problems. The members of the reflective-oriented group were provided opportunities to discuss their feelings and problems, while the leaders conveyed the importance of feelings of empathy, acceptance, and understanding in dealing with their children. In terms of six success criteria, the behaviorally-oriented program resulted in significantly more improvement than did the reflective model (Tavormina, 1975). The evidence indicated that parents of the mentally retarded profited most by instruction and training in dealing with the specific problems they faced in rearing their children.

Some of the advantages of group counseling of the parents of exceptional children are:

1. The group gives the parents emotional support. Groups of people with common experiences and similar needs feel free to express their feelings,

attitudes, and beliefs. The group identification which typically develops as the result of shared experiences and common feelings seems to lessen the individual's emotional burden. The mere discovery that many other reasonably normal and adequate parents have similar conflicts and frustrations helps many parents to put their own problems in a different perspective.

In the group situation the parent is free to proceed at his own rate. He can bring up and focus on problems that are most significant to him. In group discussion he is able to clarify his ideas and feelings. Self-pity, guilt, and shame diminish when a parent discovers that others have shared and surmounted his problems.

2. In the group situation, parents educate each other. The typical group of parents of exceptional children have, *in toto,* accumulated a tremendous amount of information about exceptional children and the resources available for their diagnosis, care, and treatment. They are able to save each other a tremendous amount of time, money, and emotional stress by the exchange of information and experiences. And parents are generally more receptive to information, advice, and counseling coming from people like themselves than they are to the same information provided by professionals.

3. Programs for action are more likely to succeed as the result of group endeavors than when individuals act alone.

Many times the greatest service that a counselor can provide the parents of exceptional children is to put them in touch with a local group of parents, and perhaps to follow through and see that they meet with the group at least once. Such parents can also profit from membership in the state and national organizations concerned with exceptional people.

F. Weiner (1973) has written a very good book for parents, teachers, physicians, and others who may be called on to make referrals for handicapped children. It indicates resources available on the community, state, and national levels, both public and private. It is clearly written and convenient to use. R. L. Kroth (1975) has also provided a good discussion of the problems involved in communicating with the parents of exceptional children.

Counseling as a continuing process   Whenever possible, counseling services should be continuously available. Parents who are not receptive to counseling at one time may be so later. The problems of exceptional children change with their age. A program for a handicapped child which is adequate so long as the child is of school age must be replaced by another when he is older. Changes in the family constellation bring new problems. While the aim of counseling is to help the parents help themselves, an overdependency on counselors is discouraged. Parents should leave counseling with the feeling that they can return if subsequent problems become overwhelming.

THE SELF-HELP ORGANIZATIONS

Paralleling professionally organized and directed group counseling, a self-help movement has grown in the United States. Some of these groups were started in the 1930s, but their tremendous growth has occurred largely in the last two decades. Two general types of self-help are distinguishable. One type is composed of the deviant individuals themselves who have the same problems and are seeking help from each other; Alchoholics Anonymous, Gamblers Anonymous, Neurotics Anonymous, Overeaters Anonymous, Recovery Inc., and Synanon are illustrative of this group. The second type consists of family members or friends of the persons with the primary personal-social problems; Alon, Alateen, and Parents of Retarded Children are examples of organizations of this type. Almost every category of deviants has organizations of both types.

While the functions of the two categories overlap, the latter type more often engages in advocacy, social action, and program development, whereas the former is more likely to focus on its more immediate problems. A tremendous number of people are involved in these programs. One survey of self-help organizations for the physically handicapped alone found over 1,200 such groups in the United States (Massachusetts Council of Organizations of the Handicapped, 1973). In 1973, Alcoholics Anonymous reported a membership of 405,858 in 14,037 chapters in the United States (Jaques & Patterson, 1974). Many of the values of such self-help groups are the same as those provided by professionally organized group counseling and psychotherapy:

1. Gaining facts and information concerning their conditions and problems
2. Exchanging information concerning ameliorative and coping devices
3. Providing mutual motivation and support
4. Receiving feedback from others to assist in evaluating one's status and progress
5. Gaining a group identification that reduces one's feelings of isolation and alienation
6. Obtaining satisfaction from members' mutual altruistic concern

THE CHILD-ABUSING PARENT

When stresses exceed the parents' endurance levels, it is inevitable that they will direct their resentment and hostility at the child himself. When this hostility becomes overt, the result may be a battered or abused child.

While child abuse is not primarily a problem of the deviant child or parent, deviancy in either may be a contributing cause or a consequence of the abuse. Child abuse involves a vulnerable child, a predisposed abusing parent, and a stress situation which triggers the abuse (Nazzaro, 1974; Spinetta & Rigler, 1972). Other things being equal, a handicapping condition in a child will significantly increase the level of family stress. The increased ambivalence in parental feelings engendered by a child who is handicapped increases the probability that such a child will become a scapegoat for overt acts of resentment and hostility. Finally, child abuse often results in head injury, which involves a likelihood of brain damage (Apthorp, 1970). One study estimates that 28 percent of battered children with head injuries suffer permanent brain damage (Brandwein, 1973); in this researcher's opinion, child abuse is a significant cause of mental retardation. D. Zadnik (1973) claims that many children are visually impaired or blinded by child abuse. One study of fifty-one cases of child abuse found that one-quarter of the children were low-birth-weight infants (Klein & Stern, 1971), more likely than infants of normal birth-weight to suffer from a multiplicity of problems. Such problem children add to the parents' burden and are vulnerable in two ways: They are vulnerable as objects of overt hostility, and since they are more fragile they are also more likely to be damaged by physical abuse. However, most abused children are not handicapped (Apthorp, 1970; Shanas, 1975; Soffing, 1975).

Characteristics of the child-abusing parent

Child-abusing parents come from all socio-economic levels. However, the reported cases (the only ones studied) come disproportionately from families experiencing economic and social stress. Abusing families also have a high incidence of unstable marriages, separation, and divorce as well as of minor criminal offenses. The abused child is often the outcome of an unwanted pregnancy. The familes are commonly described as "multiproblem families" in which an interplay of socio-economic, mental, physical, and emotional factors condition the abuse (Helfer & Kempe, 1974; Shanas, 1975).

Abusing parents themselves, as children, were often neglected or abused either physically or emotionally. They were reared and treated in much the same way that they treat their own children. They are reacting to their children in keeping with their own experiential history of cruelty and lack of love. In addition, abusing parents often make unrealistic demands on their children. When the child's performance fails to meet their high level of expectations, they justify the abuse as a

proper disciplinary measure and strongly defend their right to use physical force (Green, Gaines, & Sandgrund, 1974).

At one time a high incidence of neurotic or psychotic behavior was
assumed to be characteristic of abusing parents. Today the consensus
seems that to be that, while direct and deliberate murder of a child often
indicates a frankly psychotic parent, few abusing parents are clinically
psychotic or neurotic. They are most often characterized as "lacking in
impulse control" (Spinetta & Rigler, 1972).

E. J. Merrill (1962) has identified three clusters of traits characteristic
of abusing parents: (1) Such parents are beset with a generalized and
pervasive hostility and aggressiveness usually directed at the world in
general but sometimes focused on a vulnerable child. (2) Such parents
are characterized by rigidity, compulsiveness, and perfectionism. They
expect their children to be clean, orderly, and obedient far beyond their
years. These parents insist that they are entirely right in the ways they
treat their children and defend their right to act as they do. They seem
to be concerned primarily with their own pleasures and blame the children for the troubles they are having. (3) Child-abusing parents may be
immature, passive, dependent, moody, unhappy, and despondent. Generally passive and unaggressive, they occasionally break out with uncontrolled violence directed toward their children.

Since the battered child syndrome was first recognized in the 1950s,
considerable progress has been made in dealing with the problem. A
Child Abuse Prevention and Treatment Act was passed by Congress and
signed by President Gerald Ford on January 31, 1974. It established a
National Center on Child Abuse within the Office of Child Development
of the Children's Bureau. By April 1975 the bureau had awarded grants
and contracts totaling $4.5 million to increase and improve services for
the prevention, identification, and treatment of child abuse and neglect
(News and Reports, *Children Today,* 1975). All fifty states now have
child abuse report laws which require physicians to report suspicious
cases.

When victims of child abuse are simply returned to their parents,
one-third of them will subsequently be seriously injured or even killed.
Consequently, many communities now provide psychiatric and/or counseling services for the parents and protection and care for the children.
For example, San Francisco has an Extended Family Center which serves
families referred by the courts and by public health, mental health, and
social welfare agencies. The state of Florida has a "hot line" which has
been receiving about 20,000 calls a year in cases of child abuse and/or
neglect. In Oregon, a volunteer group—the Child Abuse Study Committee, Inc.—is focusing on the area of public education. The United
States Office of Education is awarding grants for the development of

models for teacher training (Broeck, 1974; Nazzaro, 1974; Shanas, 1975). Predictably, an organization of child-abusing parents calling itself Parents Anonymous has been formed.

SUGGESTIONS FOR PARENTS OF EXCEPTIONAL CHILDREN[1]

Assert and maintain your right to know and to be involved. Since you are the primary planner, decision-maker, advocate, and monitor for your child, insist that you be treated as such. Your success in doing this will depend upon how well informed you are and your ability to work and cooperate with the other people involved. Resistance to your inclusion in the decisions concerning your child can be met by persuasion, by insisting that you know many things about your child that the others do not know, and finally, by insisting on your legal rights. Obtain and retain copies of your child's records. If possible, make tape recordings of diagnostic and interpretive conferences. Keep records of visits with dates, addresses, persons present, and, if other records are not available, your recollections and understandings of what was said and recommendations made.

Become informed. Familiarize yourself with the professional literature and terminology used by specialists in the area of your child's exceptionality. Make sure that you understand the terminology used by professionals. If in doubt, ask them to translate into lay language and give examples of what they mean. Talk with as many professionals as you can. Talk with other parents, join parent groups, and share your information with them. Visit, observe, and ask questions about programs that may be of help to your child.

Work hard at trying to de-stigmatize the category to which your child belongs. Insist on and impart to your child and others the notion that differentness is not bad. Encourage the idea that these deviants are individuals with certain special problems, rather than defective persons. Do not hide your child just because he is different. It is important for both you and your child to learn to cope with the inevitable questions and/or stares of others.

Help your child become maximally independent. Do not do for him, and do not permit others to do for him, those things he can do or learn to do for himself. Firmness and the setting of limits combined with patience and persistence are as necessary for the development of the handicapped as for the nonhandicapped.

[1] Adapted and modified from Hobbs, 1975; Sevigny & Sevigny, 1974; and Ouellet, 1972.

Give your child as normal a life as possible. Think in terms of what he *can* do rather than what he cannot do. It is easy to be so impressed with his limitations that you fail to see his possibilities.

Your problems are not unique. The problems of the parents of exceptional and nonexceptional children are basically the same. It is of course necessary for the parents of exceptional children to exert special effort in dealing with the increased emotional and physical strain engendered by the child's differentness. Fear, anguish, anger, and resentment vie with faith, hope, and love in the matrix of all parent-child relationships. It is harder for the latter to overbalance the negative emotions which have a greater likelihood of cropping up because of the exceptional circumstances of the deviant child.

SUMMARY

The individual exceptional child can best be understood in terms of the entire family constellation. Family and child exert reciprocal effects on each other, and changes in either affect both. Parental and family reactions to the advent of a child with a disability do not differ in kind from people's reactions to other types of stress. Parental reactions to the problems of the exceptional range from complete denial to realistic coping with the situation. Self-pity, ambivalence, projection, guilt, shame, depression, self-punishment, and the development of patterns of mutual dependency are common parental reactions to the presence of a less-than-adequate child in the family.

The general reactions of children to a handicapped sibling largely reflect those of the parents, but must always be considered in counseling the families of exceptional children. Working with the families of exceptional children involves no unique counseling techniques or principles. However, the nonprofessional counselor is admonished to heed these precepts:

1. Let the counselee talk.
2. Use the terminology of the counselee.
3. Accept the counselee as an individual but do not necessarily approve of and endorse his ideas, practices, and plans.
4. See both parents, preferably the entire family.
5. Deal with feelings and attitudes as well as with intellectual matters.
6. Keep interpretation on a fairly elementary and superficial level.
7. Give diagnostic information according to the individual's ability to understand and accept it.
8. Include specific plans for the future.

9. Remember that group counseling is often useful for the parents or families of exceptional children.
10. Keep your door open. Counseling should be a continuing process.

Suggestions for parents include:

1. Assert and maintain your right to know and to be involved in all plans and decisions concerning your handicapped child.
2. Become informed concerning the category of your child's disability.
3. Help your child to become maximally independent.
4. Give your child as normal a life as possible.
5. Remember that your problems are not unique just because your child is deviant.

REFERENCES

ANDERSON, K. A., & A. M. GARNER, "Mothers of Retarded Children: Satisfaction with Visits to Professional People," *Mental Retardation*, 1973, *1* (4), 36–39.

APTHORP, J. S., "The Battered Child," in C. R. Angle & E. A. Bering, Jr., eds., *Physical Trauma as an Etiological Agent in Mental Retardation* (Washington, D.C.: U.S. Department of Health, Education and Welfare, 1970).

BEHRENS, M. L., "Child Rearing and the Character Structure of the Mother," *Child Development*, 1954, *25*, 225–38.

BENNETT, J. M., "Proof of the Pudding," *The Exceptional Parent*, 1974, *4* (3), 7–12.

BOLES, G., "Personality Factors in the Mothers of Cerebral-palsied Children," *Genetic Psychology Monographs*, 1959, *59*, 159–218.

BRANDWEIN, H., "The Battered Child: A Definite and Significant Factor in Mental Retardation," *Mental Retardation*, 1973, *11* (5), 50–51.

BROECK, E. T., "The Extended Family Center: 'A Home Away from Home' for Abused Children and Their Parents," *Children Today*, 1974, *3* (2), 2–6.

CALDWELL, B. M., "The Effects of Infant Care," in M. S. Hoffman & L. W. Hoffman, eds., *Review of Child Development Research* (New York: Russell Sage Foundation, 1964).

EISENPREIS, B., "My Child Isn't Like That," *The Exceptional Parent*, 1974, *4* (2), 5–9.

GOLDEN, D. A., & J. G. DAVIS, "Counseling Parents After the Birth of an Infant with Down's Syndrome," *Children Today*, 1974, *3* (2), 7–11, 36–37.

GREEN, A. H., R. W. GAINES, & A. SANDGRUND, "Child Abuse: Pathological Syndrome of Family Interaction," *American Journal of Psychiatry*, 1974, *131*, 882–86.

GREGORY, R. W., "Family Forum," *The Exceptional Parent*, 1972, 2 (2), 30.

HAYDEN, V., "The Other Children," *The Exceptional Parent*, 1974, *4* (4), 26–29.

HEISLER, V., *A Handicapped Child in the Family: A Guide for Parents* (New York: Grune & Stratton, 1972).

HELFER, R. E., & C. H. KEMPE, eds., *The Battered Child*, 2nd ed. (New York: Brunner/Mazel, 1974).

HOBBS, N., *The Futures of Children* (San Francisco: Jossey-Bass, 1975).

JACKSON, D. D., *Communication, Family, and Marriage* (Palo Alto, Ca.: Science and Behavior Books, 1970).

JAQUES, M. E., & K. M. PATTERSON, "The Self-help Group: A Review," *Rehabilitation Counseling Bulletin*, 1974, *18* (1), 49–58.

JOHNSON, R. C., & G. R. MEDINNUS, *Child Psychology: Behavior and Development*, 3rd ed. (New York: John Wiley, 1975).

KANTOR, D., & W. LEHR, *Inside the Family* (San Francisco: Jossey-Bass, 1975).

KEITH, D. V., "Use of Self: A Brief Report," *Family Processes*, 1974, *13* (2), 201–6.

KLEIN, M., & L. STERN, "Low Birth Weight and the Battered Child Syndrome," *American Journal of Diseases of Children*, 1971, *122*, 15–18.

KLEIN, S. D., "Brother to Sister: Sister to Brother," *The Exceptional Parent*, 1972, *2* (1) , 10–15; (2), 26–27.

KOGAN, K. L., & N. TYLER, "Mother-child Interaction in Young Physically Handicapped Children," *American Journal of Mental Deficiency*, 1973, *77*, 492–97.

KROTH, R. L., *Communicating with Parents of Exceptional Children* (Denver: Love Publishing Co., 1975).

LAXER, R. M., "Relation of Real Self-rating to Mood and Blame and Their Interaction in Depression," *Journal of Consulting Psychology*, 1964, *28*, 539–48.

LOVE, H. D., *The Mentally Retarded Child and His Family* (Springfield, Ill.: Charles C Thomas, 1973).

MASSACHUSETTS COUNCIL OF ORGANIZATIONS OF THE HANDICAPPED, INC., *A Directory of Organizations of the Handicapped in the United States* (Hyde Park, Mass., 1973).

MERRILL, F. J., "Physical Abuse of Children: An Agency Study," in V. DeFrancio, ed., *Protecting the Battered Child* (Denver: American Humane Association, 1962).

MICHAELS, C. T., "Chip on My Shoulder," *Exceptional Parent*, 1974, *4* (1) , 31–35.

NAZZARO, J., "Child Abuse and Neglect," *Exceptional Children*, 1974, *40*, 351–54.

"News and Reports: New Child Abuse Grants," *Children Today*, 1975, *4*, 34–35.

OUELLET, A. M., "Michelle: A Long Way to Kindergarten," *The Exceptional Parent*, 1972, *2* (2), 31–33.

PENDER, B., "A Parent's View," *Children Today*, 1975, *4* (1), 34–35.

RADKE, M. J., "The Relation of Parental Authority to Children's Behavior and Attitudes," University of Minnesota Institute of Child Welfare Monograph, Series 22 (Minneapolis, 1946).

REITER, G. F., & P. R. KILMANN, "Mothers as Family Change Agents," *Journal of Counseling Psychology*, 1975, *22*, 61–65.

ROGERS, C. R., *Clinical Treatment of the Problem Child* (Boston: Houghton Mifflin, 1939).

SCHAEFER, E. S., "A Circumplex Model for Maternal Behavior," *Journal of Abnormal and Social Psychology*, 1959, *59*, 226–45.

SCHAEFER, E. S., "Converging Models for Maternal Behavior and for Child

Behavior," in J. E. Glidewell, ed., *Parental Attitudes and Child Behavior* (Springfield, Ill.: Charles C Thomas, 1961).

SEARS, R. R., G. E. MACCOBY, & H. LEVIN, *Patterns of Child Rearing* (New York: Harper & Row, 1957).

SEVIGNY, R., & L. SEVIGNY, "Who Gives a Damn?" *The Exceptional Parent,* 1974, *4* (3), 22–23.

SHANAS, B., "Child Abuse: A Killer Teachers Can Help Control," *Phi Delta Kappan,* 1975, *56* (7), 479–82.

SMITH, E., B. M. RICKETTS, & H. SMITH, "The Recommendations for Child Placement by a Psychiatric Clinic," *American Journal of Orthopsychiatry,* 1962, *32,* 42–52.

SOFFING, M., "Abused Children and Exceptional Children," *Exceptional Children,* 1975, *42,* 126–33.

SPINETTA, J. J., & D. RIGLER, "The Child-abusing Parent: A Psychological Review," *Psychological Bulletin,* 1972, *77,* 296–304.

TAVORMINA, J. B., "Relative Effectiveness of Behavioral and Reflective Group Counseling with Parents of Mentally Retarded Children," *Journal of Consulting and Clinical Psychology,* 1975, *43,* 22–31.

WEINER, F., *Help for the Handicapped Child* (New York: McGraw-Hill, 1973).

WITMER, H., "The Outcome of Treatment in a Child Guidance Clinic," *Smith College Studies in Social Work,* 1933, *3,* 399–408.

WULBERT, M.; S. INGLIS; E. KREIGSMANN; & B. MILLS, "Language Delay and Associated Mother-child Interactions," *Developmental Psychology,* 1975, *11,* 61–70.

ZADNIK, D., "Social and Medical Aspects of the Battered Child with Visual Impairment," *The New Outlook for the Blind,* 1973, *67,* 241–50.

ZUK, G. H., "The Cultural Dilemma and Spiritual Crises of the Family with a Handicapped Child," *Exceptional Children,* 1962, *28,* 405–8.

2

Intellectual exceptionality

Photo by Sybil Shackman, Monkmeyer Press Photo Service

Chapter 6

The intellectually superior

The specific nature of outstanding ability demanded by society tends to vary over the years, but the demand for the contributions of the intellectually superior is always high. The ever-increasing complexity of society and the expanding horizons of scientific investigation have emphasized the necessity for early identification and training of the very brilliant. It is theorized that early identification and subsequent training will help bring about more complete use of their potential for making significant contributions to the culture and will also be of personal benefit to the brilliant themselves. The contributions of the very bright portion of the population should enhance the quality of existence for all. Concern for the human condition will not allow us to overlook or fail to develop this potential for human betterment.

SOME BACKGROUND

Concern for the identification and training of the gifted is not recent. Plato wanted to discover the most able youth so that they might be educated for state leadership and suggested tests of native ability for their selection.

The scientific investigation of the gifted can be readily traced to F. Galton's (1869) reports of his genetic and statistical studies of the gifted. These were really the first quantitative studies of human abilities. Galton attempted to show that people's natural abilities derived from inheritance in much the same way as did such features as height and other physical attributes. Carefully examining the biographies of individuals of outstanding achievement, he concluded that the principal elements contributing to achievement were "ability, zeal, and readiness to work." He felt that each of these was in part a result of inheritance, but that the most important factor was the "gift of high ability." He devoted his book to the study of the ability of gifted people. From his studies he recognized two kinds of ability. The more important one was a single "general ability" that was basic to all thoughts and actions. A number of "special aptitudes," each of limited scope, were also recognized, but Galton insisted that these special factors were of secondary importance and contributed only slightly to the attaining of eminence. He asserted that without a special gift for a particular kind of achievement one would not achieve in that area, but that to become great in a given area one needed a high degree of general ability. He emphasized the great versatility that he found in the early years of the future genius. This point has been emphasized more recently, and it has been indicated that the *direction* of endeavor results chiefly from interest or accident (Burt, 1962). According to Galton, those of outstanding ability to achieve possess a greater *quantity* of their particular abilities. They possess the same *qualities* as do others, but they have them in greater quantity.

Much interest was aroused by these reports and by subsequent investigations of social influences on the gifted as well as the role of genetic factors in giftedness (Ward, 1906; Cattell, 1915). Reports of leadership, mental health, and ability were made, and genius was presented as superior mental ability by L. M. Terman (1904, 1905, 1906).

With the advent of the Binet tests, it was soon discovered that the range of performance on intelligence tests was great and that those scoring very high on the tests were, indeed, exceptional. Early investigations by Terman (1915, 1925) initiated the attack on many of the then current beliefs about the brilliant and on the attitudes toward them. The reports of Terman et al. (1925) constitute an important landmark in the investigations of giftedness. He investigated more than a thousand gifted children and reported on their development and behavior. These children were studied well into adulthood, and these investigations have provided a large volume of data about the gifted (Terman & Oden, 1947, 1959; Oden, 1968). Investigations of the gifted have been numerous, and a substantial body of literature in this area has accumulated. A general view of the gifted, their problems, and their promise will be presented in this chapter.

PROBLEMS OF DEFINITION AND TERMINOLOGY

Definitions of intelligence have been offered by a great number of investigators. These definitions have perhaps reflected the divergence of interests and theoretical orientations of persons interested in intelligence as much as they have contributed to any clarification of the concept. The way in which intelligence is defined is a partial determinant, at least, of the way in which the intellectually gifted or exceptionally intelligent will be defined. It is to be expected, then, that uniformity of definition of the exceptionally brilliant will not be found. This problem is further confounded when the same criterion is used differently by various investigators. This is the case in attempting to delineate the brilliant.

A commonly used method of defining the brilliant is in terms of scores on a test of intelligence. This is not as simple a method as it might appear at first glance. Not all investigators have employed the same tests of intelligence. Some have used individual tests while others have employed group tests of ability. Those using individual measures have not always used the same instrument, and a tremendous variety of group measures has been employed. In addition, the investigators have differed about the score above which an individual would be designated as brilliant, gifted, talented, or superior.

In Terman's notable investigations, the IQ as measured by the Stanford-Binet intelligence test (Terman et al., 1925) was the criterion used. The minimum score originally set for the gifted was 140, although some children scoring as low as 135 were later included in his group. Subsequently, other investigators have employed other scores as being the minimum for the gifted child. Perhaps the most popular figure has been an IQ of 130 but IQ's lower than 130 have been used to select children for special classes. A. O. Heck (1953) indicated that an IQ of 125 was an approximate point for determining admission to classes for the intellectually superior, and children with IQ's of 120 whose performance is consistently outstanding in areas of value to society have been considered as eligible for special classes (Otto, 1957). The normally bright child has been considered to have a minimum IQ of 110 (Bentley, 1937).

The use of the IQ in defining the gifted has the advantage of objectivity. It can also be applied relatively early in life. This gives it an advantage over the earlier definitions, which categorized the gifted as those who had achieved outstanding stature in one of the professions and thus identified them after their education and training were completed. Although L. S. Hollingworth (1931) has asserted that the IQ is the only way to identify gifted children with certainty, using it as the sole basis has come under severe attack. Children from low socio-economic backgrounds and from certain ethnic backgrounds tend not to score well on verbal tests and may be excluded when such instruments are used as the basis for selection. Some children who do not score exceptionally high on tests of intelligence later tend to excel in music and the arts. To include these individuals, the definition of the gifted was broadened to include the "talented" and those whose performance is consistently remarkable in some potentially valuable activity (Witty, 1958). Further elaboration of the definition to include creativeness as a part of giftedness has become popular (Frierson, 1969). Creativeness has received sufficient investigative attention to be treated in a separate chapter of this text. Research on the gifted published in professional journals shifted from 61 percent dealing with gifted children in 1961 to 64 percent dealing with creativity in 1966 (Frierson, 1969). The 1970s are witnessing a return to interest in the gifted.

The profusion of definitions of the brilliant is great. W. Abraham (1958) reported that one of his students uncovered 113 different definitions of the gifted while preparing a term paper. Despite this diversity and the confusion in terminology, there is some general agreement as to who constitutes the exceptional. Despite the shortcomings of conventional IQ tests, scores on these instruments provide a handy frame of reference for thinking about the gifted, and most investigations of the gifted have dealt with children with high IQ's. As a working hypothesis, we shall consider those with high IQ's or those who in other areas of performance are consistently outstanding. The words *gifted, brilliant,* and *exceptional* will be used interchangeably.

IDENTIFICATION OF THE GIFTED

Before any systematic effort can be made to provide adequate educational programs or personal guidance for those with high levels of intellect, they must be identified. If gifted students require different curricula and methods of instruction than do average students, these people must be discovered so that appropriate measure can be taken for their academic welfare. The same thing is true in the personal and social realms. If development of the gifted as persons is to receive unique consideration, they must be known to those who can make the necessary provisions.

For educational purposes, a systematic program for identification can be developed. Classroom teachers can use measuring devices with all of their students as a first crude step. Such a preliminary screening program can save time and effort, and reduce the complex task of final selection by well-trained personnel.

Standardized tests of achievement can be employed systematically in the school. Those who score high enough above the norms for their age or grade to be considered outstanding can be further examined. A danger in the use of tests of achievement as the sole criterion for selection for special attention is that a number of children who are not particularly brilliant, but who are highly motivated to do good work in school, will be found to score high. These children may be doing very well in their current situation, and should not be expected to excel beyond their current status. Tests of educational achievement do not detect the individual who has the *potential* for high-level achievement but who is not achieving at a rate beyond that of his classmates.

Group tests of intelligence can be employed as a rough device in the discovery of those individuals who are not achieving at a high level. At the same time, those who are achieving at high levels but do not score high on the group tests of intelligence can be referred for more intensive investigation.

Reliance on group tests of intelligence for adequate classification is sometimes necessary because of the lack of adequately trained personnel. When this procedure is employed, several dangers are encountered (Martinson & Lessinger, 1960; Pegnato & Birch, 1959). R. A. Martinson and L. M. Lessinger found that less than half of a group of 332 pupils scoring over 130 on the Stanford-Binet scored as high as 130 on a group test of intelligence. C. V. Pegnato and J. W. Birch reported similar findings: to identify 92 percent of those scoring above 135 on an individual test, it was necessary to consider all who had exceeded 115 on the group test. This discrepancy between the results of employing group and individual intelligence tests points up the necessity for thorough examination if the detection procedures are to be effective.

Individual intelligence tests are to be administered by trained individuals. Interpretation of test results is not a routine matter. The trained psychologist has available the use of more valid measuring instruments than does the untrained individual. The psychologist also has had special training in the interpretation and use of such scores once they have been derived. The sophistication of trained psychologists makes their services in this area imperative. They have knowledge of a variety of tests and testing devices, and can make better estimates of the procedures to be used in an individual evaluation. Individual examination is usually to be preferred over group testing as a procedure. Many of the group tests depend for their validity upon their agreement with the individually administered ones, and greater attention can be paid to the examining situation when it is done on a one-to-one basis.

An interesting attempt to identify the gifted by evaluating school children's creative responses has been reported (Martinson & Seagoe, 1967). In this investigation a high IQ group (Stanford-Binet IQ mean = 142.7) produced more products that were rated as creative than did a lower-IQ group (mean = 107.5). In this investigation the traditional IQ proved to be a better predictor of creative production than did a measure of divergent thinking!

School grades have also been employed as a rough device for screening. As a generalization, it is safe to say that students who obtain a preponderance of A and B grades are more likely to be brilliant than are those who get lower grades, but school grades reflect many things besides achievement. (It has already been indicated that achievement measures, by themselves, are not adequate.) High grades are sometimes given to increase morale and motivation, and biases are bound to creep into the situation as a result of personality, as well as of social and cultural factors involved in the complex schoolroom situation.

Teachers' ratings have also been used. When teachers have been asked to designate the children in their classes who are gifted, however, they have not been able to do so very accurately. This is particularly true when no operational definition of giftedness is supplied and each teacher is left free to use personal judgment in determining giftedness. One investigation (Pegnato & Birch, 1959) found that teachers did not refer about 55 percent of the children who were later found to be gifted by the criteria established by the investigators. Thirty-one percent who were not gifted by the criteria employed were referred. If checklists of behavioral characteristics of the gifted are supplied, however, the teachers' ratings improve. Peer nominations by elementary school children have been found to correlate highly with teacher nominations (Granzin & Granzin, 1969). Rather extensive lists (Abraham, 1958; Kough & De-Haan, 1955) cite characteristic behavior of the gifted, either defined by the constructors of the lists or based on large numbers of investigations of the characteristics of gifted individuals. Precocity in a number of physical and intellectual areas combined with breadth of activities and interests is usually indicative of brilliance.

The value to the culture of stimulating, directing, and educating the brilliant is so great that the importance of the task of identifying them should not be underestimated. The use of the best available techniques for this purpose is to be encouraged. A variety of procedures can be employed and the best trained personnel available should employ them.

INCIDENCE[1]

The frequency of occurrence of the brilliant depends on the definition used. The frequency of occurrence in the general population is automatically determined if the brilliant are defined as comprising a given percentage of the population. On such a basis, estimates of frequency among school children have ranged from 0.5 to 20 percent. If the estimate includes those who are not necessarily intellectually superior but do have unusual skill in some particular area, such as the musically and artistically talented or those with mechanical or motor skills, it will be higher, of course. Using such a definition, 15 percent of a group of Illinois chil-

---

[1] Although epidemiologists define *incidence* as the occurrence of new cases during some specified time period and *prevalence* as the total number of active cases in the population at a specified time, we shall use the terms interchangeably as referring to the total number in the population.

dren were found to be gifted (DeHaan & Havighurst, 1957). Workers using other criteria that included creativity estimate that between 5 and 10 percent of the student population should be considered gifted (Sumption & Luecking, 1960).

Operational definitions of the gifted based on intelligence test scores have been followed by a great amount of research. Obviously, the number of persons considered gifted will be determined by the location of the score which constitutes the criterion. If an IQ of 130 on the Wechsler Intelligence Scale for Children is employed, about 2 percent will be considered gifted; if the cutoff score is reduced, this percentage will increase. It has been estimated (Conant, 1959) that as many as 15 to 20 percent should be considered gifted.

Differences among schools in the number of brilliant students enrolled have been found to be rather extensive. E. H. Malherbe (1921), examining a group of private school children with the Stanford-Binet, found that 13 percent of the students in grades 1 to 8 had IQ's over 140. Terman (1916) reported that only .55 percent of a group of 905 public-school children in the same grades scored 136 or over.

The socio-economic level of the community has been found to be an important variable in determining the percentage of children who score at various levels on tests of intelligence. In an average community, 16 to 20 percent of the elementary school population can be expected to have IQ scores above 115, whereas in a high-income area 45 to 60 percent will be found above the same score. If a higher IQ is considered, the same general proportion of difference is found. For children with IQ's above 140, the percentages for the average community are between 0.5 and 1 percent; for the favored community, between 2 and 3 percent (Gallagher, 1959). It seems that between three and six times as many children in the elementary schools in a superior community will have IQ's above either 115 or 140 than will children in a school in an average area.

There are no definitive answers to the question of how many children in the schools should be considered to be brilliant or gifted. The particular operational definition of giftedness to be employed is likely to be determined by the educational facilities available and by the amount of interest and enthusiasm for providing education and training for the superior groups. If the school district under consideration is relatively small, a larger percentage of the population must be included to justify the cost of special classes or facilities; if there is a larger student population from which to select, a smaller percentage will fill whole special schools. Variability of prevalence data is to be expected when practical programs must be devised in school districts of various sizes and socioeconomic classifications employing various definitions of giftedness.

CHARACTERISTICS OF THE GIFTED

In discussing the characteristics of the gifted as a group, there is always the danger of falsely assuming that individual differences among them are small. There are many differences between one highly intelligent individual and the next, which are not to be ignored when considering the gifted as a group. To assume homogeneity among the gifted would be to ignore the fact that the restriction of any one variable does not have an equally restrictive effect on other variables, even though they may be highly correlated. For example, if a group of people, all of whom are 6 feet or over in height, is selected for investigation, it is true that there will be also some selection on the basis of weight. Tall people tend to weigh more than short ones. But the restriction of the variability of weight will not be as great as the restriction imposed on height, even though the two are positively correlated.

Variability in factors other than intelligence is to be expected among the gifted as a group. Among the gifted will be found the short, tall, active, and lethargic, as well as high achievers and low achievers. It should be remembered, in reading the following paragraphs, that the intellectually superior are being considered as a group and that the characteristics indicated are not all applicable to each and every gifted person.

Physical characteristics

As a group, the gifted tend to exceed the average on measures of physical traits (Terman et al., 1925; Witty, 1930; Miles, 1954). B. S. Burks, D. W. Jensen, and L. M. Terman (1930) report that a study of Terman's gifted group showed them to have superior ratings on thirty-four anthropometric measures, including height, weight, and general physical development. Witty's (1930) six-year investigation of another group of gifted children found them to be of better than average bodily development. Superior neuromuscular capacity (Monahan & Hollingworth, 1927) and infrequent physical defects (Jones, 1925) among children of superior intelligence have been reported.

Terman and P. A. Witty both secured health histories of their samples. Consistently health examinations showed that the general physical health of both the child and his parents was better than average. The children were slightly heavier at birth. They cut their first tooth about two months earlier, and walked and talked about two months earlier than the average child. The children in these investigations were more precocious in speech development than they were in other areas. Later development seems to follow an accelerated program, and pubescence is reached earlier by the gifted.

Both major and minor physical defects are found less frequently among groups of gifted children than among the unselected population. They are, in general, fine physical specimens who enjoy good growth and health. These findings, when they were first reported, were in sharp disagreement with popular opinion. It had been thought that the brilliant were typically frail and weak. Research has indicated that, in fact, they are likely to be large, robust, and healthy.

Sex

The question of whether giftedness occurs more frequently in girls or boys really has not been satisfactorily answered. In some of the investigations of children with high IQ's, an excess of boys over girls is reported. Terman et al. (1925) found 121 gifted boys and 100 gifted girls in a sample of 643 preschool and elementary school children. A. M. Jones (1925) reports a similar finding. M. D. Jenkins (1936) reported an excess of girls over boys in a Negro population. The adequacy of the sampling procedures in all these studies can be questioned, if they are to be used for investigating the frequency of the sexes among the gifted. In the Terman studies, volunteers were permitted and teachers were asked to nominate individual students for examination. Such a procedure apparently produces a disproportionately large number of boys. Some evidence of this can be garnered from the fact that when all children of given birth dates were examined in Scotland, the sample was found to contain a ratio of 4 boys to 5 girls with IQ's of 140 and over (MacMeeken, 1939). Other investigators using samples more adequate for this purpose have reported similar findings (Lewis, 1940). After reviewing a number of investigations, C. C. Miles (1954), and Terman and L. E. Tyler (1954), concluded that there appeared to be consistent difference in the frequency of the sexes among the gifted, and that the sex ratios found depended on the content of the test used.

In view of the conflicting data, it would seem safe to assume that there is no large discrepancy in the frequency with which the sexes occur among the gifted. This is particularly true in view of the fact that the experiences of the sexes become more and more divergent with age, so that we cannot be certain of the fairness of a given test for both sexes. E. E. Maccoby and C. N. Jacklin (1974) have made a thorough examination of sex differences and intellect. Early examination of intelligence is contaminated by different development schedules for the sexes and the lower reliability of the scales at the earlier ages.

Educational achievement

The importance of educational achievement among the intellectually superior has been emphasized. The highly superior can make considerable and significant contributions to the culture, and it is felt that they must become educated to a relatively high degree to maximize their productivity and possibly to ensure their personal happiness and welfare.

The results of research on the educational attainment of the gifted indicate that, as a group, they achieve highly in most areas. They do not tend to be one-sided, as had been thought. They tend to be remarkably versatile, and their accomplishments in educational areas are found to be rather universally high. This tends to refute the old supposition of the compensation of abilities. The mass of research data indicate that there is no compensating area of weakness for the areas of demonstrated strength in educational achievement.

Early studies of the school progress of the gifted have been in general agreement that they make rapid strides in academic areas (Terman et al., 1925; Witty, 1940). Terman reports that three out of five of his gifted group attended kindergarten before entering the elementary grades at an average age of six years and three months. This was in the early 1920s, when kindergartens were not as prevalent as they are currently. One out of ten in his sample was placed in the second grade on beginning school, and one out of five skipped half of the first grade. By the end of grade school, his group was found to have skipped one entire grade. Still, the gifted children were found to be below the placement that would be made on the basis of mental age. This is commonly found among gifted children in school. It has been pointed out (Miles, 1954) that if the average gifted child were promoted according to his mental age (MA), he would be at least 2.8 years advanced by the age of seven and 5 or more years accelerated by the age of eleven. This would seem to be an unwarranted expectation of performance by these students, however. It has been pointed out that the MA progressively overestimates the potential of students as their IQ increases, and that this may be due to the lack of opportunity to receive either school or life experiences essential to performance at their level of MA. It has been suggested that 0.3 of a year of achievement be subtracted from the MA prediction for each 10 IQ points above 100 (Los Angeles City School Districts, 1955; Lucito, 1963). This would materially reduce the predictions made from MA alone. Even then, the predicted acceleration may be difficult for superior students to attain.

Whether the achievement of the gifted is assessed by the grades assigned to their schoolwork or by achievement tests, the results tend to be the same (Witty, 1940). They tend to excel in the academic aspects of education. Teachers rate them as superior in such areas as reading, arithmetic, grammar, science, literature, composition, history, and geography. They excel to a lesser degree in areas that are not correlated so highly with intelligence, such as penmanship, shopwork, sewing, and art. The gifted tend to receive a larger proportion of A's and B's than do the students of average intellectual ability. This seems to hold true even when the children have been accelerated and are competing for grades with older classmates (Barnette, 1957; Shannon, 1957).

On standardized tests of achievement, the gifted have consistently scored higher than their classmates of average intellectual ability. Terman et al. (1925) pointed out that the measured achievement of the gifted in grade school correlates more highly with intelligence when age is held constant than it does when years of attendance in school are used. Correlations between achievement and intelligence have been found to be higher for moderately superior children than for highly superior children (Cohler, 1941; Johnson, 1942). This is to be expected in view of the increasing overestimation of achievement as IQ increases. When classroom instruction is about the same (Hollingworth & Cobb, 1928) or when groups with lower IQ's receive special coaching (Hildreth, 1938), the differences in IQ continue to affect the achievement scores. Those with high IQ's tend to retain their superior status on measures of achievement, especially on tests measuring more complex abilities.

In the winning of honors and scholarships, the same general picture of superior achievement is apparent. The gifted are more often winners in essay contests and of class honors in elementary and high school. They obtain more scholarships to college than do the less adept, and once in college they contribute a disproportionately higher number of members to honor rolls and honorary organizations. A higher percentage of the gifted group pursues work at the graduate level in college than is characteristic of the average college graduate (Terman & Oden, 1947).

Extracurricular activities

Gifted children learn to read earlier than do children of average ability. Roughly half the children in both Terman's (1925) and Witty's (1930) groups of gifted children learned to read before attending school. Reading is a favored pastime of gifted children, and one of their favorite school subjects. The gifted read twice as many books as a control group over a two-month period (Terman et al., 1925).

The gifted express as much liking for games and for playing with other children as do average boys and girls. They are likely to prefer playmates somewhat older than themselves. They spend somewhat less time in active play with other children than do the average, and somewhat more time at games that involve reading and greater mental maturity. H. C. Lehman and Witty (1927) report that gifted girls engage in a somewhat larger number of play activities than average girls and that the reverse is true for boys. This finding is supported by the notion that high activity level appears to be a negative factor among boys for intellectual performance (Maccoby & Jacklin, 1974). The gifted engage less frequently in certain kinds of vigorous physical games, and more often in games and activities in which reading is an element. The games and activities that are enjoyed most and played most frequently by the gifted are about the same as those of the average child, with some preference being given by the gifted to thinking games and those that tend to be mildly social.

Gifted children typically display a very strong liking for school and are active in the various sponsored clubs, organizations, and special-interest groups. They enjoy games and sports and rate them highly as school activities. This, again, is contrary to the long-held notion of the solitary and sedentary nature of the gifted.

Personal and social characteristics

The personality traits and character development of the gifted have been investigated in some detail. There seems to be general agreement among the early investigators that the gifted, as a group, differ in a favorable direction from unselected children. Terman et al. (1925), using a wide range of tests and rating devices, investigated the personal and social characteristics of a group of 500 gifted children and a like number of children in an unselected control group. Witty (1930) studied the characteristics of 100 gifted children. The results of these studies were equally favorable to the gifted, challenging the once widely held belief that intellectual superiority was associated with social and personal maladjustment.

Terman et al. (1925) report that gifted children have much more favorable social characteristics than the control group. The gifted showed more favorable social preferences, less boastful exaggeration, less cheating, and greater trustworthiness under stress. From 60 to 80 percent of the gifted exceeded the median scores on the separate tests of the battery employed. The gifted were found to be significantly freer from psychopathic trends and significantly more emotionally stable than were control children. The superiority of the gifted in emotional stability was maintained for a number of years when they were reexamined (Burks, Jensen, & Terman, 1930; Oden, 1968).

Teachers' and parents' ratings of the personal characteristics of the gifted tend to agree with the results of measures of intellectual and volitional traits and are somewhat less in agreement on physical and social traits. Teachers report gifted children to be above average in many desirable traits (Specht, 1919), including courtesy, cooperation, willingness to take suggestions, and sense of humor (Johnson, 1923). The superiority on personality traits of the gifted as a group is given support by other investigations of personality traits in intellectually superior children as compared with children of average IQ. Social adjustment of the gifted as a group tends to be above average. Even children who have been accelerated in school and are young for their grade placement have been reported as well adjusted (Miller, 1957). Sociometric studies indicate that the gifted are more frequently chosen by their peers in regular classes (Gallagher 1958). On projective tests as well as on rating scales, the lower frequency of emotional problems has held up (Gallagher & Crowder, 1957). Investigations using teachers' rating, sociometric procedures, personality inventories, and projective techniques have reported superiority in emotional stability of the gifted as a group. There is evidence that this superiority continues into adulthood (Barbe, 1957; Terman & Oden, 1959).

The studies so far cited have dealt with gifted children as a group, and various other factors have not been controlled. M. Bonsall and B. Stefflre (1955), working with a group of gifted and a group of nongifted high school boys, found the usual pattern of superiority for the gifted as a group. However, when they analyzed the data so that only gifted and nongifted students from the same economic levels were compared, little or no differences were found between the two groups. Although it is without doubt true that the intellectually superior make better personal and social adjustments than do the intellectually average, part of this superiority is apparently due to class differences.

Social and cultural background

The social and cultural background of the gifted as a group tends to be considerably better than that of the general population. Gifted children tend to come from homes where the socio-economic level is above average (Terman et al., 1925; Gallagher & Crowder, 1957). Results of investigations uniformly indicate that the parents of gifted children are found most frequently among professional and managerial groups. (Cole,

1956). In Terman's sample, 81.4 percent of his subjects had parents whose occupational status was classified as professional, semiprofessional, or business, and only 6.8 percent had parents who came from the ranks of semiskilled and unskilled labor. This was an interesting finding, in that it had been known for some time that the occupational status of parents was positively correlated with the achievement of the offspring. But this investigation was not dealing with the later achievement of the offspring, but rather with their measured intelligence while they were still in early childhood. Such measures of intelligence during early childhood should not reflect the cumulative results of opportunity for achievement to nearly the same extent as they would be reflected in adult achievement. It was found (Cattell & Brimhall, 1921) that 43.1 percent of the fathers of 885 leading American scientists came from among the professions, and that the same was true for the fathers of 49.2 percent of 666 American men of letters (Clarke, 1916). Terman and Oden (1947) report that the fathers of their gifted group came from the professions in 31.4 percent of the cases.

These investigations are not, of course, directly comparable, because different means of classifying occupational status were employed and the ages of the children in the samples were different. It is interesting to note, however, that from 12 to 18 percent more of the parents of the prominent individuals investigated came from the professions than was true of the gifted sample. There is no doubt that social influences were operative on children examined by Terman and his associates, but it could hardly be argued either that social influence on eventual accomplishment ceases at rather early ages or that the social influence on Terman's sample was as extensively involved in the measures of intelligence employed as it was in the development of adult achievement. If one looks at these data uncritically, one might interpret them as suggesting the relative influence of intelligence and social factors in the production of outstanding individuals in the culture. Such a ratio would be at least 2 to 1 or 3 to 1 in favor of the factor of high-level intelligence. When Terman divided his group into high and low achievers on the basis of achievement in early adulthood and examined the family background of the two groups, a marked discrepancy was noted (Terman & Oden, 1947). The proportion of professional fathers of the high achievers was 38 percent, and only 18.5 percent of the low achievers. The parental education of these two groups was really quite different. Over three times as many fathers of the group of high achievers had graduated from college. These data indicate that occupational and educational background are much more important than the data just cited would tend to indicate. At the present state of our knowledge about the relative influence of high-level intelligence and socio-economic background on achievement, no very accurate statement can be made. H. Munsinger (1975), after reviewing "all the reliable published data," concludes that, while there is disagreement about the precise values to be assigned to genetic and environmental effects, the available data indicate that heredity is more important than environment in producing individual differences in IQ. That social, educational, and occupational background does have a profound influence on the adult achievement of the gifted cannot be denied, but its ratio of contribution to outstanding achievement remains unknown.

If the gifted are treated as a group, the superiority of their general social and cultural background is rather apparent. Terman's sample of gifted had parents whose average formal education exceeded that of the general population by four or five years. These parents had more often graduated from college and received Ph.D. degrees. The median income of families in a random sample of gifted was twice as high as that of California families in general, although extremely high incomes were infrequent. The families of the gifted were rated as superior by investigators (4.5 on a 6-point scale). The homes themselves were distinctly superior to the other homes in their neighborhoods, and the incidence of divorce and broken homes was less among the gifted than among an unselected sample. The gifted tend to come disproportionately from urban, as opposed to rural, environments. This may indicate that urban homes provide more intellectual stimulation.

Intellectually superior children come, in relatively high proportions, from parents who have a good education and high-prestige occupations. The upper and upper-middle classes, jointly, produce nearly twice as many children with IQ's in the top quartile as are produced by the average family, and less than one-half as many children in the lowest quartile (Havighurst, 1962). The home environments from which the intellectually superior come can be described as more intellectually stimulating than the average, and superior on a number of bases. The families tend to be less autocratic, read more and better books and magazines, travel more, and in general have greater energy and stability. The cultural patterns of the families tend to encourage education and achievement (Stouffer & Shea, 1959).

The importance of general cultural influence on achievement and on opportunity is indicated by the fact that a librarian's son is one thousand times more likely to win a National Merit Scholarship than is a laborer's son (Bond, 1957). Studies in England and in New Zealand lend further support to the important role of general cultural factors in the production of scholars (Burt, 1962). Follow-up measures of intellect of the Terman group indicate that as adults they rank about as far above the mean of the population as they did in childhood (Oden, 1968). When 1,571 of their offspring were examined, a mean IQ of 133.2 was obtained (Oden, 1968).

An interesting investigation of differences between lower- and upper-status gifted children has been reported by E. C. Frierson (1965), who studied four groups of elementary school children from Cleveland, Ohio. His four groups were: upper socio-economic status, gifted ($N = 88$); lower socio-economic status, gifted ($N = 56$); upper socio-economic status, average ($N = 86$); and lower socio-economic status, average ($N = 55$). Gifted children were defined as those of IQ 125 or greater on the Stanford-Binet Intelligence Scale. Socio-economic status was assigned by use of the Shevky-Bell Social Rank Index (Shevky & Bell, 1955). Average children were designated as those scoring between 85 and 115 on the Kuhlman-Anderson Intelligence Test.

The children were compared on measures of personality, interests activities, creativity, height, and weight. Although the gifted differed from the average children in most of the ways previously reported, significant differences also were found between the two gifted groups. Upper-status gifted children were aware of parental aspirations for their college education; this was not true of many lower-status gifted. Lower-status gifted did not like school as well, read as much, or achieve as highly in science as the upper-status gifted; competitive team sports were preferred more by lower-status gifted than by upper-status gifted. Upper-status gifted children were superior to the lower-status gifted group on measures of creativity.

Socio-economic background must be an area of consideration in the educational program for individual gifted children (Renzulli, 1973). It is not to be expected that differences in children from contrasting socio-economic backgrounds will be educationally insignificant for the gifted. The learning style of disadvantaged gifted students has been described as likely to be content-centered, externally-oriented, physical in nature, problem-oriented, slow, and patient (Riessman, 1962). Disadvantaged gifted children have been described as visual as opposed to abstract learners who are dependent on concrete rather than abstract exposure (Gallagher, 1968). Successful teachers of the gifted differ from the less successful in several significant dimensions (Bishop, 1968). Teachers of the gifted should be conscious of the characteristics of the various gifted groups as well as informed of the preferred procedures in working with them (Jordan, 1974).[2]

---

[2] The literature in this area is extensive. Several excellent articles have appeared in a volume of *The Journal of Special Education* (Anastasi, 1975; Astin, 1975; Fox, 1975; Keating, 1975; Stanley, 1975).

EDUCATION OF THE GIFTED

Gifted students typically do well in school, and there has been little concern about such matters as their keeping up with the class. They usually have little or no trouble measuring up to age or grade levels for achievement. This, combined with their general tendency to be well-behaved and emotionally controlled, may cause them to go unnoticed in the classroom. They create no particular classroom disturbances. They have plenty of ability. They can be left to fend for themselves and will still do all right in school. A common attitude seems to be "Don't worry about the gifted; they will do all right anyway!"

There is no immediate and apparent characteristic of the gifted that serves as a basis for an emotional appeal for special consideration. Special consideration for the gifted does not have the emotional appeal or the urgency of training for the physically handicapped, the blind, the deaf, or the mentally retarded. Rarely does one hear a plea for special facilities or programs for the exceptionally brilliant based on democracy in education. Democracy in education has a strong appeal in this country and has been employed as an argument for special facilities for those who are handicapped in some way. Contrariwise, it has been argued that special consideration for the gifted would be undemocratic, in that it would give advantage in training and education to those who are already ahead of their classmates and result in a kind of intellectual aristocracy or privileged group. *Guarding against privilege has perhaps absorbed more attention and effort in our educational structure than have plans and procedures for providing for individual differences.* Actually, a desirable slogan for the individual education of students might be "special privilege for all." In the final analysis this is what a program based upon meeting the educational needs of individuals, as well as the culture, strives to do.

In recent years many professionals and laymen have become genuinely concerned about the education of the gifted, in part because of the rapid advancements in science and technology of the past decade or so. The necessity to train scientists is obvious in a rapidly expanding scientific world. Few would deny that we must provide educational facilities that will develop achievement in these areas, as well as in the areas of social and literary accomplishment. However, there is a great deal of disagreement as to how this can best be done. Disagreement among so-called experts in the area of curriculum and methods is easy to find. This no doubt stems from our current lack of information in these fields. Research in this area is proceeding. An unfortunate delay in doing anything about the problem stems from our not knowing what to do. In the meantime, various programs are being developed out of a perceived necessity for doing something to insure that better use of ability is made by society. It seems to be much wiser to develop such programs than to delay doing anything for fear of not doing the "right" thing.

Some interesting results that should encourage giving special attention to the education of the gifted have been reported by R. A. Martinson (1961). The findings of her investigation of various education and administrative programs, special classes, cluster grouping, and independent study are encouraging. In measured results, including academic achievement and social adjustment, children given special services exceeded those who did not receive them. Perhaps any systematic program considered adequate by professionals familiar with the characteristics of the gifted produces better results than no program at all. The percentage of gifted children in the United States, however, who are in special programs or for whom any systematic program is provided has been reported to be amazingly small (Dunn, 1963). Research has indicated that gifted students can develop new problem-solving skills through the use of auto-instructional materials, and teachers can teach gifted students to approach problems creatively (Parnes, 1966). The United States Office of Education has, by policy statement, recognized the education of the gifted and talented as being an integral part of our educational system, and advocates increased educational opportunities for these students. Improvement in evaluative thinking abilities of gifted children who received special instruction for only one month has been reported (Hauck, 1967). Testing the achievement of those of high ability presents special problems and is being given special attention (Keating, 1975b). Although measures of academic skills are used to determine access to many educational opportunities, they tend to lack utility for predicting professional achievement (Wallach, 1976).

Education and underachievement

It has long been recognized that within school groups in general there are students whose academic achievements are more nearly appropriate to their potential for contributing to the culture. It has been fairly well recognized, and it seems to be a reasonable enough expectation, that those of average or nearly average intelligence should achieve at a grade level approximately equal to the expected attainment as predicted from their MA's. Those who score above the average range (who have IQ's over 110) have not, however, achieved at the level predicted by their

MA's with any degree of consistency. It is true that these children manage to reach school standards relatively easily, and even exceed age-grade expectancy in most instances. They do achieve at high levels, but the question is whether their achievement is close enough to the level to be expected on the basis of their mental age. It has been argued that as long as these individuals are achieving adequately for their chronological age and grade placement and even exceeding this level, there is little to be concerned about. Others have deplored the lag between the achievement to be predicted on the basis of the bright child's mental age and his actual achievement. If MA is used as the criterion for estimating achievement (without any correction to compensate for the tendency of this group not to meet this criterion), the gifted can be labeled as underachievers. Formulas for making some correction for this tendency have been developed (Horn, 1941), and tables which make corrections for the limitation in experience of very bright children have been constructed (Los Angeles City School Districts, 1955). These tables make a downward adjustment in expected achievement of about 0.3 of a year for each 10 IQ points beyond 100 for age groups common to the elementary school. The rationale for reducing the level of performance predicted by the MA for gifted children has to do with the difficulties of providing the stimulation and experience that might result in such rapid achievement. The MA offers a standard for achievement that is not typically found among the gifted. For example, an eight-year-old child with an IQ of 150 would have an MA of twelve, and would thus be expected to function in school at a level comparable to the average twelve-year-old with an IQ of 100 who has made normal progress in school and is now in the seventh grade. But eight-year-old children with IQ's of 150 do not function at the beginning seventh-grade level. It is argued that they cannot reasonably be expected to do so, and that the MA does not yield a valid estimate of their potential achievement.

Although even gifted children who have been accelerated by a year earn better grades than their older classmates (Barnette, 1957; Shannon, 1957), there has been concern over a number who are definitely underachievers. M. Meeker (1968) reported that gifted children from a special program in the elementary school tended to do much less well when they moved into a traditional secondary school where they received less than adequate attention.

The number of gifted who do not attend college has been considered alarmingly high (Wolfle, 1960), and there are others who do not live up to the cultural standards expected of them (Terman & Oden, 1947). The loss to society that occurs when some of the gifted become definite underachievers and the loss that may be occurring because insufficient challenge, stimulation, opportunity, or facilities are provided for still more of the gifted, have produced some interesting investigations of achievement and underachievement.

Terman and Oden (1947) and Oden (1968) report some interesting data on achievement from their follow-up investigations of gifted children at adulthood. They divided their gifted group into what they called an *A* group on the basis of adult achievement and what they called a *C* group on the same basis. The *A* group was comprised of those who had lived up to their earlier promise; the *C* group was comprised of those who for one reason or another were not dong as well as earlier data had indicated. The principal criterion for assignment to one of the two groups was the extent to which a subject had made use of his superior intellectual ability. Comparisons were made on the basis of 200 items of information secured for 150 subjects in each group between 1921 and 1941.

Both the *A* and *C* groups had been outstandingly good elementary school students. Their achievement test scores had fallen above the norms in about one-third of the instances, and the overall achievement of the groups had tended to be highly similar in every school subject except language use and art information, in both of which the *A* group slightly exceeded the *C* group. The *C* group was about a third of a year older at the time of completion of the eighth grade. The *A* group was reliably younger when they graduated from high school (9.6 months) and when they graduated from college (15.6 months). Differences in achievement had not really become apparent until they attended high school, and then the grades attained by the *A*'s were significantly better than those of the *C*'s. This difference was also found to exist among those who went to college.

In adulthood, the *A*'s were found to have higher levels of vocational interest and broader interests than the *C*'s. They were particularly more interested in politics, social life, and literature. The family backgrounds of the two groups were somewhat different. The parents of those in the *C* group had less formal education, as did their brothers and sisters, than was characteristic of the *A* group. The proportion of those whose fathers had graduated from college was three times as high in the *A* group as in the *C* group. The fathers' occupational status was also different. The fathers of those in the *A* group were professionals over twice as frequently as the *C* group fathers. The additional education of the fathers of the *A* group was reflected in the number of books reported to be in the home library. Nearly twice as many books were reported to be in the libraries of parents of those in the *A* group. The educational tradition of the families of those in the *A* group was also much stronger.

Separation and divorce were about twice as common among the parents of those in the *C* group as among the parents of those in the *A* group. On measures of both personal and social adjustment, the *C* group itself did not do as well as did the subjects in group *A*. These findings, coupled with the stronger educational tradition in the families of those in the *A* group, may account for a considerable amount of the differences in achievement. Factors other than intellect appear to be highly involved in achievement, and among these factors social and personal adjustment seem to be relatively important.

An investigation of tenth- and twelfth-grade students of high ability sheds additional light on the problem of achievement among the gifted (Pierce, 1962). The upper 30 percent of children who took ability tests in a midwestern high school were chosen for investigation. These 222 boys and girls were divided into four groups: high-achieving tenth-grade boys; high-achieving tenth-grade girls; low-achieving twelfth-grade boys; and low-achieving twelfth-grade girls. High and low achievers were designated as being above or below the median of a sample drawn from each grade and sex.

When adjustment was measured by the California Psychological Inventory (CPI), the high achievers were found to be better adjusted than the low achievers. The ratings of peers and teachers confirmed that the high achievers had greater qualities of leadership and were less aggressive. All three of these methods of evaluating adjustment indicate that the high achievers tend to be better adjusted than the low achievers. From interviews with the students it was concluded that high-achieving students were more scholastically ambitious, liked school better, read more, and identified themselves more often with an adult of the same sex who valued education. The high achievers were more positive toward school-related activities and toward individuals who value education.

When the subjects were examined for motivation to achieve by analyzing stories they had written, the high-achieving boys scored somewhat higher than the others, but the difference is rather small. The same was found to be true for twelfth-grade girls, but it was reversed for tenth-grade girls. That is, tenth-grade girls who were high achievers scored as having less motivation to achieve than did the low achievers. This instrument has not proved useful in discriminating between high- and low-achieving girls.

The parental attitudes differed. Mothers of high-achieving boys were found to be less authoritarian and controlling than mothers of low-achieving boys. Mothers of low-status, low-achieving boys were the most authoritarian and controlling of the mothers studied. There is no evidence that mothers of high- and low-achieving girls differed with respect to authoritarianism and control. These maternal attitudes do not keep girls of low social status and high ability from achieving to the same extent that they seem to deter the boys.

Differences have been found in the child-father relationships of underachievers and overachievers. In a rather extensive investigation of 223 children in grades 2 through 5 who had IQ's of 120 and above, M. B. Karnes et al. (1963) found some interesting data. They selected the top and bottom 16 percent of their sample on the basis of achievement in relation to ability, and compared them. The attitude and relationship of the child to the father appeared to play a significant role. The fathers of the underachieving children showed more hostility toward and rejection of their children than did the fathers of the overachievers.

In an extensive investigation of underachievers in grades 4, 7, and 10 in thirteen districts of one California county, underachievers with IQ's of 115+ on the California Test of Mental Maturity were selected for study (Shaw, 1961). Those with a B average or better were called achievers. The groups were given various personality tests, from which it was discerned that the underachievers exhibited a greater negative self-concept and a generally more negative outlook on life. Overt expressions of aggression and hostility were greater among the underachievers. The overachievers apparently experienced feelings of hostility, but tended to suppress them. Underachievers tended to have general feelings of inadequacy which were not characteristic of the achievers.

Individual differences in performance among the gifted are great. It is well established that a certain level of general intelligence is essential for high-level performance in socially useful areas. The level of intellect necessary has not been agreed on, but it is known that individuals with IQ's of 120 have sufficient intellect for most pursuits if they possess the requisite motivation and opportunity is provided. There are enough individuals of very high intellect who do not perform at high levels to indicate that general intelligence alone does not ensure performance commensurate with ability. The problem of the grossly underachieving among the gifted is one for social concern, as well as one of individual welfare and happiness. It is thought that individual welfare is enhanced by many of the same kinds of achievement that are of benefit to the culture. It is to these ends that educational provisions of various kinds have been made. If the gifted all achieved well up to their level of ability in the usual school situation, there would be no problem about their education. But underachievement does exist and there is considerable concern about it. Therefore, the problems of education have been investigated and provisions of one kind or another have been made for special attention to the education of the gifted.

Educational provisions

The empirical data provided by research on the gifted have yielded some basis for planning for their education. It would be better if more were known about the individual personal characteristics of the gifted.

More research needs to be done before we can have definitive ideas about the most appropriate educational processes, procedures, and plans for the education of the gifted, but as we have already observed, many programs have been effectuated nevertheless. Unfortunately, in some instances the administrative structure has been decided on before either educational objectives or procedures were adopted. Both the objectives and educational experiences that are deemed desirable should be determined first, so that administrative procedures that are most compatible with the kind of educational program desired can be developed.

Educational provisions for exceptional children have been discussed in an earlier chapter, and it is encouraging to note that attempts are being made to evaluate the relative effectiveness of certain procedures. An investigation of the effectiveness of two plans for increasing the achievement of underachieving intellectually gifted children has yielded some differences (Karnes et al., 1963). Children from grades 2 to 5 who had Stanford-Binet IQ's in excess of 120 and who were achieving one standard deviation or more below the mean of their grade level were selected. The group was divided into two treatment conditions. The members of one group were placed in what were called homogeneous groups (classes with only gifted, high-achieving students). Members of the other groups were placed in heterogeneous groups (classes with children ranging from dull normal to intellectually gifted). After two or three years, the gifted underachievers in the homogeneous arrangement were found to have gained in academic achievement more than the heterogeneously placed children. They also were found, through a test of creativity, to have gained more in fluency. Interestingly, although the children in the homogeneous classes gained greater parental acceptance, both groups lost some acceptance by their peers.

This kind of investigation is difficult to execute, and unfortunately the number of gifted underachievers in each treatment condition was small. However, the results suggest that there may be advantages to the homogeneous grouping of the gifted, as opposed to their placement in regular classes. It is possible that the added stimulus provided by being surrounded by achievers is an important factor in increasing the educational progress of gifted underachievers as well as gifted achievers.

It has been found that special provisions for the education of the gifted tend to enhance their achievement. It would seem that almost any program conceived and executed by enlightened and trained personnel enhances the educational achievement of the gifted (Martinson, 1961).

The effectiveness of grouping has been given much investigative effort. The extensive reviews of these investigations present a confusing pattern of advantages and disadvantages. Most reviewers indicate that grouping, in and of itself, is of little advantage unless the academic program is designed to accommodate the various ability levels.

SUMMARY

A brief history of the interest in and investigations of giftedness was presented in this chapter, and some problems of definition and terminology were discussed. Concern for the gifted child is not of recent vintage, but quantitative studies of the gifted are a relatively recent development. The pioneering work of Terman and his associates, who investigated the characteristics of gifted children and conducted extensive follow-up studies at later periods in life, has contributed a large body of data to the area. The various definitions of the gifted have contributed to some of the confusion that exists in terminology employed in this area. The definition of the gifted is partially determined by the definition of intelligence that is employed. Intelligence has, of course, been defined in a variety of ways.

The importance of the possible contributions of the gifted to the culture, as well as a cultural concern for individual welfare, make the problem of identifying the gifted among us an imperative one. Ability and talent cannot be adequately used unless they are identified. The early detection of superiority among children is essential to make the earliest provisions for their development and education.

Intellectually superior children tend to be superior in a number of ways that are not closely related to intellectual performance. In general they tend to be larger, healthier, happier, and have more extensive interest and hobbies than their normal peers. They particularly enjoy reading and develop this skill rather early and with a minimum of difficulty. Their educational achievement tends to be uniformly high, and they engage in extracurricular activities rather extensively. The gifted tend to have better-educated parents than the average, to come from better socio-economic backgrounds, and to have parents with higher occupational levels.

The providing of special educational programs and facilities for the gifted has not developed as rapidly or as extensively as have special programs for the handicapped. The gifted do not create serious problems in the home or school. They are not as noticeable as certain of the handicapped groups, nor do they arouse compassion. Concern has developed for the welfare of the highly gifted underachiever, and some research in this area has been reported. Programs for the education of the gifted need to be undertaken at the earliest possible moment and should be sufficiently flexible so that they can be changed when additional research findings so indicate.

REFERENCES

ABRAHAM, W., *Common Sense about Gifted Children* (New York: Harper & Row, 1958).

ANASTASI, A., "Commentary on the Precocity Project," *The Journal of Special Education,* 1975, *9,* 93–103.

ASTIN, H. S., "Sex Differences in Mathematical and Scientific Precocity," *The Journal of Special Education,* 1975, *9,* 79–91.

BARBE, W. B., "What Happens to Graduates of Special Classes for the Gifted," *Educational Research Bulletin,* 1957, *36,* 13–16.

BARNETTE, W. L., "Advance Credit for the Superior High-school Student," *Journal of Higher Education,* 1957, *28,* 15–20.

BENTLEY, J. E., *Superior Children* (New York: W. W. Norton, 1937).

BISHOP, W., "Successful Teachers of the Gifted," *Exceptional Children,* 1968, *34,* 317–25.

BOND, H. M., "The Productivity of National Merit Scholars by Occupational Class," *School and Society,* 1957, *85,* 267–68.

BONSALL, M., & B. STEFFLRE, "The Temperament of Gifted Children," *California Journal of Educational Research,* 1955, *6,* 195–99.

BURKS, B. S., D. W. JENSEN, & L. M. TERMAN, *The Promise of Youth: Follow-up Studies of a Thousand Gifted Children (Genetic Studies of Genius,* vol. 3) (Stanford, Ca.: Stanford University Press, 1930).

BURT, C., "The Gifted Child," in B. Bereday & P. Lauwerys, eds., *The Yearbook of Education* (New York: Harcourt Brace Jovanovich, 1962).

CATTELL, J. M., "Families of American Men of Science," *Popular Science Monthly,* 1915, *86,* 504–15.

CATTELL, J. M., & D. R. BRIMHALL, "Families of American Men of Science," in *American Men of Science,* 3rd ed. (New York: Science Press, 1921).

CLARKE, E. L., "American Men of Letters: Their Nature and Nurture," *Columbia University Studies in History, Economics and Public Law,* 1916, *72,* 1–169.

COHLER, M. J., "Scholastic Status of Achievers and Nonachievers of Superior Intelligence," *Journal of Educational Psychology,* 1941, *32,* 603–10.

COLE, C. C., JR., *Encouraging Scientific Talent: A Report to the National Science Foundation* (Princeton, N. J.: College Entrance Examination Board, 1956).

CONANT, J. B., *The American High School Today* (New York: McGraw-Hill, 1959).

DeHAAN, F., & R. J. HAVIGHURST, *Educating Gifted Children* (Chicago: University of Chicago Press, 1957).

DUNN, L. M., ed., *Exceptional Children in the Schools* (New York: Holt, Rinehart and Winston, 1963).

FOX, L. H., "Facilitating Educational Development of Mathematically Precocious Youth," *The Journal of Special Education,* 1975, *9,* 63–77.

FRIERSON, E. C., "Upper and Lower Status Gifted Children: A Study of Difference," *Exceptional Children,* 1965, *32,* 83–90.

FRIERSON, E. C., "The Gifted," *Review of Educational Research,* 1969, *39,* 25–37.

GALLAGHER, J. J., "Social Status of Children Related to Intelligence, Propinquity, and Social Perception," *Elementary School Journal,* 1958, *58,* 225–31.

GALLAGHER, J. J., *The Gifted Child in the Elementary School* (Washington, D.C.: National Education Association, Department of Classroom Teachers, 1959).

GALLAGHER, J. J., "The Disadvantaged Gifted Child," in A. J. Tannenbaum, ed., *Special Education and Programs for Disadvantaged Children and Youth* (Washington, D.C.: NEW, CEC, 1968).

GALLAGHER, J. J., & T. H. CROWDER, "Adjustment of Gifted Children in the Regular Classroom," *Exceptional Children,* 1957, *23,* 306–12, 317–19.

GALTON, F., *Hereditary Genius* (London: Macmillan, 1869).

GRANZIN, K. L., & W. J. GRANZIN, "Peer Group Choice as a Device for Screening Intellectually Gifted Children," *Gifted Child Quarterly,* 1969, *13,* 189–94.

HAUCK, B. B., "A Comparison of Gains in Evaluation Ability Between Gifted and Nongifted Sixth-grade Students," *Gifted Children,* 1967, *11,* 166–71.

HAVIGHURST, R. J., *Growing Up in River City* (New York: John Wiley, 1962).

HECK, A. O., *The Education of Exceptional Children* (New York: McGraw-Hill, 1953).

Higher Education and National Affairs. Washington, D.C.: American Council on Education, 1975, *24* (41), 5.

HILDRETH, G., "The Educational Achievement of Gifted Children," *Child Development,* 1938, *9,* 365–71.

HOLLINGWORTH, L. S., "How Should Gifted Children Be Educated?" *Baltimore Bulletin of Education,* 1931, *50,* 196.

HOLLINGWORTH, L. S., & M. V. COBB, "Children Clustering at 165 IQ and Children Clustering at 145 IQ Compared for Three Years in Achievement," *Yearbook of the National Society for the Study of Education,* 1928, *27,* 3–33.

HORN, A., *Uneven Distribution of the Effects of Specific Factors,* Southern California Education Monograph, 12 (Los Angeles: University of Southern California Press, 1941).

JENKINS, M. D., "A Socio-psychological Study of Negro Children of Superior Intelligence," *Journal of Negro Education,* 1936, *5,* 175–90.

JOHNSON, H. G., "Does the Gifted Child Have a Low AQ?" *Journal of Educational Research,* 1942, *36,* 91–99.

JOHNSON, O. J., "Teachers' Judgments of Qualities of Gifted Pupils as Related to Classroom Activities," *School and Society,* 1923, *17,* 466–69.

JONES, A. M., "An Analytical Study of One Hundred and Twenty Superior Children," *Psychological Clinic,* 1925, *16,* 19–76.

JORDAN, J. B., "Foundation for Exceptional Children Addresses the Needs of the Culturally Gifted Child," *Exceptional Children,* 1974, *40,* 279–83.

KARNES, M. B., et al., "The Efficacy of Two Organizational Plans for Underachieving Intellectually Gifted Children," *Exceptional Children,* 1963, *29,* 438–46.

KEATING, D. P., "The Study of Mathematically Precocious Youth," *The Journal of Special Education*, 1975a, *9*, 45–62.

KEATING, D. P., "Testing Those in the Top Percentiles," *Exceptional Children*, 1975b, *41*, 435–36.

KOUGH, J., & R. F. DEHAAN, *Teacher's Guidance Handbook* (Chicago: Science Research Associates, 1955).

LEHMAN, H. C., & P. A. WITTY, *The Psychology of Play Activities* (New York: A. S. Barnes, 1927).

LEWIS, W. D., "A Study of Superior Children in the Elementary School," *Peabody College Contributions to Education*, No. 266 (Nashville, Tenn.: Peabody College Press, 1940).

LOS ANGELES CITY SCHOOL DISTRICTS, EVALUATION AND RESEARCH SECTION, "Expected Achievement Grade Placement Tables," Division of Instructional Services Publication G. C.–6 (Los Angeles, 1955).

LUCITO, L. J., "Gifted Children," in L. M. Dunn, ed., *Exceptional Children in the Schools* (New York: Holt, Rinehart and Winston, 1963).

MACCOBY, E. E., & C. N. JACKLIN, *The Psychology of Sex Differences* (Stanford, Ca.: Stanford University Press, 1974).

MACMEEKEN, A. M., "The Intelligence of a Representative Group of Scottish Children," *Publication of the Scottish Counsel on Research in Education*, 1939 (15).

MALHERBE, E. H., "New Measurements in Private Schools," *Survey*, 1921, *46*, 272–73.

MARTINSON, R. A., *Educational Programs for Gifted Pupils* (Sacramento: California State Department of Education, 1961).

MARTINSON, R. A., & L. M. LESSINGER, "Problems in the Identification of Intellectually Gifted Pupils," *Exceptional Children*, 1960, *26*, 227–31.

MARTINSON, R. A., & M. V. SEAGOE, *The Abilities of Young Children* (Washington, D.C.: Council for Exceptional Children, 1967).

MEEKER, M., "Differential Syndromes of Giftedness and Curriculum Planning: A Four-year Follow-up," *Journal of Special Education*, 1968, *2*, 185–94.

MILES, C. C., "Gifted Children," in L. Carmichael, ed., *Manual of Child Psychology* (New York: John Wiley, 1954).

MILLER, V., "Academic Achievement and Social Adjustment of Children Young for Their Grade Placement," *Elementary School Journal*, 1957, *57*, 257–63.

MONAHAN, J. E., & L. S. HOLLINGWORTH, "Neuromuscular Capacity of Children Who Test Above 135 IQ (Stanford-Binet)," *Journal of Educational Psychology*, 1927, *18*, 88–96.

MUNSINGER, H., "The Adopted Child's IQ: A Critical Review," *Psychological Bulletin*, 1975, *82*, 623–59.

ODEN, M. H., "The Fulfillment of Promise: 40-Year Follow-up of the Terman Gifted Group," *Genetic Psychology Monographs*, 1968, *77*, 3–93.

OTTO, H. J., "Curriculum Adjustment for Gifted Elementary School Children in Regular Classes," Bureau of Laboratory Schools Publication 6 (Austin: University of Texas Press, 1957).

PARNES, S. J., "Programming Creative Behavior," U.S. Department of Health,

Education and Welfare, Office of Education, Cooperative Research Project No. 5–0716 (Buffalo: New York State University, 1966).

PEGNATO, C. V., & J. W. BIRCH, "Locating Gifted Children in Junior High Schools," *Exceptional Children,* 1959, *25,* 300–304.

PIERCE, J. V., "The Bright Achiever and Under-Achiever," in B. Bereday & P. Lauwerys, eds., *The Yearbook of Education* (New York: Harcourt Brace Jovanovich, 1962).

RENZULLI, J. S., "Talent Potential in Minority Group Students," *Exceptional Children,* 1973, *39,* 437–44.

RIESSMAN, F., *The Culturally Deprived Child* (New York: Harper & Row, 1962).

SHANNON, D. C., "What Research Says about Acceleration," *Phi Delta Kappan,* 1957, *39,* 70–73.

SHAW, M. C., "The Inter-relationship of Selected Personality Factors in High Ability Underachieving School Children: Final Report," Project 58–M–1 (Sacramento: California State Department of Public Health, 1961).

SHEVKY, E., & W. BELL, *Social Area Analysis* (Stanford, Ca.: Stanford University Press, 1955).

SPECHT, L. F., "A Terman Class in Public School No. 64, Manhattan," *School and Society,* 1919, *9,* 393–98.

STANLEY, J. C., "Intellectual Precocity," *The Journal of Special Education,* 1975, *9,* 29–44.

STOUFFER, S. A., & P. D. SHEA, *Your Educational Plans* (Chicago: Science Research Associates, 1959).

SUMPTION, M. R., & E. M. LUECKING, *Education of the Gifted* (New York: Ronald Press, 1960).

TERMAN, L. M., "A Preliminary Study in the Psychology and Pedagogy of Leadership," *Pedagogical Seminary,* 1904, *11,* 413–51.

TERMAN, L. M., "A Study of Precocity and Prematuration," *American Journal of Psychology,* 1905, *16,* 145–83.

TERMAN, L. M., "Genius and Stupidity," *Pedagogical Seminary,* 1906, *13,* 307–73.

TERMAN, L. M., "The Mental Hygiene of Exceptional Children," *Pedagogical Seminary,* 1915, *22,* 529–37.

TERMAN, L. M., *The Measurement of Intelligence* (Boston: Houghton Mifflin. 1916).

TERMAN, L. M., & M. H. ODEN, *The Gifted Child Grows Up* (Stanford, Ca.: Stanford University Press, 1947).

TERMAN, L. M., & M. H. ODEN, *The Gifted Group at Mid-life* (Stanford, Ca.: Stanford University Press, 1959).

TERMAN, L. M., & L. E. TYLER, "Psychological Sex Differences," in L. Carmichael, ed., *Manual of Child Psychology,* 2nd ed. (New York: John Wiley, 1954).

TERMAN, L. M., et al., *Mental and Physical Traits of a Thousand Gifted Children* (Stanford, Ca.: Stanford University Press, 1925).

WALLACH, M. A., "Tests Tell Us Little About Talent," *American Scientist,* 1976, *64,* (1) 57–63.

WARD, L. F., *Applied Sociology* (Boston: Ginn, 1906).

WITTY, P. A., "A Study of One Hundred Gifted Children," *University of*

Kansas Bulletin of Education, State Teachers College Studies in Education, 1930, *1* (13).

WITTY, P. A., "A Genetic Study of Fifty Gifted Children," *Yearbook of the National Society for the Study of Education,* 1940, *39,* 401–8.

WITTY, P. A., "Who Are the Gifted?" in N. D. Henry, ed., *Education for the Gifted: Yearbook of the National Society for the Study of Education,* 1958, *57,* Part 2.

WOLFLE, D., "Diversity of Talent," *American Psychologist,* 1960, *15,* 535–45.

Chapter 7

Creativity

Creativity has been an area of considerable concern over the past two decades. Previous research that might now be called investigation of creativity was conducted under different topic headings, and reported in the psychological literature under such labels as "insight," "imagination," "artistic ability," and "special abilities."

Many people believe that our culture is becoming less and less tolerant of independent or socially divergent behavior. The social and cultural dangers of overconformity in both the ideational and overt behavioral realms have been emphasized by social theorists. The rewards for conformity, and the relative absence of rewards for independent thinking and acting, have been a possible stifler of individuality and a deterrent to self-expression (Sawrey & Telford, 1975).

Recent technological advances have made it possible to solve within minutes problems that previously would have taken years. Electronic computers and data-processing equipment not only have taken the drudgery out of certain kinds of problem solution, but they have made it possible for people to formulate problems that heretofore were not even considered. Human ingenuity can now be applied to using machines to perform further analyses, the results of which may lead to still further hypotheses to be investigated. Our modern electronic age seems more and more to reject people as performers of routine tasks and solvers of routine problems. Machines can perform a great number of tasks and solve many problems with much greater efficiency than can people. Such a technological culture, if it is to continue its growth, demands less of human physical energy and more of ideational processes. Unique ideas, and original problems and new ways of solving them, are the grist of an innovating society. At the same time, we cannot allow our lives and our culture to become as mechanistic and controlled as our very efficient technology must be. Humans must be the controllers of the technology, not vice versa. Continued social, political, industrial, and educational progress is dependent, in large part, on the creativity of the members of society.

DEFINING CREATIVITY

Definitions of creativity are numerous, and they vary according to the particular emphasis given to the concept. If one focuses on the process or processes of creating, his definition might be at variance with that of one who focuses on the end-product of creative endeavor. If one is concerned with the personal or phenomenological aspects of behavior, his definition will include the behavior and feelings that were unique to a particular individual under specified conditions. If the focus of concern is the socially significant and unique responses of individuals, an external frame of reference evolves and leads to a different kind of definition, one which involves a comparison with some cultural norm.

For a response to a problem to be termed original, the probability of its occurring must be low (Maltzman, 1960; Mednick, 1962). I. Maltzman has added that it must also be relevant to the situation; S. Mednick that it must also be useful. By these standards, a person may be highly original, but not qualify as highly creative. This is obviously true as these concepts are considered by Mednick. Maltzman contends that creativity depends not only on originality, but also on societal recognition and approval. And because creativity is dependent on society's approval, he contends that originality is the facet of creativity that is most readily investigated in the laboratory.

J. P. Guilford (1959) distinguished between originality and creativity on the basis of his factor analytic investigations of creativity. Originality is one of several traits contributing to creativity. Creativity is a more general trait that includes not only originality, but flexibility, fluency, and motivational and temperamental traits as well.

The personal or phenomenological definitions of creativity involve novelty or uniqueness, but place it in a personal frame of reference. A product may be a creative one if it is new or novel to the individual involved, if it is his creation, if it is expressive of himself rather than dictated by someone else. It need be neither useful nor unique. Its social recognition and cultural impact may be zero, but if it is a unique personal experience, it is creative (Maslow, 1959, 1970; Rogers, 1959; Barron, 1968). A. H. Maslow (1970) distinguishes between *special-talent* creativeness of the Mozart type and the creativeness of all people. He indicates that creativeness is a universal characteristic of persons, that each has originality or inventiveness with unique characteristics. The creativeness of the self-actualized person he compares to the naive creativeness of unspoiled children. All people possess the potential for creativeness at birth, but most lose it as they become enculturated. J. G. Nicholls (1972) has discussed, in some detail, the concept of creativity as a normally distributed trait.

Those who use a cultural frame of reference insist that a creative product must be novel to both the individual and the society and that, in addition, it must be useful. To be called "creative," an activity must result in something that is culturally, as well as individually, novel and useful (Torrance, 1962).

INVESTIGATING CREATIVITY

There are three basic approaches to the investigation of creativity: focus can be on the *creative product,* the *creative person,* or the *creative process* (Rock, Evans, & Klein, 1969).[1]

The creative product

It is agreed that a production must be novel to be called creative. The criterion of novelty or unusualness is, of course, a relative matter. To an internationally knowledgeable adult, originality or novelty of product may be a painting, a musical composition, a scientific theory, or a mechanical invention. A child judges originality in terms of the extent of his experience; something may be original to him if he is unaware that similar productions have been made many times before. Depending on the comparison group, a creation may be original in one context and common in another. The originality of a product is relative to a norm that serves as a judgmental standard for evaluation of its uniqueness. Within such a variable context, uniqueness is the initial prerequisite of a creative product.

However, individual originality by itself is not a sufficient condition for creativity. If mere unusualness were the sole criterion, we would identify a strange collection of objects as creative, including everything odd, bizarre, or statistically improbable. The verbal flow from persons making up a psychiatric population will contain more novel or unique combinations than will the speech of the same number of more "normal" individuals; however, few people would label these products creative.

At some point the second criterion of appropriateness is either explicitly or implicitly applied: To be creative, a product must fit or be useful within its relevant context. It must be relevant to the situation and to

[1] For additional documentation for the following discussion of these three areas of focus, see Kagan (1967), Arasteh (1968), Ward (1968), Kogan & Pankove (1972), Vance (1973), and Harris & Evans (1974).

the purposes of the producer. The popular stereotype of the slightly mad scientist randomly mixing substances in his laboratory in the attic and accidentally stumbling on the discovery of the age is, of course, sheer fantasy. A creative product is actively produced, not passively self-generated or accidentally fabricated. Creative products are fabricated from a number of ingredients, one of which is a personal and/or social need. The incentive may range from a desire for self-expression or catharsis to a wish for monetary rewards, social acclaim, or the reduction of one's intellectual or perceptual uncertainties. The motivation of creative activities may vary greatly.

Appropriateness may be in terms of a social or environmental need, or it may be related to the internal motives of its producer. The combination of colors selected by an artist may fit because they harmonize with their surroundings or because they appropriately express the artist's momentary mood. Many people insist that unusualness and appropriateness are not only necessary but also sufficient criteria for the identification of creative products. However, P. W. Jackson and S. Messick (1967) have proposed two additional criteria: the transcendence of constraint (transformation), and condensation. Jackson and Messick consider creativity to be a matter of degree, and great creative products must be sufficiently unique and appropriate to provide new perspectives on some aspect of human experience. The masterpiece involves a major transformation of material, concept, or interpretation. The creative product breaks through the strong restraint imposed by previous ways of thinking, types of solutions to a practical problem, or ways of interpreting events. Examples of creative products in the field of science which rank high in their transformational properties are Charles Darwin's concept of the evolution of species, Sigmund Freud's ideas concerning the nature and significance of unconscious psychological processes, Albert Einstein's theory of relativity, and the transformation that was involved in the transition from the microscope that made use of the magnifying properties of a lens to the magnification of an entirely different order of magnitude used in the electron microscope. As creative products in the realm of art are more common examples, you will doubtless be able to think of several.

The creations mentioned above also qualify for Jackson and Messick's other prerequisite for higher-order creativity—condensation. Contributions which produce transformations and form one concept which can be significantly applied to a wide area of thought are of a higher order of creativity than contributions having a limited frame of reference and are more specific in conceptualization or practical utility. The two universally identified characteristics of creativity—originality and appropriateness— together with the two additional ones proposed by Jackson and Messick— transformation and condensation—provide criteria that can also be ordered with reference both to their importance and to their developmental sequence. Each of the four criteria in order can be considered an additional requirement for higher-order creativity.

The creative person

Highly creative or potentially creative individuals have been identified by their peers and by means of batteries of tests of creativity. The techniques used in assessment and identification will be discussed later. We will now summarize what seems to be the consensus concerning the personal characteristics of individuals so identified.

Ideational flexibility   Creativity involves the transcending of traditional ways of perceiving and thinking. Perceptual categories must be fluid. On the broad cognitive level, this flexibility has been called openmindedness. Creative activity requires an individual to move freely back and forth between fantasy and reality. He must be able and willing to entertain seriously ideas and hypotheses which may violate "common sense." The creative person enjoys the fanciful, and even the playfully entertaining, elements of bizarre and unusual possibilities. A fluid and wide-ranging generation of possibilities provides a large pool of hypotheses for later, more critical evaluation. Highly creative individuals reporting on their own experiences, as well as research studies of the characteristics of creative people, agree that a high level of tolerance for wild conjecture, a certain willingness to extend and even enjoy transcending the commonplace or the real, and a penchant to entertain the highly improbable and the impossible are necessary ingredients of creativity.

Personal independence   The creative individual is relatively free of conventional restraints and restrictions. He is a limited nonconformist. However, his nonconformity and unconventionality are typically limited to the area of his creative productivity. He is really neither a conformist nor a nonconformist—he is independent, in the sense that he is not particularly concerned about what others think and say. He is not preoccupied with the impression he makes on others. He is relatively free to be himself. He is highly task- rather than self-oriented. Creative people are nonconformists in their areas of creative endeavor. However, they are not deliberate nonconformists. They are genuinely independent and are often conventional in areas peripheral to their creative activities. It has become popular in contemporary educational and psychological circles to decry conformity and to elevate nonconformity to one of the supreme virtues. Both conformity and nonconformity are characteristics of the truly independent person. Such a person recognizes that certain degrees of conformity are essential for life in organized society. The solution to the problem posed by the conformity–nonconformity dichotomy involves maintaining a proper balance between the two extremes so as to facilitate one's functioning in society, to stimulate the growth of the individual, and to tolerate nonconformity in the individual's particular area of creative competence.

Sex role of the creative person   There is a consistent tendency for creative males to score higher in femininity than do their less creative peers on tests designed to indicate the relative strength of the masculine and feminine components of personality. This shift toward femininity in creative males results from their conforming less rigidly to the traditional male sex role than does the average male. The creative male is able to develop and manifest intellectual and cultural interests that are either male or female without feeling threatened. The creative male is able to participate in and give expression to both his masculine and feminine traits. He is less completely identified with and limited by his male identification, and in this sense he is also more independent than are his more rigidly sex-typed male contemporaries.

Tolerance of ambiguity   The independence of the highly creative individual is manifested in a high level of tolerance for ambiguities in life and a willingness to accept the uncertainties and complexities of existence. The creative individual does not feel impelled to force closure on questions, to be blind to apparent paradoxes, and to impose a perceptual and conceptual simplicy on life's problems. Creative people are especially disposed to recognize, accept, and even welcome complexity. Their perceptual preferences are much farther toward the complex and asymmetrical end of a complex–simple and symmetrical asymmetrical continuum. Creative people appear to be challenged by disordered complexity. They are not unduly anxious about apparent chaos and are able to do without the satisfaction of ordering anarchy by distorting reality or by imposing artificial and unreal simple and immediate "solutions" to problems.

Tolerance for errors   For an individual to be original and innovative in thought and action, he must not be afraid to err. The production of a wide range of alternative solutions to a problem and the maintenance of an attitude of relaxed contemplation which are a characteristic of creative people require a minimal concern with the danger of error. This does not mean that creative people consider errors to be nonsignificant, but they view evidence that a hypothesis or conclusion is in error as information rather than as a personal disgrace or defeat. A person with great capacity for generating possibilities and freedom to express his feelings regarding these possibilities will have a high level of tolerance for being wrong.

Intelligence and creativity   Most researchers consider creativity to constitute a cluster of traits resembling and, to some extent, overlapping general intellectual ability. Studies of creative individuals have indicated that creative activity, like intellectual productivity in general, is the result of a dynamic interaction among a group of characteristics including a certain minimum of intellectual ability together with such things as high drive, cognitive flexibility, open-mindedness, and tolerance of ambiguity. Although there is practically no correlation between intelligence test scores and creativity among individuals judged highly creative by their peers, no one doubts that over the entire range of intelligence, from the mentally retarded to the most intellectually gifted, a positive relationship exists.

Sociability and creativity   Highly creative individuals are not high in sociability. In general, the creative person is neither asocial nor antisocial; he simply has less than normal regard for the pleasant security of positive peer approval. The threat of negative evaluation or social rejection is not cause for personal alarm. The creative individual is much more inner- than outer-directed. The highly creative person can be a minority of one without being unduly disturbed. He may be more sensitive to the demands of a problem than to the evaluations of the social environment. The highly creative person does not highly value "togetherness," is not greatly concerned with smooth interpersonal relations, and consequently may be perceived as asocial or antisocial.

The anxieties of creative people   Many previously mentioned personality traits of creative people are generally considered characteristic of the "healthy minded." From this, we would expect their anxiety levels to be low (Ward, Kogan, & Pankove, 1973). However, on a conventional test of anxiety, creatve individuals score considerably above normal. However, the anxiety of creative individuals is different from that of the personally disturbed neurotic individual. The high anxiety of the highly creative individual is the result of two things, the first of which might be called a "divine discontent" with his status or rate of progress in comparison with his self-expectations or aspirations. Studies have demonstrated that self–ideal self discrepancies are related to the maturity and cognitive levels of the individual rather than indicative of pathology, as previously believed (Mullener & Laird, 1971). There is a general tendency for this discrepancy to increase with age, and there is evidence that this increase is the result of the individual's increasing capacity for becoming sensitive to and incorporating into his ideal-self-concept a definitely delineated set of values. The more cognitively mature person, having conceptualized his ideal-self on the one hand and recognized his own self-concept on the other, makes greater self-demands and, when unable to fulfill them, is more aware of the disparity between the two than is the less mature person, who has not conceptualized either. The general notion is that self–ideal self discrepancy results from the attainment of a certain level of cognitive development, which itself has brought about the conceptualization of the self and the ideal-self and the realization of a discrepancy between them (Mullener & Laird, 1971).

It has been suggested that creativity may be associated with alpha waves. Ordinarily, alpha activity is inhibited during concentration; however, among artists alpha wave production was found to increase during creative periods (Martindale, 1975).

The positive relationship between anxiety and development level indicates that maturity increases the discriminative capacities of the individual, his awareness of self and ideal-self, and also his anxiety as he becomes aware of their disparity. The attainment of higher intellectual and cognitive levels carries with it higher levels of self-expectation and an increased likelihood of self-discontent, with its concomitant anxiety. The important thing is not the presence or absence of anxiety, but the level of anxiety and the individual's reaction to it. The highly creative individual keeps his anxiety within manageable limits and uses it in productive ways.

The value systems of the highly creative   The highly creative are much more interested in broad conceptual meanings and significances than are "ordinary" people. They are relatively uninterested in small details or in facts for their own sake. They are more concerned with the meanings, the interrelationships, and the implications of data than with the data themselves. On the AVL Study of Values, a test designed to indicate the relative strength of six values or interest areas—theoretical, economic, aesthetic, social, political, and religious   highly creative people from a wide variety of fields score highest in the theoretical and aesthetic areas.

Reading the biographical accounts of highly creative people and the research studies that try to delineate their characteristics creates a conviction that creativity stems more from a way of life than from unique learning and perceptual experiences. These people have a characteristic broad set of attitudes and values, not merely a set of techniques or devices for solving problems.

DIVERGENT AND CONVERGENT THINKING

The ideation involved in creative thinking is often described as divergent, as contrasted with the convergent thinking which takes place in ordinary problem-solving (Guilford, 1959). The distinction between divergent and convergent thinking can be shown by some examples taken from commonly used tests of creativity. A task designed to assess *divergent thinking* may involve the listing of as many uses as possble for some common article such as brick or a paper cup. Performance on such tasks is evaluated in terms of the number of separate uses and categories of uses given. Performance on word-association tests is determined by the number of different associations evoked by a list of common words. An individual may be asked to formulate as many different problems as possible from information and data provided by the examiner, or he may be required to think of all the possible questions about a picture shown to him. An unusual-uses test requires the subject to indicate as many unusual uses as possible for a familiar object such as a tin can, a toy, or a book (Torrance, 1962, 1966; Getzels & Jackson, 1962). Tests of this kind are not scored for the "correct" answer but according to the number, diversity, and uniqueness of the responses. The thought processes required to score well on such tests as these have been labelled *divergent,* as contrasted with the *convergent thinking* involved in situations where the production of the one correct solution or answer is required, as, for example, in a multiple-choice test. One, and only one, answer is appropriate in such situations. Divergent thinking is required when one is confronted with a problem that has many possible solutions.

Divergent thinking has been considered more characteristic of highly creative individuals than of those not rated as highly creative. However, some have questioned the practice of identifying divergent thinking as indicative of creativity (Hudson, 1966; Nicholls, 1972; Sawrey & Telford, 1975; Kogan & Pankove, 1974). M. A. Wallach (1971) has been critical of the assumption that aspects of divergent thinking as measured by tests of creativity are closely related to "real world" creativity. N. Kogan and E. Pankove (1974) found no evidence to support the assumption that divergent thinking assessed in the later years of elementary school was prognostic of later creativity in high school when the criterion for creativity was nonacademic attainment in secondary school. The question of the validity of such measures has not been adequately resolved and must still be thoroughly investigated before such tests are of great educational utility.

The processes required by divergent, as opposed to convergent, thinking may appear very different at first glance, but they probably have many elements in common. The emphasis placed on divergent thinking in early speculations about the nature of creativity may have produced a tendency to attribute less importance to convergent processes than they possess. Divergent and convergent components are both to be found in most forms of thinking. For example, in a completion type of question, where the problem is to provide the best completion (convergence), the individual reads the statement and a large number of associations occur as he reads it (divergence). When the subject completes the reading of the statement and realizes the nature and form of the required completion, typically several possible ones emerge (divergence). The subject then tries out and rejects each one in turn until the one which seems to fit best is discovered. This item is accepted and used (convergence). The divergent aspect of this process may not be as obvious as it is when the instructions require the individual to give as many different associations or uses as possible; however, a wide variety of possible completions provides a larger pool of hypotheses from which to select. There are some divergent components even in the most formal problem.

Convergent components are apparent in creative thinking, if some criterion of success other than number and diversity of responses is applied. If personal acceptability or social usefulness is desired, convergence will occur before the creative process is completed. Typically, the creative process does not terminate with the emission of as many associations, hypotheses, or solutions as possible. Some implicit or explicit standard of acceptability is applied, and one of the alternatives is used as the most appropriate basis for decision or action.

In actual life, the creative process does not end, as it does in the test situation, with the listing of all the possible uses of a brick or the verbal solution of a problem. One may think of many uses for a brick because a brick is at hand and one desires to make use of it. Thought, then, is given to all the possible uses for it, so that the most appropriate one can be selected. This process involves both divergent and convergent ideational processes. Even in the production of the most free and self-expressive art, where social standards may be largely disregarded, there is some convergence in terms of the artist's sense of appropriateness. Out of the infinite array of possible combinations of colors, forms, and figures is finally selected and produced the one combination which best expresses the artist's feelings or ideas. Self-imposed selectivity still involves convergence. And when the creative process involves the development of a new process, convergence occurs in terms of the relative utility of the many ideas, propositions, or hypotheses available. Most ideation contains both divergent and convergent components.

The dichotomy of divergent and convergent elements is analogous to the older dichotomy of inductive and deductive reasoning. Inductive reasoning is said to proceed from particular instances to general rules, while deduction supposedly begins with the generalizations and derives specific conclusions therefrom. Inductive reasoning is said to proceed from the particular to the general, while deductive reasoning moves from the general to the particular. In certain respects, induction is divergent thinking and deduction is convergent thinking.

In practice, of course, reasoning is neither purely inductive nor purely deductive; it always has elements of each. The interested lay person or scientist may begin with repeated observations of a related nature and then generalize from these specific instances (convergence, hypothesis formation, or inductive reasoning). From the generalization, a number of inferences are then drawn. If *A* is true, then *B, C, D,* and *E* should follow (divergence or deductive reasoning). If inferences *B, C, D,* and *E* are verified, the generalization is confirmed.

IDENTIFYING THE HIGHLY CREATIVE

Problems of central importance in the investigation of creativity involve identifying the creative person and determining his level of creativity (Taylor, 1959, 1960; Stein & Heinze, 1960). If the highly creative are to be studied in a scientifically meaningful fashion, they must be identified. To do this, some criterion of creativity must be invoked. The particular criterion employed must be culturally significant and have considerable reliability. It is generally agreed that creativity is not an all-or-none phenomenon, but a characteristic possessed by all individuals in varying degrees. Obviously, those individuals who are renowned for their creative work must be investigated if we are to determine the possible characteristics that contributed to their creativity. Not only must these characteristics be determined, but if we are to encourage the development of creative potential in the young, we must discern those patterns of early treatment that contributed to or detracted from their eventual creativity. If the potentially highly creative can be identified early in life, it may be possible to provide them with the kinds of experiences that will ensure the best development of their creative talent.

Identifying highly creative adults

A general approach to the study of creativity is to investigate the characteristics of individuals who are recognized by others in their field as being highly creative. Groups of scientists, writers, architects, artists, and so forth can be asked to nominate individuals within their discipline who are the most highly creative, and the nominees can be investigated. Such a procedure has been followed by the Institute for Personality Assessment and Research (IPAR) at the University of California at Berkeley (MacKinnon, 1953, 1962; Barron, 1963). IPAR has been particularly active in the investigation of creativity in adults, and the general methods of their investigation reflect the considerable creative ability of the investigators.

An investigation of creative architects (MacKinnon, 1962) is reported to be typical of the procedures employed at IPAR (Barron et al., 1965). Subjects were selected for this investigation by a nomination and voting procedure. Five senior architects of the faculty of the College of Architecture at the University of California, Berkeley, were each asked to nominate the forty most creative architects in the United States. A loose definition of creativity in architecture was provided the nominators as a working guide:

> Originality of thinking and freshness of approach to architectural problems; constructive ingenuity; ability to set aside established convention and procedures when appropriate; a flair for devising effective and original fulfillments of the major demands of architecture, the demands of technology, visual form, planning, human awareness, and social purpose.

The nominated architects as well as control groups were invited to come to Berkeley for a weekend of intensive study in the Institute for Personality Assessment and Research. They were housed in a comfortable house, along with the investigators, for a weekend of intensive evaluation. They were studied in groups of ten with standard psychometric devices as well as with instruments developed for the specific study. They were searchingly interviewed about their life histories and present functioning, and they were observed in contrived, stressful social situations. The general method has been described as a "living-in assessment method." The results of the tests, ratings, interviews, and observations were analyzed by appropriate statistical techniques to discern the characteristics of the creative, as opposed to the less creative, groups.

The successful architect has a complicated task to perform that combines many of the aspects of other professions. He has to exercise the diverse skills of the author, psychologist, journalist, educator, business person, lawyer, and engineer to become a successful and effective architect. His expression of creativity must have many aspects if he is to become a noticed architect. Thus the choice of architects for the study of creativity was probably a very wise one.

Creative writers, scientists, mathematicians, and artists also have been studied by these techniques of selection and assessment. Such investigations provide descriptions of the highly creative and give a retrospective glimpse of their development. Of particular importance is the personalized picture of the highly creative that is thus obtained. The characteristics of those who are presently designated as highly creative can yield hypotheses about the background and development of creativity that can be investigated through longitudinal studies.

Historical methods have been employed in the investigation of the intelligence of individuals of eminence (Cox, 1926). Biographical investigations of the personalities of contemporary scientists have also been reported (Cattell & Drevdahl, 1955). Though this method of investigation is different from that employed at IPAR, the conclusions drawn about the personal characteristics of the individuals investigated are markedly similar.

Identifying highly creative children

If proper procedures for the nurturing of creativity are to be developed, it is necessary to identify those who have the greatest creative potential. It has long been known that when procedures are instituted for the development of a particular facet of performance, those individuals already possessing some skill profit proportionately more from a given amount of training than those who are relatively unskilled. Therefore, the highly creative youngster might be expected to develop rapidly. It is reasoned, too, that those with strong tendencies toward creativity have a greater capacity for making culturally useful innovations.

If the characteristics of children who will later become highly creative adults can be determined, it may be possible to provide them, at a very early age, with experiences that will develop those characteristics and minimize those that lead to low productivity and creativity. A great deal of effort has been expended in attempts to discern the cognitive (Kogan, 1973) and other personality variables in children that might be predictive of adult creativity. Tests designed to measure various aspects and correlates of creativity in children have been developed. One of the serious problems encountered in the development of such instruments is that of validity. Test questions that tend to evoke novel or unusual responses or solutions to problems, and questions that are designed to measure originality or uniqueness of response, may or may not be indicative of later creative activity.

Long-range studies of people who, as children, were designated as highly creative have not been reported in the research literature. L. M. Terman and M. H. Oden's (1959) follow-up studies of gifted children at adulthood have indicated that the highly *intelligent,* as determined by IQ, tend to become highly productive adults, but we do not know whether these individuals were creative either as children or as adults.

Developing tests of creativity

An elaborate battery of tasks has been developed by J. P. Guilford and his associates (Guilford & Merrifield, 1960) for the assessment of creativity. Guilford has attempted a factorial analysis of the intellect and its measurement. In his presidential address to the American Psychological Association (1950), he outlined a group of objections to existing measures of intellect and indicated that the "structure of intellect" was complex, and required a variety of measures. He hypothesized that the thinking abilities involved in creativity were those he had defined as "divergent productions and transformations," as opposed to the "convergent functions" that he indicated were being measured by the then-current measures of intellect. Although Guilford has subsequently modified his thinking on this issue, much emphasis was given to *convergent versus divergent thinking.* Guilford's subsequent designation of components of creative thinking includes not only divergent productions, but the redefinition of abilities of the convergent-production category of his structure of intellect as well as sensitivity to problems which fall in his "evaluation" category. Thus a great number of thinking abilities are designated as involved in creativity, and a goodly number of tests have been designed for their measurement (Guilford, 1959; Guilford & Merrifield, 1960; Taylor & Holland, 1962).

J. W. Getzels and Jackson (1962) used five different measures of creativity in their research. Some of their ideas were borrowed from Guilford, and others were of their own creation. One measure was a word-association test in which subjects were required to give as many definitions as possible of a fairly common word, such as *bolt* or *sack.* The score depended on the absolute number of definitions and the number of different categories into which they could be placed. A second measure was a uses-of-things test. This test is similar to tests used by Guilford in his studies of cognitive ability. The subject gives as many uses as he can for a common object, such as a brick or a toothpick, and he is scored on the basis of both the number and the originality of the uses given. "Brick can be used as a bed warmer" is a more original answer than "bricks can be used to build houses." A third measure was the hidden-shapes test, from a previously developed test battery (Cattell, 1956). In this test, the subject is shown a card with a simple geometric figure on it. He is then required to find that figure hidden in a more complex form or pattern. A fourth measure was a fables test. In this test, the subject is presented with short fables from which the last line is missing, and is required to compose three different endings for each fable: a "moralistic" one, a "humorous" one, and a "sad" one. The score depends upon the number, appropriateness, and originality of the endings. A final test was termed *make-up problems.* In this situation, the subject was presented with a number of complex paragraphs. Each paragraph contained many numerical statements, and the subject was required to make up as many mathematical problems as possible with the information given. The score depended on the number, appropriateness, complexity, and originality of the problems.

The Torrance tests of creative thinking (Torrance, 1966) have been used rather widely as measures of creativity. Some of the tasks are an ask-and-guess test, a product-improvement test, an unusual-uses test, and a just-suppose test. These tests present problems that emphasize unusual or clever ideas. The battery also contains the picture-construction test, the incomplete-figures test and the parallel-lines test. There are four scoring criteria for the Torrance tests: fluency—the number of relevant responses made; flexibility—the number of shifts from one category of meaning to another; originality—the infrequency of the responses offered; and elaboration—the detail and specificity of the responses. All of the tasks call for the production of divergent solutions, multiple possibilities, and some type of thinking theoretically involved in creative behavior.

E. P. Torrance (1972) has reported considerable validational evidence for his tests of creativity, but the positive character of that evidence has been seriously questioned (Crockenberg, 1972). An investigation of the predictive validity of tests of divergent thinking was conducted over a five-year period with ambiguous results (Cropley, 1972). This longitudinal study was based in part on Torrance's procedures but leaves the question of validity rather vague. Kogan and Pankove (1972, 1974) have raised again the question of the validity of tests of divergent thinking in the assessment of creativity. The correlation between scores obtained on the Torrance tests of creative thinking and scores on intelligence tests are rather high (Wallach, 1968). It has been indicated that the use of these tests as measures of creativity, as the tests are currently scored, is really open to serious question (Harvey et al., 1970). Fluency, defined as number of responses elicited, has been described as a pervasive element in measures of creativity. This measure may, in part, account for the high correlations found among measures of creativity (Clark & Mirels, 1970).

IQ AND CREATIVITY

Many reports of limited relationships between creativity and intelligence have been made by generalizing from samples containing a restricted range of both intelligence and creativity. The meaning of correlation under such circumstances is difficult to discern. It has long been known that the IQ, above a given level, is essentially unrelated even to such an intellectually challenging area as collegiate success. Many factors are involved. Such things as health, motivation, study habits, and family finances are considerations. On the other hand, unless there is a certain minimum level of measured intelligence, academic failure becomes highly predictable. There *are* individual differences among the highly intelligent. Restriction of the range of one variable does not equally restrict other variables, even though they are highly correlated in the general population. Creativity, if it is a complex of individual differences among the highly intelligent, should not be expected to correlate highly with IQ. The study of individual differences is most desirable, and studies of individual differences among the highly intelligent, including creativity as a variable, are to be encouraged. The concept of creativity should enhance our knowledge of people and their performances. Enthusiasm for the concept should not be carried to the point of making it into a panacea for the woes of society. The implied, and sometimes stated, abandonment of the concept of general intelligence may be a matter of throwing the baby out with the bath. Although it may well be true that we must look beyond the limits of the IQ to understand creativity (Guilford, 1950), it does not follow that intelligence can be ignored in our quest for such understanding. Creativity has been defined as involving social usefulness, and it appears logical that most of the useful creative ideas are likely to come from the most intelligent. High intelligence does not guarantee creative activity, but low intelligence certainly militates against it.

Correlational investigations and speculations

It has been estimated, as the result of correlational studies of creativity and intelligence among subjects designated highly creative, that the correlation between the two variables is low but positive (Barron et al., 1965). In these instances, the range of both creativity and intelligence has been restricted. The amount of restriction of ranges is variable from one investigation to the next, and the exact curtailment of range of creativity is really not known. For highly creative writers, the correlation between IQ and creativity has been estimated to be around .40 (Barron, 1963). In a study of architects designated as creative, a correlation of near zero is reported, but the author speculates that, over the entire range of creativity and intelligence, there is a positive relationship between the two variables (MacKinnon, 1962). From a study of the upper 1 percent of high school students, it has been estimated that intelligence has little or no relationship to creative performance in arts and science (Holland, 1961). In addition to the problem of curtailment of range, it has been pointed out that creativity in a given area may require different abilities than creativity in another. Among architects, creativity may reflect the ability to engineer structural innovations, in which case it should be a correlate of intelligence. If the creativity depends on new artistic designs, intelligence would probably be less important (McNemar, 1964). The kind of creativity involved, then, may be a factor in the size of correlation to be expected. Highly creative writers were reported to have an average IQ of about 140. Creative writers apparently are very bright! From groups of so restricted a range of intelligence, conclusions about the general relationship of intelligence and creativity cannot be drawn.

The serious problem of attempting to predict later creativity from tests of creativity in childhood has been mentioned. Actually, the childhood characteristics of creative adults have been studied only retrospectively. Tests administered during childhood, and scored for uniqueness and novelty of response, may or may not be highly related to adult creative activity. We do not now have creative adult subjects who, as children, were given the current tests of creativity. This problem of validity is difficult, but it cannot be ignored. However, if tests of creativity are administered to children, and if these subjects are subsequently investigated as adults, data on validity will then be available.

Users of tests of creative thinking for elementary school children and adolescents have reported little relationship between scores on such measures and scores on tests of intelligence (Torrance, 1962; Getzels & Jackson, 1962). The extensive investigation of Getzels and Jackson (1962) has been cogently criticized by a number of other workers (Burt, 1962; De Mille & Merrifield, 1962; Marsh, 1964; McNemar, 1964; Ripple & May, 1962). Their statistical procedures and their manner of describing their research have been attacked. They used, as a measure of creativity, the sum of scores of five tests of creativity. Using their reported data, Q. McNemar (1964) discerned that creativity and the IQ's in their sample correlate to the extent of .40. This r has been greatly attenuated by the usual measurement errors, by the restriction of the IQ range (the mean was 132), and by the variety of intelligence test scores employed. McNemar concluded that their creativity tests and intelligence tests have far more common variance than is indicated by the authors' report. Getzels and Jackson's use of Chi Square as a statistical procedure has been criticized by R. W. Marsh (1964) because of Chi Square's insensitivity to interaction. Marsh concluded that the IQ may still be the best single criterion for creative potential.

An empirical demonstration of the possible effect of restriction of the range of IQ's has been reported by R. E. Ripple and F. B. May (1962). By correlating Otis IQ's and scores on creative thinking tests administered to several seventh-grade groups, homogeneous or heterogeneous with respect to their IQ's, they demonstrated that the low correlation of these measures reported by other investigators may well be due in part to the restricted range of the IQ's in their samples. F. Barron (1968) asserts that beyond a minimum IQ, creativity is not a function of intelligence as measured by IQ tests. A minimum IQ would appear to be about 120, which has to be considered a rather high IQ.

An unfortunate designation of the groups investigated and reported by Getzels and Jackson has contributed to the confusion. Basically, they reported on two groups of adolescents. One group was composed of individuals scoring in the top 20 percent on measures of intelligence but not in the top 20 percent on measures of creativity. The other group scored in the top 20 percent on measures of creativity, but not on measures of intelligence. They excluded those who were in the top 20 percent on both. The group scoring in the top 20 percent on measures of creativity but not on intelligence was labeled the *high-creative* group, and the other group was labeled the *high-IQ* group. The mean IQ of the high-IQ group was 150, whereas the mean IQ of the high-creative group was 127. Now an IQ of 127 most certainly is not as high as an IQ of 150, but it is still a high IQ when the total range is considered; their high-creative group was still fairly bright. The labeling of the two groups as *high-IQ* and *high-creative* has probably contributed to the tendency to overlook their high level of intelligence.

The correlation between IQ and creativity obtained in an extensive investigation of a carefully chosen sample of 7,648 fifteen-year-old boys and girls in Project Talent (Shaycoft, et al., 1963) was reported to be .67 This *r* becomes .80 when corrected for attenuation (McNemar, 1964).

It would seem that the extent of the relationship between IQ's and measured creativity depends on the nature of the tests of creativity employed, among other things. The nature and size of the relationship remains speculative, however. It would appear that the early speculations that the relationship is slight may have been exaggerated and may have led to considerable confusion. Creativity of certain kinds may be highly related to intelligence, while creativity in certain other areas may not be so highly dependent on intelligence. That some intelligence is essential for the production of cultural, scientific, technological, or artistic innovation would appear obvious.

HIGHLY CREATIVE ADULTS

Adults designated as highly creative by one means or another have been studied rather intensively by several groups of investigators by the methods already described. Perhaps the most usual means of designation as highly creative has been that of nomination by contemporaries. As a consequence of the investigations of creative scientists, writers, artists, architects, and mathematicians, a rather large body of descriptive material is available. However, a general picture of the highly creative person is difficult to discern, because of the complexity of bright adults in general and because of the diversity of creative endeavor. Individual differences among the highly creative are to be expected.

There does seem to be some agreement among various investigators as to the characteristics of outstanding scientists. They are generally described as being highly intelligent, emotionally sensitive, self-sufficient, of independent judgment, dedicated, introspective, confident, ideationally productive, and somewhat unconventional. On the Allport-Vernon-Lindzey Scale of Values, they score high in "Theoretical and Aesthetic" values and low in "Religious, Social, and Economic" values (Gough, 1961). Barron (1965) presents a unified picture of the productive scientist gleaned from the research of a number of individual investigators. Productive scientists are depicted as having a high degree of intelligence, emotional stability, ego strength, personal dominance, forcefulness of opinion, and liking for precision and order. They are challenged by the unknown, by contradictions, and by apparent disorder. They appear to be somewhat distant and detached in personal relations, and prefer to deal with things or abstractions rather than with people. Productive scientists are further depicted as having a strong need for independence and autonomy. They appear to be self-sufficient and self-directing, and they enjoy abstract thinking. They resist pressure to conform in their thinking. In brief, they seem to be personally strong, dedicated, independent, somewhat adventurous, and scholarly. These characteristics of the productive scientist appear to be those that would rationally be expected (Taylor & Barron, 1963). To be productive or creative, the scientist must be bright, orderly, and thorough. If he is to make a contribution to science, his efforts must be unique and at the frontiers of knowledge. Novelty and uncertainty are of necessity involved in such endeavors. The scientist must be willing to take risks and be enthusiastically dedicated to the pursuit of his ideas and directions.

An earlier investigation (Cox, 1926) of the characteristics of 300 geniuses, divided into several subgroups according to area of accomplishment, provides some interesting data for comparing scientists and imaginative writers. Their personal and moral qualities, as well as their intellectual ones, were depicted.

The scientific geniuses were estimated to have an average IQ of over 170. This represents a very high level of intellect, as might be expected. Compared with eminent individuals from all of the subgroups, the scientists had very great strength or force of character and balance, and were very active. They were less sociable, excitable, and sensitive to criticism than the other subgroups. These scientists were described as the strongest, most forceful, and best balanced people in the study.

The artists in the study were estimated to be of somewhat lower, but still very high, intelligence, their average IQ probably being well over 135. They were rated as having a high degree of aesthetic feeling, desire to excel, belief in themselves, originality of ideas, and ability to strive for distant goals.

Imaginative writers (poets, novelists, and dramatists) were judged to have an average IQ of 165. These people were notably high in imaginativeness and aesthetic feeling, effort directed toward pleasure, originality of ideas, strength of memory, and keenness of observation. They ranked lower on common sense and the degree to which their actions and thoughts were dependent on reason than did the other groups.

The descriptions of eminent people in science and the arts have some common, as well as some distinguishing, features. Individual differences among the highly creative are to be expected as much as are individual differences among the highly intelligent, and it is difficult to put together a composite picture of creative adults. In one rather large investigation of physical scientists (Taylor et al., 1961), a list of 150 criteria of scientific productivity and creativity was developed. Even when this number was reduced to 48 categories, and then by factor analysis further reduced to 14, picture of potential creativity remained extremely complex. Torrance (1962) compiled a list of 84 characteristics found in one or more studies to differentiate highly creative persons from less creative ones. This list includes such apparently contrasting items as courageous and timid; self-assertive and introversive; appears haughty and self-satisfied at times and is outwardly bashful; reserved and spirited in disagreement; receptive to the ideas of others and stubborn; emotional and somewhat withdrawn; and, finally, quiescent, self-satisfied at times, and discontented. With such diverse descriptions of productive and creative people at hand, one is tempted to say that the only communality discernible in persons designated as creative is that they have attained eminence—that is, adults designated as creative have been creative. The complexity of the category or the vagueness of the concept tends to make a composite description of the "creative" extremely tenuous.

The most consistent findings in the literature appear to be those of D. W. MacKinnon (1960). Other investigators have since reported essentially the same patterns of interest on the Strong Vocational Interest Blank and the Allport-Vernon-Lindzey Scale of Values. The more original or highly creative rated high on the interest scales for architect, psychologist, author-journalist, and specialization level. They scored low on scales for purchasing agent, office manager, banker, farmer, carpenter, veterinarian, policeman, and mortician. MacKinnon interprets these findings as indicating that creative individuals are less interested in small details or the practical, concrete facets of life, and more concerned with meanings, implications, and the symbolic equivalents of things and ideas.

All of MacKinnon's highly creative groups scored high on theoretical and aesthetic values and high on several scales of the Minnesota Multiphasic Personality Inventory. His groups of highly creative males scored high on the masculinity–femininity scale, athough they were *not* effeminate in manner or appearance. Their elevated masculinity–femininity scores apparently derived from their openness to their feelings and emotions, a sensitive awareness of self and others, and a wide range of interests. Their interests included many which are regarded as feminine in our culture.

Various researchers have emphasized conflicting motives among the highly creative (MacKinnon, 1960; Palm, 1959; Torrance, 1962) and their ability to tolerate the tensions arising from such conflicts. Torrance depicts the creative person as one who enjoys intense, sustained, and vigorous effort to surmount difficulties and who has a need to dramatize and display his ideas and prove his personal worth. These tendencies are held in check by the creative individual's self-awareness, awareness of the feelings and experiences of others, and detached intellectualization. The total picture is one of a person alive and open to his and others' experiences, who tries to organize and see meaning in them.

HIGHLY CREATIVE ADOLESCENTS

In the study of the personal characteristics of creative children and adolescents, an assumption must be made about the future creativity of the subjects. Retrospective studies of the childhood of creative adults yields some justification for assuming that creativity in childhood and adolescence is predictive of adult creativity. Such an assumption seems warranted, too, in the light of investigations of other psychological variables. Most psychological variables in adults can be seen to have their roots in earlier development and experience. In essence, the quest is for answers to the question, "What are the early signs of adult creativity?"

An investigation of the personality characteristics of highly creative adolescents was conducted by Getzels and Jackson (1962). In this investigation, the adolescents selected for study and comparison were in grades 7 through 12. They were separated into a high-creative group (26 children) and a high-IQ group (28 children), in the manner previously described. When the two were contrasted, some interesting findings resulted.

The values of the two groups appeared to be grossly different. Both groups were given an Outstanding Traits test. Thirteen descriptions of hypothetical children displaying a desirable personality quality or trait were given to the subjects. They were required to rank the thirteen descriptions of children in three ways. First, they ranked the descriptions according to the degree to which they would like to be like the child described. The data from this procedure provided a measure of the "self-ideal" of the subjects. Second, they ranked the descriptions according to the degree to which they believed the various children would succeed in adult life. A "success image" of the subjects was thus obtained. Third, they ranked the descriptions according to the degree to which they believed the children described would be liked by their teachers. This provided a measure of the subjects' "teacher perception."

Analyses of the data revealed that both groups agreed on the qualities that make for adult success in our society and on the qualities which teachers prefer in their students. However, there was little agreement between the two groups about what qualities they wanted for themselves, despite their agreement about the qualities considered desirable by the adult world. The high-IQ group preferred for themselves the personal traits believed to be predictive of adult success. The high-creative group had but little preference for these traits. In other words, the high-creative group seemed not to be highly success-oriented. The high-IQ group preferred traits for themselves that were highly similar to those personal traits they believed to be favored by teachers. Not so the high-creative group. They tended to place high personal value on qualities which they felt teachers value least! "Sense of humor" was ranked near the top, above "high marks," "high IQ," and "goal directedness." The high-IQ group ranked "sense of humor" near the bottom, below high marks, high IQ, and goal directedness. A sense of humor seems to be highly characteristic of creative adolescents and it is expressed in a variety of ways, but both groups perceived the teachers as ranking it rather low. The highly creative adolescents know what makes for conventional success and what teachers like, but there are not necessarily the qualities they want for themselves.

The attempt to determine something of the ultimate goals and aspirations of the two groups made it apparent that there were differences here as well. The techniques used by Getzels and Jackson uncovered differences in both the quantity and quality of occupational goals. The number of occupational possibilities mentioned by the high-creatives was significantly greater than the number mentioned by the high IQ's, nearly twice as many. And the occupational choices of the high-IQ group were more conventional (doctor, lawyer, professor), while the high-creative group made unconventional choices (adventurer, inventor, writer) a significantly greater proportion of the time. In other words, the highly creative adolescents had more diffuse occupational goals. They appeared to be more willing to deal with a greater range of career possibilities, and with careers in which success is problematic. The results of the Getzel and Jackson research with adolescents are fairly generally supported by other workers who find that highly creative adolescents tend to be more intelligent, adventurous, and self-confident than less creative ones. They have a less favorable attitude toward school, with highly creative boys

being more accepted by their peers than are highly creative girls (Kurtzman, 1967).

The same general area of research has been explored by other means
with highly similar findings (Halpin, Payne, & Ellett, 1973). G. Halpin
et al., using biographical data, found that the more creative adolescent
girls regularly read news magazines and other nonrequired reading and
that they often watched television news and special reports. These creative girls enjoyed courses in the sciences and music, and were active in
dramatic and musical groups. They liked their teachers and felt their
high school education had been adequate. They did not often go out on
dates, something which was characteristic of their less creative age mates.
They daydreamed, sometimes felt downcast, and brooded over the
meaning of life more than did their less creative peers.

The results obtained with the male sample were somewhat at variance with those of the girls. The more creative adolescent boys disliked
their teachers and school, did less homework, and were not as academically interested as the girls. They seldom engaged in team sports or
physical activities and disliked physical education. They did enjoy discussion courses and actively took part in questioning the teacher about
topics under discussion. They often wanted to be alone to pursue their
thoughts and were regarded as rather radical and unconventional.

A further investigation (Payne et al., 1975), using the Cattell and
Eber (1962) Sixteen Personality Factor Questionnaire (16PF) and the
What Kind of Person Are You? test (WKPAY) (Torrance & Khatena,
1970), found that the most significant characteristics on the self-report
basis, for an academically talented group of gifted youth, were those of
willingness to experiment, assertiveness, less intelligence, shrewdness,
and reserve. The artistically talented group described themselves as experimenting, assertive, tender-minded, and expedient. The combined
group could be described in these terms as experimenting, assertive, less
intelligent, shrewd, and reserved.

Family background of highly creative adolescents

Data on their subjects' families were obtained by Getzels and Jackson
(1962) with a questionnaire directed at parents and by a two- to three-
hour conference with each mother. Parents of the high-IQ children
tended to have somewhat more education than the parents of high-creative children. Mothers also tended to be housewives more exclusively,
that is, without holding any other jobs. It was the opinion of the interviewers that the parents of the high-IQ children were more insecure than
the parents of the high-creative children, and thus were more concerned

about correct and proper child rearing. Finances and financial hardship were mentioned more frequently in the mother's memory of her own home by the mothers of the high-IQ children than by the mothers of the high-creative children.

Questions about reading habits revealed that the homes of the high-IQ group subscribed to and read more magazines. Specifically they subscribed to more children's magazines and fewer magazines of liberal political comment. The authors observed that the families of the high-IQ children were more conventional, more child-centered, and put greater pressure on the child to do well scholastically.

The mothers of the high-IQ group tended to be somewhat more satisfied with their child-rearing practices than the mothers of the high-creative sample. Getzels and Jackson indicate that these mothers have a right to self-satisfaction if their intent was to rear children who do well in school, accept conventional values, are liked by their teachers, and aspire to careers in the prestige professions. The two groups of mothers differed about the kinds of friends they preferred for their children. The mothers of the high-IQ group tended to emphasize such external factors as good family, good manners, and studiousness. The mothers of the high-creative children valued such attributes in their children's friends as a sense of values, interests, openness, and maturity of interpersonal relations. The family of the high-IQ child was characterized by Getzels and Jackson as one in which individual divergence is limited and risks minimized; the family of the high-creative child as one in which individual divergence is permitted and risks accepted.

A rather extensive study of the biographical correlates of creative personality among gifted adolescents yielded some interesting findings (Halpin, Payne, & Ellett, 1973). They found the parents of the creative gifted adolescents to be less strict, critical, and punitive than the parents of less creative adolescents. They also found that parents of the creative allowed greater freedom. The parents tended to come from high educational, income, and occupational levels. The socio-economic factor was not as important for girls as it was for boys. This suggests that different background factors may have varying influence on the development of creative personality for young men and women.

A detailed study of five creative adolescent artists who were compared with two groups (equally limited in size) of young artists who were not rated as being truly creative, yields descriptions of creative individuals that essentially conform to the data on creative adults and to the Getzels and Jackson reports on creative adolescents (Hammer, 1961). The highly creative young painters, as opposed to the merely facile young painters, showed greater depth of feeling, greater need for self-expression, a greater range of emotions, stronger determination and ambition, more tolerance for discomfort, more independence, more rebelliousness, more self-awareness, and a balance of feminine and masculine components in their natures.

HIGHLY CREATIVE CHILDREN

Studies of the personality characteristics of children who either score high on tests of creativity or are rated high in creativity by their teachers are of great interest to parents, psychologists, and educators. It is understood full well that many young children who are creative will no longer be so at adulthood and that some children who are not classified as creative may turn into creative adults. However, it would seem that children designated as highly creative have a better chance of being creative in later life than those not so designated. If children classified as creative do not turn out to be creative adolescents or young adults, it would also be interesting to determine why this is so. Either way, the study of creativity in children certainly seems justified.

J. S. Renzulli (1973) has suggested the use of various measures of creativity to identify and develop talent among the culturally different and disadvantaged. This relatively untapped reservoir of talent holds great potential for cultural and individual development.

An investigation of the personalities of highly creative children by P. S. Weisberg and K. J. Springer (1961) is reported by Torrance (1962). This was an extensive investigation, using materials from the Minnesota test battery, psychiatric interviews, Rorschachs, and the Draw-a-Family Technique. As compared with less creative children, the highly creative scored higher on strength of self-image, ease of early recall, humor, availability of Oedipal anxiety, and uneven ego development. The more creative children could recall their earlier experiences more readily even when they were unpleasant. Torrance reports that the same highly creative child might love Shakespeare and dolls, and that self-control appropriate to a young adult might be interspersed with impulsive, almost infantile behavior, during one interview.

Projective tests showed a tendency toward unconventional responses and fanciful, imaginative treatment of the material. The results were interpreted as reflecting both a greater independence from the environment and a greater readiness to respond emotionally to it. The creative children were seen as more sensitive and independent than the less creative children. These findings are in essential agreement with those of subsequent investigations of creative children (Singer & Rummo, 1973).

The families of the highly creative children were described as not overly close, with little clinging to one another. There was little stress on conformity to parental values, and the parents' marriage was not a particularly well-adjusted one. Emotion was often openly expressed. Both parents interacted strongly with the creative child, who was allowed to regress. The mothers were sometimes ambivalent toward their children. There was no overevaluation of the child's abilities.

Torrance (1962) conducted a well-controlled investigation of the personalities of a group of elementary school children. He chose the most creative boy and girl from each of twenty-three classes in grades 1 through 6, and matched them with control subjects in sex, IQ, race, classroom teacher, and age. He states, from an analysis of his data, that certain personality characteristics differentiate the highly creative from the less creative children. Teachers and peers agree that the highly creative, especially boys, have wild and silly ideas. Their work is characterized by the production of ideas "off the beaten track, outside the mold," and by humor, playfulness, relative lack of rigidity, and relaxation. These findings are in essential agreement with those of other investigations of the personality traits of creative children and adolescents.

DEVELOPMENT AND FOSTERING OF CREATIVITY

The course of the development of creativity in children in our culture is not an easy one. Torrance (1962, 1965) has been particularly interested in the development of creativity and has studied developmental patterns throughout the elementary grades. Creative children in the early grades often have the reputation among their peers for having silly or naughty ideas and are thought of as wild by their teachers. By the end of the third grade, they have usually learned to keep their wild ideas to themselves and thus some of their originality goes unrecognized and unrewarded. During the subsequent few years, they learn to conform more or less to the conventional demands of the school, but without enthusiasm for the conformity demanded.

Highly creative individuals have a hard time in our school systems. There is much in our culture which puts a premium on conformity and discourages the divergence necessary for creative activity. C. R. Rogers (1959) has listed two general conditions which he considers to be favorable to creative activity: "psychological safety" and "psychological freedom." Acceptance of the individual is one of the most important factors conducive to psychological safety as conceived by Rogers. Creative children, as a group, are aware of those traits which their culture, teachers, and peers value highly, but they do not want these traits for themselves (Getzels & Jackson, 1962; Torrance, 1962). Highly creative individuals recognize that they deviate from the cultural norm. It follows from the very nature of creativity that creative activity must be different; it must be deviant behavior. When acceptance of the person is conditional upon conformity, creative people will be devalued as individuals, and their deviant ideas will be discouraged. A society that provides a wide variety of socially approved roles for its citizens will be acceptant of the deviant creative individual. In a culture that is highly tolerant of a minority of one, the deviant individual can be himself without posing or pretending. He does not feel less worthy because he is different. In a nonthreatening social environment, the creative individual will have a low level of anxiety, and his principal sources of motivation will be the positive satisfactions of exploration and discovery rather than the reduction of anxiety. When the individual feels psychologically safe, he is not afraid to develop and express divergent ideas.

When creative individuals associate with people who are able to understand and appreciate their world, they can be comfortable and need not waste time and energy protecting themselves. They can be divergent without being defensive, nonconformist without suffering social disapproval.

"Psychological freedom" as described by Rogers (1959, 1963) is in many ways a consequence of "psychological safety." The person who is psychologically free:

1. Is able to accept himself for what he is without fear of being laughed at or ridiculed.
2. Can give at least symbolic expression to impulses and thoughts without having to repress, distort, or hide them.
3. Can handle percepts, concepts, and words playfully and in unusual ways without feeling guilty.
4. Sees the unknown and the mysterious either as a serious challenge to be met or as a game to be played.

Studies of highly creative people indicate that the cultural and educational climates in America today are not rewarding creative people commensurately with their potential value to society. These studies suggest that to promote creativity, we need to provide a more friendly and rewarding environment; we must cease equating ideational divergence with mental illness. We will have to recognize the value of a wide diversity of talents, encourage children to perceive things in unconventional ways, increase our tolerance of people who perceive and think in ways that are different from our own, and develop specific methods for teaching and for encouraging creativity.

J. L. Freedman and A. N. Doob (1968) have studied, in an interesting series of experiments, the effects of deviance per se on individual behavior. These investigations were described in chapter 3. Exactly where individuality turns into anxiety-arousing deviancy varies tremendously in different people, circumstances, and dimensions. However, at some point most people begin to be concerned about their deviancy (Steffensmeier & Terry, 1975).

A series of studies by I. Maltzman and his students (Maltzman, Bogarty, & Breger, 1958, 1960; Maltzman, 1960) have experimentally demonstrated that certain procedures consistently facilitate original (uncommon) responses. Specifically, they found that practice in giving unusual responses in free association to a list of words produced an increase in the number of unusual associative responses to a different list of words presented at a later time. They also showed that instructions to give unusual or original responses produced a significant increase in such associative responses. Training in giving unusual word-associative responses also increased performance on an Unusual Uses Test in which the subjects were asked to give as many different uses as they could think of (other than their common, everyday uses) for six common objects. Practice and instructions were both effective in increasing the number of original responses. Practice in giving the same associative responses to words produced a smaller number of original responses to different words at later times. Apparently certain training techniques can significantly decrease originality; different techniques can increase it. Reinforcing unusual responses by saying "good" increases the number of such responses. Similar results have been obtained in a large number of experiments on verbal conditioning. Experimental studies on the training of originality indicate that originality in school children can be increased by instructions, encouragement, and reinforcement. Teacher, parent, peer, and community approval of genuinely original efforts, as suggested by H. Mearns (1958), may be extended to other types of creative endeavor.

SUGGESTIONS ON NURTURING CREATIVITY

To be most effective, the circumstances encouraging creativity must be built into the total context of life. Highly creative activities are nurtured as a way of life rather than by the use of a set of specific devices. Creative activities are fostered by the social climate of the individual's life and are mediated by a complex set of perceptual, conceptual, linguistic, motivational, and attitudinal processes. Some suggestions for the fostering of creative activities follow.[2]

---

[2] Adapted from Sawrey & Telford (1973) Harris & Evans (1974), and others.

Perpetuate curiosity

Children high in curiosity are also generally high in self-esteem. Initially active and highly curious, they have a wealth of experience with their environment, develop competencies, interact successfully with their external world, develop confidence in themselves, and hence have high self-esteem and are potentially creative. Of course, children with initially equivalent levels of active curiosity may find exploration and manipulation of novel situations and objects differentially rewarding because of their environmental circumstances. Children rewarded for curiosity will continue experimenting. Conversely, children who are punished or, for whatever reason, negatively reinforced when investigating new experiences tend to restrict activity, to limit the experiential world, and to fail to develop those competencies that contribute to self-confidence and creativity. Curiosity, self-esteem, and creativity in children are positively related and probably grow and develop together (Maw & Maw, 1970).

Free people from fear of error

Anxiety about the likelihood of making errors hampers originality. Emphasis on the ways in which we learn from errors encourages the playful experimentation with possibilities which is a necessary ingredient of creativity. A relaxed and permissive attitude toward initial errors which are subsequently evaluated and rejected in terms of relevant appropriateness encourages the experimentation with alternative possibilities which is a part of being creatively productive. Labeling errors without providing information leading to correction is minimally useful educationally. Instructional procedures should encourage adventuresomeness and minimize the risks attendant upon exploration. Educational procedures should also maximize the informativeness and minimize the failure component of error.

Encourage fantasy as well as reality-oriented cognition

Just as severe criticism of errors hampers originality, so an insistence that all judgments be closely tied to reality may discourage the play and fanciful experimentation with wild possibilities that are often fruitful. Periods of relaxed, fanciful concoction of extreme possibilities followed by critical evaluation are reported by most creative people as being highly productive. Free movement from fantasy to reality and a mixture of wild spontaneity and critical evaluation should be encouraged.

Encourage contacts with creative people

High levels of creativity require that people accept and appreciate innovations and innovative people. Contact with such people will contribute to this end. Children will strive to maximize their similarity to others who possess traits or command goals they admire. The child desiring intangible goals and not knowing how to realize them will try to attain these goals by becoming like adult models who possess or command these characteristics or goals (Harris & Evans, 1974). Although the highly creative children are less sociable than others, they will often profit from the permissive and rewarding atmosphere provided by the laboratory, workshop, or studio of a highly accomplished and admired person.

Encourage diversity and individuality

Evidence indicates fairly consistently that most people find their own and others' deviancies in thought and action threatening. A culture, subculture, and family which by precept, as well as by verbal commitment, value diversity and accept and appreciate differences will provide a social environment conducive to high creativity.

Encourage individual initiative

Providing maximum opportunities for individual study, permitting each learner to proceed at his own rate, and providing flexibility in laboratory and field experiences all nurture the basic components of creative activities.

Avoid stereotyping the potentially creative

It is hard to see the member of a socially stigmatized group as having potential for creativity. However, while it is true that the statistical probability that recognized creativity will occur in the disadvantaged is less than the probability of its occurrence among the more advantaged, the history of mankind repeatedly documents that a potential Leonardo da Vinci, Isaac Newton, Ludwig von Beethoven, or Albert Einstein may exist in a Hindu untouchable, the son of a slave, or a child in the ghetto. A realization of our verbal commitment to equality of social, economic, and educational opportunity will increase the likelihood that such potential will be realized.

SUMMARY

Concern with the development and encouragement of creativity has become widespread in our culture. Government, industry, and education all want to identify and develop creativity. Rapid technological advances have made routine problem-solving the province of machines. People can be free from this drudgery to engage in more productive and creative enterprise.

Creativity may be defined in two essentially differing frames of reference. The personal and phenomenological frame of reference results in an emphasis on the subjective originality of response: If it is novel, new, or different for the individual, it is creative. Creativity may also be defined in the light of its end-product: To be creative, the innovation must not only be novel to the individual, but useful and novel to the culture as well. The emphasis in this chapter has been largely on the latter concept. Originality is usually designated as being an essential part of creativity, but it does not involve social recognition. Originality becomes, then, more amenable to laboratory investigation than does creativity.

A variety of means have been employed to identify highly creative individuals. In the identification of creative adults, a method of nomination by peers can be used or a listing of culturally relevant productions can be made. Identifying creative children is more tenuous. Teachers may make nominations, or tests designed to measure originality can be employed. A great deal of effort has gone into the development of tests of creativity for both children and adults. The criteria for creativity seem to be elusive, especially for creativity among children and adolescents. Long-range studies should improve the validity of measures being developed.

The relationship between measured intelligence (IQ) and creativity over the entire range of both variables is not known. Low positive estimates of the size of the correlation may be unrealistically low. Some intelligence is obviously essential for creative activity, but a high level of intelligence does not guarantee creativity. The concept of creativity may encompass a host of individual differences among the gifted.

The personalities of creative adults have been investigated by a number of researchers. The descriptions of the highly creative are complicated, and attention must be paid to the area of creative activity in order to present a meaningful composite of creative persons, even within a given discipline. Tests of creativity have been devised and given to groups of children and adolescents. Descriptions of children and adolescents thus designated as highly creative were presented.

Procedures for fostering creativity in children and adults were suggested. These procedures should interest parents and educators.

REFERENCES

ARASTEH, J. D., "Creativity and Related Processes in Young Children: A Review of the Literature," *Journal of Genetic Psychology*, 1968, *112*, 77–108.

BARRON, F., *Creativity and Psychological Health* (New York: Van Nostrand Reinhold, 1963).

BARRON, F., "The Dream of Art and Poetry," *Psychology Today*, 1968, 2 (7), 18–23, 66.

BARRON, F., et al., *New Directions in Psychology*, vol. 2 (New York: Holt, Rinehart and Winston, 1965).

BURT, C., "Creativity and Intelligence," *British Journal of Educational Psychology*, 1962, *32*, 292–98.

CATTELL, R. B., *Objective-Analytic Test Battery* (Champaign, Ill.: Institute for Personality and Ability Testing, 1956).

CATTELL, R. B., & J. E. DREVDAHL, "A Comparison of the Personality Profile of Eminent Researchers with That of Eminent Teachers and Administrators and That of the General Population," *British Journal of Psychology*, 1955, *46*, 248–61.

CATTELL, R. B., & H. W. EBER, *Handbook for the Sixteen Personality Factor Questionnaire* (Champaign, Ill.: Institute for Personality and Ability Testing, 1962).

CLARK, P. M., & H. L. MIRELS, "Fluency as a Pervasive Element in the Measurement of Creativity," *Educational Measure*, 1970, 7, 83–86.

COX, C., "The Early Mental Traits of 300 Geniuses," in *Genetic Studies in Genius*, vol. 2 (Stanford, Ca.: Stanford University Press, 1926).

CROCKENBERG, S. B., "Creativity Tests: A Boon or Boondoggle for Education," *Review of Educational Research*, 1972, *42*, 27–46.

CROPLEY, A. J., "A Five-year Longitudinal Study of the Validity of Creativity Tests," *Developmental Psychology*, 1972, *6*, 119–24.

DE MILLE, R., & P. R. MERRIFIELD, "Creativity and Intelligence," *Educational Psychology Measurement*, 1962, *22*, 803–8.

FREEDMAN, J. L., & A. N. DOOB, *Deviancy: The Psychology of Being Different* (New York: Academic Press, 1968).

GETZELS, J. W., & P. W. JACKSON, *Creativity and Intelligence* (New York: John Wiley, 1962).

GOUGH, H. G., "Techniques for Identifying the Creative Research Scientist," in D. W. MacKinnon, ed., *The Creative Person* (Berkeley: University of California Extension, 1961).

GUILFORD, J. P., "Creativity," *American Psychologist*, 1950, *5*, 444–54.

GUILFORD, J. P., "Traits of Creativity," in H. H. Anderson, ed., *Creativity and Its Cultivation* (New York: Harper & Row, 1959).

GUILFORD, J. P., & P. R. MERRIFIELD, *The Structure of Intellect Model: Its Uses and Implications*, Report of the Psychology Laboratory, No. 24. (Los Angeles: University of Southern California, 1960).

HALPIN, G., D. A. PAYNE, & C. P. ELLETT, "Biographical Correlates of the Creative Personality: Gifted Adolescents," *Exceptional Children*, 1973, *39*, 652–53.

HAMMER, E. G., *Creativity* (New York: Random House, 1961).

HARRIS, M. B., & R. C. EVANS, "The Effects of Modeling and Instruction on Creative Responses," *Journal of Psychology*, 1974, *86*, 3–11.

HARVEY, O. J., J. K. HOFFMEISTER; C. COATES; & B. J. WHITE, "A Partial Evaluation of Torrance's Test of Creativity," *American Educational Research Journal*, 1970, *7*, 359–72.

HOLLAND, J. L., "Creative and Academic Performance Among Talented Adolescents," *Journal of Educational Psychology*, 1961, *52*, 136–47.

HUDSON, L., *Contrary Imaginations* (London: Methuen 1966).

JACKSON, P. W., & S. MESSICK, "The Person, the Product, and the Response: Conceptual Problems in the Assessment of Creativity," in J. Kagan, ed., *Creativity and Learning* (Boston: Houghton Mifflin, 1967).

KAGAN, J., ed., *Creativity and Learning* (Boston: Houghton Mifflin, 1967).

KOGAN, N., "Creativity and Cognitive Style: A Life Span Perspective," in P. B. Baltes & K. W. Schaie, eds., *Life-span Developmental Psychology: Personality and Socialization* (New York: Academic Press, 1973).

KOGAN, N., & E. PANKOVE, "Creative Ability for a Five-year Span," *Child Development*, 1972, *43*, 427–42.

KOGAN, N., & E. PANKOVE, "Long-term Predictive Validity of Divergent-thinking Tests: Some Negative Evidence," *Journal of Educational Psychology*, 1974, *68*, 802–10.

KURTZMAN, K. A., "A Study of School Attitudes, Peer Acceptance and Personality of Creative Adolescents," *Exceptional Children*, 1967, *34*, 157–62.

MACKINNON, D. W., "Fact and Fancy in Personality Research," *American Psychologist*, 1953, *8*, 138–46.

MACKINNON, D. W., "What Do We Mean by Talent and How Do We Test for It?" in *The Search for Talent* (Princeton, N.J.: College Entrance Examination Board, 1960).

MACKINNON, D. W., "The Nature and Nurture of Creative Talent," *American Psychologist*, 1962, *17*, 484–95.

McNEMAR, Q., "Lost: Our Intelligence? Why?" *American Psychologist*, 1964, *19*, 871–82.

MALTZMAN, I., "On the Training of Originality," *Psychological Review*, 1960, *67*, 229–42.

MALTZMAN, I., W. BOGARTY, & L. BREGER, "A Procedure for Increasing Word Association Originality and Its Transfer Effects," *Journal of Experimental Psychology*, 1958, *56*, 392–98.

MALTZMAN, I., W. BOGARTY, & L. BREGER, "Experimental Studies in the Training of Originality," *Psychological Monograph*, 1960, *74* (493).

MARSH, R. W., "A Statistical Re-analysis of Getzels and Jackson's Data," *British Journal of Educational Psychology*, 1964, *34*, 91–93.

MARTINDALE, C., "What Makes Creative People Different," *Psychology Today*, 1975, *9* (2), 44–50.

MASLOW, A. H., "Creativity in Self-actualizing People," in H. H. Anderson, ed., *Creativity and Its Cultivation* (New York: Harper & Row, 1959).

MASLOW, A. H., *Motivation and Personality*, 2nd ed. (New York: Harper & Row, 1970).

MAW, W. H., & E. W. MAW, "Self Concepts of High and Low Curiosity Boys," *Child Development*, 1970, *41*, 123–29.

MEARNS, H., *Creative Power: The Education of Youth in the Creative Arts* (New York: Dover Publications, 1958).

MEDNICK, S., "The Associative Basis of the Creative Process," *Psychological Review*, 1962, *69*, 220–32.

MULLENER, N., & J. I. LAIRD, "Some Developmental Changes in the Organization of Self Evaluation," *Developmental Psychology*, 1971, *5*, 233–36.

NICHOLLS, J. G., "Creativity in the Person Who Will Never Produce Anything Original and Useful: The Concept of Creativity as a Normally Distributed Trait," *American Psychologist*, 1972, *27*, 717–27.

PALM, H. J., "An Analysis of Test-score Differences Between Highly Creative and High Miller Analogies Members of the Summer Guidance Institute," Research Memo., BER-59-13 (Minneapolis: Bureau of Educational Research, University of Minnesota, 1959).

PAYNE, D. A.; W. G. HALPIN; C. D. ELLETT; & J. B. DALE, "General Personality Correlates of Creative Personality in Academically and Artistically Gifted Youth," *The Journal of Special Education*, 1975, *9*, 105–8

RENZULLI, J. S., "Talent Potential in Minority Group Students," *Exceptional Children*, 1973, *39*, 437–44.

RIPPLE, R. E., & F. B. MAY, "Caution in Comparing Creativity and I.Q.," *Psychological Reports*, 1962, *10*, 229–30.

ROCK, D. A., F. R. EVANS, & S. P. KLEIN, "Predicting Multiple Criteria of Creative Achievements with Moderator Variables," *Journal of Educational Measurements*, 1969, *6* (4), 229–36.

ROGERS, C. R., "Toward a Theory of Creativity," in H. H. Anderson, ed., *Creativity and Its Cultivation* (New York: Harper & Row, 1959).

ROGERS, C. R., "Learning to Be Free," *National Education Association Journal*, 1963, *52*, 28–31.

SAWREY, J. M., & C. W. TELFORD, *Educational Psychology*, 4th ed. (Boston: Allyn & Bacon, 1973).

SAWREY, J. M., & C. W. TELFORD, *Adjustment and Personality*, 4th ed. (Boston: Allyn & Bacon, 1975).

SHAYCOFT, M. F., et al., *Project Talent: Studies of a Complete Age Group Age 15* (Pittsburgh: University of Pittsburgh, 1963; mimeographed).

SINGER, D. L., & J. RUMMO, "Ideational Creativity and Behavioral Style in Kindergarten-age Children," *Developmental Psychology*, 1973, *8*, 154–61.

STEFFENSMEIER, D. J., & R. A. TERRY, eds., *Examining Deviance Experimentally* (Port Washington, N.Y.: Alfred, 1975).

STEIN, M., & S. HEINZE, *Creativity and the Individual* (New York: Free Press, 1960).

TAYLOR, C. W., ed., *The Third (1959) University of Utah Research Conference on the Identification of Creative Scientific Talent* (Salt Lake City: University of Utah Press, 1959).

TAYLOR, C. W., "Identifying the Creative Individual," in E. P. Torrance, ed., *Creativity: Second Minneapolis Conference on Gifted Children* (Minneapolis: Center for Continuation Study, University of Minnesota, 1960).

TAYLOR, C. W., & F. BARRON, *Scientific Creativity: Its Recognition and Development* (New York: John Wiley 1963).

TAYLOR, C. W., & J. S. HOLLAND, "Development 32 and Application of Tests of Creativity," *Reviews of Educational Research,* 1962, *32,* 91–102.

TAYLOR, C. W., et al., "Explorations in the Measurement and Predictions of Contributions of One Sample of Scientists," USAF ASD technical report, 61–96 (Washington, D.C., 1961).

TERMAN, L. M., & M. H. ODEN, *The Gifted Group at Mid-life* (Stanford, Ca.: Stanford University Press, 1959).

TORRANCE, E. P., *Guiding Creative Talent* (Englewood Cliffs, N.J.: Prentice-Hall, 1962).

TORRANCE, E. P., *Rewarding Creative Behavior* (Englewood Cliffs, N.J.: Prentice-Hall, 1965).

TORRANCE, E. P., *Torrance Tests of Creativity* (Princeton, N.J.: Personnel Press, 1966).

TORRANCE, E. P., "Predictive Validity of the Torrance Tests of Creative Thinking," *Journal of Creative Behavior,* 1972, *6,* 236–52.

TORRANCE, E. P., & J. KHATENA, "What Kind of Person Are You?" *Gifted Child Quarterly,* 1970, *14,* 71–75.

VANCE, E. T., "Social Disability," *American Psychologist,* 1973, *28,* 498–511.

WALLACH, M. A., "Review of Torrance Tests of Creative Thinking," *American Educational Research Journal,* 1968, *5,* 272–81.

WALLACH, M. A., "Creativity," in P. H. Mussen, ed., *Carmichael's Manual of Child Psychology,* vol. 1 (New York: John Wiley, 1971).

WARD, W. C., "Creativity in Young Children," *Child Development,* 1968, *39,* 737–54.

WARD, W. C., N. KOGAN, & E. PANKOVE, "Incentive Effects in Children's Creativity" *Child Development,* 1973, *43,* 669–76.

WEISBERG, P. S. & K. J. SPRINGER, "Environmental Factors Influencing Creative Function in Gifted Children" (Cincinnati: Department of Psychiatry, Cincinnati General Hospital, 1961; mimeographed).

Chapter 8

The mentally retarded:
Some general considerations

DEFINITIONS

The American Association on Mental Deficiency proposes the following definition of mental retardation: "Mental retardation refers to significantly sub-average general intellectual functioning existing concurrently with deficits in adaptive behavior, and manifested during the developmental period" (Grossman, 1973). This definition is very different from the older ones. F. A. Doll (1941), in a widely quoted statement, indicated six criteria essential to an adequate definition of mental deficiency: (1) Social incompetence, (2) due to mental subnormality, (3) resulting from developmental arrest, which (4) obtains at maturity, (5) is of constitutional origin, and (6) is essentially incurable.

Although Doll's definition is more than a quarter of a century old and official definitions and conceptions of mental subnormality have been greatly changed in the interval, many popular ideas of mental retardation reflect this type of definition. This is particularly true of the last two components—constitutional origin and incurability.

According to the AAMD all three conditions—subnormal intellectual functioning, originating during the developmental period, and impairment of adaptive behavior—must be present for a person to be designated mentally retarded. Persons cannot be labeled mentally retarded just because their adaptive behavior is impaired. There are many causes other than mental retardation for slow maturational development, poor school progress, and inadequate social and vocational adjustment. Persons likewise cannot be designated as mentally retarded solely because of a low IQ. A low IQ, plus impaired adaptive behavior, which originates before maturity, are all required.

The AAMD's definition is stated in functional terms—impairment in adaptive behavior and low level of intellectual functioning. This impairment may take the forms of: (1) maturational retardation as in-dictated by slowness in acquiring skills such as sitting, crawling, standing, walking, talking, habit training, and interacting with age peers; (2) deficiencies in learning, principally poor academic achievement; and (3) inadequate social adjustment, principally adult social and economic inadequacy. The individual's adequacy of adjustment must be judged in relation to that of his peers. This definition makes "mental retardation" a term descriptive of the current status of the individual's adaptive behavior and functional level, irrespective of etiology or curability.

This AAMD definition, as well as several older ones, refers to the current functional status of the individual rather than to any inferred "potential" or future condition. A person may function sufficiently subnormally to meet the criteria at one time in life and not do so at some other time. A person's status may change as the result of changes in his level of intellectual functioning, changes in his level of adaptive behavior, or changes in the demands and expectations of the culture in which he lives. Retardation is purely descriptive of current condition and does not necessarily imply either prognosis or etiology.

Mental retardation is neither a disease nor a medical syndrome with a specific cause. There are more than a hundred specific identified causes. Mentally retarded individuals may function subnormally because of genetic factors (single gene, polygenes, or chromosomal aberrations); organic deficits of environmental origin (infections, toxins, physical trauma, diet, gestational disorders, or irradiation levels); or the social and psychosocial conditions of their lives. Even though the etiologies of mental subnormality are numerous, in the majority of cases the exact causes are not known. In most cases, care, treatment, and educational training procedures are not related to etiology. They are related more directly to the individual's level of functioning and his unique patterns of abilities and disabilities than to what caused his condition. Of course, etiology is of paramount importance when the primary concern is prevention rather than remediation and treatment.

Current definitions and conceptions of mental retardation say nothing about curability. Only within the framework of a medical model of mental retardation is this term appropriate. Remediation is always relative to current medical, rehabilitative, and educational methodology. All current programs for the care, treatment, training, and education of the mentally retarded assume that, by appropriate means, the functional levels of these individuals can be significantly altered. Present information concerning a child's current level of functioning, as well as test scores, are used in choosing or devising treatment programs which will maximize the individual's personal and social effectiveness.

IDENTIFICATION OF THE MENTALLY RETARDED

The AAMD definition of mental retardation assumes a psychometric criterion for the determination of the level of intellectual functioning, developmental information to indicate maturational status, school records to indicate learning ability, and evidence of social and economic competence to serve as an index of social adjustment when the person involved is an adult. Socio-economic competence may also be evaluated by various adaptive behavior scales.

The psychometric criterion

With the advent of intelligence testing, psychometric criteria came to the fore as diagnostic of mental retardation. The first individual intelligence tests were developed as a means of identifying the mentally retarded so that instructions could be adapted to their stage of mental development. Although at one time mental retardation was defined in terms of either perceived adaptive behavior or test scores, this is no longer true. In practice, psychometric criteria are invoked only when deficiencies of adaptive behavior are judged to be sufficient to indicate possible mental retardation.

The adaptive behavior criterion

Adaptive behavior is defined as "the effectiveness or degree with which the individual meets the standards of personal independence and social responsibility expected of his age and cultural group" (Grossman, 1973). During infancy and early childhood, deficits in adaptive behavior may be reflected in:

1. Sensori-motor skills (turning, creeping, walking, manual manipulations).
2. Communication skills (social smiling, gesturing, speaking).
3. Self-help skills (eating, dressing, toileting, bathing).
4. Socialization (playing imitatively, playing with others cooperatively or in parallel depending upon age).

During childhood and early adolescence, deficits in adaptive behavior may be reflected in:

1. Academic learning.
2. Judgment and reasoning in dealing with the environment.
3. Social skills (participation in group activities and effective interpersonal relationships).

In late adolescence and adulthood, deficits in adaptive behavior may be reflected in:

1. Vocational competence.
2. Family and social duties.

Adaptive behavior　　Many current discussions imply that the concept of adaptive behavior as a criterion of mental retardation is new (Hobbs, 1975; Leland, 1974; Nihira, 1973). However, a historical survey of definitions and descriptions of this condition discloses that it is essentially a new term for an old concept. Almost from the beginnings of professional concern with subnormal intellectual functioning, there has been either an implicit or an explicit assumption that personal-social competence, the level of behavioral adaptation to one's environment, is the ultimate criterion of mental retardation. In essence, this means that irrespective of the extent of neural damage or deficits in the intellectual sphere, no person can be considered mentally retarded (mentally deficient, mentally defective, mentally subnormal, or feebleminded) unless his personal and socio-economic competence is significantly inferior to that of the majority of his peers. Of course, there is always the assumed or stated limitation that such demonstrated incompetence is the result of intellectual retardation. In other words, historically as now, the dual standard of both personal-social incompetence *and* mental subnormality was necessary to warrant a diagnosis of mental retardation.

The British psychiatrist, Charles Mercier, remarked in 1890 that though a person be extremely dull and stupid, he cannot be considered mentally retarded if he is able by his own efforts to maintain a standard of living appropriate to his social class. Only when his intellectual deficiency is so extreme as to make him socially incompetent can he be judged mentally retarded. A. F. Tredgold (1908), the author of what was for half a century the most influential English-language textbook in the field, defined mental retardation—he called it *amentia*—as "a state of incomplete mental development of such a kind and degree that the individual is incapable of adapting himself to the normal environment of his fellows in such a way as to maintain existence independent of supervision, external control or support." Even after the advent of mental testing, Tredgold (1952) rejected educational and intelligence test scores as adequate criteria of mental retardation. He insisted that social competence was the only logical criterion that the community can justly impose. Before the use of intelligence tests, the various degrees of deficiency were identified purely in terms of personal competence and achievement.

Thus, according to Tredgold, adult idiots are unable to guard themselves against common dangers, understand only the simplest commands, and cannot articulate beyond a few monosyllables (Tredgold, 1952). A. Binet and T. Simon similarly characterized an idiot as a person who is not able to communicate with his fellows by means of language: "He is unable to learn to talk and does not understand language" (quoted in Peterson, 1925). Tredgold stated that imbeciles, although superior to idiots, are incapable of managing themselves or their affairs. "They are capable of learning to perform simple tasks under supervision, but incapable of earning their living or contributing materially toward their own support." According to Binet and Simon, "The imbecile is a person who is incapable of communicating with his fellows by means of written language: he is unable to read, comprehend the written word, or to write meaningfully" (Peterson, 1925).

Morons—"feebleminded" in British terminology—are individuals whose mental defectiveness is less than that of imbecility but who require care, supervision, and control for their own protection (Tredgold, 1952). Tredgold further characterizes them as capable of earning a living under favorable circumstances, but incapable because of mental limitations of competing on equal terms with their fellows, or of managing themselves and their affairs with ordinary prudence. Binet's description of this degree of defectiveness is essentially the same. Personal-social incompetence has repeatedly been claimed to be the basically definitive characteristic of mental retardation.

Despite the claim commonly made that mental test scores are today the *primary definitive data* used in identifying and diagnosing mental retardation, we do not believe this to be true. Except in rare instances, the initial identification of an individual as possibly or probably mentally retarded is never based on test performance. In practice, marked developmental retardation during the preschool period, repeated school failure during the school years, and evidence of gross personal-social incompetence as an adult are the initial observations which lead to the administration of mental tests to determine if levels of intellectual and achievement test performances *are consistent with* a diagnosis of mental retardation. Although verification, by means of psychometric devices, of the initial assessment of the individual as mentally retarded because of his achievement deficiencies is perceived as a kind of medical-model diagnosis, its real purpose is to determine eligibility for special treatment. This treatment may be special educational placement or assistance, social services, vocational rehabilitation programs, supervised living in a group home, sheltered workshop placement, or—when referred by courts because of delinquency—diminished responsibility and institutionalization instead of a prison sentence. The following case is typical of individuals in which the observed deficiency in adaptive behavior is in the preschool period (developmental retardation).

Developmental retardation in mental subnormality

Karen's mother recalls that as an infant her daughter seemed to be quite normal physically. However, at six months she felt that Karen did not respond as her older sister had at the same age. She did not sit up by herself and when her mother sat her up, she just toppled over. At her next regular medical check-up, Karen's mother asked her pediatrician if something was wrong. He assured her that Karen was possibly a little slow in maturing, but it was nothing to worry about. Karen was slow in creeping and crawling and when she could neither stand alone nor walk at eighteen months she was taken to another pediatrician, who told her mother that her bones were too weak to support her weight. Thyroid therapy was tried, but it did not help.

Karen's parents really began to worry when at age two, when other children her age were beginning to talk, their daughter was still cooing and gurgling but had no real speech. Frantically, they trundled Karen from physician to physician and from clinic to clinic seeking reassurance that she was normal. They received no real assistance nor a positive diagnosis, possibly because they focused on speech and walking as the areas of concern. Karen's mother spent endless hours trying to teach her to walk and talk.

Karen's parents were pleased when she was toilet trained effortlessly at three years. At the same age Karen took her first halting steps. Between three and four she began to say single words. At this time Karen's parents really suspected that she was mentally retarded, but no one who had examined her had mentioned the word. When they finally asked their pediatrician if she was retarded, he said he really did not know and referred them to a psychologist. When the pediatrician received the word from the psychologist that the patient was severely retarded—her Stanford-Binet IQ was 46—his advice was immediate institutionalization.

Karen's mother says, "Although for the past two years I was sure that something was wrong, I had focused on the physical disabilities alone. None of the doctors had mentioned mental retardation and I don't know when I first started linking the concept with my child's condition, but I finally asked my pediatrician if she was mentally retarded. I hoped he wouldn't say 'yes' but at the same time I wanted to know, one way or the other."

When the pediatrician told Karen's mother of the psychologist's diagnosis, she left his office in tears. Heartsick, she took her daughter home. The parents accepted the diagnosis but rejected the suggestion to institutionalize. Friends and relatives continued to hint that Karen would be better off in an institution. However, her parents coolly ignored the hints and made plans to take care of her at home.

The learning-ability criterion

Formal education is part of our culture, and intellectual achievement has considerable prestige value. Intellectual skills are also a prerequisite to admittance to many trades and professions. The individual who does not progress in school has failed in an important social area. The school situation is also the first place in which objective comparisons are systematically made, and the child finds himself in a rather definite position in a prestige hierarchy based largely on intellectual achievements.

Failure in school is often the first symptom of inadequate intellectual functioning. In view of this, school failure, when not the result of sensory or motor handicaps, severe emotional disturbance, or absence from school, is considered to indicate mental retardation. Two or three years' retardation in school achievement, in the absence of other causes, has traditionally been considered indicative of possible mental retardation. The following case is fairly typical of such individuals.

Kirk was not diagnosed as mentally retarded until he was eleven years old. His developmental history was not exceptional. There were minor feeding problems in infancy. He did not walk until he was nineteen months old. He had frequent earaches during early childhood and his hearing in one ear is moderately impaired. His preschool behavior seems to have been within the normal range. Explicit limitation became evident only in school achievement. Kirk's school history was an accumulation of school failures, repeated grades, and social promotions. There were no special disciplinary problems.

In the first grade, Kirk's teacher noted "immaturity, slowness, and inattentiveness to school tasks." In the second grade his school record indicated "failure to learn to read and lack of number concepts." The parents agreed to Kirk's retention in the second grade. However, his repetition of second grade did not improve his reading and arithmetic skills. He was promoted yearly for the next three years, but his school performance continued on a low level. Kirk was kept in the regular classroom with no special remedial help during this period.

Kirk was described by his teachers as personable and well accepted by the other students. His attitude toward teacher and school was cooperative. He seemed to have no special personality or emotional problems. His first- and second-grade teachers felt that he was capable of doing better than he did. However, the notes left by teachers for the next three years indicated that they suspected mental retardation. At the age of eleven, after a conference of his present and former teachers, the school nurse, and his principal, Kirk was referred to the school psychologist as possibly mentally retarded.

The psychologist found that Kirk read at about a second-grade level. His sight vocabulary was third-grade. His spelling was commensurate with his reading. His spelling errors showed little appreciation of letter-sound associations. He had little understanding of vowel sounds—a second-grade skill. His arithmetic skills were also about second-grade.

On the Stanford-Binet test he obtained an IQ of 62. His specific weaknesses noted in the test situation were (a) general comprehension, (b) inability to handle abstract concepts, (c) difficulty in reasoning and in drawing inferences, and (d) deficiency in dealing with relationships. His strengths were his cooperativeness, his persistence in tasks even after he became aware of errors, and his eagerness to please. Kirk was judged eligible for special class placement, and following a case conference with his parents he was so placed.

At ages fourteen and seventeen Kirk's status was reassessed. At the latter age his academic achievement level was about fourth grade and his IQ was 65—a nonsignificant change. In the three-year interim between fourteen and seventeen Kirk had shown no significant change in achievement level. It was evident that he had reached a plateau in achievement level, and his parents agreed that he should drop out of school. During the following year, Kirk stayed at home. He then returned voluntarily to be placed in the work-study program, a cooperative program between the local schools and the state division of vocational rehabilitation.

Because of Kirk's advanced age and positive personality assets he was assigned full-time job placement with weekly evening training-counseling sessions under adult education auspices. His work-training placement was as stockboy in a grocery store. The school psychologist and counselor agreed that his training should include the development of specific arithmetic skills, improving his handwriting, budgeting, learning how to establish and maintain a savings account, and general work habits. Kirk was jointly supervised by the school's vocational program coordinator and the vocational rehabilitation counselor. Kirk seemed to be doing well. His attitude toward his work and supervisors was excellent. After three months on the job, Kirk felt he should be making more money and began talking about getting a better job. Kirk's counselors encouraged him to stay where he was for a while, and he now seems satisfied to do so. We would predict reasonable success for Kirk in similar work situations.

Kirk's case is typical of the mildly mentally retarded. Physically, they do not differ significantly from their more academically able peers. They may be a little slow, but within the range of normal preschool development. They become identified as mentally retarded only after marked and persistent academic deficiencies and verification by test scores. They continue to be so labeled until they leave school by dropping out or by "graduating." Most of them manage to find jobs, and to a degree they succeed and merge into the general population. Kirk's intellectual limitations are counterbalanced by his pleasing personality, good grooming, and good work habits. He will probably attain and maintain an acceptable minimal level of socio-economic competence.

The social-adjustment criterion

Although it has limitations, the test of social adequacy is the most basic of all. It is the elementary datum from which we start in establishing the fact of mental retardation.

Technically, the subject of the following case wou d not be mentally retarded according to the current AAMD definition, since her condition did not develop before maturity. However, historically, such individuals have been so classified since they function similarly to those retarded from childhood, so we shall use it as an example.

Mrs. J. was referred to the senior author by the Social Welfare office because of suspected mental subnormality. The record showed Mrs. J. to be fifty-five years of age, but she looked and acted at least twenty years older. According to the case worker, Mrs. J.'s husband had recently died and she had been left alone and destitute. Consequently, she had been placed on welfare under the supervision of the caseworker.

The social worker found that Mrs. J. was unable to care for herself. Physical examinations had disclosed nothing organically wrong. She seemed fairly well oriented and showed no psychotic symptoms. So, largely by a process of exclusion, mental retardation was suspected and she was referred for psychological evaluation.

The behavior that was considered indicative of mental deficiency included failure to keep herself and her house clean or to cook, inability to keep accounts or to make change, tendency to become lost when she went uptown alone, and the habit of talking childishly. Mrs. J. was brought to the office by her social worker and told to stay there until the social worker returned to take her home. The interview and tests verified the social worker's characterization of the client, except for some inconsistencies. Her vocabulary was largely that of an adult, but the things she said were childish. She could talk about her daughter who had married and moved away, but could not remember her current address. She could remember correctly her place and date of birth, but not her social worker's name. She could remember her recipe for making a cake, but, according to her social worker, would forget that she had placed it in the oven to bake.

The author's initial impression was that Mrs. J. acted like a senile person, and he asked the social worker to verify her age. She seemed closer to eighty than to fifty. Her age was verified as fifty-five.

When a Stanford-Binet test was administered, Mrs. J. obtained a mental age of five years and four months. However, her vocabulary was only slightly below the twelve-year level. On the Goodenough Draw-a-Man test she obtained a mental age of six. Her test scores were consistent with a diagnosis of mental retardation, and her score pattern was characteristic of a person who had previously functioned at a higher level but had deteriorated.

The test performances and subjective impression were indicative of marked mental retardation sufficient to require care and supervision. There was evidence that the client had previously functioned at a much higher level and seemed to be suffering from a premature senility. At that time the author was unfamiliar with Alzheimer's and Pick's diseases, both of which are premature senile conditions characterized by progressive mental deterioration (Burian, 1974). Both are associated with the deterioration of localized areas of the brain; the causes are unknown. Mrs. J. seemed to fit the clinical descriptions of these disorders.

This case is typical of those in which the initial assessment of possible mental retardation in adulthood is made on the basis of deficiencies in personal-social competences, which are then verified or refuted by tests.

MEASURES OF ADAPTIVE BEHAVIOR

Those persons who perceive of the adaptive behavior criterion of mental retardation as being of recent origin are thinking of the formal AAMD 1959 definition and the development of scales for its measurement. The first of these scales was the Vineland Social Maturity Scale developed by Doll (1936, 1953). The Vineland scale is a schedule of 117 items of habitual activities ranging from infantile behavior, such as a baby's laugh and coo, to adult levels involving community activities. The items are arranged into eight loosely defined categories: general self-help, self-help in dressing, self-help in eating, communication, self-direction, social-ization, locomotion, and occupation. The required information is elicited in a semistructured interview with a parent, teacher, attendant, or other person who is intimately acquainted with the child. A social quotient (SQ) comparable to the intelligence quotient (IQ) can be obtained. The standardization of the scale is inadequate; however, because of the need for information of the sort the scale was devised to measure, it has been widely used. There is a substantial correlation between Stanford-Binet IQ's and Vineland SQ's, ranging from .40 to .80 depending on the heterogeneity of the group (Hurst, 1962).

In 1963 L. F. Cain, S. Levine, and F. F. Elzey published a social competency scale for use with trainable mentally retarded children (roughly, IQ's from 25 to 59). It was standardized on 716 mentally retarded children aged five to fourteen. The Cain-Levine Scale consists of 44 items divided into four subscales: self-help, initiative, social skills, and communication. Subscore and total scores can be converted into percentile scores based on the norms for trainable mentally retarded children.

A project sponsored by the AAMD produced two adaptive behavior scales, one for children three through twelve and the other for those thirteen through adult. These scales deal with the areas of independent functioning (feeding oneself, toilet training, dressing oneself); personal responsibility (staying alone in the house, playing without direction or supervision, running errands, taking care of pets); and social responsibility (observing traffic lights, looking out for the safety of others) (Nihira et al., 1969; Leland, 1974). The scales provide scores on separate aspects of adaptive behavior, which can be combined to provide a measure of an individual's overall level of adaptive behavior. Adaptive level is categorized into four subgroups ranging from almost complete lack of adaptation to near normal (Grossman, 1973). N. M. Lambert, M. R. Wilcox, and W. P. Gleason (1975) have provided a standardization of this scale. One study using this scale found a correlation of +.75 between IQ and adaptive scale score for 126 institutionalized mentally retarded persons. Correlation between achievement test scores and IQ ranged from .26 to .50. Adaptive behavior scale scores did not correlate significantly with achievement test scores (Malone & Christian, 1974).

E. E. Balthazar (1971) has constructed a scale of adaptive behavior for use with the severely and profoundly mentally retarded that covers a wider range of behavior than do the other scales. It also differs from the others in insisting upon the use of direct observation rather than second-hand information. Scores on this scale can be translated into percentile scores based on the performances of 451 institutionalized individuals ranging in IQ from below 20 to 35. Balthazar suggests that the scale be used in planning training programs designed to increase the functional level of the mentally retarded. This scale correlates between .59 and .67 with the Vineland Scale, indicating a moderate degree of commonality.

A Social Competency Inventory for adults has been published by K. M. Banham (1968). Comprehensive Behavior Checklist, compiled by J. M. Gardner (1970); Adaptive Behavior Checklist, by R. M. Allen, A. D. Cortazzo, and C. Adams (1970); and Fairview Self-Help Scale, by R. T. Ross (1969), are similar instruments which are now available. J. R. Mercer (1973) more recently has developed a measure of adaptive behavior (Adaptive Behavior Inventory for Children) consisting of 28 age-grade subscales. This scale draws heavily on the work of Doll (1953) and A. Gesell (1948), especially for the younger years.

Uses of the adaptive behavior scales

While the original purpose of the scales of adaptive behavior may have been diagnostic, their greatest usefulness will probably be that of identifying the starting points for training-educational programs (Malone

& Christian, 1974). These scales can supplement family-reported evidence of developmental retardation in the young child, educational records of the school learning characteristics of the school-age child, and social welfare or court reports of personal-social deficiencies of the adult, and they can indicate specific domains of behavior and particular skills in need of training. Periodic surveys with such scales can be used to indicate improvements and to evaluate remedial programs (Schwartz & Allen, 1974). This was the principal use being made of a similar instrument developed in England by H. C. Gunzburg, at a much earlier period. The senior author found Gunzburg's scale in use routinely at the Monybull Hospital, Birmingham, England, when he visited there in 1967 (Gunzburg, 1958, 1973).

Unfortunately, there has been relatively little longitudinal validation of the various scales of adaptive behavior. They seem to have been accepted because of their face validity (apparent reasonableness). Those who are familiar with the poor reputation of conventional developmental scales as predictors of later intellectual functioning for the general population may be reluctant to place faith in the newer behavior adaption scales for young children. However, there is considerable evidence that at the lower end of the developmental continuum, marked retardation is highly related to later intellectual performance and general educational-social-economic competence (VanderVeer & Schweid, 1974). S. Anderson and S. Messick (1974) have provided a critical discussion of the theoretical and practical problems involved in defining and assessing the precursors of social competence in young children.

The assessment of mental retardation

The assessment of the mentally retarded individual is an inevitable process. It goes on informally and haphazardly when done by relatives, friends, and acquaintances. It becomes more systematic and formal when done by teachers, counselors, and psychologists for purposes of school promotion, demotion, or retention, or for placement in special classes or institutions.

Except for very special purposes, the immediate occasion for the assessment of mental status is some social circumstance, and the ultimate purpose of diagnosis is the solution of some social problem. In addition, the final test of the accuracy of diagnosis and the effectiveness of treatment is the extent to which the social circumstance is improved.

The relation of identification to criteria

It is obvious that identification of the mentally retarded individual involves the acceptance of certain criteria. We have already indicated that, in practice, multiple criteria are commonly used. The relative weight given to the psychometric, educational, social, economic, and developmental criteria will vary with the purpose of the assessment process. Whereas combined school achievement (educational criteria) and mental test scores (psychometric criteria) are most valid for the identification of the mentally retarded of school age when other specialized programs are being considered, the broader criteria of adequate social adjustment and economic sufficiency are more crucial in the evaluation of the out-of-school adult, and general developmental status is the most relevant information for the preschool child.

Since the various criteria do not correlate highly with each other, we can have the paradox of a child who was classed as intellectually retarded while in school and who, as an adult, functions in a socially adequate way. The available data on the incidence of mental retardation according to chronological age suggest that this happens with a fairly large number of individuals. Table 8–1 shows such data based on two different surveys.

Table 8–1 shows that relatively few children below school age are diagnosed as mentally retarded, that the percentage of defective individuals increases tremendously during the school-age period, and that in adulthood the percentage drops to a comparatively low level. Part of the large difference between children and adults is attributed to the higher death rates among the mentally subnormal and the greater ease of case-finding while the children are of school age, but it is probable that the biggest single factor is the lesser weight given to abstract verbal facility in the adult situation. Many retarded individuals of the higher mental levels (the mildly mentally retarded), who probably make up 75 percent of the children of school age so diagnosed, find formal education an unsurmountable hazard, but once they are out of school a large percentage of them are not defective in terms of social and economic criteria (Tarjan et al., 1973; Granat & Granat, 1973). Other surveys are consistent with the data presented in table 8–1, showing that the reported incidence of mental retardation rises with increasing age, reaches a peak at about fourteen, and then drops off sharply (Granat & Granat 1973).

These observations help explain some apparent paradoxes concerning the number of individuals who are "really" mentally retarded. The literature has long asserted that approximately 3 percent of the population are mentally retarded. However, the limited population surveys that have been made show incidences far below this figure. Whenever surveys have been made of "identified" or "certified" cases, the incidence has been found to be nearer 1 percent (Granat & Granat, 1973; Tarjan, 1973; Mercer, 1973). When educational and treatment programs are initiated and justified on the basis of the 3 percent figure and it is found that this number is only about one-third those actually identified as

Table 8–1

Incidence of mental retardation and chronological age
(per 1,000 of the general population)

Age in Years	England and Wales*	Baltimore†
0–4	1.2	0.7
5–9	15.5	11.8
10–14	25.6	43.6
15–19	10.8	30.2
20–29	8.4	7.6
30–39	5.7	8.2
40–49	5.4	7.4
50–59	4.9	4.5
60 and older	2.9	2.2

* Based on Wood Report as reported by N. O'Connor and J. Tizard (1956, p. 22).
† Data from P. C. Lemkau, C. Tietze, and M. Casper (1942).

retarded, administrators wonder where the other two-thirds are. These individuals are assumed to exist as undiscovered or unidentified cases.

Actually, the 3 percent figure is obtained only from the statistics of test construction and interpretation. As figure 8–1 indicates, the percentage of individuals in the general population scoring two standard deviation units below the mean is slightly less than the 3 percent figure commonly cited. Assuming that the standard deviation of the test is approximately 15 IQ points, minus two standard deviation units yields an IQ of 70, the conventional psychometric cutting-off point for mental retardation. Note that this figure will actually be obtained only if the *purely statistical single psychometric criterion is applied.*

We have already stated that in practice, the double criteria of significant impairment in intelligence (indicated by low test scores) *and* below-normal general adaptation (developmental retardation, school failure, or socio-economic incompetence) are applied. The lower incidence figures are obtained because many of the individuals who meet the psychometric criterion (IQ below 70) are functioning adequately in the classroom as children or are meeting the minimum socio-economic standards of society as adults and so fail to qualify in terms of general adaptation. Conversely, many individuals who are judged sufficiently impaired in general adaptation to qualify as mentally retarded score too high psychometrically to qualify on this basis.

The senior author, serving as a school psychologist, has found that approximately one-third of the children referred to him by teachers as probably mentally retarded fail to meet the psychometric criteria. D. I. Ashurst and C. E. Meyers (1973), in their study of 269 students referred by teachers as suspected mental retardates, found that 116 were not so classified by school psychologists. In this study, the psychological assessments were not purely psychometric but were based on school records and classroom observations, as well as on test scores.

If we assume that 3 percent of the population meet the psychometric criterion (IQ's below 70), at least half of these are not significantly impaired in general adaptation. In Sweden, where all nineteen-year-old males undergo examinations (including an intelligence test) for placement in military service, 1.5 percent obtained test scores sufficiently low as to qualify as mentally retarded, but had never been so identified. It was also found that 0.71 percent of the men had been certified mentally retarded. The two groups combined yield a *psychometrically-defined* prevalence of 2.21 percent, as compared with 0.71 percent certified on the basis of the *double criterion* (Granat & Granat, 1973). Mercer (1973) found that when the double criterion is used, the rates of mental retardation are cut to about half those found by the psychometric criterion alone. Table 8–2 portrays these relationships. If we round out these figures, we obtain values not far from about 50 percent of the cases (1.5

Table 8–2

The use of a double criterion for identifying the mentally retarded

	Adaptive Level (Educational-Social Criterion)	Psychometric Level (Test Performance Criterion)	Judgments Rendered
1	–	+	Suspected, referred, and identified as not mentally retarded
2	–	–	Suspected, referred, and identified as mentally retarded
3	+	–	Not suspected or referred, and identified as not mentally retarded
4	+	+	Referred for other than suspected mental retardation, but tested and identified as not mentally retarded

– = below critical levels
+ = above critical levels

percent of the general population) in category 3 (psychometrically eligible but socially adequate), and possibly about equal numbers of the other 50 percent in categories 1 and 2. These figures should not be taken too seriously, as they are only rough approximations based on very limited data.

TERMINOLOGY AND CLASSIFICATION

The American Association on Mental Deficiency has recommended a standard set of terms, but there is still great variation in the terminology used in the field of intellectual subnormality both in the Uinted States and abroad. In the older American terminology, *feebleminded* was the generic term for all persons sufficiently intellectually subnormal to warrant special consideration, and the terms *moron, imbecile,* and *idiot* designated various degrees of subnormality. At a later date, *mental deficiency* replaced *feebleminded* as the generic term, while the older terms were retained for the three subcategories. The AAMD more recently has proposed that *mental retardation* become the preferred generic term, and that the various degrees of subnormality be indicated as *mild, moderate, severe,* and *profound.* Additional sets of roughly equivalent terms are used in Great Britain, by the World Health Organization, and by the American Psychiatric Association. There are also separate educational terminologies, both in Great Britain and in America. Table 8–3 indicates the relationships among these various sets of terms.

The diversity of roughly equivalent terms is the result of the different criteria used to define and identify individuals with intellectual impairments, the varying purposes served by the diagnosis, and the never-ending attempt to get away from the negative connotations of the names given to handicapping conditions. The older terms—*feebleminded, moron, imbecile,* and *idiot*—came to have a clinical and psychometric frame of reference. Definitions were largely in terms of IQ ranges, heredity was considered to be the primary causal factor, and the prognosis was considered to be poor. These terms, descriptive of significant intellectual impairment with the connotations of hopelessness, became emotionally toned and stigmatizing. The newer terms—*mental retardation* as the general term and *mild, moderate, severe,* and *profound* as varying degrees— are less emotionally toned and commonly involve the use of multiple criteria. The terms *educable, trainable,* and *custodial* to indicate degrees of mental retardation obviously refer largely to the practical problems of administrative classification. All these terms refer to classes of intellectual subnormality which relate to the degree of impairment. A second classification, which the AAUD calls a biomedical classification, is based on the principle *causes* of the low level of intellectual functioning.

Table 8-3

Some terminology for mental retardation

Organization	Generic Terms	More Specific Designation			
American clinics (earlier)	Feebleminded	Moron	Imbecile	Idiot	
American clinics (later)	Mental deficiency	Moron	Imbecile	Idiot	
World Health Organization	Mental subnormality	Mild	Moderate	Severe	
American Psychiatric Association	Mental subnormality	Mild	Moderate	Severe	
British clinics	Amentia	Feebleminded	Imbecile	Idiot	
American, educational	Mentally retarded	Educable	Trainable	Custodial	
British, educational	Amentia	Educational subnormal	Backward		
Approximate IQ-equivalent of British educational terminology	0–70	50–70	20–50	Below 20 or 30	
American Association on Mental Deficiency	Mentally retarded	Mild	Moderate	Severe	Profound
Recommended IQ-equivalent of AAMD	0–70	55–69	40–54	25–39	Below 25
Standard score ranges of AAMD	Below −2.00	−2.01 to −3.00	−3.01 to −4.00	−4.01 to −5.00	Below −5.00

Two etiological populations of mentally retarded

Current discussions emphasize that the definition and assessment of mental retardation are independent of etiology and prognosis. However, there is a *statistical relationship* between certain etiological categories, on the one hand, and scholastic aptitude, socio-economic status, and adaptive behavior levels, on the other. For example, some workers have differentiated between a "familial" and an "organic" population of the mentally retarded. Members of the familial population have no demonstrable organic damage or deficit. They represent the lower portion of the normal curve of intellectual ability. These persons are a part of the normal distribution of abilities produced by the multigenic-environmental interactions. (A corresponding number of persons constitute the upper extreme of the normal curve because of more favorable combinations of these same factors.) The majority of the low-level individuals have IQ and adaptive behavior ratings in the mildly retarded levels. Very few score below 50 in IQ (Mercer, 1973).

The "organics," on the other hand, have marked physiological defects and tend to have IQ's and adaptive scale SQ's below 50. The causes of these individuals' deficiencies are relatively infrequently occurring single genes, chromosomal abnormalities, and/or major neurological defects from such things as dietary deficiencies, infections, toxins, and physical trauma of similar infrequent occurrence.

The "organics" and the small number of "familials" combine to form a disproportionate number of individuals functioning at very low levels. This produces a great excess of low-level cases beyond those theoretically expected from the shape of the "normal curve." While the two populations are not entirely discrete and the relationships are not sufficient to warrant individual diagnosis and prognosis on the basis of etiology alone, some inferences can be drawn from the etiological categories to which a person belongs. The "organics" are much more likely to be severely or profoundly impaired in intellectual functioning and adaptive behavior than are the "familials." Conversely, individuals with IQ's below 50 and those with correspondingly low levels of adaptive behavior will show markedly more organic impairment than will persons scoring higher in intellectual and adaptive behavior (Mercer, 1973). We shall return to this etiological distinction in chapter 9.

Genetic causation

Mental retardation caused by a dominant gene   Mental retardation due to a single defective dominant gene is rare. Some conditions apparently of this type are Huntington's chorea, tuberous sclerosis, neurofibromatosis, hereditary cerebellar ataxia, and Freidreich's ataxis (Roberts, 1963). It is obvious that severe mental defectiveness due to a single dominant gene will be self-limiting because the parents must also be defective. Since most of the severely mentally retarded do not reproduce, because of either sterility or lack of opportunity, the transmission of the defective dominant gene from one generation to the next is very limited. No recipient of a dominant "lethal" gene can beget offspring. Some of these genetically determined conditions may occur in a mild form in one generation or in certain members of a family, and in a more severe form in other generations or in other members of the same family. The less severely affected individual can produce and transmit the defective genes to succeeding generations. The occurrence of sporadic cases is sometimes attributed to a mutation in a germ cell (Kugelmass, 1954). The average age of onset of Huntington's chorea is thirty-six (Gottesman, 1963), so that this condition can be perpetrated indefinitely and in some cases unknowingly. But if we are to be consistent with the AAMD definition, we should not call those conditions of mental subnormality which appear after maturity "mental retardation."

The characteristics of mental subnormality which is determined by a single dominant gene are as follows:

1. The affected and unaffected members of a family are usually sharply differentiated.
2. Every defective individual has at least one affected parent.
3. Where only one parent is affected, and is heterozygous, approximately one-half of the offspring will be affected; when the affected parent is homozygous, all the offspring will be mentally defective.
4. When both parents are affected and are heterozygous, approximately three-fourths of the offspring will be defective (Penrose, 1963; McCusick, 1971). Figure 8–1 diagrams these relationships.

Mental retardation caused by a recessive gene   Much more often, mental retardation is due to a single recessive gene. Such defective children typically come of apparently normal parents. The defect is typically the result of the child's receiving two similar recessive genes, one from each parent. The phenotypically normal parents are carriers of the defective gene but are not themselves affected. Some conditions which are generally considered to be due to a single defective recessive gene are: Tay-Sachs disease, gargoylism, galactosuria, phenylketonuria, and genetic microcephaly. Most of these types of mental retardation are found rarely and the sum of all of them does not represent a very large proportion of the total population of the mentally deficient. However, many types have been discovered quite recently, and new ones are currently being identified, which indicates that this category may be larger than was formerly realized.

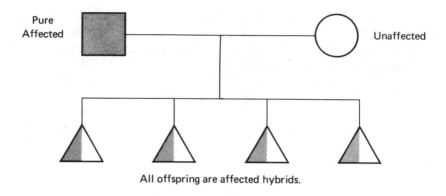

All offspring are affected hybrids.

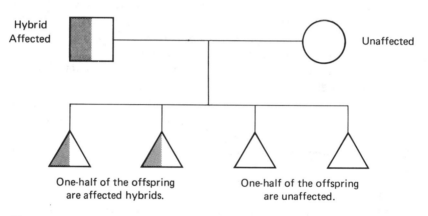

One-half of the offspring   One-half of the offspring
are affected hybrids.   are unaffected.

Figure 8–1   The transmission of simple autosomal dominant traits.

Many genetically determined mental deficiencies are, in turn, due to inborn defects of metabolism. The genes produce defective metabolism which in turn affects the development and functioning of the nervous system (possibly through other agencies), resulting in lowered mentality.

Where mental deficiency is the result of a single recessive gene,

1. The affected and unaffected members of a family are usually clearly differentiated;
2. Many times the parents and immediate ancestors are unaffected;
3. The offspring are more often affected when the parents are related to each other by blood than when they are not;
4. When neither parent is himself affected, but some of the offspring show the defect, approximately one-fourth of the children will be defective (Penrose 1963; McCusick 1971). Figure 8–2 diagrams the results of various combinations of recessive traits.

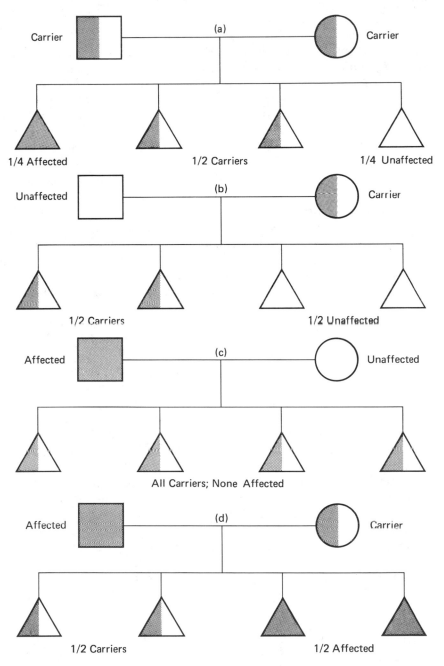

Figure 8–2   Autosomal simple recessive traits. Triangles indicate that offspring can be either sex. (a) is the most common type of mating which produces affected offspring. This mating produces 1/4 affected and 3/4 normal, 1/2 of whom are carriers.

Chromosomal aberrations   Improved techniques for studying chromosomes led to the discovery, in 1956, that the true number of chromosomes in humans was forty-six rather than forty-eight (Tjio & Levan, 1956). Soon after this it was disclosed that mongols (Down's syndrome) had forty-seven chromosomes in place of the normal complement of forty-six (Lejeune & Turpin, 1961). It has since been established that mongolism is associated with an extra chromosome (trisomism) at pair number 21. Cases of extra chromosomes in positions other than number 21 have been reported, but almost none of these individuals, although usually mentally retarded, are mongols (Lilienfeld, 1968). Three etiological subtypes of mongolism—nondisjunction, translocation, and mosaicism—have been identified. These will be discussed in chapter 9. It is now possible to diagnose Down's syndrome prenatally. Carrier prospective parents can be provided genetic counseling concerning the statistical risks of their offspring being defective and concerning alternative means of satisfying parental needs (Nitowski, 1973; Dorfman, 1972).

Mental retardation involving many genes   The ordinary familial, undifferentiated, nonclinical, or common garden variety mental defectives are at the low end of the distribution curve of intelligence. The factors determining the intelligence of these individuals are the same as those affecting the intelligence level of the normal and the superior. It is certainly a mistake to treat this group of mentally retarded as a well-defined and isolated category, for in reality they are simply the arbitrarily defined tail end of a normally distributed population.

Unlike the mentally retarded whose deficiency results from a single gene, the ordinary familial mentally retarded do not differ markedly from their parents or siblings. They have no obvious distinguishing physical characteristics. They are more likely to be smaller in stature, lighter in weight, have defective vision and hearing, poor health, and greater susceptibility to disease than their peers of normal or superior mentality, but many individuals in this group are actually superior in these areas. Postmortem gross and microscopical examinations of the nervous systems have failed to disclose significant special characteristics of the brains of the typical familial mental defective. Most of the histological studies showing characteristic neural pathology in mental defectives have been carried out upon the low-grade cases who are predominantly of the secondary, or exogenous, types.

CHANGING CONCEPTIONS OF THE IMPORTANCE OF HEREDITY

Following the rediscovery of Gregor Mendel's work in 1900 and its uncritical application to humans, heredity came to be stressed as the primary factor in the etiology of mental retardation. Estimates of the incidence of mental retardation in which heredity was considered to be the principal cause averaged around 80 percent. A. F. Tredgold, in 1929, gave 80 percent; L. S. Hollingworth, in 1920, 90; and H. H. Goddard, in 1914, 77 (Hutt & Gibby, 1965). Around 1930 there was a reaction against the extreme hereditarian emphasis, and it has since been carried to the point that some workers in the 1960s and even '70s seem to be denying that heredity plays any significant role in determining the mental level of the ordinary familial type of mental retardation (Sarason & Gladwin, 1958; Mercer, 1972).

J. E. Wallin (1956), in a review of some twenty-three studies in which estimates of the extent of hereditariness among the mentally deficient were made, found values ranging from 90 percent to 1.7 percent. One noticeable trend in the studies is the decreasing emphasis on the role of heredity in the more recent reports. The wide diversity of views and percentages given in the studies of this topic arises partly from the nature-versus-nurture bias of the individual authors, partly from the different kinds of cases constituting the groups studied, and partly from the varying criteria used in assigning causative factors in individual cases.

A. R. Jensen (1973) and Mercer (1972) are examples of the frequent opposing interpretations of the same data. To Mercer, the fact that conventional tests are less predictive of general socio-economic competence for members of the lower-class than for middle-class individuals indicates the inappropriate cultural bias of the tests. Jensen cites this same fact as evidence for the different distribution of Level II (higher-level cognitive) abilities across classes and races.

ENVIRONMENTAL CAUSES OF MENTAL RETARDATION

There is a wide variety of possible environmental causes of mental retardation. It is easy to list these and to indicate how they may conceivably lower the mental level. It is also possible to find individual cases in which each of these alleged causes is apparently operative. However, when quantitative studies start with a fairly large, heterogeneous group of mentally deficient individuals, and comparisons are made of the incidence of the alleged causes in the deficient group and in a comparable group of intellectually normal people, significant differences often fail to appear. In other words, that various environmental factors produce mental retardation seems to be fairly convincing on the clinical, individual case level, but their functioning as statistically significant factors in causing mental retardation in general is often hard to establish.

Prenatal environmental causes

The differentiation of cases of mental retardation due to prenatal environmental causes from those produced by rare genetic determiners is very difficult. Both groups are congenital. Presumably a genetically normal fetus or embryo can be injured by mechanical, chemical, nutritional, glandular, actinic, and infectious agents, but there are few data and few informed guesses about the extent to which any or all of these factors actually produce mental retardation. I. N. Kugelmass (1954) estimates that such prenatal factors produce 10 percent of the mental retardates.

Prenatal physical trauma   It is very possible that unsuccessful attempts at abortion and accidents to the pregnant mother may so injure the fetus as to lower the child's mental level. There are clinical records of defective children being born to mothers following such occurrences. However, a causal relation between the two events is very difficult to establish. Workers in the field feel that direct injury to the embryo or fetus from blows, falls, or unsuccessful attempts at abortion by means of mechanical instruments is relatively unimportant in producing mental deficiency (Adams & Salam, 1970).

Prenatal nutrition   Many authors recognize the possibility that "nutritional amentia" may occur (Tredgold & Soddy, 1956; Fraser, 1964).

The evidence that inadequate nutrition can affect both physiological and psychological development in humans is convincing (Kaplan, 1972). Gestation, a critical period in the growth of brain tissue, is the time of greatest vulnerability to malnutrition. We would theoretically expect malnutrition of the pregnant mother to be related to mental retardation of the offspring. The evidence that maternal restriction of calories and protein as well as other essential dietary components retards the growth of the human fetus seems definitive (Rosso, 1975).

A larger number of studies, but without controls, suggest that the nutritional status of the pregnant mother may significantly affect the mental level of the offspring. Two decades ago it was shown that congenital malformations in mammals could be experimentally produced by putting the pregnant mother on a deficient diet. The first such congenital malformations were produced by vitamin deficiencies. Since that time a bewildering array of congenital malformations has been produced by feeding to the pregnant mothers diets which were deficient in any one of the following: vitamin A, vitamin D, riboflavin, folic acid, thiamin, niacin, and pantothenic acid. On the other hand, deficiencies of pyridoxine, choline, biotin, or vitamin K have failed to produce congenital malformations. Paradoxically, congenital anomalies have been produced by feeding animals excessive amounts of vitamin A (Zamenhof, Van Markens, & Grauel, 1971).

The role of specific nutritional deficits is well documented. It has long been known that insufficient iodine in a pregnant mother's diet can cause her child to be a cretin with accompanying mental retardation (Kaplan, 1972). Extreme iron deficiencies in the pregnant mother's diet may produce iron deficiency anemia in the offspring. Such children suffer from a significantly higher rate of serious congenital abnormalities than children born of nonanemic mothers (Kaplan, 1972). Little information seems to be available on the mental status of such children. However, it seems that in at least one large-scale study of humans, a measurable intellectual deficit was produced in children by deficiencies in the diets of the pregnant mothers (Harrell, Woodward, & Gates, 1956).

Surveys of human populations have no definitive value because of their lack of controls, but they are suggestive. Reports of a high rate of congenital malformation among the offspring of Jewish women who spent periods of internment in German concentration camps prior to World War II are common. One study of 1,430 offspring born from 1946 to 1948 of Jewish mothers who had gone through the hardships of concentration camp life prior to their marriages showed a disproportionate number of congenital defects (Benda, 1952). Mongolism, hydrocephalus, club feet, polydactylism, anencephaly, and other, similar conditions occurred many times as often as would be expected. Such data are difficult to interpret because of the multiple factors involved—such as the influence of general starvation, specific dietary deficiencies, mental and emotional stress, and possibly age (Warren, 1973).

Prenatal infections   The evidence that diseases of the mother during pregnancy may affect the physical and mental development of the fetus is convincing. Congenital syphilis has long been recognized as a clinical entity. The child may be infected prenatally, through the placental circulation, or in the passage through the birth canal during delivery. It has been established that a syphilitic mother undergoing treatment *can* give birth to an uninfected child.

The proportion of mentally retarded children resulting from syphilitic infection has long been in dispute, but it has certainly declined in recent years. Prenatal infection with syphilis from infected mothers is today a relatively infrequent cause of mental deficiency in children. Surveys conducted before 1935 showed that about 6 percent of institutionalized mental defectives had a history of congenital syphilis. This figure had fallen to about 4 percent in the 1950s (Wolf & Cowen, 1959). After a decade of decline, there has been an increase in the incidence of syphilis in the United States during the 1970s. Because of the general availability of treatment, this is not likely to result in an increase in neurosyphilis.

Rubella, or German measles, in the first trimester of pregnancy has also been established as a cause of multiple maldevelopments in the fetus. The most common congenital defects so caused are those of the eyes, the heart, and the central nervous system. Microcephaly, deafness, blindness, and epilepsy have all been reported (Dodrill, Macfarlane, & Boyd, 1974). Mental retardation may be but usually is not an accompaniment of such maldevelopment. It is not known just how rubella affects the developing embryo, but the critical time is the organogenic period—the first three months of pregnancy.

The studies of the extent to which maternal rubella is responsible for congenital malformations are divergent, depending upon whether they are among the earlier reports, which were largely retrospective (starting with the malformations and working back in attempting to determine possible causes), or prospective (starting with a medical diagnosis of maternal rubella and determining the incidence of malformation in the resulting offspring). The earlier studies reported 50 to 100 percent of maldeveloped offspring; the later, better controlled, studies claim only about 10 to 15 percent of congenital defects (Gregg, 1941; Swan, 1947; Wolf & Cowen, 1959; Skinner, 1961). There is a sharp gradient in susceptibility. One study (Michaels & Mellin, 1960) found 47 percent, 22 percent, and 7 percent of injured infants born to mothers infected in the first, second, and third months of pregnancy respectively.

A vaccine for rubella is now available which makes it possible to eliminate this source of potential damage to the unborn child. The use of this vaccine was effective in preventing another epidemic otherwise predicted for the 1970s. The last major epidemic, in 1964–65, resulted in an estimated 20,000 damaged children being born, an additional estimated 30,000 were stillborn, and an unknown number were spontaneously aborted (Dodrill, Macfarlane, & Boyd, 1974).

Prenatal infection of the fetus by protozoa does occur, but it is apparently a relatively uncommon phenomenon caused by a one-cell parasite in the mother's blood. The parasite may enter the fetus through the placental barrier. It has been observed in the lower animals since about 1900, and was first reported in humans in 1942. Since that time several hundred cases have been reported. An infected mother may infect her fetus and give birth to a child with various abnormalities of the nervous system, including hydrocephalus, microcephalus, and intracerebral calcification. Any organ or tissue of the body may be affected, but the central nervous system suffers most severely in the congenital condition (Weinman & Chandler, 1956).

Congenital cases are often stillborn; others show obvious symptoms at birth but survive for various periods; and sometimes symptoms do not appear for weeks, months, or even years. Most of the congenital cases are mentally retarded. The few surveys which have included a search for toxoplasmosis indicate a very few cases of mental deficiency apparently caused by toxoplasmosis, even though serological studies indicate that the population is widely infected (Minto & Roberts, 1959; Masland, Sarason, and Gladwin, 1958).

Various other protozoan, bacterial, and infectious viral diseases have been suspected either of being transmitted from the pregnant mother to the developing embryo or fetus, or of otherwise interfering with normal development. Among these are Asiatic cholera, typhus, typhoid, Asian influenza, malaria, and mumps. That a fetus can apparently be injured by a virus which caused no evident maternal illness greatly complicates the task of assessing the importance of maternal infections during pregnancy as etiological factors in mental retardation. It is claimed that a virus can injure a fetus via the pregnant mother's blood stream, even when the mother herself is immune to the virus (Masland, Sarason, & Gladwin, 1958).

Cytomegalovirus is said to be the most common *viral* cause of mental retardation (Marx, 1975). It is estimated that one of every 1,000 infants—more than 3,000 per year in the United States—is seriously mentally retarded as the result of prenatal infection with this virus. The virus is a major cause of various birth defects including mental retardation, blindness, and deafness. Systematic surveys have shown that about 1 percent of all infants are infected with this virus at birth. About 2 percent of low socio-economic infants, as compared with 0.5 percent of high socio-economic infants, are born with cytomegalovirus infection. Investigators are now trying to develop a vaccine to protect against such infection. Cytomegalovirus is widely distributed in human populations throughout the world. In the United States about 80 percent of adults age 35 to 40 have acquired antibodies indicative of infection with the virus (Marx, 1975).

Blood incompatibility   Since 1939, it has been known that Rh incompatibility between the maternal and fetal blood may result in the newborn child's being severely jaundiced, and that mental deficiency is a possible accompaniment.

It is estimated that Rh incompatibility is the cause of the mental retardation of 3 to 4 percent of the institutionalized mentally retarded (Yannet & Lieberman, 1948). The proportion of Rh-negative mothers in a large group of undifferentiated mentally retarded is significantly larger than that reported in the literature for large random samplings (Glasser, Jacobs, & Schain, 1951). There seems to be one case of Rh incompatibility in every 150 to 200 births (Waters, 1958).

Replacement blood transfusions for the jaundiced Rh-positive child born of an Rh-negative mother are now saving many of these children from the more serious effects of Rh incompatibility (Waters, 1958). However, one study found that children who had had severe anemia and jaundice, and who had received replacement transfusions so that there was no detectable nervous system defect, still scored 23.1 IQ points below their normal siblings. The lowering of the IQ was significantly related to the degree of jaundice (Day & Haines, 1954).

Additional help is now available for Rh-negative women whose husbands have Rh-positive blood. Anti-Rh gamma globulin can be used to block the sensitizing process which produces antibodies to an Rh-positive baby's incompatible blood. The administration of the appropriate gamma globulin immediately following the birth of each Rh-positive baby gives the mother a temporary passive dose of antibodies which destroy any Rh-positive blood cells which may get into the mother's blood stream during the delivery. This prevents the mother from producing permanent antibodies. If the mother has already built up antibodies, the gamma globulin will not protect future children. Currently the supply of gamma globulin is a problem since it can be obtained only from rare blood donors whose blood plasma has a high level of Rh-positive antibodies.

The development of spectrophotometric methods for the examination of the amniotic fluid, making possible more accurate determinations of the severity of the condition; the use of exchange transfusions at birth; the institution of premature delivery in critical cases; the use of new techniques of intrauterine transfusion; combined with the use of gamma globulin have all helped reduce the mental retardation, deafness, and cerebral palsy previously common in the Rh-positive offspring of Rh-negative mothers.

Mother-child blood incompatibility in the classical major blood groupings (A, B, and O) may also be a factor in causing some cases of mental deficiency (Yannet & Lieberman, 1948).

Radioactivity   In the late 1920s it was discovered that X ray irradiation of human mothers during pregnancy resulted in abortions or in a wide array of congenital defects including *spina bifida* (cleft spine), deformed skulls, and microcephaly (Murphy, 1928; Goldstein & Murphy, 1929). Studies by the United States Bomb Casualty Commission have shown that one of every six unborn children who received substantial does of radiation at Hiroshima were delivered malformed (Oughterson, 1956). These malformations were caused by the direct effect of high levels of irradiation on the young fetus. Present evidence indicates that high levels of irradiation to the pelvic regions of pregnant mothers in the first three weeks of pregnancy are usually fatal to the embryo. However, if the embryo survives, it is normal. Comparable irradiation during the next eight weeks results in the most severe abnormalities involving the entire body (dwarfism) but often centering on the brain (microcephaly) and the sense organs (blindness and/or deafness). Between the fifteenth and the twentieth weeks of pregnancy, irradiation produces minor defects and lesser brain damage. After the twentieth week the fetus usually suffers no apparent damage. All of these studies have involved mothers undergoing irradiation for cancer of the pelvic regions, who either did not realize they had become pregnant or their conditions were so serious the doctors and the mothers took the risks of damaging the fetuses in an attempt to save the mothers (Cushner, 1968).

A second way in which irradiation may produce mental retardation is by the production of mutations. A mutation is presumably an alteration in the complicated chemical nature of the gene. Mutations occur spontaneously and may be either beneficial or detrimental so far as the propagation of the species is concerned. However, the mutant genes in the vast majority of cases produce some kind of harmful effects (Drake, 1975).

The possible effects of the increased irradiation of the people of the earth from synthetic sources is receiving a great deal of attention. It seems that radiation may affect the germ cells in three ways: they may be killed; their chromosomes may be broken up; or they may mutate. The death of the germ cells would, of course, simply reduce the fertility of the individual. Breakage of the chromosomes may induce abortion or malformation of the offspring, if conception takes place within a few months of irradiation. The last and most important is the increased mutation rate already mentioned (Drake, 1975).

Since most mutations are deleterious, an increase in the number of mentally retarded is to be expected from any significant increase in the general level of radiation. Although the amount of irradiation required to produce malformations such as microcephaly is large, the effects of irradiation are cumulative. For this reason, there is considerable concern over the possible combined effects of natural radiation, X rays used for dental and medical diagnosis or treatment, and the increased radiation incident to the use of atomic energy for industry and war. The studies of the Hiroshima and Nagasaki atomic bomb explosions show that there was a marked increase in microcephaly and mental retardation as well as in fetal and infant mortality among children born to pregnant mothers exposed to radiation. Many of the survivors of all ages were also found to have chromosomal abnormalities (Miller, 1969; Boffey, 1970). The conservative use of X ray by dentists and medical doctors in diagnosis, and the use of ultrasensitive film and image intensifiers in X ray procedures, minimize the amount of exposure to radiation from these sources.

Toxic agents   Virtually all drugs, hormones, and potentially toxic agents pass through the placental barrier and enter the fetal circulation

(Ward, 1972). Thalidomide taken during pregnancy produces mostly limb deformities. However, heart, eye, and ear defects are also common in the offspring of mothers ingesting this drug while pregnant. Apparently little, if any, brain damage occurs. The fetus is particularly vulnerable to toxins because the enzyme systems involved in the metabolic detoxication and elimination of dangerous substances are poorly developed. Consequently toxins can attain high concentrations in fetal tissues. Antithyroid agents such as radioactive iodine administered to the mother, after ten to twelve weeks of pregnancy, when the fetal thyroid has the ability to take up the radioactive iodine, may produce potential cretinism in the offspring. Morphine withdrawal effects are seen in babies born to morphine-addicted mothers; if they are not recognized and treated promptly, the infants may die. Infants of methadone-addicted mothers display symptoms (Zelson, 1973). One follow-up study of thirty infants born to heroin-addicted mothers showed a disproportionate incidence of impaired growth, hyperactivity, and attentional deficits in the offsprings. The authors found these deficits to be independent of the socio-economic status of the parents and other environmental factors (Wilson, Desmond, & Verniaud, 1973).

Natal causes of mental retardation

The major hazards of the birth process are prematurity, traumatic injury, and asphyxia.

Prematurity   Extensive long-range studies, with fairly adequate control groups, have established that an abnormal number of people born prematurely are mentally retarded (Masland, Sarason, & Gladwin, 1958; Wright, 1972).

One comparative study of over a thousand mentally retarded children and the same number of controls (matched for age, sex, race, place of birth, maternal age, and social and economic status), found that the incidence of prematurity was independent of whether the prematurity was the result of a complication of pregnancy or parturition (Pasamanick & Lilienfeld, 1955). This same study found that complications of pregnancy, prematurity, and congenital abnormalities were all associated with mental retardation. These same factors were also shown to be associated with stillbirth, neonatal deaths, cerebral palsy, epilepsy, and childhood behavior disorders. The association of these factors is greatest with cerebral palsy and epilepsy, next with mental retardation, and least with childhood behavior disorders.

One group of seventy-three prematurely born children, five to ten years of age, was compared with their siblings who were not premature. The mean IQ of the premature children was 94, as compared with 107 for their full-term siblings. The difference was statistically significant. Nineteen of the premature group were mentally retarded, five were in institutions. None of the normal siblings were mentally retarded (Dann, Levine, & New, 1958). Other studies have reported comparable findings (Towbin, 1969).

It seems that there is a definite association between prematurity and mental retardation, and that this association persists even when those cases are excluded in which the prematurity and mental deficiency might both be due to some common factor such as disease or accident (Drillien, 1961; Fitzhardinge & Stevens, 1972). Fetuses, otherwise normal, delivered prematurely by Cesarean section develop more normally than do those born equally prematurely by either spontaneous or instrumental delivery. This indicates that the stresses of the birth process are greater and potentially more damaging when both mother and fetus are less ready for the delivery. Over 300,000 premature children are born annually in the United States. The evidence indicates that improved medical procedures have been more successful in increasing the survival rates of premature infants than in preserving the infant from neurological damage (Begab, 1974). Evidently the premature fetus, unready for birth and fragile, born through a physiologically unprepared, unrelaxed birth canal, is highly vulnerable to anoxic and mehanical damage sufficiently serious to produce a high incidence of mental retardation, cerebral palsy, epilepsy, and other neuropsychiatric disorders in such children (Wright, 1972).

Asphyxia   Asphyxia, a term often used interchangeably with anoxia and hypoxia, refers to a reduction of oxygen level below the physiological requirement of the baby. Asphyxia during the birth process may occur if the placenta separates too soon, if the umbilical cord kinks, if the child aspirates excessive amniotic fluid, or if the child, for any reason, does not breathe for some time after delivery. There is considerable difference of opinion about the importance of natal asphyxia in producing neural damage and subsequent mental retardation. Present evidence indicates that the newborn is capable of tolerating a relatively severe degree of oxygen deprivation. Anoxia seems to produce a lowering of body temperature and metabolic level which may operate as a protective mechanism (Gottfried, 1973).

The studies which have attempted to relate oxygen deprivation at birth to mental level yield inconclusive results. One follow-up study of infants who were known to have a severe degree of asphyxia at birth, but who by the end of the neonatal period were considered to have been normal, showed that they had mean Stanford-Binet IQ's of 88.05 as compared with 100.47 for the control subjects. This difference is statistically significant (Darke, 1944).

On the other hand, in one sample of 250 subjects, no significant correlations were obtained between their IQ's in their preschool years and the oxygen content of their blood during the first three hours after birth (Apgar, 1955). The apparently discrepant data may be due either to the very low correlation between preschool and later IQ scores or to the large percentage of infants having oxygen levels above the critical level. Apparently practically all newborns experience some degree of oxygen restriction, but most suffer no measurable aftereffects (Gottfried, 1973).

Severe mental retardation often results when resuscitation follows prolonged asphyxia (coma due to oxygen deficiency) from respiratory arrest, carbon monoxide poisoning, or near drowning (Bering, 1969). Protracted coma due to brain concussion results in psychological deficits the severity of which is directly related to the duration of unconsciousness (Bering, 1969). At the present time, both the bulk of the studies and expert opinion indicate that asphyxia is a cause of mental retardation— but just how important it is has yet to be determined (Gottfried, 1973).

Traumatic birth injury   It is estimated that birth injuries are responsible for somewhere between 1 and 5 percent of the mentally retarded (Penrose, 1963). Traumatic birth injury and prematurity are related. The brain structure òf the premature infant is more fragile than that of the full-term infant, and therefore more easily damaged. The mother is also not entirely prepared for the birth process; her pelvic structure is not as elastic and does not yield so readily to the pressure of the infant as when the child is born at full term. The increase in pressure necessary to expel the child, and the increased vulnerability of the premature child, result in a high incidence of stillborn and birth-injured children. Mechanical pressure applied directly to the head or strong uterine contractions may injure the brain, may occlude the umbilical cord, and may impede the venous outflow or arterial outflow of the brain. The size of the maternal pelvis, position of the fetal head, and forceps delivery are all correlated with neuropsychological impairment of the infant (Bering, 1969; Willerman, 1970).

Where complications of delivery are related to mortality rates and mental level of the surviving infants, breech delivery (particularly with large infants), as compared with spontaneous normal vertex, forceps delivery, and Caesarian section, showed a very high mortality rate and low mental level (Russell, Neligan, & Millar, 1970).

It is claimed that most infants, even after a normal birth, show some signs of slight intracranial injury. In most cases the signs of injury rapidly disappear, with no apparent aftereffects.

Postnatal causes of mental retardation

Many of the prenatal and natal causes of mental retardation also operate postnatally. However, there are some additional factors whose effects are primarily postnatal.

Traumatic brain injury   Traumatic brain injury from such things as gunshot wounds, automobile accidents, and falls is a rare cause of mental retardation. The incidence of head trauma among children is positively related to such things as low socio-economic status, single-parent family, and sex. Males have several times the incidence of head injuries as do females. The peak incidence for both sexes is in the three- to six-year age group (Meyer, 1970). The National Center for Health Statistics conservatively estimates the annual incidence of significant head injuries in infants and young children at 3.3 percent of the population under six years of age: 794,000 cases in 1967 (Caveness, 1970). The fate of children sustaining severe head trauma is not promising (Natelson & Sayers, 1973). Estimates of the extent of mental deficiency resulting from such postnatal injuries range from 1 to 2 percent.

Postnatal infections   All brain infections involve the hazard of permanent brain damage and mental retardation. These infections include encephalitis of various types, meningitis from various causes, and syphilitic brain infections, as well as some other, rare types. The total number of cases of mental deficiency resulting from these various viruses and bacteria is much greater than those produced by traumatic brain injury.

Encephalitis (inflammation of the brain) is caused by a group of neurotropic viruses, as well as by some viruses which normally have no particular affinity for the nervous system. Its incidence is unknown, but it is believed that many mild cases (some estimate 80 percent of the total) go unrecognized. The postencephalitic symptoms include a large number of motor disturbances (including cerebral palsy and the Parkinsonian syndrome), personality changes, and general mental retardation or deterioration. One study reports a deficit of 16 IQ points in a group of postencephalitic children when compared with their normal siblings (Dawson & Conn, 1929). Follow-up studies of such children show that they suffer defects in visual, motor, and perceptual function, and are educationally retarded (Sabatino & Cramblatt, 1969).

About 90 percent of the neurological complications of measles, chicken pox, mumps, and scarlet fever are encephalitic. The prognosis for postencephalitics is not good, since there is a tendency for their intelligence level to decline.

Meningitis (literally an inflammation of the coverings of the brain) may be caused by almost any pathogenic microorganisms. The most common organisms involved are the meningococcus, streptococcus, pneumococcus, and the tubercle bacillus. There is also a viral form of meningitis. The permanent aftereffects of meningitis are varied, but blindness, deafness, and arrest of mental development are common (Eichenlaub, 1955; Nickerson & MacDermot, 1961). The incidence of mental retardation caused by meningitis is not known, but it is probably a less important cause than encephalitis. Meningitis responds to treatment with modern antibiotics. Protozoa may also occasionally invade the brain (Cerva, Zimals, and Novak, 1969). A vaccine for the prevention of meningitis was developed after six years of research at the Walter Reed Army Institute of Research in Washington, D.C. and is now available for general use. The yearly number of diagnosed cases of meningitis is estimated to be about 500 among military recruits and 3,000 among civilians.

Diet   When the discussion of mental retardation caused by dietary deficiencies is limited to a few specific types of mental retardation, the evidence is clear and convincing. For example, endemic cretinism due to iodine deficiency has been known for a long time. In most of the regions of the world where endemic cretinism is likely to develop, the ingestion of iodized salt usually prevents its occurrence (Klein & Kenny, 1972).

The presence of normal amounts of phenylalanine in the diet of a phenylketonuric child will result in his being mentally retarded, while the reduction or elimination of phenylalanine from the diet of such a child makes possible normal mental development. Lactose, in the diet of a galactosemic child, operates in a similar fashion. There may be other dietary elements that operate this way. However, the importance of the more general nutritional factors in determining intellectual level is not so clear.

Research studies of restriction of food intake in rats and mice have shown that a diet quantitatively inadequate, to the extent that it produces considerable bodily stunting, does not decrease the learning ability of the animals. When differences in learning rates have been found, the stunted animals have usually been found to be *superior* to the normal animals (Morgan, 1965). If the risks of inference from rats to humans are not too great, reduced food intake, in itself, would not be expected to reduce mental level. The numerous reports of apparent lowering of human mental level due to a low food intake have practically all involved specific deficits of essential food elements in addition to low caloric intake.

Evidence from experimental studies of the lower animals as well as observational and clinical reports of humans indicates that insufficient intake of protein during early neural development affects adult mental level. The diet of children afflicted with Kwashiorkor may be adequate in calories, but it is grossly deficient in protein. The intellectual levels of children who have apparently recovered from severe episodes of protein deficiency are consequently below those of comparable individuals with adequate diets (Eichenwald & Fry, 1969; Richardson, Birch, & Hertzig, 1973).

General nutritional status correlates positively with IQ (Jones, 1946). However, the correlations largely disappear when the social and economic status is held constant. One exception to this seems to occur with children living close to subsistence. One study of a fairly homogeneous group of children from a slum area found a correlation of only .18 ± .04 between their nutritional status and their IQ (O'Hanlon, 1940). M. Winick, K. K. Meyer, and R. C. Harris (1975) found that severely malnourished Korean children, adopted and reared in middle-class American homes, had mean IQ's of 102 and achievement test scores equal to the norms for American children when tested approximately six years later. These children were adopted at a mean age of eighteen months and had resided in their American homes for at least six years. While numerous studies have demonstrated that malnutrition during the first two years of life, when accompanied by the other socio-economic deprivations that usually accompany it, is associated with retarded physical and mental development which persists into adulthood, this study indicates that malnourished children subsequently reared in a relatively "enriched" environment, and provided the diet of an average middle-class American home, have developed normally in terms of mental level and school achievement.

Research studies have demonstrated clearly that vitamin B complex deprivation reduces the learning ability of rats (Morgan, 1965). However, deficiencies of vitamins A and D have *failed* to produce any consistent decrease in the learning of rats (Moore & Mathias, 1934; Bernhardt, 1936; Maurer, 1935; Frank, 1932).

The few data available from studies of variations in vitamin intake using human beings are conflicting. One researcher (Harrell, 1947) reports that thiamin administration increases learning and intelligence, but the improvements found were small and not statistically significant. Other research workers (Balken & Maurer, 1934; Bernhardt, Northway, & Tatham, 1948; Guetzkow & Brozek, 1946; Morgan, 1965) have been unable to demonstrate significant effects of the vitamin B complex on learning in humans. None of these studies have dealt with groups suffering from *acute* deficiencies of this vitamin complex. Likewise, no one has studied the effects of experimentally induced acute deficiencies of these vitamins in human subjects.

Lowering of both mental and physical functioning is said to be part of the syndrome of pellagra and beriberi, which are the result of chronic vitamin deficiencies. The mental deterioration found in these chronic conditions is probably comparable to the decreased learning ability of rats suffering from severe vitamin deficiency. The relative infrequency of pellagra and beriberi in Western culture today indicates that vitamin deficiencies are probably not an important cause of mental retardation.

Lead poisoning   A wide variety of toxic agents, which in large quantities may be fatal, produce neurological damage and mental defects in lesser amounts. Currently, lead poisoning is of most concern. Outbreaks of lead poisoning have occurred from time to time since antiquity. Within recent times it has been known as a hazard only in certain occupations (painter's colic). Yet it remains a serious threat, principally among children in urban slums.

A particularly high-risk group are young children living in old houses, who eat chips of leaded paint, plaster, and putty containing lead. A few small chips of old paint can contain more than 100 milligrams of lead. A safe daily intake is less than half a milligram. The mortality from severe lead poisoning is about 30 percent, with permanent brain damage occurring in more than a quarter of those who survive.

Lead poisoning has been estimated to affect as many as 225,000 young children each year (Snowdon & Sanderson, 1974). While the ingestion of substances containing lead is commonly thought to be the result of the young child's natural predilection for placing in his mouth nonfood as well as edible substances, there is evidence dietary deficiencies—particularly calcium and iron deficits—may operate as predisposing factors. For example, weanling rats, provided a low calcium diet, voluntarily ingested lead acetate solution in much greater amounts than did the normal controls (Snowdon & Sanderson, 1974).

Lead as an air pollutant also adds to the hazard. Recent studies have revealed an extremely high lead content in street dust and surface soil in some areas. Additional sources of lead are the culinary use of improperly glazed earthenware, acidic food stored in certain lead pewterware, the lead content of solder used in some canning processes, the coating previously used on toothpaste tubes, the lead-based ink used by some printers, and the inhalation of lead fumes produced by the burning of lead-impregnated materials such as battery casings.

In December 1973, President Richard Nixon signed into law the Lead-Based Paint Prevention Act of 1973, which will do much to reduce the extent of lead exposure. Several cities have instituted screening and treatment programs for children residing in the inner cities. Close cooperation among health professionals, community workers, housing authorities, and parents and continuing public education concerning the hazards of lead poisoning are needed to deal with the problem (Barnes, 1973; Lin-Fu, 1973).

General cultural factors   The research studies of the past thirty years have shown that intellectual level as measured by conventional tests is influenced by the child's family, social class, and general cultural background. It seems likely that most attempts to determine the proportional contribution of heredity and environment in the determination of intellectual level have oversimplified the problem. There is evidence that the influence of each factor depends upon the other. Thus, the contribution of heredity to the variance of a given trait will itself vary according to the environmental conditions.

Similarly, environmental difference may produce considerable change in the functional level of a person with one level of inherited potential and practically none in someone with a much lower potential.

In addition to the facts that the contribution of environment to functional level varies with inherited potential and that cultural stereotypes may artificially limit the expression of such potential, the weight to be assigned to a given environmental change may vary with the age of the child. Studies have shown that the child's exposure to a superior environment may have a greater effect at an earlier age than at a later age (Freeman, Holzinger, & Mitchell, 1928). For example, the regular administration of thyroid extract to a potential cretin, if started at birth, may result in a reasonably normally developed individual. If similar medication is delayed until after adolescence, the individual will be mentally deficient. Cretinism usually is not inherited, but it illustrates the point. Both nature and nurture contribute to all behavior traits, and their respective contributions can never be specifically weighted.

On the other hand, in a general way, we are probably justified in speaking of certain given conditions, such as the single-gene-determined mental deficiencies, as inherited. In these conditions, the range of environmentally produced variations is very narrow. In the ordinary familial, higher-level types of mental defectives, both heredity and environment affect the ultimate level of attainment over a considerable range. We never feel that we can speak of these deficiencies as either environmental or inherited, since variations in either can have a significant effect on functional level.

When the heredity is presumably normal, but an environmental factor such as brain injury so lowers the individual's capabilities that he functions defectively both socially and psychometrically, we can legitimately speak of the deficiency as environmentally induced. In these cases the range of variation has been so narrowed by an environmental factor that the person's original inheritance has relatively little influence on his functional level.

In the last group are those individuals who, because of environmental restrictions, emotional conditioning, or personality disorganization, function at a level comparable to the mental retardates in the other groups. These individuals still have potential, and their deficiencies are presumably remediable. Adequate training or psychotherapy can often greatly increase their functional level. Such people are discussed more fully in the chapter on the culturally deviant.

The nature-nurture controversy revisited in the 1970s

The questions of the relative heritability of intelligence and the validity of inferring the causes of cross-cultural differences from measures of heritability were raised anew in the late 1960s by the publications of Arthur Jensen of the University of California. Jensen (1968, 1969, 1973) derived heritability values from the statistical analysis of intelligence test scores and claimed that these values were sufficiently high to indicate that intelligence is overwhelmingly the result of genetic inheritance rather than environmental influences. Jensen also contended that compensatory educational programs, such as Head Start, had failed to reduce the educational deficits of the disadvantaged children, particularly of the blacks, because these children were incapable of the higher levels of conceptual learning as the result of their genetic limitations. Predictably, the appearance of Jensen's articles in the *Harvard Educational Review* evoked many critical reactions.[1]

In the years that have intervened since Jensen's original publications, the controversy has accelerated rather than abated. According to E. M. Hetherington and C. W. McIntyre (1975), at least fifteen books and collections of readings dealing with the issue were published in 1974. The complex issue of the interactive roles of nature and nurture in the determination of intellectual functioning has been oversimplified and dichotomized in the popular press. One result of this controversy has been a movement to restrict the use of mental tests, particularly in situations involving minority groups.

Our major objections to Jensen's interpretations and extrapolations are implicit in the preceding discussion. However, since Jensen has raised the racial issue, we will summarize the research findings which cause us to question the Jensen genetic interpretation of the origin of racial differences in intelligence.

1. Heritability values are based on individual differences within a specific group and have nothing to do with mean differences between

---

[1] For two of the more objective evaluations, see Layzer (1974) and Loehlin, Lindzey, & Spuhler (1975).

groups. Therefore, the percent of heritability based on the variances within one population cannot be extrapolated to another population or to differences between populations. The values obtained on one population or subpopulation may differ markedly from those on another. A heritability figure is not a value that can be applied to a trait in general but only to a trait as found in a particular population and under a particular set of environmental circumstances (Feldman & Lewontin, 1975).

2. The ranges of environmental and genetic variations in the groups and environs investigated are also critical variables in determining heritability values. A given behavioral characteristic may be uninfluenced by environmental variations within a particular range but be extremely sensitive to changes outside that range. For example, R. M. Cooper and J. P. Zubek (1958) found that the large difference between "bright" and "dull" strains of rats disappeared entirely when the rats were reared in either a very restricted or an enriched environment. Large, genetically determined differences in rates of learning present under one set of environmental circumstances disappear entirely under different developmental conditions.

3. A given environmental change may exert marked effects at one stage of development but have relatively little influence if present during other developmental periods—the critical-period phenomenon. A child born without a functional thyroid gland (a potential cretin), who receives a small amount of thyroxin from birth, can develop into a mentally normal adult instead of a low-grade mentally retarded individual. However, the same amount of thyroxin will have no appreciable effect on mental level when administered to an adult cretin. B. S. Bloom (1964) and others believe that the first four years of a child's life constitute a critical period for mental development and that environmental enrichment or improvement has a much greater effect during this period than later in life.

4. The overall difference between the mean intelligence tests scores of blacks and whites in America is about one standard deviation or 15 IQ points (Jensen, 1968). Jensen believes that this difference cannot be accounted for in terms of environmental differences. However, it has been shown that environmental differences commonly encountered in contemporary society can produce larger differences. The mean difference between the IQ's of identical twins reared under contrasting "favorable" and "unfavorable" conditions is about 20 points (Newman, Freeman, & Holinger, 1937; Bloom, 1964). Siblings reared apart under similar conditions differ by approximately the same amount (Sontag, Baker, & Nelson, 1958). Bloom (1964) believes that 20 points is a conservative estimate of the effects of extreme social environments on measured intelligence. Thus it seems that the social, economic, educational, and

color-related caste differences between blacks and whites in America *can* account for the black–white intelligence-test-score differences and do not necessitate the postulation of intellectually-related genetic differences.

5. The heritability of a trait within a population and the hereditary origin of a difference between two populations are not the same and are not necessarily related. Some extreme examples will make this point clear. The genetic variability of pure strains (identical twins, etc.) is zero and the heritability values obtained within such strains are also zero. All variations within strains are due to environment. However, if the contrasting strains have been selectively bred and developed for differing specific behavioral characteristics such as maze "brightness" and "dullness," the differences between the two populations, reared under the same environments, are entirely hereditary. Heritability values are zero but group differences are entirely hereditary. Conversely, if two groups of identical genetic endowment are reared under very different circumstances, the resulting group differences will be entirely of environmental origin with zero heritability within each group. The etiology of differences between two populations has no necessary relation to the heritability within the populations and cannot be inferred from it (Feldman & Lewontin, 1975).

6. The fact that a large percentage of the variance of a trait within a population is attributed to hereditary factors does not preclude the production of significant group changes due to changing environmental variables. Estimates of the percentage variance in height due to genetic factors run as high as 90 percent. However, this does not prevent major illness or inadequate diet during critical growth periods from exerting significant effects on adult height. In the early years of this century, children born in the United States after their immigrant parents had resided here for four or more years were considerably taller than their siblings born and reared partly or completely in Europe (Boas, 1911). The second- and third-generation American-born children of pure Japanese extraction are several inches taller than their parents or grandparents born and reared in Japan (Tanner, 1973).

7. The available evidence suggests that if all relevant environmental variables could be equated, the black–white difference in intelligence tests scores would disappear. Some evidence supporting this contention is as follows:

a. The first intelligence test (Army Alpha) administered to a nationwide sample showed that the average score of Northern World War I black army recruits was considerably above that of Southern blacks. The median scores of blacks in Pennsylvania, New York, Illinois, and Ohio were above those of white recruits in Mississippi, Kentucky, Arkansas, and Georgia. However, the latter differences were small and based on small numbers of cases and attracted little attention when first reported. (Yerkes, 1921).

b. The superiority of Northern as compared with Southern blacks, found consistently in the early studies, was shown not to be a result of a selective migration of the superior individuals to the North (Klineberg, 1935; Lee, 1951).

c. The children of black migrants from the South showed increases in intelligence test scores directly proportionate to length of residence in the North (Klineberg, 1935, Lee, 1951). Earlier studies had found a similar relationship between the Army Alpha test scores of foreign-born immigrants and length of residence in the United States (Brigham, 1923).

d. The more closely the socio-economic and educational backgrounds of black and white comparison groups are equated, the smaller the test score differences become (McCord & Demerath, 1968).

e. When groups are equated on such specific things as proportions of broken homes, time spent with children in educational-related activities, and housing crowdedness factors, in addition to the conventional indices of socio-economic and educational status, the customary test-score discrepancies practically disappear (Tulkin, 1968).

f. One group of 130 black children, adopted and reared by superior white parents (mean IQ's of 120), scored above the national average on conventional intelligence tests (their mean IQ was 106). The earlier the children were adopted, the higher their IQ's. The lowest score of any adopted black was 86—close to the national average for all black children. The school achievement of these black children was above the national average (reading and math at the fifty-fifth percentile) (Grow, 1975; Scarr-Salapatek & Weinberg, 1975). A similar study of 141 Korean children who were adopted into their middle-class American homes before the age of three (the mean age was eighteen months) obtained intelligence and achievement test scores equal to, or above, the norms for American children six years later (Winick, Meyer, & Harris, 1975).

During the last fifty years, opinion has shifted from a preponderance in support of heredity as being the major cause of the superior achievements in test-score performances of whites as compared with blacks, to a small dissonant minority who still hold this belief. Arguments in support of the contentions of this latter group are given by H. E. Garrett (1962), A. M. Shuey, (1966), and Jensen (1973).[2]

DIVERSITY AMONG THE MENTALLY RETARDED

Mental retardation is not a disease, although diseases may accompany or cause it. It is not a unitary thing. Etiologically it is many things and has a bewildering array of causes. Its physical accompaniments are either many and diverse or practically nil, depending upon the etiological type

---

[2] For recent, more balanced reviews of the problem, see Loehlin, Lindzey, & Spuhler (1975), and Feldman & Lewontin (1975).

and the level of retardation. The personalities and temperaments of the mentally retarded are almost as diverse as are those of groups of the population at large. Even when the mentally retarded are placed in so-called homogeneous groups for educational purposes, tremendous scholastic differences still exist within these classes. The mentally retarded are a heterogeneous group who are identified, and to some degree segregated and given special consideration because of one characteristic—inadequate adaptive behavior resulting from impairment of intellectual functioning.

When people ask "What are mentally retarded people like?" they are asking a meaningless question. They would not ask "What are short or fat people like?" Most people would agree that about the only thing that such physically deviant individuals have in common is their diminutive stature or their obesity. While being mentally retarded has more widespread behavioral consequences than being tall or being fat, the similarities between mental retardates and intellectually normal people exceed their differences. The mentally retarded are almost as statistically variable and individually distinctive as are people whose intelligence is within the normal range.

SUMMARY

The causes of mental retardation are both hereditary and environmental. A few rare types of mental retardation are caused by a single dominant gene. A larger number of types apparently are due to a single recessive gene. Chromosomal anomalies account for certain types of mental retardation. The hereditary components of the ordinary "familial," or nonclinical, class of mental retarded are multifactorial or polygenetic and interact with environmental factors.

The importance assigned to the genetic factor in the determination of mental level has varied tremendously from time to time and from researcher to researcher. The period from 1900 to 1930 was a time when great emphasis was placed on the hereditary component. From 1930 to 1950, the emphasis shifted to environment as the principal determinant of intellectual level. The problem of assigning specific weights or values to heredity and environment as they influence the intelligence level is almost beyond solution because of the many variables. The concept of a "range of variation" within which either heredity and environment may operate is suggested as a useful frame of reference.

Environmental causes of mental retardation are prenatal physical trauma, nutritional or toxic infections, blood incompatibility, and radio-activity. Natal causes include prematurity, asphyxia, and physical trauma. Postnatal causes are physical trauma, infections, dietary and extreme sensory deprivation, or general environmental deprivation.

Mental retardation is not a unitary thing. It is not a disease. It has diverse causes and physical accompaniments and embraces a rather wide range of mental levels.

REFERENCES

ADAMS, R. I., & M. Z. SALAM, "General Aspects of the Pathology of Cranial Trauma in Infants and Children," in C. R. Angle & E. A. Bering, Jr., eds., *Physical Trauma as an Etiological Agent in Mental Retardation* (Washington, D.C.: U.S. Department of Health, Education and Welfare, 1970).

ALLEN, R. M., A. D. CORTAZZO, & C. ADAMS, "Factors in an Adaptive Behavior Checklist for Use with Retardates," *Training School Bulletin*, 1970, *67*, 144–57.

ANDERSON, S., & S. MESSICK, "Social Competence in Young Children," *Developmental Psychology*, 1974, *10*, 282–93.

APGAR, V., "Neonatal Anoxia: I. A Study of the Relation of Oxygenation at Birth to Intellectual Development," *Pediatrics*, 1955, *15*, 652–62.

ASHURST, D. I., & C. E. MEYERS, "Social System and Clinical Model in School Identification of the Educable Mentally Retarded," in G. Tarjan, R. K. Eyman, & C. E. Myers, eds., *Sociobehavioral Studies in Mental Retardation* (Washington, D.C.: American Association on Mental Retardation, 1973).

BALKEN, E. R., & S. MAURER, "Variations of Psychological Measurements Associated with Increased Vitamin-B Complex Feeding in Young Children," *Journal of Experimental Psychology*, 1934, *17*, 65–92.

BALTHAZAR, E. E., *Balthazar Scales of Adaptive Behavior* (Champaign, Ill.: Research Press, 1971).

BANHAM, K. M., *A Social Competence Inventory for Adults* (Durham, N.C.: Family Life Publications, 1968).

BARNES, B., "Lead Poisoning in Remodeling of Old Homes," *Children Today*, 1973, 2 (5), 7–10.

BEGAB, M. J., "The Major Dilemma of Mental Retardation: Shall We Prevent It?" *American Journal of Mental Deficiency*, 1974, *78*, 519–29.

BENDA, C. E., *Developmental Disorders of Mental Retardation and Cerebral Palsies* (New York: Grune & Stratton, 1952).

BERING, E. A., JR., "Mental Retardation Caused by Physical Trauma," *Science*, 1969, *164*, 460–66.

BERNHARDT, K. S., "Vitamin A Deficiency and Learning in the Rat," *Journal of Comparative Psychology*, 1936, *22*, 277–78.

BERNHARDT, K. S., M. L. NORTHWAY, & C. M. TATHAM, "The Effect of Added Thiamin on Intelligence and Learning with Identical Twins," *Canadian Journal of Psychology*, 1948, *2*, 58–61.

BLOOM, B. S., *Stability and Change in Human Characteristics* (New York: John Wiley, 1964).

BOAS, F., *Changes in Bodily Form of Descendants of Immigrants* (Washington, D.C.: U.S. Senate Document No. 208, 1911).

BOFFEY, P. M., "Hiroshima/Nagasaki: Atomic Bomb Casualty Commission Perseveres in Sensitive Studies," *Science,* 1970, *168,* 679–83.

BRIGHAM, C. C., *A Study of American Intelligence* (Princeton, N.J.: Princeton University Press, 1923).

CAIN, L. F., S. LEVINE, & F. F. ELZEY, *Manual for the Cain-Levine Social Competency Scale* (Palo Alto, Ca.: Consulting Psychologists Press, 1963).

CAVENESS, W., "Epidemiologic Studies in Head Injury," in C. A. Angle & E. A. Bering, Jr. eds., *Physical Trauma as an Etiological Agent in Mental Retardation* (Washington, D.C.: U.S. Department of Health, Education and Welfare, 1970).

CERVA, L., V. ZIMALS, & K. NOVAK, "Amoebic Meningoencephalic: A New Amoebic Isolate," *Science,* 1969, *163,* 575–76.

COOPER, R. M., & J. P. ZUBEK, "Effects of Enriched and Restricted Environments on the Learning Ability of Bright and Dull Rats," *Canadian Journal of Psychology,* 1958, *12,* 159–64.

CUSHNER, I. M., "Irradiation of the Fetus," in A. C. Barnes, ed., *Intra-uterine Development* (Philadelphia: Lea & Febiger, 1968).

DANN, M., S. Z. LEVINE, & E. V. NEW, "The Development of Prematurely Born Children with Birth Weights or Minimal Postnatal Weights of 1,000 Grams or Less," *Pediatrics,* 1958, *22,* 1037–53.

DARKE, R. A., "Late Effects of Severe Asphyxia Neonatonum," *Journal of Pediatrics,* 1944, *24,* 148–52.

DAWSON, S., & J. C. CONN, "Effects of Encephalitis Lethargica on the Intelligence of Children," *Archives of Diseases of Childhood,* 1929, *1,* 357–89.

DAY, M. F., & A. HAINES, "Erythroblastosis Caused by Rh Incompatibility," *Pediatrics,* 1954, *13,* 333–38.

DODRILL, C., D. MACFARLANE, & R. BOYD, "Effects of Intrauterine Rubella Infection and Its Consequent Physical Symptoms on Intellectual Abilities," *Journal of Consulting and Clinical Psychology,* 1974, *42,* 251–55.

DOLL, E. A., *The Vineland Social Maturity Scale: Revised Condensed Manual of Directions* (Vineland, N.J.: Training School, 1936).

DOLL, E. A., "The Essentials of an Inclusive Concept of Mental Deficiency," *American Journal of Mental Deficiency,* 1941, *46,* 214–19.

DOLL, E. A., *The Measurement of Social Competence: A Manual for the Vineland Social Maturity Scale* (Minneapolis: Educational Testing Bureau, 1953).

DORFMAN, A., ed., *Antenatal Diagnosis* (Chicago: University of Chicago Press, 1972).

DRAKE, J. W. (Committee Chairman), "Environmental Mutagenic Hazards," *Science,* 1975, *187,* 503–14.

DRILLIEN, C. M., "The Incidence of Mental and Physical Handicaps in School-age Children of Very Low Birth Weights," *Pediatrics,* 1961, *27,* 452–64.

EICHENLAUB, J. E., "Meningitis," *Today's Health,* 1955, *52,* 40–42.

EICHENWALD, H. F., & P. C. FRY, "Nutrition and Learning," *Science,* 1969, *163,* 644–48.

FELDMAN, M. W., & R. C. LEWONTIN, "The Heritability Hang-up," *Science,* 1975, *190,* 1163–67.

FITZHARDINGE, P. M., & E. M. STEVENS, "The Small-for-date Infant," *Pediatrics,* 1972, *50,* 50–57.

FRANK, M., "The Effects of a Rickets-producing Diet on the Learning Ability of White Rats," *Journal of Comparative Psychology,* 1932, *13,* 87–105.

FRASER, F. C., "Teratogenesis of the Central Nervous System," in H. A. Stevens & R. Hebens, eds., *Mental Retardation: A Review of Research* (Chicago: University of Chicago Press, 1964).

FREEMAN, F. N., K. J. HOLZINGER, & B. C. MITCHELL, "The Influence of Environment on the Intelligence, School Achievement, and Conduct of Foster Children," *Yearbook of the National Society for the Study of Education,* 1928, *27,* 103–218.

GARDNER, J. M., *The Comprehensive Behavior Checklist: Manual* (Columbus, Ohio: Columbus State Institute, 1970).

GARRETT, H. E., "The SPSSI and Racial Differences," *American Psychologist,* 1962, *17,* 260–63.

GESELL, A., *The First Five Years of Life* (New York: Harper & Row, 1948).

GLASSER, F. B., M. JACOBS, & R. SCHAIN, "The Relation of Rh to Mental Deficiency," *Psychiatric Quarterly,* 1951, *25,* 282–87.

GOLDSTEIN, L., & D. P. MURPHY, "Microencephalic Idiocy Following Radium Therapy for Uterine Cancer During Pregnancy," *American Journal of Obstetric Gynecology,* 1929, *18,* 189–95.

GOTTESMAN, I. I., "Genetic Aspects of Intelligent Behavior," in N. R. Ellis, ed., *Handbook of Mental Deficiency* (New York: McGraw-Hill, 1963).

GOTTFRIED, A. W., "Intellectual Consequences of Perinatal Anoxia," *Psychological Bulletin,* 1973, *80,* 231–42.

GRANAT, K., & S. GRANAT, "Below-average Intelligence and Mental Retardation," *American Journal of Mental Deficiency,* 1973, *78,* 27–32.

GREGG, M. M., "Congenital Cataract Following German Measles in the Mother," *Transactions of Ophthalmic Society of Australia,* 1941, *3,* 35.

GROSSMAN, H. J., ed., *Manual on Terminology and Classification in Mental Retardation* (Baltimore: American Association on Mental Deficiency Special Publication Series, No. 2, 1973).

GROW, L., *Black Children—White Parents: A Study of Transracial Adoption* (New York: Child Welfare League of America, 1975).

GUETZKOW, H., & J. BROZEK, "Intellectual Functions with Restricted Intakes of B-complex Vitamins," *American Journal of Physiology,* 1946, *59,* 358–81.

GUNZBURG, H. C., "Vocational and Social Rehabilitation of the Feebleminded," in A. M. Clarke & A. D. Clarke, eds., *Mental Deficiency: The Changing Outlook* (London: Methuen, 1958).

GUNZBURG, H. C., *Social Competence and Mental Handicap* (London: Baillière Tindall, 1973).

HARRELL, R. F., "Further Effects of Added Thiamine on Learning and Other Processes," *Teachers College Contributions to Education*, 1947, *928*, 102.

HARRELL, R. F., E. WOODWARD, & A. I. GATES, "The Influence of Vitamin Supplementation of the Diets of Pregnant and Lactating Women on the Intelligence of Their Offspring," *Metabolism*, 1956, *5*, 552–61.

HETHERINGTON, E. M., & C. W. McINTYRE, "Developmental Psychology," in M. R. Rosenzweig & L. W. Porter, eds., *Annual Review of Psychology*, vol. 26 (Palo Alto, Ca.: Annual Reviews, Inc., 1975).

HOBBS, N., *The Futures of Children* (San Francisco: Jossey-Bass, 1975).

HURST, J. F., "The Meaning and Use of Difference Scores Obtained Between the Performance on the Stanford-Binet Intelligence Scale and the Vineland Social Maturity Scale," *Journal of Clinical Psychology*, 1962, *18*, 153–60.

HUTT, M. L., & R. G. GIBBY, *The Mentally Retarded Child*, 2nd ed. (Boston: Allyn & Bacon, 1965).

JENSEN, A. R., "Social Class, Race, and Genetics: Implications for Education," *American Educational Research Journal*, 1968, *5*, 1–42.

JENSEN, A. R., "How Much Can We Boost IQ and Scholastic Achievement?" *Harvard Educational Review*, 1969, *39*, 1–123.

JENSEN, A. R., *Educability and Group Differences* (New York: Harper & Row, 1973).

JONES, H. E., "Environmental Influences on Mental Development," in L. Carmichael, ed., *Manual of Child Psychology* (New York: John Wiley & Sons, 1946).

KAPLAN, B. J., "Malnutrition and Mental Deficiency," *Psychological Bulletin*, 1972, *78*, 321–34.

KLEIN, A. H., & F. M. KENNY, "Improved Prognosis in Congenital Hypothyroidism Treated Before Age Three Months," *Journal of Pediatrics*, 1972, *81*, 912.

KLINEBERG, O., *Negro Intelligence and Selective Migration* (New York: Columbia University Press, 1935).

KUGELMASS, I. N., *The Management of Mental Deficiency in Children* (New York: Grune & Stratton, 1954).

LAMBERT, N. M., M. R. WILCOX, & W. P. GLEASON, *The Educationally Retarded Child* (New York: Grune & Stratton, 1975).

LAYZER, D., "Heritability Analyses of IQ Scores: Science or Numerology?" *Science*, 1974, *183*, 1259–66.

LEE, E. S., "Negro Intelligence and Selective Migration: A Philadelphia Test of the Klineberg Hypothesis," *American Sociological Review*, 1951, *16*, 227–33.

LEJEUNE, J., & R. TURPIN, "Chromosomal Aberrations in Man," *American Journal of Human Genetics*, 1961, *13*, 175–84.

LELAND, H., "Adaptive Behavior and Mentally Retarded Behavior," in R. K. Eyman, C. E. Meyers, & G. Tarjan eds., *Sociobehavioral Studies in Mental Retardation* (Washington, D.C.: American Association on Mental Deficiency, 1974).

LEMKAU, P. C., C. TIETZE, & M. CASPER, "Mental Hygiene Problems in an Urban District: Third Paper," *Mental Hygiene*, 1942, *26*, 275–88.

LILIENFELD, A. M., *Epidemiology of Mongolism* (Baltimore: Johns Hopkins Press, 1968).

LIN-FU, J. S., "Preventing Lead Poisoning in Children," *Children Today*, 1973, 2 (1), 2–6.

LOEHLIN, J. C., G. LINDZEY, & J. N. SPUHLER, *Race Differences in Intelligence* (San Francisco: W. H. Freeman, 1975).

McCORD, W M., & N. J. DEMERATH, "Negro Versus White Intelligence: A Continuing Controversy," *Harvard Educational Review*, 1968, *28*, 120–35.

McKUSICK, V. A., *Mendelian Inheritance in Man: Catalogs of Autosomal Dominant, Autosomal Recessive, and X-linked Phenotypes* (Baltimore: Johns Hopkins Press, 1971).

MALONE, D. R., & W. P. CHRISTIAN, JR., "Adaptive Behavior Scale as a Screening Measure for Special Education Placement," *American Journal of Mental Deficiency*, 1974, *79*, 367–71.

MARX, J. L., "Cytomegalovirus: A Major Cause of Birth Defects," *Science*, 1975, *190*, 1184–86.

MASLAND, R. L., S. B. SARASON, & T. GLADWIN, *Mental Subnormality* (New York: Basic Books, 1958).

MAURER, S., "The Effect of Acute Vitamin A Depletion upon Maze Performance in Rats," *Journal of Comparative Psychology*, 1935, *20*, 456–58.

MERCER, J. R., "IQ: The Lethal Label," *Psychology Today*, 1972, *6*, 44.

MERCER, J. R., "The Myth of 3% Prevalence," in G. Tarjan, R. K. Eyman, & C. E. Meyers, eds., *Sociobehavioral Studies in Mental Retardation* (Washington, D.C.: American Association on Mental Retardation, 1973).

MERCIER, C., *Sanity and Insanity* (London: Walter Scott, 1890).

MEYER, R. J., "The Epidemiology of Head Trauma in Childhood," in C. R. Angle & E. A. Bering, Jr., eds., *Physical Trauma as an Etiological Agent in Mental Retardation* (Washington, D.C.: U.S. Department of Health, Education and Welfare, 1970).

MICHAELS, R. H., & G. W. MELLIN, "Prospective Experience with Maternal Rubella and Associated Congenital Malformations," *Pediatrics*, 1960, *26*, 200–209.

MILLER, R. W., "Delayed Radiation Effects in Atomic Bomb Survivors," *Science*, 1969, *166*, 569–74.

MINTO, A., & F. J. ROBERTS, "The Psychiatric Complications of Toxoplasmosis," *Lancet*, 1959, *1*, 1180–82.

MOORE, H., & E. MATHIAS, "The Effect of Vitamin A and B Deficiency on the Maze-learning Ability of the White Rat," *Journal of Comparative Psychology*, 1934, *16*, 487–96.

MORGAN, C. T., *Physiological Psychology*, 3rd ed. (New York: McGraw-Hill, 1965).

MURPHY, D. P., "Ovarian Irradiation: Its Effects on the Health of Subsequent Children," *Surgery, Gynecology, and Obstetrics*, 1928, *47*, 201–15.

NATELSON, S. E., & M. P. SAYERS, "The Fate of Children Sustaining Severe Head Trauma During Birth," *Pediatrics*, 1973, *51*, 169–70.

NEWMAN, H. H., F. H., FREEMAN, & K. J. HOLINGER, *Twins: A Study of Heredity and Environment* (Chicago: University of Chicago Press, 1937).

NICKERSON, G., & P. N. MACDERMOT, "Psychometric Evaluation and Factors Affecting the Performance of Children Who Have Recovered from Tuberculous Meningitis," *Pediatrics*, 1961, *27*, 68–82.

NIHIRA, K., "Importance of Environmental Demands in the Measurement of Adaptive Behavior," in G. Tarjan, R. K. Eyman, & C. E. Meyers, eds., *Sociobehavioral Studies in Mental Retardation* (Washington, D.C.: American Association on Mental Retardation, 1973).

NIHIRA, K.; R. FOSTER; M. SHELLBAAS; & H. LELAND, *Adaptive Behavior Scales Manual* (Washington, D.C.: American Association on Mental Deficiency, 1969).

NITOWSKY, H. M., "Prescriptive Screening for Inborn Errors of Metabolism: A Critique," *American Journal of Mental Deficiency*, 1973, *77*, 538–50.

O'CONNER, N., & J. TIZARD, *The Social Problems of Mental Deficiency* (New York: Pergamon Press, 1956).

O'HANLON, G. S., "An Investigation into the Relationship Between Fertility and Intelligence," *British Journal of Educational Psychology*, 1940, *10*, 196–211.

OUGHTERSON, A. W., *Medical Effects of the Atomic Bomb in Japan* (New York: McGraw-Hill, 1956).

PASAMANICK, B., & A. M. LILIENFELD, "The Association of Fetal Factors with the Development of Mental Deficiency," *Journal of American Medical Association*, 1955, *159*, 155–60.

PENROSE, L. S., *The Biology of Mental Defect*, 3rd ed. (New York: Grune & Stratton, 1963).

PETERSON, J., *Early Conceptions and Tests of Intelligence* (Chicago: World Book, 1925).

RICHARDSON, S. A., H. G. BIRCH, & M. E. HERTZIG, "School Performance of Children Who Were Severely Malnourished in Infancy," *American Journal of Mental Deficiency*, 1973, *77*, 623–32.

ROBERTS, J. A., *An Introduction to Medical Genetics* (London: Oxford University Press, 1963).

ROSS, R. T., *Fairview Self-help Scale* (Costa Mesa, Ca.: Fairview State Hospital, 1969).

ROSSO, P., "Maternal Malnutrition and Placental Transfer of D-aminoisbutric Acid in the Rat," *Science*, 1975, *187*, 648–49.

RUSSELL, J. K., G. A. NELIGAN, & D. G. MILLAR, "Obstetric Trauma in Newcastle-upon-Tyne," in C. A. Angle & E. A. Bering, Jr., eds., *Psycical Trauma as an Etiological Agent in Mental Retardation* (Washington, D.C.: U.S. Department of Health, Education and Welfare, 1970).

SABATINO, D. A., & H. CRAMBLATT, "A Longitudinal Study of Children with Learning Disabilities Subsequent to Hospitalization for Viral Encephalitis," *Journal of Learning Disabilities*, 1969, *2*, 62–72.

SARASON, S. B., & T. GLADWIN, "Psychological and Cultural Problems in Mental Subnormality," in R. L. Masland, ed., *Mental Subnormality* (New York: Basic Books, 1958).

SCARR-SALAPATEK, S., & R. A. WEINBERG, "The War over Race and IQ: When Black Children Grow Up in White Homes," *Psychology Today*, 1975, *9* (7), 80–82.

SCHWARTZ, B. J., & R. M. ALLEN, "Measuring Adaptive Behavior: The Dynamics of a Longitudinal Approach," *American Journal of Mental Deficiency*, 1974, *79*, 424–33.

SHUEY, A. M., *The Testing of Negro Intelligence*, 2nd ed. (New York: Social Science Press, 1966).

SKINNER, C. W., JR., "The Rubella Problem," *American Journal of Diseases of Children*, 1961, *101*, 104–12.

SNOWDON, C. T., & B. A. SANDERSON, "Lead Pica Produced in Rats," *Science*, 1974, *183*, 92–94.

SONTAG, L., C. BAKER, & V. NELSON, "Mental Growth and Personality: A Longitudinal Study," *Monograph of the Society for Research in Child Development*, 1958, *23* (2), 1–143.

SWAN, C., "Rubella and Congenital Malformations," *Medical Annual*, 1947, 303–10.

TANNER, J. M., "Growing Up," *Scientific American*, 1973, *229*, 34–54.

TARJAN, G.; S. W. WRIGHT; R. K. EYMAN; & C. V. KEERAN, "Natural History of Mental Retardation: Some Aspects of Epidemiology," *American Journal of Mental Deficiency*, 1973, *77*, 369–79.

TJIO, J. H., & A. LEVAN, "The Chromosomal Number of Man," *Hereditas*, 1956, *42*, 1–6.

TOWBIN, A., "Mental Retardation Due to Germinal Matrix Infraction," *Science*, 1969, *164*, 156–61.

TREDGOLD, A. F., *Mental Deficiency* (London: Ballière, Tindall & Cox, 1908).

TREDGOLD, A. F., *A Textbook of Mental Deficiency (Amentia)*, 8th ed. (Baltimore: Williams & Wilkins, 1952).

TREDGOLD, A. F., & K. SODDY, *Mental Deficiency*, 9th ed. (Baltimore: Williams & Wilkins, 1956).

TULKIN, S. R., "Race, Class, Family, and School Achievement," *Journal of Personality and Social Psychology*, 1968, *9*, 31–37.

VANDERVEER, B., & E. SCHWEID, "Infant Assessment: Stability of Mental Functioning in Young Retarded Children," *American Journal of Mental Deficiency*, 1974, *79*, 1–4.

WALLIN, J. E., *Mental Deficiency* (Brandon, Vt.: Journal of Clinical Psychology, 1956).

WARD, I. L., "Prenatal Stress Feminizes and Demasculinizes the Behaviors of Males," *Science*, 1972, *175*, 82–84.

WARREN, N., "Malnutrition and Mental Development," *Psychological Bulletin*, 1973, *80*, 324–28.

WATERS, W. J., "The Prevention of Bilirubin Encephalopathy," *Journal of Pediatrics*, 1958, *52*, 559–65.

WEINMAN, D., & A. H. CHANDLER, "Toxoplasmosis in Man and Swine: An Investigation of the Possible Relationship," *Journal of American Medical Association,* 1956, *161,* 229.

WILLERMAN, L., "Fetal Head Position During Delivery and Intelligence," in C. A. Angle & E. A. Bering, Jr., eds., *Physical Trauma as an Etiological Agent in Mental Retardation* (Washington, D.C.: U.S. Department of Health, Education and Welfare, 1970).

WILSON, G. S., M. M. DESMOND, & W. M. VERNIAUD, "Early Development of Infants of Heroin-addicted Mothers," *American Journal of Diseases of Children,* 1973, *126,* 457–62.

WINICK, M., K. K. MEYER, & R. C. HARRIS, "Malnutrition and Environmental Enrichment by Early Adoption," *Science,* 1975, *190,* 1173–75.

WOLF, A., & D. COWEN, "Perinatal Infections of the Central Nervous System," *Journal of Neuropathology and Experimental Neurology,* 1959, *18,* 191–243.

WRIGHT, F. H., "A Controlled Follow-up Study of Small Prematures Born from 1952 Through 1956," *American Journal of Diseases of Children,* 1972, *124,* 506–21.

YANNET, H., & R. LIEBERMAN, "Further Studies of ABO Secretion Status and Mental Deficiency," *American Journal of Mental Deficiency,* 1948, *52,* 314–17.

YERKES, R. M., ed., "Psychological Examining in the United States Army," *Memoirs, National Academy of Science,* 1921, *15,* 890.

ZAMENHOF, S., E. VAN MARKENS, & L. GRAUEL, "DNA (Cell Number) in Neonatal Brain: Second Generation (F²) Alteration by Maternal (F⁰) Dietary Protein Restriction," *Science,* 1971, *172,* 850–51.

ZELSON, C., "Current Concepts: Infants of Addicted Mothers," *New England Journal of Medicine,* 1973, *288,* 1393–95.

Chapter 9

Mental retardation:
Mild and severe

In this chapter we discuss degrees of mental retardation ranging from *mild* to *severe*. We shall use an IQ of 50, associated with a comparable level of adaptive behavior, the most commonly used dividing line between the *educable* and *trainable* mentally retarded, as an arbitrary boundary line between these categories. In doing this, we are including the AAMD *profound, severe,* and part of the *moderate* groupings in our *severely retarded* category. The AAMD *mild* and part of the *moderate* categories are combined into our *mild mental retardation* group.

MILD RETARDATION

Mentally retarded children with IQ's above 50 have enough in common to warrant discussing them all together. First, the subgroups within this range merge imperceptibly into each other in terms of most social and educationally significant variables. Second, they represent an arbitrarily designated low end of the normal distribution curve of intelligence. Third, their low intellectual status is generally caused by an interacting combination of handicapping multigenic and/or environmental factors. Fourth, although individuals in this broad category are statistically below average in physique and general health, they are not perceptibly different in these respects from the general population. More specifically, they usually lack the physical stigmata often found in the severely retarded. Fifth, most of the mildly mentally retarded are first identified as educational retardates and only after extensive study are labeled mentally retarded. Follow-up studies of children in this category indicate that most of them, as adults, merge into society and adjust to out-of-school situations only slightly less satisfactorily than do their intellectually normal age-mates from the same socio-economic background.

This category of the mentally retarded has traditionally included many of the children now designated *educationally handicapped* or *culturally disadvantaged*. These individuals are handicapped principally by their low academic aptitudes and the ever-increasing demands of their culture.

Identification of the mildly mentally retarded

In the previous chapter we indicated that the severely mentally retarded child is likely to be identified first by the family or the physician because of his marked developmental failures. The extent and significance of the retardation may then be verified or questioned psychometrically. The dynamics of the family largely determine whether the child becomes a candidate for foster-home or institutional placement or remains in his natural home. We also pointed out that the bulk of the mentally retarded (the mildly or educable mentally retarded) are identified by the school systems. The identification and labeling of the mildly mentally retarded in sizable numbers occurred only when it was deemed desirable to establish special school programs or assistance for certain children, most of whom were essentially normal in most other respects, but who were showing marked and persistent educational retardation. The identification of these children as mentally retarded in a psychological and/or medically clinical sense came about as the result of guidelines and standards made necessary by legislation mandating special educational programs and/or assistance for these children. Clinical—largely psychometric —guidelines were set up to determine eligibility for these excess-cost programs. Note that these populations are never first surveyed to determine which children are clinically eligible and then placed in special educational programs. Only when the child fails to perform adequately within a special segment of his social system—the school system—is his intellectual adequacy questioned. When he fails to fulfill his role expectancies as a school learner, he *may be referred* to a psychologist to determine whether his intellectual deficiencies are sufficiently global in nature and degree to *make him eligible* for educational classification as educably mentally retarded. The psychologist is practically never called upon to confirm mental retardation solely on the basis of low test performances, and the current definitions require that both adaptive behavior and psychometric criteria be used.

INCIDENCE

From our earlier discussions, it is clear that estimates of the number of mentally retarded are meaningful only in terms of the criteria applied at a particular time and in a given culture or subculture. Purely psychometric criteria place about 2.5 percent in this category. A combined psychometric and adjustive behavior criterion reduces this figure by about one-half. Figure 9–1 shows this percentage distribution according to a normal probability curve.

When theoretical expectations are compared with actual counts from various sources, the two agree very well for the borderline and mildly mentally retarded, but the estimated prevalence greatly exceeds theoretical expectations for the severely mentally retarded, as shown in table 9–1. The theoretical expectancies are based on the assumption that a person's mental level is produced by a large number of factors combining on the basis of chance. The deviation from normal expectancies at the lower mental levels is thought to reflect the operation of disease, accidents, single dominant or recessive genes, and other infrequently occurring deleterious factors which have massive effects and produce a disproportionate number of severely mentally retarded individuals.

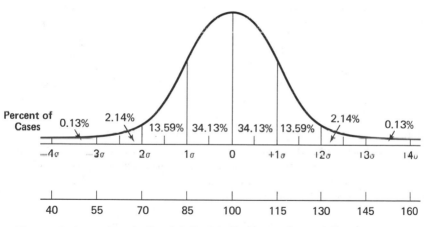

Figure 9–1   Borderline intellect in the general population

PHYSICAL CHARACTERISTICS

We have already indicated that in appearance, physique, and general health the mildly mentally retarded are not noticeably different from their intellectually normal age-mates. However, there is a statistically significant, but low, correlation between intellectual level and various indices of organic status and health (Liese & Lerch, 1974). All studies show the life expectancy of the mentally retarded to be below that of the general population. The incidence of sensory defects and motor

Table 9–1

Departures from expectations based on the normal distribution curve
when 3 percent are considered mentally retarded

IQ	Theoretical Expectancy	Estimated Prevalence	Excess Beyond Theoretical Expectancies	Percentage of Excess
0–20	50	92,750	92,700	185,400
20–50	164,861	371,000	206,139	125
50–70	5,537,710	5,593,360	55,650	1

Data from Dingman & Tarjan (1960), and Robinson & Robinson (1976).

disabilities is greater, and the medical histories of the mentally retarded show a higher incidence of disease and development defects than do those of persons of average or more intelligence (Mercer, 1973; Bruininks, 1974).

The mentally retarded approach the normal much more closely in physique and general health than they do intellectually, but they do show some inferiority. The physical handicaps of the mentally subnormal are the result of a variety of causes. In some cases, the mental and physical inferiorities have a common basis such as accident, disease, and maldevelopment, which produce widespread organic and intellectual deficits. Some of the organic deficits of the retarded are the result of their generally low socio-economic status. A wide variety of health-related factors such as poor diet, inadequate medical care, and greater contact with and less resistance to common communicable diseases and infections are associated with low socio-economic status.

WORK AND JOB EXPECTANCY

Despite the ever-increasing emphasis on academic training for employment in a good number of situations, it is still safe to say that a large number of employment opportunities are open to those who possess less formal training. A vast number of industrial jobs can be performed by a person with limited intelligence with a minimum of formal training. Some of the industrial jobs involve a great deal of repetition. With the rapid increases in work mechanization and simplification, the increase in simple jobs has been, and should continue to be, great. The low-level, semiskilled jobs that are constantly created in turn create a great demand for workers of relatively low mental ability. Many workers of relatively limited intelligence do not become bored by the repetitive nature of the task. They gain a high degree of proficiency and tend to stay on the job longer than some people of high intelligence. Research studies indicate that the dull-normal have sufficient intelligence to successfully pursue a large variety of occupations. Large numbers of automotive mechanics, carpenters, cooks, barbers, miners, farmers, and laborers of various kinds have been found to have intelligence test scores equivalent to the dull-normal and borderline categories.

Jobs requiring little training are usually lower-paying jobs, but there are a lot of them. During times of maximum employment, the dull should encounter no particular difficulty in finding jobs. During slack periods, more of these people will be without jobs, and they will probably be less skillful at finding jobs than the more intelligent workers. However, A. S. Halpern (1973) points out some factors which attenuate the perception of the mentally retarded as marginal workers—the last to be hired and the first to be fired. First, the mentally retarded are not always poor workers; second, some employers are committed to employing the handicapped and assume a protective stance toward them. Halpern cites two studies which indicate that when economic conditions deteriorate and unemployment increases, the employed mentally retarded are *not* in jeopardy in disproportionate numbers.

Over the last decade there has been a tremendous proliferation of school, on-the-job, and workshop programs for the mentally retarded. Most of these are cooperative programs operated jointly by school systems and state departments of vocational rehabilitation (Gold, 1973).

COGNITIVE DEVELOPMENT

Although the mentally retarded have often been considered abnormal in some unique way, they are perceived today as developmentally retarded. According to this view, the mentally retarded are generally perceived as proceeding developmentally through the same cognitive stages as nonretarded children but at a slower rate. It is also thought that because of this slower development, retarded individuals reach a lower cognitive ceiling. Evidence indicates that after about the age of fourteen new cognitive structures are not acquired; thus the slower-developing child will not reach the cognitive capacity of the faster-developing, nonretarded child.

The data on language development support this position. For example, concrete words are readily learned by EMR children, whereas the construction of more abstract words such as *then* and of more difficult logical constructions such as *if-then* are not mastered by EMR children until three or four years after their nonretarded peers have made this acquisition (Anastasiow & Stayrook, 1973). Retardates and nonretardates of equal mental ages do not differ significantly on most indices of educational and linguistic competence. However, the retardate's use of the more abstract grammatical categories is inferior to that of the nonretardate of comparable mental age (Bartel, Bryen, & Seehn, 1973).

ACADEMIC EXPECTANCY

The mildly mentally retarded group is considered *educable*. If the instruction is appropriate and the atmosphere for learning is adequate, these people can be expected to acquire academic skills ranging in level from the second to the fifth or sixth grade. Their maximum academic achievement can be expected to equal that of the average seven- to ten-year-old child. As has been indicated elsewhere (Sawrey & Telford, 1973), the mentally retarded child should not be expected to attain this level of accomplishment at the same chronological age as normal children. The rate of mental growth is not the same for mentally retarded children as it is for normal ones. The normal child of eleven has a mental age of eleven, whereas the mildly mentally retarded child of eleven has a mental age of seven. This is the conventional age for first or second graders, and in all probability the retarded child will be ready to do first or second grade work by the time he is ten or eleven years old.

The academic progress of a group of 163 children with a median IQ of 60.6 who were admitted to special classes at the age of twelve years and seven months yields what are probably typical data for academic progress (Phelps, 1956). Most of these people left school at sixteen, with work certificates, or at eighteen, without them. The median time spent in the class was three years and four months. A small percentage (2.5) graduated from the eighth grade, and a still smaller percentage (1.2) from junior high school. The median reading grade level on leaving school was 3.9, and the median arithmetic grade level was 4.3. The median age of 12.7, when they were admitted to the special classes, may seem rather high, but it is likely that many of them were not mature enough to have profited much from academic instruction before that age.

MAINSTREAMING THE MENTALLY RETARDED

The mainstreaming or normalization trends discussed in chapter 3 have focused primarily on the mildly mentally retarded—the educable. Since the first special schools and classes were established in the United States, segregated facilities have been the most popular settings for educating the mildly mentally retarded. However, during the past decade, discontent with segregated facilities has increased and a variety of alternatives have been developed. One focus of this discontent was the "over-representation" of disadvantaged minority children in the classes for the mentally retarded. Militant minorities brought pressure on state and local educational agencies to remedy the situation. The courts also played a major role in the "decertification" of minority children previously classified as mentally retarded. These developments, a variety of intertwined political and ethical issues, as well as the deinstitutionalization trend already under way, have led to a widespread movement to provide the most "normalizing" and least restrictive educational programs possible for all the handicapped. This movement is bolstered by a wide array of legal precedents, moral mandates, and philosophical arguments (Anderson, 1973b; Birch, 1974; Kindred et al., 1975).

An inquiry addressed to the states and territories of the United States in mid-1973 elicited a list of over eighty programs then in operation for mainstreaming the mentally retarded. The number is now likely to be in the hundreds. These programs vary greatly in detail, but they are all distinguished by the amalgamation of regular and special education into one system which provides a spectrum of services for all children according to their unique educational needs. This makes special education a set of special resources for the entire school population rather than a separate administrative unit providing programs for specific groups designated "special." A basic assumption of the mainstreaming movement is that the regular class teachers can provide for the special needs of all children—deviant as well as normal—with the supplemental services of the special educational personnel.

Mentally retarded children formerly spent most of their school day in their special classes and infrequently joined the other children in joint activities or classes. With mainstreaming, the mentally retarded child is assigned to a regular classroom where the regular instructional program is supplemented by his going to a resource room or learning center for small-group instruction or individual tutoring, according to the program designed for him individually. In ideal situations, the resource teacher, a specialist in teaching the mentally retarded, together with the regular teacher and school psychologist, work out an individual program for each pupil. Pupils may stay in the resource room from a few minutes to several hours, but usually for less than a majority of each school day. The regular and resource teachers share responsibility for instructing the children and planning their programs. Student–teacher ratios usually vary according to the number of deviant children in the class and the nature of the children's special educational needs. The number of pupils assigned to a resource teacher is also limited—often to about twelve or fifteen. Practically all programs provide special in-service training for the regular teachers.

Because the mainstreaming movement has focused so largely on the educable mentally retarded, it may be appropriate to repeat some of the misgivings concerning the trend mentioned in chapter 3. N. Hobbs (1975) and G. M. Clark (1975) have summarized them as follows: (a) Mainstreaming is no more a panacea for the educational problems of the mentally retarded than was the special classroom. If mainstreaming is to be successful, it will require fundamental staffing and structural changes in school programs. The quality of the people who work with the handicapped as well as the nonhandicapped is the central determinant of a program's educational outcomes. The special classes often fail because they are not only a dumping ground for problem children, but also a repository for incompetent teachers. When gifted and involved teachers are supported by sympathetic and helpful administrators and colleagues, the children in special classrooms are genuinely interested in their educational activities, cooperative parents are delighted with their children's placements, and children in the regular classrooms say they wish they could be in the special classrooms. (b) The movement toward integration of the mentally retarded into the regular classrooms will fail if the attitudes of students and teachers are not made a focus of concern. Most teachers have had little, if any, experience with the mentally retarded and share the negative attitudes of the general public with regard to them. We often forget that formal certification of the mentally retarded did not institute the labeling and stigmatizing process for these children. Mentally retarded children in the regular classrooms, who have experienced repeated educational failure, are typically frustrated and have been socially ignored and isolated if not actively rejected. Many teachers will need special assistance if they are to accept, interact effectively with, and successfully integrate handicapped children into their classes. (c) Mainstreaming the mentally retarded will succeed only if they are included in educational programs designed and administered to meet the needs of individual children—handicapped or not. Instruction may be singly, in small groups, or all together, as the situation requires. Such an arrangement will result in the handicapped being separated from the nonhandicapped more often and for longer periods of time, but the governing principle of responsiveness to the learning requirements of individual children will apply to all. (d) The principle of "normalization"—to come as close as possible to normal living and educational procedures for the retarded in light of individual intellectual, physical, and social capacities (Dybwad, 1973)—does not dictate the educational mainstreaming of *all* the mentally retarded (Weismann, 1974). There are many mentally retarded whose problems and/or conditions require total care and/or treatment. Special segregated facilities for the severely retarded and multipally handicapped will still be needed. The wholesale elimination of all special programs and segregated facilities will be as big a mistake as unnecessary and inappropriate placement. The elimination of special classes and other segregated facilities will be helpful only if and when more effective alternatives are available. (e) Mainstreaming the mentally retarded will not solve problems which originate in the culture, the home, and the general educational programs. Practices and values in these areas largely determine which children experience educational difficulties sufficiently great to become candidates for special educational programs or services. Mainstreaming in itself will not change these conditions.

Currently there are few research data concerning the relative effectiveness of mainstreaming the previously segregated mentally retarded. N. G. Haring and D. A. Krug (1975) conclude from their study of a limited number of subjects that a large number of educable mentally retarded children in segregated special education classes are capable of making normal growth in regular programs. However, if the high-risk children are to be successfully mainstreamed, they must be academically and socially prepared for such reentry. Intensive individualized instruction is required to bring these children to a level which enables them to function successfully in regular classes. R. B. Edgerton and C. P. Edgerton (1973), in a largely subjective evaluation of the mainstreaming of mentally retarded children with a "learning lab" program, claim results favorable to such a setting.

SEVERE RETARDATION

Many of the problems centering on social attitudes and programs for the mentally retarded arise from the tendency of many people to perceive the mentally retarded as a single homogeneous group. Increasing recognition of the great diversity of the category is evidenced by the misgivings being expressed over the consequences of deinstitutionalizing and/or mainstreaming the severely handicapped.[1]

Distinguishing characteristics

Whereas most of the mildly mentally retarded are of the ordinary familial type and have few if any distinguishing physical characteristics,

[1] This was the concern of a diverse group of people who recognized that the severely/profoundly retarded have unique needs. They met in November 1974 to organize the American Association for the Education of the Severely/Profoundly Handicapped.

most of the severely mentally retarded are physically deviant. Most of the "clinical types" of mental retardation, which are typically characterized by distinctive patterns of physical symptoms, are severe mental retardation. The causes or accompaniments of severe mental retardation consist, in most cases, of organic brain injury, endocrinological and biochemical deviations of either genetic or environmental origin, and single pathogenic genes.

SOME GENETIC SYNDROMES

Chromosomal aberrations

Down's syndrome (mongolism)   Mongolism constitutes the largest single clinical category of the severely mentally retarded. From 10 to 20 percent of severely retarded children are of this type. In many cases, from a fourth to a third of the students in the classes for severely mentally retarded are mongoloids. Approximately 1 in every 600 to 900 live babies is a mongoloid. The incidence of mongoloid births varies markedly with the age of the mother: 1 in 1,500 for mothers between fifteen and twenty-four years; 1 in 1,000 for mothers between twenty-five and thirty-four; 1 in 150 for mothers over thirty-five; 1 in 70 for mothers forty to forty-four; to 1 in 38 for mothers over forty-five. Even though young mothers run relatively little risk of having a mongoloid child, 1 in every 4 is born to a mother under thirty. This discrepancy between relative incidence and total number occurs because so many more children are born to younger mothers (Lilienfeld, 1969, Koch & de la Cruz, 1975).

More than fifty physical signs have been listed as characteristic of mongolism. The problem is that none of these stigmata is peculiar to mongoloids, and no single sign is found in all of them. In addition, some of these characteristics do not appear until the child is several years old, while others disappear with aging (Dicker, 1972; Falk et al., 1973). D. Gibson, L. Pozony, and D. E. Zarfas (1964), by applying standards of age stability and assessment reliability, have reduced the number of significant diagnostic signs to the following thirteen: (1) a flattened skull which is shorter than it is wide; (2) abnormally upturned nostrils caused by undeveloped nasal bones; (3) abnormal toe spacing (increased space particularly between the first and second toes); (4) disproportionate shortness of the fifth finger; (5) a fifth finger which curves inward; (6) a fifth finger which has only one crease instead of the usual two; (7) short and squared hands; (8) epicanthic fold at the inner corners of the eye; (9) large fissured tongue; (10) a single crease across the palm of the hand (simian crease); (11) abnormally "simplified" ear; (12) adherent ear lobule; and (13) abnormal heart.

J. E. Wallin (1949) considers the presence of three or more of these physical anomalies to be indicative of mongolism. If four or more of these anomalies are present, the individual is "almost certainly a mongolian type of imbecile." Despite considerable variability in the individual identifying characteristics, the overall physical impression in mongolism is usually one of striking similarity.

While rare cases with borderline intelligence have been reported (Wunsch, 1957), most mongoloids are severely mentally retarded (Stemlicht & Wandever, 1962). The mean IQ for various groups is in the 20 to 40 range.

As we indicated earlier, mongolism was first demonstrated to involve a chromosomal abnormality in 1959. Since then, three principal types of chromosomal deviations have been identified in mongolism:

1. A trisomy of chromosome number 21 resulting from *nondisjunction*. This is a genetic disorder but not an inherited one. This type is rarely familial. It is the form most commonly born to older mothers.
2. A *translocation* of a chromosome involving the attachment of an extra number 21 chromosome onto another (usually number 15). This type is familial and occurs in the children of younger parents.
3. A rare chromosomal anomaly in mongolism is known as *mosaicism*. The range of symptoms, including mental level, varies greatly in this condition.

There is evidence that individuals in the three chromosomal subcategories of mongolism differ in learning ability, mental level, and temperament, as well as in certain biochemical characteristics (Gibson, 1973; Jeremiah, 1973; Ikeda, 1973; Koch & de la Cruz, 1975).

Since the discovery of the chromosomal abnormality in mongolism a large number of chromosomal deviations have been identified. It is estimated that 1 percent of people have such chromosomal deviations (Carrel, Sparkes, & Wright, 1973). Apparently most chromosomal abnormalities result in early embryonic death. Studies of aborted embryos indicate that approximately one-third display chromosomal aberrations (Bloom, 1970). At least 6.5 percent of newborns possess major chromosome abnormalities sufficient to impair their effectiveness in society (Lubs & Ruddle, 1970).

Samples of amniotic fluid containing cells from the developing fetus can be taken to detect chromosomal abnormalities during the first twelve to sixteen weeks of pregnancy. Translocations of chromosomes in "carrier" parents can also be detected by cytogenic study of suspected individuals (Dorfman, 1972). A mother who carries the appropriate chromosomal translocation for mongolism has a 33 percent chance of having a mongol child. An infant chimpanzee with clinical, behavioral, and chromosomal features similar to those in mongolism has been described in one study (McClure, Belden, & Peiper, 1969).

Mental retardation caused by a single gene

Some of these types were listed in chapter 8, and limitations of space permit only a brief characterization of a few of them. Most are relatively rare. They appear most often in the children of consanguineous marriages and display the other features of single-gene-determined conditions listed earlier. There is no consistency in the naming of the clinical types of mentally retarded. Some are named after the men who first identified and described the syndrome. Others are identified by their etiology. Still others are given the label of some physical stigma which is a part of the syndrome.

Biochemical anomalies

Biochemical causes of mental retardation may involve abnormal carbohydrate metabolism or storage, anomalies of protein (amino acid) metabolism or excretion, and similar defects involving lipoid material (fats).

Carbohydrate metabolism   Galactosaemia is the best known of the conditions involving abnormal carbohydrate metabolism. Individuals suffering from this condition are unable to metabolize galactose. This leads to a high level of galactose in the blood and urine, and in some unknown way results in mental retardation. Infants placed on a galactose-free or lactose-free diet before the onset of permanent tissue damage can develop normally. Since lactose is a constituent of milk, such a regime requires the elimination of milk from the child's diet (Rundle, 1964; Fishler et al., 1972). A single recessive gene seems to be the cause of galactosaemia. Carriers of the recessive gene show an abnormal tolerance for galactose and can therefore be identified (Lee, 1972).

Additional abnormalities of carbohydrate metabolism which may produce mental retardation are:

1. *Sucrosia,* an inability to metabolize sucrose (ordinary beet or cane sugar)
2. *Idiopathic hypoglycaemia,* an error of carbohydrate metabolism producing abnormally low blood-sugar levels
3. *Glycogenosis,* a disturbance of the metabolism of glycogen.

Protein metabolism   Phenylketonuria (PKU) was the first of the metabolic disorders shown to cause mental retardation. It is the result of a single-gene-determined defect of amino acid metabolism. The genetic anomaly produces a deficiency of the liver enzyme which normally catalyzes the breakdown of the amino acid phenylalanine to tyrosine. In this condition, phenylalanine accumulates and is eventually metabolized by an alternate pathway, producing *ketonuria,* the characteristic excretion in the urine of above-average amounts of phenylketones (Menkes, 1967). Approximately 60 percent of untreated PKU children have IQ's under 20, more than 80 percent have IQ's below 40, while a few are average or above in intelligence (Menkes, 1967). Behavior syndromes similar to those of untreated PKU children have been produced in monkeys by feeding them high levels of phenylalanine from birth to three to six months of age (Chamove, Waisman, & Harlow, 1970).

Phenylketonuria is caused by a single recessive gene, although carriers of the defective gene can be detected (Hsia, Paine, & Driscoll, 1957). Tests of the blood and urine can detect the condition, and if a diet low in phenylalanine is instituted early enough, development apparently can be normal. Some states now require routine testing of infants for this condition (Frankenburg, Goldstein, & Olson, 1973).

Additional conditions involving abnormal protein or amino acid metabolism are discussed by A. T. Rundle (1964) and Holt & Coffey (1968).

Metabolism of fats   The best-known group of related conditions involving abnormal lipoid metabolism is *amaurotic familial idiocy.* Various forms of this condition have been given different names, depending primarily on the age of onset. The infantile form (Tay-Sachs disease) has an early onset and progresses rapidly. It is characterized by progressive spastic paralysis, blindness, convulsions, and death by the third year. Juvenile forms have a later onset (three to ten years), with mental deterioration and death within ten to fifteen years. A single recessive gene seems to be the primary cause of this condition (Lou & Kristensen, 1973; Pampeglione, Privett, & Harden, 1974).

Additional conditions involving abnormal lipoid metabolism are *Niemann-Pick disease, Gaucher's disease,* and *Gargoylism (Hurler's disease)* (Milunsky, 1973).

Mental retardation resulting from endocrine disturbances

Cretinism   Cretinism is the best-known disorder of endocrine function resulting in mental retardation. Cretinism results from insufficiency of thyroid, which causes irreversible damage to the central nervous system. There is evidence that a fetus suffering from insufficient thyroid may sustain such brain damage prenatally (Lawson, 1955). Cretinism can be either genetic or environmental in origin. The endemic type of cretinism is the result of an iodine-deficient diet and occurs in geographic regions in which the soil, water, and vegetation are deficient in iodine.[2] Cretinism of this type can be prevented by iodine supplements to the diet. Using iodized salt is one way of accomplishing this. Most sporadic cretinism is not genetic.

However, there are at least three separate genetic types of cretinism. All involve recessive genes which seem to interfere with the different enzyme systems of the body involved in the synthesis and secretion of thyroxin. The degree of mental retardation is roughly proportional to the extent of hypothyroidism.

The complex physical syndrome of cretinism involves physical dwarfism and marked delay in bone development, muscular flaccidity, and a shuffling and waddling gait. The head is large, extremities are short and fat, and the fingers are square at the ends. The neck is short and thick, the skin is dry and scaly, the tongue is thick, and the abdomen protrudes. Basal metabolism and blood pressure are both low. The typical cretin is placid, inactive, apathetic, and severely mentally retarded.

Early identification, and immediate and properly controlled thyroid medication, can prevent the more severe symptoms. In most cases the physical symptoms can be prevented by thyroid treatment, but normal intelligence is seldom attained (Smith, Blizzard, & Wilkins, 1957). Intellectual and physical impairment are generally more severe in the endemic and sporadic forms of cretinism, which are of environmental origin, than in the genetic types. Cretins of the genetic type practically always have goiters, indicating the presence of some thyroid tissue. The genetic types also have not suffered from thyroid deficiency *in utero,* because the normal mother supplies the needs of the fetus.[3]

Other endocrine disorders   Some additional endocrine disturbances sometimes associated with mental retardation are *hypoparathyroidism, nephrogenic diabetes insipidus,* and *sexual infantilism and dwarfism* (Rundle, 1964; Kirman et al., 1956).

Cranial anomalies of genetic origin

Microcephaly   Microcephaly may be either genetic or environmental. The genetic form is transmitted by a single recessive gene. The secondary, or exogenous, form results from massive irradiation of the fetus or embryo (Plummer, 1952), or possibly from maternal infections

---

[2] See Fierro et al. (1969) for a report on an Andean region where cretinism is still endemic.
[3] For a good discussion of the genetic basis of cretinism, as well as many of the other metabolic disorders, see Stanburg (1960).

(Wesselhoeft, 1949). Microcephalic individuals are characterized by small, conical skulls; the lower jaw recedes; the skin of the scalp is often loose and wrinkled. The individuals are small in stature but not dwarfed, with a curved spine and stooping posture. The appearance of microcephalics is often like that of monkeys, and their quick, jerky movements remind one of a bird. Genetic microcephalics are severely mentally retarded, but those with the acquired type are more variable both in physical characteristics and mental level (Warkany & Dignan, 1973).

Other cranial abnormalities   Two other cranial anomalies of possible genetic origin are *acrocephaly* or *oxycephaly*, a tower- or steeple-shaped skull, with a narrow forehead which slopes up to a point to form a dome-shaped vertex (Crome, 1973,); and *anencephaly*, a partial or complete absence of the cerebrum and cerebellum. Since these individuals live for only short periods of time, their mental level cannot be determined (Wortis, 1973).

SYNDROMES OF EXOGENOUS ORIGIN COMMONLY ASSOCIATED WITH SEVERE MENTAL RETARDATION

Hydrocephaly

Hydrocephaly (water on the brain) consists of an excessive accumulation of cerebrospinal fluid either in the ventricles of the brain (internal hydrocephalus) or on the outside of the brain in the subarachnoid space (the external form). If the internal form develops before the bones of the skull have fused, the head gradually enlarges, sometimes attaining tremendous size. The extreme conditions of hydrocephalus produce various sensory, motor, and intellectual symptoms—of which mental retardation is one. If the excessive accumulations of fluid develop after the cranial bones are mature and the sutures have fully ossified, enlargement of the head cannot occur, but pressure builds up inside the brain. This pressure produces a thinning of the neural tissue, with resulting motor disability, including paralysis and convulsions, mental deterioration, and eventual death if the condition is progressive.

The mentality of hydrocephalics ranges all the way from low-grade idiocy to superior intelligence. A slight degree of hydrocephaly, which becomes arrested, may be consistent with normal or superior mentality. One of the authors has studied two individuals who, as children, showed pathological head expansion with all of the classical symptoms of hydrocephalus. In neither of these children did the condition progress to a point where any mental effects were noticeable. At maturity, both had test scores comparable to their normal siblings, and the only residual symptoms were poor motor coordination of a nonspecific, generalized sort—including poor articulation. At the other extreme are the severely affected, progressive cases which end up in hospitals and institutions as severely retarded, helpless individuals whose life span is typically short.

Several operative procedures have been developed for early correction of the defect, and treatment with drugs has met with some success (Young et al., 1973). Hydrocephaly is often associated with myelomeningocele, a congenital cleft of the spinal column with spinal cord in protrusion (Gressang, 1974; Anderson, 1973a).

Cerebral palsy

Cerebral palsy may occasionally be of genetic origin, but it is usually caused by environmental factors. It is characterized by disturbances of motor function due to brain damage. Cerebral palsy is by far the most common single syndrome associated with severe mental retardation of exogenous origin. Estimates of the total number of cases are in the hundreds of thousands, with an estimated ten thousand new cases added each year (Bailey, 1958). While not all of these are mentally retarded, a sizable percentage are. Since cerebral palsy always involves motor disabilities, this condition is discussed in a later chapter on the orthopedically handicapped.

Epilepsy

Epilepsy may have either a genetic or an environmental etiology. It is sometimes associated with mental retardation, but when the retardation is severe both the epilepsy and the mental retardation are usually the result of extensive brain damage or maldevelopment, as in microcephaly or cerebral palsy.

Brain infections

Severe mental retardation may be caused by brain infections, as we indicated earlier. Meningitis, encephalitis, and syphilitic brain infections can all result in mental retardation. Untreated syphilitic brain infection is progressive (except for remissions), with a wide variety of physical, personality, and intellectual accompaniments. There is nothing unique about mental defect of syphilitic origin, and with the modern methods of treatment it has become a minor cause of mental retardation.

Meningitis Meningitis usually responds to the modern antibiotics and seldom causes severe mental subnormality. Defects of vision and hearing are probably caused by meningitis more often than is severe mental retardation (Pate et al., 1974). One follow-up study of thirty-seven cases of neonatal meningitis showed ten to be apparently normal. The others all had obvious abnormalities of vision, hearing, speech, and motor processes, and intelligence levels below normal (Fitzhardinge, Kazemi, & Stern, 1974).

Encephalitis Encephalitis more often results in permanent brain damage and mental retardation than do syphilis and meningitis. Mental deterioration and other postencephalitic effects may follow immediately after the acute attack or they may appear several years later. These chronic effects either remain stationary or become progressively worse.

Paradoxically, the severity of the delayed aftereffects is not closely related to the severity of the acute attack. In fact, many times the symptoms and immunity reactions of postencephalitis develop in the absence of any recognized acute attack. For example, 149 of one group of 507 postencephalitics had no history of an acute phase (Wallin, 1949).

The postencephalitic symptoms include a large number of motor disorders and character and personality changes, as well as general mental deterioration. The motor symptoms include all of those found in cerebral palsy—paralysis, muscular rigidity, tremors, tic, athetoid and choreiform movements, and the Parkinsonian syndrome. The latter syndrome is said to develop in about 20 percent of postencephalitics. Parkinsonism includes the expressionless, immobile, masklike face, tremors, a stiff and eventually stooped posture, and propulsive gait. Hydrocephalus, epilepsy, and deafness are infrequent sequelae. The incidence of serious aftereffects varies from 10 to 40 percent.

Personality and intellectual changes are more likely to develop when the encephalitis is contracted in infancy or early childhood (DeJong, 1959). In fact, it has been claimed that no child who has encephalitis before the age of three ever escapes some intellectual deficit. About half of the postencephalitics are reported as suffering some mental deficit when encephalitis was contracted before age fourteen. Behavioral and personality changes include increased emotional instability, hyperactivity, sleep reversals, impulsiveness of action, and even psychosis. Some 20 percent are reported to develop psychotic symptoms.

There have been few well-controlled studies of the extent of mental deterioration or arrested intellectual development in postencephalitics. Enough case studies have been reported to indicate that the term *arrested mental development* can appropriately be applied to some of these cases. The mental deficit resulting from encephalitis ranges all the way from no apparent decline to complete arrest or even marked deterioration (Fitzhardinge, Kazemi, & Stern, 1974).

In one survey of ten studies, mean IQ's ranged from 73 to 91 and individual scores ranged all the way from low-grade custodial to superior (Pintner, Eisenson, & Stanton, 1940). One study reports a deficit of 16 IQ points in a group of postencephalitic children as compared with their normal siblings (Dawson & Conn, 1926). There seems to be a tendency for the intelligence level to decline in successive testings. The prognosis for postencephalitics is not very good (Lurie et al., 1937; Brown, Jenkins, & Cisler, 1940).

EDUCATIONAL PROGRAMS FOR THE TRAINABLE

Since it is expected that most of the trainable mentally retarded will be dependent or semidependent all their lives, the objectives of their school programs are limited. In general terms, their training programs are devised to develop self-help skills, socialization, and elementary oral language. The materials and methods are not far removed from those of Jean Itard and Edouard Seguin, discussed in chapter 3, although there is greater emphasis on socialization through group activities—especially group play.

The self-help skills taught are such things as independent eating, dressing, toileting, washing, combing hair, brushing teeth, and using a handkerchief. The children are taught to follow directions and to perform simple tasks. In the area of social skills, the children are taught consideration for others (for example, taking turns), common courtesy, and obedience. A good deal of basic sensory and motor training is provided to improve sensory discrimination and develop motor skills. Such household skills as dusting, sweeping, setting and clearing the table, washing and drying dishes, washing and ironing, sewing, elementary homemaking, using common tools, telephoning, and limited traveling in familiar areas are also taught. Considerable time is spent on the development of oral language. Health and safety rules are also taught. The major purposes of these classes are to develop the ability of the child to look after himself and to perform simple tasks about the home or the immediate neighborhood.

Follow-up studies of former students of the special classes for the trainable indicate that the outcomes are extremely varied. Practically none of the studies included control or comparison groups of children who did not attend such classes. These studies indicate that, in the years immediately following the termination of their school attendance, about one-fourth of the children are ultimately institutionalized and most of the others live under supervision at home. Interviews with parents indicate that they believe the school programs have been a help in reducing the child's dependency on the family.

One follow-up study of 120 graduates of classes for the trainable mentally retarded found that, when these individuals were nineteen to twenty-one years of age, 94 percent were living at home with their families. About half (48 percent) were in special workshop programs earning less than ten dollars a week for full-time work. The remaining 52 percent were not involved in any post-school work or rehabilitation programs. The parents' stated principal reasons for their children's non-involvement were the extent of the individual's handicap (50 percent), transportation difficulties (30 percent), and lack of proper post-school programs (20 percent). The parents reported that 94 percent of the handicapped individuals could care for their personal needs. Twenty-three percent of the parents felt confident in leaving their handicapped child for extended periods of time, 56 percent had reservations, and the rest would not leave them. Ninety percent of the children had specific responsibilities for household chores in their homes, 60 percent were in-dependently mobile within the immediate neighborhood, but only 10 percent left their neighborhoods to travel alone. Forty percent never went beyond the front yard of their homes (Stanfield, 1973).

The sheltered workshops have demonstrated that some of the train-able mentally retarded can be productively employed. N. O'Connor and J. Tizard (1956) have provided some optimistic reports of success attained by boys of this mental level in factory work, following systematic on-the-job training. There is some evidence that Great Britain and certain other countries of Europe are more successful with their work programs, which are oriented toward industrial production, than is the United States, which uses a more educational, mental-hygiene, and social-learning ap-proach (O'Connor & Tizard, 1956). One report of an industrial-produc-tion oriented workshop in the United States indicates that many of the trainable mentally retarded can function adequately in such a situation (Blue, 1964).

M. W. Gold (1973) has shown that severely mentally retarded persons can be successfully trained to perform simple workshop tasks using con-ventional operant conditioning procedures. The tasks were broken down into elementary components, and each component, in turn, was taught using modeling and operant reinforcements, both physical and verbal.

A study of the work characteristics of mentally retarded adults in workshop-like situations has shown that: (1) productivity is significantly related to IQ; (2) an IQ of 20 constituted an approximate limit below which such work is not practical; and (3) tolerance for work is positively related to intellectual level, with the most retarded showing the greatest work decrement from boredom and fatigue (Tobias & Gorelick, 1963).

Custodial treatment (IQ's below 20–30)

Until recently, the only alternatives open to parents of the custodial-level mentally retarded child (IQ below 20 to 30) were home care and institutionalization. Day hospitals, day care centers, and boarding or nursing homes are now also becoming alternatives. Public and private residential institutions still take care of the largest group of those profoundly mentally retarded who live outside their own homes.

A 1965 survey of state institutions for the mentally retarded in the United States showed that approximately 192,000 people were residing in such institutions. Table 9–2 shows the resident populations, classified according to degree of retardation.

Table 9–2

Distribution of institutional residents according to degree of mental retardation, compared to estimated prevalence (192,493 cases)

Degree of Retardation	IQ	Percentage of Residents	Estimated Percentage Prevalence
Profound	Below 20	27	1.4
Severe	20–35	33 ⎫	6.0
Moderate	36–50	22 ⎭	
Mild	51–67	13	92.6*
Borderline	68–83	5	

* IQ's of 50 to 70.
Data from Scheerenberger (1965), and Dingman & Tarjan (1960).

The data in Table 9–2 indicate that the resident population is predominantly of the lower mental levels. Eighty-two percent are classified as having IQ's below 50, whereas this group represents only 7.4 percent of the estimated total number of mentally retarded. This means that the below-50 IQ group contributes to the resident population between eleven and twelve times its proportional numbers, whereas the above-50 IQ category contributes only 15 percent of its proportional numbers. If we extrapolate from these data and obtain 464,000 as the approximate number of individuals in the United States with IQ's below 50 in 1965, and 157,-800 as the resident population, only about one-third of the total number were in public institutions for the mentally retarded. Since public institutions house about 90 to 95 percent of the total institutionalized population in the United States, almost two-thirds of this group reside at home. The proportion residing in boarding homes and other similar facilities until recently has been negligible.

The role of the residential institution

In the last ten years, emphasis on the residential institution as the place to take care of the bulk of the mentally retarded has declined. Several developments have contributed to this trend. One, as previously indicated, was the recognition that segregation was not the solution to the problem of mental defectiveness. Another was the increasing cost of institutional care and the practical impossibility of obtaining funds sufficient to provide institutions for any large percentage of the mentally handicapped. It was also recognized that the large residential institution was not the best place to provide care and training for most of the mentally retarded. It is estimated that only about 4 percent of the mentally retarded were ever institutionalized (McCarver & Craig, 1974).

Advances in medicine, as well as social changes, have contributed to the change in the makeup of our institutional population. Medical advances now keep alive many low-grade mental defectives who would earlier have died. For example, the death rate in New York State institutions for the mentally retarded decreased from 34.9 per thousand in 1926 to 13.5 per thousand in 1944. Coupled with this decline in death rate are an increase in the proportion of first admissions in the lower mental level and a reduction in the age of first admissions. These three factors (increased longevity, reduced admission age, and increasing proportions of admissions from the lower mental level requiring life-long custodial care) all combined to give the institutions a predominantly static, custodial, resident population. As a result, the days of trying to provide institutionalization for the bulk of the mentally retarded have passed.

This does not mean that public and private institutions will cease to exist. Institutions of this type will continue to be needed in any comprehensive program for the care and training of the mentally retarded. They are needed to receive selected cases requiring custodial, or total, care. Most of these cases will be the severely mentally retarded which the family is unable or unwilling to care for at home, as well as the mentally deficient who have additional handicaps.

If current trends continue, we can expect the public residential institutions, which account for 95 percent of the total residential population, to become more custodial centers for the totally dependent. The per capita cost will increase as the number of higher-grade cases decreases. The increase in cost will result from the need for more attendants to perform the tasks formerly done by the high-grade patients as well as for an increased number of professionals (M.D.'s and nurses) to care for the large number of custodial cases with organic pathology.

Almost from their inception, institutions have made widespread use of patients for the performance of many routine tasks involved in institutional management and upkeep. The performance of such tasks was labeled "work therapy," the patients received little or no pay, and total institutional costs were considerably reduced. However, such peonage was formally outlawed in state hospitals as the result of a 1974 United States District Court ruling in *Souder* v. *Brennan,* which directed institutions to pay all patient-workers minimum wages or at least a portion of the minimum wage contingent upon their productivity (Scharr, 1975). The result of this ruling is that many institutions eliminated "work therapy" jobs altogether and replaced patient help with outside employees. This trend, together with court-mandated improvements in physical facilities and level of treatment which have resulted from the the "right to treatment" lawsuits, have markedly increased institutional costs. Since the financial situation of most state mental health institutions has always been bleak, the additional financial burdens may contribute to the continued decline of the residential institutions.

Training the custodial mentally retarded

The conditioning methods that have been used to study learning in the lower animals have also been applied with some success to the training of the low-level custodial mentally retarded. N. R. Ellis (1962, 1963) developed a theoretical analysis of how toilet training could be accomplished using regular operant procedures. M. Dayan (1964) later reported some success with the method. P. Roos (1965) has described an "intensive habit-training unit" established to apply these methods systematically to the training of the profoundly mentally retarded. G. J. Bensberg (1965) has reported considerable success with these methods.

The methods vary from simple toilet training, in which each person was placed on the commode every two hours and was rewarded each time he eliminated while he was on the commode (Dayan, 1964), to the development of many self-care habits by a systematic rewarding of successive approximations to the desired behavior—called "behavior shaping" (Bensberg, 1965). N. H. Azrin (1973) has described in detail a procedure which successfully toilet trained ten profoundly mentally retarded individuals in three days.

In the latter methods, simple verbal directions and appropriate gestures were used as cues, and successive approximations of the desired behavior were immediately rewarded. At first food (pieces of cookies and candy) was used. The food reward was always preceded or accompanied by a social reward (such as saying "good boy" or patting the head). As learning progressed, the social rewards were continued but the food was gradually withheld until longer units of behavior occurred and closer approximations to the desired response were attained. Finally the edible rewards were discontinued and only the social rewards were used.

These studies indicate that the principles of operant conditioning used in training lower animals in research laboratories and by such commercial organizations as Animal Behavior Enterprises, Inc., of Hot Springs, Arkansas, can be successfully applied to the low-level custodial mentally retarded. These methods can be used by regular institutional personnel after instruction in behavior-shaping methods (Bensberg, 1965). Studies indicate that intensive training programs can significantly improve the functional levels of the severely retarded. For example, whereas under routine institutional care only 16 percent of the severely retarded improved their ambulatory skills in a three-year follow-up period, 50 percent of those included in an intensive special program did so. Comparable improvement was obtained from toilet training (Tarjan et al., 1973).

SUMMARY

In discussing the mentally retarded as a group, there is the ever-present danger of minimizing or ignoring individual differences among them. Although their range of intellectual ability is limited, there is still room for great individual variance. The restriction in range of intelligence does not restrict other important variables in direct proportion.

The exact extent of mental retardation is not known. If a purely psychometric criterion is used—IQ's below 70—we arrive at a figure of about six million. However, if we use the combined standard of an IQ below 70 and an equally low relative level of adaptive behavior, the figure obtained is closer to two or three million. Between 80 and 90 percent of these are mildly retarded. An additional one-fifth of the school population is probably sufficiently educationally handicapped to require special consideration.

The mentally retarded are generally found to be under par in physical health and stature. Their life span is shorter and their death rate higher than those of the normal population.

Currently, most mildly mentally retarded school children are either being returned to or retained in regular classes. If these mainstreaming programs are successful in meeting the special needs of these children, the mentally retarded as an educational category may disappear. The educational needs of mentally retarded children as well as of children with "learning disabilities" (to be discussed in chapter 10) are probably

different only in degree from those of "normal" children, and may likewise be taken care of by more individualized, diagnostic-prescriptive
teaching.

Most individuals with IQ's below 50 are either *severely* or *profoundly*
mentally retarded, according to the AAMD classification, and are either
trainable mentally retarded or *custodial,* in educational terminology.
The bulk of the "clinical types" of mentally retarded, the single-gene-
determined cases, and most of the more severely environmentally damaged (the exogenous mentally retarded) also fall into these categories.

The genetic syndromes are the result of either chromosomal aberrations or pathogenic single genes. Mongolism (Down's syndrome) is the
most common type of chromosomal anomaly accompanying mental retardation. Three subtypes of mongolism are differentiated in terms of
the chromosomal mechanism involved. These are nondisjunction, which
results in the embryo's having three number-21 chromosomes (trisomy)
instead of the normal two; translocation, in which an extra number-21
chromosome is attached to another one—usually a number-15; and mosaicism, in which at an early stage of embryonic development one cell
which will develop into a particular type of tissue (such as skin) receives
an extra number-21 chromosome. In mosaicism, some of the person's
body tissues are made up of cells having 47 chromosomes and others
consist of cells with the normal number of chromosomes (46).

Mongolism is characterized by a long list of physical stigmata, and
mongoloid persons are usually severely mentally retarded. Biochemical,
physical, and mental characteristics seem to vary somewhat, according to
chromosomal type.

Biochemical anomalies caused by single genes with accompanying
mental retardation may affect carbohydrate, protein, or lipoid (fat) metabolism. Galactosaemia—an inability to metabolize galactose or lactose
(milk sugar); phenylketonuria—a failure to properly metabolize phenylalanine (one of the amino acids which is a constituent of most proteins);
and amaurotic familial idiocy—involving abnormal lipoid metabolism,
are representative of these three categories. Specific dietary restrictions,
if instituted sufficiently early in life, can prevent the physical stigmata
and mental retardation characteristic of certain types of untreated cases.

Familial cretinism is a form of severe physical and mental retardation
resulting from insufficient thyroid. Cretinism can be of either genetic or
environmental origin. Untreated cretins display a characteristic physical
syndrome and are severely mentally retarded. Most cretinism can be
prevented by early and continued administration of supplementary thyroid extract.

Microcephaly (in which the person has an extremely small head) can
be either genetic or environmental in origin. Microcephalics are severely
mentally retarded and have many characteristic physical stigmata.

Hydrocephaly (water on the brain) is a syndrome which is usually environmentally caused. The most common cause is an obstruction in the ventricular system of the brain which prevents the normal circulation of the cerebrospinal fluid. The abnormal accumulation of cerebrospinal fluid produces an enlarged head, atrophy of brain tissue, and mental retardation. Some cases can be treated surgically.

Severe mental retardation may accompany or be caused by cerebral palsy, epilepsy, and brain infections. General familial and cultural deprivation is not considered an important cause of severe mental retardation, since the familial-cultural background of this type is fairly typical of that of the general population.

The bulk of the severely mentally retarded are cared for in residential institutions, special classes, and at home. A relatively small number work in sheltered workshops and under close supervision in industry. Some are taken care of in boarding homes, halfway houses, and day care centers. Even the low-level custodial mentally retarded can be trained if appropriate methods are employed.

REFERENCES

ANASTASIOW, N. J., & N. G. STAYROOK, "Miscue Language Patterns of Mildly Retarded and Nonretarded Children," *American Journal of Mental Deficiency*, 1973, 77, 431–34.

ANDERSON, E. M., "Cognitive Deficits in Children with Spina Bifida and Hydrocephalus: A Review of the Literature," *British Journal of Educational Psychology*, 1973a, 43, 257–68.

ANDERSON, E. M., *The Disabled School Child: A Study of Integration in Primary Schools* (London: Methuen, 1973b).

AZRIN, N. H., "On Toilet Training the Severely and Profoundly Retarded," *Journal of Research and Training*, 1973, 1, 9–13.

BAILEY, C. J., "Interrelationships of Asphyxia Neonatorium, Cerebral Palsy, and Mental Retardation: Present Status of the Problem," in W. F. Windle, ed., *Neurological and Psychological Deficits of Asphyxia Neonatorium* (Springfield, Ill.: Charles C Thomas, 1958).

BARTEL, N. R., D. BRYEN, & S. SEEHN, "Language Comprehension in the Moderately Retarded Child," *Exceptional Children*, 1973, 39, 375–82.

BENSBERG, G. J., "Teaching the Profoundly Retarded Self-help Activities by Behavior Shaping Techniques," *American Journal of Mental Deficiency*, 1965, 69, 674–79.

BIRCH, J. W., *Mainstreaming: Educable Mentally Retarded Children in Regular Classes* (Minneapolis: Leadership Training Institute/Special Education, University of Minnesota, 1974).

BLOOM, S. E., "Trisomy–3–4 and Triploidy (3A–ZZZW) in Chick Embryos," *Science*, 1970, 170, 457–58.

BLUE, C. M., "Trainable Mentally Retarded in Sheltered Workshops," *Mental Retardation*, 1964, *2*, 97–104.

BROWN, A. W., R. W. JENKINS, & L. E. CISLER, "Influence of Lethargic Encephalitis on the Intelligence of Children as Determined by Objective Tests," *American Journal of Diseases of Children*, 1940, *59*, 238–54.

BRUININKS, R. H., "Physical and Motor Development of Retarded Persons," in N. R. Ellis, ed., *International Review of Research in Mental Retardation* (New York: Academic Press, 1974).

CARREL, R. E., R. S. SPARKES, & S. W. WRIGHT, "Chromosome Survey of Moderately and Profoundly Retarded Patients," *American Journal of Mental Deficiency*, 1973, *77*, 616–22.

CHAMOVE, A. S., H. WAISMAN, & H. F. HARLOW, "Abnormal Social Behavior in Phenylketonuric Monkeys," *Journal of Abnormal Psychology*, 1970, *76*, 62–68.

CLARK, G. M., "Mainstreaming for the Secondary Educable Mentally Retarded: Is It Defensible?" *Focus on Exceptional Children*, 1975, 7 (2), 1–5.

CROME, L. *Pathology of Mental Retardation*, 2nd ed. (Baltimore, Md.: Williams & Wilkins, 1973).

DAWSON, S., & J. C. CONN, "Effects of Encephalitis Lethargica on the Intelligence of Children," *Archives of Diseases in Childhood*, 1926, *1*, 357–89.

DAYAN, M., "Toilet Training Retarded Children in a State Residential Institution," *Mental Retardation*, 1964, *2*, 116–17.

DEJONG, R. N., "Diseases of the Nervous System," in D. A. Rytard & W. P. Greger, eds., *Annual Review of Medicine* (Palo Alto, Ca.: Annual Reviews, 1959).

DICKER, L., "Dermatolyphics and Level of Retardation in Down's Syndrome," *American Journal of Mental Deficiency*, 1972, *77*, 143–48.

DINGMAN, H. F., & G. TARJAN, "Mental Retardation and the Normal Probability Distribution Curve," *American Journal of Mental Deficiency*, 1960, *64*, 991–94.

DORFMAN, A., ed., *Antenatal Diagnosis* (Chicago: University of Chicago Press, 1972).

DYBWAD, G., "Basic Legal Aspects in Providing Medical, Educational, Social, and Vocational Help to the Mentally Retarded," *Journal of Special Education*, 1973, *7*, 39–51.

EDGERTON, R. B., & C. P. EDGERTON, "Being Mentally Retarded in a Hawaiian School," in G. Tarjan, R. K. Eyman, & C. E. Meyers, eds., *Socio-behavioral Studies in Mental Retardation* (Washington, D.C.: Monograph of the American Association on Mental Deficiency, 1973).

ELLIS, N. R., "Amount of Reward and Operant Behavior in Mental Defectives," *American Journal of Mental Deficiency*, 1962, *66*, 595–99.

ELLIS, N. R., "Toilet Training the Severely Defective Patient: An S–R Reinforcement Analysis," *American Journal of Mental Deficiency*, 1963, *68*, 98–103.

FALK, R. E.; R. E. CARREL; M. VALENTE; B. F. CRANDALL; & R. S. SPARKES, "Partial Trisomy of Chromosome: II. A Case Report," *American Journal of Mental Deficiency*, 1973, *77*, 383–88.

FIERRO, B.; R. W. PENAFIEL; L. J. DEGROAT; & I. RAMIREZ, "Endemic Goiter and Endemic Cretinism in the Andean Region," *New England Journal of Medicine,* 1969, *280* (6), 296–302.

FISHLER, K.; G. N. DONNELL; W. R. BERGREN; & R. KOCH, "Intellectual and Personality Development in Children with Galactosemia," *Pediatrics,* 1972, *50,* 412–19.

FITZHARDINGE, P. M., M. KAZEMI, & L. STERN, "Long-term Sequelae of Neonatal Meningitis," *Developmental Medicine and Child Neurology,* 1974, *16,* 3–10.

FRANKENBURG, W. K., A. D. GOLDSTEIN, & C. O. OLSON, "Behavioral Consequences of Increased Phenylalanine Intake by Phenylketonuric Children," *American Journal of Mental Deficiency,* 1973, *77,* 524–32.

GIBSON, D., "Karyotype Variation and Behavior in Down's Syndrome," *American Journal of Mental Deficiency,* 1973, *78,* 128–33.

GIBSON, D., L. POZONY, & D. E. ZARFAS, "Dimensions of Mongolism: II. The Interaction of Clinical Indices," *American Journal of Mental Deficiency,* 1964, *608,* 503–10.

GOLD, M. W., "Research on the Vocational Rehabilitation of the Retarded," in N. R. Ellis, ed., *International Review of Research in Mental Retardation,* vol. 6 (New York: Academic Press, 1973).

GRESSANG, J. D., "Perceptual Processes of Children with Myelomengingocele and Hydrocephalus," *American Journal of Occupational Therapy,* 1974, *28,* 226–30.

HALPERN, A. S., "General Unemployment and Vocational Opportunities for EMR Individuals," *American Journal of Mental Deficiency,* 1973, *78,* 123–27.

HARING, N. G., & D. A. KRUG, "Placement in Regular Programs: Procedures and Results," *Exceptional Children,* 1975, *41,* 413–17.

HOBBS, N., *The Futures of Children* (San Francisco: Jossey-Bass, 1975).

HOLT, K. S., & V. P. COFFEY, eds., *Some Recent Advances in Inborn Errors of Metabolism* (London: E. & S. Livingstone, 1968).

HSIA, D. Y., R. S. PAINE, & K. W. DRISCOLL, "Phenylketonuria," *Journal of Mental Deficiency Research,* 1957, *1,* 53.

IKEDA, Y., "Intellectual Development of Chromosomal Mosaic Children with Down's Syndrome," *Japanese Journal of Special Education,* 1973, *10* (3), 44–59.

JEREMIAH, D. E., "Down's Syndrome and Diabetes," *Psychological Medicine,* 1973, *3,* 455–57.

KINDRED, M; J. COHEN; D. PENROD; & T. SHAFFER, *The Mentally Retarded Citizen and the Law* (Riverside, N.J.: Free Press, 1975).

KIRMAN, B. H., et al., "Familial Pitressin-resistant Diabetes Insipidus with Mental Defect, *Archives of Disabled Children,* 1956, *31,* 59–61.

KOCH, R., & F. DE LA CRUZ, eds., *Down's Syndrome (Mongolism): Research, Prevention, and Management* (New York: Brunner/Mazel, 1975).

LAWSON, D., "On the Prognosis in Cretinism," *Archives of Diseases in Childhood,* 1955, *30,* 75.

LEE, D. H., "Psychological Aspects of Galactosaemia," *Journal of Mental Deficiency Research,* 1972, *16,* 173–91.

LIESE, J. E., & H. A. LERCH, "Physical Fitness and Intelligence in TMR's," *Mental Retardation,* 1974, *12* (5), 50–51.

LILIENFELD, A. M., *Epidemiology of Mongolism* (Baltimore: Johns Hopkins Press, 1969).

LOU, H. C., & K. KRISTENSEN, "A Clinical and Psychological Investigation into Juvenile Amaurotic Idiocy in Denmark," *Developmental Medicine and Child Neurology*, 1973, *15*, 313–23.

LUBS, H. A., & F. H. RUDDLE, "Chromosomal Abnormalities in the Human Population," *Science*, 1970, *189*, 495–97.

LURIE, L. A., et al., "Late Results Noted in Children Presenting Post-encephalitic Behavior: A Follow-up Study of Fifty Cases," *American Journal of Psychiatry*, 1937, *95*, 171–79.

McCARVER, R. B., & E. M. CRAIG, "Placement of the Retarded in the Community," in N. R. Ellis, ed., *International Review of Research in Mental Retardation*, vol. 7 (New York: Academic Press, 1974).

McCLURE, H. M., K. H. BELDEN, & W. A. PEIPER, "Autosomal Trisomy in a Chimpanzee: Resemblance to Down's Syndrome," *Science*, 1969, *165*, 1010–11.

MENKES, J. H., "The Pathogenesis of Mental Retardation in Phenylketonuria and Other Inborn Errors of Amino-acid Metabolism," *Pediatrics*, 1967, *39*, 297–308.

MERCER, J. R., "The Myth of 3% Prevalence," in G. Tarjan, R. K. Eyman, & C. E. Meyers, eds., *Sociobehavioral Studies of Mental Retardation* (Washington, D.C.: American Association on Mental Deficiency, 1973).

MILUNSKY, A., *The Prenatal Diagnosis of Hereditary Disorders* (Springfield, Ill.: Charles C Thomas, 1973).

O'CONNOR, N., & J. TIZARD, *The Social Problem of Mental Deficiency* (New York: Pergamon Press, 1956).

PAMPEGLIONE, G., G. PRIVETT, & A. HARDEN, "Tay-Sachs Disease: Neurophysiological Studies in 20 Children," *Developmental Medicine and Child Neurology*, 1974, *16*, 201–8.

PATE, J. E.; W. W. WEBB; S. H. SELL; & F. M. GASKINS, "The School Adjustment of Post-meningitic Children," *Journal of Learning Disabilities*, 1974, *7*, 21–25.

PHELPS, H. R., "Post-school Adjustment of Mentally Retarded Children in Selected Ohio Cities," *Exceptional Children*, 1956, *23*, 58–62.

PINTNER, R., J. EISENSON, & N. STANTON, *The Psychology of the Physically Handicapped* (New York: Appleton-Century-Crofts, 1940).

PLUMMER, G., "Anomalies Occurring in Children Exposed in Utero to the Atomic Bomb in Hiroshima," *Pediatrics*, 1952, *10*, 687–93.

ROBINSON, H. B., & N. M. ROBINSON, *The Mentally Retarded Child*, 2nd ed. (New York: McGraw-Hill, 1976).

ROOS, P., "Development of an Intensive Habit-training Unit at Austin State School," *Mental Retardation*, 1965, *3*, 12–15.

RUNDLE, A. T., "Etiological Factors in Mental Retardation: I. Biochemical," *American Journal of Mental Deficiency*, 1964, *67*, 61–68.

SAWREY, J. M., & C. W. TELFORD, *Educational Psychology*, 4th ed. (Boston: Allyn & Bacon, 1973).

SCHAAR, K., "Minimum Wage Regs Pose Problems," *APA Monitor*, March 1975, *6* (3), 10–11.

SCHEERENBERGER, R. C., "The Current Census of State Institutions for the Mentally Retarded," *Mental Retardation,* 1965, *3,* 4–6.

SMITH, D. W., R. M. BLIZZARD, & L. WILKINS, "The Mental Prognosis in Hypothyroidism of Infancy and Childhood," *Pediatrics,* 1957, *19,* 1011–20.

STANBURG, J. B., *The Metabolic Basis of Inherited Disease* (New York: McGraw-Hill, 1960).

STANFIELD, J. S., "Graduation: What Happens to the Retarded Child When He Grows Up," *Exceptional Children,* 1973, *39,* 548–52.

STEMLICHT, M., & Z. W. WANDEVER, "Nature of Institutionalized Adult Mongoloid Intelligence," *American Journal of Mental Deficiency,* 1962, *66,* 301–2.

TARJAN, G.; S. W. WRIGHT; R. K. EYMAN; & C. V. KEERAN, "Natural History of Mental Retardation," *American Journal of Mental Deficiency,* 1973, *77,* 369–79.

TOBIAS, J., & J. GORELICK, "Work Characteristics of Adults at Trainable Level," *Mental Retardation,* 1963, *1,* 338–44.

WALLIN, J. E., *Children with Mental and Physical Handicaps* (Englewood Cliffs, N.J.: Prentice-Hall, 1949).

WARKANY, J., & P. DIGNAN, "Congenital Malformations: Microcephaly," in J. Wortis, ed., *Mental Retardation and Developmental Disabilities: An Annual Review,* vol. V (New York: Brunner/Mazel, 1973).

WEISMANN, A. B., "Some Aspects of Special Education in Scandinavia," *Journal of Special Education,* 1974, *8,* 247–57.

WESSELHOEFT, C., "Rubella (German Measles) and Congenital Deformities," *New England Journal of Medicine,* 1949, *210,* 258–61.

WORTIS, J., *Mental Retardation and Developmental Disorders* (New York: Brunner/Mazel, 1973).

WUNSCH, W. L., "Some Characteristics of Mongoloids Evaluated at a Clinic for Children with Retarded Mental Development," *American Journal of Mental Deficiency,* 1957, *62,* 122–30.

YOUNG, H. F.; F. G. NIELSEN; M. H. WEISS; & P. THOMAS, "The Relationship of Intelligence and Cerebral Mantle in Treated Infantile Hydrocephalus," *Pediatrics,* 1973, *52,* 38–47.

Chapter 10

Learning disabilities

HISTORICAL ORIGINS

The Straussian legacy

The category of learning disabilities as known today has developed out of the concept of the "brain-damaged child," formulated by Alfred A. Strauss and Heinz Werner while they were associated for more than a decade at a Michigan institution for the mentally retarded then known as the Wayne County Training School. Heinz Werner, a developmental and comparative psychologist, and Alfred A. Strauss, a neuropsychiatrist, both refugees from Nazi Germany, worked together at this school for approximately thirteen years studying the impact of brain injury on the behavior and psychological development of children. Strauss and Werner differentiated the endogenous (largely genetic) from the exogenous (largely brain-damaged) mentally retarded and focused their attention on the latter.

During this period a number of young psychologists and educators including Newell Kephart, Ruth Melcher Patterson, William Cruickshank, Charlotte Philleo, and Samuel A. Kirk worked in various capacities at Wayne County Training School and became interested in the problems of the brain-injured child. Of this group, Kephart and Cruickshank have most directly perpetuated the work of Werner and Strauss. Most other workers in the area of learning disabilities have, knowingly or unknowingly, borrowed from these pioneers. Werner and Strauss, of course, drew upon the work and concepts of their predecessors. They acknowledge their indebtedness to Jean Itard and Edouard Seguin's early work with the mentally retarded. They also borrowed more directly from the earlier work of Kurt Goldstein with brain-injured adults.

The behavioral symptoms alleged to characterize the minimally brain-damaged child, which came to be known as the Strauss syndrome, had the following principal components: perceptual disorders, perseveration and distractibility, thinking and conceptual disorders, and motor disorders—especially awkwardness, hyperactivity, and disinhibition. These components have been expanded, subdivided, and made more specific but still form the core of the behavioral characteristics of children with "learning disabilities."

Goldstein's contributions

Goldstein (1939), a neurologist, drawing on his experience principally with brain-injured veterans of World War I, advanced the notion that cortical injury, particularly when it involved the frontal lobes, resulted in marked changes in personality and in cognitive and behavioral functioning. The primary deficit stressed by Goldstein was loss of abstract concepts. This deficit resulted in concretistic thinking accompanied by an inability to abstract and generalize from experience, an inability to plan ahead, a deficit in symbolic thought, and in more extreme cases, generalized linguistic disabilities. Goldstein described the acute emotional upset which his patients showed as reactions to apparently trivial stresses, such as changes in the physical arrangements of their wards or modifications of the daily routines. These reactions were seen as indications of the patients' need for a well-structured, highly predictable environment. A complex and constantly changing environment required a degree of flexible planning and anticipation and the invoking of higher and more abstract ideational processes, and of this they were not capable (Goldstein, 1939). Many of the characteristics of the "Strauss syndrome" which eventually were incorporated into the category of learning disabilities were identified by Goldstein.

Early work on dyslexia and aphasia

Strauss paid relatively little attention to linguistic defects in his characterizations of the brain-injured child. However, the professional literature in the fields of speech, hearing, and neurology had long associated certain linguistic and other types of symbolic representational impairment with brain injury. An impressive list of formidable-sounding terms had been coined to refer to a wide variety of linguistic defects associated with brain injury. These included aphasia and dyslexia. *Aphasia* refers to an impairment of language functions due to brain injury. Aphasias were subdivided into sensory or reception aphasia—when the disorder involved the understanding of the written or spoken word; expressive or motor—when the disability centered on the speaking or writing functions; and semantic aphasia—when the loss involved the finer meaning components of language (Ewing, 1930; Ajax, 1973). *Dyslexia* refers to a neurogenic reading disability. The symptoms of dyslexia, in addition to the defining inabilities to read, include difficulties in writing and spelling, memory disorders, inadequate auditory and visual imagery, deviant motor behavior patterns, and other signs of neurological disturbances (Orton, 1937; Mykelbust & Johnson, 1962; Naidoo, 1971; Miles, 1971).

S. T. Orton, one of the pioneers in the area of dyslexia, believed that the study of language losses in brain-damaged adults disclosed the neurological pattern governing reading and other language functions. Orton concluded that linguistic and reading disorders could result from disturbances of cerebral *function* as well as from the destruction of cerebral tissue. He believed that the most severe cortical damage would result in *cortical blindness,* in which there was no conscious vision although the subcortical optic neural mechanism was unimpaired. Less severe damage could produce *mind blindness,* in which the patient could see objects but was unable to recall their use. With still less cortical damage, *word blindness* could occur, in which only the printed or spoken word had no meaning. This third category constitutes sensory aphasia, according to the more conventional terminology.

Although Orton's studies began with the reading problems of children, his interest expanded to special writing disabilities (agraphia), developmental "word deafness," delayed speech (motor aphasia), childhood stuttering, generalized motor discoordination (developmental apraxia), and various combinations of these syndromes.

Orton's book was written in 1937 and he died in 1948; however, his descriptions of children's linguistic problems and the techniques he proposed for their remediation still serve as the basis for much that is current. His influence is also perpetuated by the Orton Society, which publishes the *Bulletin of the Orton Society.* Orton contributed significantly to the legacy of the organic basis of specific behavioral, linguistic, and cognitive malfunctioning. While the direct antecedents of the category of learning disabilities are the contributions of Werner and Strauss, the notion that specific educational and particularly linguistic handicaps were neurogenic was found in these earlier works on aphasia by A. Ewing, and on dyslexia by Orton in the 1930s.

The concept of dyslexia has undergone essentially the same changes as that of "learning disabilities," and dyslexia is now usually considered a subclassification of this category. The disorder was originally defined as a specific linguistic disability of organic origin. Then, because its organic basis could seldom be independently verified, dyslexia came to be defined as a behavioral syndrome which was assumed to be the result of a postulated, but not demonstrated, neural impairment. Because many emotionally disturbed and environmentally disadvantaged children showed symptoms indistinguishable from those of dyslectic individuals with demonstrated brain damage, dyslexia came to be considered not a specific disease entity but a behavioral syndrome which can result from a number of different factors—both organic and functional. The concept came to be divorced from etiology (Lillywhite, Young, & Olmsted, 1970; Miles, 1971; Naidoo, 1971; Klasen, 1972; Satz & Friel, 1974; Marshall & Newcombe, 1973).

Behavioral tests for the identification of the neurologically impaired

Strauss and others characterized the behavior patterns of the brain-damaged child and suggested that when the behavior of a given child *resembles that of diagnosed neurologically impaired children,* the child can be presumed to be brain-damaged even though his medical history is negative and no positive neurological signs are present. Such a proposal opened the way for the development of purely behavioral tests for the identification of children of this type.

Goldstein and M. Scheerer (1941) developed a battery of tests for the identification of the conceptual deficits of the brain-injured individual. A series of studies started by W. C. Halstead in the 1930s culminated in the development of a battery of tests consisting of twenty-seven behavioral indicators of brain damage (Halstead, 1947). Neither of these test batteries came into general use, but they did contribute to the conviction that it was possible to identify the brain-injured individual by means of behavioral data. It remained for L. Bender (1938, 1946) to make available a simple and easily administered test which, while not claiming to be limited in purpose to the identification of the neurologically impaired, came to be used predominantly for this purpose. The Bender-Gestalt test made use of nine designs previously developed by K. N. Wertheimer (1923) to demonstrate the principles of Gestalt psychology involved in perception. Bender postulated that the perception and reproduction of the Gestalt figures are determined by organic factors dependent on the growth patterns and maturational level of the individual and on his neurological impairment, either functionally or organically induced.

These tests were important in themselves, but they also significantly contributed to the notion that the neurologically impaired constituted a fairly distinct category of people with differentiating behavioral characteristics. The existence of such tests also indicated that brain-damaged individuals can be differentiated from "normals." The educational program described by Strauss and L. Lehtinen (1947) was specifically designed to remedy the perceptual, cognitive, and behavioral limitations of this category of handicapped children. The category of the brain-injured child thus became, even under its original exponents, a broad, elastic category including children with neurological impairment demonstrated by positive neurological signs as well as those with perceptual and conceptual difficulties with no evidence of brain damage but which were assumed to be the result of a postulated neural impairment. The reasoning behind these assumptions seemed to be as follows: since some children with brain injury show certain perceptual, cognitive, and behavioral characteristics, those children with these same characteristics can be assumed to be brain-damaged.

THE DIVORCEMENT OF THE CATEGORY OF
LEARNING DISABILITIES FROM ETIOLOGY

Skeptics have long insisted that children with functional emotional disturbances display many of the components of the Strauss syndrome. More recently, a large number of "culturally disadvantaged" children have also been shown to have deficiencies in perceptual discrimination, concept formation, and sustained attention and are hyperactive and emotionally labile, much like the diagnosed brain-damaged. Critics have argued convincingly that these behavioral symptoms do not necessarily indicate central nervous system damage.

Many people today believe that there will be no loss if the concept of presumed neurological impairment as an intervening variable is dropped and each child's particular perceptual, cognitive, and motor deficits and assets are described or defined so that appropriate psycho-educational programming can be developed for him. Irrespective of etiology, the critical problem is to determine the individual's areas of relative strength and handicap and then to capitalize on the strengths and remove, diminish, or circumvent the deficits so that the child's intellectual and behavioral functioning may reach the optimal practical level.

The need for a new category

Since the 1940s it has been generally accepted by educators, school psychologists, psychiatrists, and neurologists that there is a group of children of normal or superior intelligence who fail to learn because of neurogenic learning disabilities. These children have been variously characterized as minimally brain-damaged, chronic brain syndrome, minimal brain dysfunction, or psychoneurological learning disabilities. However, paralleling these organically-oriented designations there has been a corresponding set of *behavioral* terms used to identify these groups of children. Dyslexia (marked impairment of the ability to read), dysgraphia (inability to express ideas in written form) and perceptual handicap, difficulties in figure-ground differentiation, and letter and number reversals in reading and writing (poor form recognition) are behavioral syndromes presumably associated with cerebral dysfunction. Although originally the correlation of behavior syndromes and neural impairments was assumed, the evidence supporting this assumption was always tenuous. It soon became clear that: (a) many children with known brain damage do not exhibit the patterns of behavior presumably characteristic of the brain-damaged child; (b) many children exhibiting these behavior patterns do not show independent signs of neurological impairment; (c) most of the behavior characteristics ascribed to the brain-damaged are common manifestations of emotional and presumably functional psychiatric disorders, so these behavior syndromes can arise from *either* functional or organic causes; (d) attaching the qualifying adjective *minimal* to the term *brain damage* does not increase the appropriateness of the organically-oriented designation; (e) there is little to be gained by postulating the existence of nondemonstrable neurological impairment to account for the observed behavioral deficits.

In the early 1960s the term *learning disabilities* began to appear regularly as a substitute for "brain injured." This term referred to behavior rather than to etiology. Although the new term still carried the implications of brain damage, it seemed more logical to call children who displayed symptoms similar to those with certain neurological impairments learning-disabled rather than brain-damaged. Although originally the term *learning disability* became the educational alternative to the etiological category of minimal brain dysfunction, there is an increasing tendency to divorce it from etiology and define it entirely in behavioral and educational terms (Hobbs, 1975).

The sudden popularity of the concept

Before the 1960s the term *learning disabilities,* if used at all in special education, referred in a generic way to all children who were educationally handicapped for whatever reason. In the early 1960s the term began appearing with regularity largely as a substitute for *minimally brain-injured.* Within a few years the acceptance of the term *learning disabilities* by people in the field of special education was widespread. In the early '60s the term *learning disorders* competed with learning disabilities for acceptance. In 1965 J. Hellmuth published *Learning Disorders,* volume one. The following year the *Review of Educational Research* for the first time reviewed the topic of "Learning Disorders" (Bateman, 1966). The 1969 review of the same area is titled "Learning Disabilities"

(Kass, 1969). At the 1965 annual convention of the Council for Exceptional Children, the topic of learning disabilities was second only to mental retardation in the number of sessions and papers dealing with it. The entire December 1964 issue of *Exceptional Children* was devoted to the topic of learning disabilities. In 1965, when the local and state organizations of parents of minimally brain-damaged children formed a national organization, they adopted the name "National Association for Children with Learning Disabilities," and by 1969 they had over two hundred local and state affiliates (McCarthy, 1969). In 1968 the first issue of the *Journal of Learning Disabilities* appeared. During the 1970s the literature on the topic has continued to multiply (Tarnopol, 1974).

Legal recognition of the category

Early in the 1960s the state legislatures began recognizing the category and started providing additional financial aid for programs so designated. California began providing such state aid in 1963. The designation used for the programs in that state is *educationally handicapped* (EH). What happened in California is probably typical of what happened elsewhere. The California Association for Neurologically Handicapped Children, consisting largely of the parents of minimally brain-damaged children, sponsored and obtained passage of a bill in the state legislature providing special state aid for the establishment of special classes for such children. A 1968 national survey of programs for children with learning disabilities found that over half of the programs were started largely as the result of the activities of parent pressure groups (Clark & Richards, 1968). Since the differentiation between the neurologically handicapped and the emotionally disturbed is not easily made, the authorized programs for the educationally handicapped in California included both categories. California may be unique in the use of the term *educationally handicapped* to refer to this group which, by code, includes both the emotionally disturbed and the neurologically handicapped as etiological categories in the same classes. National legislative recognition for the educational category was first given when HR13310, the Children with Learning Disability Act of 1969, passed the U.S. House of Representatives by a roll call of 350 to 0. The bill provided $6 million for the fiscal year 1971, $12 million for 1972, and $18 million for 1973 to support research, training programs, model centers, and demonstration programs in the area. By 1967 it was reported that over thirty-five states had legislation providing financial assistance to school districts for the development of support of special classes or programs for children described as educationally handicapped, perceptually handicapped, neurologically impaired, minimally brain-damaged, and/or emotionally disturbed (Blom, 1969). All such children are now being encompassed within the category of learning disabilities. By the 1970s no area of special education was receiving as much attention as that of learning disabilities. However, some doubts about the usefulness of the category were being expressed (Hobbs, 1975).

DEFINITIONS AND DELINEATIONS

The distinguishing behavioral characteristics of the category of neurologically impaired children—described by Strauss as *brain-injured,* later known as *Strauss-syndrome children,* and known still later as *children with learning disabilities*—were hyperactivity, distractibility, disinhibition, and perseveration. Educational measures proposed to overcome or compensate for these behavioral disturbances or deficits included spacious rooms to accommodate small groups of children without crowding, bare walls with all extraneous sights eliminated, translucent rather than transparent windows, screens to hide extraneous objects, and sound-absorbent walls and ceilings to reduce distracting sounds. Masking screens for printed matter, which permitted only one line of print to be seen at one time, were used to reduce the distracting effects from the rest of the page. The significant figures in visual material were darkly outlined to aid in the differentiation of figure and ground, in accordance with the principles of Gestalt psychology.

Strauss mentioned the necessity of directed and controlled motor activity to reduce the disinhibition and diffuse hyperactivity. However, it remained for N. C. Kephart (1960) and R. H. Barsch (1965) to develop educational programs which centered primarily around motor activities. Drill was kept to a minimum because of the tendency of these children to perseverate. The teaching of rhythm was recommended. Speech training was required but should be done by specialists.

The Strauss-Lehtinen program and concepts set the patterns and, with shifts in emphasis, still dominates the thinking and practice in the field. Some programs for the neurologically impaired or Strauss-syndrome child were established during the 1940s and 1950s, but it was not until the next decade, as already indicated, that the concept really came into its own. Several things had developed during these years which made the period of the 1960s propitious for this great surge of interest. One was the enlarging of the category.

Definitions

In 1967 the Association for Children with Learning Disabilities adopted the following definition:

> A child with learning disabilities is one with adequate mental ability, sensory processes, and emotional stability who has a limited number of specific deficits in perceptual, integrative, or expressive processes which severely impair learning efficiency. This includes children who have central nervous system dysfunction which is expressed primarily in impaired learning efficiency.

The following year, the National Advisory Committee to the Bureau of Education for the Handicapped, Office of Education, formulated the following definition, which provided the basis for the subsequent Children with Specific Learning Disabilities Act of 1969:

> Children with special learning disabilities exhibit a disorder in one or more of the basic psychological processes involved in understanding or in using spoken or written language. These may be manifested in disorders of listening, thinking, talking, reading, writing, spelling, or arithmetic. They include conditions which have been referred to as perceptual handicaps, brain injury, minimal brain dysfunction, dyslexia, developmental aphasia, etc. They do not include learning problems which are due primarily to visual, hearing, or motor handicaps, to mental retardation, emotional disturbance or to environmental disadvantage.

Except for the exclusionary provisions, such a concept is divorced from etiology and is characterized largely by a significant educational discrepany between the individual's capacity for learning and his actual functional level. Such a definition will include a sizable group of children in need of special assistance who have previously been denied such help because they failed to meet the specifications of the older conventional categories of exceptional individuals eligible for special aid.

Taking care of one category of "left-over" children

Educators, psychologists, psychiatrists, and pediatricians, as well as parents, have long recognized that there is a group of children of average or above-average intelligence who fail to actualize their potential in school learning. Such children have been a source of puzzlement and frustration to all concerned. They all demonstrate a failure to learn despite apparently adequate intellectual abilities, sensory acuity, and educational opportunities. These are the children who are referred from service to service and from agency to agency in the hope of finding a conventional category for special educational or rehabilitative service where they "fit" and can receive help. The psychologist finds that they are not mentally retarded, the psychiatrist can find no evidence of emotional blockings or other serious disturbance, the neurologist finds no evidence of neural impairment, the internist's findings are negative, and the child is handed back to the regular classroom teachers and/or parents with the admonition, "I guess it is your problem." One reason for the tremendous popularity of the category *learning disabilities* is that a large number of people were waiting in the wings who were eligible and anxious to take advantage of the help that such an additional service offered. It promised to reduce the total number of "left-over" children in need of special help. N. Hobbs (1975) refers to "learning disabilities" as a catch-all category. Cruickshank (1972) states that some forty terms have been used to describe the conditions encompassed by the category.

THE EDUCATIONAL APPEAL OF THE TERM

Another reason for the popularity of the term and concept of learning disabilities derives from the implications of the term itself. The term and category are educationally oriented. Most of the conventional groupings of children for rehabilitative and special educational purposes have derived from medical and psychological rather than from primarily educational sources. For the most part, quantitative medical, psychological, and legal definitions and criteria have been used in defining and establishing eligibility requirements for educational services. In many cases these criteria and definitions are not maximally useful for identifying educational needs. This often results in interpreting eligibility criteria loosely or strictly and otherwise stretching or redefining terms to make them educationally relevant. This means that many children may be legally and administratively eligible for programs which they do not need while others more in need of the special services are deprived of them because they do not fit the category and are therefore ineligible. The trend toward mainstreaming and noncategorical funding will mitigate this problem.

If the category of learning disabilities can be divorced from etiology, it frees special education from being limited by the "medical model," which is probably no more appropriate for special education than it is for mental health.

The term *learning disability* implies diagnosis that is primarily educational and remediation that is teacher-learner oriented. The term also suggests a program of positive action: appropriate teaching. It does not suggest an inherent and largely static condition, as does the term *mental retardation.* The name contains a plea for good teaching based on the child's specific needs.

The term is relatively nonstigmatizing, designates a specific deficit in children who are essentially normal, and focuses attention on identifying the child's specific needs and applying appropriate remedial procedures rather than becoming excessively concerned with etiology and proper labeling. Hobbs (1975) says that for cosmetic reasons, it is a "nice" term to have around.

Because the same people are intimately involved in both processes, identification and classification will be more closely tied to the corrective, remedial, educative process. A continuing study and analysis of the child's classroom behavior and his assets and deficits in learning is crucial in the identification of and his response to remedial procedures. Rehabilitative efforts become part of a continuous diagnostic, evaluative process. Diagnosis is concerned with identifying the areas of educational deficit, and response to the proposed educational procedures becomes an integral part of the diagnostic and classifying procedures.

The concept and category of learning disabilities will not break down the rigid artificial barriers between the categories of exceptional individuals for whom special services are provided, nor will they entirely divorce special education from its medical and psychological roots and its excessive concern with formal diagnosis and defining etiologies. Nevertheless, it does constitute a major step in this direction. The broad category of learning disabilities will assist in providing a full circle of services for all who need them. It constitutes a move in the direction of providing a comprehensive, integrated program extending over the entire range of deviants in need of special services and covering the entire age range.

EDUCATIONAL PROGRAMS FOR CHILDREN WITH LEARNING DISABILITIES

The training and educational techniques involved and the rationale for most of the programs designed for children with learning disabilities are either derived or extrapolated from Strauss and Lehtinen (1947) (McCarthy & McCarthy, 1969; Tarnopol, 1974). The programs are specifically designed to remedy or diminish the behavioral deficits arising from the characteristics of such children, presumed to be caused by their postulated, but often nondemonstrable, neural impairment. Breaking down and adding to the original list of the behavioral characteristics provided by Strauss, researchers and writers in the field have listed almost a hundred specific behaviors. J. J. McCarthy and J. F. McCarthy (1969) list the eight most frequently cited:

1. Hyperactivity
2. Perceptual-motor deficits
3. Emotional lability
4. General orientation and laterality defects
5. Disorders of attention, such as distractibility and short attention span
6. Impulsivity
7. Disorders of memory and conceptual thinking
8. Specific learning defects, particularly language deficits

These are the deficits we associate today with learning disabilities. Strauss and Lehtinen (1947) wrote separate chapters on the pathologies of perception, language, concept formation, and behavior and related these deficits to educational or training techniques designed to remedy them.

Because of the diversity of behavioral manifestations and the equally wide difference of opinion as to the etiology of learning disabilities, it was inevitable that a great many diagnostic-remedial programs would be developed. We shall mention most of these and discuss some typical ones.[1]

Typical programs which focus on the sensory-motor systems are the Strauss-Lehtinin, the Cruickshank, the Getman, the Barsch, and the Doman-Delacato. Programs with a perceptual emphasis are the Frostig and the Fitzhugh. Programs stressing the development of language and cognition have been less prominently associated with particular individuals; however, D. J. Johnson and H. R. Myklebust (1967) have described programs with such emphases. Of course, Ortman's work on dyslexia also belongs in this category. There are also a great number of eclectic diagnostic-remedial programs, of which L. Witmer's and G. M. Fernald's were forerunners of the many now available.

The Strauss-Lehtinen-Cruickshank perceptual-motor program

We have already indicated that the Strauss-Lehtinen conceptualization of the brain-damaged child and their development of a program of education for these children provided the basis for the programs associated today with learning disabilities. Most of the programs in existence today have been largely refinements of this program or of particular components of this program.

[1] For a more extended treatment, see Lerner (1976), and Cruickshank & Hallahan (1975).

Cruickshank, one of the original group of workers with Werner and Strauss, has written extensively and developed a program of his own which largely follows the Strauss-Lehtinen proposals. Cruickshank et al. (1961), and Cruickshank (1967, 1975a) emphasize that individuation of instruction is essential to an appropriate educational program. This requires a small teacher–student ratio. Even with a relatively homogeneous group, a full-time teacher and teacher's aide should have no more than eight children. The major element which must be incorporated into the educational programs for brain-injured children is "structure," and many of the details of methods consist of ways in which structure can be used in the training and education of the child. The various components of structure identified by Cruickshank are relationship structure, environmental structure, program structure, and structured teaching material. Motor training is also an essential part of the program.

Relationship structure   Relationship structure refers to the personal relationship between teacher and child. A satisfactory relationship requires that the teacher understand the child sufficiently well to deal with him in ways that will maximize his development. Properly structured personal relationships are the basis from which all other structuring emanates. If this relationship is satisfactory the child eventually identifies with his teacher, internalizes his goals, and strives to live up to his expectations. Cruickshank believes that this can best be achieved in a structured teaching situation—an adult-dominated teaching situation. Such a situation is not dominated in the sense of constricted, but dominated in terms of carefully planned procedures based on the unique needs and nature of the individual child. The adult is the most significant element in the entire concept of structure, and too much emphasis cannot be placed on the nature of this personal relationship. Essential elements incorporated into this child–teacher relationship are (a) The setting of limitations for appropriate behavior. The child must know just what is and what is not acceptable behavior. (b) Within these limitations the teacher must accept the child and his behavior at all times in terms of the meaning of the situation to the child. (c) The final essential is that of consistency of attitude and behavior on the part of the teacher.

Environmental structure   The classroom must be a nonstimulating or nondistracting environment. This is achieved by removing as many visually and auditorily distracting stimuli as possible. Walls, woodwork, and furniture are all painted the same color. No bulletin boards or pictures are on the walls. Indirect lighting or translucent rather than transparent window glass is used. Wall-to-wall carpeting and sound-treated walls and ceilings are used to reduce extraneous sounds.

Individual cubicles for each child are recommended. The sound-deadened cubicle is large enough to permit the child and the teacher to sit side by side. The cubicle prevents the child from visual distraction by the other children.

Children in such programs should be in a self-contained classroom with their own toilet and lunchroom facilities immediately at hand. The factor of stimuli-reduction is a significant one for the brain-injured child (Cruickshank, 1975a).

Program structure   Program structuring is a further attempt to bring order into the child's "life space." It is essential that the child's daily program be simplified and definitely structured so that routines can be anticipated. With the school program sufficiently simplified and precisely structured, the child and teacher can work together comfortably within a context which ensures the child some degree of success. The program structuring extends to such things as the specific ways in which hats, coats, and overshoes are put on, taken off, and stored; ways of signaling the teacher or assistant for help; the routines established for lunch, toilet, and rest activities; and all the other innumerable routines involved in the course of a normal school day.

Structured teaching material   Teaching materials and their use must be adapted to the child's individual characteristics regarding attention-span, perceptual and conceptual limitations, perseverative and dissociative tendencies, and motor capacities. Much of the material used by the child will be prepared by the teacher or assistant to meet the child's specific needs. Most of it is expendable. As with all disabled, it is necessary to "teach to the disability." Where figure-ground perceptual difficulties are present, the stimulus value of the perceptual components which require emphasis must be increased by the use of heavy outlining or contrasting colors. Tasks must be geared to the child's attention span. For example, to minimize the distracting effects of extraneous stimuli, masking screens which expose only one line of print at a time are prescribed, and instead of giving the child a single page with ten arithmetic problems to be done, he is provided ten pages, one at a time, with one problem on each page.

Motor training   In addition to the personal relationship and environmental structuring, motor training is an integral part of the educational program of the brain-injured child. Daily motor training carried out on an individual basis for approximately thirty minutes is prescribed. It is suggested that properly supervised volunteers can assist in the motor-training program. It is also recommended that the total educational program include a speech development or correction program carried out by personnel ancillary to the educational program.

The Kephart program

Newell Kephart (1960, 1975) and Cruickshank (1967, 1975b) have probably most completely perpetuated the work of Werner and Strauss. While Kephart's program is a perceptual-motor one, he, more than Cruickshank, made the motor component the primary focus of treatment and the perceptual component somewhat derivative. His program is also more developmentally organized. Kephart stresses the effects of motor processes on perception and the effects of perception on the higher cognitive processes in a kind of hierarchical relationship. Kephart also emphasizes the need to develop skills in their "natural order." He believes that perceptual-motor deficits are primarily organic in nature and are best remedied by the development of such basic skills as eye-hand coordination, temporal-spatial relationships, and form perception. Kephart relates the effects of perceptual-motor practice to changes in the central nervous system without as much speculating concerning specific brain mechanism as C. H. Delacato (1966) has done. The Delacato program is discussed later in this chapter.

On the physiological side, Kephart believes that perceptual and motor processes are inseparably tied to each other because there is always a motor component accompaniment or consequence of perception. Movements are modified and perceptions molded by the visual and kinesthetic feedback involved in these processes.

Kephart provides a number of nonstandardized tests for measuring the child's stage of perceptual-motor development and for evaluating the child's progress in improving these skills. He also provides specific instructions and procedures for the development of form perception, space and form discrimination, ocular control, and general sensorimotor integration. Kephart's program uses chalkboard training, rail walking, balancing, tracing templates, and music. The Straussian heritage is evident in much of Kephart's work with primary emphasis being placed on the motor and developmental aspects.

Barsch's "movigenic" program

While the effects of his early work with Strauss are evident, R. H. Barsch (1965) seems to have developed some unique techniques and an orientation to learning which is somewhat novel. "Movigenics" is the study of the origins and development of the movement patterns which are necessary for ideational learning. Barsch's physiologically-oriented curriculum is based on an elaborate set of eight major constructs or hypotheses. (Interested readers are referred to the original source for the details of constructs.) Using these constructs as a theoretical framework, Barsch has developed his movigenic program consisting of a planned sequence of activities by means of which the child explores his world, orients himself in space, and integrates his activities and experiences into progressively more complex patterns and relationships.

A movigenic classroom is very different from the ordinary one. All furniture is removed to provide maximum open space for activity. Lines on the floor guide the child upon entering and leaving the room, for work at the chalkboard, and for other activities. A strip of carpeting across one end of the room provides a surface for crawling, creeping, and rolling. The children in class go barefoot or in stocking feet.

Although activities are carefully planned, no rigid schedules are followed. A good deal of equipment such as walking and balancing rails, scooter and teeter boards, and tracing templates are used. Visuo-motor practice involving first one eye, then the other, and then both eyes, with the body in various positions, is provided. Practice in visual tracking in darkness is a part of the program. Tachistoscopes are used in visual training. Analogous exercises in auditory processes are also included. While one can recognize the possible influences of Itard, Seguin, and Maria Montessori and much that is derived directly from Strauss, many of Barsch's ideas about movement and vision seem novel.

Getman's visuo-motor emphasis

Whereas Barsch emphasized visual and general motor training about equally, G. N. Getman and his associates (1964, 1965, 1966) have worked out a program of visuo-motor training with development of the general motor system as necessary but subsidiary to the former. For Getman, visual perception is the culmination of a developmental motor sequence consisting of seven levels. These levels are suggestive of Delacato's (1966) model to be discussed later. It is necessary to understand all the physiological systems of the body and their developmental sequence if we are really to understand how the child learns. Learning is a process involving the entire body.

The first developmental level of Getman's seven-step model is the *Innate Response System*. This is primarily a reflex alerting mechanism, including such things as the light reflex, the grasp reflex, the reciprocal reflexes involved in bilaterality and antagonistic muscular responses, the statokinetic reflexes involved in maintaining postures, and the myotatic reflexes providing muscles with kinesthetic guidance. These response systems are species specific and are innate. However, Getman believes the maximum effective relationship between the different reflex systems is established through activity, awareness of movement, and conscious control of movements which are learned.

Getman's second level is that of the *General Motor System,* which includes creeping, crawling, walking, running, and jumping. These activities extend and further develop laterality and provide for the exploration of the child's world.

The third developmental level is that of the *Special Motor Systems.* This level involves the incorporation and elaboration of the systems of the first two levels in more complex patterns. The special motor systems include visual-motor combinations such as eye-hand coordinations, foot-hand relationships, and an infinite number of postural-hand-foot-gesture-voice combinations.

The fourth level involves predominantly the development of the *Ocular Motor System.* This system includes the coordinate and balanced movements of the two eyes. Other components of the ocular system are eye-fixations, saccadic movements (back and forth movements of the eyes), visual pursuit movements, and eye rotations (moving both eyes in all directions).

The fifth level of Getman's system is that of the *Speech Motor Systems.* This includes the verbal skills of babbling, imitative, and original oral speech.

The sixth developmental level is that of the *Visual System*—really visual imagery. This system involves imagery which is cross-sensory in the sense that one can visualize something that one feels. This imagery also involves recall of the events of yesterday and the projection of similar events into the future. This provides the basis for the recognition of past-present-future relationships. At this level perception occurs.

Single perceptual events generate constructs. Relegating individual percepts to appropriate constructs results in *Cognition,* the seventh and highest developmental level in Getman's model.

Getman's discussion focuses dominantly on visual perception and the ocular mechanism. The exercises proposed by him and his associates (Getman et al., 1964) include practice in general coordination, balance, eye-hand coordination, eye movements, form recognition, and visual memory (visual imagery).

The Delacato program

One of the most controversial of the motor approaches to learning disabilities was developed by Glenn Doman, a physical therapist, and Carl Delacato, an educator.

The Delacato (1966) approach, like the Getman model, is developmental and physiological but in a more specific and limited sense. Although Delacato's concepts seem to have developed independently of the Strauss formulations, he agrees with their contention that the neurologically impaired retardate displays clinically observable behavioral symptoms which are characteristic of his organic deficits. However, Delacato has developed a much more specific and elaborate theoretical superstructure to rationalize his diagnostic and remedial procedures. His conceptions of both neurological and behavioral growth and function are hierarchical and developmental. According to Delacato, neurological development progresses vertically from the spinal cord, through the medulla, pons, and midbrain to the cerebral cortex. The developmental progression to this level is also found in animals below humans in the phylogenetic scale. However, the normally developed human goes one step beyond that of the lower animals and achieves unilateral cerebral dominance. When this is achieved, the two cerebral hemispheres, while mirroring each other anatomically, have differentiated functionally. Left-hemisphere-dominant individuals are right-handed, right-footed, and right-eyed. The dominant cerebral hemisphere also controls language. The evolution of *Homo sapiens* into an ideating, language-oriented human being was the consequence of his development of cortical laterality. Failure to attain this highest level of human neurological development (unilateral cortical dominance), or brain damage which disturbs this functional dominance, manifests in impaired linguistic processes. Aphasia, delayed speech, stuttering, retarded reading, poor spelling and handwriting, and reading which may be within the normal range but below the individual's level of mathematical performance, are in this descending order reflections of corresponding degrees of decreasing neurological impairment or failures of development of cerebral unilateral dominance. Individuals who have normal language development have achieved this uniquely human level of neurological development.

Lack of adequate neurological development at each of the lower (spinal cord, medullary, pontine, brain-stem, or cortical) levels shows a specific syndrome of behavioral deficits. To illustrate: Spinal cord and medullary deficits result in failures to make the normal precreeping and precrawling movements. The remedial procedures recommended for these deficits consist in passively imposing these movements upon the body of the child until he begins making them spontaneously. For example, while one person holds the child's head, another moves the body in undulating, fish-like movements.

The inability to execute homolateral crawling movements at an appropriate age (six months) and "improper" sleep postures are indicative of inadequate neural organization at the pontine level. For this deficit, homolateral "patterning" is administered by putting the child through the appropriate arm and leg movements. When the child is able to execute these movements spontaneously, daily practice in crawling with the stomach in contact with the floor is prescribed. The child is also taught the "proper" sleep posture which consists of the homolateral position, that is, arm and leg on the same side flexed and the head turned toward the flexed limb.

Failures of neurological integration at the midbrain level manifest themselves as deficits in the cross-pattern activities such as making simultaneous opposite arm and leg movements in creeping. These behavioral defects are treated similarly by imposing the appropriate patterning movements on the child.

Bilateral cortical deficits manifest themselves in the child's failure to develop cross-pattern walking (what other kind is there?). Play exercises involving the large muscles of the body and practice in walking are recommended to remedy this defect.

Failures to develop consistent laterality and "confused" laterality indicate a failure in the development of unilateral cortical dominance. The accompanying symptoms include a long list of linguistic deficiencies; the particular ones found depend on the degree of the lack of cortical dominance of one side of the brain.

According to Delacato, the ontogenetic development of each individual recapitulates the phylogenetic evolutionary development of *Homo sapiens*. This recapitulation of the evolutionary development begins at conception and normally is complete at six and one-half years of age. The orderly development of neural controls in humans progresses, as indicated, from the spinal cord up to the cerebral cortex and parallels the evolutionary origins of their structures. Adequate development of all lower levels is a prerequisite to the functioning of higher levels and normal behavior requires that each higher level dominate and supersede all those below it. Any obstruction to this ontogenetic recapitulation arrests behavioral development and prevents the development of the higher functions. The recommended procedures are designed to bring about this neurological organization and when this is accomplished the behavioral deficits disappear.

In addition to the "patterning" activities which are unique to the Delacato model, the entire training schedule includes much that is found in the other programs proposed for educationally handicapped children. These recommended procedures include creeping and crawling, walking and trampoline jumping, training in visual and auditory discrimination and perception, reading aloud to the child, encouraging talking, and play activities involving the large muscles. These exercises have much in common with those used by physiotherapists in aiding the cerebral palsied.

The Marianne Frostig visual perception approach

Marianne Frostig has published a test of visual perception (1961), has developed a specific remedial program for the perceptually handicapped (Frostig & Horne, 1964), and directs the Frostig Center of Educational Therapy for children with learning disabilities. The test is designed to differentiate the various kinds of visual-perceptual disabilities and to serve as the basis for specific remedial programs. It is a paper-and-pencil test designed to assess five areas of visual perception: eye-motor coordination, figure-ground, constancy of shape, position in shape, and spatial relationships.

The perceptual training materials developed by Frostig are designed to ameliorate the specific disabilities disclosed by the tests and to provide readiness training in the perceptual abilities normally developed prior to school entrance (Frostig, 1975).

The Fitzhugh program

Kathleen Fitzhugh and Loren Fitzhugh (1966) have produced a series of eight workbooks consisting of exercises designed as a remedial or readiness program. The program covers visual-perceptual problems in two workbooks and language and numbers in the remaining five. The workbooks are essentially self-teaching. The visual-perception exercises deal principally with spatial organization and attempt to increase the child's ability to perceive and manipulate shapes and objects in time and space.

The language and number workbooks are designed to improve the child's ability to identify letters, numbers, words, and pictures. They also are intended to increase the child's understanding of language symbols and arithmetic operations.

Some general diagnostic-remedial approaches

In the 1890s Lightner Witmer at the University of Pennsylvania and Grace Fernald in the Clinic School at the University of California at Los Angeles were treating educationally handicapped children in a diagnostic-remedial way.

Witmer's psycho-educational approach   The establishment by Witmer in 1896 of the first psychological clinic in the world, at the University of Pennsylvania, marked the beginning not only of clinical psychology but also of the diagnostic-remedial approach to problem school

children. Each child served by the clinic received an educational program specifically designed for him by an interdisciplinary team in which
the teacher was the central figure. Clinical studies were supplemented by
classroom observation. Diagnosis was a continuing process growing out
of clinical data, classroom experience, and the child's response to treatment. Psychologists, teachers, social workers, and physicians were all involved in the process.

Witmer believed that children with educational problems could not
be understood without periods of systematic observation in the school
setting during which attempts were made to improve their behavior.
Particular emphasis was put on special types of remedial and educative
efforts. Much of what Witmer wrote in the journal, *The Psychological
Clinic,* which he founded and edited, sounds quite modern and many of
his procedures are applicable to the child today designated as having
learning disabilities. Like many present-day psychologists, Witmer was
interested in the physical and neurological aspects of the cases referred to
him (Wolman, 1965).

The Fernald contribution   Grace Fernald, the first psychologist to
work in a child guidance clinic, was dealing in a diagnostic-remedial way
with children with learning disabilities in the University of California
clinic school long before these children were separately categorized
(Fernald, 1943). She insisted that all educational difficulties in children
of normal or superior intelligence can be removed or compensated for
if proper techniques are employed.

Fernald is best known for her kinesthetic method of teaching reading,
which is still used with children who have failed to learn to read by
other methods. The first step in Fernald's method consists in writing in
large letters on a card a word chosen by the child. The child then traces
the word with his finger while saying it. He repeats the process until he
is able to write the word from memory. It is important that the child
trace the word with his finger, and have cutaneous contact with the
paper while saying the word in a natural way. This procedure combines
visual, kinesthetic, cutaneous, and auditory factors. In the next step, the
tracing is dropped, and the child merely looks at and says the word.
From then on, the method is fairly conventional except that Fernald believes that children should select the words they want to learn and
should begin writing and reading with their own stories rather than
those adults have written for them.

Other diagnostic-remedial approaches

Currently, a large number of pragmatic diagnostic-remedial approaches to the problems of children with learning disabilities are being

developed (Blanco, 1974; Gearheart, 1973; Hallahan & Cruickshank, 1973; Moran, 1975). As the field of learning disabilities evolves, the pragmatic general diagnostic-remedial approaches may prove to be the dominant ones. The entire range of children designated as having learning disabilities may prove to be so varied that educational programs stemming from a single orientation may not be applicable to more than a small segment of the total population. For children with perceptual-motor problems and children whose problems verge in that direction, programs with this emphasis will be most appropriate. Matching each child's disability to the appropriate program is technically feasible but does involve many practical problems.

The majority of children currently being referred to programs for the educationally handicapped are recommended for individualized instruction in a small class setting. The specific recommendations usually include perceptual training and counseling (Keogh & Becker, 1973). These children show a fairly consistent constellation of classroom behavior. A Pupil Identification Scale based on the classroom behavior of such children has been developed to assist in identifying these problem children (Novack, Bonaventura, & Merendo, 1973). B. K. Keogh and L. D. Becker (1973) provide some cautions and guidelines for the early identification of children with learning problems.

EVALUATIVE STUDIES

A few studies have been concerned with the claim of Strauss and his coworkers that brain-damaged children do actually learn differently from non-brain-damaged children. C. D. Barnett, N. R. Ellis, and M. Pryor (1960) matched brain-damaged and non-brain-damaged children on a variety of variables and compared their learning of six different types of skills in which differences in favor of the neurologically unimpaired group would support the Straussian theory. The brain-damaged children performed less well on two of the learning tasks but no differences were found on the other four. The authors concluded that the proposition that the brain-damaged learn differently from the neurologically unimpaired must be questioned.

D. B. Cruse (1961) found no differences in distractibility between brain-injured and ordinary familial retardates of equal mental levels. Cruickshank et al. (1961) and K. J. Rost (1967) found that the use of isolation booths during one semester had no measurable effect on the classroom learning of brain-injured children.

J. W. Somerville, L. S. Warnberg, and D. E. Bost (1973) compared the performances of first grade boys judged to be either distractible or nondistractible either in cubicles or with increased levels of stimulation and found no effects of the different conditions for either group. They conclude that "the acceptance of stimulus reduction as desirable for distractible children is, at best, premature."

Cruickshank (1975a) has reviewed the research studies evaluating the effects of structuring on the learning of learning disabled children. He concludes that although the research support for the efficacy of structuring is meager, the theoretical basis for advocating structuring for these children is so compelling that he continues to recommend it.

On the other hand, M. Levine, G. Spivak, and G. Fernald (1962) did find differences in visual discrimination learning between groups of brain-injured, emotionally disturbed, and normal children, favoring the normal and emotionally disturbed. N. Haring and E. L. Phillips (1962) found that a group of emotionally disturbed, but presumably not neurologically damaged, children profited significantly by a program which was structured along the lines recommended by Cruickshank for the brain-damaged. This study provides support for the proposition that the highly structured programs designed for the brain-damaged are useful for children with behavioral characteristics similar to those who are positively identified as brain-injured.

D. D. McCormick, J. N. Schnobrick, and S. W. Footlik (1966) provide some support for the Straussian hypothesis. They compared two equated groups of first graders, one of which received perceptual-motor exercises systematically for nine weeks, the other of which received an equivalent amount of physical education activity. Subsequent testing revealed no significant differences between the means of the reading achievement scores of the two groups. However, a subgroup of underachievers in the perceptual-motor-trained group did show significant greater improvement in reading than did those whose achievements were more in keeping with their aptitudes.

L. Goodman and D. Hammill (1973) reviewed forty-two studies which had used the Kephart and Getman training techniques. These authors considered the two programs sufficiently similar to be lumped together. Both programs focus on the development of motor and visual skills and both embody the concept of the importance of a developmental sequence of visual-motor skills. From their evaluative survey of these studies, Goodman and Hammill conclude:

> The results of attempts to implement the Kephart and Getman techniques in the schools for the most part have been unrewarding. Particularly disappointing were the findings which pertain to the effects of such training on perceptual-motor performance itself. . . . The results of the intervention studies using the Kephart and Getman techniques, taken collectively, suggest that such training is not particularly effective. Participation in the training

programs produced little improvement in the children's visual-motor functioning. . . . Moreover, the effect of training on intelligence or academic achievement was not clearly demonstrated.

D. D. Campbell (1973) found that the evidence indicates that well-developed psychomotor skills are not essential for educational competence or reading proficiency. While the incidence of poor psychomotor skills among learning-disabled children is high, the significance of this fact is unknown.

The results of studies designed to test the Delacato hypothesis have also been equivocal. M. P. Robbins (1966) could find no evidence that a group of children receiving Delacato exercises in creeping and crawling, maintaining specified writing positions, and engaging in sidedness and cross- and homolateral patterning activities did any better in reading and arithmetic than did a control group which continued its normal classroom activities or a group which engaged in activities which were the opposite of those recommended by Delacato. J. R. Kershner (1968), in a slightly different type of study, reports results which tend, in part, to support the Delacato approach. E. Zigler and V. Seitz (1975), in a critical review of sensorimotor patterning, conclude that the positive results claimed for the procedures are unwarranted.

M. S. Jessen (1970) found that training with the Frostig visual-perceptual training materials and additional auditory and kinesthetic training significantly improved the reading readiness of kindergartners and the reading skills of first graders. However, after a two-year interval, the perceptually trained children did not have significantly higher reading achievement test scores than comparable children who received no training.

D. Hammill and J. L. Wiederholt (1972) comprehensively reviewed the Frostig Visual Perception Test and its related training program, and concluded that the training programs were not effective in increasing children's perceptual competencies. They also were ineffective in increasing the children's educational or intellectual functioning. P. Buckland and B. Balow (1973) found that children low in reading readiness, given forty days of training with the Frostig program, profited no more from the program than did comparable children who engaged in activities which were largely listening and verbal in nature.

The limited research on the effectiveness of the various programs developed for the children with learning disabilities is inconclusive. E. M. Koppitz (1971), in a follow-up study of learning disabled children attending special classes for such children, obtained results reminiscent of the finding concerning such classes for the educable mentally retarded or the "slow learners." Some administrators thought of these classes as remedial, short-term assignments; the children would return to their regular classes after they had "caught up." Other administrators perceived of these placements as last resorts for nonlearners and the unmanageable, while still others considered these classes to be places where vulnerable children could be placed early enough to prevent the development of serious learning, emotional, and behavior problems. Koppitz found that only 17 percent of children so placed (30 of 177) returned successfully to their regular classes. The corresponding figure for the mentally retarded is about 10 percent (Kirk, 1974). Those children who returned to their regular classes had practically all "lost" a year—they did not "catch up." The teachers of these special classes uniformly resented having their classes used as "dumping places" for the incorrigibles. The author believed that such assignments could best serve as preventative measures for "high-risk children" before their problems have become serious.

There is little in the evaluative studies to guide the practitioner in selecting the most effective one to use. Perhaps children with learning disabilities are too heterogeneous a group for all to be helped by any program that is dominantly linguistic, perceptual, or motor. It is possible that further research and practice should be directed at the problem of matching student needs and appropriate remediation.

THE FUTURE OF THE CATEGORY

Hobbs and his co-workers (1975) see little value in incorporating the term and category of learning disabilities into the lexicon of exceptional children. However, the recognition that the large number of children usually encompassed by this broad category need special help, may contribute to the development of individualized instruction based on diagnostic-remedial procedures from which all children may benefit. If, and when, noncategorical funding and treatment programs become the rule, the need for special categories such as this will decrease.

Cruickshank (1975) states that "learning disabilities" has become a catch-all term for those children with educational and/or psychological problems, the etiology and treatment of which are unclear. He believes that the term should be dropped and that more specific terms such as "perceptual disabilities," which are more descriptive of the problem, should be used instead.

SUMMARY

An increasingly large segment of the schools' special education population is being designated as "children with learning disabilities." The term was seldom heard before the 1960s, but by the 1970s the group was probably receiving more professional attention than any other category of exceptional children. The term *learning disabilities* first appeared as a substitute for *brain-injured* in the sense in which the term was used by Strauss. The brain-injured, according to Strauss, was a broad and elastic category including children with positive neurological signs and/or a history of neural trauma on the one hand but also applicable to children characterized by purely behavioral, perceptual, and conceptual deficits *similar to* those with demonstrated neural pathology. There is an increasing tendency to divorce the category from etiology entirely and to define it in purely behavioral and educational terms.

Strauss and Lehtinen proposed a specific methodology for the education of the brain-injured child; most subsequent programs developed for children with learning disabilities have been derived, either directly or indirectly, from their proposals. Cruickshank's program follows very closely the original Strauss model and emphasizes the importance of "structure." Kephart developed a more action- and developmentally-oriented program. Barsch also emphasized the role of movement but put particular stress on the ocular mechanisms.

The most controversial program is that of Delacato, which claims to modify the nervous system directly. Delacato insists that by imposing certain activities on the child, one can modify the underlying neural mechanisms in predictable ways. Marianne Frostig and the Fitzhughs have developed programs which emphasize visual perception and provide sets of training materials to be used in their proposed educational procedures. Although not historically related to Strauss and his co-workers, there are available several general diagnostic-remedial approaches which are applicable to the remediation of learning disabilities.

REFERENCES

AJAX, E. T., "The Aphasic Patient: A Practical Review," *Diseases of the Nervous System*, 1973, *34*, 135–42.

BARNETT, C. D., N. R. ELLIS & M. PRYOR, "Learning in Familial and Brain-injured Defectives," *American Journal of Mental Deficiency*, 1960, *64*, 894–97.

BARSCH, R. H., *A Movigenic Curriculum* (Madison, Wis.: Bureau for Handicapped Children, 1965).

BATEMAN, B., "Learning Disorders," *Review of Educational Research*, 1966, *36*, 93–119.

BENDER, L., "A Visual Motor Gestalt Test and Its Clinical Use," American Orthopsychiatric Association Research Monograph, no. 3, 1938.

BENDER, L., *Bender Motor Gestalt Test: Cards and Manual of Instructions* (New York: American Orthopsychiatric Association, 1946).

BLANCO, R. F., *Prescriptions for Children with Learning and Adjustment Problems* (Springfield, Ill.: Charles C Thomas, 1974).

BLOM, G. E., "The Concept 'Perceptually Handicapped': Its Assets and Limitations," *Seminars in Psychiatry*, 1969, *1*, 253–61.

BUCKLAND, P., & B. BALOW, "Effects of Visual Perception Training on Reading Achievement," *Exceptional Children*, 1973, *39*, 299–304.

CAMPBELL, D. D., "Typewriting Contrasted with Handwriting: A Circumvention Study of Learning-disabled Children," *Journal of Special Education*, 1973, *7*, 155–68.

CLARK, A. D., & C. J. RICHARDS, "Learning Disabilities: A National Survey of Existing Public School Programs," *Journal of Special Education*, 1968, *2*, 223–28.

CRUICKSHANK, W. M., "The Education of the Child with Brain Injury," in W. M. Cruickshank & G. O. Johnson, eds., *Education of Exceptional Children and Youth*, 2nd ed. (Englewood Cliffs, N.J.: Prentice-Hall, 1967).

CRUICKSHANK, W. M., "Some Issues Facing the Field of Learning Disabilities," *Journal of Learning Disabilities*, 1972, *5*, 380–88.

CRUICKSHANK, W. M., "The Learning Environment," in W. M. Cruickshank & D. P. Hallahan, eds., *Perceptual and Learning Disabilities in Children* (Syracuse, N.Y.: Syracuse University Press, 1975a).

CRUICKSHANK, W. M., "The Psychoeducational Match," in W. M. Cruickshank & D. P. Hallahan, eds., *Perceptual and Learning Disabilities in Children* (Syracuse, N.Y.: Syracuse University Press, 1975b).

CRUICKSHANK, W. M.; F. A. BENTZEN; F. H. RATZEBURG; & M. T. TANNHAUSER, *A Teaching Method for Brain-injured and Hyperactive Children* (Syracuse, N.Y.: Syracuse University Press, 1961).

CRUICKSHANK, W. M., & D. P. HALLAHAN, eds., *Perceptual and Learning Disabilities in Children* (Syracuse, N.Y.: Syracuse University Press, 1975).

CRUSE, D. B., "Effects of Distraction upon the Performance of Brain-injured and Familial Retarded Children," *American Journal of Mental Deficiency*, 1961, *66*, 86–90.

DELACATO, C. H., *Neurological Organization and Reading Problems* (Springfield, Ill.: Charles C Thomas, 1966).

EWING, A., *Aphasia in Children* (New York: Oxford University Press, 1930).

FERNALD, G. M., *Remedial Techniques in Basic School Subjects* (New York: McGraw-Hill, 1943).

FITZHUGH, K. B., & L. FITZHUGH, *The Fitzhugh Plus Program* (Galien, Mich.: Allied Education Council, 1966).

FROSTIG, M., *Manual for the Marianne Frostig Developmental Test of Visual Perception* (Palo Alto, Ca.: Consulting Psychologists Press, 1961).

FROSTIG, M., "The Role of Perception in the Integration of Psychological Processes," in W. M. Cruickshank and D. P. Hallahan, eds., *Perceptual and Learning Disabilities in Children* (Syracuse, N.Y.: Syracuse University Press, 1975).

FROSTIG, M., & D. HORNE, *The Frostig Program for the Development of Visual Perception* (Chicago: Follett, 1964).

GEARHEART, B. R., *Learning Disabilities: Educational Strategies* (St. Louis: C. V. Mosby, 1973).

GETMAN, G. N., "The Visuomotor Complex in the Acquisition of Learning Skills," in J. Hellmuth, ed., *Learning Disorders*, vol. 1 (Seattle: Special Child Publications of the Seattle Seguin School, 1965).

GETMAN, G. N., *How to Develop Your Child's Intelligence* (Luverne, Minn.: Announcers Press, 1966).

GETMAN, G. N.; E. R. KANE; M. R. HALGREN; & G. W. McKEE, *The Physiology of Readiness* (Minneapolis: P.A.S.S., Inc., 1964).

GOLDSTEIN, K., *The Organism* (New York: American Book, 1939).

GOLDSTEIN, K., & M. SCHEERER, "Abstract and Concrete Behavior: An Experimental Study with Special Mental Tests," *Psychological Monographs, 239*, 1941, 151.

GOODMAN, L., & D. HAMMILL, "The Effectiveness of the Kephart-Getman Activities in Developing Perceptual-motor and Cognitive Skills," *Focus on Exceptional Children,* 1973, *4* (9), 1–9.

HALLAHAN, D. P., & W. M. CRUICKSHANK, *Psychoeducational Foundations of Learning Disabilities* (Englewood Cliffs, N.J.: Prentice-Hall, 1973).

HALSTEAD, W. C., *Brain and Intelligence* (Chicago: University of Chicago Press, 1947).

HAMMILL, D., & J. L. WIEDERHOLT, "Review of the Frostig Visual Perception Test and the Related Training Program," in L. Mann & D. Sabatino, eds., *The Review of Special Education* (King of Prussia, Pa.: Buttonwood, 1972).

HARING, N., & E. L. PHILLIPS, *Educating Emotionally Disturbed Children* (New York: McGraw-Hill, 1962).

HELLMUTH, J., ed., *Learning Disorders,* vol. 1 (Seattle: Special Child Publications, 1965).

HOBBS, N., *The Futures of Children* (San Francisco: Jossey-Bass, 1975).

JESSEN, M. S., "Reflections on Research Related to Reading Readiness," *Journal of California State Federal Council for Exceptional Children,* 1970, *19,* 19–21.

JOHNSON, D. J., & H. R. MYKLEBUST, *Learning Disabilities: Educational Principles and Practices* (New York: Grune & Stratton, 1967).

KASS, C. E., "Learning Disabilities," *Review of Educational Research,* 1969, *39,* 71–82.

KEOGH, B. K., & L. D. BECKER, "Early Detection of Learning Problems: Questions, Cautions, and Guidelines," *Exceptional Children,* 1973, *40,* 5–11.

KEPHART, N. C., *The Slow Learner in the Classroom* (Columbus, Ohio: Charles E. Merrill, 1960).

KEPHART, N. C., "The Perceptual-motor Match," in W. M. Cruickshank & D. P. Hallahan, eds., *Perceptual and Learning Disabilities in Children* (Syracuse, N.Y.: Syracuse University Press, 1975).

KERSHNER, J. R., "Doman-Delacato's Theory of Neurological Organization Applied with Retarded Children," *Exceptional Children,* 1968, *34,* 441–45.

KIRK, D. L., "The Great Sorting Machine," *Phi Delta Kappan,* 1974, *60* (8), 521–25.

KLASEN, E., *The Syndrome of Specific Dyslexia* (Baltimore: University Park Press, 1972).

KOPPITZ, E. M., *Children with Learning Disabilities: A Five-year Follow-up Study* (New York: Grune & Stratton, 1971).

LERNER, J. W., *Children with Learning Disabilities* (Boston: Houghton Mifflin, 1976).

LEVINE, M., G. SPIVAK, & D. FERNALD, "Discrimination in Diffuse Brain Damage," *American Journal of Mental Deficiency*, 1962, *67*, 287–91.

LILLYWHITE, H. S., N. B. YOUNG, & R. W. OLMSTED, *Pediatrician's Handbook of Communication Disorders* (Philadelphia: Lea & Febiger, 1970).

McCARTHY, J. J., & J. F. McCARTHY, *Learning Disabilities* (Boston: Allyn & Bacon, 1969).

McCARTHY, J. M., "Learning Disabilities: Where Have We Been? Where Are We Going?" *Seminar in Psychiatry*, 1969, *1*, 354–61.

McCORMICK, D. D., J. N. SCHNOBRICK, & S. W. FOOTLIK, *The Effects of Perceptual Motor Training in Reading Achievement* (Chicago: Reading Research Foundation, 1966, mimeographed).

MARSHALL, J. C., & F. NEWCOMBE, "Patterns of Paralexia: A Psycholinguistic Approach," *Journal of Psycholinguistic Research*, 1973, *2*, 175–99.

MILES, T. R., "More on Dyslexia," *British Journal of Educational Psychology*, 1971, *41*, 1–5.

MORAN, M. R., "Nine Steps to the Diagnostic Prescriptive Process in the Classroom," *Focus on Exceptional Children*, 1975, *6* (9), 1–14.

MYKLEBUST, H. R., & D. JOHNSON, "Dyslexia in Children," *Exceptional Children*, 1962, *29*, 14–25.

NAIDOO, S., "Specific Developmental Dyslexia," *British Journal of Educational Psychology*, 1971, *41*, 19–21.

NOVACK, H. S., E. BONAVENTURA, & P. F. MERENDO, "A Scale for Early Detection of Children with Learning Disabilities," *Exceptional Children*, 1973, *40*, 98–105.

ORTON, S. T., *Reading, Writing, and Speech Problems in Children* (London: Chapman & Hall, 1937).

ROBBINS, M. P., "A Study of the Validity of Delacato's Theory of Neurological Organization," *Exceptional Children*, 1966, *32*, 517–22.

ROST, K. J., "Academic Achievement of Brain-injured and Hyperactive Children in Isolation," *Exceptional Children*, 1967, *28*, 103–7.

SATZ, P., & J. FRIEL, "Some Predictive Antecedents of Specific Disability: A Preliminary Two-year Follow-up," *Journal of Learning Disabilities*, 1974, *7*, 437–41.

SOMERVILLE, J. W., L. S. WARNBERG, & D. E. BOST, "Effects of Cubicles versus Increased Stimulation on Task Performance by First-grade Males Perceived as Distractible and Nondistractible," *Journal of Special Education*, 1973, *7*, 169–85.

STRAUSS, A. A., & L. LEHTINEN, *Psychopathology and Education of the Brain-injured Child* (New York: Grune & Stratton, 1947).

TARNOPOL, L., *Learning Disabilities: Introduction to Educational and Medical Management* (Springfield, Ill.: Charles C Thomas, 1974).

WERTHEIMER, K. N., "Studies in the Theory of Gestalt Psychology," *Psychologische Forschungen*, 1923, *4*, 230–41.

WOLMAN, B. B., "Clinical Psychology and the Philosophy of Science," in B. B. Wolman, ed., *Handbook of Clinical Psychology* (New York: McGraw-Hill, 1965).

ZIGLER, E., & V. SEITZ, "On an Experimental Evaluation of Sensorimotor Patterning: A Critique," *American Journal of Mental Deficiency*, 1975, *79*, 483–92.

Chapter 11

The bicultural individual

As we indicated earlier, behavioral and developmental deviations have significance only within a given cultural context. Variations in physique, intellect, and personality are universal; society dictates which of these constitute disabilities or assets, impairments or enhancements of personal worth. Each culture assigns tasks, attaches meanings to deviations, and classifies people according to the demands and expectancies of that culture. Thus, individuals able to function adequately in one culture, subculture, or family situation may be handicapped in another. It is these individuals who have been described as "culturally deprived," "culturally disadvantaged," caught in "cross-cultural streams," "culturally deviant," or "culturally different."

Some of the individuals so labeled object to all such descriptive terms as unjustly stigmatizing. Indeed, the prefix *dis* does mean "negation" or "absence of," *de* means "away from," "separation," or "reversal." Consequently, any terms that include these prefixes will have negative connotations. We said in chapter 1 that deviations can be either desirable or undesirable, malignant or benign. However, since unspecified deviance is usually perceived negatively, all of the terms whose denotative meanings signify difference also have acquired the connotation of stigma. This leaves us with no connotatively neutral terms for identifying such categories of people. We have adopted the terms *culturally deviant* and *culturally different* as the most acceptable of the alternatives. Our major concern is with persons whose cultural background is sufficiently different from that of the dominant society to cause them to function disadvantageously in the society in which they elect or are forced to live. In effect, the individuals with whom we are concerned are principally those whose academic achievement is low and whose employment prospects are poor because of their cultural differentness.

SOME HISTORICAL CONCEPTS

Historically, there have been varied explanations of social class and ethnic group differences. For generations, each ethnocentric culture and subculture accounted for its perceived superiority as the result of inherent biological differences. Consequently, the dominant Euro-American culture originally explained the unfortunate conditions of its disadvantaged minorities on the basis of genetic inferiority. However, in the 1940s geneticists, educators, and social scientists challenged the biological explanations, proposing more feasible social explanations.

The first alternative to the biological interpretation of ethnic and social class differences was in terms of an alleged "cultural deprivation." According to this conception, white middle- and upper-class children had the benefit of exposure to a more enriched environment than did less advantaged children. The implication of this interpretation was that disadvantaged children should have their lives enriched by being exposed to a larger, more varied environment. This concept was consistent with studies of the apparently irreversible deleterious effects of rearing certain species of lower animals in "impoverished environments" (Wallace, 1974).

This explanation was sharply challenged by those who insisted that many of the disadvantaged minorities have a full, rich, multifaceted culture—they are not culturally deprived. The culturally-deprived explanation was then replaced by that of "cultural disadvantage." According to this conception, the minority ethnic, the inner-city ghetto child, and the isolated rural groups had cultures or subcultures which were sufficiently deviant from that of the dominant culture to place them at a disadvantage.

The cultural-disadvantage explanation was countered by those who claimed that the perceived "disadvantage" was simply a reflection of the biased ethnocentricism of the dominant culture. It was pointed out that these "disadvantaged" ethnic group and ghetto children readily acquired coping mechanisms necessary for their survival and adequate functioning in their own social milieu. Within the context of their lives, they were advantaged.

To counter critics of the concepts of cultural deprivation and cultural disadvantage, the more specific concept of "educational disadvantage" was proposed: that what minority children learned in their homes, communities, and subcultures handicapped them in the academic arena as compared with children reared within the framework of the dominant culture. One rejoinder to this claim is that blame for the disadvantage belongs with the dominant culture: that, for a variety of reasons, minority children have been *deprived* of appropriate education by the dominant majority. Lower-social-class and disadvantaged ethnic children have been both unintentionally and willfully *excluded* from the system of formal education and from the major rewards of the larger society. The implication of this interpretation is that society, rather than the disadvantaged, should be changed. (This is the same claim that has been advanced earlier concerning the education of the more conventional categories of the handicapped. Many people perceive the current educational and vocational disadvantage of the blind, the deaf, and the orthopedically handicapped as a measure of the extent to which society has been unable or unwilling to devise and make available to these groups of citizens adequate alternative means of learning and making a living.) Such critics insist that it is the obligation of the larger social group to change rather than to compel the currently disadvantaged to change. The proposed change is in the direction of a more complete and conscious "cultural pluralism": the assumption that ethnic and subcultural groups have the right to preserve and live within the context of their own cultural heritage, with full acceptance by all other groups, and with equal opportunities to contribute to and benefit from American political, social, and economic life. Ideally this would provide a condition of cultural parity among ethnic and cultural groups within a single society.

SOME SOCIAL AND EDUCATIONAL IMPLICATIONS OF CULTURAL PLURALISM

Some of the consequences of a commitment to the concept of cultural pluralism are indicated by the following quotations: "To make the schools a vehicle for cultural pluralism, the institutional values of male superiority, white European superiority, and the superiority of people with money must be abandoned" (Sizemore, 1974). "Appropriate education in a pluralistic society would begin with the development of programs that use the cultural context of the populations served by the schools to determine the values, goals, and content of education" (Epps, 1974). These statements advocate a kind of ideal democratic cultural pluralism, a system that posits the right of each ethnic group and each individual to maintain his ethnic or communal identity and cultural values. The option of either maintaining one's ethnic identity or entering and becoming a part of the dominant culture should be available for both groups and individuals. As they mature, individuals should be allowed to choose freely whether to remain within the bounds of the communality of their origins or to change and move into the dominant society. In the ideal pluralistic situation, differing life styles, languages, values, and ways of earning a living should not only be mutually accepted and appreciated, but should lead to equal personal and social rewards and satisfactions. To be more specific: (1) Standard English and deviant English dialects, all standard "foreign" languages and their deviant forms, and all combinations of these should be equally acceptable and useful. (2) The various human relations styles, such as the extended or limited family, the degree of democratic procedures versus authoritarianism, the nurturing of togetherness versus independence in the family, and permissive versus restrictive parent–child relationships, should all have equivalent personal and social outcomes. (3) The various incentive-motivation styles—competition versus cooperation, internal versus external locus of control, immediate versus delayed gratification of needs, future versus present time orientation—should all be equally acceptable and rewarding. (4) All patterns of cognitive organization—preferred modes of perceiving, thinking, and problem-solving—should be equally effective educationally, socially, and economically. B. A. Sizemore (1974) apparently envisions something like this when he insists that groups disadvantaged in terms of the dominant value system must change the social system which disadvantages them: "Minority groups can no longer allow majority groups to define their problems, create their values and devise their norms. . . . Each group should have a position of parity and power in decision making." It is hard to imagine the society in which these ideals would attain.

The closest approximation to such a condition would probably be a mosaic of separate ethnic, religious, and social class groups, each with its life style, values, and patterns of rewards. Each culture consists, in part, of the standards which are applied in its evaluative and rewarding processes. If each group is to maintain its value systems, it must maintain its self-contained society. It seems that the preservation of certain minority cultural components will perpetuate educational and social inequalities in free competition with other cultures. Such a separatism has been advocated by a few black leaders and has been attained to a degree by a few religious communes. However, the concept of cultural pluralism advocated most often envisions assimilation, pluralism, and separatism in varying amounts. These attitudes are reflected in the following statements: "A central issue in cultural pluralism concerns the right of the minority ethnic group to preserve its cultural heritage without at the same time interfering with the carrying out of standard responsibilities to general American civic life" (Castaneda, 1974). "Public policy should manifest a commitment to cultural pluralism, to the appreciation of enriching values to be found in the ways of life of diverse ethnic and racial backgrounds. Public policy should support the right of the individual to be different, and encourage not mere tolerance but a positive valuing of difference. [However] . . . these arguments should not be construed as advocating the abandonment of common and shared cultural standards and expectations. We argue for difference, not for cultural division and fragmentation. Nor should the argument be construed as discouraging entry into the dominant culture by members of minority groups" (Hobbs, 1975).

This ambivalence—retaining the unique characteristics of the minority ethnic culture while fulfilling one's responsibilities and obligations and reaping the benefits of participation in the majority culture—is stated or implied by many modern social critics. However, when there are genuine incompatibilities between the two cultures, one must be sacrificed to the other. Growing up and becoming socialized in a particular cultural context often involves the acquisition of some restrictive attitudes, values, and practices antithetical to those required for effective participation in certain other cultures. For example, most of the various human-relations styles paired above are antithetical to each other. Likewise, the paired incentive-motivation styles are equally incompatible. It seems likely that these incompatibilities are the basis for many of the disadvantages experienced by various ethnic and social-class groups in America today.

Reducing the inequities between social classes and ethnic groups will require not only increasing opportunities—opening previously closed doors—but also changing the attitudes, beliefs, expectations, and value systems of the advantaged majority, the disadvantaged minorities, or both. Historically this change has been required predominantly from the minorities. In practice, most societies have one dominant culture which largely provides the norms and evaluative processes in terms of which its rewards and punishments are bestowed.

The only alternative seems to be one suggested by Sizemore (1974) and others. This is the notion that the current values of wealth, productivity, social power, and economic power should be abandoned and be replaced by the ideals of maximum individual self-fulfillment and self-realization. Regardless of an individual's usefulness to society, he should be respected, valued, and rewarded according to the extent that he has developed and expanded his human potential.

THE COGNITIVE AND LINGUISTIC ACCOMPANIMENTS OF CULTURAL DIFFERENCE

The changing conceptions of the cognitive and linguistic characteristics of the culturally deviant child have paralleled the conception of the nature of cultural disadvantage itself. As we said earlier, the lower-class and ethnically disadvantaged child was originally perceived as having impoverished perceptual and conceptual systems. Linguistic limitations were considered to reflect the child's cognitive limitations; his limited language was thought to reflect and impose limitations on the use of cognitive skills. This was a "deficit" interpretation of cognitive and language handicaps which supposedly reflected an impoverished experiential background. We have explained that this interpretation was challenged by those who insisted that most disadvantaged children do not suffer from an impoverished or culturally deprived environment. Linguists also insisted that within their native cultures or subcultures, "disadvantaged" children's language was fluent and highly complex. Not only were the supposedly handicapped children's language skills well developed, but the content of their language demonstrated a rich cognitive structure capable of dealing with abstract and logically complex hypothetical questions. Linguists insisted that there is no such thing as a good lan guage or a bad language, a superior language or an inferior language: Each language is appropriate for its time and circumstance. The languages of ghetto blacks, poor whites, and Spanish-Americans are systematic, regular in their rules of construction, and constitute as good a basis for thinking and conceptualization as any other form of language. The only distinguishing characteristic of the language of these disadvantaged minorities is that it is *different from Standard English*—the dialect of the schools. This, in essence, is the *difference* interpretation of the language "handicap" of the culturally different child. The contrast between the conventional "deficit" and the "difference" interpretations of the nature of the deviant child's linguistic handicap is often stated as follows: If the deficiency is in the child we must change the child, but if the child is only different and not deficient then we must change the culture or at least our educational procedures.[1]

The "difference" interpretation of the nature of the disadvantaged child's linguistic problem holds that the deficit is in the ears of the hearer rather than in the language of the speaker. The problem is really the ethnocentricism of the majority who perceive their own speech as the best and all others as defective. Extreme critics insist that our monocultural and monolingual society and schools are responsible for assigning whole generations of minority children to lives of poverty and social disadvantage (Kobrick, 1972). However, more moderate writers, while accepting the validity of the "difference" interpretation of both cultural and linguistic disadvantage, and recognizing that firmly ingrained values, attitudes, and social practices are involved, believe that this disadvantage is likely to persist for a long time. Consequently, the immediate problem is how to minimize the disadvantage that accompanies cultural and linguistic differences in the current generation.

Language as a vital component of culture is highly value-laden. Differ-

---

[1] For further discussion, see Williams (1971); Cazden, John, and Hymes (1972); Gonzalez (1974); Bryen (1974); and Hall and Turner (1974).

ing cultural values attach to sets of alternative terms *within conventional English*. Most English words of Greek or Latin origin have connotations of superiority as compared with their Anglo-Saxon equivalents. This difference dates from 1066, when Duke William of Normandy—later William the Conqueror—conquered England and superimposed an alien French and Latin language upon the land. William and his victorious barons, who spoke French, came to dominate the upper classes, while the serfs clung to their Anglo-Saxon dialect. Philosophical and scientific vocabularies also derived from Greek and Latin, so the highly educated learned these languages and the dominant aristocrats spoke French—a Latin language. There developed two linguistic codes relating to many functions, the more patrician one of Greek and Latin origin, and the more plebian one its Anglo-Saxon equivalent. Many components of the latter are still perceived, in English-speaking countries, as uncouth or obscene. Similar values attach to many nonstandard English dialects and accents.

A large number of observational and experimental research studies indicate that, in American society, some forms of language are blocks to academic and economic success and high social status. For example, two such studies found that within various ethnic groups (blacks, whites, and Mexican-Americans), the speech of middle-class American children was favored over that of lower-class children by both middle- and lower-class listeners. The same listeners showed higher evaluations of speakers of Standard than of Spanish-accented English. Although listeners rated the Spanish-accented speakers higher in their home contexts than in the school context, Standard English speakers were regularly evaluated higher in both contexts (Ryan & Carranza, 1975; D'Anglejan & Tucker, 1973). Another study (Hurt & Weaver, 1972) showed that when unseen speakers used either Standard English on the one hand, or black dialect, French-accented English, or Jewish dialect on the other, listeners rated the speakers of Standard English as better looking, taller, more sociable, and more intelligent than the speakers of any of the others. Listeners who scored high on a scale of ethnocentricism rated a speaker of a black dialect lower than did less ethnocentric listeners. However, listeners, whether ethnocentric or not, tend to use dialect as an important attribute in classifying a speaker. A related study (Williams & Shamo, 1972) found that persons playing the role of personnel interviewers were consistent in assigning speakers to occupations they considered appropriate to the social levels indicated by certain characteristics of their speech. From a relatively short list of speech characteristics (incidence of silent pauses, use of complete clauses relative to use of sentence fragments, and length of sentences) it was possible to predict accurately when adult listeners would consider another unseen adult or child to be "culturally disadvantagcd." In all cases the use of nonstandard English was related to ratings of presumed cultural disadvantage. In another study, untrained judges were able to assign correct social status to speakers solely on the basis of a very short sample of their speech (Callary, 1974).

Because accented and other forms of nonstandard English evoke prejudicial and stereotypical attitudes and expectancies in listeners and thereby reduce one's chances for educational and occupational success, schools are striving to make Standard English available to the linguistically deviant student.

BILINGUAL EDUCATION

The question of how to deal in school with the language of minority groups—particularly of blacks, Mexican-Americans, Puerto Ricans, American Indians, and poor whites—has been of concern to educators since the early 1960s. Although there is still considerable difference of opinion concerning the many theoretical and practical issues involved, some consensus on the following points seems to be emerging.

First, it is important that teachers understand the nature of the conflict that arises when children's language and culture are rejected either implicitly or explicitly by their teachers and by the school. Such acts are viewed by the children as a rejection of themselves, their families, and their way of life. Rejection has considerable negative impact on the child's motivation and attitudes. To learn well in school, children must feel genuinely respected and valued for what and who they, their families, their language, and their culture are.

Second, to maintain the children's self-respect and expectations of success, children's first experiences in school must be positive rather than negative. This means that children must begin their schooling in the language they know best. When English is the sole medium of instruction, the five million children who speak a language other than English in their homes and neighborhoods are asked to assume a double burden. In addition to acquiring academic skills, disadvantaged children whose preferred language is not English must learn to understand and make themselves understood in a language which they know little or not at all. For many such children the situation soon becomes hopeless. They are immediately retarded in their schoolwork, the retardation increases as they grow older, and they soon become either psychological or physical drop-outs.

Third, the only feasible program for children whose preferred language is other than English is a bilingual program. Bilingual programs teach children to read in their own language, and then to speak, read, and write English, in that order.

Fourth, it is claimed that learning to read in his own language enhances rather than retards the child's ability to learn to read English. Children are more confident in their ability to learn to read in a language they already know. Having mastered the mechanics of reading in their preferred language, they can then apply their skill to learning to read another language—English.

A review by P. L. Engle (1975), for the Ford Foundation, surveyed the extensive literature from other countries (the Philippines, South Africa, Uganda, Mexico, Canada, Russia, Ireland, Peru) and concluded that although the third and fourth propositions above have been accepted as axiomatic, they are still open to debate. They are accepted because of their apparent reasonableness, not because they have substantial research support.

Federal support for bilingual education was incorporated into Title VII of the Elementary and Secondary Education Act of 1965 by an amendment in 1967 (Public Law 90–247). This act appropriated funds for programs designed to deal with the problems of the bilingual child in pre-school through grade twelve, the education of his parents, the development of curricular materials and guides, and appropriate teaching techniques. Since that time, many states have passed laws permitting local school districts to provide bilingual programs, while other states require school districts to provide such programs for children whose native language is other than English (Kobrick, 1972; Kolm, 1974).

The language problems of disadvantaged children whose families and peers speak Spanish, Italian, Chinese, or Japanese are much more clear-cut than are those of lower-class black and white children who come to school speaking nonstandard English. The language-deficit versus language-difference explanation of the nature of the disadvantaged child's handicap, mentioned earlier, focused on the latter children. The initial question involved is whether the dialect of the ghetto black or white child is sufficiently different from Standard English to impair oral and written communication in school. If so, the bilingual approach is appropriate for these children, just as it is for the Mexican-American or Japanese-American child, and Standard English should be taught as a second language. On the other hand, if the differences between Standard English and the dialects of the lower-class whites and blacks are only superficial and are analagous to the Anglo-Saxon–Latin difference mentioned earlier, the bilingual—English-as-a-second-language—approach is inappropriate.

While some people claim that the nonstandard English black dialect is essentially a slightly deviant Southern speech pattern, and others maintain that it is essentially an autonomous language with specific African origins, the consensus seems to be that the dialects of lower-class blacks and whites are similar and that the differences are surface phonological ones (differences in pronunciation) rather than matters of basic grammatical structure. V. C. Hall and R. R. Turner (1974), after an extensive survey of the studies available up to that time, found no evidence that the dialects spoken by lower-class black and white children cause any problems in their *comprehension* of standard English. It has long been recognized that comprehension of any language always precedes and exceeds production. This means that children can learn to understand a language they hear without using it themselves, particularly when a more favored alternative is available. Evidence indicates that lower-class children's understanding of Standard English is sufficient for them to understand it as well as the dialect which they speak. Speakers of nonstandard English readily translate Standard English into their dialect for their own use. This automatic translation occurs so uniformly that Hall and Turner contend that it serves no useful purpose to teach English as a second language to speakers of nonstandard English, if the goal is to improve their *comprehension* of standard English.

Many who accept Hall and Turner's claim that the average lower-class black's comprehension of Standard English is not deficient believe that the dominant culture's nonacceptance of the deviant speech and culture of such a child has contributed to his poor academic performance. Although there have been some instances of resistance in both black and white communities, a growing number of educators and linguists insist that teachers should develop a more tolerant attitude toward nonstandard English. They should also become knowledgeable concerning the specifics of nonstandard English and should let children, particularly those beginning school, use their dialects in the classroom (Somervill, 1975).

However, there is still considerable difference of opinion concerning the role of nonstandard English in formal reading instruction. It is pointed out that many reading "errors" are really dialect differences; the child simply reads in terms of his own language patterns. There is a mismatch between his spoken nonstandard English and the written language of the texts. M. A. Somervill (1975) lists several alternatives for dealing with the inconsistency between the written language of Standard English and the nonstandard oral English of deviant groups: (*a*) teaching oral Standard English before and simultaneously with formal reading instruction; (*b*) allowing or encouraging a dialect rendition of regular text material; (*c*) neutralizing the texts by deleting material that is not the same in dialect and Standard English; (*d*) using beginning readers written in nonstandard English; and (e) having the children dictate stories and then using, for reading, the exact content and language style of the children. It should be noted that those who advocate (d) and (e) suggest using the dialect material *only as an introductory measure,* to be followed by a transition to the use of Standard English material. It is suggested that the deviations from Standard English be made in grammar and in word order but not in spelling, since in Standard English many words are not spelled phonetically.

Because nonstandard-English-speaking children will typically understand the Standard English of their regular textbooks when they begin to read, they will usually translate the text into their own dialect. For example, instead of reading, "Here is a boy," the black child says, "Her go a boy." When the book reads," I am playing," the child says, "I playin' ." Although these translations are grammatically and technically incorrect, the child's comprehension is complete. When children are able to translate the text into their own language, they are reading— decoding printed symbols into oral language that is meaningful. They grasp the important principle that written words are symbols for oral words.

It is sometimes considered desirable to teach the child Standard English later on. Standard English can be taught as an additional dialect rather than as a replacement for the language of the home and community. It can be taught as "another way" which is used in school and in other places, rather than as "the right way." In the upper elementary grades and high school, students can be told that the ability to speak Standard English will help them to realize their full potential in many social and vocational situations in the larger society, in much the same way that knowing a second language such as Spanish may open up other types of vocational outlets (Seymour, 1973).

According to Somervill (1975), most investigations in the area have been demonstration projects; very little research has been conducted, and only a few of the alternatives suggested above have been investigated. Currently no firm recommendations can be made concerning which of the alternatives is most effective.

The question of the nature and causes of the basic academic-achievement differences between children of parents with low incomes, low-level skills, little education, and belonging to certain ethnic groups, and their more advantaged classmates, are still matters of debate. According to the language- and cultural-difference explanation, lower-class children and members of educationally and vocationally disadvantaged ethnic groups are not deficient in their basic intellectual or language skills, nor are they unmotivated. They merely have intellectual repertoires, linguistic dialects, and dominant motive systems which are sufficiently different from those expected and rewarded in the dominant culture to cause them to be disadvantaged in terms of the norms of that society. However, J. McV. Hunt and his co-workers have carried out a series of studies whose results question this claim (Kirk & Hunt, 1975; Kirk, Hunt, & Lieberman, 1975; Hunt, Kirk, & Volkmar, 1975; Hunt, Kirk, & Lieberman, 1975; Kirk, Hunt, & Volkmar, 1975). Limitations of space preclude a detailed description of their studies. However, the results consistently showed that the lower-social-class Head Start children showed deficits in the semantic mastery of all the abstract concepts of color, position, shape, and numbers. This is essentially a deficiency in the child's ability to translate perceptual experiences into verbal symbols. Semantic mastery requires the development of central (ideational) processes which represent objects, relationships, and perceptual and conceptual abstractions.

These researchers consider their findings inconsistent with the contention of many psycholinguists that lower-class children, particularly black children, have no deficits in their basic cognitive-linguistic abilities and fail in school because they must cope with the unfamiliar dialect of Standard English at the same time they are learning to read and to master other school tasks. Hunt and his co-workers grant that social class and race differences in dialect do exist, but insist that these do not constitute the principle handicaps of these children. Lower-class children, both black and white, show substantial deficiencies in their semantic mastery of elementary abstractions which are basic to school learning. Hunt et al. contend that these cognitive and linguistic abilities are learned, and that the deficits of the disadvantaged children result from the experiences, or lack of them, provided in their homes and communities during their preschool years. Social-class differences in educationally relevant cognitive skills regularly appear around the third year of life (Seltzer, 1973).

It is noteworthy that these studies found no significant differences between lower-class white and black children. While the evidence is not entirely consistent, the bulk of it indicates that most, if not all, educationally relevant racial and ethnic-group differences can be reduced to social class-related and economic status–related factors (Peisach et al., 1975). There are few if any uniquely ethnic or racial components of social advantage. For example, the cognitive, linguistic, and educational characteristics of black and white disadvantaged children are practically identical with those of more advantaged children a few years younger (Jensen, 1974; Peisach et al., 1975). In other words, the causes of most educationally-relevant differences between racial, ethnic, and different social-class groups are essentially the same as the causes of the differences between individuals within each group.

Longitudinal studies of the use of nonstandard English found that children, both black and white, show a significant increase in Standard English use and a corresponding decrease in nonstandard English use as they pass through the elementary grades. For example, one study of black and white children attending the same integrated St. Louis County school system found that (1) children of both races used more Standard than nonstandard English; (2) black and white males used more nonstandard English than did their female classmates; and (3) children of both races increased their use of Standard English as they advanced in grade (Marwit & Marwit, 1976).

It seems that although dialect and color differences may result in stereotyping and prejudicial attitudes which are restrictive, the disadvantaged child also displays a broad array of semantic and cognitive characteristics which hamper educational achievement. These restrictive educational characteristics develop as the result of a variety of limiting environmental conditions, as suggested by H. M. Levin (1974), S. R. Tulkin (1968), and K. T. Alvy (1973).

There is some evidence that language serves different functions for the lower-class than for the typical middle- or upper-class person. For the lower-class individual, language serves to control others and to express feelings more than to convey information, and the force of the language derives from the power and status of the speaker rather than from the information it imparts. Behavior is regulated not by the probable consequences of the act itself, but according to the relationship of the speaker and the listener. The child obeys not because of the instructional content of what he is told, but because the speaker is his father, mother, teacher, police officer, or someone else with power or authority. What is said is less important than who says it. When the child responds to a demand by saying, "Who says I have to?" he is making an explicit reference to this. When the child's "Why?" is answered either implicitly or explicitly by, "Because I say so," or "Because I am your mother," the emphasis is on a status or power relationship rather than on the rationality of the request. The following conversational exchange illustrates several of these characteristics.

Son:	"Can I go to town tonight?"
Father:	"No, you certainly cannot!"
Son:	"Why not?"
Father:	"You are always going to town."
Son:	"Well, why shouldn't I?"
Mother:	"Didn't you hear your father?"
Son:	"Yes, but there is no reason why I shouldn't go."
Father:	"I said you are not going and that's reason enough. Now shut up!"

Such a verbal exchange is characterized by the total lack of information exchanged, the emphasis on authority, and the use of language to control behavior rather than to instruct.

Alvy (1973) terms social relationships which are regulated predominantly by status considerations "role-to-role relationships." The typical lower-class child's family relationships are more role-to-role than person-to-person. Alvy shows that the teaching styles of typical lower-class mothers result in their children's completing assigned tasks less successfully and being less able to explain what they did while working on the assigned tasks. Lower-class as compared with middle-class mothers rely on a higher proportion of status (role-to-role) appeals, their language output is less extensive, and they use less general and less abstract verbal categories.

There are other social class differences which may partially account for the language differences of lower- and higher-social-class children. Lower-class parents spend less time talking with their infants and young children than do middle-class parents. Poor families live in more crowded quarters where all family members are within each other's view, and communication can be more nonverbal (pointing, gesturing, and grimacing); this may lessen the need for children to communicate precisely in words. Democratic forms of discipline in which the consequences of alternative courses of action and their relative desirability are discussed are also more characteristic of upper- than lower-class families (Kirk & Hunt, 1975). As the result of social-class differences in living and child-rearing practices, lower-class children have trouble in school because they attend to educationally irrelevant things. Children develop hierarchies of relative importance in terms of which they attend to and respond to various dimensions and characteristics of sensory experience. Language has several dimensions, such as intensity, tonal quality, gestural component, and semantic contents. Disadvantaged children use the semantic component (word meaning) less than do their more advantaged counterparts, and nonsemantic but less educationally-oriented channels with less precise and explicit meanings more. (He hears me only when I get angry and scream.)

MENTAL TESTS AND THE CULTURALLY DIFFERENT CHILD

Over the past decade, people involved in the assessment of children from deviant cultures for possible placement in special education programs have become concerned about the possible "unfairness" of conventional tests. Tests and test scores in themselves are, of course, neither fair nor unfair. Tests have reliability and validity and are appropriate or inappropriate for particular purposes. It is only the treatment of individuals pursuant to the obtaining of test scores that can be appropriately labeled fair or unfair. Discussions concerning the use and misuse of psychological tests usually focus on intelligence tests. It is unfortunate that they were ever called intelligence tests. They are really scholastic aptitude tests. If we conceive of intelligence as the effective dealing with one's environment, scholastic aptitude tests are devised to indicate an individual's level of competence in dealing with the academic environment, the subworld of formal education. Intelligence is not an entity but an attribute of an individual, like beauty or speed. People function more or less adequately, that is, intelligently, in terms of the demands and expectancies of the culture and situations in which they live.

Starting over a quarter-century ago, and continuing to the present, there have been periodic attempts to develop "culture free," "culture fair," or "culture specific" tests.

Culture free, culture fair, and culture specific tests

The makers of *culture free* tests try to devise test items free of cultural content and to eliminate those that are culturally loaded. *Culture fair* tests are those which contain items which are common, and preferably equally common to all cultures. While these test concepts seem feasible, in practice their use has been disappointing. Attempts to develop culture free tests have convinced most test makers that there is no such thing. There is no way to measure scholastic aptitudes such as memory, learning, perceiving, conceiving, and problem-solving apart from content, and content is always culturally related. In this sense, all tests are, to a degree, content or culture specific. Attempts to develop culture fair tests have been no more successful. It was found that in reducing the specifically culturally related content of tests, one also decreases their usefulness in specific social contexts. It was surprising and disappointing to many to discover that disadvantaged children score as low on the supposedly culture free and culture fair tests as they do on the conventional, culturally loaded ones (Grossman, 1972; Jensen, 1974; Barnes, 1973; Arvey, 1972; Williams, 1974).

The most recent proposal is the development of *culture specific* tests (Barnes, 1973; Mercer, 1973; Williams, 1974). These tests would be written from the contexts of particular minority cultures and subcultures and validated in terms of their accuracy in predicting educational, vocational, and social competence within those specific cultures and subcultures. Such tests, of course, will not predict success within the mainstream of society as well as do conventional tests based on mainstream culture (Hobbs, 1975). The argument for culture specific tests is based on the contention that since Anglo-American culture is not necessarily superior to others, modern America should develop alternative "mainstreams" and individuals should have the option of selecting the one within which they will live. The differing life styles, languages, and values would be equally acceptable, and those participating in minority cultures and subcultures would not be considered deprived or disadvantaged (Hobbs, 1975). However, until such an ideal condition exists, individuals will continue to be rewarded largely according to the values of the dominant culture; test scores, to be meaningful, must be based on and reflect the requirements of that society.

It is clearly possible to decrease the specific cultural content in the development and validation of a given test, but in doing so we diminish its usefulness in the social context where it is designed to be used. No single set of aptitudes is the prerequisite for survival and adaptability in all environments. Every society requires individuals capable of performing the necessary social and economic functions of that society, and inevitably will favor and reward aptitudes, behavior, and values contributing to those capabilities.

The intelligent and highly valued person in a hunting society is the person with keen vision and hearing, great strength and endurance, and good motor coordination so that he can detect, track down, and either capture or kill the animals of prey. These are the aptitudes upon which his survival depends. Successful living on the terms dictated by current industrialized society increasingly requires a background of success in school. Scholastic aptitude tests are designed to tap the scholastically relevant characteristics of the individual for use in educational placement and guidance.

In the school, welfare, or court situations where questions of intellectual competence arise, we do not start with mental test scores. We start with inadequacies in adaptive behavior. These inadequacies most often take the form of marked retardation in the development of sensori-motor, language, and self-help skill in the preschool period, failures in school learning during the school age period, and gross inadequacies in the broad social and economic competence realm in adulthood. We start with the observation that some individuals have acquired markedly fewer socially useful skills or have learned them significantly less well than their peers. Systematic sampling of the individual's perceptual, learning, memory, and reasoning processes and the products of past learning (his repertoire of information and linguistic skills) by means of standardized tests helps determine whether these demonstrated failures are due to deficiencies in the cognitive-learning realm.

In the senior author's experience screening children referred by teachers as probably mentally retarded, 20 percent of the children so referred score within normal ranges on conventional mental tests. The educational inadequacies of such children are the result of something other than lack of scholastic aptitude. Scoring within normal ranges on such tests means that: (1) the perceptual, memory, judgmental, and reasoning aptitudes, (2) the fund of information acquired as the result of experiences common to children of comparable age and circumstances, and (3) the repertoire of specifically taught skills and information which are a necessary prerequisite to additional school learning are on too high a level for the individual's difficulties to be due to lack of intellectual competence. Today, children scoring within normal ranges on scholastic aptitude tests but who are markedly retarded in school achievement may be classified as "educationally handicapped" or as having "learning disabilities" and may be provided help, as we indicated in earlier chapters. When failures in adaptive behavior are accompanied by evidences of gross cognitive-intellectual inadequacies, the child may be identified as mentally retarded and become eligible for special assistance in a program more appropriate to his competencies and level of functioning.

The problem of the relative usefulness of culturally loaded, culture free, culture fair, and culture specific tests usually becomes involved with the question of the *causes* of individual and group differences in test scores. The practical usefulness of test scores in determining children's present status for educational purposes has nothing to do with how they happen to obtain those scores except for pure "chance" factors. Tests can be useful in indicating the individual's *current repertoire* of educationally relevant linguistic, cognitive, and motor skills as well as his fund of information and meanings as a starting point for either remediation or further educational development. Except for social and/or biological engineering programs designed to reduce the deficits or improve the functional levels of future generations, the question of the etiology of the deficits is largely irrelevant. Tests should be validated and used in terms of their relevance for their treatment-remediation implications rather than the *causes* of test performances. Very often the causes of a low test score and school failure are the same—organic or social or both—but the determination of the causes is not to be found either in the test or in the lack of achievement.

Devising tests tailored to particular minority ethnic groups or to various disadvantaged subcultures will, of course, show differences in favor of the members of the various minorities. Although proposals to develop such tests have recently been presented anew, the senior author is familiar with an "intelligence test" based on the culture of southwestern American Indians, developed in the late 1920s or early 1930s. However, we have been unable to locate a reference to it in the literature. This test, when administered to whites and American Indians, produced the anticipated differences in favor of the Indian children. More recently R. I. Williams (1973) has developed a Black Intelligence Test of Cultural Homogeneity, a hundred-item multiple-choice vocabulary test which was standardized on separate black and white groups, retaining only those words which were easy for blacks and difficult for whites. Test results consequently show a consistent superiority of urban blacks over whites. The Dove Counter-Balance General Intelligence Test is based on general information drawn from a mixture of Mexican-American, black-American, and ghetto white cultures. Scores on this test reflect familiarity with these cultures. It is hard to tell to what extent the authors of these tests are seriously trying to develop genuinely useful tests for educational use within these specific cultures, and to what extent they simply wish to demonstrate that tests can be devised which show differences in favor of the supposedly disadvantaged groups.

If the authors of such tests were serious they would use the methods of industrial psychologists who set out to devise a test for selecting employees for a particular job. They start with a job analysis to determine the specific tasks the job requires, then develop a list of specific personal skills and aptitudes required for successful job performance. They next select or devise a test or a scale of tests to determine the extent to which a given person possesses these characteristics. Finally they validate the proposed tests or test items in terms of how well they discriminate between good and poor workers currently employed. The most discriminating items are retained and administered to new employees, and revalidated to determine how well they discriminate among these individuals in terms of their subsequent job performance. The test items which still stand up in the cross-validation are retained and used for selection purposes. Periodic revalidation of such tests is necessary whenever jobs or types of job applicants change.

In a relatively unsophisticated way, this was Alfred Binet's method in developing his first scholastic aptitude test for the purpose of identifying children who were high-risk students and likely to become educational casualties. Such children were to be placed in separate classes and taught by specially trained teachers using methods more applicable to learning problems. Binet believed that the early identification and appropriate treatment of these children would prevent them from becoming so discouraged by their repeated failures that they cease trying and function below their potential. These tests were designed to help teachers adapt instruction to the individual child's level of mental development. Then, as now, teachers recognized that effective learning requires a mixture of old and new experiences. Children are challenged by new experiences and tasks which are within their comprehension; they reject that which completely eludes their grasp, and are bored by repetitions of the completely understood. Tests can assist in determining children's current level of skills and their repertoire of information so that a proper mixture of novelty and familiarity can be maintained. The current shift from norm-referenced tests (comparisons with others) to criterion-referenced tests (relative achievement of educational objectives) is in keeping with this emphasis (Goodstein, 1976).

SUMMARY

Individuals may function inadequately either because they lack the potential for learning or because of inadequate or inappropriate experiential backgrounds. The latter are the culturally different, often called disadvantaged. Cultural disadvantage is always relative to the demands and expectancies of the dominant culture of the society in which the person either elects or is required to live.

The culturally deviant who find themselves disadvantaged in contemporary American culture consist predominantly of certain minority groups with different national origins (American Indians, blacks, Puerto Ricans, Mexican-Americans); people inhabiting culturally impoverished rural areas; and most of the big, heterogeneous group of poverty-stricken slum dwellers. While most of the culturally disadvantaged are poor, not all of the poor are culturally disadvantaged.

The lower and lowest classes in America constitute the largest subgroups of the disadvantaged. Many of the ethnically different share the handicaps associated with low social class. Some of the roots of, or concomitants of, the disadvantages experienced by these groups are:

1. The constantly increasing educational and occupational demands and expectancies of the culture.
2. The increased urbanization of the population resulting from mechanized, large-scale scientific farming, which has forced the marginal farm owners, sharecroppers, and farm laborers to migrate to the cities.
3. The people's distrust of impersonal agencies such as educational systems, public health departments, fire departments, public and private welfare agencies, and police departments designed to help them.
4. The relatively low level of formal education as well as a lack of appropriate occupational skills.
5. The emphasis on fate or bad luck or the connivance of other people as the causes of their misfortunes.
6. A more present- than future-time orientation.
7. The restriction of their perceptual and cognitive categories and systems.

8. A language system that (*a*) is more imperative than instructive, intended to control other people rather than to instruct them; and (*b*) is power- and status-oriented. The power of the language derives from the age, position, size, or strength of the speaker, rather than from the information imparted. Children learn to relate to the status of the speaker more than to the logic of the propositions or to the probable consequences of the acts.

Programs for the remediation of social and cultural disadvantage include:

1. Diminishing the restrictive influences of poverty, discrimination, and segregation.
2. Providing more and better educational and vocational training programs.
3. Establishing preschool programs which intervene early enough in the child's life and continue long enough to have a major effect on the child's perceptual, conceptual, linguistic, and motivational systems.

These programs are designed to increase the social competence of children: their effectiveness in dealing with their environment. This competence includes a reasonable degree of educational performance, the capacity for independent living, and vocational competence. The prerequisites for such effective functioning change with the times and circumstances. Consequently, there is probably no single general aptitude, the possession of which will sustain general social competence under all circumstances. In defining goals and developing indices (tests) of social competence, we are always confronted with the inevitable value- and culture-laden nature of the tests. Because of this, attempts to devise culture (value) free, culture fair (value neutral), and culture specific (deviant culture relevant) criteria of competence (tests) have been largely unsuccessful.

REFERENCES

ALVY, K. T., "The Development of Listener Adapted Communications in Gradeschool Children from Different Social-class Backgrounds," *Genetic Psychology Monographs*, 1973, *87*, 33–104.

ARVEY, R. D., "Some Comments on Culture Fair Tests," *Personnel Psychology*, 1972, *25*, 433–48.

BARNES, E. J., "IQ Testing and Minority School Children: Imperatives for Change," *Journal of Non-White Concerns in Personnel and Guidance*, 1973, *2*, 4–20.

BRYEN, D. N., "Special Education and the Linguistically Different Child," *Exceptional Children*, 1974, *40*, 589–99.

CALLARY, R. C., "Status Perception Through Syntax," *Language and Speech*, 1974, *17*, 187–92.

CASTANEDA, A., "Persistent Ideological Issues of Assimilation in America," in E. G. Epps, ed., *Cultural Pluralism* (Berkeley, Ca.: McCutchan Publishing Corp., 1974).

CAZDEN, C. B., V. P. JOHN, & D. HYMES, eds., *Functions of Language in the Classroom* (New York: Teachers College Press, 1972).

D'ANGLEJAN, A. V., & G. R. TUCKER, "Sociolinguistic Correlates of Speech Style in Quebec," in R. Shuy & R. Fashold, eds., *Language Attitudes: Current Trends and Prospects* (Washington, D.C.: Georgetown University Press, 1973).

ENGLE, P. L., "Language Medium in Early School Years for Minority Language Groups," *Review of Educational Research*, 1975, *45*, 283–325.

EPPS, E. G., "The Schools and Cultural Pluralism," in E. G. Epps, ed., *Cultural Pluralism* (Berkeley, Ca.: McCutchan Publishing Corp., 1974).

GONZALEZ, G., "Language, Culture, and Exceptional Children," *Exceptional Children*, 1974, *40*, 565–70.

GOODSTEIN, H. A., "Assessment and Programming in Mathematics for the Handicapped," *Focus on Exceptional Children*, 1976, 7 (7), 1–11.

GROSSMAN, H. J., *Manual on Terminology and Classification in Mental Retardation* (Washington, D.C.: American Association on Mental Deficiency, 1972).

HALL, V. C., & R. R. TURNER, "The Validity of the 'Different Language Explanation' for Poor Scholastic Performance of Black Students," *Review of Educational Research*, 1974, *44*, 69–82.

HOBBS, N., *The Futures of Children* (San Francisco: Jossey-Bass, 1975).

HUNT, J. McV., G. E. KIRK, & C. LIEBERMAN, "Social Class and Preschool Language Skill: IV. Semantic Mastery of Shapes," *Genetic Psychology Monographs*, 1975, *92*, 115–29.

HUNT, J. McV., G. E. KIRK, & F. VOLKMAR, "Social Class and Preschool Language Skill: III. Semantic Mastery of Position Information," *Genetic Psychology Monographs*, 1975, *91*, 317–37.

HURT, H. T., & C. H. WEAVER, "Negro Dialect and the Distortion of Information in the Communication Process," *Central States Speech Journal*, 1972, *23*, 118–25.

JENSEN, A. R., "How Biased are Culture-loaded Tests?" *Genetic Psychology Monographs*, 1974, *90*, 185–244.

KIRK, G. E., & J. McV. HUNT, "Social Class and Preschool Language Skill: I. Introduction," *Genetic Psychology Monographs*, 1975, *91*, 281–98.

KIRK, G. E., J. McV. HUNT, & C. LIEBERMAN, "Social Class and Preschool Language Skill: II. Semantic Mastery of Color Information," *Genetic Psychology Monographs*, 1975, *91*, 299–316.

KIRK, G. E., J. McV. HUNT, & F. VOLKMAR, "Social Class and Preschool Language Skill: V. Cognitive and Semantic Mastery of Number," *Genetic Psychology Monographs*, 1975, *92*, 131–53.

KOBRICK, J. W., "The Compelling Case for Bilingual Education," *Saturday Review*, April 29, 1972, 54–58.

KOLM, R., "Ethnic Studies and Equality," in A. Kopan & H. Walberg, eds., *Rethinking Educational Equality* (Berkeley, Ca.: McCutchan Publishing Corp., 1974).

LEVIN, H. M., "Equal Educational Opportunity and the Distribution of Educational Expenditures," in A. Kopan & H. Walberg, eds., *Rethinking Educational Equality* (Berkeley, Ca.: McCutchan Publishing Corp., 1974).

MARWIT, S. J., & K. L. MARWIT, "Black Children's Use of Nonstandard Grammar: Two Years Later," *Developmental Psychology*, 1976, 12, 33–38.

PEISACH, E.; M. WHITEMAN; J. S. BROOK; & M. DEUTSCH, "Interrelationships Among Children's Environmental Variables as Related to Age, Sex, Race, and Socio-economic Status," *Genetic Psychology Monographs*, 1975, 92, 3–18.

RYAN, E. B., & M. A. CARRANZA, "Evaluative Reactions of Adolescents Toward Speakers of Standard English and Mexican-American Accented English," *Journal of Personality and Social Psychology*, 1975, 31, 855–63.

SELTZER, R. E., "The Disadvantaged Child and Cognitive Development in the Early Years," *Merrill-Palmer Quarterly*, 1973, 19, 241–52.

SEYMOUR, D. Z., "Black English in the Classroom," *Today's Education*, February, 1973, 123, 63–64.

SIZEMORE, B. A., "Making the Schools a Vehicle for Cultural Pluralism," in E. G. Epps, ed., *Cultural Pluralism* (Berkeley, Ca.: McCutchan Publishing Corp., 1974.

SOMERVILL, M. A., "Dialect and Reading: A Review of Alternative Solutions," *Review of Educational Research*, 1975, 45, 247–62.

TULKIN, S. R., "Race, Class, Family, and School Achievement," *Journal of Personality and Social Psychology*, 1968, 9, 31–37.

WALLACE, P., "Complex Environments: Effects on Brain Development," *Science*, 1974, 185, 1035–37.

WILLIAMS, F., ed., *Language and Poverty: Perspectives on a Theme* (Chicago: Institute for Research on Poverty Monograph Series, 1971).

WILLIAMS, F., & G. W. SHAMO, "Regional Variations in Teacher Attitudes Toward Children: Language Control States," *Speech Journal*, 1972, 23, 73–77.

WILLIAMS, R. I., *Black Intelligence Test of Cultural Homogeneity* (St. Louis: Williams & Associates, 1973).

WILLIAMS, R. I., "Black Pride, Academic Relevance, and Individual Achievement," in R. W. Tyler & R. M. Wolf, eds., *Crucial Issues in Testing* (Berkeley, Ca.: McCutchan Publishing Corp., 1974).

3

The sensorially handicapped

Photo by J. Berndt, Stock, Boston

Chapter 12

The visually handicapped

In many respects the blind have always been a favored group, compared with the other categories of the handicapped. Historically, they have sometimes been assigned useful roles such as serving as guides in the dark and as memorizers and oral transmitters of tribal and religious lore. They were often assumed to have the power of "second sight" in compensation for their lost vision and were revered as prophets and soothsayers. While blindness has occasionally been perceived as a divine visitation, interpreted as benign, more often it was seen as punishment for sin—one's own or one's parents'—and blind people were stigmatized.

Because of the high visibility and the obvious nature of the handicap, blindness has effectively elicited the sympathy and concern of the non-handicapped. Consequently, despite their relatively small number, it is estimated that ten times more legal, social, and educational services have been provided for the blind than for any other handicapped group (Bauman, 1972). R. A. Scott has estimated that in 1960 there were over eight hundred separate organizations, agencies, and programs for the blind in the United States. The total annual expenditures of these agencies were nearly $470 million (Scott, 1969). The first special educational programs established were for the visually handicapped.

EARLY HISTORICAL CONCERNS

Several early Christian monasteries and hospitals showed some concern for the blind (Best, 1934). In the fourth century, St. Basil at Caesarea, in Cappadovia (a Roman province in Asia Minor) established a hospice for the blind. In the following century, similar facilities (refuges, asylums, or retreats) were established in Syria, Jerusalem, France, Italy, and Germany. In 1254 Louis IX created an asylum in Paris in which several hundred blind persons found refuge. This asylum was established mainly to care for the large number of blind crusaders returning to Western Europe. Many were said to have lost their sight as punishment at the hands of the Saracens (Best, 1934). This large refuge for the blind attracted considerable attention and similar facilities were subsequently established in many cities of Western Europe.

In the sixteenth century Girolinia Cardano, a physician in Pavia, Italy, conceived the idea that the blind might be taught to read through the sense of touch and attempted to provide some instruction in this way. About the same time, Peter Pontanus, a blind Fleming, and Padre Lana Terzi of Brescia, Italy, wrote books on the education of the blind. A third contemporary anonymous publication on the same subject appeared in Italy. In the eighteenth century, a book on the teaching of mathematics to the blind was published by Jacques Bernovilli in Switzerland. During this time several attempts were made to devise a means for the blind to read the printed word (Best, 1934).

Valentin Haüy of Paris is thought to have established the first school for the blind. In 1784 Haüy took a blind boy he found begging on the streets as his first student. He paid the boy to compensate for his lost alms. Haüy soon increased the number of his students to twelve. In 1791 the school was taken over by the state and continued as a public institution. Other countries soon followed the lead. Between 1891 and 1909 seven schools were started in Great Britain and early in the nineteenth century schools for the blind were started in many of the large cities of Europe.

In 1826 Dr. John D. Fisher of Boston visited the school founded by Haüy in Paris. He was sufficiently impressed to agitate for establishment of a similar school in Massachusetts. As a result, the Massachusetts legislature in 1832 incorporated the New England Asylum for the Purpose of Educating the Blind, later to be known as Perkins Institute and Massachusetts School for the Blind. This school started with six students. Gridley Howe was its first superintendent. About the same time, New York established a similar school (now the New York Institute for the Education of the Blind); Pennsylvania did likewise (now the Overbrook School for the Blind) (Lowenfeld, 1971, 1973). These schools were all private institutions, but shortly thereafter, the first state school for the blind was started in Ohio. Subsequently all of the states established residential public schools where education for the blind was provided essentially free of charge. The first special classes for the blind in American public schools were established in Chicago in 1900 (Lowenfeld, 1971). Thus, private benevolence gave way to public support, and restrictive admission and tuition were replaced by free education for all the blind.

The first private and public schools for the blind were residential, but since the turn of the century, day schools and/or classes for the blind have become an integral part of most school systems. The tendency to integrate the blind into the regular classes has accelerated, and today most blind children enrolled in the public schools are partly or completely integrated into regular classes.

SOME DEFINITIONS

There are both quantitative and functional definitions of the visually handicapped. When quantitative definitions are required for legal and administrative purposes, blindness is usually defined as "visual acuity of 20/200 or less in the better eye with proper correction, or a limitation in the fields of vision such that the widest diameter of the visual field subtends an angular distance no greater than 20 degrees" (American Foundation for the Blind, 1961). A person is said to have a visual acuity of 20/200 if he must be at a distance of twenty feet to read the standard type which a person with normal vision can read at a distance of two hundred feet. The restriction of the visual field to an angular distance of twenty degrees or less is sometimes called tunnel vision. An individual with such a condition may have normal visual acuity for the area on which he can focus, but his field of vision is so restricted that he can see only a limited area at a time. A person suffering a restriction of either visual acuity or field to this extent is typically considered legally and medically blind (Liska, 1973).

There has been little demand for medical and legal definitions of *partial blindness* or *partially sighted*. However, the quantitative standard most often accepted is "visual acuity of between 20/70 and 20/200 in the better eye after maximum correction," or comparable visual limitations of other types. Some eye specialists have proposed more complex quantitative measures of "visual efficiency" in which visual acuity plays only a part (Hoover, 1963).

Functional definitions vary according to the purposes they are intended to serve. Thus we have "travel vision," "shadow vision," "near vision," and "distance vision," as well as "educational blindness" and "occupational blindness." Because of its practical importance, *educational blindness* has been most systematically studied. The educationally blind are those people whose vision is so defective that they cannot be educated via vision. Their education must be primarily through the auditory, cutaneous, and kinesthetic senses. The educationally blind must read and write in Braille. Functional definitions of the partially sighted or partially blind—we shall use the two terms interchangeably—are less precise. The partially sighted are able to use vision as their main avenue of learning and do not require Braille. But they read only enlarged print, or require magnifying devices, or can read only limited amounts of regular print under special conditions.

Many studies have documented the lack of a close relationship between the quantitative medical and legal definitions and the more functional definitions of visual handicaps. Many legally blind children can read large or even ordinary print. Many more can distinguish large objects sufficiently well to enable them to move around and have a sense of orientation (travel vision), and most have some light perception (shadow vision). Of over seven thousand children enrolled in over six hundred classes for the partially sighted, less than one-third had vision within the limits of visual acuity commonly used in defining partial sight —between 20/70 and 20/200 in the better eye after maximum correction (Kerby, 1952). Table 12–1, based on another study (Jones, 1962), also shows the discrepancies between the quantitative and functional criteria.

Table 12–1
Reading practice as related to visual acuity

	Percentages of Children		
Visual Acuity	Reading Print	Reading Braille	Reading Both Braille and Print
20/200*	82	12	6
15/200*	67	27	6
10/200*	59	32	9

* The fractions indicate that the person must be 20, 15, or 10 feet distant from standard type to read the material which a person with normal vision can read at 200 feet. All these groups are legally blind. Data from Jones (1962).

SYMPTOMS OF VISUAL IMPAIRMENT

Since regular and complete eye examinations for all children are seldom feasible, initial identification of children for more complete examinations is usually based on behavioral symptoms or rough screening tests. The more common symptoms of visual impairment are as follows:

1. Has chronic eye irritations as indicated by watery eyes or by red-rimmed, encrusted, or swollen eyelids.
2. Experiences nausea, double vision, or visual blurring during or following reading.
3. Rubs eyes, frowns, or screws up the face when looking at distant objects.
4. Is overcautious in walking, runs infrequently and falteringly for no apparent reason.

5. Is abnormally inattentive during chalkboard, wall chart, or map work.
6. Complains of visual blurring and attempts to brush away the visual impediments.
7. Is excessively restless, irritable, or nervous following prolonged close visual work.
8. Blinks excessively, especially while reading.
9. Habitually holds the book very close, very far away, or in other unusual positions when reading.
10. Tilts the head to one side when reading.
11. Can read only for short periods at a time.
12. Shuts or covers one eye when reading.

TESTS OF VISUAL IMPAIRMENT

The National Society for the Prevention of Blindness recommends, as a minimum test for school-age children, an annual test with the Snellen chart. The Snellen test chart consists of rows of letters, or *E*s, in various positions in lines of different size print. Each row of letters of a given size has a distance designation. For example, the twenty-foot row can be read by people with normal vision at a distance of twenty feet. A person reading the twenty-foot row at this distance is said to have 20/20 vision. A person who can read nothing smaller than the seventy-foot line at the standard twenty-foot distance has 20/70 vision.

The Snellen test is the most widely used because it is simple and can be quickly administered by a nurse or a teacher. Despite its widespread use, however, the Snellen test has decided limitations. It tests central vision only. It does not detect hyperopia (farsightedness), presbyopia (impairment of vision due to diminution of the elasticity of the crystalline lens), or strabismus (a deviation of one of the eyes from its normal direction). While most authorities strongly recommend that visual screening programs include tests such as the Massachusetts Vision Test, the Telebinocular, the Sight Screener, and the Ortho-Rater, studies indicate that, when used by teachers, the Snellen chart does about as well as these much more complicated and expensive devices (Crane et al., 1952; Foote & Crane, 1954).

N. C. Barraga (1970) has developed a functionally-oriented test—the Visual Efficiency Scale—designed to assess visual discrimination of low-vision children for educational purposes. It is claimed that the test facilitates the selection of appropriate individualized training programs for these children. Preliminary results indicate that the test has acceptable internal consistency and validity for this purpose (Harley & Spollen, 1973).

CAUSES OF IMPAIRED VISION

Table 12–2 indicates various causes of visual defects among children of school age, as well as changes in etiology, over a twenty-five-year period. The category of "excessive oxygen" is of special interest because it accounts for one-third of the 1958–59 total. The condition or disease known as retrolental fibroplasia (RLF) was practically unknown before the 1940s. It was identified as a clinical entity and named by Dr. T. L. Terry, a Boston ophthalmologist, in 1942. The condition occurred only in premature infants and its incidence increased rapidly until, in 1952–53, it accounted for over half the blindness of preschool children. In 1952 it was established that the increased concentrations of oxygen to which premature infants were being subjected was the cause. Since the cause was discovered, and it was found that the concentration and duration of oxygen administration could be reduced below the critical level without increasing the mortality rate, blindness of this type has occurred only rarely. However, the impact of the several thousand blind children of this type was felt in the educational systems through the early 1970s, when they had largely completed their education.

In some respects the RLF blind children are different from children comparably blind from other causes. One study of 263 such children—all legally blind—found that a large number suffered excessive developmental retardation, multiple disabilities, and various behavior disorders including autistic symptoms and "blindisms" (various repetitive hand or body movements, such as rubbing the eyes, waving the fingers before the face, and swaying) (Chase, 1974). When the cause of RLF was discovered, it was thought that oxygen could be administered at levels which would keep the mortality rate and the incidence of hyaline membrane disease and anoxic brain damage low and still not produce blindness. Unfortunately, this has not been found to be true. Consequently there has been a recent increase in RLF blindness when it has been found necessary to keep oxygen levels high enough to prevent brain damage or death (Chase, 1974).

Table 12–2 indicates that, except for the marked increase in the 1958–59 figures due to retrolental fibroplasia, the total incidence of blindness has not changed significantly. However, the relative importance of certain etiologies has changed. Blindness due to infectious diseases has progressively declined, from 6.1 per 100,000 in 1933–34 to 1.3 in 1958–59. There has also been a progressive decline in blindness due to injuries. Unspecified prenatal causes remain the major etiological category of the blind. Heredity is undoubtedly the primary cause in many of these cases.

Table 12–2
Estimated prevalence of legal blindness of different etiologies in school children (per 100,000)

Causes	1933–1934	1943–1944	1954–1955	1958–1959
Infections	6.1	5.0	1.5	1.3
Injuries	1.6	1.5	1.0	0.8
Excessive oxygen	—	—	3.8	11.3
Tumors	0.5	0.8	1.0	0.6
Prenatal causes	10.8	12.1	11.1	16.2
Cause unreported	1.9	2.2	1.3	2.6
Totals per 100,000	21.2	21.9	19.9	34.1
Number of cases	2,702	3,749	4,429	7,757

Data from Hatfield (1963).

C. E. Kerby (1958) estimates that 14 to 15 percent of blindness results from genetic factors. Heredity as a cause is difficult to establish, but it is thought to be an important etiological agent.

As the age composition of the population changes, the incidence of blindness and the relative importance of the various causes of visual impairment change. With increased longevity, glaucoma, cataracts, and diabetic retinopathy increase in importance as causes of blindness. By the mid-1970s these three conditions accounted for one-half of all blindness (Ginsberg, 1973–74). In the late 1960s and early 1970s, the blind population was increasing at a rate nearly twice that of the general population. Between 1940 and 1970 the known blind population of the United States increased 70 percent, while the total population increased 45 percent. In the mid-1970s three out of four blind persons were over forty-five years of age (Ginsberg, 1973–74). (See table 12–3.) Except for

Table 12–3
Blindness rates and age in adults

Age Range	Rate per 100,000
45–64	200
65–74	440
75–84	900
85+	2600

Data from Ginsberg (1973–74).

retrolental fibroplasia, most of this increase is the result of the high incidence of glaucoma (2 percent of the adult population are affected) and cataracts (25 percent of the total blind). With more effective controls for diabetes an increasing number of affected persons live to advanced ages, develop diabetic retinopathy, and pass on the genetic potential to succeeding generations. Maturity-onset diabetes (onset after age forty) has a strong genetic component: 60 percent of the children of two such diabetics will develop the condition by age sixty (Lowenstein & Preger, 1976). The number of diabetics in the United States has increased from 1.2 million in 1950 to 5 million in 1975, an increase of more than 300 percent, while the population has increased less than 50 percent (Maugh, 1975). A diabetic is twenty times more likely to become blind than a nondiabetic of the same age. However, the precise course of events leading from diabetes to blindness is not known (Kupfer, 1973; Lowenstein & Preger, 1976).

INCIDENCE OF VISUAL IMPAIRMENT

The incidence of mild visual defects is very high. It is estimated that one-fourth of schoolchildren have some visual anomaly. In a survey of over 5,000 children in California, 22 percent of the elementary school children and 31 percent of the high school students were found to have visual defects (Dalton, 1943). Of course, the great majority of these defects are correctable and constitute no particular educational or vocational handicap.

There are no dependable statistics on the prevalence of blindness and partial sight as herein defined (Hurlin, 1962). The medicolegal criterion for blindness (corrected vision of 20/200 or less in the better eye) is generally considered to give an incidence of approximately 1 in 3,000 (0.03 percent) of school-age children. The number of children with visual acuity between 20/70 and 20/200 (the partially sighted) is estimated to be 1 in 500 (0.2 percent). These figures are much larger than the number of children judged to need special educational services because of visual impairment (the educationally blind or partially sighted). The United States Office of Education estimates that a total of 0.09 percent of school children need special education facilities for the visually impaired. Of these 0.09 percent, two-thirds (0.06 percent) are educationally partially sighted, and one-third (0.03 percent) are educationally blind. As of January 1973, 24,195 blind students were enrolled in educational facilities below college level (Morris, 1974). While this is a sizable group, the visually impaired probably constitute the smallest area of exceptionality. The incidence of blindness increases dramatically with age—particularly beyond early adulthood. Consequently, the total estimated prevalences greatly exceed those given above for children. In 1972, the estimated prevalence of blindness for the United States (including Puerto Rico and the Virgin Islands) was 225 per 100,000 population; that is, a total of 475,200 persons are legally blind. The rates of blindness are appreciably higher for nonwhites than for whites in America—252.7 as compared with 127.1. Geographic differences are also marked. The highest rate is 370.1 per 100,000 for Washington, D.C., and the lowest is Hawaii with 139.1 per 100,000 (Hatfield, 1973).

THE HANDICAPS OF THE BLIND

Like all disabilities, the total handicap of the blind person consists of the cumulative effects of the disability itself and its inherent limitations, the social stigma manifesting itself in cultural stereotypes of the blind, and the self-concept of the blind person.

The inherent limitations of any disability are relative to the extent to which current technology has made available to the handicapped compensatory devices and procedures. Blindness (*a*) prevents direct access to the printed word, (*b*) restricts independent mobility in unfamiliar surroundings, (*c*) limits a person's direct perception of his distant environment as well as of objects too large to be apprehended tactually, and (*d*) deprives the individual of important social cues.

The stigmas of blindness which contribute to the total handicap of blindness consist of a set of popular conceptions or misconceptions which result in social practices that are sufficiently consistent with and supportive of these misconceptions to constitute a self-fulfilling prophecy. The popular stereotypes of blindness contain contradictory components. On the one hand are the presumed traits of docility, dependency, helplessness, and despondency. This stereotype is implicit in the application of the term to the nonhandicapped as typified by expressions such as "You are as helpless as a blind man," "Are you blind?" "He is blind with rage." Blindness also has connotations of "lacking in perceptiveness or judgment," "without intelligent control," and "random." A nationwide poll indicated in 1970 that Americans fear blindness second only to cancer (David, 1970).

The stereotype of helplessness is typified by the blind person on the street corner holding a tin cup. On the other hand, we also have the less common popular conceptions of the unusual and almost miraculous aptitudes of blind people—their alleged insights which more than compensate for their lack of vision, the supposed increased acuity of their other senses, or their possession of a special extra sense or extrasensory perceptiveness. As mentioned earlier, blinded individuals have historically been especially revered as prophets and sages. Because of the dominantly negative stereotype of blindness and the stigmatizing connotations of the term, many people prefer alternative terms such as *sightlessness, visual handicap,* or *visual impairment.* Reflecting this tendency, the International Conference on Education of Blind Youth recently became the International Council for Education of the Visually Handicapped, and the American Association for Instructors of the Blind became the Association for Education of the Visually Handicapped (Bourgeault, 1974).

Since the popular stereotype of helplessness and dependency is the dominant one, the treatment of the blind individual often results in social practices which preclude his developing and exercising the skills and competences which will enable him to become independent. There is nothing uniquely inherent in the nature of blindness that requires a person to be docile, helpless, and dependent. He only becomes so through the same basic processes of learning as do the sighted who develop these same characteristics.

R. A. Scott (1969) shows how the blind beggar, complying to the popular stereotype of helplessness by superficially conforming to the popular conceptions of the sighted, persuades people to give him money. He behaves as others expect him to and, in exchange, extracts money from the normal. Blind beggars, while capitalizing on the stereotype of helplessness, are usually independent, capable, and employable. They typically travel independently using public transportation, move about freely as street crowds shift, maintain their orientation in crowds, remain composed under stress, and are self-reliant. The causes for which money is solicited by the blind beggar, such as an operation or a new guide dog, are usually fictitious. Some of the blind beg because it is lucrative, they prefer begging to other jobs that are available to them, and they enjoy more freedom than they have when they become or remain the client of official agencies (Scott, 1969). The blind person may succumb to the social pressures and expectancies engendered by the cultural stereotype by internalizing the role and becoming a helpless, dependent individual requiring and entitled to extensive aid, and/or by deliberately exploiting for his own economic gain the compassion and guilt feelings of the sighted via begging.

On the other hand, one study suggests that those blind persons who are able to accept friends and participate in the organizational activities sponsored by agencies for the blind while maintaining their individual autonomy are most likely to be employed and to be independent in social roles (Lukoff & Whiteman, 1970; Wright, 1974). Those who succumb, becoming dependent upon the agencies, on the one hand, or reject social relationships and organizational activities within the blind community and are aggressively independent in their relationships with the sighted, on the other, have low rates of employment and are more dependent in their social roles. There is evidence that the "blind system," both here and abroad, has responded to Scott's (1969) claim that it has been self-serving, has nurtured dependency upon the agencies, and has exploited the blind. Several authors insist that these organizations must become more concerned with service accountability and integrate more into the communities they serve (Brown, 1974; Westaway, 1973; Davidson, 1973).

Vision plays an important role in interpersonal communication, but the blind person is deprived of important social cues. Instead of maintaining eye contact, as the sighted normally do when conversing, the blind person may turn his better ear toward the speaker, thus turning his face away. Turning the face and/or eyes away from the speaker suggests inattentiveness and evasiveness and is disconcerting to the sighted. The blind person is also deprived of the socially communicative cues provided by the facial expressions, gestures, and movements of the other person. His failure to observe and use conventional gestures in communication may result in less complete communication or in the use of gestures which are perceived by others as either contradictory to the oral message or distracting. The blind person uses facial expressions and gestures less often and less appropriately than do the sighted and more often develops stereotyped body movements called "blindisms" which detract from the individual's communicative effectiveness.

MOBILITY OF THE BLIND

One of the most, if not the most, difficult task for the blind person is that of independent travel. However, until recently the problem has never been systematically investigated. The only aspect of the mobility of the blind that has been comprehensively researched is "obstacle sense," which is discussed in the next section. Since in moving about independently, the blind person makes use of other senses—especially audition—seldom used by the normally sighted for this purpose, the mobility of the blind is influenced markedly by additional handicaps, particularly auditory impairment. It is therefore not surprising to find a significant relationship between the auditory thresholds of blind subjects and their relative mobility. The highest correlations are found with thresholds for the higher frequencies (Riley, Luterman, & Cohen, 1964; Warren & Kocon, 1974). This relationship probably derives from the crucial role of the higher frequencies in the detection of obstacles (echo reception).

Sight provides us with cues for distance and direction such as motion, color, brightness, contrast, depth, and perspective, all of which are involved in the mobility of the sighted. The most obvious limitation of the blind is their limited capacity to perceive distant objects. Other, less obvious causes are in the areas of motivation. The young blind child cannot see objects or people, which he would then set out to reach as does the sighted child. He has to wait for contact, sound, or smell to arouse his curiosity. The blind child cannot see other children moving toward and reaching for toys and other interesting objects. He is deprived of visual models to imitate. The visual incentives which stimulate the sighted child to learn to crawl, creep, stand, walk, and run are not present to the blind. The visually impaired child is much more dependent on auditory, principally verbal, sources for his motivation to move. The many bumps and bruises he cannot avoid arouse the anxiety of those about him because of the real as well as the exaggerated danger he invites. This and the overprotection afforded him add to his inherent disability and increase his handicap. Although independent locomotion —the ability to move about freely and independently at home, in the neighborhood, and in traffic—is of primary importance to the blind, it has only recently begun to receive the attention it warrants. It is obvious that these skills, which the sighted individual learns largely incidentally and with little formal instruction, must become a matter of primary concern in the training of the blind.

Such training begins in the home, where situations must be deliberately contrived to encourage the blind child to become curious and explore his world. The blind child needs a wealth of sounds, objects within reach, and even odors which he is encouraged to find and explore. Stimulation to move about the house, rather than to sit quietly in the crib or playpen, is more essential for the blind than for the sighted child. Keeping furniture in the same places and teaching the child the safe routes around the house will minimize the number of bumps and bruises which may discourage independent exploration of his world. Permitting him to follow family members about, and encouraging him to use furniture, utensils, and tools and to smell and taste vegetables and fruit are a necessary part of the blind child's education.

Normal playground activities require some modification, but with adequate supervision the blind child can participate in most such programs. The blind child can use the sandbox, jungle gym, and most other playground equipment. He can swim, dance, wrestle, and participate in many forms of athletics.

Surveys indicate that most blind adults have relatively little ability to travel independently, are dissatisfied with their level of performance, have not been systematic or purposeful in their mode of travel, have seldom had travel training of any duration, and have no active plans for improvement (Finestone, Lukoff, & Whiteman, 1960).

The goals of programs to aid the blind are not limited to independent travel, but also involve training in dressing, eating, and personal relations. Specific travel training includes instruction in the use of the cane and experience with the seeing-eye dog, as well as more general training in motor and mental orientation in travel. Mobility has come to be recognized as vital to personal independence, independent travel, and vocational success. Consequently, many formal programs have been developed to promote and teach independent mobility to the blind (La-Duke, 1973). The first such program was the "Seeing Eye," founded by Dorothy Harrison Eustis. The use of guide dogs by the blind has received a good deal of popular interest, but its practicability has probably been exaggerated. It is estimated that the use of guide dogs is practical for only about 5 percent of the blind (Robson, 1974). The seeing-eye dog does not guide the blind person to a destination. The person must know his destination and how to get there. His is still the task of orientation. The dog, like the cane, only indicates the spaces into which the blind person can safely move.

The second organized program to teach orientation and increase the independent mobility of the blind was the armed services program developed during and following World War II. The Hines Center in the suburbs of Chicago concentrated on mobility training. One of the products of the Hines program was the introduction of the long cane, sometimes called the "Hoover cane" after Dr. Richard Hoover, a former physical education instructor, who devised it. Although the introduction of the Hoover cane initially generated considerable resistance among the blind, it is almost universally accepted today as an important aid to mobility. The initial resistance arose because the blind felt that their public and self-images suffered when the cane publicized their disability. Some also argued that the long cane clearing a path through a crowd would endanger the sighted public. These claims have been mostly forgotten, and the Hoover technique is an important part of most programs of mobility training today.

When properly used, the Hoover cane becomes almost an antenna for sensing the environment. It can provide information concerning several things the blind especially fear, such as holes in the ground and ground surfaces which suddenly change steeply upward or downward, like a flight of stairs (Fjeldsenden, 1974). The recommended technique for using the Hoover cane is as follows: The dominant hand is held near the center of the body with the index finger pointing straight down along the cane. The wrist is pivoted so that the tip of the cane describes an arc in front of the user, touching the ground lightly on each side as it describes the arc. The tip should just clear the ground so that low protruding objects may be detected. The arc must be equidistant from the center on each side to allow for proper coverage of the entire body. The cane tip is moved in a rhythmic motion across the body in step with the feet: when the left foot steps forward, the cane makes its arc to the right, and vice versa (Uslan & Manning, 1974). One study demonstrated that intensive, directed training in the long cane can save about one-half the time usually spent in learning this skill (Peel, 1974).

Many formal programs provide orientation and mobility training for the visually impaired. In 1973 there were approximately four hundred trained people involved in providing such instruction in the United States (LaDuke, 1973). These programs were reaching out to meet the multipally handicapped, the aged, and those with low vision as well as blind children (Corbett, 1974). J. Armstrong (1975) provides a good survey of current programs.

More than twenty electronic devices have been developed to aid the blind, but only a few have become commercially available. Some which were designed specifically to aid in orientation and mobility include: (a) the "Pathsounder," developed by Lindsay Russell, a unit about the size of a small camera which is suspended from the neck at chest height. It emits warning sounds when an object comes within three to six feet of the user. (b) Ultrasonic spectacles were devised by Dr. Lesley Kay. This device, which uses the principle of sonic radar employed by bats, consists of a modified spectacle frame housing ultrasonic sending and receiving units. The emitted sound is reflected from objects in its path, amplified, and conducted to the user's ears via two plastic tubes inserted in the ears. (c) A laser cane, developed by J. M. Benjamin, Jr., makes use of laser beams. This instrument projects three laser beams up, away, and down from the cane, held in front of the user. The presence of an object is signaled by means of a vibrating pin located in the cane's head or by a high-pitched tone. (d) Another mobility aid, which operates somewhat like the laser cane, is a device which projects a narrow beam of invisible infrared rays directly ahead of the user's head. An object within the detection range reflects the rays back to the glasses and is detected by a receiver. The reflected signal is amplified and passed in the form of a musical tone to the ear via a plastic tube. This device weighs less than three ounces and is mounted on ordinary eyeglass frames.[1] L. Kay (1975) analyzes a questionnaire filled out by users of his device and reports that 88 percent found it useful. These electronic aids all make use of hearing. Some other mobility aids use touch as the mediating sense.

Some experimental work has been done with tactual maps of an area which a blind person may wish to traverse. Preliminary work indicates that such maps can use variations in the elevation of symbols as effective

[1] For more complete descriptions of these devices, see Mims (1973).

coding dimensions. Plastic sheets have been found to work better than paper for such mapping. Raised figures are interpreted more readily than incised ones. Performance can be significantly improved by teaching the subject to scan a map in a systematic way. Overlays on the maps which present supplementary information in Braille have also been tried. Sometimes the Braille is placed on the underside of the map (Gill, 1974; Geldard, 1974). According to J. M. Gill, one limitation of the Braille supplement is that 60 percent of the registered blind population of England cannot read Braille. B. B. Blasch, R. L. Welsh, and T. Davidson (1973) have suggested that an "auditory map" consisting of a tape-recorded description of a particular route or geographic area, indicating landmarks relevant to orientation and independent travel, may supplement the use of a long cane or a guide dog.

Dependence on human guides is seldom satisfactory. It is often costly, and it makes the blind person's mobility contingent on the good health, dependability, and availability of a second person. If he can travel independently, the blind person is freed of his dependence on the convenience and disposition of family members and friends, or the availability and competence of hired guides (Spar, 1955). Studies show that blind persons using human guides travel much less than those who use canes or dogs. The blind who use dogs as guides actually travel more than either of the other groups (Finestone, Lukoff, & Whiteman, 1960).

Independent travel involves mental orientation as well as physical locomotion (Lowenfeld, 1971; Warren & Kocon, 1974). Mental orientation is the recognition of an area in terms of its spatial and temporal relations to onself. This recognition typically consists of a "mental map" or "schema" of the area, within which the blind person orients himself as he moves toward his destination. As he moves about, he picks up cues—noises, echoes, changes in ground level, air currents, odors—which either confirm or cast doubt on the accuracy of his mental orientation. The blind person also makes use of his "motor memory." This is his sense of direction and distance, a kind of "muscular memory." A destination is perceived as at a certain distance in terms of time or movement. The blind person perceives distances, not by counting steps, but more in terms of time and movement (Kay, 1974).

The obstacle sense of the blind

Many totally blind individuals can sense obstacles in their paths. It is this ability which has generated the belief that the blind have a supernormal sensory capacity of some sort. Theories to explain the obstacle sense have ranged from the occult, bordering on the supernatural, through a heightened responsiveness of either known or unknown sense organs, indirect response to remote sensory cues (unrecognized cues arouse fear which produces contractions of the pilomotor muscles of the skin, and the person experiences the muscular contractions as an obstacle in his path), to theories which assume a simple direct response to cues from one or more sense organs (auditory, thermal, or pressure).

A series of experiments started in the 1930s and continued over a period of twenty-five years demonstrated fairly well that the "obstacle sense" is largely a reaction to small, unrecognized auditory cues (principally echoes) which warn the individual of obstacles. There is nothing supersensory or mysterious about this responsiveness. It is something that a person with vision could accomplish equally well if he had the motivation, training, and experience. In fact, it is probable that a blind person cannot accomplish anything with his remaining senses that a seeing person could not accomplish equally well if his incentives and experiences were the same. The obstacle sense can function only when conditions are favorable. The noise of wind, rain, and other things interferes with its functioning. When a person is moving rapidly, the auditory cues often can not be perceived and reacted to quickly enough to be useful.

PERSONAL AND SOCIAL ADJUSTMENT

The earlier discussion of the relationship of exceptionality in general to personal and social adjustment applies to the visually impaired. There is no special "psychology of the blind." The blind are characterized by no special personality characteristics or types. The adjustment problems of the visually disabled, like those of the normal, range all the way from those of everyday social contacts to those of economic dependence. Congenitally blind children left to themselves do not live in a world of blackness or eternal night. They do not yearn for light or feel sorry for themselves because they cannot see. The few that do express such attitudes have acquired them from other people. The social and personal effects of impaired vision are nonspecific, most often taking the form of immaturity and insecurity (Bauman, 1964; Schindale, 1974). The phantasies of the blind concern social acceptance, personal achievement, and withdrawal to a simpler and less demanding life. These are analogous to the phantasies of the normally sighted (Cutsforth, 1951).

Certain "blindisms" are commonly listed as occasionally found in the blind. Blindisms are socially irrelevant and often bizarre repetitive activities which are distracting to other people. The most common ones are rocking or weaving, fingering or rubbing the eyes, waving the fingers before the face, and bending the head forward, as well as the twisting, squirming, and posturing which are characteristic of many nervous or mentally retarded sighted children. None of these activities is peculiar to the blind, and they are important only because they add to the person's exceptionality and decrease his social acceptability. In most cases these activities disappear as the child grows up, although they persist longer in blind children who are also emotionally disturbed or mentally retarded. The socialization and personal development of the blind are being augmented by such things as special museums, exhibits, and gardens designed especially for them, such as the Mary Duke Biddle Gallery for the Blind, a part of the North Carolina Museum of Art in Raleigh, North Carolina; the Garden of Fragrance in San Francisco's Golden Gate Park; and the traveling museum for the blind sponsored by the California Arts Commission.

INTELLIGENCE OF THE VISUALLY IMPAIRED

Except in the few instances in which blindness and intellectual subnormality are genetically linked (Tay-Sachs disease) and in those cases where mental deficiency and blindness may result from common environmental causes (disease or accidents), any intellectual deficits which accompany visual impairment are presumably due to the uncompensated limitations of sensory input and mobility. An individual's mental potential is neither raised nor lowered by blindness. His functional level may be lowered to the extent to which society has not provided experiences which can offset the limitations imposed by his sensory deficit. The neuromuscular maturation and postural achievements of blind infants are within the normal range for sighted children (Adelson & Fraiberg, 1974).

SENSORY ACUITY OF THE BLIND

The popular notion that the blind are endowed with hyperacute hearing, touch, taste, and smell or with phenomenal memory is largely erroneous. Studies have consistently shown that persons with vision are either equal or superior to the blind in their ability to identify the direction or distance of the source of a sound, to discriminate the relative intensities of tones, to recognize tactual forms, and to discriminate relative pressures, temperatures, or weights, as well as in their acuteness of smell, taste, and the vibratory sense. The blind have likewise displayed no superiority in either rote or logical memory (Seashore & Ling, 1918; Hayes, 1941; Axelrod, 1959; Lowenfeld, 1963; Emart & Carp, 1963). Any superiority of the blind in the perceptual areas is the result of increased attention to small cues and greater use of such cues as a source of information and guidance. It is apparently not the result of a lowering of sensory thresholds.

PERCEPTUAL AND CONCEPTUAL PROCESSES OF THE BLIND

It is obvious that the congenitally blind person experiences (perceives) the objects of the universe and builds up his knowledge of the world in ways that are different from those of seeing children. That is, his percepts and concepts derive from different types of stimuli—which does not mean that this cognition is necessarily less adequate or useful.

It is as impossible for the seeing person to experience the world of the congenitally blind as it is for the congenitally blind to conceive of visual experiences, but it does not necessarily follow that the blind individual thereby has a significantly restricted range of concepts. It is obvious that a person lacking visual perception will have no visual imagery. Studies indicate that adults who became blind before the age of five have no visual imagery (Lowenfeld, 1973; Warren, 1974). However, such people do develop and use concepts of forms, space, and distance beyond the range of touch and movement. They function efficiently in conceptual areas which sighted people derive primarily from visual experiences. It is not known if these percepts and concepts, derived primarily from tactual, kinesthetic, and auditory sources, remain on these levels or whether there is a coalescence of impressions and an emergence of concepts from such experiences into something akin to that which the sighted derive from visualization.

The duration of early visual experience prior to becoming blind is also important in the acquisition of manipulatory and locomotor skills. If the child has vision during the period when his manual activities normally come under visual control, he acquires a basic integration of the manual and visual modes. This provides the basis for a later extrapolation from motor to visual processes in those persons blinded later in life. Vision during the early years of life also seems critical in the development of locomotion (Warren, 1974).

Knowledge of the spatial qualities of objects is gained by the blind largely through touch and kinesthesis. Audition provides clues to the direction and distance of objects which make sounds, but it gives no idea of the objects as such. Tactual and kinesthetic experiences require direct contact with, or movement around, objects. Thus, distant objects, such as the heavenly bodies, clouds, and the horizon, as well as very large objects such as mountains and other geographical units, or microscopic objects such as bacteria, cannot be perceived and must be conceived only by analogy and extrapolation from objects actually experienced. While this is a limitation, it is probably comparable to the way in which the sighted person conceives of the size of the world and the other planets which he cannot directly perceive or of interplanetary distances which are far beyond his direct experience. When interplanetary distances are stated in terms of light years, for example, one's conception of such magnitudes depends largely on verbal or written symbols, or is an extrapolation from distances actually traversed. They are hardly perceived in the way that the distant mountaintop or the corner grocery store are perceived (Kephart, Kephart, & Schwartz, 1974).

It is surprising that we have few studies directly concerned with the concept formation or the conceptual levels attained by the blind as compared with the normally sighted. One study compared "early blind" and "late blind" children with sighted children on various tactile and auditory tasks (Axelrod, 1959). "Early blind" subjects were inferior to seeing subjects in: (1) abstracting a characteristic common to consistently rewarded members of pairs of objects; (2) solving matching problems involving spatial or temporal sequences; and (3) transferring a principle of solution from one sensory area to another—auditory to cutaneous or vice versa. The "late blind" subjects showed no inferiority to the normally sighted. The differences obtained, while statistically significant, were small and, according to the author, do not suggest marked intellectual impairment. The author also indicates that possible brain damage to the early blind cannot be ruled out.

Research studies have documented the deficiencies of the visually handicapped in the development of spatial concepts (Nolan & Ashcroft, 1969). There is also research evidence indicating that blind persons do not use abstract concepts to the degree that sighted people do, but think much more on a concrete level (Nolan & Ashcroft, 1969; Suppes, 1974).

Blind children score below their sighted peers in the mastery of Piagetian tasks such as seriation, classification, and conservation. Their relative deficits become greater as they grow older (Friedman & Pasnak, 1973). However, it has been shown that with intensive training, blind children are able to improve these abilities sufficiently to catch up with their sighted peers (Friedman & Pasnak, 1973).

In one study, eighty-one blind children six to twelve years old attending regular classes were found to be more verbally fluent, flexible, and original as measured by the Torrence Tests of Creative Thinking than were comparable sighted children (Halpin, Halpin, & Torrence, 1973). These authors postulate that the blind child is more fluent because he relies heavily on verbal output to compensate for the limitations imposed by blindness. The blind may also have to be more flexible and adaptable to cope with the demands of living in a world designed for the sighted. The blind may have to rely more on imagination than do the sighted, and what they imagine may be more unusual, unique, and original than reality.

EDUCATIONAL ACHIEVEMENT OF THE VISUALLY IMPAIRED

Visual defects of the type found in 25 to 35 percent of schoolchildren, most of which are not sufficiently severe to require special educational programs, do not seem to affect educational achievement. While hyperopia (farsightedness) and astigmatism (irregularity of the curvature of the cornea) are associated with less than normal progress in reading, myopia (nearsightedness) is associated with above-normal progress in reading (Farris, 1936; Eames, 1955, 1959).

As early as 1918, an educational achievement test was developed for the blind (Hayes, 1941). Since then many achievement tests have been adapted for use with the blind. In addition to offering the tasks in Braille, these tests come with more detailed preliminary instructions, and two and one-half or three times the time is allowed for taking them. Some tests have been adapted for oral administration. Because of these differences, direct comparisons with the norms obtained on the regular tests with the sighted are rather hazardous. However, we can only take achievement test scores as we find them. When seeing and blind children are compared grade by grade, the two groups are about equal except in arithmetic, in which the scores of the blind are generally lower. However, blind children are on the average about two years older than seeing children of the same grade. Consequently, comparisons by either chronological or mental age indicate considerable educational retardation (Hayes, 1941; Lowenfeld, 1973). The greater age of blind children seems to result largely from their late entry to school, their absence from school because of treatment for eye trouble, the lack of appropriate school facilities, and their slower rate of obtaining information from Braille, large type, or audition. Persons interested in testing the blind will find *A Manual for the Psychological Examination of the Adult Blind* (Bauman and Hayes, 1951) very valuable.

Some incidental facts relevant to the school achievement of the blind are:

1. The cause of blindness and the age of becoming blind are unrelated to school achievement (Hayes, 1934).
2. Age of school entrance is negatively correlated with school success (Hayes, 1934).

3. Blind children have particular difficulties in arithmetic (Nolan, 1959a).

Currently Braille and large-type editions of the New Stanford Achievement Test series are available for grades 2 through 12. These are power rather than speed tests (Morris, 1974).

EDUCATION OF THE VISUALLY IMPAIRED

The aims, content, and subject matter involved in the education of the visually impaired are not essentially different from those involved in normal education. They need a good general education, plus a vocational type of instruction which is in keeping with their special requirements. The education of the visually impaired, like all special education, requires special training of teachers, special facilities and equipment, and some curricular modifications. Because the educations of the educationally blind and the partially sighted are somewhat different, we will discuss them separately.

Special educational needs of the blind

It is estimated that ordinary educational experiences are 85 percent visual. Since the blind child is deprived of this type of experience, the adaptation required for his education requires a shift from vision to the auditory, tactual, and kinesthetic senses as avenues of instruction, learning, and guidance. These needs have been met by teaching Braille reading and writing, using many audio aids, and constructing and using models, as well as embossed and relief maps, graphs, and geometric designs. Because of the importance of independent mobility for the blind child, instruction in orientation and training and experiences designed to increase his control of the environment and of himself in relation to it are becoming part of special education programs for the blind.

The teaching of Braille   Learning and developing facility in the Braille system of reading and writing is the greatest single curricular modification required for the education of the blind. In 1829 Louis Braille, a young blind student and later a teacher at the Paris School for the Blind, modified a military code used for night communication so that it could be used by the blind. The system has been further modified under various auspices. At one time there were three major systems in use—the New York point system, American Braille, and British Braille. In 1932 a modified British Braille became the Standard English Braille, and since 1950 it has been used consistently as the preferred system. In

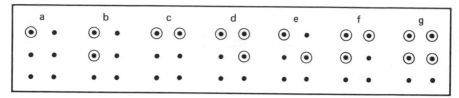

Figure 12–1   Sample of the Braille letter codes

1950, UNESCO adapted a Braille system for all languages, but many of its details still have to be worked out.

Braille is the most efficient and useful means of reading and writing yet devised for the blind. Using the sixty-three possible combinations of six raised dots in the Braille cell, virtually any literary, numerical, or musical material can be presented. Since unmodified Braille takes a lot of space—each Braille cell requires a quarter-inch of line—many abbreviations, contractions, and signs have been developed.

The proficient Braille reader must be familiar with the twenty-six letters of the alphabet, 189 contractions and short-form words, and 31 punctuation and composition marks—a total of 246 different basic elements (Brothers, 1974). The American Printing House for the Blind produces an instructional kit and a set of Braille Code Recognition materials to assist in the development of Braille reading skills.

Mathematics makes use of a special Braille notation system, and most scientific symbols can be written in Braille. A type of Braille shorthand for the blind stenographer has also been developed.

Although Braille is a modified military code, it is not merely a code for the blind reader. It is a complete medium for reading and writing. Braille is taught, learned, and read much the same as ordinary writing and reading. Reading Braille is, in many ways, similar to visual reading. The proficient Braille reader uses both hands in reading, but the two function independently, one ahead of the other. The hands move regularly and smoothly, and horizontally along the line, with few vertical regressive movements. The touch is light, the pressure uniform. The activity is not particularly fatiguing, and there seems to be no decrease in the sensitivity of the touch even after several hours of reading.

Developing facility in reading Braille involves a unifying process in which larger and larger units of material are apprehended at a time in a manner similar to the reading of print by sighted persons. Some Braille readers use lip movements or silent speech, just as do some visual readers (Fertsch, 1946).

The limitations of Braille as compared with visual reading are its relative slowness, the large size of books printed in Braille, and the restricted range of material available. A plane geometry textbook, when put into Braille, required over one thousand pages and cost more than ten times the same text in print. Carl Sandburg's biography of Abraham Lincoln is ten volumes in Braille (Heck, 1953). Braille reading is comparatively slow—about one-third or one-fourth the rate of visual reading. Blind high school students read approximately 90 words per minute in Braille. A really good Braille reader may attain a speed of 150–200 words a minute (Lowenfeld, 1973). Two studies have shown that relatively short periods of rapid reading instruction and practice can double a blind person's rate of reading Braille (Crandell & Wallace, 1974; Mc-Bride, 1974).

Braille can be written either by using a mechanical Braille writer or with a slate and stylus. Most schools start children writing with the Braille writer, which is relatively easy and fun to operate. The use of the slate and stylus is more difficult and requires fine motor coordination. The slates come in both pocket and desk sizes. Writing is done by punching holes with a stylus in a paper inserted between two metal strips. Since the material must be read from the underside of the paper, it must be written in reverse by starting at the right margin and writing toward the left. Blind children are also taught to use a standard typewriter, usually in the third or fourth grade. They find it very difficult to write with pen or pencil, and this is no longer emphasized except to teach each child to write his name.[2]

Other forms of tactile communication

Of the score or more systems—other than Braille—that have been devised for tactile communication, only a few have survived (Sherrick, 1975; Geldard, 1974). The best known of these devices is the Optacon, developed by J. C. Bliss and made commercially available by Telesensory Systems in 1971. According to Bliss, there were over a thousand Optacons in use in 1973 (Bliss & Moore, 1974). This machine is still being improved and modified, and plans are underway for a self-contained one-hand model (Harland, 1974). The Optacon enables the blind to read ordinary printed matter, exposed to a camera and transmitted to the finger pad as an array of vibrating pins which is a tactile facsimile of the printed symbols. However, M. J. Tobin and R. K. James's (1974) evaluation of the Optacon is not very encouraging. They provided thirty-six blind subjects with twelve hours of practice on the Optacon, and a smaller group of seventeen subjects with up to forty-eight hours of prac-

2 See Lowenfeld, Abel, and Hatten (1969) for a good survey of the studies on Braille reading.

tice. The subjects were sixteen to fifty-four years of age and were all professional or semiprofessional people. Most of the subjects could read only ten to twelve words per minute after training. Some, for short periods of time, could reach forty words per minute. Tobin and James conclude that reaching a useful level of reading with the Optacon is a long, hard process. They claim that reading machines, such as this one, are only "peripheral aids" where speed is not important, and when no other help is available.

Audio aids for the blind   The education of the blind requires many audio aids. Tape recorders and record players are necessary parts of his school life. Resource or itinerant teachers may give assignments or special instructions on tape. Text material not available in Braille may be taped or recorded. Recordings are normally read at rates of 150 to 170 words per minute—considerably faster than reading Braille. Most of the "talking books" available are fiction or magazines, but school texts are made available through the American Printing House for the Blind, the Library of Congress, and a few private agencies.[3]

A "harmonic compressor" now makes it possible to compress human speech so that it can be played back at twice the normal rate without the usual "Donald Duck" effect which occurs when conventional recordings are reproduced at higher than their recording speeds. Aside from its speed, the reproduction sounds like natural speech. One comparison of Braille reading and listening to both normal and compressed speech recordings showed that Braille reading took twice as long as listening to normal recordings and three times as long as listening to compressed speech. With materials of four different levels of difficulty, no differences in comprehension were found among the three methods. Compressed speech was the most efficient (Tuttle, 1974).

Arithmetic aids for the blind   Mental arithmetic is used extensively in the education of the blind. For higher levels of mathematics, calculators, rulers, slide rules, compasses, and protractors have all been adapted for use by the blind. The Braille writer is also used in arithmetical calculations, as are an arithmetic board and adaptations of the abacus. Modeling clay, pins, and rubber bands are used in constructing geometric designs and graphs (Walter, 1974).

Additional educational aids   Braille relief and embossed maps and relief globes are useful in teaching geography as well as orientation and space perception to the blind child. Maps of the room, the school grounds, and the town help the blind child develop a mental map of his surroundings, assist him in his orientation, and aid his independent travel. In addition to mobility training and the special equipment men-

---

[3] For full information concerning these services, see Field (1974).

tioned, special physical education, art, and handicraft activities for the blind are required.

Vocational training for the blind

The educational needs of the blind person are more adequately met today than are his vocational needs. In most of the more advanced countries of the world today, no blind child of normal intelligence need grow up without academic, prevocational, and even some vocational training. Some programmed texts, modified for audio presentation to the blind, have been developed (Dunham & Shelton, 1973). However, many blind people are unable to obtain employment appropriate to their capacities. It is estimated that less than half of the blind individuals capable of working in general occupations are doing so and that only about 20 percent of those who could function adequately in sheltered workshops are so employed (Barnett, 1955; Wilson, 1974).

Specialized vocational training—the teaching of specific skills and knowledge required for employment in regular trades or professions—is seldom provided by agencies for the blind. Only in a few limited areas, such as work with other blind, in the operation of service stands, and in the teaching of special skills such as chair caning, broom-making, and weaving have the agencies for the blind developed vocational training programs. For the most part, blind people must obtain their vocational training along with the sighted. No special techniques for placing skilled or professional workers have been developed. The only special problem involved in vocational placement is dealing with the unrealistic prejudices of employers and with unwarranted physical qualifications which may preclude the hiring of the blind.

There are relatively few occupations and professions in which the blind are not successfully employed. For example, the National Blind Teachers Association listed eighty blind teachers of the sighted in 1970 (Boykin, 1974). However, the sheltered workshop is still the largest single source of employment for blind people. In the most successful instances of industrial job placement, commitments have been obtained from top management for the employment of a given number of blind workers. It is understood that the workers will meet regular production schedules and standards and be paid at regular rates. As long as the company has jobs which can be satisfactorily performed by blind workers, employment opportunities will be maintained for a specified number or percentage of blind workers. Union commitments are sometimes needed to exempt these people from the seniority provisions of union contracts. Agreements to employ a certain *number* of blind, rather than a particular group of blind workers, prevent the loss of those jobs to other blind workers when a particular employment is terminated. To prevent the blind workers from isolating themselves from the larger working group, many placement officers prefer not to place several blind workers in the same department. H. Rusalem (1973) has provided a good discussion of the vocational problems of the blind.

Education of the partially sighted

The education of the partially sighted is much less a problem than is that of the blind. For the most part, the partially sighted are basically seeing people and are educated with and prepared for life as such. At one time a large number of "sight saving" classes were conducted for the partially sighted. The notion of sight saving has been largely discarded because it is generally recognized that the maximum use of even defective eyes will not cause them to deteriorate. Vision is not saved by not using it. The child with poor vision is now encouraged to use his vision to its maximum, to learn to read print, to write, and to acquire as much of his education as possible by sight. In contrast with the sight-saving emphasis of the old classes for the partially sighted, we now find programs, or at least proposals, for their "sight development" or "sight utilization." In such programs, the children are "learning to see," to make full use of their residual vision (Lowenfeld, 1973).

People working with the visually impaired are becoming increasingly concerned with the most effective use of any residual vision. Many legally blind children have potentially useful but undeveloped near vision. Many such children can develop considerable functional vision even though they have very low measured visual acuity. However, these children require planned opportunities and programs to achieve this end. Teaching procedures specifically directed at this end can significantly increase the visual efficiency of partially sighted children (Barraga, 1964; 1970).

The education of partially sighted children makes those adjustments in curriculum and equipment necessary for the education of the handicapped child, but otherwise his education is not unique. He does not have to learn Braille reading and writing. He is capable of independent travel without acquiring special techniques. His spatial orientation and concepts are not unique.

Educational aids for the partially sighted   For the child with borderline vision, minor adjustments, such as sitting near the blackboard, placing his desk in a good light, and being allowed to move about so as to be as close as possible to charts and other wall displays, may be all that is necessary.

For the more severely handicapped child, books in large type and magnifying devices of various types are necessary. Two companies—American Printing House for the Blind and Stanwix Publishing House—publish books in large type for the partially sighted, and a fairly wide variety of reading material is becoming available.

The simplest way to obtain magnification of print is to bring the book closer to the eyes. To see people holding reading very close to the eyes is disturbing to many persons because they believe such close reading damages the eyes. Most authorities believe that reading material may safely be held as close to the eyes as necessary. For many partially sighted individuals, however, holding print close to the eyes is not adequate and other means of magnification may be needed.

Optical magnification is achieved in several ways. Magnifying projectors and special lenses—both contact and in conventional frames—are available. Telescopic effects are achieved by using contact lenses along with special lenses in conventional frames. A wide variety of special magnifying devices is produced.

Simple enlargement of print or magnification does not make a normal reader out of the partially sighted person. All means of enlarging print reduce the effective field of vision. This means that the amount of material that can be perceived at one time is reduced, and the rate of reading is correspondingly slow. It is therefore necessary to find the most appropriate type and degree of magnification for each person.

Blind college students

Blind college students have special needs. They need to read a large number of technical and highly specialized books. Obtaining access to these books either in Braille or as recordings is often difficult. Recordings for the Blind, Inc., makes tape recordings of such books and is constantly enlarging its free lending library. It serves over 80 percent of the blind college students in the United States and supplies them with several thousand tapes annually. Limited financial support for the organization comes from businesses, foundations, and private contributors. However, the more than 4,000 unpaid volunteers who contribute their time and talent are the greatest asset. The organization is always in need of additional qualified volunteers to keep abreast of the expanding and ever-changing literature. Persons interested in donating their services should contact the organization at 215 East 58th Street, New York, New

York 10022. Recording centers are located throughout the United States.

For materials which are not available in taped form, the blind have to depend on readers. In most states limited funds are available to pay such readers. In many cases sighted fellow-students volunteer their services.

A few years ago, the majority of blind persons graduating from college were limited to professional opportunities in the field of work for the blind as home teachers, counselors, and instructors in centers for the blind. Today most of them are finding employment in the world of the sighted.

Residential versus regular classes

The residential schools were the first, and for a long time practically the only, facilities for the education of the visually impaired. With the development of many local facilities, however, the role of the residential schools has lessened. Most educators today believe that the maximum degree of integration of the handicapped child into the regular school and community is the most desirable arrangement. This means that those children who can be educated in regular, unsegregated classrooms should be so placed. Children who can be educated in special classes, or by resource or itinerant teachers, should not be institutionalized. The residential school aims to return the handicapped child to the regular school as quickly as possible. The majority of visually impaired children are in integrated classrooms with their sighted peers, with supplementary services supplied by resource teachers (Hull & McCarthy, 1973; Lappin, 1975).

EDUCATION OF THE BLIND WITH ADDITIONAL HANDICAPS

The negative effects of multihandicaps tend to be multiplicative rather than simply additive. Specifically, the total effects of blindness and deafness together are far more detrimental than the simple additive effects of either occurring separately (Kennedy, 1973). One basic difference between a deaf-blind child and a child who is *either* blind *or* deaf is that the former has no concept of the function of language. The deaf child can see other people communicating and can see the effects of communicating. While initially he does not understand the process, when language training is started the nature of the oral communication process soon becomes apparent. The blind child, of course, hears and acquires speech as does the sighted. He understands the use of language as an expressive and manipulative device. In contrast, the congenitally deaf-blind child has no awareness of language—either its existence or its functions. So, in addition to acquiring the mechanics of communication, the deaf-blind child must first develop an awareness of communication and a concept of its purposes and functions. He must also be motivated to participate in communicative activities.

Dr. Samuel G. Howe and Ann Sullivan Macy's pioneering work with Laura Bridgman and Helen Keller, respectively, focused attention on the education of the deaf-blind in America. The first systematic program for these children was provided at the Perkins Institute for the Blind in Watertown, Massachusetts. Over the past decade there has been a decrease in the proportion of handicapped individuals with single disabilities and an increase in the proportion with multiple handicaps (Nezol, 1975). The rubella epidemic of 1964-65 produced many deaf and blind children and has resulted in an increasing concern for these children in the United States.[4] Whereas in 1970 there were fewer than a dozen programs in the United States specifically for deaf-blind children, by 1975 there were nearly one hundred (Hammer, 1975).

The education of these children is a very demanding, one-to-one, teaching-learning process. The teacher typically becomes a companion to his student and provides constant and intensive social contact and stimulation as well as formal instruction. Education is initially directed at establishing contacts with the world via the cutaneous, kinesthetic, gustatory, and olfactory senses, and arousing a desire for learning. The isolation of the deaf-blind individual is great, and it is only after effective contact is established and his isolation is reduced that formal instruction is possible (Tweedie, 1974).

A device potentially useful to the deaf-blind has recently been developed. The instrument applies the "speech feeling" technique made famous by Helen Keller and taught for many years at the Perkins Institute (Kirman, 1973). When using this technique, the deaf-blind person places his hand on the face of the speaker in such a way that one or more fingers can detect lip and jaw movements and oral air pressure. One finger detects throat vibrations, and one finger feels the nasal vibrations. By learning to differentiate these complex cutaneous patterns, the trained person's perception of language becomes remarkably accurate.

The device developed by J. D. Miller, E. M. Engebretson, and C. L. DeFilippo (1974), using this principle, transmits nasal vibrations, throat vibrations, and pressure variations near the speaker's lips to three locations on the skin in the form of tactile vibrations. Initial reports of the use of this device are encouraging (Sherrick, 1975).

One interesting program is provided by the Hadley School for the Blind, founded in 1920 in Winnetka, Illinois, as a correspondence school.

---

[4] For details, see Guldager (1969) and Robbins & Stenquist (1967).

The school offers a course called "Independent Living Without Sight and Hearing," designed by Hadley's president, Dr. Richard Kinney, and taught by Geraldine Lawhorn. Both Kinney and Lawhorn are deaf and blind. Hadley has an enrollment of several thousand students. Tuition is free for the legally blind (Crist, 1975; Kinney, 1972).

Special educational programs for the blind–mentally retarded have also been established. While these programs require much less modification than do those for the deaf-blind, the instruction is largely individualized and classes must be limited to three to five children (Williams, 1964).

SELF-HELP AIDS AND SUGGESTIONS FOR SIGHTED-PERSON ASSISTANCE

Those who live or work with the blind will find useful the wealth of practical suggestions provided by such books as B. Lowenfeld's *Our Blind Children,* now in the third edition, as well as the catalogs and information supplied by The American Foundation for the Blind (15 West 16th Street, New York, New York 10011). Special items invented or modified for the blind by the Foundation include watches with raised dots for numbers, safety-insulated spoons which hook onto the cooking pot, knives with built-in slicing guides for cutting such foods as meat and cheese at desired thicknesses, needle threaders, a hem gauge, pie-cutting guides, carpenter's levels with audible indicators, measuring devices with raised dots indicating dimensions and unit divisions, and a large number of modified popular games.

Suggestions for the sighted who wish to aid the blind include the following: (a) Teach children to use the Continental technique of eating (holding the fork in the left hand and the knife in the right at all times) rather than the American "cross-over" convention. The former makes the act of eating neater and simpler for the blind. (b) Maintain a routine in table arrangements, tell the location of things "by the clock," and use salt and pepper shakers of different sizes or shapes. Teach children to shake salt and pepper into their hand before putting them on food, so as to estimate the amount. Name and indicate the location of food as it is served. (c) To assist in walking, ask the blind person if he would like to take your elbow. A gentle but firm grip just above your elbow is best. The blind person can then walk about half a step behind you. Start and stop gradually rather than abruptly, and walk in as straight a line as possible. (d) Let the blind person enter a car by himself after you have placed his hand on the car door. A blind friend of the senior author has humorously described the various ways in which he has been "manhandled" by persons trying to "put" him into a car or bus. (*e*) In a restaurant, place the blind person's hand either on the chair back or on the seat, and read the menu aloud unless he already knows it. Let him give his order to the waiter. Either touch his hand or tell him the location of such things as ash trays, sugar bowls, salt and pepper shakers. Tell him what his bill is and let him pay the waiter or cashier. (*f*) When you meet a blind person, shake his hand if he makes a gesture in your direction. Speak directly to him; do not use his sighted companion as an "interpreter." Do not raise your voice.

SUMMARY

The blind were the first handicapped group for whom social provisions were made. Although the numbers involved are comparatively small, they have enjoyed more public concern and special legislation than any other category of the handicapped. Today the quantitative definitions of blindness and partial sight are being either supplemented or replaced by more situationally relevant, functional definitions. While the blind are easily identified, the partially sighted require examinations by specialists.

A wide variety of both genetic and environmental causes produce blindness. Infections and accidents are decreasing in importance as causes, whereas a larger percentage of blindness is attributed to prenatal factors the exact nature of which is largely unknown. It is estimated that among school-age children, one in three thousand meet the medicolegal criterion of blindness, and that one in five hundred have vision in the 20/70 to 20/200 range commonly designated as partially sighted. The United States Office of Education estimates that about half the medico-legally blind children (one out of six thousand) are educationally blind (requiring the bulk of their education to be other than visual) and that about twice this number (one in three thousand) require the special education provided for the partially sighted.

The three major problems of the blind are social understanding, education by other than visual means, and independent mobility. Some type of educational program is available to practically all of the blind in the United States. The problems of social understanding and acceptance of the blind are gradually being reduced. Systematic assistance and training for independent travel are only recently becoming available.

The "obstacle sense" of the blind has been shown to be fundamentally the location of echoes by auditory means. The language of the blind is not noticeably different from that of normal people. Language defects are probably more common, but they are not noticeably different in type from those of the sighted. The same things are true of the personal and social maladjustment of the visually impaired. Their basic intellectual capacities are probably normal. Their restricted sensory input, limited mobility, and greater dependence on other people probably account for any deficits they show in intelligence and on scholastic achievement tests. The blind seem to be capable of compensating for their visual deficit in the perceptual and conceptual areas. While the congenitally blind lack visual percepts and concepts, they do not suffer any significant overall deficiency in this area.

All of the different types of administrative arrangements are used in educating the blind. Most blind school children attend regular integrated classrooms. The special educational needs of the blind are the learning of Braille; the extensive use of auditory, tactual and kinesthetic experiences; and special mobility training. The partially sighted are educated essentially as are the normally sighted, but with the aid of large print and magnification of various types.

REFERENCES

ADELSON, E., & S. FRAIBERG, "Gross Motor Development in Infants Blind from Birth," *Child Development,* 1974, *45,* 114–26.

AMERICAN FOUNDATION FOR THE BLIND, *A Teacher Education Program for Those Who Serve Blind Children and Youth* (New York: American Foundation for the Blind, 1961).

ARMSTRONG, J., "Blind Mobility: Current Research Programs," *American Foundation for the Blind: Research Bulletin,* June 1975, *29,* 145–48.

AXELROD, S., *Effects of Early Blindness: Performance of Blind and Sighted Children on Tactile and Auditory Tasks* (New York: American Foundation for the Blind, 1959).

BARNETT, M. R., "Current Problems of the Blind," in M. E. Frampton & E. D. Gall, eds., *Special Education for the Exceptional,* vol. 2 (Boston: Porter Sargent, 1955).

BARRAGA, N. C., *Increased Visual Behavior in Low Vision Children* (New York: American Foundation for the Blind, 1964).

BARRAGA, N. C., "Teaching Children with Low Vision," in R. L. Jones, ed., *New Directions in Special Education* (Boston: Allyn & Bacon, 1970).

BAUMAN, M. K., "Group Differences Disclosed by Inventory Items," *International Journal of the Education of the Deaf,* 1964, *13,* 101–6.

BAUMAN, M. K., "Research on Psychological Factors Associated with Blindness," in R. E. Hardy & J. G. Cull, eds., *Social and Rehabilitation Services for the Blind* (Springfield, Ill.: Charles C Thomas, 1972).

BAUMAN, M. K., & S. P. HAYES, *A Manual for the Psychological Examination of the Adult Blind* (New York: The Psychological Corporation, 1951).

BEST, H., *Blindness and the Blind in the United States* (New York: Macmillan, 1934).

BLASCH, B. B., R. L. WELSH, & T. DAVIDSON, "Auditory Maps: An Orientation Aid for Visually Handicapped Persons," *The New Outlook for the Blind,* 1973, *67,* 145–58.

BLISS, J. C., & M. W. MOORE, "The Optacon Reading System," *Education of the Visually Handicapped,* 1974, *6,* 98–102.

BOURGEAULT, S. E., "Blindness: A Label," *Education of the Visually Handicapped,* 1974, *6,* 1–6.

BOYKIN, A. O., "There's a Unicorn in the Classroom," *Phi Delta Kappan,* 1974, *60* (8), 593–94.

BROTHERS, R. J., "Classroom Use of the Braille Code Recognition Materials," *Education of the Visually Handicapped,* 1974, *6,* 6–13.

BROWN, C. E., "Defining and Measuring Services to Improve Their Effectiveness," *The New Outlook for the Blind,* 1974, *68,* 241–46.

CHASE, J. B., "A Retrospective Study of Retrolental Fibroplasia," *The New Outlook for the Blind,* 1974, *68,* 61–71.

CORBETT, M. P., "Professionalism in Mobility," *The New Outlook for the Blind,* 1974, *68,* 104–7, 123–25.

CRANDELL, J. M., & D. H. WALLACE, "Speed Reading in Braille: An Empirical Study," *The New Outlook for the Blind,* 1974, *68,* 13–19.

CRANE, M. M., et al., "Study of Procedures for Screening Elementary School Children for Visual Defects," *American Journal of Public Health,* 1952, *42,* 1430–39.

CRIST, L. M., "One Who Has Learned to 'See' and 'Hear' Guides Others," *The Christian Science Monitor,* 21 April 1975, 23.

CUTSFORTH, T. D., *The Blind in School and Society,* rev. ed. (New York: American Foundation for the Blind, 1951).

DALTON, M. M., "A Visual Survey of 5,000 School Children," *Journal of Educational Research,* 1943, *37,* 81–94.

DAVID, W. D., "Your Health: Eye Care," *Today's Education,* 1970, *59* (3), 40.

DAVIDSON, O. R., "The Accountability of Nonprofit Institutions in a Free Society," *The New Outlook for the Blind,* 1973, *67,* 389–95.

DUNHAM, J., & H. SHELTON, "Machine Presented Audible Programmed Instruction for the Blind," *Education of the Visually Handicapped,* 1973, *5,* 117–19.

EAMES, T. H., "The Influence of Hypermetropia and Myopia on Reading Achievement," *American Journal of Ophthalmology,* 1955, *39,* 375–77.

EAMES, T. H., "Visual Defects in Reading," *Journal of Education,* 1959, *141,* 1–34.

EMART, A. G., & F. M. CARP, "Recognition of Tactual Forms by Sighted and Blind Subjects," *American Journal of Psychology,* 1963, *76,* 488–91.

FARRIS, L. P., "Visual Defects as Factors Influencing Achievement in Reading," *Journal of Experimental Education,* 1936, *5,* 68–70.

FERTSCH, P., "An Analysis of Braille Reading," *New Outlook for the Blind,* 1946, *40,* 128–31.

FIELD, G., "Recorded and Braille Textbooks: Everything the Blind Student Needs to Know," *The New Outlook for the Blind*, 1974, *68*, 151–56.

FINESTONE, S., I. LUKOFF, & M. WHITEMAN, *The Demand for Dog Guides and the Travel Adjustment of Blind Persons* (New York: Research Center, Columbia University, 1960).

FJELDSENDEN, B., "Translation of Visual Information into Auditory Cues," *Research Bulletin: American Foundation for the Blind*, October 1974, *28*, 19–56.

FOOTE, F. M., & M. M. CRANE, "An Evaluation of Visual Screening," *Exceptional Children*, 1954, *20*, 153–61.

FRIEDMAN, J., & R. PASNAK, "Accelerated Acquisition of Classification Skills by Blind Children," *Developmental Psychology*, 1973, *9*, 333–37.

GELDARD, F. A., ed., *Conference on Cutaneous Systems and Devices* (Austin, Tex.: The Psychonomic Society, 1974).

GILL, J. M., "Tactual Mapping," *Research Bulletin: American Foundation for the Blind*, October 1974, *28*, 57–80.

GINSBERG, E., "Preventive Health: No Easy Answers," *The Sight-Saving Review*, 1973–74, *43*, 187–95.

GULDAGER, L., "The Deaf-blind: Their Education and Their Needs," *Exceptional Children*, 1969, *36*, 203–6.

HALPIN, G., G. HALPIN, & E. P. TORRANCE, "Effects of Blindness on Creative Thinking Abilities of Children," *Developmental Psychology*, 1973, *9*, 268–76.

HAMMER, E. K., "What Is Effective Programming for Deaf-blind Children?" *The New Outlook for the Blind*, 1975, *69*, 25, 31.

HARLAND, H., "An Experimental One-Hand Optacon," *Research Bulletin: American Foundation for the Blind*, October 1974, *28*, 165–68.

HARLEY, R., & J. SPOLLEN, "A Study of the Reliability and Validity of the Visual Efficiency Scale with Low Vision Children," *Education of the Visually Handicapped*, 1973, *5*, 110–14.

HATFIELD, E. M., "Causes of Blindness in School Children," *Sight-Saving Review*, 1963, *33*, 218–33.

HATFIELD, E. M., "Estimates of Blindness in the United States," *Sight-Saving Review*, 1973, *43*, 69–80.

HAYES, S. P., "Factors Influencing the School Success of the Blind," *Teachers Forum (Blind)*, 1934, *6*, 91–99.

HAYES, S. P., *Contributions to a Psychology of Blindness* (New York: American Foundation for the Blind, 1941).

HECK, A. O., *The Education of Exceptional Children*, 2nd ed. (New York: McGraw-Hill, 1953).

HOOVER, R. E., "Visual Efficiency as a Criterion of Service Needs," *Research Bulletin*, 1963, *12* (3), 116–19.

HULL, W. A., & D. G. McCARTHY, "Supplementary Program for Visually Handicapped Children," *Education of the Visually Handicapped*, 1973, *5*, 97–114.

HURLIN, R. G., "Estimated Prevalence of Blindness in the United States and in Individual States," *Sight-Saving Review*, 1962, *32*, 162–65.

JONES, J. W., "Problems Involved in Defining and Classifying Blindness," *New Outlook for the Blind*, 1962, *56*, 115–21.

Kay, L., "Orientation for Blind Persons: Clear Path Indicators as Environmental Sensor," *The New Outlook for the Blind,* 1974, *68,* 289–96.

Kay, L., "The Sonic Glasses Evaluated," *The New Outlook for the Blind,* 1975, *67,* 7–11.

Kennedy, A., "Language Awareness and the Deaf-blind Child," *Teaching Exceptional Children,* 1973, *6,* 99–102.

Kephart, J. G., C. P. Kephart, & G. C. Schwartz, "A Journey into the World of the Blind Child," *Exceptional Children,* 1974, *40,* 421–27.

Kerby, C. E., "A Report on the Visual Handicap of Partially Seeing Children," *Exceptional Children,* 1952, *43,* 137–42.

Kerby, C. E. "Cause of Blindness in Children of School Age," *Sight-Saving Review,* 1958, *28,* 10–21.

Kinney, R., *Independent Living Without Seeing and Hearing* (Winnetka, Ill.: Hadley School for the Blind, 1972).

Kirman, J. H., "Tactile Communication of Speech," *Psychological Bulletin,* 1973, *80,* 54–74.

Kupfer, C., "Evaluation of the Treatment of Diabetic Retinopathy: A Research Project," *The Sight-Saving Review,* 1973, *43,* 17–28.

LaDuke, R. O., "An Analysis of Current Issues and Trends in Orientation and Mobility," *Education of the Visually Handicapped,* 1973, *5,* 20–27.

Lappin, C. W., "At Your Service: The Instructional Materials Reference Center for the Visually Handicapped," *Teaching Exceptional Children,* 1975, *5,* 74–76.

Liska, J. S., "What Does It Mean to Be 'Legally Blind'?" *The New Outlook for the Blind,* 1973, *67,* 19–20.

Lowenfeld, B., "The Visually Handicapped," *Review of Educational Research,* 1963, *33,* 38–41.

Lowenfeld, B., *Our Blind Children,* 3rd ed. (Springfield, Ill.: Charles C Thomas, 1971).

Lowenfeld, B., ed., *The Visually Handicapped Child in School* (New York: John Day, 1973).

Lowenfeld, B., G. L. Abel, & P. H. Hatten, *Blind Children Learn to Read* (Springfield, Ill.: Charles C Thomas, 1969).

Lowenstein, B. E., & P. D. Preger, Jr., *Diabetes: New Look at an Old Problem* (New York: Harper & Row, 1976).

Lukoff, J. F., & M. Whiteman, *The Social Sources of Adjustment to Blindness* (New York: American Foundations for the Blind, Research Series No. 21, 1970).

McBride, V. G., "Explorations in Rapid Reading in Braille," *The New Outlook for the Blind,* 1974, *68,* 8–12.

Maugh, T. H., II, "Diabetes: Epidemiology Suggests a Viral Connection," *Science,* 1975, *188,* 347–51.

Miller, J. D., E. M. Engebretson, & C. L. DeFilippo, "Preliminary Research with a Three-channel Vibrotactile Speech-reception Aid for the Deaf," *Journal of the Acoustical Society of America,* 1974, *55,* Supplement 564.

Mims, F. M., "Sensory Aids for Blind Persons," *The New Outlook for the Blind,* 1973, *67,* 407–14.

Morris, J. E., "The 1973 Stanford Achievement Test Series as Adapted for Use by the Visually Handicapped," *Education of the Visually Handicapped,* 1974, *6,* 33–40.

Nezol, A. J., "Reading and the Multipally Handicapped Blind Child," *The New Outlook for the Blind,* 1975, *69,* 39–41.

Nolan, C. Y., "Achievement in Arithmetic Computation: Analysis of School Differences and Identification of Areas of Low Achievement," *International Journal of Education of the Blind,* 1959a, *8,* 125–28.

Nolan, C. Y., & S. C. Ashcroft, "The Visually Handicapped," *Review of Educational Research,* 1969, *39,* 52–70.

Peel, J. C. F., "Psychological Aspects of Long Cane Orientation Training," *Research Bulletin: American Foundation for the Blind,* October 1974, *28,* 111–24.

Riley, L. H., D. M. Luterman, & M. F. Cohen, "Relationship Between Hearing Ability and Mobility in a Blind Adult Population," *New Outlook for the Blind,* 1964, *58,* 139–41.

Robbins, N., & G. Stenquist, *The Deaf-Blind "Rubella" Child* (Watertown, Mass.: Perkins School for the Blind, 1967).

Robson, H., "The Practice of Guide Dog Mobility in the United Kingdom," *The New Outlook for the Blind,* 1974, *68,* 72–78.

Rusalem, H., *Coping with the Unseen Environment: An Introduction to the Vocational Rehabilitation of Blind Persons* (New York: Teachers College Press, 1973).

Schindale, R., "The Social Adjustment of Visually Handicapped Children in Different Educational Settings," *Research Bulletin: American Foundation for the Blind,* October 1974, *28,* 125–44.

Scott, R. A., *The Making of Blind Men* (New York: Russell Sage Foundation, 1969).

Seashore, C. E., & T. L. Ling, "Comparative Sensitiveness of Blind and Seeing Persons," *Psychology Monographs,* 1918, *25,* 148–58.

Sherrick, C. E., "The Art of Tactile Communication," *American Psychologist,* 1975, *30,* 353–60.

Spar, H. J., "Some Special Aspects of an Adequate Vocational Training and Employment Program for the Blind," in M. E. Frampton & E. D. Gall, eds., *Special Education for the Exceptional,* vol. 2 (Boston: Porter Sargent, 1955).

Suppes, F., "A Survey of Cognitions in Handicapped Children," *Review of Educational Research,* 1974, *44,* 145–76.

Tobin, M. J., & R. K. James, "Evaluating the Optacon: General Reflections on Reading Machines for the Blind," *Research Bulletin: American Foundation for the Blind,* October 1974, *28,* 145–57.

Tuttle, D. W., "A Comparison of Three Reading Media for the Blind: Braille, Normal Recording, and Compressed Speech," *Research Bulletin: American Foundation for the Blind,* April 1974, *27,* 217–30.

TWEEDIE, D., "Behavioral Change in a Deaf-blind Multihandicapped Child," *Volta Review*, 1974, *76*, 213–18.

USLAN, M. M., & P. MANNING, "A Graphic Analysis of Touch Technique Safety," *Research Bulletin: American Foundation for the Blind*, October 1974, *28*, 175–80.

WALTER, M., "Use of Geoboards to Teach Mathematics," *Education of the Visually Handicapped*, 1974, *6*, 59–62.

WARREN, D. H., "Early vs. Late Vision: The Role of Early Vision in Spatial Reference Systems," *The New Outlook for the Blind*, 1974, *68*, 157–62.

WARREN, D. H., & I. A. KOCON, "Factors in the Successful Mobility of the Blind: A Review," *Research Bulletin: American Foundation for the Blind*, October 1974, *28*, 191–218.

WESTAWAY, D. L., "Alternatives to the Blindness System in Australia," *The New Outlook for the Blind*, 1973, *67*, 65–71.

WILLIAMS, D., "Sunland's Program for the Blind," *Mental Retardation*, 1964, *2*, 244–45.

WILSON, E. L., "Assessing the Readiness of Blind Persons for Vocational Placement," *New Outlook for the Blind*, 1974, *65*, 57–60.

WRIGHT, B. A., "An Analysis of Attitudes: Dynamics and Effects," *New Outlook for the Blind*, 1974, *68*, 105–18.

Chapter 13

The aurally handicapped

THE SIGNIFICANCE OF AURAL HANDICAPS

Because of the low visibility of auditory defects, and because the hard-of-hearing are often suspected of being unmotivated, inattentive, or mentally retarded, the general public has lacked interest in and sympathy for the aurally handicapped. The normal person can close his eyes and move about in total darkness and achieve some conception of the nature of blindness. The average individual has been temporarily orthopedically handicapped and has obtained some idea of the problems of the crippled. However, one cannot close his ears. Even inserting ear plugs does not approximate the condition of the average person with a serious auditory deficit. The nonhandicapped individual typically is either apathetic or impatient with the acoustically handicapped person.

In many respects, the deaf are a misunderstood, disadvantaged minority. For example, while there are legal precedents requiring courts to provide interpreters without cost for the deaf as well as for those who do not speak English, only a few states have legislated this requirement for the deaf. Even with competent interpreters the language gulf presents serious problems. The sign language of the deaf lacks precise equivalent words for many commonplace legal terms. When literal translation is impossible, interpreters attempt to convey the sense of the statements. This often raises the objections of judges and opposing lawyers.

The young child with defective hearing often does not realize the nature of his problems, and few nonhandicapped adults are aware of the breadth of the problems of the aurally handicapped. The failure of the congenitally deaf child to acquire speech in the ordinary way, and his inability to hear the speech of others, are his most obvious handicaps. However, the oral and aural handicaps of the deaf and the severely hard-of-hearing are much broader than this. Sharing a common language is a prerequisite to full integration of a child into family, community, and society. To a degree, the problems of the deaf resemble those of minority group members who lack adequate command of English. Adequate hearing and speaking are tremendous aids to cooperative behavior. Sounds—

even nonverbal ones—act as guides to behavior and to understanding. Hearing is normally a major source of pleasurable social experience. A common language is our principal means of social interaction. In addition to being two of our prime avenues of information, hearing and speech contribute to social acceptance as well as to one's feeling of personal security, and they also aid in the learning and maintaining of nonverbal skills. That severely and profoundly deaf but otherwise normal children sit up, crawl, and walk later than their normal siblings indicates the importance of hearing and speech in the development of nonverbal habits. The severely aurally handicapped child lacks much more than his ability to hear other people and to acquire speech in the ordinary developmental way. Loss of hearing not only results in an impoverished informational environment; it also entails a restriction of the child's incentives to explore his world, a reduction in the things to become curious about.

DEFINITIONS

Within special education, the deaf and the hard-of-hearing are usually differentiated. These two subgroups are not homogeneous, and further subclassifications are often made. Such subgroups are usually based on the degree of hearing impairment, the cause of the deficit, or the age of the person at the onset of the disability.

The two types of definitions of exceptionality mentioned in earlier chapters—the quantitative and the psychological, educational, and social —are found in the literature on the aurally handicapped. The quantitative definitions typically indicate auditory disability as the degree of hearing loss measured audiometrically in terms of decibels (db). (Hearing loss refers to the deficit in the better ear in the speech range of frequencies.) The following definitions and categorizations are representative of this type.

> *Class 1. Mild losses (20 to 30 db).* People with hearing losses in this range learn to speak by ear in the ordinary developmental way, and are borderline between the hard-of-hearing and the normal.
> *Class 2. Marginal losses (30 to 40 db).* People with such losses usually have some difficulty in hearing speech at a distance of more than a few feet, and in following conversation. Speech can be learned by ear.
> *Class 3. Moderate losses (40 to 60 db).* With amplification of sound and the assistance of vision, people with hearing in this range can learn speech aurally.
> *Class 4. Severe losses (60 to 75 db).* People with hearing losses in this range

will not acquire speech without the use of specialized techniques. Most such people are considered "educationally deaf." They are borderline between the hard-of-hearing and the deaf.

   Class 5. Profound losses (greater than 75 db). People with hearing in this range seldom learn language by ear alone, even with maximum amplification of sound.

People in classes 1, 2, and 3 are considered to be *hard-of-hearing,* while those in classes 4 and 5 constitute the *deaf.* The use of subgroups is a recognition that there are tremendous differences between the hard-of-hearing and the deaf, as audiometrically defined.

An alternative proposal, by a committee of the American Medical Association (1961), is to indicate hearing loss in terms of percentages rather than in decibels.

The more functionally-oriented definition proposed by the White House Conference on Child Health and Protection (1931) distinguishes between the hard-of-hearing and the deaf primarily in terms of the *age of onset of the hearing loss.* This formulation defines as deaf: (1) those persons who are born with sufficient hearing loss to prevent the spontaneous acquisition of speech; (2) those who became deaf before language and speech were established; and (3) those who became deaf so soon after speech and language were acquired that these skills have been practically lost. The *hard-of-hearing* are defined as those persons who acquired useful speech and the ability to understand speech *prior to their hearing loss,* and who have continued to use these skills.

This conception violates the common-sense use of "deaf" and "hard-of-hearing," which refers to the degree of loss rather than to the age at which the sense of hearing was lost. According to this definition, an individual with an 80-decibel, congenital loss of hearing is called "deaf"; another person, with the same loss but dating from the age of ten, is called "hard-of-hearing." Such use does unnecessary violence to the common-sense meanings of the terms.

The definition of the Committee on Nomenclature of the Conference of Executives of American Schools for the Deaf (1938) is simpler and more practical. In their terms, the deaf are those people in whom the sense of hearing is nonfunctional for the ordinary purposes of life, while the hard-of-hearing are those in whom the sense of hearing, although defective, is functional with or without a hearing aid. The deaf are then subdivided into: (1) the congenitally deaf; and (2) the adventitiously deaf, who were born with normal hearing but whose hearing became nonfunctional through accident or disease. We shall use the nomenclature of the Executives of American Schools for the Deaf in our discussion.

The aurally handicapped are sometimes subdivided according to whether the hearing loss is purely conductive (conduction deafness) or is the result of sensory-neural impairment (neural deafness). Since conduction deafness usually can be greatly aided by sound amplification systems (hearing aids), whereas sensory-neural impairment is less amenable to such treatment, the difference between the two is of social and educational, as well as of medical, significance.

It is often necessary, for legal and administrative purposes, to use audiometric definitions and classifications of aural impairment. However, the functional criteria, though vague, are more educationally and psychologically meaningful. Of course, there is a fairly high correlation between the two criteria. For example, it is possible to say that most people with hearing losses within designated, pure-tone, audiometrically defined limits have specified functional limitations. But there are exceptions. Individuals with the same threshold for pure tone often vary greatly in their behavioral (social, psychological, and educational) impairment. It is possible for almost any degree of residual hearing to become functional for most of the "ordinary purposes of life." Possibly only total loss of hearing, which is extremely rare, precludes any functional usefulness. This means that functional utility is a matter of degree, and cannot be divided into two discrete categories. With intensive auditory training, children reported to have "99 percent bilateral loss of hearing" have learned to speak spontaneously and to interpret speech aurally (Wedenberg, 1951, 1955). Conversely, children who experience only a partial hearing loss after speech and language are well established may, under unfavorable conditions, have these skills deteriorate and become functionally deaf and unintelligible. In other words, it is possible, with proper training, for small amounts of residual hearing to become socially and educationally useful. It is also possible for individuals with auditory potential well within the useful range to fail to use it, or to cease to use previously acquired language skills and become functionally deaf. Degree of hearing loss is only slightly related to employment status (Miller, Kunce, & Getsinger, 1972). The range of individual differences among the aurally impaired is as significant as is the mean difference between the normal and the aurally impaired. Persons with identical audiometric characteristics get along very differently in daily life (Ewertson & Birk-Nielsen, 1973). Labels and formal categories have some usefulness, but they can never be substituted for information concerning the individual person under study.

The aurally impaired, like all other categories of the handicapped, are referred to by a variety of terms with various degrees of stigmatizing connotations. One study found that of several labels commonly used— *deaf, deaf-mute, deaf and dumb, hard-of-hearing,* and *hearing impaired—*

the last term, *hearing impaired*, was the least stigmatizing (Wilson, Ross, & Calvert, 1974).

SYMPTOMS OF HEARING LOSS

An infant severely or profoundly deaf from birth experiences emotion, cries, and initially vocalizes much as does a baby whose hearing is unimpaired. Because such a child seems dominantly normal, his auditory defect may not be suspected—or, if it is suspected, it may not be definitely established for some time. Not until the deaf infant is six months old and starting to babble do his sound patterns become differentiated from those of infants who can hear. Often, the failure of the child to speak at the normal age first causes parental concern. Symptoms such as the infant's failure to jump or blink his eyes are often not noticed. Being oblivious to ordinary noises may be perceived as evidence that the infant is a "good" baby.

One mother has described her discovery of deafness in her nine-month-old son: "My child was stirring from his nap. His back was toward me and he was looking out the window. I called out to him but he did not respond. Drawing nearer, I called his name louder. Still no response! I approached on the run and by the time I reached the end of his crib I was shouting, but he still did not turn. Then he saw me and held out his arms. Ronnie was deaf!" (Rhodes, 1972).

Many of the symptoms of deafness, such as poor articulation, delayed speech, and lack of responsiveness, are found in mentally retarded, emotionally disturbed, and brain-damaged children, as well as in some otherwise normal children. In the absence of physical signs of pathology, such as malformations of the ears, absence of the ear canal, or chronic discharge from the ears, it is not easy for parents to discover deafness in a child before the age when he normally begins to talk.

The general symptoms of auditory deficit in older children are:

1. Apparent chronic inattention
2. Frequent failure to respond when spoken to
3. Marked delay in age of speaking or unusually faulty articulation
4. Apparent backwardness in school despite adequate tested intelligence

TESTS FOR IDENTIFYING THE AURALLY IMPAIRED

Studies have uniformly shown that a relatively small proportion of children who are aurally impaired are identified by behavioral symptoms alone. One research report indicates that teachers do only slightly better than chance in detecting hearing losses among their students (Curry, 1954). Many studies document the need for audiometric testing for the identification of the majority of children with significant hearing losses (Kodman et al., 1959; Nagafuchi, 1974). The range of testing devices and procedures used in the detection and measurement of auditory loss is very wide.

Unstandardized tests of hearing

Noise makers of various types, the oldest devices for testing hearing, are still widely used. For the very young child, a cowbell, a metal cricket which produces a loud snap, or a castanet may be used. The intensity level of the sounds should be fairly high. Responses such as the following are considered indicative of hearing: momentary cessation of random movements, body start (Moro reflex), blinking of the eyes, finger or toe spreading or clenching, and turning the head or eyes in the direction of the sound (Thompon & Weber, 1974).

The old "watch" and "whisper" tests attempted to standardize sounds and procedures to some extent. In the former, the old "Ingersoll" pocket watch was held four feet from each ear in turn, with the other ear plugged. The watch was then gradually withdrawn until the person could not hear it. The reverse procedure was then followed; the average of the two minimum distances at which the tick could be heard provided a rough measure of auditory acuity.

In the whisper test, the person tested stands twenty feet away with his back to the tester and repeats what is whispered. If the testee fails at twenty feet the tester moves closer until the testee is able to repeat the words whispered. Auditory deficit is estimated from the relative reduction in distance required for the repetition to be correct.

Appropriately tuned tuning forks were also used to present different-pitched tones to the person to be tested. However, unless calibrated, mechanical activating devices are used, relative loudness is uncontrolled and such devices can provide only rough approximations of auditory defect. One noise maker of known frequency and intensity characteristics is now available commercially (Lillywhite, Young, & Olmsted, 1970).

A refinement of this type of test has been developed and used by F. B. Simmons at the Stanford University School of Medicine. The test involves an automated device for recording an infant's movements in its crib when a test sound is applied. The automated system uses an inexpensive motion detector mounted on the frame of the crib, which records the infant's activity on a paper tape before, during, and after a test sound is emitted from a microphone located in the nursery ceiling. The system currently monitors thirty-two cribs simultaneously and is capable of testing six hundred babies an hour. The average cost of screening with this device is said to be only eighty-five cents per child (News and Reports, Children Today, 1974).

Pure-tone audiometers

The modern audiometers most frequently used are electronic devices which produce tones of variable frequency (pitch) and intensity (loudness) over a wide range. Today, practically every complete test and analysis of a person's hearing involves the use of the pure-tone audiometer. The testing consists of the systematic sounding of a series of tones varying in pitch and loudness. The person being tested hears the tones through earphones and responds by saying "Now" or by pressing a button whenever the tone is heard. The test results are typically plotted on an audiogram which provides a graphic representation of the acuity of each ear for various frequencies. Many audiologists have replaced the manual audiometer with an automatic one devised by G. von Békésy (Sala & Babeghian, 1973).

The phonographic audiometer

These devices are phonographs with the desired number (from ten to forty) of telephone receivers attached. Calibrated recordings of both male and female voices are played, and the voices grow gradually less distinct until the material spoken—usually digits or words—can be heard only by people with normal or superior hearing. Each ear is tested separately. The child being tested responds by writing in appropriate blanks, checking the proper word, or marking the picture of the object named. Tests with the phonographic audiometer are calibrated and standardized, and make possible the rapid screening of large numbers of children. More recent developments along this line are usually known as "speech perception tests."

Speech perception tests

Speech perception tests measure perception for speech in a manner somewhat like the whisper test and older phonographic audiometric tests. The American Medical Association has developed tests of the threshold of speech perception. These tests use standardized speech material which is presented either on commercial recordings or via the live voice, monitored and controlled for intensity (O'Niell, 1964). The Central Institute for the Deaf in St. Louis has developed a Social Adequacy Index to indicate the degree of difficulty an aurally impaired individual has in ordinary communication (Davis, 1948; O'Neill, 1964). H. Davis (1973) claims that speech audiometry provides a much better indication of the *functional level* of the ear than does pure-tone audiometry.

A large repertoire of tests have been devised to supplement conventional audiometric methods. These are used largely to test the hard-to-test child, such as the very young, suspected malingerers, persons apparently functionally deaf (psychic deafness), mentally retarded, the hyperactive, and the multi-handicapped (Galkowski, 1974). One group of these tests, like some mentioned earlier, depend on the motor response to sound. However, instead of depending on overt movements, the tests often use the *stapedial reflex response*. An audible sound causes a reflex contraction of the tiny stapedius muscle within the middle ear. This muscle attaches to the stapes, the smallest of the three tiny bones spanning the middle ear which transmit the sound vibrations to the inner ear. To detect this contraction, an acoustic probe must be inserted into one ear to make contact with the stapedius muscle (Beagley, 1973). J. Jerger et al. (1974) claim that this method agrees with ordinary audiometric procedures in 96 percent of the cases tested.

Electroencephalogram (EEG) or brain-wave audiometry has also been used. This consists of observing changes in the amplitude of the EEG in response to sound. However, because of the large amplitude and high variability in the background EEG and the lack of specificity of the response, EEG audiometry has been largely replaced by less variable methods.

The psychogalvanic skin response has also been used as an index of hearing in hard-to-test children.

Evoked response audiometry developed from the EEG audiometry described above. This fairly complicated technique involves summing the electrical variations (evoked potentials) which are produced when audible short bursts of sound are heard. A small digital computer or similar device sums or averages these sound-evoked electrical variations while largely ignoring the ongoing background EEG (Cody & Sownsend, 1973). H. A. Beagley (1973) claims that evoked response audiometry can yield audiograms which agree well with those obtained in the usual way.

Electrocochleography is a direct measurement of the electrical output of the cochlea. This technique requires a penetration of the ear drum under local or general anesthesia and the placing of an electrode in contact with the inner wall of the middle ear. From this electrode the electric output of the cochlea can be recorded.

Differential diagnostic auditory tests

Bone conduction tests have been employed since the early part of the nineteenth century to differentiate conduction from sensori-neural hearing losses. In these tests a tuning fork or bone-conduction vibrator transmits sounds to the forehead. If the auditory impairment is due to defects in the conduction apparatus (peripheral to the inner ear), hearing by bone conduction will be better than by air conduction. In bone conduction the ordinary air conduction components are bypassed and the vibrations are conducted by the bones of the skull directly to the fluids of the inner ear. If the defect is sensori-neural (in the cochlea or the auditory nerve), bone conduction is no more effective than air conduction. In a modern version of this test, a bone-conduction vibrator is applied to the forehead, held by a headband. The vibrator is activated by words spoken into a microphone and transmitted to the vibrator. The patient repeats the words he hears and raises his right or left hand to indicate on which side he hears them. Lateralization is made toward the deafer ear with a conduction loss and toward the better ear with a sensori-neural hearing loss (Davis, 1973).

Several researchers have also devised tests to assist in determining the locations of lesions in sensori-neural auditory impairment (Shulman & Edelman, 1973; Brasier, 1973).

Other testing methods

A large number of ingenious variations of both formal and informal methods of testing auditory acuity have been developed. For example, warbled pure tones have been found to be more effective than steady tones with children who have difficulty in attending (Douglas, Fowler, & Ryan, 1961). One test for children uses a simple Go-Game, in which they make a simple motor response whenever the word "Go!" is heard (Dale, 1962). Music, noise makers, and animal sounds have been used as stimuli, both for measurement and for warm-up exercises which provide rough preliminary assessment of the child's hearing (Reichstein & Rosenstein, 1964).

Conditioned response methods, in which the appropriate response is rewarded, have taken several forms (Waldon, 1973). In one of these, the child looks into a darkened house. When he hears a tone, he pushes a button which illuminates the interior of the house and revolves a group of dolls (Dix & Hallpike, 1947). Another such device yields candy and knickknacks when the child responds to the auditory stimuli (Meyerson & Michael, 1960). Studies indicate that children whose responses are rewarded perform significantly better than children who are not rewarded (Reichstein & Rosenstein, 1964). Two Danish researchers have constructed a social-learning handicap index to indicate hearing handicap in daily life (Ewertsen & Birk-Nielsen, 1973).

CAUSES OF AUDITORY DEFECTS

Some auditory defects are inherited. There is a hereditary type of degenerative nerve deafness which may be present at birth or develop later in life. Infections such as German measles (rubella) in early pregnancy, as well as influenza and mumps, may cause congenital deafness which is not hereditary. Occasionally, a child is born with an absence or malformation of the ear canal, ear drum, or the ossicles of the middle ear. Although the development of a vaccine for the prevention of rubella may result in its elimination, there are currently many rubella-deafened children in special education and rehabilitation programs. While hearing loss is the most common defect associated with rubella, other anomalies such as cataracts, heart disease, microcephaly, diffuse brain damage, and motor disabilities are also common (Jensema, 1974). Consequently, most of these children have very special educational and rehabilitation needs.

Postnatal causes of auditory defects include most of the childhood diseases—scarlet fever, mumps, measles, and whooping cough. Occasionally, typhoid fever, pneumonia, influenza, and meningitis result in injury to the auditory mechanism. A common but decreasingly important cause of auditory loss is chronic infection of the middle ear (*otitis media*). Among adults, intracranial tumors, cerebral hemorrhage, prolonged exposure to tones of high intensity, and degenerative processes in the auditory mechanism are increasingly important causes of deafness. In approximately one-third of all cases, the causes of deafness are unknown (Vernon, 1968a; Schein & Delk, 1974). It is estimated that occupational noise is responsible for more sensori-neural hearing loss than all other causes combined (Glorig, 1972). Continual or repeated high-intensity noises in the frequency range above 500 Hz (Hz = Hertz = cycles per second) do the most damage to the ear. The passage of the 1970 Occupational Safety and Health Act encouraged employers to become concerned about potentially hazardous noises in their plants (Glorig, 1972). Recent surveys in the British Isles and in Australia find genetic and environmental causes of profound deafness to be of about equal importance (Fraser, 1974).

THE INCIDENCE OF AUDITORY DEFECTS

From 1830 through 1930 the United States Bureau of the Census included an enumeration of deaf persons in each decennial census. Prevalence rates provided by these data were so erratic (a rate of 32.1 per 100,000 in 1900, compared with 67.5 in 1880) that the Bureau discontinued the enumeration of deafness and other disabilities after 1930 and recommended that a separate agency be established for that purpose. Not until forty years later was a federal grant provided to the National Association of the Deaf to make a national census of the deaf population. (Schein & Delk, 1974). According to J. D. Schein and M. T. Delk, Jr., experts had considered the prevalence rates for deafness to be about 1 per 1,000. The Schein and Delk survey estimates deafness at about 2 per 1,000—twice the assumed rate. The Bureau of the Census counted 47 deaf persons per 100,000 in 1930; the Schein and Delk survey estimates 203 per 100,000. The authors doubt that this increase is due to inaccuracies in the two enumerations: "There seems little doubt that there are proportionally, as well as actually, more deaf people today than forty years ago." The 1974 national survey of the deaf estimates that 13.4 million persons in the United States have a significant impairment of hearing. Of these, 1.8 million are deaf. These data indicate that impairment of hearing is the single most prevalent chronic disability in the United States (Schein & Delk, 1974).

Among adults, progressive nerve deterioration (prebycusis) is the most common type of auditory defect. The relationship between age and the incidence of impaired hearing (principally prebycusis) is shown in table 13–1.

The aging process is said to produce a hearing loss of 160 cycles per year from the upper frequency limits, so that most individuals past

Table 13–1
Incidence of impaired hearing as related to age (per 1,000)

Age	Incidence
45–54	36
55–64	64
65–75	125
Above 75	226

Data from United States Department of Health, Education and Welfare (1961).

middle age have little hearing above 10,000 cycles. There is a more or less normal course of maturation and decline of hearing abilities. Maturation is a gradual process which reaches its maximum between ten and thirteen years with no significant change until late maturity. Statistically the entire population of elderly people have a hearing loss of approximately one decibel a year. This means that between the ages of 65 and 85, when this loss becomes significant, the average person will experience a cumulative hearing loss of 20 decibels (Rupp, 1971; Fior, 1972).

PERSONAL CHARACTERISTICS
OF THE ACOUSTICALLY HANDICAPPED

Questions concerning the intellectual, personality, and behavioral characteristics of children with auditory defects sound deceptively simple. Such questions typically assume some specific but unspecified criterion for identifying people who are deaf or hard-of-hearing. But "hard-of-hearing" sometimes includes people with measurable but not necessarily handicapping losses in one or both ears (if a pure-tone audiometric test is used). Sometimes the same term refers to people whose perceptions of speech are functional but defective (a social-utility criterion). Some who follow the recommendations of the White House Conference use the term to refer to any impaired individual who, regardless of the degree of auditory impairment, has developed speech and language in the ordinary developmental way. When we deal with data about groups variously defined, and assume that they are the same population, we get many different and apparently contradictory answers to our questions. In the absence of a single acceptable criterion of deafnes, information about the characteristics of the deaf has limited usefulness.

Obtaining adequate samplings of a defined population is also difficult. Investigators with limited time, money, and facilities have had to study groups that were available. These groups have practically always been selected populations—students in special schools, special classes, or patients referred to clinics or practitioners. It is probable that children in residential schools contain a disproportionate number of people with multiple handicaps. In addition to their auditory defects, these children are often brain-damaged, aphasic, epileptic, emotionally disturbed, and may have impaired vision bordering on blindness. While these children all have auditory defects, the impairment of hearing is often not their greatest problem, nor is it the primary cause of their placement in residential schools. With the development of more special classes for the acoustically handicapped within the regular schools and the increased integration of handicapped students with the normal, the population of residential schools is changing to such a degree that the students of to-day are not comparable to those of twenty years ago. Children who attend residential schools are more severely aurally handicapped, are less academically able, have lived in less favorable psychological environ-ments, and have more multiple handicaps than children attending special day-school classes or ordinary public or private schools. Special resi-dential schools and special education classes probably enroll a dispro-portionate number of problem children, regardless of the degree of auditory impairment.

Assuming that we have access to a defined group of unselected acous-tically handicapped, typical of a designated population, what are the proper questions to ask concerning them? Do we want to know the edu-cational, personality, intellectual, and social characteristics of the acous-tically handicapped as a group, irrespective of kind or degree of auditory impairment, linguistic ability, social origins, or place of residence? When the average person asks what people with auditory handicaps are like, he seems to be asking some such question. However, the answer would probably be meaningless. Suppose we find, as we usually do, that the acoustically handicapped are somewhat below the average of the non-handicapped population in all of these areas. What would it mean? Anal-ysis might show that the deficit in these areas is contributed almost entirely by a comparatively small group of severely impaired, multipally handicapped, institutionalized individuals. The rest of the acoustically deficient are essentially normal in other respects.

Perhaps the more appropriate question is: "What are the character-istics of people with various degrees of impaired hearing and no other disability?" The authors have found no studies which answer this ques-tion. However, if we had an answer, we might then ask, "What, if any, are the additional handicapping effects of institutionalization, and of various degrees of physical and other sensory impairments?" Conversely, we can also ask what types of medical care and treatment, home situa-tions, social provisions, and educational programs minimize these dele-terious influences. With these limitations in mind, we will briefly summarize the present state of our information concerning people with impaired hearing.

Intelligence level of the acoustically handicapped

Studies of handicapped groups have typically begun with attempts to determine how the intelligence of the group compares with comparable nonhandicapped persons.

Over a half-century ago, R. Pintner and D. G. Paterson (1915) used a modification of the Goddard Revision of the Binet-Simon Scale to test eighteen deaf children. They obtained a mean IQ of 63. Since that time, dozens of studies have compared the intelligence test performances of various groups of acoustically impaired people with the acoustically normal. Because of the language handicap of the majority of the severely aurally impaired, verbal tests of intelligence have seldom been used in such studies. Surveys of available studies show a great diversity of results. For example, L. Meyerson (1963) surveyed twenty-five studies. Ten, using individual performance tests, reported lower than normal IQ's for deaf children. The median IQ of the means reported in the ten studies is 91. In twelve studies, no significant differences between the deaf and the acoustically normal were reported. In three, the deaf were found to have higher IQ's. Studies using *group tests* have reported slightly lower mean IQ's for the aurally impaired than have those using individual tests. In the same review, Meyerson surveyed twelve studies using *group* non-verbal or nonlanguage tests. He found the median IQ of the reported means of eight studies to be 85. Four studies reported insignificant differences, and none of them found higher IQ's for the deaf children. Since the 1930s and '40s, interest in the general question of the intelligence of the aurally handicapped seems to have decreased. The authors' tabulation of thirty-six major studies according to year of publication is shown in table 13–2.

There are probably several reasons for the declining interest in the question of the general intellectual level of people with sensory deficits. Workers in the field have decided that a simple statement of the mean IQ of all people with auditory defects is neither meaningful nor useful. To be meaningful, measurements must be of people with a specified type of handicap, degree of impairment, age of onset of the disability, degree of language deficit, chronological age, and background. The tests used must also be specified as group or individual, language or non-language, omnibus or analytical. The problem of the intellectual level of the acoustically impaired breaks down into dozens of smaller, more specific, but more meaningful subproblems.

Our changing conceptions of the nature and components of intelligence have also reduced interest in the general question of the intellectual level of people with auditory defects. Before the 1930s, intelligence was generally considered to be primarily a genetically determined, innate ability to learn. If a child was born with little potential, there was not much to be done about it. Heredity was thought to place definite limits on achievement, and environmental influences were thought to operate only within these limits.

Starting in the late '20s and continuing through the '30s and '40s, a long series of studies demonstrated that environmental changes have

Table 13–2
Years of publication of studies of the intelligence test scores
of the aurally impaired

Year	Number of Studies
1910–1919	1
1920–1929	4
1930–1939	16
1940–1949	12
1950–1959	3
	Total = 36

significant effects on intelligence test scores. This change from an extreme hereditarian to a more environmental emphasis was accentuated during the '50s and '60s by a series of studies of the effects of environmental deprivations on intellectual level. Intelligence, as measured, is currently recognized to be a product of both genetic and environmental factors. It is partially a social product. Intelligence test scores are rough indices of functional level, implying no particular information about the determinants of that level.

In the absence of evidence that inferior intelligence and hereditary deafness are genetically linked, we assume that the hereditary determinants of the intellectual level of deaf children are not significantly different from those of their siblings with normal hearing. Differences in their intellectual functioning must then be due to environmental differences. The question of the possible intellectual inferiority of the sensorially handicapped becomes a question of the extent to which the sensory deprivation has influenced the individual's level of intellectual functioning.

Partially because of these considerations, interest has shifted from the general question to that of ways in which the restrictions of auditory input affect the level and pattern of intellectual functioning. In special education, interest focuses primarily on the question of the most effective means of compensating for the auditory deficit. The extent of deficit of intellectual and behavioral functioning in uncomplicated cases of deafness is conceived of as an index of the extent to which the culture has failed to develop or use devices and methods for compensating for the sensory limitations. Special education assumes that specific methods of training and educating handicapped children do make a difference in their functional level. Deaf children learn, or fail to learn, self-help and independence, as well as the fundamental educational and vocational skills, according to the adequacy and availability of the required specialized educational and training resources. In such a frame of reference, the effect of deafness on intelligence becomes part of the question of its effect on achievement (Reynolds, 1965).[1]

Some researchers believe that although the general intellectual level of the aurally impaired child may not be inferior to that of comparable children with normal hearing, the perceptual and conceptual processes of congenitally deaf children fail to develop in a comparable way (Myklebust, 1953, 1960; Farrant, 1964). This view is supported by some studies (Hughes, 1959) dealing primarily with *verbal* conceptualization, but the bulk of the investigations indicate that in processes not requiring verbalization, or when the verbalizations required are within the vocabulary range and experience of the subjects, the deaf do as well as hearing subjects in abstract conceptualization (Bornstein & Roy, 1973; Henderson & Henderson, 1973; Furth, 1971, 1973; Suppes, 1974; Ross & Hoemann, 1975; Kates, 1967). Deaf subjects have less adequate verbalization than do hearing subjects, and a larger proportion of adequate conceptual categorizations which are accompanied by inadequate verbalizations than do hearing subjects of the same age and IQ. These differences in verbalization disappear when hearing and deaf subjects are equated as to age, IQ, and educational achievement. Educational attainment probably equates verbalization. These studies also find no evidence of greater rigidity (less flexibility in the strategies of concept attainment) in the deaf subjects.

Educational achievement of the aurally impaired

The studies of educational achievement have uniformly shown the deaf to be retarded from three to five years. The absolute amount of educational retardation increases with age (Schein & Delk, 1974). H. G. Furth (1971) states that the average reading level of deaf pupils is only about grade 3. Only 10 percent of the deaf read above the fourth-grade level. Educational retardation is less in the more mechanical skills, such as arithmetic computation and spelling, than in the more intellectual areas, such as paragraph meanings, word meanings, and arithmetic comprehension. Language and communication lag behind the motor and computational skills (Furth, 1971, 1973).

Students applying for admission to the preparatory class at Gallaudet College, who probably represent the best students graduating from the residential schools for the deaf, have a mean age of eighteen years and nine months and obtain a median grade of 9.2 on the Stanford Achievement Test. This level is attained by the average fifteen-year-old hearing child

[1] For more detailed discussion, see Vernon (1968b) and Vernon and Miller (1974).

(Fusfeld, 1954). This group of students, probably highly selected in terms of educational achievement, is retarded by three to four years. About 12 percent of the deaf population twenty-five to sixty-four years of age have gone to college, and half of these earned baccalaureate degrees. These figures are about one-third that of the general population (Schein & Delk, 1974). The educational retardation of deaf children may be partially the result of the excessive amount of school time required for them to learn to speak and their subsequent language deficiencies. The development of improved methods for teaching these children, and the increasing number of children who acquire language in the home, nursery school, and kindergarten prior to beginning their academic education, may help reduce the extent of their educational retardation. M. Vernon (1971) claims that deaf persons who from the first use finger spelling and sign language do better academically than do those children who have been limited to oral communication.

Personal and social adjustment of the aurally impaired

The statements made in earlier chapters concerning the personal and social adjustment of handicapped people in general hold true for the deaf and the hard-of-hearing. Research studies of the personal and social traits of the aurally impaired show a higher degree of emotional instability, neuroticism, and social maladjustment than do the appropriate norm groups (Fiedler, 1952; Levine, 1960; Schein, 1975). The barriers of deafness and limited language certainly increase the total incidence of frustration, loneliness, helplessness, and despair. However, the deaf child need not be psychologically different from the child who hears. Although the aurally handicapped are more maladjusted than are the normal, they show no distinctive forms or patterns of maladjustment. The adjustment patterns in deaf and hard-of-hearing children are as varied as they are in hearing children. Most of these problems do not derive directly from the hearing loss; they are accentuated by the child's primary handicap but cannot be traced directly to his hearing.

Like most other disadvantaged groups, the deaf display a greater tendency than normals to limit their levels of aspiration in the interest of avoiding failure rather than striving for the approval of high achievement (Stinson, 1974). L. R. Bowyer and J. Gillies (1972) find no significant difference between deaf and partially deaf children in terms of their social and emotional adjustment.

When hearing people are unable to communicate with deaf people in a mutually satisfactory way, they often stop trying to do so and either ignore or avoid them altogether. This leaves the auditorily handicapped alone and encourages their retreat into isolation. We pointed out in chapter 2 how the nonhandicapped avoid the handicapped out of a combination of self-consciousness and uncertainty about the right way to act with a deviant person (Thayer, 1973).

SOCIAL ORGANIZATIONS OF THE DEAF

The deaf have been the most active of the handicapped groups in organizing independently on their behalf. The many communities of deaf adults are largely the natural result of people joining with their own kind for mutual pleasure and benefit. The prime reason deaf adults assemble together is the relatively free and easy communication they can enjoy. Like most such groups, their mutual problems and interests hold them together. Deaf adults rarely find it possible or enjoyable to integrate wholly with the hearing. The commonalities which bind them together also account for the fact that 95 percent of deaf marry other deaf (Jacobs, 1974).

Many national and state organizations of the deaf have local chapters. In 1967 the federal government sponsored the formation of the Council of Organizations Serving the Deaf as a central coordinating agency. There are many local social clubs with their own athletic teams and leagues. In nearly every large city, there is at least one organization of the deaf which rents social halls for various activities; the only qualification for membership in most of these clubs is deafness.

In many large cities, religious services for the deaf range from providing interpreters to having full-time ministers for deaf members. The Lutheran Church in Los Angeles has provided a successful housing program for deaf senior citizens. In New York City the Jewish deaf have their own synagogues, social clubs, and a senior citizens housing unit (Tanya Towers). Several television programs are either translated or produced for the deaf. Annually, the *American Annals of the Deaf* publishes a directory of special services and programs.

A device now commercially available allows the deaf to converse on the telephone. It consists of a regular telephone connected to a teletype machine. A light indicates to the deaf person that someone on the other end has picked up the receiver. The caller then types his message on his teletype and waits for the reply. Calls can, of course, be made only to parties with similar devices. There is a portable machine that can be hooked up to any telephone (Leszczynski, 1975). Unfortunately, the equipment costs about $250 minimum and upkeep is fairly expensive (Schein & Delk, 1974).

MEDICAL ASPECTS OF HEARING LOSS

Medical care and surgery can do a lot to improve certain types of hearing loss. Individuals with middle-ear damage have a very good chance of obtaining improved hearing as a result of appropriate surgery or appropriate hearing aids.

Surgery

Some of the more common surgical operative procedures are:

1. *Fenestration of the labyrinth.* A new oval window is made into the horizontal semicircular canal of the inner ear. The artificial window is closed with a membrane which acts as a sound-sensitive surface, picking up the sound waves directly and bypassing the bones of the inner ear.
2. *Mobilization of the stapes.* The plate of the stapes (the bone which attaches to the oval window) is loosened by breaking away the excess bone impeding its action. About 80 percent of these operations are said to be successful (Gildston & Gildston, 1972).
3. *Artificial replacement of the stapes.*
4. *Covering tympanic drum perforations with skin grafts.*

Today, the otological surgeon can change the shape of the middle ear; rebuild the ossicular chain (the three bones spanning the middle ear); repair, move into a new position, or make a new tympanic membrane; construct new functional membranous windows into the inner ear; and make a bony canal into the middle ear when an infant is born without one (Proctor, 1961).

At present, there is no known medical or surgical means of significantly improving nerve deafness. The approximately 20 percent of deaf children who are deaf because of meningitis, mumps, acute fevers, or other forms of injury to the inner ear or auditory nerve cannot be helped surgically. Because of the constant development of new surgical procedures, however, every person with a serious hearing loss should have a complete otological examination and be advised of the possibilities of medical or surgical treatment.

Hearing aids

Modern hearing aids can be used in place of, or in addition to, surgical procedures to improve the hearing of a large percentage of people with conduction deafness. A hearing aid is primarily a sound amplifier. The earphone simply increases the loudness of sounds; a person must have some residual hearing to profit by sound amplification. The person with conduction deafness (outer or middle-ear impairment) can profit more from hearing aids than can the person with perceptive or nerve deafness (injury to the middle ear or auditory nerve).

Improvements in hearing aids are being made continuously, and every person with some residual hearing should probably consider their use. It is estimated that not more than one person in three who could be helped by a hearing aid owns and uses one (Van Itallie, 1962; Schein & Delk, 1974; Maltzman, 1949; Gentile, Schein, and Hasse, 1967). People with aural impairments fail to use hearing aids for several reasons. Some are unaware of the possibilities offered by modern hearing aids. Many are restrained by vanity or self-consciousness. Some of the deaf and hard-of-hearing have become resigned to their restricted world and are either apathetic or resistant to help. Many people have tried hearing aids and then discarded them. Most of these people can profit from counseling. The first group may simply need information concerning the nature and availability of hearing aids. Those restrained by vanity may be helped to realize that when a person needs and can profit by a hearing aid, he is probably more conspicuous when he does not wear one than when he does. The social blunders of the person who hears only half of what is said are much more obvious than is an inconspicuous hearing aid. The adolescent girl who will not wear a hearing aid when she needs one makes social errors, the consequences of which are far greater than being recognized as a person with a hearing loss sufficient to require a hearing aid, but otherwise normal. Many people who discard their hearing aids after a short trial expect too much and do not realize that a considerable period of adjustment and new learning is required before a hearing aid can be tolerated and used effectively.

The limitations of hearing aids   Some people cannot profit sufficiently from hearing aids to warrant their use, some expect too much from them, and some have developed habits which preclude their effective use. There are people with certain kinds of inner-ear (nerve) deafness who cannot tolerate hearing aids. The person with nerve deafness often has an irregular pattern of auditory loss. A hearing aid with equal amplification of all frequencies will make some sounds unbearably loud while it is making others just audible. Some earphones provide greater amplification of higher tones, but this often produces intolerable distortion. The accentuation of high tones and suppression of the low frequencies sometimes produce such a radical change in patterns of stimulation that the person's habitual patterns of auditory perception are severely disrupted (Anderson, 1967).

Several attempts have been made to shift or transpose high-frequency speech sounds to lower ranges so as to make them more audible to people with residual hearing in the low frequencies. Since most deaf individuals have some residual hearing in the very low frequencies, the successful devising of practical means of doing this would be of considerable significance (Quigley, 1969). Preliminary studies indicate that selective amplification of particular frequencies to fit individual hearing losses is practical and is superior to the flat amplification of a broad band of frequencies as found in most conventional hearing aids (Reddell & Calvert, 1966; Quigley, 1969).

P. Kuyper (1972) claims that a person with two equally impaired ears should wear two hearing aids. This produces better directional hearing and suppression of acoustical sound shadows. It also produces better understanding of language in an environment of interfering sounds (the "cocktail party effect"). With two-ear hearing, the individual in a crowd feels himself to be in the center of the sources of sound. All sounds do not seem to come from one side, and he feels less threatened by possible unforeseen occurrences. In a group he can quickly identify the person who is speaking and employ lip-reading as an aid to understanding.

The average person has to learn to use a hearing aid. Amplification does not restore hearing to normal. It does not necessarily make a hard-of-hearing person hear better. It only provides him with the possibility of hearing better. The deafened person (one who has lost his hearing after having heard normally) has often lost his habits of selective hearing. The congenitally deaf person has never acquired these habits. The deaf or hard-of-hearing person must learn or relearn to screen out irrelevant sounds and "hear out" the sounds that are important to him. The deafened person must also develop a tolerance for the distortions of sound imposed by a hearing aid.

It is advantageous for a person with progressive impairment to begin using a hearing aid before he loses the habits of listening and of selective hearing. Distortions imposed by a hearing aid may be tolerated if the device is used with progressively greater amplification as the hearing loss develops, whereas the degree of distortion ultimately involved may be intolerable if the aid is used for the first time after a loss has become acute. Similarly, babies with congenital hearing losses may be fitted with hearing aids so that they will learn in the ordinary developmental way to use sounds as guides to behavior and to understanding. The severely handicapped child, without a hearing aid, may learn to ignore sounds that he can hear because they are too faint to attract his attention and serve as useful guides. He does not become interested in sounds and remains unaware of their significance. If effective amplification is provided, the child will learn to notice and respond to sound. The child who has learned to live in a soundless world is likely to find some sounds disagreeable, and must change from having dominantly visual and cutaneous perception to having dominantly visual and auditory perception.

Economic factors may limit the use of hearing aids. Among the deaf, hearing aid use is directly related to income. Hearing aids are expensive to purchase and maintain (Schein & Delk, 1974).

THE AURALLY IMPAIRED CHILD IN THE FAMILY

In addition to the family problems of handicapped children in general, there are some situations peculiar to the aurally impaired. If the child has any residual hearing—and most children do—every attempt should be made to capitalize on it. After complete otological and audiometric examinations have been made and any surgical or medical treatments completed, hearing aids may be used if there is any useful residual hearing, and training should start immediately.

The child should be raised in a speaking environment. Special efforts should be made to reinforce both the child's responses to sounds and his spontaneous vocalizations. If parents look at the child, go to him, attend to his needs, and play with him when he cries, coos, and gurgles, he will tend to repeat his vocalizing. Talking carefully, distinctly, and slowly to the child when he is watching one's face and when the face is in full light will encourage him to combine looking and listening as sources of cues to meanings. The aurally handicapped child needs the same kind of opportunities to learn and understand speech as the normal child, but he needs more of them. Special situations may have to be contrived to emphasize the relationship of dimly heard sounds and visual cues to their meanings by concrete reference to persons, objects, activities, and situations.

When treatment directed at maximizing the child's use of his residual hearing and his potential for speech is combined with a good home-training program, most aurally handicapped children can come to school as talking children. The majority of deaf children who learn to talk have had good home training from their earliest years (Ewing & Ewing, 1958). If the child is one of the few who are totally deaf, he must learn to understand speech and to talk via sight and touch.

Phrases and short sentences using the pattern of normal speech—spoken a little more slowly and clearly—while maintaining the normal rhythmic pattern of the sentence are more easily followed than are single words. The home is the place where auditory training, lip reading (or the more recent terms *speech reading, visual communication* and *visual listening*), and learning to speak all begin (O'Niell, 1964). Proper home training with hearing aids is making it possible for a large percentage of aurally handicapped children to learn to understand language and to talk in the ordinary, developmental way.

A list of suggestions to encourage oral speech for the parents of children with severe auditory impairments follows:

1. Talk to your child constantly. Provide a rich speaking atmosphere. Don't use signs with him, and when the child uses a sign, supply the proper word.
2. Expect your child to learn speech reading and to speak. Start with simple phrases or meaningful words in specific situations or with reference to concrete objects and activities.
3. Work constantly to increase his vocabulary. Systematically introduce new words and teach different words for the same thing to avoid the development of a stilted, limited speech pattern.
4. Insist that the child speak for himself, first to members of his family, then to friends and relatives, and later to casual acquaintances and strangers. Don't step in to speak and interpret for your child. Encourage independence and self-confidence.
5. Require and expect the handicapped child to accept responsibility, perform household duties, and participate in family life essentially like the nonhandicapped. Send him on errands as soon as he has sufficient vocabulary to make himself understood.
6. Discourage the use of pencil and paper or signs in place of oral speech.
7. Provide as much pleasure and feeling of satisfaction as possible with the use of language. Speech training in the house should never become dull, monotonous, repetitious drill.

Language used spontaneously, in natural situations where it serves a purpose and is meaningful, with the attention, acceptance, and understanding of others operating as rewards, is the ideal situation for the acquisition of speech by the aurally impaired child, just as it is for the nonhandicapped. Success in teaching him to understand and to use oral speech depends on the whole family, the characteristics of the child himself, and the use of specialized facilities and help. But of all these factors, the most important is the parents' attitude toward the child and his handicap (Ewing & Ewing, 1958).

EDUCATION OF THE AURALLY HANDICAPPED

Although no clear division can be made between the deaf and the hard-of-hearing, many of the problems of their education are sufficiently different to warrant their being educated either separately or by different methods (Ewing, 1960). The primary difference in the education of these two groups is in their learning to speak and to understand speech. The deaf child with no useful residual hearing must depend entirely on vision and the other senses for his education. He must learn to understand speech solely by seeing (lip reading, speech reading, visual communication, or visual listening), and he learns to speak via the visual, cutaneous, and kinesthetic senses. If the child with useful residual hearing is taught, like the deaf child, to rely largely or entirely on visual, cutaneous, and kinesthetic cues for understanding speech and for learning to speak, he will eventually neglect his auditory potential and become functionally deaf. The profoundly deaf child acquires oral speech by learning to reproduce what he sees on the lips and faces of people talking to him. He can monitor his speech only via the cutaneous and kinesthetic sensations from his vocal apparatus. The hard-of-hearing child needs auditory training along with his speech reading to increase his use of his residual hearing, so that he develops a combined visual and auditory perceptual system. Except for the ways in which they acquire their communication skills, the education of the profoundly deaf and the hard-of-hearing is not significantly different.

In France, Abbé de L'Épée (1710–1789) established the first school for deaf children and educated them by the use of signs (manual communication). In Germany, Samuel Heinicke (1723–1790) started the first public school for the deaf, using and teaching the oral methods of communication. By 1800, as the result of these two early developments, there were two opposing schools of thought in Europe on the question of how best to teach deaf children—the French or sign system (manual) and the German, oral system (Butterfield, 1971). For over two hundred years the debate concerning these two competing means of communication has continued (Vernon, 1971).

Until recently the education of the deaf in the United States followed the early German lead and was primarily oral. Manual communication was discouraged under the assumption that children who used signs would not be motivated to learn to speak, to use their residual hearing, or to speech-read. Manual communication was largely reserved for the "oral failures"—those who failed to develop oral skills. However, this assumption has been challenged; since 1969, a growing number of programs in the United States have used both oral and manual communication (Moores, Weiss, & Goodwin, 1973).

The shift from purely oral to combination methods has resulted from the accumulating research evidence indicating that: (a) children taught by purely oral methods use manual communication with their peers despite instructions not to and despite punishment for doing so; (b) only a small percentage— about 17 percent—of students taught by purely oral methods ever become fluent orally; (c) only about 25 percent of the deaf can follow a normal conversation by speech reading, while nearly 75 percent communicate fluently manually, even when use of signs is prohibited in the classroom; (*d*) early manual communication facilitates, rather than retards, the later development of oral language; (*e*) children who use finger spelling and sign language do better academically than do comparable children who have been limited to oral communication; (*f*) deaf children of deaf parents outperform the deaf children of hearing parents on measures of English language skills, suggesting the beneficial effects of early experience with manual communication (Vernon, 1971; Moores, Weiss, & Goodwin, 1973; Hoemann, 1974; Charrow & Fletcher, 1974).

Today there are few advocates of pure "manualism," and the number of pure oralists is also decreasing. The number who advocate the use of oral speech together with finger-spelling, sign language, and speech-reading (total communication) is increasing (Vernon, 1971; Northcott, 1973; Furfey, 1974; Suppes, 1974).

Speech reading and oral language for the deaf

Teaching a profoundly deaf child to be fluent in speech-reading and in oral speech is one of the most demanding instructional tasks, on the one hand, and the most satisfying accomplishments, on the other. Such instruction requires intensive individualized teaching by a dedicated and resourceful instructor.

Some problems of speech- or lip-reading   Speech-reading can never be a complete substitute for normal hearing. But lip-reading, especially when combined with some residual hearing—either with or without a hearing aid—does promote better communication. The profoundly deaf child often develops some rudimentary lip-reading skills spontaneously. However, monitored practice with a trained teacher is necessary for proficiency in lip-reading. Most authorities agree that lip-reading can benefit people with hearing losses as low as 25 decibels (Broberg, 1971).

Some of the more obvious difficulties the deaf person has in learning speech-reading and in oral speech follow. (*a*) The absence of the auditory feedback—which is necessary for speech acquisition in the normal developmental way—during the early developmental period when the child is apparently optimally capable of language learning, is most handicapping. (*b*) Whereas hearing children monitor their own speech and perceive the speech of others largely through audition, the deaf must depend mainly on vision to perceive the speech of others and on the cues provided by the feedback from their motor (kinesthetic) and skin (cutaneous) senses to monitor their own speech. (*c*) Normal speakers cannot observe their mouth and face while talking and consequently do not understand the ambiguities of the visual cues their speech provides. (*d*) The visual cues provided by oral speech are only the byproducts of articulation and are manipulated so as to produce appropriate sounds rather than visually distinguishable ones.

The person with only minimally useful residual hearing has a great advantage over the profoundly deaf individual in speech-reading and the acquisition of oral speech. For such individuals, the auditory and the visual can complement each other. With training, the visual cues can fill in the missing auditory links and the trained ear can bridge the visual gaps. The person with minimally useful residual hearing can often perceive low-pitched sounds. He can therefore distinguish most consonants and can understand many words (Erber, 1974). The profoundly deaf person perceives only time and intensity changes in speech and probably does this largely through the vibrotactile receptors in the ears.

Special aids

Many devices have been developed to detect and amplify or code certain features of oral speech as special aids for the deaf (Erber, 1974; Boothroyd & Decker, 1972; Babcock & Wallen, 1974). Some of these devices transform speech into a visual form; others shift the high-frequency components of speech to a lower frequency range and thus bring speech within the perceptual range of those whose auditory losses are primarily for the higher frequencies. A third group of instruments provide articulatory cues to the deaf person via coded light signals. In one of these a microphone picks up sound waves and causes miniature lights set in a frame of glasses to light up in different patterns. These cues provide the wearer with information to supplement the cues provided by the speaker's lips and face.

Manual communication

Two systems of manual communication are used by the deaf. One is the manual alphabet, or finger-spelling, in which the configurations of the hand correspond to the letters of the alphabet. In this system a spoken language is spelled out manually. The other system consists of sign language, in which a set of manual configurations, movements, and gestures correspond to particular words or concepts. There are national and regional variations in sign language that are comparable to those of spoken languages. The American Sign Language (ASL), with certain regional variations, is used by the deaf in North America and has recently been the subject of formal analysis. The ASL is somewhat like pictograph writing, in which some symbols are arbitrary and some are representational. For example, the sign for "always" is made by holding the hand in a fist, index finger extended as in pointing while rotating the arm at the elbow. This is purely arbitrary. The sign for "flower" is more representational. It is made by holding the fingers of one hand extended, all five fingertips touching (the tapered hand), and touching the fingertips first to one nostril and then to the other as if sniffing a flower. All such signs are arbitrary to a degree. The literate deaf individual typically uses a combination of ASL and finger-spelling in manual communication.

Special educational provisions for the child with impaired hearing are provided, to some degree, from kindergarten through college. Residential schools, special day schools, special classes in the regular schools, resource teachers, and itinerant teachers are all used for the education of the aurally impaired child.

Nursery schools for the aurally impaired child

The young child with useful residual hearing, fitted with a hearing aid and equipped with good home training, will probably develop best in a normal environment where he experiences oral speech all day long and where special efforts are made to talk to him as much as possible. The profoundly deaf child will require supplementary training by a special teacher of the deaf. The special teacher can also instruct and train the mother and the regular teacher so that they can provide supplementary speech and speech-reading training for the child. A good, natural, normal nursery-school program, with the aurally handicapped child using his hearing aid, if indicated, and the teachers making special efforts to reach and stimulate him, is probably the best supplement to the home-training program for the three- to five-year-old.

The special school for the deaf

Deaf children are educated in four settings: residential schools, special day schools, special day classes, and regular classes (Vernon, 1975). In 1960 there were seventy-two public residential schools for children with auditory impairments in the United States, enrolling about 16,000 children. Historically, the residential school was the first type of facility established for the education of the deaf. The advantages and disadvantages of the residential school for the child with auditory impairment are essentially those listed earlier for residential institutions in general. As is true for most other categories of exceptional people, there is a decrease in the percentage of children with hearing impairments being sent to the special schools—both residential and day. In 1972 about half of the deaf aged twenty-four to sixty-four had been educated entirely in residential schools while about one-fourth had attended regular classes for at least part of their education (Schein & Delk, 1974), and about 10 percent had never attended a special school or class for the hearing impaired. The special day school for the aurally impaired child has not been a practical facility except in a few large cities. The relatively low incidence of severe auditory impairment (perhaps 2 per 1,000) requires a school to draw from such a large geographical area that transportation becomes a serious problem.

The residential school will probably always be needed, although attendance at such schools is decreasing. Children with severe hearing impairments living in isolated rural areas, aurally impaired children with additional disabilities, children with unfavorable home situations, and others with special problems can best be educated in residential schools. For some children, short-term programs may be sufficient to develop their special oral and aural skills to the point where they can function satisfactorily in the regular classroom (Poulos, 1961). Since nearly half the children attending residential schools for the hearing impaired go home each weekend, and 12 percent of the children attending such schools are really day students, the majority of the students maintain contact with their homes, communities, and families (Schunhoff, 1964).

The special class in a regular school

The special class, with some integration with the regular classes or a still greater degree of integration with the assistance of resource teachers, consultants, or itinerant teachers, is rapidly becoming the most common educational arrangement for children with auditory impairments. With maximum surgical remediations and the use of improved hearing aids, many children previously considered hopelessly deaf and placed in residential schools can now function adequately in the regular schools.

Although there is a paucity of large-scale and well-controlled studies, the evidence indicates that children in the ordinary school environment mixing with the normally hearing children are superior to institutionalized children, except possibly in the areas of personal adjustment. When institutionalized and integrated groups of children are equated for degree of auditory impairment, age of onset of the disabilities, and mental level, the children educated in integrated classes are generally superior in fluency of speech and in educational achievement (Johnson, 1962; Brereton,

1957). Recent experience indicates that children can manage in the ordinary school with more severe hearing impairments than has been generally considered possible. Such children do require special help (Hehir, 1973; Northcott, 1973).

When the special class for aurally impaired children is part of a regular school, varying degrees and rates of integration can be achieved according to the child's needs. There is evidence that abrupt complete integration may overwhelm some aurally handicapped children (Motto & Wawrzaszek, 1963); for such children, gradual integration is indicated. Alice Streng (1958) recommends that most handicapped children begin school in a special class. They can later be assigned to a regular classroom—preferably one to a classroom—for a limited time each day, largely for socialization. Still later, they can take such courses as art and physical education with the regular students. As they grow older, they are assigned to regular classes in selected additional subjects in which they excel. In high school, the average aurally impaired child can take home economics, industrial arts, physical education, and art, and each year add one additional regular academic subject to his program. By the senior year, such students would be taking all their work in regular classes. There is evidence that the increasing integration of the deaf into regular educational settings and programs is increasing their social acceptance by their more "normal" classmates (Kennedy & Bruininks, 1974).

The aurally impaired college student

In the United States, the deaf high school graduate has a choice of attending a college for the deaf—Gallaudet—or one of the two thousand regular universities and colleges. Gallaudet, a federally sponsored college for the deaf in Washington, D.C., is the only college exclusively for the deaf in the world.

Many of the problems of the deaf student are magnified in the regular college. There are no special facilities or aids available to him. Classroom instruction is often more oral—sometimes purely lecture or lecture and discussion. The handicapped student is only one among many nonhandicapped, and usually no special consideration is provided him. Students with severe auditory impairments usually watch the lecturer to get the general ideas, but depend upon a carbon copy of the notes of helpful classmates and their own outside reading for details. It is very difficult for people who must read speech to follow the rapid flow of conversation in group discussions. They usually have to rely on the help of a thoughtful friend in such situations, for this problem seems insurmountable.

VOCATIONAL OPPORTUNITIES OF THE AURALLY IMPAIRED

The deaf find employment in almost all vocational areas. Table 13–3 indicates the occupational distribution of the employed deaf in the United States in the late 1950s.

Table 13–3 indicates that the deaf are employed in all major occupational groups. They are underrepresented in the higher professional, managerial, and clerical and sales areas, probably because of the greater necessity for facile communication in these occupations. There are relatively greater numbers employed in the intermediate occupational levels (craftspersons and semiskilled "operatives"), and a decidedly smaller percentage working as unskilled laborers, as compared with the general population. In the study cited (Lunde & Bogman, 1959), 85 percent of the deaf workers were rated "successful" in their occupations.

Table 13–3
Percent distribution of principal occupations of employed deaf 16 to 64 years of age in the United States, 1972

Occupation	Percent
Professional and technical	8.8
Nonfarm managers and administrators	1.4
Sales	0.5
Clerical	15.0
Craftspersons	21.3
Operatives, nontransit	34.7
Operatives, transit	1.2
Laborers, nonfarm	6.2
Farmers and farm managers	0.8
Farm laborers	0.8
Service workers	9.2
Private household workers	0.2

Data from Schein and Delk (1974).

Studies of the occupational success of girls who had attended the Lexington School for the deaf indicate that achievement in the language skills was the keystone to successful careers (Connor & Rosenstein, 1963).

The vocational training of the aurally handicapped is not essentially different from that designed for those who hear. Individual differences in special talents and general intelligence are as great among people with hearing defects as among those with normal hearing. Interests, motivation, and realistic levels of personal aspirations and social expectation are no less important to the aurally impaired than to the acoustically normal, and their occupational possibilities are only slightly more restricted.

We mentioned earlier that job success seems to be only slightly related to degree of defect, but is more closely related to personal characteristics (Miller, Kunce, & Getsinger, 1972). In 1972, 3 percent of deaf males were unemployed as compared with 4.9 percent of all males (Schein & Delk, 1974). The overwhelming majority of the deaf are employed. Unfortunately, the deaf are employed predominantly in industrial enterprises, which have a predicted relative decrease of workers, and are underrepresented in the personal service fields, where increasing demands are predicted (Vernon, 1975).

Each state has a vocational rehabilitation office and most states have many branch offices, most of which employ personnel trained to work with the deaf and hard-of-hearing. Also, in many state departments of employment people are selected and trained to work with the handicapped.

THE SOCIAL LIFE OF THE DEAF

The social life of most of the deaf and hard-of-hearing is essentially the same as that of those with normal hearing. The average deaf person has a job, owns his home, marries someone of his choice, raises a family of reasonably normal children, and participates in the social life of his community. More than other types of handicapped people, they tend to favor social groups of their own kind. Many deaf people are more relaxed and find great satisfaction from associating with those who share their problems and interests. One evidence or consequence of the tendency of the deaf to associate with those similarly impaired is found in a study of ten thousand married adult deaf, which showed that less than 5 percent had married hearing people (Meadow, 1975).

In addition to social clubs, the deaf have organized the National Fraternal Society of the Deaf, which writes insurance in the millions, publishes a monthly paper, and has a large ladies' auxiliary (Elstad, Frampton, & Gall, 1955). The deaf have organized the National Association of the Deaf, with offices in Silver Spring, Maryland. The Association publishes a monthly magazine. The deaf hold a national basketball tournament yearly; less often, they have bowling and football tournaments. They also stage the World Deaf Olympics.

Since 1967 there has been a National Theater of the Deaf. Cast members communicate on stage by a "sign-mime" language, and two translators speak words for the hearing members of the audience.

The deaf have been a very self-conscious group. They have opposed all types of begging by the deaf. In several states, they have established homes for the aged deaf. The deaf have opposed special preferential legislation for the aurally impaired, just as they have opposed legislation which they feel unrealistically restricts their activities (Elstad, Frampton, & Gall, 1955). The deaf, like many other disadvantaged minorities, have recently become militant in making demands in their own behalf (McCay, 1974; Vernon, 1975). Compared with other categories of the handicapped, the deaf do well economically. The median income of families of employed deaf persons is 85 percent as much as the United States average (Schein & Delk, 1974). Personal earnings are directly related to age at the onset of deafness. Those born deaf have the lowest average.

PROSPECTS FOR THE AURALLY IMPAIRED

If we extrapolate from the recent past, the prospect for additional amelioration of the condition of the deaf is good. We can expect continued developments in the medical treatment and surgical remediation of the aurally impaired. Further reduction in the incidence of severe aural impairment can result from the decreasing incidence of those diseases of the pregnant mother, or of the child, which may damage the auditory apparatus. We can reasonably expect improvements in hearing aids which reduce the handicap of those with impaired hearing.

There is always the possibility that some major breakthrough may occur—the more effective use of the other senses in perceiving speech, or even bypassing the ordinary sensory inputs to get appropriate neural impulses to the brain.

The social understanding and vocational outlooks for the deaf are improving.

SUMMARY

Studies of attitudes toward handicapped persons show that while the blind, the orthopedically disabled, the physically ill, and the like are viewed with compassion, the majority of lay people are either indifferent to the deaf or react unfavorably toward them. The individual deprived of hearing from birth, in addition to being unable to hear the speech of other people and to acquire speech in the ordinary developmental way, lacks an important tool for the acquisition of nonverbal skills, a major source of pleasurable social experience, as well as one of the principal means of social interaction. The deaf and the hearing are most meaningfully differentiated according to whether they have hearing which is functional for the ordinary purposes of life.

Because only a small proportion of the deaf and the hard-of-hearing are identified by parents and teachers unaided, a wide variety of tests has been developed for this purpose. These consist of the watch test, the whisper test, the phonographic audiometer and its modern counterpart, the speech perception tests, tuning fork tests, the galvanic skin response test, and finally and most important, the pure-tone audiometers.

Auditory defects are both endogenous (hereditary) and exogenous (environmental or adventitious) in origin. The causes of a large percentage of cases of impaired hearing are unknown. The exact incidence of impaired hearing is unknown, but conservative estimates indicate that some 300,000 children and 2,300,000 adults are sufficiently aurally impaired to warrant special care and treatment.

There are no personal characteristics or personality patterns peculiar to the aurally impaired. The deaf typically score below the hearing on most intelligence tests, but this can be accounted for in terms other than differences in inherent capacity. The educational retardation of two to three grades commonly found among the severely aurally impaired indicates the extent to which society has failed to develop alternative methods of educating these people. The conceptual deficiencies of the aurally impaired seem to be principally in the verbal areas. Deafness produces no peculiar patterns of personal or social adjustment or maladjustment but, like any other handicap, it creates an excessive number of adjustment problems. Special care and treatment of the acoustically impaired involves medicine, surgery, education, and social work, as well as other disciplines. People with middle- or outer-ear damage (conduction deafness) have a very good chance of having their hearing improved by corrective surgery, appropriate hearing aids, and aural rehabilitation. Those with damage to the inner ear or the auditory nerve have a smaller chance of obtaining help in these ways.

The education of the aurally impaired child begins in the home and is continued in residential schools, special day schools, special classes in regular schools, and integrated classes. The consensus seems to be that the aurally handicapped, like most other exceptional children, should not be sent to special schools if they can be suitably educated in ordinary schools, and that they should not go to boarding schools if they can be suitably educated in day schools near their homes. The acquiring of adequate language and communication skills constitutes the major problem of the aurally handicapped, whether these are acquired by oral speech and speech-reading alone or by speech with the aid of finger-spelling, either with or without the language of signs.

There is increasing interest in and respect for what can be achieved by manual methods of communication beginning with the very young child. It has been found that learning sign language does not retard the development of speech or speech-reading skills. There seems to be little evidence to support the claim that oral speech is necessary for adjusting to a hearing society. Deaf children who learn sign language early in life perform better than those who do not develop these skills, on speech, speech-reading, and psychological adjustment measures.

The deaf find employment less often than the aurally unimpaired in the professional, managerial, clerical and sales, and personal service areas, and more often in the skilled crafts and in the technical areas. Some find employment in practically all areas.

The social life of the deaf is essentially the same as that of the rest of the population, although there is a greater tendency for them to form social groups of their own kind than is true for the other types of handicapped people. The prospect for improved surgical, remedial, and educational programs for the aurally impaired is good.

REFERENCES

A.M.A. COMMITTEE ON MEDICAL RATINGS OF PHYSICAL IMPAIRMENT, "Guide to the Evaluation of Permanent Impairment of Ear, Nose, Throat, and Related Structures," *Journal of the American Medical Association,* 1961, *177,* 489–501.

ANDERSON, V. M., "The Incidence and Significance of High-frequency Deafness in Children," *American Journal of Diseases of Children,* 1967, *113,* 560–65.

BABCOCK, R., & M. K. WALLEN, "Visible Speech: Toward Improved Speech for the Hearing Handicapped," *Educational Technology,* 1974, *11,* 52–54.

BEAGLEY, H. A., "Electro-physiological Tests of Hearing," *British Journal of Disorders of Communication,* 1973, *8,* 115–19.

BOOTHROYD, A., & M. DECKER, "Control of Voice Pitch by the Deaf," *Audiology,* 1972, *11,* 343–53.

BORNSTEIN, H., & H. L. ROY, "Comment on 'Linguistic Deficiency and Thinking: Research with Deaf Subjects,'" *Psychological Bulletin,* 1973, *79,* 211–14.

BOWYER, L. R., & J. GILLIES, "The Social and Emotional Adjustment of Deaf and Partially Deaf Children," *British Journal of Educational Psychology,* 1972, *42,* 305–8.

BRASIER, V. J., "A Binaural Integration Test," *Audiology,* 1973, *12* (1), 40–43.

BRERETON, B. L., *The Schooling of Children with Impaired Hearing* (Sydney, Australia: Commonwealth Office of Education, 1957).

BROBERG, R. F., "You've Come a Long Way, Baby: Lipreading in the Early 1970's," *Hearing and Speech News,* 1971, *39* (1), 20–23.

BUTTERFIELD, P. H., "The First Training Colleges for Teachers of the Deaf," *British Journal of Educational Studies,* 1971, *19* (1), 51–69.

CHARROW, V. R., & J. D. FLETCHER, "English as the Second Language of Deaf Children," *Developmental Psychology,* 1974, *10,* 463–70.

CODY, D. T. R., & G. L. SOWNSEND, "Some Physiological Aspects of the Averaged Vertex Response in Humans," *Audiology,* 1973, *12* (1), 1–13.

CONFERENCE OF EXECUTIVES OF AMERICAN SCHOOLS FOR THE DEAF, "Report of the Conference Committee on Nomenclature," *American Annals of the Deaf,* 1938, *83,* 1–3.

CONNOR, L. E., & J. ROSENSTEIN, "Vocational Status and Adjustment of Deaf Women," *Volta Review,* 1963, *65,* 585–91.

CURRY, E. T., "Are Teachers Good Judges of Pupils' Hearing?" *Journal of Exceptional Children,* 1954, *21,* 42–48.

DALE, D. M., *Applied Audiometry for Children* (Springfield, Ill.: Charles C Thomas, 1962).

DAVIS, H., "The Articulation Area and the Social Adequacy Index for Hearing," *Laryngoscope,* 1948, *58,* 761–78.

DAVIS, H., "Sedation of Young Children for Electric Response Audiometry (ERA)," *Audiology,* 1973, *12* (2), 55–57.

DIX, M., & C. S. HALLPIKE, "The Peep Show," *British Medical Journal,* 1947, *2,* 719–23.

DOUGLAS, F. M., E. P. FOWLER, JR., & G. M. RYAN, *A Differential Study of Communication Disorders* (New York: Columbia Presbyterian Medical Center, 1961).

ELSTAD, L. M., M. E. FRAMPTON, & E. D. GALL, *The Deaf in Special Education for the Exceptional* (Boston: Porter Sargent, 1955).

ERBER, N. P., "Visual Perception of Speech by Deaf Children: Recent Developments and Continuing Needs," *Journal of Speech and Hearing Disorders,* 1974, *39,* 178–85.

EWERTSEN, H. W., & H. BIRK-NIELSEN, "Social Hearing Handicap Index," *Audiology,* 1973, *12,* 180–83.

EWING, A. G., ed., *The Modern Educational Treatment of Deafness* (Washington, D.C.: Volta Bureau, 1960).

EWING, I. R., & A. G. EWING, *New Opportunities for Deaf Children* (Springfield, Ill.: Charles C Thomas, 1958).

FARRANT, R. H., "The Intellective Ability of Deaf and Hearing Children Compared by Factor Analysis," *American Annals of the Deaf,* 1964, *109,* 306–25.

FIEDLER, M. F., *Deaf Children in a Hearing World* (New York: Ronald Press, 1952).

FIOR, R., "Physiological Maturation of Auditory Function Between 3 and 13 Years of Age," *Audiology,* 1972, *11,* 317–21.

FRASER, G. R., "Epidemiology of Profound Childhood Deafness," *Audiology,* 1974, *13,* 335–41.

FURFEY, P. H., "Total Communication and the Baltimore Deaf Survey," *American Annals of the Deaf,* 1974, *119,* 377–80.

FURTH, H. G., "Linguistic Deficiency and Thinking: Research With Deaf Subjects, 1964–1969," *Psychological Bulletin,* 1971, *96,* 58–72.

FURTH, H. G., "Further Thoughts on Thinking and Language," *Psychological Bulletin,* 1973, *79,* 215–16.

FUSFELD, I. S., "A Cross Section Evaluation of the Academic Program of Schools for the Deaf," *Gallaudet College Bulletin,* 1954, no. 3.

GALKOWSKI, T., "Auditory Reactions in Mentally Retarded Children by Means of Psychogalvanic Reflexes," *Audiology*, 1974, *13*, 501–5.

GENTILE, A., J. D. SCHEIN, & K. HASSE, *Characteristics of Persons with Impaired Hearing*, Publication No. 1000, Series 10, no. 35 (Washington, D.C.: U.S. Department of Health, Education and Welfare, Public Health Service, 1967).

GILDSTON, H., & P. GILDSTON, "Personality Changes Associated with Surgically Corrected Hypo-acusis," *Audiology*, 1972, *11*, 354–67.

GLORIG, A., "Thunderation," *Hearing and Speech News*, 1972, *40* (1), 6–7, 23–26.

HEHIR, R. G., "Integrating Deaf Students for Career Education," *Exceptional Children*, 1973, *39*, 611–18.

HENDERSON, S. E., & L. HENDERSON, "Levels of Visual-information Processing in Deaf and Hearing Children," *American Journal of Psychology*, 1973, *86*, 507–21.

HOEMANN, H. W., "Deaf Children's Use of Finger-spelling to Label Pictures of Common Objects: A Followup Study," *Exceptional Children*, 1974, *40*, 515–20.

HUGHES, R. B., "A Comparison of Verbal Conceptualization in Deaf and Hearing Children" (unpublished Doctoral dissertation, University of Illinois, 1959).

JACOBS, L., "The Community of the Adult Deaf," *American Annals of the Deaf*, 1974, *119*, 41–46.

JENSEMA, C., "Post-rubella Children in Special Educational Programs," *The Volta Review*, 1974, *76*, 466–73.

JERGER, J., P. BURNEY, L. MAULDIN, & B. CRUMP, "Predicting Hearing Loss from the Acoustic Reflex," *Journal of Speech and Hearing Disorders*, 1974, *39*, 11–22.

JOHNSON, J. C., *Educating Hearing-impaired Children in Ordinary Schools* (Manchester, England: Manchester University Press, 1962).

KATES, S. L., *Cognitive Structures in Deaf, Hearing, and Psychotic Individuals* (Northampton, Mass.: Clarke School for the Deaf, 1967).

KENNEDY, P., & R. H. BRUININKS, "Social Status of Hearing Impaired Children in Regular Classes," *Exceptional Children*, 1974, *40*, 336–42.

KODMAN, F., et al., "Socioeconomic Status and Observer Identification of Hearing Loss in School Children," *Journal of Exceptional Children*, 1959, *26*, 176–79.

KUYPER, P., "The Cocktail Party Effect," *Audiology*, 1972, *11*, 277–82.

LESZCZYNSKI, L., "Device Allows Deaf to Converse on Phone," *San Jose* (California) *Mercury News*, 13 April 1975, 20.

LEVINE, E., *The Psychology of Deafness* (New York: Columbia University Press, 1960).

LILLYWHITE, H. S., N. B. YOUNG, & R. W. OLMSTED, *Pediatrician's Handbook of Communication Disorders* (Philadelphia: Lea & Febiger, 1970).

LUNDE, A. S., & S. K. BIGMAN, *Occupational Conditions Among the Deaf* (Washington, D.C.: Gallaudet College Press, 1959).

McCAY, V., "Deaf Militancy," *American Annals of the Deaf*, 1974, *119*, 15.

MALTZMAN, M., *Clinical Audiology* (New York: Grune & Stratton, 1949).

MEADOW, K. P., "The Deaf Subculture," *Hearing and Speech Action*, July–August 1975, *13* (9), 16–19.

MEYERSON, L., "A Psychology of Impaired Hearing," in W. M. Cruickshank, ed.,

Psychology of Exceptional Children and Youth, 2nd ed. (Englewood Cliffs, N.J.: Prentice-Hall, 1963).

MEYERSON, L., & J. L. MICHAEL, *The Measurement of Sensory Thresholds in Exceptional Childen* (Houston: University of Houston, 1960).

MILLER, D. E., J. T. KUNCE, & S. H. GETSINGER, "Prediction of Job Success for Clients with Hearing Loss," *Rehabilitation Counseling Bulletin,* 1972, *16* (1), 21–28.

MOORES, D. F., K. L. WEISS, & M. W. GOODWIN, "Receptive Abilities of Deaf Children Across Five Modes of Communication," *Exceptional Children,* 1973, *40,* 22–28.

MOTTO, J., & F. J. WAWRZASZEK, "Integration of the Hearing Handicapped: Evaluation of the Current Status," *Volta Review,* 1963, *65,* 124–29.

MYKLEBUST, H. R., "Towards a New Understanding of the Deaf Child," *American Annals of the Deaf,* 1953, *98,* 345–57.

MYKLEBUST, H. R., *The Psychology of Deafness* (New York: Grune & Stratton, 1960).

NAGAFUCHI, M., "Filtered Speech Audiometry in Normal Children and in the Mentally Retarded," *Audiology,* 1974, *13,* 66–77.

"News and Reports: Detecting Infant's Hearing Loss," *Children Today,* 1974, *3* (1), 30–31.

NORTHCOTT, W. H., ed., *The Hearing Impaired Child in a Regular Classroom: Preschool, Elementary, and Secondary Years* (Washington, D.C.: The Alexander Graham Bell Association for the Deaf, 1973).

O'NIELL, J. J., *The Hard of Hearing* (Englewood Cliffs, N.J.: Prentice-Hall, 1964).

PINTNER, R., & D. G. PATERSON, "The Binet Scale and the Deaf Child," *Journal of Educational Psychology,* 1915, *6,* 201–10.

POULOS, T. H., "Short-term Rehabilitation Programs for Hard of Hearing Children," *Hearing News,* 1961, *29,* 4–7.

PROCTOR, B., *Chronic Progressive Deafness* (Detroit: Western Michigan University Press, 1961).

QUIGLEY, S. P., "The Deaf and the Hard of Hearing," *Review of Educational Research,* 1969, *39,* 103–23.

REDDELL, R. C., & D. R. CALVERT, "Selecting a Hearing Aid by Interpreting Audiologic Data," *Journal of Auditory Research,* 1966, *6,* 445–52.

REICHSTEIN, J., & J. ROSENSTEIN, "Differential Diagnosis of Auditory Deficits: A Review of the Literature," *Journal of Exceptional Children,* 1964, *30,* 73–82.

REYNOLDS, M. C., "The Capacities of Children," *Journal of Exceptional Children,* 1965, *31,* 344–55.

RHODES, M. J., "Invisible Barrier," *The Exceptional Parent,* 1972, *1* (6), 10–14.

ROSS, B. M., & H. HOEMANN, "A Comparison of Probability Concepts in Deaf and Hearing Adolescents," *Genetic Psychology Monographs,* 1975, *91,* 61–120.

RUPP, R. R., "The Specter of Aging," *Hearing and Speech News,* 1971, *39* (6), 10–13.

SALA, O., & G. BABEGHIAN, "Automatic Versus Standard Audiometry," *Audiology,* 1973, *12* (1), 21–27.

SCHEIN, J. D., "Deaf Children with Other Disabilities," *American Annals of the Deaf,* 1975, *120,* 92–99.

SCHEIN, J. D., & M. T. DELK, JR., *The Deaf Population of the United States* (Silver Spring, Md.: National Association of the Deaf, 1974).

SCHUNHOFF, H. F., "Bases of a Comprehensive Program in the Education of the Deaf," *American Annals of the Deaf,* 1964, *109,* 240–47.

SHULMAN, A., & F. EDELMAN, "Site of Lesion Testing," *Audiology,* 1973, *12* (2), 90–100.

STINSON, M. S., "Relations Between Maternal Reinforcement and Help and the Achievement Motive in Normal-Hearing and Hearing-Impaired Sons," *Developmental Psychology,* 1971, *10,* 348–53.

STRENG, A., "Public School Programs for Children with Impaired Hearing in Small School Systems," *Volta Review,* 1958, *60,* 304–6.

SUPPES, F., "A Survey of Cognitions in Handicapped Children," *Review of Educational Research,* 1974, *44,* 145–76.

THAYER, S., "Lend Me Your Ears: Racial and Sexual Factors in Helping the Deaf," *Journal of Personality and Social Psychology,* 1973, *28,* 8–11.

THOMPSON, C., & R. A WEBER, "Responses of Infants and Young Children to Behavior Observation Andrometry (BOA)," *Journal of Speech and Hearing Disorders,* 1974, *39,* 140–47.

UNITED STATES DEPARTMENT OF HEALTH, EDUCATION AND WELFARE, *Health Statistics from the United States National Health Survey,* Publication 584 B–27 (Washington, D.C., 1961).

VAN ITALLIE, P. H., *How to Live with a Hearing Handicap* (New York: Paul S. Erickson, 1962).

VERNON, M., "Current Etiological Factors in Deafness," *American Annals of the Deaf,* 1968a, *113,* 103–15.

VERNON, M., "Fifty Years of Research on the Intelligence of Deaf and Hard-of-hearing Children: A Review of Literature and Discussion of Implications," *Journal of Rehabilitation of the Deaf,* 1968b, *1,* 1–12.

VERNON, M., "Myths in the Education of Deaf Children," *Hearing and Speech News,* 1971, *39* (4), 13–17.

VERNON, M., "Major Current Trends in Rehabilitation and Education of the Deaf and Hard of Hearing," *Rehabilitation Literature,* 1975, *36,* 102–7.

VERNON, M., & W. G. MILLER, "Language and Nonverbal Communication in Cognitive and Affective Processes," *Psychoanalysis and Contemporary Science,* 1974, *2,* 124–35.

WALDON, E. F., "Audio-reflexometry in Testing Hearing of Very Young Children," *Audiology,* 1973, *12* (1), 14–20.

WEDENBERG, E., "Auditory Training of Deaf and Hard of Hearing Children," *Acta Oto-laryngologica* Supplement, 1951, *21* (94).

WEDENBERG, E., "Auditory Training of Severely Hard of Hearing Preschool Children," *Acta Oto-laryngologica* Supplement, 1955, *25* (110).

WHITE HOUSE CONFERENCE ON CHILD HEALTH AND PROTECTION, "The Handicapped and the Gifted" (New York: Appleton-Century-Crofts, 1931).

WILSON, G. B., M. ROSS, & D. R. CALVERT, "An Experimental Study of the Semantics of Deafness," *The Volta Review,* 1974, *76,* 408–14.

4

Motor and speech handicaps

Chapter 14

The orthopedically handicapped

Children and adults with orthopedic handicaps have all varieties and degrees of difficulty in physical movement (walking, coordination, and speech). The physical impairment may be due to accidents, disease, or congenital anomalies. Children with cerebral palsy are usually included among those with orthopedic difficulties for educational purposes, because of the severe nature of the physical involvement in cerebral palsy.

It is obvious that the term *orthopedically handicapped* designates such a broad category of individuals that to attempt to find psychological and other characteristics of them as a group may be an exercise in futility. This extremely heterogeneous category of exceptionality includes individuals who are alike in not being average in physical ability. Beyond this, their likenesses become fewer and fewer because of the tremendous variety of disabling conditions that occur. However, some general characteristics can be gleaned from research findings and from clinical observations, although generalizations from these findings are difficult.

INCIDENCE OF ORTHOPEDIC HANDICAP

Any estimate of the number of orthopedically handicapped in the population is dependent on the manner of their definition. The United States Office of Education (1970) estimates that 0.5 percent of school-age children in the nation are afflicted with crippling conditions or health impairments. Different definitions and different sources of estimates yield varying numbers. The White House Conference Report (1958) summarized the data from surveys on the prevalence of crippling disabilities. Some surveys indicate 0.91 per 1,000 of the general population for certain areas and cities, while others go as high as 9.79 per 1,000.

Physically handicapped students have long been recipients of special treatment by the elementary and secondary schools, and special provisions for handicapped college students have received increasing attention, although it is reported that 27 percent of four year universities and colleges in the United States indicate that they cannot accept students in wheel chairs (Mahan, 1974).

There has been a continuous increase in the percentage of crippled children being helped by crippled children's programs since 1937 (Saffian, 1962). In 1960, slightly fewer than half the number listed on the states' registers were involved in such programs. The nature of the disabilities of children being served by the programs was varied, with congenital malformations being the most frequent. Handicaps resulting from bone disorders and organs of movement were the second most frequently mentioned, and cerebral palsy was third. Certain crippling factors have noticeably declined. Poliomyelitis accounted for 14.5 percent of children in official programs in 1950, but by 1960 this figure had declined to 7 percent and soon it will disappear entirely if immunization programs become universal. However, in the mid-1970s public health officials expressed concern about the declining numbers of children being vaccinated against polio, and warned that a resurgence of the disease was possible. Vaccine has reduced the incidence of poliomyelitis drastically, and other medical advances hold promise of still further reduction in the incidence of crippling diseases. At the same time, increased medical skill may result in saving from death some orthopedically handicapped infants who heretofore would have died. Some of these children suffer neural damage that results in physical disability of one kind or another.

There has been a significant decrease in the crippling conditions which result from infectious diseases. Such conditions as poliomyelitis, osteomyelitis, tuberculosis of the bones and joints, and arthritis due to infection have been reduced over the years by advancing medical science. Congenital defects, which include a large variety of disorders, have increased among the newborn. However, because of the early correction of many deformities and the development of effective prosthetic devices, large numbers of congenital defects can no longer be considered handicapping.

Although impairment of visual perception is frequent among motor-impaired children, it has been suggested that there may be sufficient independence of the two systems that visual impairment should be measured independently of motor functions in the handicapped (Newcomer & Hammill, 1973). An unfortunate trend has been toward increased impairment due to accidents of various kinds (Boyles & Calovini, 1960). The National Safety Council (1975) indicates that accidents claim more lives of children aged one to fourteen than the five leading diseases combined. Between 11,000 and 15,000 children are accidentally killed in the United States each year, and it is estimated that over 50,000 other children are permanently crippled and disabled by accident. Over half the crippling accidents occur to children under five years of age (Garrison & Force, 1965).

EMOTIONAL AND SOCIAL ADJUSTMENT

Investigations of the adjustment of physically handicapped people are never very satisfactory, for several reasons. The extent and nature of physical disability within a group of the orthopedically handicapped are extremely variable. It is difficult to determine the intellectual level of the handicapped, and therefore matching them with control groups is always tenuous. Brain damage may be present in some individuals and not in others, and the extent of damage usually is unknown.

The problems of formulating an adequate self-concept are many for the physically handicapped. Self-concept has been considered to be intimately related to adjustment (Wright, 1960; Sawrey & Telford, 1975). The orthopedically handicapped child is different by reason of his disability. He may suffer pain, fatigue from undue exertion, accidents, and fear of injury or social rejection. These factors make it difficult for him to form realistic perceptions of his adequacies and limitations. As a result of too much parental attention, emotional rejection by parents, or condescending attitudes on the part of society in general, the handicapped child may come to feel inferior and inadequate. The resulting behavior may be maladaptive.

A number of investigators have indicated significant differences in the psychological adjustments of crippled and nonphysically handicapped children, while others have reported that the adjustments of the two groups can be favorably compared (Cruickshank, 1972). There is little doubt that the adjustive problems of crippled children take on different proportions than do those of noncrippled children. That their adjustive problems are different in kind or process is doubtful. An investigation of the emotional needs of crippled children (Cruickshank & Dolphin, 1949) found that there were no statistically significant differences between them and a group of normal children. Cruickshank (1972) later concluded that many of the objective tests used in the early studies of adjustment of crippled and noncrippled children were not sensitive enough to point up differences even if they did exist. More subtle and less personally threatening projective tests found differences between crippled and normal children (Broida, Izard, & Cruickshank, 1950; Smock & Cruickshank, 1952). The differences reported tend to support the hypothesis that a desire for, and a fear of, social participation constitutes a source of anxiety and fear in crippled children. It is probable that there are characteristic differences in adjustments between crippled and normal children. Delicate measuring instruments and sophisticated research procedures are needed to determine the nature and extent of these differences. Researchers in the field have emphasized that parental and home attitudes may be more significant factors in the adjustment of crippled children than they are for normal children. Such speculations appear to be reasonable, since the handicapped child is likely to spend more time in the home and be more dependent on the family for social contacts.

The parents with attitudes toward crippled children considered to be most constructive (Coughlin, 1941) are those that have sufficient understanding to accept the child's handicap and turn their attention and energies toward finding means to compensate for it. Such parents fully realize the implications of the orthopedic problem and can accept the problem and the child both intellectually and emotionally.

LIMITING COVERAGE

There are a great number of crippling conditions from which both children and adults suffer. Cerebral palsy, poliomyelitis, osteomyelitis, arthritis, muscular dystrophy, multiple sclerosis, spina bifida, skeletal deformities, birth defects, and various other debilitating conditions are of concern to the student of exceptionality. Children and adults with special health problems, such as epilepsy, heart conditions, asthma, eczema, and diabetes, are of concern to educators and psychologists.

It is not our intention to cover each of these conditions and their special problems. We indicated earlier that many problems are shared by normal persons as well as by persons with orthopedic and special health abnormalities, and to cover each of these conditions is beyond the scope of the text. We shall focus our attention on cerebral palsy.

CEREBRAL PALSY

A considerable number of children who are orthopedically handicapped have suffered from early brain damage to the motor area of the brain. This damage results in motor disturbances and incoordination of various degrees of severity. People exhibiting these motor disturbances as the result of brain damage are said to be suffering from *spastic paralysis*.

Spastic paralysis was first described by W. J. Little in 1843, hence it has been referred to as "Little's disease." Although spastic paralysis was described rather early, intensive work in the area of cerebral palsy was a long time in coming. Serious work in this area got under way during the 1930s, and since that time a great deal of research has been done. A particularly great amount of energy has gone into providing services for the cerebral-palsied.

Cerebral palsy has been defined as "a motor defect present or appearing soon after birth and dependent on pathological abnormalities in the brain" (Yannet, 1944). Localization of motor functions and sensory functions in the brain is generally accepted. When there is a motor or sensory dysfunction, it is assumed that damage has occurred to the particular part of the brain controlling this function. Damage to the motor area of the brain results in cerebral palsy. Although it is extremely difficult to determine the extent of any brain damage beyond that to the motor area and that causing concomitant sensory dysfunction, attempts continue in some areas that may be considered sensory/cognitive (Neuringer, Goldstein, & Gallaher, 1975; Adams et al., 1975).

Classification and description

Cerebral palsy may be classified in several different ways, which leads to considerable confusion. F. Stephen (1958) lists five basic ways in which cerebral palsy is classified: (1) according to type; (2) according to number of limbs involved; (3) according to time of onset; (4) according to degree of involvement; and (5) according to the extent and nature of the brain damage.

Classification according to type   Three main types are discerned: the spastic; the athetoid; and the ataxic. They are defined in terms of the dominant symptoms, which in turn are related to the area of the brain that has been damaged.

In *spasticity,* the lesions are in the motor cortex, the premotor area, and the pyramidal tract. Injury to the motor area of the brain results in loss of voluntary muscle control. There appears to be a generalized muscular response to stimulation that results in the simultaneous contraction of both the flexor and extensor muscles. The result is that coordinated movement is extremely difficult. The slightest stimulation causes the person to become very rigid. Jerky and spasmodic movements with "clasp-knife" rigidity and exaggerated reflexes are common. Hypertonicity prevails, and the person can move only with the greatest difficulty. Severe trembling, unsteadiness, and tense and irregular movements are characteristic. Making a deliberate effort to control the jerkiness and incoordination frequently causes them to be worse rather than better.

In *athetosis,* the lesions are in the extrapyramidal system, particularly in the basal ganglia. Athetosis is characterized by involuntary, slow, writhing, serpentine-like movements of the paralyzed member. The shoulders, face, feet, hands, and arms may be involved. Frequently the hands and arms are the seriously involved members. The rhythmical, writhing movement is slow and persistent. If one were to see only an arm and not the rest of the person, it could easily be mistaken for a deliberate, tense movement. The writhing may start in the shoulder and steadily move outward toward the fingers, involving progressively the elbow, the wrist and then the fingers. Frequently the muscles of the throat and diaphragm are involved, and speech becomes labored, hoarse, and unintelligible. The person may have difficulty in controlling saliva-tion, and thus add to his inconvenience and embarrassment. He may start to do something, like reach for a glass, but spill the contents. This causes excitement and an increased effort for control, which may result in increased tension and spasticity. When the patient relaxes or goes to sleep, the athetoid movements disappear. Athetosis accounts for 15 to 20 percent of the cerebral-palsied (Smith & Neisworth, 1975).

More common that a pure case of either spasticity or athetosis is a combination of the two, involving damage to both areas (Sarason, 1959).

In *ataxia,* the area of the brain involved is usually the cerebellum or cerebellar tract. The eighth cranial nerve, which is involved with hear-ing and equilibrium, is sometimes affected. Ataxia is characterized by a disturbance in balance which is reflected in posture and gait. The person moves at a gait that suggests intoxication. Movements are awkward, speech is slurred, and the person sways and staggers. Locomotion is such that he appears dizzy and uncertain.

Classification according to number of limbs involved   W. S. Wyllie (1951) has suggested a sixfold classification according to the number and manner in which the limbs are involved:

1. *Congenital symmetrical diplegia,* paralysis in all limbs
2. *Congenital paraplegia,* in which only the legs are involved
3. *Quadriplegia* or *bilateral hemiplegia,* in which the disturbance is greater in the arms than in the legs
4. *Triplegia,* a very rare condition in which three limbs are involved
5. *Hemiplegia,* in which both limbs on the same side are involved
6. *Monoplegia,* an extremely rare condition in which only one limb is affected

Stephen (1958) makes the point that such a classification implies a continuum of motor disturbance, rather than clearly defined types of disturbance, and that such a continuum offers a possible explanation for the differences in the reported frequencies of the various involvements.

Classification according to time of onset   When classification is made according to time of onset, three periods of time are usually designated: antenatal, natal, and postnatal. It is not easy to distinguish among these. The antenatal (before birth) and natal (birth) factors are difficult to separate from each other. This is true of the natal and postnatal (after birth) factors as well, when the postnatal factors occur shortly after birth.

Classification according to degree of involvement Various systems of classification according to degree or severity of involvement are used. F. E. Schonell (1956) classified her subjects as to whether they were slightly, moderately, severely, or very severely handicapped. Even with careful tabulation of the various afflictions common to cerebral-palsied children, a great deal of subjective judgment of total severity is still involved. Although such a classification is meaningful within a limited area, it would seem to be lacking in the precision that is essential to meaningful research. There are so many facets of the cerebral-palsied to evaluate that the task of arranging the complexity of variables into a single continuum of severity would seem to be extremely subjective.

Classification according to extent and nature of brain damage In that our ability to detect the extent and nature of brain damage is limited, it would seem that such a classification would have to depend largely on the sensory defects concomitant with cerebral palsy. The cerebral-palsied are brain-damaged, and they are probably not uniformly so. Our means of detection of brain damage are currently too limited to make meaningful classifications of damage other than through motor and sensory impairment.

Incidence

Reports of the incidence of cerebral palsy present a somewhat confusing picture. The usual problems of data collection, analysis, and interpretation are confounded by difficulties in defining the limits of what constitutes cerebral palsy. Milder cases present particular difficulties in this regard.

W. M. Phelps (1946) contends that the incidence of new cases is rather constant from year to year and from one part of the country to the next. He contends that for every 100,000 births, 7 cerebral-palsied children are born each year. Of these, one dies in infancy or at an early age. This leaves an expectancy of 6 new cases each year for each 100,000 population. Two of these (or one-third) are definitely mentally retarded and will require permanent custodial care. The remaining 4 will need treatment. Phelps estimates that there are 40 cases under twenty years of age for each 100,000 population.

P. Asher and F. E. Schonell (1950) and M. I. Dunsdon (1952) report the incidence of cerebral palsy in school-age children to be about 1 per

1,000 in England. Investigations in America have yielded slightly higher figures. The United Cerebral Palsy Association has accepted a rate of 3 to 3.5 per 1,000 school-age children in the United States (Baker, 1959), and the total number of children and adults in the United States with cerebral palsy has been estimated at 550,000 (Smith & Neisworth, 1975).

Etiology

Because the causative background of cerebral palsy is complex, we shall attempt only a brief summary of the outstanding features here. The causal factors can be classified as to their time of occurrence in the development of the individual.[1]

Prenatal causes   Disease in the mother and developmental lesions are considered to be important factors in the etiology of cerebral palsy. Infections of the fetal brain from diseases of the mother occur. Notable among these are syphilis, meningitis, encephalitis, and German measles. Prenatal factors predisposing the fetus to damage are numerous (Wilson, 1973). Insufficient oxygen in the mother's bloodstream may result in cerebral damage (Benda, 1952). Anoxia of the brain can occur if the fetus is turned in such a manner as to twist the umbilical cord around its neck. When the oxygen supply is thus disrupted, the brain soon degenerates or fails to develop adequately. Hemorrhages caused by blood incompatibility due to Rh factors may produce brain damage (Yannet, 1944). The most serious cases of cerebral palsy are the result of congenital brain deformities (Gauger, 1950).

Natal causes   C. E. Benda (1952) states that birth injury accounts for 30 to 40 percent of severe cases of mental deficiency occurring in families who could ordinarily expect normal offspring. The mode of birth was not found to be of any particular significance in the production of cerebral palsy. Nearly one-fourth of his sample were premature babies. Prolonged labor was reported in eight of his thirty-seven cases, but normal delivery was reported in nine. Prematurity is dangerous to the child because the mother is not actually ready to give birth, and the pressure on the infant during birth is likely to be increased. The child is less mature, and consequently less capable of resisting the increased pressure than he would be at maturity. Hemorrhages and asphyxiation occur more easily in the premature.

Various other factors are related to, or can produce, cerebral palsy. Mechanical injury at birth through difficult delivery or from the use of forceps is a factor. However, the role of forceps in the production of

---

[1] For a more thorough treatment of the background of cerebral palsy, see Benda (1952).

cerebral palsy has probably been grossly overestimated. The sudden release of pressure during Caesarean delivery may cause the rupture of blood vessels, as may too rapid a birth or too great pressure during a very difficult birth. Interruptions to the oxygen supply and hemorrhages of the brain membranes and tissue are prominent in birth injury (Wilson, 1973). Cerebral palsy resulting from birth injury of one kind or another comprises about 10 percent of the institutionalized cerebral-palsied cases (Sarason, 1959). A continuum theory of brain damage (Meyer, 1957), implying that all brains are more or less damaged at birth, indicates the difficulty involved in identifying brain injury at birth.

Postnatal causes   Injury to the brain after birth may produce cerebral palsy. Such injuries to the motor area of the brain can be produced by injury to the skull through severe accident. High temperature for a prolonged period, which results in a reduced oxygen intake, can also produce brain damage. The separating of natal from postnatal factors is very difficult when it is considered that some injuries at birth are not detectable for some length of time. Injuries occurring after birth, when the brain has more fully developed, are not associated with mental deficiency to the same extent as are prenatal anomalies.

Other factors associated with cerebral palsy

S. B. Sarason (1959) indicates that mothers of cerebral-palsied children are significantly older than the average. H. Yannet (1944) reports that the percentage of affected children who were first-born is not significantly higher than would be expected by chance, and that a greater proportion are born after the third pregnancy than would be expected by chance. Sarason and Yannet were dealing with the cerebrally-palsied mentally deficient.

Dunsdon (1952), investigating cerebral-palsied children of whatever mental level, found 66 percent of 327 cerebral-palsied children were first-born. She reported that 40 percent of her cases had suffered from asphyxia and that 39 percent were premature.

Cerebral palsy cannot be accounted for by any single etiological factor. W. M. Cruickshank and S. Raus (1955) have suggested that a genetic component may be still another variable to consider in cerebral palsy.

Intelligence of children with cerebral palsy

The task of measuring the intelligence of cerebral-palsied children is fraught with difficulties. The problem of how best to measure the intelligence of children who may have multiple sensory handicaps in addition to paralysis has been attacked by a number of investigators. Most investigators have found it necessary to alter the tasks of standardized intelligence tests in one way or another to fit the handicapped state of the subject involved. Altering standardized tests in any way no doubt has an effect on their validity. In the absence of tests developed particularly for the multiple combinations of disabilities encountered in cerebral palsy, investigators of the intelligence of the cerebral-palsied typically have used the Stanford-Binet or other such tests and have prorated the test scores. Items that are inappropriate are not used, and those that are used count an increasing amount. A certain percentage of cases are found to be untestable. H. V. Bice and Cruickshank (1955) found 15 percent to be untestable.

Studies of the intelligence of the cerebral-palsied have yielded consistent results. Two English studies and two in the United States are in fairly close agreement, and all have involved a sizable number of cases. Dunsdon (1952) studied the intelligence of 916 cerebral-palsied children, largely candidates for special school in England. She reports that the IQ's of 58.6 percent were below 70, and that only 8.25 percent scored 100 or better. Schonell (1956), after studying 354 cases of English cerebral-palsied children over three years of age, reports that 51 percent had IQ's over 70, and that 23 percent had IQ's between 50 and 69.

In America, T. Hopkins, H. Bice, and K. Colton (1954) reported on 1,000 cases in New Jersey. They reported that 48.8 percent had IQ's below 70; 20.4 percent had IQ's between 50 and 69; and 7.9 percent had IQ's of 110 or more. E. Miller and G. B. Rosenfeld (1952) studied 330 children with cerebral palsy. They report that 50 percent of their cases had IQ's below 70, and that 4 to 5 percent scored 110 or better. To assess the possibility of an increase in the percentage of mentally defective children due to the large number of children brought to the clinic from a considerable distance as a "last resort," they evaluated them separately and compared them with the total group. They found "no important differences." (A better control would have been to compare them to the remainder of the group. As it is, they were compared to a group over one-third of which consisted of themselves.)

The four studies presented tend to agree that the incidence of mental deficiency among the cerebral-palsied is high. The studies indicate that roughly 50 percent have IQ's below 70. The distribution of the intelligence of the cerebral-palsied definitely piles up at the lower end of the intellectual continuum. Only 3 or 4 percent have IQ's above 115, and less than one-fourth have IQ's between 70 and 89. The studies agree, too, that there is no significant difference between the mean IQ's of athetoids and spastics. This is in contrast with the supposition that intelligence is relatively unaffected in athetosis. The damage in athetosis is subcortical (in the basal ganglia), and intelligence was therefore thought to be less impaired. However, there appears to be no significant difference in general intelligence between the two main forms of cerebral palsy. Dunsdon (1952) and Schonell (1956) both report quadriplegics to be less intelligent than those with a lesser number of limbs involved. The reason for the lowered IQ of quadriplegics could be that their paralytic handicap keeps them from learning at the rate others learn, or it could be that in quadriplegia the extent of damage outside the motor area of the brain tends to be greater.

A. Heilman (1952) reported 59 percent of cerebral-palsied children to be mentally retarded; J. W. Wrightstone, J. Justman, and S. Moskowitz (1954) estimated 27 percent; and J. Greenbaum and J. A. Buehler (1960) 45 to 55 percent. These discrepancies no doubt reflect the selection factor operating in the schools from which the samples of students were drawn. If a school is highly selective, it is likely to have fewer low-intellect individuals among its cerebral-palsied.

In view of the range, it is difficult to characterize the intelligence of the cerebral-palsied. Intellectually they do not represent a homogeneous group, although the general trend is for intelligence to be low.

Associated defects

Other than motor paralysis and decreased intellectual efficiency, which are characteristic of the cerebral-palsied, a number of defects are commonly found. Roughly 30 percent of children with cerebral palsy are reported to have a history of one or more epileptic seizures (Floyer, 1955; Hopkins, Bice, & Colton, 1954). In a study of certified mentally defective children, B. H. Kirman (1956) reported that children with epilepsy tended to be less intelligent than those not so afflicted. Visual defects and speech disorders are common. Speech defects probably occur in about 70 percent of the cases of cerebral palsy (Stephen, 1958). Hearing disabilities have been reported as more frequent than in other populations. Sensory impairment has been reported in 50 percent of cases of hemiplegia (Tizard, Paine, and Crothers, 1954).

Cerebral-palsied children, particularly those who are mentally retarded, have a wide variety of concomitant defects. When the additional defects are added to the already existing ones, they represent a tremendous handicap. The cerebral-palsied child is typically a multiply handicapped child.

Treatment and training

Special facilities for the treatment and training of cerebral-palsied and other brain-damaged children have grown rapidly during the past 30 years. The training and subsequent rehabilitation of those who are not mentally retarded are very promising, and a number of physical therapy theories and procedures have been developed (McDonald & Chance, 1964). Adolescent youngsters have been successfully trained as para-professionals to work with the handicapped (Rouse & Farb, 1974), and approaches to management of cerebral palsy are being evaluated (Heal, 1974). The treatment of learning disabilities among the cerebral-palsied is discussed elsewhere in this book.

SUMMARY

Children and adults with orthopedic handicaps are those who have problems of physical motility. The orthopedically handicapped include people with a large variety of physical disabilities. Orthopedic handicaps can stem from innumerable causes, and the incidence of such handicaps is relatively high. The relationship between various psychological variables and physical handicap is not a close one. Emotional and social adjustment and intellective status of the physically handicapped were discussed.

Cerebral palsy has a long history, but little systematic work was done until the 1930s. Cerebral palsy is a motor defect present at birth or appearing soon after, and dependent on pathologic abnormalities in the brain. It has been classified and described in a variety of ways. The most common is according to type. Three main types are generally considered: spastic, athetoid, and ataxic. Spasticity is characterized by jerky, spasmodic movements. Athetosis is characterized by rhythmical, writhing movements, and ataxia by disturbances in balance.

The incidence of cerebral palsy is probably from 1 to 3 per 1,000 school-age children. It has been estimated that there are about 40 cases under twenty years of age for each 100,000 people.

Cerebral palsy is caused by brain damage of one kind or another. The causes of brain damage are many. They have been divided into prenatal, natal, and postnatal factors. A number of conditions giving rise to injury before, during, or shortly after birth have been studied and reported.

The intelligence of the cerebral-palsied is rather low. Roughly half have IQ's below 70. The distribution of intelligence is crowded toward the lower end. However, the range of intelligence among the cerebral-palsied is rather large. Sensory defects are common. Concomitant defects in cerebral-palsied mentally deficient are frequent. The cerebral-palsied person typically suffers from a multiplicity of handicaps.

Brain-injured children display a wide variety of physical disabilities and behavioral disorders.

REFERENCES

Adams, J., T. J. Kenny, R. A. Peterson, & A. Carter, "Age Effects and Revised Scoring of the Canter BIP for Identifying Children with Cerebral Dysfunction," *Journal of Consulting and Clinical Psychology*, 1975, *43*, 117–18.

Asher, P., & F. E. Schonell, "A Survey of 100 Cases of Cerebral Palsy in Childhood," *Archives of Diseases of Childhood*, 1950, *25*, 360–79.

Baker, H. J., *Exceptional Children*, 3rd ed. (New York: Macmillan, 1959).

Benda, C. E., *Developmental Disorders of Mentation and the Cerebral Palsies* (New York: Grune & Stratton, 1952).

Bice, H. V., & W. M. Cruickshank, "The Evaluation of Intelligence," in W. M. Cruickshank & S. Raus, eds., *Cerebral Palsy: Its Individual and Community Problems* (Syracuse, N.Y.: Syracuse University Press, 1955).

Boyles, I. J., & G. Calovini, *Statistical Report: Physically Handicapped Children in Illinois* (Springfield, Ill.: Office of Superintendent of Public Institutions, 1960).

Broida, D. C., C. E. Izard, & W. M. Cruickshank, "Thematic Apperception Reactions of Crippled Children," *Journal of Clinical Psychology*, 1950, *6*, 243–48.

Coughlin, E. W., "Some Parental Attitudes Toward Handicapped Children," *The Child*, 1941, *6*, 41–45.

Cruickshank, W. M., ed., *Psychology of Exceptional Children and Youth*, 3rd ed. (Englewood Cliffs, N.J.: Prentice-Hall, 1972).

Cruickshank, W. M., & J. E. Dolphin, "The Emotional Needs of Crippled and Non-crippled Children," *Journal of Exceptional Children*, 1949, *16*, 33–40.

Cruickshank, W. M., & S. Raus, eds., *Cerebral Palsy: Its Individual and Community Problems* (Syracuse, N.Y.: Syracuse University Press, 1955).

Dunsdon, M. I., *The Educability of Cerebral Palsied Children* (London: National Foundation for Educational Research, 1952).

Floyer, E. B., *A Psychological Study of a City's Cerebral Palsied Children* (Manchester: British Council for the Welfare of Spastics, 1955).

Garrison, K. C., & D. G. Force, Jr., *The Psychology of Exceptional Children*, 4th ed. (New York: Ronald Press, 1965).

Gauger, A. B., "Statistical Survey of a Group of Institutionalized Cerebral Palsy Patients," *American Journal of Mental Deficiency*, 1950, *55*, 90–98.

Greenbaum, J., & J. A. Buehler, "Further Findings on the Intelligence of Children with Cerebral Palsy," *American Journal of Mental Deficiency*, 1960, *65*, 261–64.

Heal, L. W., "Evaluation of an Integrated Approach to the Management of Cerebral Palsy," *Exceptional Children*, 1974, *40*, 452–53.

Heilman, A., "Intelligence in Cerebral Palsy," *Crippled Child*, 1952, *30*, 12.

Hopkins, T., H. V. Bice, & K. Colton, *Evaluation and Education of the Cerebral Palsied Child* (Washington, D.C.: International Council for Exceptional Children, 1954).

KIRMAN, B. H., "Epilepsy and Cerebral Palsy," *Archives of Disease in Childhood,* 1956, *31,* 1–7.

McDONALD, E. J., & B. CHANCE, JR., *Cerebral Palsy* (Englewood Cliffs, N.J.: Prentice-Hall, 1964).

MAHAN, G. H., "Special Provisions for Handicapped Students in Colleges," *Exceptional Children,* 1974, *41,* 51–53.

MEYER, V., "A Critique of Psychological Approaches to Brain Damage," *Journal of Mental Science,* 1957, *103,* 70–109.

MILLER, E., & G. B. ROSENFELD, "The Psychologic Evaluation of Children with Cerebral Palsy and Its Implications in Treatment," *Journal of Pediatrics,* 1952, *41,* 613–21.

NATIONAL SAFETY COUNCIL, *Accident Facts.* (Chicago: National Safety Council, 1975).

NEURINGER, C., G. GOLDSTEIN, & R. B. GALLAHER, JR., "Minimal Field Dependency and Minimal Brain Dysfunction," *Journal of Consulting and Clinical Psychology,* 1975, *43,* 20–21.

NEWCOMER, P., & D. HAMMILL, "Visual Perception of Motor Impaired Children: Implications for Assessment," *Exceptional Children,* 1973, *39,* 335–37.

PHELPS, W. M., "Recent Significant Trends in the Case of Cerebral Palsy," *Southern Medical Journal,* 1946, *38,* 132–38.

ROUSE, B. M., & J. FARB, "Training Adolescents to Use Behavior Modification with the Severely Handicapped," *Exceptional Children,* 1974, *40,* 286–88.

SAFFIAN, S., "Program Trends in Crippling Conditions: 1950–1960 (Washington, D.C.: Child Health Studies Branch, Division of Research, United States Department of Health, Education and Welfare, 1962).

SARASON, S. B., *Psychological Problems in Mental Deficiency* (New York: Harper & Row, 1959).

SAWREY, J. M., & C. W. TELFORD, *The Psychology of Adjustment,* 4th ed. (Boston: Allyn & Bacon, 1975).

SCHONELL, F. E., *Educating Spastic Children* (Edinburgh: Oliver & Boyd, 1956).

SMITH, R. M., & J. T. NEISWORTH, *The Exceptional Child: A Functional Approach* (New York: McGraw-Hill, 1975).

SMOCK, C., & W. M. CRUICKSHANK, "Responses of Handicapped and Normal Children to the Rosenzweig P–F Study," *Quarterly Journal of Behavior,* 1952, *1,* 156–64.

STEPHEN, E., "Cerebral Palsy and Mental Defect," in A. M. Clarke & A. D. Clarke, eds., *Mental Deficiency: The Changing Outlook* (New York: Free Press, 1958).

TIZARD, J. P., R. S. PAINE, & B. CROTHERS, "Disturbance of Sensation in Children with Hemiplegia," *Journal of American Medical Association,* 1954, *155,* 628–32.

UNITED STATES OFFICE OF EDUCATION, *Better Education for the Handicapped: Annual Report, Fiscal Year, 1969* (Washington, D.C., 1970).

WHITE HOUSE CONFERENCE REPORT, UNITED STATES DEPARTMENT OF HEALTH, EDUCATION AND WELFARE, *Summary of Health and Vital Statistics* (Washington, D.C., 1958).

WILSON, M., "Children with Crippling and Health Disabilities," in L. M. Dunn, ed., *Exceptional Children in the Schools,* 2nd ed. (New York: Holt, Rinehart and Winston, 1973).

WRIGHT, B. A., *Physical Disability: A Psychological Approach* (New York: Harper & Row, 1960).

WRIGHTSTONE, J. W., J. JUSTMAN, & S. MOSKOWITZ, "Studies of Children with Physical Handicaps. II: The Child with Orthopedic Limitations" (New York: Board of Education of the City of New York, Bureau of Educational Research, 1954).

WYLLIE, W. S., "Cerebral Palsies in Infancy," in A. Feiling, ed., *Modern Trends in Neurology* (London: Butterworth, 1951).

YANNET, H., "The Etiology of Congenital Cerebral Palsy," *Journal of Pediatrics,* 1944, *24,* 38–45.

Chapter 15

Communication disorders

Concern for the person with a speech defect undoubtedly preceded by centuries the development of an interest in normal speech. Several centuries before Christ, Greek physicians were prescribing cures for stuttering. However, it is largely within the present century that systematic studies of normal speech have been made, and only within the twentieth century have scientific investigations of the nature, causes, and treatment of speech defects been systematically pursued. Special community and school services for persons with disorders of communication are relatively new, compared to the services provided for the more dramatic forms of disability such as blindness and orthopedic handicaps. The first statutes in the United States providing special services for speech defectives were enacted by Wisconsin in 1913. The following year, Dr. Similey Blanton established the first university clinic for speech problems at the University of Wisconsin (Irwin, 1955).

Many different professional specialties—general medicine, plastic surgery, otology, oral surgery, dentistry, psychiatry, psychology, education, and speech therapy—are involved in the diagnosis and treatment of speech disorders. A wide variety of disciplines is necessarily involved in speech correction, because anatomical, sociological, psychological, and educational factors all contribute to speech impairment and correction. Speech defects may be caused by anatomical defects or deviant physiological functioning of the jaws, tongue, or soft palate; by disturbed feelings, emotions, or attitudes; by inadequate self-concepts; and by faulty language habits arising from unsatisfactory speech models, social pressures, and misguided efforts at speech training or correction.

DEFINITIONS OF COMMUNICATION DISORDERS

There have been few attempts to define communication impairment quantitatively. The commonly accepted definitions are all largely functional in nature. Three components seem to be common to most current answers to the question: What is defective speech? Speech is considered to be defective when the manner of speaking interferes with communication, when the person's manner of speaking distracts attention from what is said, or when speech is such that the speaker himself is unduly self-conscious or apprehensive about his way of speaking. More concisely, speech is defective whenever the deviant manner of speaking interferes with communication, calls undue attention to itself, or causes the speaker concern to such an extent that special educational or remedial measures are deemed necessary.

These criteria vary according to their social context. The listening ear defines the intelligibility and distractibility of speech. The speaker himself is the measure of his personal concern. One's culture, subculture, and status within the culture, as well as one's age, profession, and role in life, enter into a definition of defective speech. The speech of the average three-year-old is defective by adult standards, but normal for his age group. The adolescent from the slum who says "dese" for "these," "dose" for "those," and "dem" for "them" will not usually be labeled a speech defective. A southern drawl, an eastern twang, or midwestern nasality are normal in those geographic regions and become matters of concern outside these localities only to radio announcers, actors, and public speakers. The listener matches the speech that he hears against a varying standard of acceptability and intelligibility, and labels speech as normal or defective accordingly.

There are similarly marked variations in what speakers find objectionable in their own speech. Many people are unable to detect marked impairments in their own speech, while others request therapy for speech which is well within the normal range. The speaker's level of personal concern does not always agree with the listener's judgment.

IDENTIFICATION AND DIAGNOSIS OF COMMUNICATION DISORDERS

Many people are identified as speech defectives by their families, by their peers, or by themselves. Some people who go to speech clinics and speech correctionists are referred by other professional people, such as doctors, psychiatrists, psychologists, and teachers. In schools, many children are referred by their regular classroom teachers. Others are identified by systematic screening procedures. Many schools, in addition to requesting referrals by teachers, systematically screen one or two grades each year.

Individuals thus identified as probable speech defectives usually undergo more thorough diagnostic examinations before treatment is started. Depending on the nature of the referral and the amount of information available, the diagnosis may be made either by a single person—the speech correctionist—or by a team of specialists. A complete diagnostic evaluation involves a complete physical examination, including a dental examination to disclose any oral, dental, or other organic factors contributing to the disorder. An assessment of intellectual level, an audiometric evaluation of hearing, and sometimes a psychiatric examination are also made to disclose any intellectual, auditory, or personality deviations which may complicate the picture.

Several screening and diagnostic scales and tests are available to aid in speech assessment (Travis, 1971; Turton, 1973; Renfrew, 1973). Some of these are the Wood Index of Defective Articulation, the Templin-Darley Screening and Diagnostic Tests of Articulation, and the Boston University Speech Sound Discrimination Picture Test. For evaluation of the severity of speech impairment there are scales of phonographically recorded samples of defective speech graded in terms of severity, with which a particular person's speech can be compared (Curry et al., 1943; Perrin, 1954). R. S. Tikofsky and R. P. Tikofsky (1965) have shown that fairly objective ratings of speech intelligibility can be made with the aid of such devices.

Recent developments in psycholinguistics have stimulated the use of informal qualitative testing procedures (Turton, 1975). L. Lee and S. M. Canter (1971) have developed a set of measuring devices which involve both formal and informal techniques.

PREVALENCE OF SPEECH DISORDERS

Surveys of the prevalence of speech disorders are not very reliable because of the varying purpose served by the surveys, the different standards applied, the diverse populations sampled, and the biases of the investigators. When all degrees and categories of speech defects are included, the total of speech-impaired schoolchildren identified is estimated at around 10 percent. One nationwide sampling of children seven years of age in England found about 10 percent of the children to have "significant speech impairments." When these same children were eleven years old, their parents and teachers alike reported 4 percent of the children to have current speech problems (Peckham, 1973).

Several surveys have reported from 7 to 8 percent of school-age children with speech defects (Pronovost, 1951). Two committees of the American Speech and Hearing Association (1952, 1959) have independently estimated that a minimum of 5 percent of school-age children have defects of speech sufficiently serious to warrant speech correction or therapy, and that an additional 5 percent suffer from noticeable but less serious defects. A breakdown of the estimated prevalence of speech problems and accompanying disorders is given in table 15–1.

Table 15–1

Distribution of speech defects of various types and causes in public school children

Type of Defect	Percentage
Articulatory defects	81.0
Stuttering	6.5
Delayed speech	4.5
Hard-of-hearing	2.5
Voice problems	2.3
Cleft palate	1.5
Cerebral palsy	1.0
Aphasia Bilinguality Mental retardation }	0.7
Total	100.0

Data from American Speech and Hearing Association (1961).

There are more people with speech defects than with any other type of exceptionality, with the possible exceptions of the emotionally disturbed, the "slow learners," and the culturally disadvantaged. Many more males than females have speech defects—two to five times as many, depending on the type of disorders (Peckham, 1973). The full explanations of these sex differences are not known.

CAUSES OF SPEECH DEFECTS

Speech defects are caused by a wide variety of organic and functional (social and psychological) factors. The organic causes include cleft palate, maldevelopment of other parts of the mouth and jaw, dental irregularities including missing or maloccluded teeth, muscular paralysis of the larynx, tumors or ulcers in or around the larynx, loss of the larynx, brain damage (in cerebral palsy and aphasia), and nasal obstructions. C. E. Hamre (1972) and M. D. Sheridan (1973) consider the high incidence of the symptoms of neurological defects among children with marked speech defects to be evidence of a general neurodevelopmental deficit in these children.

Functional causes include failure to learn adequate speech, fixations, regressive speech patterns, and general personality and emotional disturbances.

Many speech specialists do not find the dichotomy between organic and functional a very useful one. Speech difficulties which are strictly organic in origin usually acquire a large functional component as a result of the way the person reacts to the difficulty, and prolonged functional disorders may have organic consequences. Although it is possible for organic disorders to remain on that level with relatively little functional component, and for functional disorders to continue without any specific organic components, they rarely do so; most speech defects have both functional and organic components.

Recently, attention seems to be shifting from the organic to the functional as the most significant factors in the etiology of most speech defects (Van Riper & Irwin, 1958).

Recent developments in psycholinguistics may provide a new approach or a new emphasis to the study of deviant speech and language (Turton, 1975). The more complete understanding of normal psycholinguistic processes may throw light on the nature of the disturbances of speech and language. For example, P. Menyuk (1964), using a conventional linguistic model, compared the syntactic structures of children with "infantile" speech with those of otherwise comparable normal-speaking children. Her analysis indicated that at no age level did the grammatical forms used by the deviant speakers resemble the grammar used by younger normal speakers. She concluded that "infantile speech" is a misnomer. The linguistically impaired children had disordered or disorganized rather than delayed linguistic development.

NONLANGUAGE CHARACTERISTICS OF THE SPEECH-IMPAIRED

Like most other types of handicapped people, persons with speech defects often have other disabilities. Many of them, at least more than those with normal speech, are mentally retarded, brain-damaged, or have developmental anomalies such as cleft palate and cleft lip. Therefore, in asking what the speech-impaired are like, we need to define the population. If all individuals with defective speech are included, we obtain a very heterogeneous population, some subgroups of which are characterized by deviant physiques or intellectual levels, for example, the cerebral-palsied and the mentally retarded. Since the group with defective speech conta ns a disproportionate number of physically and intellectually handicapped individuals, we would expect the mean level of the entire group to be below that of the general population. On the other hand, if we inquire into the physical, intellectual, and personal characteristics of people whose *only* handicap is their speech impairment, the answer may be different. There are few, if any, studies of such groups; consequently, our discussion must deal with the entire group of people with defective speech.

Physical characteristics of the speech-impaired

Most individuals with defective speech are apparently physically normal. That is, most speech defects are primarily functional in nature and are unaccompanied by marked organic impairments. However, about 16 percent of the children with the more serious types of speech defects also have physical disabilities, and this group is large enough to bring the entire group of speech-impaired individuals below the norm of the entire population in general physique (Eisenson, 1963).

One intensive study which compared seven-year-old children with marked speech defects and normal hearing to a comparable "normal" control group found that the speech-impaired youngsters displayed the following distinguishing characteristics (Sheridan, 1973):

1. A higher proportion were born prematurely.
2. Four times the number of the speech-handicapped were not walking at eighteen months.
3. Seven times as many of the special group as of the controls had not spoken in phrases by two years.
4. Four times as many of the handicapped as of controls were visually impaired.
5. Forty-six percent of the special group, as against 13 percent of the controls, were rated by their teachers as "appreciably clumsy."
6. Four times as many of the speech-defectives were judged by their teachers to be behaviorally maladjusted.
7. There were ten times the incidence of nonreaders among the speech defectives.
8. There were twice as many boys as girls in the defective group.

Sheridan believes that the marked prevalence of unfavorable neurological and psychological manifestations among the handicapped suggests the involvement of some general "neuro-developmental disorder." The study also found that a disproportionate number of the speech-handicapped came from the lower socio-economic classes.

Sensory capacities of the speech-impaired

We find a larger incidence of speech defects among the severely visually and aurally impaired than among the population at large. When we exclude these extreme subgroups, the relationship between speech defects and sensory capacities largely disappears. Many speech correctionists believe that speech-impaired individuals—particularly those with defective articulation—are weak in auditory discrimination. Consequently, auditory discrimination testing has become a standard part of test batteries used for the identification of speech defects (Turton, 1975).

Intelligence level of speech defectives

Studies have consistently found a positive relationship between language proficiency and intelligence level. Therefore, it is not surprising to find that children with speech defects fall below the norms in measured intelligence (Everhart, 1953; Sheridan, 1973). Defects such as the absence of speech, marked delay in acquiring speech, and poor articulation, which may be caused by the child's failure to learn, are, of course, very common among the mentally retarded. However, when the mentally retarded are excluded, there is still a slight relationship between measured intelligence and the incidence of speech defects (Eisenson, 1963). It is possible that differences in socio-economic level may be a causal factor here also.

Educational achievement of the speech-impaired

Even excluding the mentally retarded and the cerebral-palsied, children with speech defects are relatively retarded in school (Berry & Eisenson, 1956; Sheridan, 1973). Speech defectives are retarded scholastically even out of proportion to expectations based on their intelligence test scores (Eisenson, 1963). Social-class differences can hardly account for the greater educational than intellectual retardation of children with speech defects. It would seem that speech defects constitute a greater handicap in formal learning than they do in acquiring the more general intellectual skills and information required for satisfactory intelligence-test performance.

CLASSIFICATIONS OF SPEECH DISORDERS

Speech defects are classified in several ways, depending on the purpose of the classification and the interest of the researcher. As previously indicated, a broad twofold classification of speech defects into the organic and the functional is commonly used when etiology is considered. Surveys of speech problems typically classify defects according to the forms they take and according to other associated and causal factors. Accordingly, we have articulatory disorders, disturbances of rhythm, voice disorders, delayed or retarded speech, mutism, and aphonia as types of defects. In a third type of classification, we list speech disorders associated with cleft palate, brain damage (cerebral palsy and aphasia), deafness, and mental retardation.

These various classifications cut across each other. Most of the classes of disorders based on symptoms (articulatory, voice, rhythm, delayed speech, and so forth), with the possible exception of aphasia, can be either organic or functional. Speech disorders of mentally retarded, cleft-palated, or cerebral-palsied individuals may take any of the forms listed, although certain types are more common than others.

Disorders of articulation

Disorders of articulation consist of omission ("at" for "cat"), substitution ("gog" for "dog"), and distortion or additions ("furog" for "frog") of speech sounds. They may involve the mispronunciation of an entire word or words.

Certain articulatory disorders are referred to as *immature speech* (baby talk), since all children make these errors in the early stages of language development. Table 15–2 shows the age levels when children are normally able to properly articulate certain sounds. More recent studies (Mecham, Berko, & Berko, 1960) indicate that *p, b, m,* and *o* are usually the easiest sounds for children to articulate. Additional sounds, in order of chronological development, are *h, w, d, k, g, j, f, v, t, z, l, s, u,* and *r.* This order agrees well with J. P. Davis's (1938) norms. A large percentage of errors of articulation are eliminated by the time children reach the fourth grade, that is, by the age of nine or ten (Roe & Milisen, 1942). After this age, defects of articulation seldom diminish without specific remedial measures.

Table 15–2
Ages at which children are normally able
to articulate certain sounds

Age (in Years)	Sounds
3.5	b, p, m, w, h
4.5	t, d, g, k, ng, y
5.5	f, v, s, z
6.5	sh, l, th (as in then)

Data from Davis (1938).

Lisping is another common form of articulatory defect among pre-school and lower-grade children. Its frequency decreases rapidly as children get older, but its persistence beyond the first or second grade warrants corrective procedures. *Lalling* (distortions of *r* and *l* sounds) is sometimes listed as an additional form of articulatory disorder.

Disorders of articulation are the most common form of speech defects, accounting for from 60 to 80 percent of diagnosed speech disorders.

Delayed speech

The age at which normal children begin to speak varies so widely that it is impossible to set a specific age beyond which delay in speaking is exceptional. However, when a child of three or four does not talk, it should become a matter for study. There are many causes of delayed speech. Table 15–3 indicates the principal causes of delayed speech in a fairly large group of children.

Table 15–3
Delayed speech in 278 children

Cause of Delay	Number of Children
Deafness	110
Developmental aphasia	72
Mental deficiency	71
Cerebral palsy	22
Mental illness	3

Data from Morley et al. (1955).

In addition to the major causes of delayed speech listed in table 15–3, some children do not learn to speak at the usual age because of lack of motivation. When doting parents or nurses anticipate every wish, or when gestures, grunts, or cries are effective in controlling others, children may have no need for words. Children with delayed speech because of insufficient motivation may be otherwise normal. They may be well-behaved and may seem to have made a satisfactory adjustment to the world without speaking. However, some nonverbal children who are not deaf, mentally retarded, brain-damaged, or seriously mentally ill display other patterns of deviant behavior. Some isolate themselves as far as possible from other people, and others seek out close physical contact with both adults and inanimate objects. They rub their bodies along the walls or on furniture, rub their faces against toys, climb on laps and snuggle up even to strangers (McWilliams, 1959). The significance of these activities is not known, but they are often considered symptomatic of personality disorders.

Disorders of voice production: phonation

Voice disorders consist of marked deviations in the loudness, pitch, quality, duration, or flexibility of sounds. In addition to the relatively simple variations of each, there are other voice defects, such as breathiness, harshness, hoarseness, and nasality. Voice disorders have the lowest incidence of all categories of speech disorders among children. They are difficult to correct in children, principally because the speech mechanism is still developing and the voice quality is changing. Voice disorders are more often diagnosed and treated in adults than in children, whereas the opposite is true of articulatory disorders and delayed speech.

Disturbances of rhythm: stuttering, stammering, and cluttering

Although some workers (Weiss, 1964) claim that stuttering, stammering, and cluttering should be differentiated, most authors do not discriminate among them. We shall use the term *stuttering* to cover the entire range of rhythmic disorders, and leave any differentiations within the group to the specialists.

Stuttering is one of the more dramatic communication disorders. The American Hearing and Speech Association estimates that somewhere between one and two million Americans stutter. Four of five stutterers recover without professional help—mostly in childhood. The association estimates that probably no more than 10 percent of adult stutterers "recover" (Smith, 1972).

The literature on stuttering is voluminous and often contradictory. More research has been done and more material written on stuttering than on any other type of speech disorder. Theories about the causes of stuttering range from the organic, through social learning, to mental hygiene. Therapy has varied from routine drills and breathing exercises, through behavior modification, through individual and group psychotherapy, to hypnosis and faith cures (see Van Riper, 1973). There are no forms of treatment that cannot claim a sizable number of successes. We shall briefly summarize the principal research findings and indicate, as best we can, the current theories of stuttering and methods of treatment.

Definitions of stuttering   It is easier to describe stuttering than to define it. Stuttering is one of the major forms of nonfluency. It is primarily a disturbance of the normal flow and rhythm of speech. It involves blocks, hesitations, and prolongations, and repetitions of sounds, syllables, words, or phrases. It is frequently accompanied by muscular tension, rapid eye-blinking, irregularities of breathing, and facial grimacing. No two stutterers have the same secondary symptoms.

Causes of stuttering   The alleged causes of stuttering have been as diverse as the theories, and are often related to them. The earlier conceptions stressed organic factors such as heredity and lack of hemispheric brain dominance (Travis, 1931). The social learning, mental hygiene, or psychological conceptions have stressed habit, personality, and emotional factors as the primary causal factors. No one cause or set of causes has been discovered to date. Stuttering probably has multiple causation.

The types of evidence usually presented in support of the alleged organic etiology, together with some comments, are:

1. The incidence of stuttering in the family lines of stutterers is much greater than in the families of nonstutterers, suggesting a possible genetic basis (Nelson, 1939; West, Nelson, Berry, 1939). (Common family child-rearing practices, attitudes, and expectancies [the self-fulfilling prophecy] can also account for this high incidence.)
2. Stuttering is more frequent among left-handed people and among people shifted from their original left-hand preference (West, Nelson, & Berry, 1939). This fact has been used to support a lack-of-brain-dominance conception of the cause of stuttering. (The conflicts involved in changing handedness may induce tensions which may precipitate stuttering. Recent neurological findings also do not support the lack-of-cerebral-dominance concept [Gruber & Powell, 1974].)
3. Stuttering has a number of physiological components or accompaniments (Walker & Walker, 1973; Turton, 1975).
4. Stuttering is associated with multiple births (twinning, and so forth), and with prematurity (Sheridan, 1973).
5. There is a greater-than-chance incidence of central nervous system disorders among stutterers (Gregory, 1964; Sheridan, 1973).

The functional conceptions of stuttering seem to be supported by the following facts:

1. Stuttering varies tremendously as a function of situational factors (Siegel & Haugen, 1964; Turton, 1975).
2. Stuttering (secondary stuttering) has profound emotional components (Sheehan, 1958b; Walker & Walker, 1973).
3. Nondirective and psychoanalytic psychotherapy which improves general adjustment, reduces conflicts, and decreases anxieties often helps or cures stuttering.

4. Stuttering most often develops at times when the child experiences considerable social pressure (when learning to speak, on entering school, and to a lesser degree at adolescence).

5. The parents of stutterers display a characteristic pattern of traits consisting of perfectionism and high levels of aspiration for their children (Goldman & Shames, 1964; Kinstler, 1961).

W. Johnson's (1942, 1956) "diagnosogenic" conception of the origin of stuttering is typical of the functional, social-psychological point of view. According to Johnson, when the young child experiences normal nonfluencies while learning to speak, his parents often fail to recognize that he is passing through a normal transitional stage of language learning. They label the child's normal blockings, hesitations, and repetitions as "stuttering," and become concerned about his "defective" speech. The label associated with manifestations of parental anxiety becomes a stigma. The child eventually becomes concerned about his speech, believing that he is a stutterer. He then becomes fearful of not speaking properly and establishes a vicious cycle of fear–anxiety–nonfluency–increased fear–higher levels of anxiety–greater nonfluency, and so forth. According to this conception, stuttering begins in the mind or ears of the listener, and is transferred to the child as concern for his own speech. The child comes to anticipate stuttering, dreads it, tries to avoid it, becomes tense, and so stutters.

Cross-cultural studies lend some support to Johnson's contention. Certain cultures with very tolerant and accepting attitudes toward speech (Ute and Pilagra Indians and native Polynesians) are said to have little, if any, stuttering, and their languages contain no words for it. In cultures with strict standards of speech (the Cowickan and Japanese societies), the incidence of stuttering is high and there are specific names for the disorder (Stewart, 1960; Lemert, 1962; Henry & Henry, 1940).

Studies of the parents of stutterers also report results which are consistent with Johnson's "diagnosogenic" conception of the origin of stuttering. These studies indicate that the parents of stutterers and nonstutterers differ in their patterns of parent–child interaction. The parents of stutterers are more critical and intolerant of deviant behavior in their children. They are more perfectionistic and hold higher levels of aspiration for their children. Furthermore, these attitudes are specifically related to the speech area (Goodstein, 1958). Readers interested in a good presentation of Johnson's theory, as well as several other conceptions of stuttering, should read the books by H. L. Luper and R. L. Mulden (1964), and by F. B. Robinson (1964). M. E. Wingate (1962a, 1962b, 1964) in a series of three articles, and R. I. Lanyon and D. A. Duprez (1970), in a more recent study, review the evidence bearing on the Johnson diagnosogenic or evaluational theory of stuttering and question the adequacy of this conception of the etiology of stuttering. On the other hand, E. K. Sander's (1963) experiment concerned with listeners' evaluations of simulated disfluent speech yields results which are consistent with the proposition that stuttering may well have its genesis in the ears of the listener.

Continued interest in the possible organic basis for stuttering is reflected in studies such as H. H. Gregory's (1964) hypothesis that stuttering may be related to a "central auditory disturbance" and R. Martin's (1962) testing of the hypothesis that stuttering may derive from a "constitutional tendency to perseverate." However, the data derived from these studies support neither hypothesis. A recent hypothesis is Sheridan's (1973) postulation of a general neurological disorder.

Primary and secondary stuttering   The distinction between primary and secondary stuttering made by C. S. Bluemel in 1932 has proven to be a useful one even though the dichotomy has been criticized by others and has been somewhat modified by Bluemel himself (Bluemel, 1932, 1957; Bloodstein, 1961; Turton, 1975). As we have indicated, all children experience a degree of nonfluency when learning to speak. A large number —some say as many as 30 percent—of children between the ages of two and four show blockings, hesitations, and repetitions of sounds or words. From an objective standpoint, they stutter. However, at this age—the so-called primary stage—the child is not aware of his speech difficulties. He is not self-conscious about his speech. He does not experience the secondary symptoms of increased muscular tension, fear, and struggle that characterize the secondary stage of stuttering.

In the secondary stage of stuttering, the individual has been labeled by himself and others as a stutterer. He approaches speech in general, and certain words or sounds in particular, with anxiety. He is afraid that he will stutter. His fear increases the probability of his stuttering. In this stage the reactions of listeners become critical when they focus the child's attention on his disfluencies. Some speech therapists claim that only secondary stuttering is true stuttering. Primary stuttering is only "normal nonfluency."

Irrespective of their theoretical commitments, all speech specialists agree that social factors are important, if not crucial, in the development of stuttering (Adams & Dietze, 1965; Andrews & Cutler, 1974). Most of the psychogenic or social-learning conceptions of stuttering also assign a crucial role to fear or anxiety in the genesis of stuttering (Schwartz, 1974). Social attitudes and anxiety are both essential components of most functional (mental hygiene) conceptions of the origins of stuttering.

Irrespective of its cause, as the child grows older each individual stutterer develops a systematic and fairly predictable pattern of blocking and/or repeating certain sounds or words in certain locations, such as at the beginning of a sentence or phrase. The rate and severity of disfluency in most stutterers will vary with environmental stress. Some typically high-stress situations are responding orally in class, being disciplined or frustrated, and talking on a telephone. Conversely, choral reading or speaking, singing, reciting memorized poems, and casual conversation with a friend are less stressful for most disfluent speakers.

The stutterer's different sensitivities to social situations typically result in his developing patterns of specific-situation avoidance. This takes two forms. One is the avoidance of sounds and words which are hard to say. The other is the avoidance of speaking in stressful situations such as speaking orally in class or speaking in public. The individual attempts to deal with the communication problem, not by dealing with his disfluent speech, but by manipulating circumstances so as to reduce the personal and social consequences of stuttering.

The treatment of primary stuttering   Even though the distinction between primary and secondary stuttering is difficult to make, the initial hesitations, blockings, and repetitions of the two- to four-year old require different treatment than do the secondary symptoms of the confirmed stutterer. Here are some general suggestions for parents and other adults concerned about the nonfluencies of the child who is in the early stages of language acquisition:

1. Measures taken should be indirect and not concerned with the speech deviations as such.
2. Keep the child in good physical condition.
3. Provide a pleasant, relaxed home atmosphere.
4. Provide as many good speech models as possible.
5. Try to develop feeling of adequacy and self-confidence (a satisfactory self-concept) in the child by using his assets and minimizing his liabilities.
6. If referred to, child's nonfluencies should be acknowledged but accepted as normal. The impression that they are bad or that other people are anxious about them should be avoided.

Symptomatic treatment of the secondary stutterer   Symptomatic treatment may attempt to teach the person either to stutter in a way that is tolerable to himself and to others (controlled stuttering), or to talk without stuttering (inhibition of stuttering).

Controlled stuttering is attained by teaching the stutterer rate-controlled speech techniques of breathing and controlled phrasing, through the repetition of what is said, reading in unison, negative practice (practice in stuttering) and various distracting devices. Remedial procedures are intended to develop tolerance of stuttering, emotional desensitization, anxiety reduction, and controlled speech. Treatment designed to make it possible for the person to talk without stuttering consists in teaching him analytically, step by step, to articulate properly and gradually to build up fluency. Many of the same techniques used in teaching controlled stuttering may also be used to develop speech which is relatively fluent. A. Irwin (1972) and others claim that they can produce "easy stuttering" simply by slowing down speech. Such stuttering is said to be free of tension. The slow "easy stuttering" can then be speeded up until it approximates normal speech. There are a great many procedures for the control or elimination of stuttering, but no real understanding of how or why they achieve these effects.

Although punishment incident to stuttering would normally be expected to increase the disfluency, it has been shown that operant conditioning involving the administration of mild electric shock to the finger is effective in reducing and/or eliminating stuttering (Beattie, 1973). The contingent application of verbal as well as nonverbal reinforcers—both rewards and punishments—has been used in the treatment of stuttering (Watts, 1973; Patty & Quarrington, 1974).

Pacing speech with a metronome has also been used effectively in the treatment of stuttering, although there has been no satisfactory explanation offered for this. The distracting effect of the sound, the slowing up of speech, and the pacemaker effects have all been proposed as the effective variables. However, the fact that rhythmic beats are more effective than irregular ones seems to discount the distraction explanation. While slow beats (seventy-five to ninety-five per minute) are more effective than slow *a-rhythmic ones,* rate alone does not seem to be the crucial variable. It is necessary for the metronome sound to signal the initiation of each word for it to have a positive pacing effect (Berman & Brady, 1973; Watts, 1973). P. A. Berman and J. P. Brady (1973) found that over half of twenty-eight speech clinicians queried regarded metronome-conditioning to be a major advance in the treatment of stuttering. Delayed auditory feedback has also been used extensively with stutterers. In this procedure the speaker's own sounds are fed back to him after a delay of a fraction of a second. Paradoxically, delayed auditory feedback produces disfluencies in normal speakers and increased fluency in stutterers. Delayed auditory feedback may constitute a slow rate-controlled and stutter-free speech which can subsequently be increased to a normal speaking rate. R. F. Curlee and W. H. Perkins (1973) report such a delayed auditory feedback program to be effective in substantially reducing stuttering, both in the clinic and in everyday speaking situations, with adolescent and adult stutterers.

The treatment of stuttering, as well as of many other types of speech defects, seems to be shifting away from mechanical drills and devices (speech correction) toward therapeutic relationships (speech therapy). One manifestation of this shift in emphasis is a preference for the term *speech therapist* rather than *speech correctionist*.

Psychotherapy for the stutterer   Psychotherapy is used with stutterers on the assumption that the nonfluency is either a symptom of, or is accompanied by, personality maladjustment and that the way to handle the stuttering is to deal with the underlying personality defects. Speech pathologists have recommended and used psychotherapy ranging from directive counseling and group discussion to the nondirective, psychoanalytic, and hypnotic therapies. The goals of psychotherapy for stutterers are essentially the same as those for individuals with normal speech. These include the development of insight (self-understanding), changes in the self-concept (ego building), self-acceptance, emotional desensitization (the reduction of fears and anxieties), and the improvement of personal relations (Wyatt & Herzon, 1962).

Psychotherapy attempts to go beyond the removal of the symptom, and deals with the more basic problems and conflicts on the assumption that speech will improve with personality reorientation and improved adjustment. Some clinicians claim that a combination of general psychotherapy and more specific speech training provides optimum treatment potential (Goraj, 1974).

The personality traits of stutterers   Prescribing psychotherapy for stutterers implies that they need personality reorganization. However, a survey of the studies of the personality traits and characteristics of stutterers does not show them to be markedly maladjusted. L. D. Goodstein (1958), J. T. Goraj (1974), and J. G. Sheehan (1958a) surveyed the literature on the topic published over a twenty-five-year period. They found opinions ranging from the contention that stutterers are essentially normal people except in speech, to the notion that stuttering is the manifestation of a basically neurotic personality. These extensive surveys disclosed little evidence to support the contention that either children or adults who stutter have a particular pattern of personality traits, are neurotic, or are otherwise severely maladjusted. Stutterers certainly do not appear to be severely maladjusted when compared with psychiatric patients. However, they are significantly different from nonstutterers in being more tense, anxious, and withdrawn. Certainly in speaking situations and when they are struggling in a stuttering block, they feel different from others and others perceive them as different. Stutterers also have lower levels of aspiration. They have significantly more personal and social problems than nonstutterers, but it is impossible to tell whether these problems were responsible for the stuttering or developed as a consequence of social reactions to the speech defect.

Speech defects associated with neural impairment

Impairment of brain functioning may be caused by maldevelopment, traumatic injury, hemorrhage, infections, abscesses, and tumors. Such pathology may result in localized injury and the impairment of language functions (aphasia), or it may produce widespread neural damage, with language disorders constituting only a part of a total syndrome which includes widespread muscular paralysis or dysfunction and mental subnormality.

The aphasic child   *Aphasia* literally means loss of speech. As a clinical entity, it is an impairment in the understanding or expression of language due to brain injury. Aphasia is a disturbance of one's ability to handle language symbols. Traditionally, the term has been applied to adults and children who have suffered brain damage *after* language has been acquired. Here the meaning is clear, for there is a loss or impairment of a previously acquired habit system. However, the concept of "congenital aphasia" discussed in a later section implies something different.

Aphasia is typically subdivided into four types. In *sensory* or *receptive aphasia,* the person can hear and see, but cannot understand spoken or written language. The neural damage is usually in the left parietal area of the cerebrum. In *motor* or *expressive aphasia,* the vocal apparatus is not paralyzed but the individual cannot formulate speech properly or write properly. The neural lesion is usually in the left frontal cortex. In *conceptual aphasia,* the person is unable to formulate concepts (less frequently listed as a category). In *global* or *mixed aphasia,* all language forms are affected. In conceptual and global aphasia the neurological damage is more diffuse than in the first two categories (Mohr, 1973; Ajax, 1973).

The loss of the language function due to brain injury in a child who has already acquired language skills does not differ from aphasia in adults, except that the language disturbance is milder than in adults with comparable brain damage and recovery is both more rapid and more complete. However, young normal children and adult aphasics make different types of linguistic errors. This indicates that the partial loss of acquired language abilities produces a different pattern of linguistic impairment than does the incomplete acquisition of that ability by a normal child (Gardner, 1974). As expected, the degree of paraphasia (the introduction of inappropriate words into one's speech) is related to the extent of neural damage and the severity of the resulting aphasia (Beyn & Vlasenko, 1974). The prognosis for postnatally acquired aphasia in children is good (Ajax, 1973).

Congenital aphasia   As early as 1866, some cases of marked language impairment in children who were neither deaf nor mentally retarded were called "congenital aphasia," but the concept never gained general acceptance. However, the question of the existence of such a clinical entity has recently received considerable attention. Despite a persistent controversy concerning the existence of the syndrome, the term has received widespread publicity and several clinics are so labeling certain children with communication disorders (Eisenson, 1965).

Congenital aphasia is often diagnosed by a process of exclusion and inference. When certain language deficits are present in the absence of mental retardation, sensory impairments, or emotional disturbances (autisms), neural pathology is postulated as the probable cause and the child is labeled "aphasic." Some of these children show evidence of central nervous system impairment, but there are many children called "aphasic" whose language impairment is the first and only manifestation of central nervous system deficit (Benton, 1964). However, most workers feel that the term should be reserved for children with positive evidence of cerebral impairment. Failure to develop language, in and of itself, is not presumptive of congenital aphasia.

None of the behavioral symptoms listed as characteristically accompanying childhood aphasia is *peculiar to this syndrome.* The most commonly mentioned symptoms (Barry, 1955; Eisenson, 1963; Edwards, 1965) are:

1. Erratic responses to the same stimulus
2. Distractibility
3. Abnormal fixation on unimportant details
4. Perseveration
5. Hyperactivity
6. Emotional lability
7. Mixed laterality
8. Abnormal delays in responding
9. Perceptual disturbances
10. Poor motor coordination

All of these are symptoms of brain damage in general. Congenital aphasia, as compared with the postnatally acquired condition, is said to be more severe, less likely to disappear spontaneously, less readily corrected by educational and therapeutic programs, and different in the nature of the neural impairment. Ordinary postnatally acquired aphasia is supposed to result from damage to the *dominant cerebral hemisphere.* Children with demonstrable injury to the speech area of *either hemisphere alone,* either congenital or occurring in infancy, are not aphasic, so it is assumed that congenital aphasia involves damage to both hemispheres.

Educators are proposing to substitute the term *verbal communication disorders* for *aphasia,* and to avoid neurological implications by referring to these children simply as "children with learning disabilities" (Bateman, 1964; Capobianco, 1964). M. A. McGinnis (1963) has developed a language training program specifically for aphasic children.

Speech defects associated with cerebral palsy   About 90 percent of children with cerebral palsy are said to have significant speech disorders. Their speech impairments are part of a larger syndrome including abnormal sucking, chewing, swallowing, breathing, and tongue movements. Language training is typically part of their total rehabilitation program. Because of the widespread nature of the neural impairment and the number of accompanying handicaps, speech correction is often difficult. It is recommended that speech training be started when the child normally begins to speak (one to one-and-a-half years of age), and in most cases it will continue for years (Mecham, Berko, & Berko, 1960).

Tests with the Illinois Test of Psycholinguistic Abilities indicate that athetosics—a subcategory of cerebral palsy in which the neural damage is subcortical—are superior to spastics, whose brain injuries are cortical, on the representational level, while the spastics are superior to athetoids on the automatic-sequential levels (Myers, 1965). Spastics are usually superior to athetoids in general language level (Hammill & Irwin, 1965). Speech correctionists working with cerebral-palsied children will find the monograph *Speech Therapy for the Cerebral Palsied,* by H. Westlake and D. Rutherford (1961), helpful.

Speech defects associated with mental retardation

The relationship between mental retardation and speech level is high. Table 15–4 shows this relationship as indicated by a typical study.

There are several reasons for the close relationship between language proficiency and intellectual level. The most obvious is that individuals with lower levels of intelligence lack the capacity for acquiring language.

Table 15–4

Speech defects as related to degrees of mental retardation

IQ	50–69	21–49	20 and below
Percentage with speech defects	43	73	100

Data from Sirken and Lyon (1941).

Before the advent of intelligence testing, idiots were defined as those individuals who were so low in mental level that they did not learn to speak. In addition to the inability of the most severely mentally retarded to acquire speech, mental retardation and speech defects may both have a common cause: brain damage or defective development of the nervous system. Critical reviews of the relationships are given by S. Goertzen (1957) and Smith (1962). The mentally retarded seem to suffer from the same *types* of speech defects as do the mentally normal, although the frequency of defects is greater (Gens, 1951; Anastasiow & Stayrook, 1973).

Speech defects associated with cleft palate

Cleft lip and cleft palate are prenatal in origin. They represent a failure of the bones and the soft tissues of the roof of the mouth and the lips to develop normally. A complete cleft of the palate creates an abnormal opening between the mouth and the nasal cavities. This opening interferes with normal sucking, chewing, swallowing, and speaking. In speaking, the air and speech sounds normally expelled through the mouth can pass without control through the nose. The cleft may involve one or both sides of the upper lip in varying degrees. The American Dental Association estimates that 1 child in every 700 is born with cleft palate (Hull, 1963). Surveys show that the incidence varies from 1 in 276 to 1 in 1,030 in different populations (Tretsven, 1963). The causes of cleft palate are not clearly established, although a genetic factor seems to be involved (Schwartz, 1954). Maternal nutrition, the Rh factor, and maternal illness during pregnancy are among the possible environmental factors (Goodstein, 1961).

The incidence of defective hearing is higher in those with cleft palates than in the normal population. The intelligence level of these children seems to be slightly below that of comparable normal children (Goodstein, 1961; Brennan & Cullinan, 1974). The communicative disabilities, nonverbal as well as verbal, of children with cleft palate are said to be greater than those dictated by the anatomical defect alone (Brennan & Cullinan, 1974). The articulation defects of cleft palate individuals are highly similar in different nationalities (Van Demark, 1974).

Treatment for cleft palate involves surgical correction, the use of prosthetic devices, and speech therapy. Surgical closure of the cleft lip is usually done as soon after birth as possible. Closure of the cleft palate is also usually done early to take advantage of the subsequent normal growth processes. Prostheses—artificial devices which provide mechanical closure of the cleft during the intervals between surgery—are also used. Speech therapy is designed to teach the child to produce as normal speech patterns as possible. Speech therapy, which initially takes the form of counseling parents concerning appropriate language stimulation techniques, later includes exercises in blowing, sucking, and swallowing, as well as articulation therapy similar to that used with children who have normal palates but similar articulatory difficulties (Turton, 1975). Because dental problems are usually involved, the rehabilitation of cleft palates often requires the combined services of pediatricians, surgeons, dentists, orthodontists, otologists, speech therapists, and sometimes psychologists or psychiatrists (Wetlake, 1955). In 1973 there were over twenty known cleft-palate parent groups with a total membership of 1,344 in the United States (Lipski & Pannbacker, 1974).

BEHAVIOR PROBLEMS ASSOCIATED WITH SPEECH DEFECTS

What was said about the personality traits of stutterers applies equally well to speech defectives as a group. They are not typically seriously maladjusted or neurotic. However, they do have more than their share of adjustment problems. They tend to be less acceptable to their peers than are children with normal speech (Woods & Carrow, 1959; Peckham, 1973). Like stuttering, other functional speech defects are associated with a set of high standards imposed on the children by the parents in an atmosphere of emotional tension (Wood, 1946; Moncur, 1952; Marge, 1965).

Ways in which children with problems of articulation differ from children with normal speech in the areas of conduct and behavior disorders are shown in table 15–5. In the study reported in table 15–5 (FitzSimons, 1958), seventy children with normal speech were compared with a group of children with nonorganic articulatory problems.

R. M. FitzSimons (1958) and C. S. Peckham (1973) also report that more of the children with speech problems had experienced abnormal birth conditions, bottle feeding, early weaning, early toilet training, and delay in walking and talking. In school, they were inferior in reading readiness, reading, health habits, and work habits. Projective test performances indicated that they exceeded the normal children in aggressive tendencies, fears, anxieties, and in perception of parents as authoritarian.

SCHOOL PROGRAMS FOR SPEECH CORRECTION

Although speech correction is done in hospitals, clinics, and private offices, by far the bulk of speech therapy is done in the schools. Many universities operate speech clinics as both training and service centers,

Table 15–5
The relative incidence of conduct and behavior disorders among children with defects of articulation and among normal children

Conduct and Behavior Disorders	Frequency of Occurrence		
	Articulation Sample	Normal Sample	Differences Between Groups
1. Eating and food problems	39	2	37
2. Nervousness	53	22	31
3. Temper tantrums	35	8	27
4. Showing off	30	6	24
5. Refusal to obey	27	7	20
6. Thumb sucking	34	15	19
7. Shyness	31	13	18
8. Destructiveness	18	2	16
9. Fears	21	10	11
10. Jealousy*	6	3	3
11. Sleeplessness	6	1	5
12. Lying	6	1	5
13. Enuresis	9	3	6
14. Fingernail biting	7	11	4
15. Hurting pets	1	0	−1

* All differences above this level are statistically significant at or above the .05 level. Data from FitzSimons (1958).

but the largest number of speech correctionists are employed in public school systems.

The most common administrative educational arrangement is to use itinerant teachers. In this type of organization, each teacher serves several schools and the children remain in their regular schools and classes. The itinerant teacher visits each school regularly and provides group or individual therapy as frequently as the workload permits. This plan is easily administered and can be easily adjusted to meet changing needs (Steer, 1961). The teacher's maximum case load is often specified by state or local codes or regulations. The recommended maximum caseload ranges from 70 to 100. However, a survey made in 1961 found that the average caseload was 130 children. Accepting 100 as the normal caseload means that any school district enrolling 2,000 students could use the services of a speech therapist (Hull, 1963).

In some school systems, speech specialists handle the most difficult cases and train regular teachers to work with the less seriously defective children. The American Speech and Hearing Association has set standard qualifications which speech therapists should meet and has delineated the role of public school therapists in its statement on "Services and Functions of Speech and Hearing Specialists in Public Schools" (1962).

About 75 percent of the children receiving speech therapy in the average school are in the first three grades. Each child is typically seen at least weekly for individual or group work. Maximum carryover from session to session is gained when the regular teachers and the parents cooperate. Very often definite school, home, and private practice exercises are required. Studies have indicated that parents can participate effectively in speech improvement programs (Tufts & Holliday, 1959; Backus & Beasley, 1951).

School programs without a speech clinician

In-service training programs can help regular classroom teachers handle children with less serious speech defects, although they probably will not attempt formal therapy. Every teacher is, to a degree, a teacher of speech. Each teacher can be a good speech model. The classroom teacher can make referrals to private, hospital, or university clinics when they are available. The teacher can handle children with all types of speech defects in the ways suggested earlier for the general treatment of the primary stutterer. Some additional suggestions for the classroom handling of the child with a major speech defect are:

1. Complete acceptance of the child as a completely worthy individual is most important.
2. Accept the child's nonfluencies in a relaxed and unembarrassed fashion. Try to get the children to do likewise.
3. Do not look away from the child, or take over and speak for him.
4. Encourage, but do not force, the child with serious speech defects to speak before the class.
5. Provide the child with nonverbal assignments and responsibilities to keep him from capitalizing on his disability.
6. Capitalize on the child's assets and provide recognition for his accomplishments to increase his self-confidence.
7. Provide as much group participation as possible for the child. If he will not participate verbally, let him participate in a nonverbal way.
8. Provide some daily oral experience for the child, such as group singing, reading in unison, or ordinary conversation.

Language development programs

Several movements coalesced during the 1960s to produce a relatively new psycholinguistic concept of language development in general and communication problems in particular. National concern for the educationally disadvantaged—especially the culturally deviant child—and for the mentally retarded provided an atmosphere favorable to the development of new approaches to the language problems of children. A revival of the notion that language is the vehicle of thought, the development of the hypothesis that the restricted or deviant linguistic patterns of the educationally handicapped child may be a critical part of his problem, and the emergence of new theories and approaches to the problems of language acquisition, combined with a heightened public and professional awareness of developmental problems to bring forth a tremendous number of language development programs.

Some language programs constitute general stimulation approaches wherein structured or free play and socialization provide the context for facilitating language development. In these programs, the emphasis is on increasing the linguistic input and output by encouraging labeling, phrase and sentence production, and the informational function of language. Several formal programs have a perceptual-motor orientation, others emanate from generative linguistic theory, others depend primarily on operant conditioning procedures, while still others have used the Piagetian analysis of development as a basis for developing teaching-learning communication sequences (Turton, 1975). All these approaches are concerned more with facilitating the development of the child's cognitive processes than with the remediation or prevention of specific language defects. We discussed this problem in the chapter on the culturally deviant individual.

SUMMARY

Speech is defective whenever the manner of speaking interferes with communication, calls undue attention to itself, or causes the speaker concern to the degree that special remedial measures are deemed necessary. Initial identification of speech defects is made both informally and by systematic screening procedures. Diagnosis and treatment may involve parents, teachers, speech therapists, psychologists, psychiatrists, pediatricians, surgeons, dentists, and orthodontists. It is conservatively estimated that 5 percent of school-age children have speech defects sufficiently serious to require therapy, and than an additional 5 percent with less serious disorders should probably receive some speech correction. The causes of speech defects are both organic (cleft palate, auditory defects, brain damage, and so forth) and functional (learning failure and emotional blocking).

As compared with normal people, those with speech defects are slightly inferior in physical characteristics, motor facility, sensory functions, intelligence, school achievement, and general behavioral adequacy. This inferiority is partially the result of the high incidence of speech defects among the organically impaired and of the greater prevalence of speech problems (particularly defects in articulation) among persons of the lower socio-economic levels.

Speech defects are usually classified according to major symptoms, as disorders of articulation, delayed speech, voice disorders, and disturbances of rhythm. Additional classes of speech disorders are based on accompanying defects. Thus we have speech disorders associated with mental retardation, cleft palate, and brain damage (cerebral palsy, aphasia). On the basis of etiology, speech defects are classified as organic or functional.

Speech disorders are treated in hospitals, clinics, schools, and private offices. The largest number of children are treated in the public schools. Treatment is given both individually and in groups, and concerns itself primarily either with symptoms (speech correction) or with underlying causes (speech therapy). In the schools, the speech therapist typically serves several schools. His caseload should normally not exceed one hundred.

REFERENCES

ADAMS, M. R., & D. A. DIETZE, "A Comparison of the Reaction Times of Stutterers and Non-stutterers to Items on a Word Association Test," *Journal of Speech and Hearing Research*, 1965, *8,* 195–202.

AJAX, E. T., "The Aphasic Patient: A Practical Review," *Diseases of the Nervous System*, 1973, *34,* 135–42.

AMERICAN SPEECH AND HEARING ASSOCIATION, COMMITTEE ON LEGISLATION, "Need for Speech Pathologists," *Journal of Speech and Hearing Disorders*, 1959, *1,* 138–39, 161–67.

AMERICAN SPEECH AND HEARING ASSOCIATION, COMMITTEE ON THE MIDCENTURY WHITE HOUSE CONFERENCE ON CHILDREN AND YOUTH, "Speech Disorders and Speech Correction," *Journal of Speech and Hearing Disorders*, 1952, *17,* 129–37.

AMERICAN SPEECH AND HEARING ASSOCIATION, "Public School and Hearing Services," *Journal of Speech and Hearing Disorders*, 1961, Monograph Supplement 8.

AMERICAN SPEECH AND HEARING ASSOCIATION, "Services and Functions of Speech and Hearing Specialists in Public Schools," *Journal of Speech and Hearing Disorders*, 1962, *4,* 99–100.

ANASTASIOW, N. J., & N. G. STAYROOK, "Miscue Language Patterns of Mildly Retarded and Nonretarded Children," *American Journal of Mental Deficiency*, 1973, *77*, 431–34.

ANDREWS, G., & J. CUTLER, "Stuttering Therapy: The Relation Between Changes in Symptom Level and Attitudes," *Journal of Speech and Hearing Disorders*, 1974, *39*, 312–18.

BACKUS, O. L., & J. BEASLEY, *Speech Therapy with Children* (Boston: Houghton Mifflin, 1951).

BARRY, H., "Classes for Aphasics," in M. E. Frampton & E. D. Gall, eds., *Special Education for the Exceptional*, vol. 2 (Boston: Porter Sargent, 1955).

BATEMAN, B., "Learning Disabilities: Yesterday, Today, and Tomorrow," *Exceptional Children*, 1964, *31*, 167–77.

BEATTIE, M. S., "A Behavior Therapy Programme for Stuttering," *British Journal of Disorders of Communication*, 1973, *8*, 120–30.

BENTON, A. L., "Developmental Aphasia (D.A.) and Brain Damage," *Cortex*, 1964, *1*, 40–52.

BERMAN, P. A., & J. P. BRADY, "Miniaturized Metronomes in the Treatment of Stuttering: A Survey of Clinicians' Experience," *Journal of Therapy and Experimental Psychiatry*, 1973, *4*, 117–19.

BERRY, M. F., & J. EISENSON, *Speech Disorders* (New York: Appleton-Century-Crofts, 1956).

BEYN, E. S., & I. T. VLASENKO, "Verbal Paraphasias of Aphasic Patients in the Course of Naming Actions," *British Journal of Disorders of Communication*, 1974, *9*, 24–34.

BLOODSTEIN, O., "The Development of Stuttering: III. Theoretical and Clinical Implications," *Journal of Speech and Hearing Disorders*, 1961, *26*, 67–82.

BLUEMEL, C. S., "Primary and Secondary Stuttering," *Quarterly Journal of Speech*, 1932, *18*, 187–200.

BLUEMEL, C. S., *The Riddle of Stuttering* (Danville, Ill.: Interstate Publishers, 1957).

BRENNAN, D. G., & W. L. CULLINAN, "Object Identification and Naming in Cleft Palate Children," *The Cleft Palate Journal*, 1974, *11*, 188–95.

CAPOBIANCO, R. J., "Diagnostic Methods Used with Learning Disability Cases," *Exceptional Children*, 1964, *31*, 187–93.

CURLEE, R. F., & W. H. PERKINS, "Effectiveness of a DAF Conditioning Program for Adolescent and Adult Stutterers," *Behavior Research and Therapy*, 1973, *11*, 395–401.

CURRY, R., et al., "A Phonographic scale for the Measurement of Defective Articulation," *Journal of Speech Disorders*, 1943, *8*, 123–26.

DAVIS, J. P., "The Speech Aspects of Reading Readiness: Newer Practices in Reading in the Elementary School," in *Seventeenth Yearbook, Department of Elementary School Principals* (Washington, D.C.: National Educational Association, 1938).

EDWARDS, A. E., "Automated Training for a 'Matching-to-sample' Task in Aphasia," *Journal of Speech and Hearing Research*, 1965, *8*, 39–43.

EISENSON, J., "The Nature of Defective Speech," in W. M. Cruickshank, ed.,

Psychology of Exceptional Children and Youth, 2nd ed. (Englewood Cliffs, N.J.: Prentice-Hall, 1963).

EISENSON, J., "Speech Disorders," in B. B. Wolman, ed., *Handbook of Clinical Psychology* (New York: McGraw-Hill, 1965).

EVERHART, R. W., "The Relationship Between Articulation and Other Developmental Factors in Children," *Journal of Speech and Hearing Disorders*, 1953, *18*, 332–38.

FITZSIMONS, R. M., "Developmental, Psychosocial, and Educational Factors in Children with Articulation Problems," *Child Development*, 1958, *29*, 481–89.

GARDNER, H., "The Naming of Objects and Symbols by Children and Aphasic Patients," *Journal of Psycholinguistic Research*, 1974, *3*, 133–49.

GENS, A., "The Speech Pathologist Looks at the Mentally Deficient Child," *Training School Bulletin*, 1951, *48*, 19–27.

GOERTZEN, S., "Speech and the Mentally Retarded Child," *American Journal of Mental Deficiency*, 1957, *62*, 244–53.

GOLDMAN, R., & G. H. SHAMES, "Comparisons of the Goals that Parents of Stutterers and Parents of Nonstutterers Set for Their Children," *Journal of Speech and Hearing Disorders*, 1964, *29*, 381–89.

GOODSTEIN, L. D., "Functional Speech Disorders and Personality: A Survey of the Literature," *Journal of Speech and Hearing Research*, 1958, *1*, 359–76.

GOODSTEIN, L. D., "Intellectual Impairment in Children with Cleft Palates," *Journal of Speech and Hearing Research*, 1961, *4*, 287–94.

GORAJ, J. T., "Stuttering Therapy as Crisis Intervention," *British Journal of Disorders of Communication*, 1974, *9*, 51–57.

GREGORY, H. H., "Stuttering and Auditory Central Nervous System Disorders," *Journal of Speech and Hearing Research*, 1964, *7*, 335–41.

GRUBER, L., & R. L. POWELL, "Responses of Stuttering and Nonstuttering Children on a Dichotic Listening Task," *Perceptual and Motor Skills*, 1974, *38*, 263–64.

HAMMILL, D. D., & O. C. IRWIN, "Speech Differences Among Cerebral Palsy Subclasses," *Exceptional Children*, 1965, *31*, 277–80.

HAMRE, C. E., "A Comment on the Possible Organicity of Stuttering." *British Journal of Disorders of Communication*, 1972, *7*, 148–50.

HENRY, J., & Z. HENRY, "Speech Disturbances Among Pilagra Indian Children," *American Journal of Orthopsychiatry*, 1940, *10*, 99–102.

HULL, F. M., "Speech Impaired Children," in L. M. Dunn, ed., *Exceptional Children in the Schools* (New York: Holt, Rinehart and Winston, 1963).

IRWIN, A., "The Treatment and Results of "Easy-stammering," *British Journal of Disorders of Communication*, 1972, *7*, 151–56.

IRWIN, R. B., "Speech Disorders," in M. E. Frampton & E. D. Gall, eds., *Special Education for the Exceptional*, vol. 2 (Boston: Porter Sargent, 1955).

JOHNSON, W., "A Study of the Onset and Development of Stuttering," *Journal of Speech and Hearing Disorders*, 1942, *7*, 251–57.

JOHNSON, W., *Speech Handicapped School Children* (New York: Harper & Row, 1956).

KINSTLER, D. B., "Covert and Overt Maternal Rejection in Stuttering," *Journal of Speech and Hearing Disorders*, 1961, *26*, 145–55.

LANYON, R. I., & D. A. DUPREZ, "Non-fluency, Information, and Word Length," *Journal of Abnormal Psychology*, 1970, *76*, 93–97.

LEE, L., & S. M. CANTER, "Developmental Sentence Scoring: A Clinical Procedure for Estimating Syntactic Development in Children's Spontaneous Speech," *Journal of Speech and Hearing Disorders*, 1971, *36*, 315–40.

LEMERT, E. M., "Stuttering and Social Structure in Two Pacific Societies," *Journal of Speech and Hearing Disorders*, 1962, *27*, 3–10.

LIPSKI, L., & M. PANNBACKER, "Cleft Palate Parent Groups," *The Cleft Palate Journal*, 1974, *11*, 176–87.

LUPER, H. L., & R. L. MULDEN, *Stuttering Therapy for Children* (Englewood Cliffs, N.J.: Prentice-Hall, 1964).

MCGINNIS, M. A., *Aphasic Children: Identification and Education by the Association Method* (Washington, D.C.: Alexander Graham Bell Association for the Deaf, 1963).

MCWILLIAMS, B. J., "The Non-Verbal Child," *Exceptional Children*, 1959, *25*, 420–23.

MARGE, M., "The Influence of Selected Home Background Variables on the Development of Oral Communication Skills in Children," *Journal of Speech and Hearing Research*, 1965, *8*, 291–309.

MARTIN, R., "Stuttering and Perseverations in Children," *Journal of Speech and Hearing Research*, 1962, *5*, 332–39.

MECHAM, M. K., M. J. BERKO, & F. G. BERKO, *Speech Therapy in Cerebral Palsy* (Springfield, Ill.: Charles C Thomas, 1960).

MENYUK, P., "Comparison of Grammar of Children with Functional Deviant and Normal Speech," *Journal of Speech and Hearing Research*, 1964, *7*, 107–21.

MOHR, J. P., "Evaluation of the Deficit in Total Aphasia," *Neurology*, 1973, *23*, 1302–12.

MONCUR, J. P., "Parental Domination in Stuttering," *Journal of Speech and Hearing Disorders*, 1952, *17*, 155–64.

MORLEY, M., et al., "Delayed Speech and Developmental Aphasia," *British Medical Journal*, 1955, *20*, 463–67.

MYERS, P., "A Study of Language Disabilities in Cerebral Palsied Children," *Journal of Speech and Hearing Research*, 1965, *8*, 129–36.

NELSON, S. E., "The Role of Heredity in Stuttering," *Journal of Pediatrics*, 1939, *14*, 3–15.

PATTY, J., & B. QUARRINGTON, "The Effects of Reward on Types of Stuttering," *Journal of Communication Disorders*, 1974, *7*, 65–77.

PECKHAM, C. S., "Speech Defects in a National Sample of Children Aged Seven Years," *British Journal of Disorders of Communication*, 1973, *8*, 2–8.

PERRIN, E. L., "The Rating of Defective Speech by Trained and Untrained Observers," *Journal of Speech and Hearing Disorders*, 1954, *19*, 48–51.

PRONOVOST, W., "A Survey of Services for the Speech and Hearing Handicapped in New England," *Journal of Speech and Hearing Disorders,* 1951, *16,* 148–56.

RENFREW, C. E., "Prediction of Persisting Speech Defects," *British Journal of Disorders of Communication,* 1973, *8,* 37–41.

ROBINSON, F. B., *Introduction to Stuttering* (Englewood Cliffs, N.J.: Prentice-Hall, 1964).

ROE, V., & R. MILISEN, "The Effect of Maturation upon Defective Articulation in Elementary Grades," *Journal of Speech and Hearing Disorders,* 1942, *7,* 37–50.

SANDER, E. K., "Frequency of Syllable Repetition and 'Stutterer' Judgments," *Journal of Speech and Hearing Disorders,* 1963, *28,* 19–30.

SCHWARTZ, M. F., "The Care of the Stuttering Black," *Journal of Speech and Hearing Disorders,* 1974, *39,* 169–77.

SCHWARTZ, R., "Familial Incidence of Cleft Palate," *Journal of Speech and Hearing Disorders,* 1954, *19,* 228–38.

SHEEHAN, J. G., "Conflict Theory of Stuttering," in J. Eisenson, ed., *Stuttering: A Symposium* (New York: Harper & Row, 1958a).

SHEEHAN, J. G., "Projective Studies of Stuttering," *Journal of Speech and Hearing Disorders,* 1958b, *23,* 18–25.

SHERIDAN, M. D., "Children of Seven Years with Marked Speech Defects," *British Journal of Disorders of Communication,* 1973, *8,* 9–16.

SIEGEL, G. M., & D. HAUGEN, "Audience Size and Variations in Stuttering Behavior," *Journal of Speech and Hearing Research,* 1964, *7,* 381–88.

SIRKEN, J., & W. LYON, "A Study of Speech Defects in Mental Deficiency," *American Journal of Mental Deficiency,* 1941, *46,* 74–80.

SMITH, J. O., "Speech and Language of the Retarded," *Training School Bulletin,* 1962, *58,* 111–24.

SMITH, R. C., "You're Not a Person: You're a Stutterer," *Hearing and Speech News,* 1972, *40* (2), 8–9, 20–22.

STEER, M. D., "Public School Speech and Hearing Services," United States Office of Education, Cooperative Research Project 649 (8191), *Journal of Speech and Hearing Disorders,* Monograph Supplement 8, 1961.

STEWART, J. L., "The Problems of Stuttering in Certain North American Indian Societies," *Journal of Speech and Hearing Disorders,* Monograph Supplement 6, 1960, 61–87.

TIKOFSKY, R. S., & R. P. TIKOFSKY, "Intelligibility Measures of Dysarthric Speech," *Journal of Speech and Hearing Research,* 1965, *8,* 325–33.

TRAVIS, L. E., *Speech Pathology* (New York: Appleton-Century-Crofts, 1931).

TRAVIS, L. E., *Handbook of Speech Pathology and Audiology* (New York: Appleton-Century-Crofts, 1971).

TRETSVEN, V. E., "Incidence of Cleft Lip and Palate in Montana Indians," *Journal of Speech and Hearing Disorders,* 1963, *28,* 52–57.

TUFTS, L. R., & A. R. HOLLIDAY, "Effectiveness of Trained Parents as Speech Therapists," *Journal of Speech and Hearing Disorders,* 1959, *24,* 395–401.

TURTON, L. J., "Diagnostic Implications of Articulation Testing," in W. D.

Wolfe & D. J. Goulding, eds., *Articulation and Learning Diagnostics and Theory* (Springfield, Ill.: Charles C Thomas, 1973).

TURTON, L. J., "Education of Children with Communication Disorders," in W. M. Cruickshank & G. O. Johnson, eds., *Education of Exceptional Children and Youth* (Englewood Cliffs, N.J.: Prentice-Hall, 1975).

VAN DEMARK, D. R., "Assessment of Articulation for Children with Cleft Palate," *The Cleft Palate Journal,* 1974, *11,* 200–208.

VAN RIPER, C., *The Treatment of Stuttering* (Englewood Cliffs, N.J.: Prentice-Hall, 1973).

VAN RIPER, C., & J. R. IRWIN, *Voice and Articulation* (Englewood Cliffs, N.J.: Prentice-Hall, 1958).

WALKER, S. T., & J. M. WALKER, "Differences in Heart-rate Variability Between Stutterers and Nonstutterers Following Arousal," *Perceptual and Motor Skills,* 1973, *36,* 926.

WATTS, F., "Mechanisms of Fluency Control in Stutterers," *British Journal of Disorders of Communication,* 1973, *8,* 131–38.

WEISS, A., *Cluttering* (Englewood Cliffs, N.J.: Prentice-Hall, 1964).

WEST, R., S. E. NELSON, & M. F. BERRY, "The Heredity of Stuttering," *Quarterly Journal of Speech,* 1939, *25,* 23–30.

WESTLAKE, H., & D. RUTHERFORD, *Speech Therapy for the Cerebral Palsied* (Chicago: National Society for Crippled Children and Adults, 1961).

WINGATE, M. E., "Evaluation and Stuttering: Environmental Stress and Critical Appraisal of Speech," *Journal of Speech and Hearing Disorders,* 1962a, *27,* 244–57.

WINGATE, M. E., "Evaluation and Stuttering: Identification of Stuttering and the Use of a Label," *Journal of Speech and Hearing Disorders,* 1962b, *27,* 368–77.

WINGATE, M. E., "Recovery from Stuttering," *Journal of Speech and Hearing Disorders,* 1964, *29,* 312–21.

WOOD, K. S., "Parental Maladjustment and Functional Articulatory Defects in Children," *Journal of Speech Disorders,* 1946, *11,* 255–75.

WOODS, F. J., & M. A. CARROW, "The Choice-Rejection Status of Speech Defective Children," *Exceptional Children,* 1959, *25,* 279–83.

WYATT, G. L., & J. M. HERZON, "Therapy with Stuttering Children and Their Mothers," *American Journal of Orthopsychiatry,* 1962, *32,* 645–59.

5

Problems of the aged

Photo by Jeff Albertson, Stock, Boston

Chapter 16

The aged

Over the past decade there has been a great increase in concern in the United States for the economic, social, cultural, and psychological welfare of our aged population. Not only has official concern increased (White House Conference on Aging, 1972), but there have also been increases in popular concern as well as in research attention to this group of people. In 1970 the American Psychological Association formed a Task Force on Aging which later published a significant report (Eisdorfer & Lawton, 1973); adult development and aging were treated in a separate chapter in the *Annual Review of Psychology* for 1975 (Schaie & Gribbin, 1975).

Age is an important variable in determining how individuals behave in relationship to each other. Young people's behavior in interaction with young people is different from young people's behavior with middle-aged or older people. The same is true for old people. Their behavior in regard to each other differs from their behavior relative to young people or middle-aged persons.

In speaking of the behavior of the aged, we recognize that there is an interaction between age and behavior. It is true, too, that there is an interaction among the variables of sex, age, and behavior. Old men behave differently toward other old males than they do toward elderly females, and differently still in relationship to the middle-aged and young of each sex. This is true also of older females. The behavior of the aged of both sexes is influenced by the social class within which they have lived, and this influence is not identical for the two sexes. Social class is also a partial determinant of how long one will live. The interacting variables of concern have now grown to four—age, sex, social class, and behavior. Variables such as economic status, health, educational level, and others interact with age and sex in the determination of behavior and as a part of social-class determination. The interactive effects of many variables are to be found in the investigations of the aged. The effects of age alone, isolated from all other variables, are difficult to determine.

WHO ARE THE AGED?

It is well recognized that individuals differ as they develop, mature, and age. Some individuals are active, alert, and involved in this culture at seventy-five or eighty years of age, while others at these ages may be sedentary, preoccupied, and introverted. The various capacities of the individual also age at different rates. It must be recognized that age can be considered biologically, psychologically, and sociologically. There are many indices of age and aging, but for our purposes we shall take chronological age as the indicator. In the past the chronological age of sixty has been used as a convenient point at which to begin identification of the aged. More recently age sixty-five has been employed as the beginning of the period of old age, probably because it is a frequent age for compulsory retirement and eligibility for certain social benefits. We shall use sixty to sixty-five as the beginning of old age in our culture.

At mid-century there were 10 million people in the United States over sixty-five years of age; by 1960 there were about 16 million; in 1970 about 20 million; and by 1980 it is estimated that there will be more than 23 million over the age of 65. This represents a 17.2 percent increase in the number of old persons from 1970 to 1980 (United States Bureau of the Census, 1970a). By 1980, people sixty-five and over will constitute 10 percent of the total American population. As life is prolonged by advances in social and medical science, the United States is gaining a greater proportion of older citizens than ever before. There were five or six times as many people over sixty-five in the United States in 1970 as there were in 1900. The greater number of older people in the population does not reflect a prolongation of life for the aged, but rather the greater proportion of the population which lives to old age. In 1900 the life expectancy for an American male was forty-nine years. It is over seventy today. However, the life expectancy for men now at the age of sixty-five is fourteen additional years, compared to thirteen additional years in 1900. Men are not living to be older and older, but more men are living long enough to reach old age (Burger, 1969). The life expectancy for women is greater than that for men and therefore women are disproportionately represented in the aged population.

SOCIO-ECONOMIC STATUS OF THE AGED

The median annual income for the single person over sixty-five has been reported to be $1,055, with 30 percent of those over sixty-five, single or married, living in poverty (Burger, 1969). The 1963 Social Security Survey of the Aged indicated that two-thirds of the married persons over sixty-two had a median equity of $10,000 in nonfarm homes and median assets of $11,180 (including homes). Among couples with at least one partner over sixty-five, 41 percent were classified as poor (that is, they had an income of less than $2,500 per year). If all the assets of individuals are prorated as annual income over expected life, the median income for married couples over sixty-five would be $3,795 (Birren, 1970a). These data indicate that a very high proportion (30 to 40 percent) of the aged can readily be classified as poor. In 1969, there were approximately 4.8 million people aged sixty-five and over who were living in poverty, according to a United States Senate Special Committee on Aging report entitled "Economics of Aging" (Associated Press, 1971). Rapidly rising health costs also were reported as a serious problem for the elderly. Limited income is an obstacle to living the kind of life that they would like, for a high proportion of the aged. It is obvious that not enough is being done to provide for the social and economic security of our citizens over sixty-five. Progress has been made in this regard, but certainly a nation cannot be content with over a third of its elderly citizens living on budgets so limited as to produce serious problems of insecurity, un happiness, and even poor health. There seems to be little question that on the average, the aged are in a worse situation than the rest of the population. The income inequality during people's working years becomes even more exaggerated in old age. The difference in income and consequently in independence and security is greater among the aged than among the general population. Not all of the aged are poor—indeed many are well off—but too large a proportion of the aged are classifiable as poor (Strumpel, 1973).

In the past decade or so a separate subculture of the aged has emerged. Social organizations, clubs, recreational centers, retirement homes, and retirement villages are devoted specifically to those in retirement or of retirement age. Some of this increase in organizational activity reflects increased affluence in the culture, but some derives from the increasing social concern for the aged, from the flexibility of retirement age stemming from affluence, and from the increased vigor of the aged produced by better health. The subculture of the aged is now beginning to demand its share of the economic, social, and political world, as well as to insist on its members' rights to individuality, independence, and privacy.

INDIVIDUAL DIFFERENCES AMONG THE AGED

There is danger of speaking and thinking of the aged as if they really comprised a homogeneous group. The only way this could be done with any semblance of accuracy is with regard to chronological age.

An interesting and extensive investigation of old people in industrial societies reports that a large proportion of the aged in the United States, Great Britain, and Denmark are reasonably active and involved in the culture. They have continuing contacts with relatives and friends and appear to have made adequate social and personal adjustments. Their social role and declining physical status appear to have become an acceptable part of their lives. Remarkable similarities among the three industrial cultures were reported (Shanus et al., 1968). A danger in reports of such investigations may be to deemphasize the heterogeneity of the aged population. It is easy to forget that there are minorities of significant size, within the group designated as aged, that lead lives of low quality and of relative isolation (Mechanic, 1969). The heterogeneity of the aged was emphasized by the President's Council on Aging (1963), whose report was prefaced by the observation that the older American has nearly 18 million faces, those of:

Nearly 10 percent of the entire United States population
Nearly 1½ million people living on farms
More than one out of four United States Senators
Almost 2 million people working full-time
All but two of the nine United States Supreme Court Justices
More than 10,000 people over one hundred years old
Over 12½ million people receiving Social Security benefits
Over 2.3 million war veterans
More than 3 million people who migrated from Europe to the United States

In composite, the older American:

May be between sixty-five and seventy but is probably older;
May have an adequate income but probably does not;
May be working but it is unlikely;
May have a high school education but probably does not;
May be in good health but probably is not;
May not receive Social Security but probably does;
Would like to have more to do but the opportunities do not exist;
May collect a private pension but probably does not;
May have adequate health insurance but probably does not;
May live alone but probably does not;
Is probably female.

It is important that we not lose sight of individual differences when discussing the aged. Indeed, they do have in common the fact that they are in the later years of life, but wide differences exist among them.

PROBLEMS OF INVESTIGATING THE AGED

In any area of research problems are involved that either are exaggerations of problems associated with research in general or are unique to the particular research under consideration. Investigation of the aged is no exception. A very real and serious problem has to do with obtaining a sample of the aged that is large enough and representative enough so that adequate generalizations can be made. Recent research efforts have been undertaken with greater cognizance of this problem than was common a short while ago. A great number of studies of old people have been conducted using institutionalized aged as the subjects. The vast majority of older people are not institutionalized; less than 5 percent of the aged reside in institutions (Bader & Hoffman, 1966). This number is probably declining as the aged receive more attention and become more economically and socially independent. It seems obvious that public institutions for the aged house those who are alone or rejected, isolated, of less good health, and dependent more frequently than those people would be represented in the entire population of the aged. Certainly, the 5 percent who are institutionalized cannot be taken as representative of the aged in general. Such investigations, if the sampling and other research variables are adequate, can yield information about the population of institutionalized aged, but not much on the rest of the aged population.

Many older persons are unwilling to serve as subjects in research investigations. This may be because they are suspicious that some of their capacities are diminishing and they do not want to be embarrassed by such a disclosure. It may be, too, that the aged simply feel that there is little that they personally can gain from research, the results of which will not be available for some period of time.

There have been few studies that are longitudinal in nature. That is, most investigations have dealt with a population of the aged and have compared the group of aged persons studied to groups of younger people. Such cross-sectional investigations fail to take into account the influence of cultural changes. What have been interpreted as changes occurring with age may be only differences among age groups due to cultural change (Zubin, 1973). To determine accurately what psychological changes are attributable to age, aging must be studied within a group of individuals. This takes time. Investigations of the characteristics of a group of persons over time will have to be carried out by an institute or organization, since the time lapse involved will often exceed the adult life of a single investigator. The best known of the longitudinal studies is probably the one on the gifted, started by L. M. Terman at Stanford University. Terman and M. H. Oden (1959) have already reported on the gifted group at mid-life. Subsequent reports on this group should prove most enlightening. Until the results of such longitudinal investigations are reported, much of our knowledge of change due to aging must be extrapolated from cross-sectional investigations.

CHARACTERISTICS OF THE AGED

Old age is characterized as a period of slowing down; a period of decline of certain abilities; a period requiring social, psychological, and physical adaptation to changed or changing circumstance.

There is a tendency for children's lives to be about the same length as those of their parents. Even more convincing of the genetic bases for longevity are the studies of aging in twins by E. J. Kallman and L. F. Jarvik (1959). They found the causes of death to be more similar in one-egg than in two-egg twins, and the difference in age of death among those dying past the age of sixty to be less for one-egg twins than two-egg twins. Such evidence strongly suggests that longevity is a partial function of genetics. One-egg twins show a remarkable similarity in intellectual functioning as well as appearance in later life. It is well recognized that environmental circumstances tend to have greater communality in kinship groups than in the population in general, but the influence of these factors notwithstanding, the genetic influence is strongly indicated. It could be that if humans mated selectively according to ancestral age, a longer life span would evolve. The physical condition of the elderly depends upon inheritance factors, manner of living, accident, injury, disease factors, and other environmental influences.

Physical changes among the aged

Physical stature declines with age. This results primarily from the stooping of the shoulders, which gives the appearance of being smaller. There is also some shrinking of the vertebral cartilages, which reduces actual height. Arms and legs may have wrinkles and appear to be flabby. Changes in the appearance of the skin can be marked. The epidermis thins and becomes more flexible and flaccid with age. Under the skin, tissues become less elastic because of the atrophy of elastic fibers from the intercellular matrix. The skin appears to sag and wrinkle. Sweat and oil glands atrophy with age, which makes the skin somewhat dry and coarse. These factors are superimposed on those of diminution of secondary sex characteristics, loss of muscle tone, and muscular and joint stiffness. The movement of the aged is characterized by shortened stride, a widened base, and a slight leaning forward.

Tremors in the hands and faces of older people are not at all uncommon. These tremors are more noticeable when the individual is tired or emotionally aroused. Loss of hair that results in a sparsely haired scalp or in baldness, especially in men, is a common characteristic of the aged, as is loss of hair color that results in gray or white hair. Hair in the opening of the ear and in the nostrils is usually coarse and bristly. The eyebrows may become somewhat bushy and bristly as well.

Facial appearance is affected by dryness and wrinkles of the skin along with other factors. Many older people have lost their teeth or the teeth have worn down, giving a pinched expression to the mouth and face. The cheek muscles sag a bit, eyelids are baggy, and the eyes may appear lusterless and watery due to inadequate tear gland function.

The changes in physical appearance of the aged reflect changing physiological structures and functions. Changes that occur at the cellular level in the skeleton produce bones that are brittle and subject to fractures which are slow in healing. Visceral changes, particularly atrophy of the testes, liver, lungs, and kidneys, are a part of aging. The central nervous system does not go unaffected. There appears to be a decrease in brain weight with advancing age. However, great brain weight loss is probably a function of pathological processes rather than of the normal aging process (Bondareff, 1959). Loss of cells in the nervous system with aging occurs in the human cortex (Brody, 1955).

Changes in physiological functions are of great significance in the lives of the aged. There tends to be a decrease in the amount and quality of sleep among older people, and they tend to suffer from insomnia (Roffwarg, Muzio, & Dement, 1966). Difficulties with teeth and chewing coupled with a decline in taste sensitivity with age (Cooper, Bilash, & Zubeck, 1959) result in changes in food intake among the aged. They tend to eat less and to eat more frequently.

Blood pressure increase because of the rigidity of arterial walls is common (Master & Lasser, 1964). Shortness of breath and increased heart beat rate take longer to return to normal following exertion than they do for younger people. The aged cannot tolerate extremes of temperature and are particularly sensitive to reduced temperatures (Hurlock,

1968). General strength and work capacity decline in old age and re-cuperation from fatigue takes longer among those of advanced age (Hur-lock, 1968).

Sensory changes

We said earlier that changes in taste sensitivity occur with aging. In general, this is true of the other sensory functions. This decrease in sensory acuity with age is not as devastating in its consequence as might be imagined. First, in normal sensory function there is more than adequate sensory input for usual personal and social functioning. Consid-erable diminution of acuity can occur without producing incapacity. More-over, except where the loss is extreme, adaptation to reduced sensory functioning is usually possible because the decline of efficiency occurs gradually. In addition, certain of the sensory processes (vision and hear-ing) can be given assistance with mechanical devices (glasses and hearing aids).

Vision is less efficient among older people than it is among younger adults. Ability to discriminate small objects decreases in the aged, as does color sensitivity (Kleemeir, 1951); the pupil size of the eye dimin-ishes with age (Birren, Bick, & Yiengst, 1950), resulting in a reduced amount of light reaching the retina. Older persons require more light for good vision and, as a result, their vision shows more relative im-provement than does that of the younger person when illumination is increased. Visual accommodation (the ability to focus on objects at vary-ing distances) is less good among the aged. The eye accommodates to nearby objects by shortening the focal distance of the lens. With age the muscular system weakens and the lens loses its elasticity, thus decreasing accommodation to objects close to the eye.

Loss of hearing efficiency is as common with aging as are changes in vision. Deterioration in hearing is greater for high frequencies than it is for others. Such loss of efficiency may be produced by prolonged expo-sure to high-level noise, but loss of sensitivity in the aged cannot be wholly explained by such injury. Reduced acuity is found among the aged who have no history of either acoustic injury or disease. Most of the aged, even though they do have reduced auditory acuity, can hear speech and have little difficulty in personal conversations. Loss of hear-ing is greater for males than for females in advanced years, and older people are likely to blame their hearing deficiencies on the "mumbling" of others rather than on their own loss of hearing (Schaie, Bates, & Strother, 1964). Sensitivity to pain diminishes with age. Beginning about age fifteen and becoming marked after age sixty (Schulderman & Zubek, 1962), this loss of pain sensitivity may be sufficient so that pain as a danger signal may become impaired. Psychomotor responses are generally slowed among the aged. Apparently because of the slowing of higher integrative functions, reaction time doubles between age thirty and seventy. In general, the more complex the response, the more markedly it is slowed (Bierman & Hazzard, 1973).

The aged must adapt to the physical changes that occur with aging. Changes in physical appearance that may be profound can be of particular importance in a culture such as ours, with its emphasis on youthful beauty. The general decrease in sensory acuity that comes with aging must be accommodated for by the aged. This may prove more difficult than a first glance would indicate. Information about the world is filtered through the sensory equipment. Moreover, much of the enjoyment of living is derived from sensory functioning. If sights, sounds, and tastes are diminished or distorted, much of their enjoyment is gone. If sensory efficiency becomes sufficiently reduced, social isolation is likely to occur and the aged must then adjust to social isolation in addition to reduced physical capacity and sensory efficiency.

Intellective functioning of the aged

Changes in intellectual functioning with age may not be as great (Baltes & Labouvie, 1973; Bayley, 1965; Bayley & Oden, 1955) or as important as is popularly assumed. While it is true that the performance of the aged on certain tests of intellectual functioning is not at as high a level as is the performance of younger persons, the importance of high performance in these areas in the lives of the aged has not really been established. Intelligence tests have been devised largely to predict academic success. It is the young who attend school and must achieve academically. It is not clear that the same complex of abilities that contributes to the academic success of the young contributes equally to successful adult living in the later years. The cultural role of the aged is grossly different from that of the young, and the complex of abilities required for success in the culture no doubt is different for the two groups.

The study of changes in intellect is best accomplished in studies of the same individuals over time (longitudinal studies) rather than by comparing one age group with another at the same time (cross-sectional studies). Longitudinal investigations of mental abilities generally report significant decline in individuals after seventy years of age. Recent research findings have supported the hypothesis that decrements in learning among older people are not simply a function of structural changes in the central nervous system. The decrement, partially at least, is associated with heightened arousal of the autonomic nervous system that occurs when the learning situation is presented (Eisdorfer, Nowlin, & Wilkie, 1970). Of course, there are pronounced individual differences in both rate and amount of decline. There is relatively less loss of mental efficiency among those of initially high intellect than among those of initially lower levels (Birren, 1961; Owens, 1966), and those who continue to be engaged in work tend to do better on intelligence tests than those who do not (Busse, 1955). It would seem that those who keep actively involved in their culture rather than become disengaged from it tend to maintain better intellective functioning (Bottwinick, 1967). Rate of decline among those who continue to engage in learning tasks is not as great as it is among those who do not continue to practice learning (Berkowitz & Green, 1965).

Tests of general intelligence indicate a slight general decline as individuals approach sixty years of age (Owens, 1966). In tasks involving learning, older subjects tend to be more cautious, to require more time to integrate their responses, and not to deal so readily with novel material as do younger ones (Birren, Jerome, & Chown, 1961). As task complexity increases, older subjects require more time and sometimes do not understand the complex instructions that are required. Slowness of behavior sets limits for older persons in a variety of intellective functions (Birren, 1970). They do less well even when they slow down (Birren, Allen, & Landau, 1954). When tests of inductive and deductive reasoning are administered, there is a decline in performance with age that has been interpreted as partially due to an increase in cautiousness with age (Birren, Jerome, & Chown, 1961; Bottwinick, 1964, 1966, 1969). Memory for recent events is said to decline in old age, while memory for more remote events remains good. Motivation is an important factor in memory and recall; older people may not be motivated as strongly to remember as are the young. Because of lack of interest, poor habits of attention, and decline of sensory efficiency, older people may not form as distinct an impression of what they see and hear as they should. This would contribute to apparent forgetting (Friedman, 1966). Greater difficulty is encountered in *recall* than in recognition by the aged, with the loss in ability to recall being considerable (Schonfield & Robertson, 1966; Smith, 1974; Taub, 1975). Of all of the measures used in tests of general intelligence, the one showing the least decline is vocabulary (Bottwinick, 1964; Fox & Birren, 1950). Intellectual activities that are dependent on verbal comprehension and language are affected less by aging than are those activities that are less language and vocabulary dependent. Tasks involving speed are particularly affected by aging. It has been suggested that the general decline in performance on speed measures is more than the slowing down of physical functioning and that they imply changes in control over the way stored information is used (Birren, Riegel, & Morrison, 1962).

The accumulated evidence clearly indicates that there is a decline in sensory and perceptual functioning with aging. These changes may involve neural modification with time (Corso, 1971). Although neuronal loss is irreversible, there may be some functional reorganization of neurons, but little is known of the utility of this possibility (Jarvik & Cohen, 1973). Longitudinal studies are beginning to show that, except for speeded performance tasks, there may be little or no change in performance of cognitive tasks, at least until age eighty or beyond (Jarvik, Eisdorfer, & Blum, 1974).

A certain amount of inflexibility or rigidity of perception as well as approach to problems is characteristic of older people. Such conceptual rigidity may begin in middle age and become more and more pronounced as age advances (Bottwinick, 1964; Corso, 1971).

It may be that lack of environmental pressure for elderly persons to employ sophisticated problem-solving approaches, rather than neural degenerative processes, may account for their problem-solving deficits (Denny & Denny, 1974).

Creative work and scientific publication tend to be concentrated more among younger than older populations. H. C. Lehman's (1953) important studies of age and achievement indicate that both quality and quantity of output decline with age, and that quality is likely to deteriorate more rapidly than is quantity of production. W. Dennis and E. Girden (1954) report that scientists in their sixties publish about half as much as those in their thirties and forties.

Interests and activities of the aged

Changes in physical strength, sensory acuity, health, and general level of energy of the aged are reflected in a decrease of activities requiring energy and exertion and an increase in sedentary activities (Kent, 1966). The narrowing of interests among the aged is a partial function of social class. Lower-class individuals do not have as great a variety of interests as do those from higher social classes (Rose, 1966). Lower-class aged have less interest in community organizations and their forms of recreation are more limited (Rosenblatt, 1966). Interests and activities of the aged tend to be extensions of the interests and activities that were common at an earlier age. Those interests that offer the greater satisfactions tend to be retained as circumstances permit. Women tend to have a wider range of interests during adulthood and old age than do men. This could be due to the more frequent focusing of interests on vocational pursuits by men than by women. Men frequently have difficulty in occupying their time when their vocational lives are interrupted by retirement (Rose, 1966; Rosenblatt, 1966).

Self-interest and self-centeredness tend to increase as people grow older. Thoughts about themselves, how they feel, and what they want to do occupy a significant portion of the life of the aged (Henry & Cummings, 1959). Concern for themselves, their health, and the past are parts of being self-centered that may contribute to unfavorable attitudes toward older people (Henry & Cummings, 1959). Despite the tendency toward self-interest with age, there appears to be, at least for many, a decrease in interest in clothing and appearance. The lack of interest in appearance results in carelessness in grooming habits and in a failure to make the best possible appearance. Older men, probably because of previous habits of careful grooming as a vocational asset, tend to be more concerned for personal appearance than do older women. Socially active older people, of course, tend to be more appearance-conscious and more interested in clothing than are those who are socially withdrawn. Styles and fashions seldom are as appropriate for the physiques of the older citizen as they are for the younger person, and old people may become discouraged with attempts to improve appearance with clothing that is ill-designed or ill-fitting for the figure that has been changed by aging (Ryan, 1966). Though some older people are much interested in dressing in the latest fashion, they tend to be a small minority of the aged. Many of the elderly are deterred from manifesting their interest in clothing and appearance by limited income that is sufficient for the purchase of only the absolute essentials. Such poverty mitigates against interest in clothing and motivation to make an attractive appearance (Ryan, 1966). Despite the difficulties of maintaining attractive appearance, some older people realize that lack of neatness and good grooming are more easily overlooked in the young than in the aged and maintain high motivation to be neatly and appropriately dressed. Many older people, from both rural and urban settings, read fashion magazines and shop around to see what are the latest fashions (Ryan, 1966).

It is popularly believed that as people become elderly they become more religious. For the average elderly person this is not particularly true. There is no strong tendency for an increase in religiousness of people as they grow older (Havighurst & Albrecht, 1953; Orbach, 1961). Most older people tend to maintain their religious beliefs and habits formed earlier in life (Orbach, 1961; Covalt, 1965).

RETIREMENT

An outstanding feature of American culture has been that of striving for social and economic gain. A real dedication to the idea that upward social, educational, and economic mobility were available to those who would strive has been a part of Americans' traditional belief system. Emphasis on gainful employment, hard work, individual effort, and striving as conditions or qualities to be revered has long been part of the culture. Such a dedication to upward social and economic mobility is understandable when coupled with the fact that this nation is one that possesses good natural resources for the rewarding of effort. Paid employment ("having a good job") comes to be not only a symbol of success, but also a moral value. The revered position that work has held in the lives of elderly people makes it understandable that the older person may feel a considerable loss of meaning in his life when he is forced into retirement. Dedication to the values of work and employment has not served the same desirable ends for the elderly in retirement as it did when they were young. It matters little if the aged worker's pension is adequate if paid employment is the only kind that he considers meaningful. Retirement, particularly if it is compulsory, can present serious problems of adjustment for those who live in a work- and production-oriented culture. Significant attitude changes toward work, employment, and productivity became noticeable in some of the "youth cultures" of the 1960s and early '70s. The affluence of society was partially rejected by some of the subgroups within the culture. This rejection of the values of cultural involvement, work, and material productivity, if maintained and if it should become a real part of the broad culture, no doubt would bring about significant attitudinal changes toward retirement and reduce many of the adjustment difficulties currently associated with the retirement of those having lived under very different work orientation.

The young or middle-aged worker involved in rearing a family and living a busy social and personal life may look upon early retirement as a time for the real enjoyment of leisure. He may look forward to having time to do the many things for which time has been lacking in the past. He can remove himself from the competitive rat-race and sit back and enjoy the remainder of his years in quiet contentment. This picture changes considerably, however, for those for whom retirement is imminent. The rosy picture of retired life may change markedly. Will there be adequate funds to continue to live in the manner to which one has grown accustomed? Will one be able to find part-time work if it is desired and necessary? What will one do with the time heretofore devoted to work? Changing lifetime patterns of living is not easy for most, and they have had little experience with uncommitted time (Kent, 1966).

Retirement as a social problem is of relatively recent vintage in the culture. Compulsory retirement at a pre-established age is in part a result of scientific and technological development in the culture. Compulsory retirement systems have derived from attempts to control the labor supply, from humanitarian concerns, and from technological advances that require adjustments of which the young are deemed most capable (for example, new production methods and emphasis on speed of performance). There has been a trend away from self-employment and toward the development of larger enterprises that employ great numbers of people on fixed or relatively fixed incomes. The requirements of work and the conditions of retirement are under control of associates and employers and only remotely and partially controlled by the individual. Only those who are successfully engaged in business for themselves or are successfully self-employed in the professions can decide, individually, when they want to retire. Not only are more and more people retiring, but the length of the retirement period grows longer as well (Report of President's Council on Aging, 1963; White House Conference on Aging, 1972). It has been estimated that a twenty-year-old male worker in 1975 may expect to spend ten years in retirement. In 1940 that worker could expect to spend five-and-one-half years in retirement, and in 1900 only three years (Claque, 1949). Whether significant changes in the length of time spent in retirement will continue in the near future is dependent upon changes in the age of compulsory or voluntary retirement, changes in longevity of the working population, and the affluence of society in general.

Attitudes toward retirement

Many attitudes toward retirement exist, from highly favorable to very unfavorable. For many of the currently retired, who were born into, grew up, and matured in a work-oriented culture, retirement from work is something they do not value. Many would prefer to work, even at a less satisfactory job than their previous employment (Report of President's Council on Aging, 1963; White House Conference on Aging, 1972). Some of this reluctance to retire or the desire to return to work stems from the economic situation in which the elderly find themselves. Many retired persons need money to provide for the necessities of life and must depend upon economic aid from government sources, charitable institutions, friends, or relatives. This is not a very attractive prospective way of life.

Some of the attitudes toward retirement of those who are retired can be examined openly. Retirement may be resisted and resented if it means a drastic reduction in living standard for the individual, particularly true if the money available in retirement is only enough to meet the necessities of existence, or even less.

While some older workers look forward to being freed from the routines and pressures of work, they do not want to quit work completely. To do so would deprive them of income, feelings of usefulness, social contacts, and various other values associated with work. For many, a partial retirement plan or even reassignment is preferable to complete retirement as such. Being forced into retirement by reaching compulsory retirement age, by dismissal, or by illness is emotionally disturbing and constitutes a serious problem in adjustment to retirement. Voluntary retirement leads to better adjustment in retirement (Thompson, Streif, & Kosa, 1960). This is probably because those who voluntarily retire have planned for it, are psychologically ready for it, and can afford it. Many workers do not want to retire, resist the whole idea of retirement, and do not prepare themselves psychologically, socially, or economically for retirement. Attitudes toward retirement vary all the way from angry resentment at "being discarded" or "being unjustly kicked out of the working world," through "turning the old horse out to pasture" (a reward for the no longer useful), to welcome relief from the work-a-day world and its steady pace (just reward for valuable services rendered).

Adequate planning for retirement in terms of the social, psychological, economic, and vocational factors of life after retirement should bring about more favorable attitudes toward retirement and enhance adjustment to the role of the retired person. The cessation of work for the person who has derived much of life's satisfaction from work is difficult. Plans that include activities designed to compensate, in part at least, for the satisfactions heretofore realized from work 'should be a part of retirement plans. Idleness and inactivity for the previously active can be a traumatic experience. Leisure time when it is not planned for can lead to boredom and indifference to life and living. Adult education programs designed to encourage the development of interests and skills that will enable the retired person to feel his life is meaningful and useful should be encouraged (Chown & Heron, 1965). The role of the retired person must be such that social contacts and companionship are available, feelings of usefulness result, and prestige is provided (Kent, 1966).

Just "finding something to do" becomes a problem for some men in retirement. They may become involved in assisting with household tasks. These activities are usually not too satisfactory, but do provide at least a feeling of being useful (Kent, 1966). One of the more overrated activities in terms of real satisfactions or substitute for satisfaction derived from work is the hobby. Hobbies, often advocated as aiding adjustment during adult life and as a solution to retirement problems, seldom prove to be work substitutes and do not necessarily facilitate adjustment in retirement, because they usually result in solitary activity. Hobbies tend to be "time-killers" and do not usually contribute to feelings of usefulness, to prestige, or to the economic welfare of the retired (Johnson,

1958). Men adjust less well to the role changes produced by retirement than do women (Kent, 1966), probably because of the more intimate involvement of women in the tasks of homemaking, which must be performed even in retirement. Then, too, the woman has usually had more experience with the domestic role than has the man. The role, therefore, is not so foreign to her and does not involve as much of an adjustment. As a result of changes in sex roles which developed during the 1970s, men's and women's adjustments to retirement will become increasingly alike in the future.

When there are healthy attitudes toward aging as well as toward retirement on the part of the worker and his family, the chances of satisfactory adjustment to retirement are the greatest (Turner, 1955). Retired persons who live in homes for the aged have more opportunities for social contacts and recreational activities than do those who remain in their own homes or live with relatives. These homes, in addition to providing social contacts and recreational facilities, must also provide opportunities for the aging to engage in tasks that will provide prestige and feelings of usefulness, to promote good adjustment. Those who remain in their home community after retirement and have adequate money to live about as they lived before retirement make the best adjustments because they have fewer adjustments to make.

SEXUAL ROLE OF THE AGED

Sexual activity among the aged, when opportunity for sexual expression is at hand, is probably more common than is popularly believed. It is a common belief that with old age comes a loss of interest in sex as well as sexual impotence. It is true that men as well as women undergo physical changes in bodily functions, but this does not mean that either sexual interest or potency is destroyed. Sexual activity is a function of a number of factors besides those of health and physical condition. Particularly for the aged, compatibility with the spouse is an important factor in the maintenance of sexual activity. The aged have difficulty in obtaining sex partners if they do not have a spouse, and few single aged maintain an active heterosexual life (Christenson & Gagnon, 1965; Swartz, 1966). Patterns of sexual behavior developed earlier in life have important influences on sexual behavior in old age. Those that have been relatively sexually active continue to be relatively more active in old age than those who were less active earlier (Freeman, 1961; Kinsey et al., 1953).

Sexual behavior among the aged is no doubt inhibited by some popular attitudes toward sex and aging. Many of the aged expect to be impotent. Psychological factors are sufficiently important in sexual functioning that such an expectancy frequently leads to impotence (Kinsey, Pomeroy, & Martin, 1948). Then, too, attitudes toward sexual functioning of the elderly frequently are antagonistic. Some believe that by the time they are past middle age they ought to be through with sex. Many aged people feel that showing any interest in sex is inappropriate for them, that sex should be limited to the young who are capable of reproduction. There is a tendency among some people to regard sexual interests and behavior after middle age as pathological despite its being widespread and recognized as a legitimate function by those with the most information (Geriatric Focus Report, 1966a). Sexual intercourse for the aged has its advocates as being therapeutic (Horn, 1974).

Intercourse among men and women in their sixties and seventies is to be expected for most couples in good health. Frequency of sexual relations decreases with age, but when intercourse is discontinued it is usually because of illness of one of the spouses or because of diminished desire in the husband. When health conditions are adequate, there is a gradual diminution of sexual activity in the aged rather than a sudden cessation (Christenson & Gagnon, 1965).

A great deal of interest in and emphasis on sexual freedom and functioning has arisen in the past decade or so. With an increase in the acceptance of sexual behavior as not involving shame and guilt and as being a legitimate means of human expression, continuance of sexual activity into the period of old age should be expected to increase. Even the news media have picked up this notion, and articles have appeared discussing the sexuality of the aged (Stephen, 1975).

Widowhood

Learning to live without a spouse after years of being married presents serious problems for the aged, who have more difficulty adjusting to changes than do younger persons. When death or divorce of the spouse comes at a late age, the results can be particularly traumatic and require a good deal in the way of adaptive behavior for the widowed to continue to live an adequate life. Loneliness becomes an important problem for the aged and particularly for the widowed (Kent, 1966).

Men tend to marry women their own age or younger than they are, and women tend to live longer than men. When these two factors are combined it can be expected that there will be a great deal more women than men who are widowed in their advanced years. There is a ratio of better than five females for every four males in the older populaton. It is estimated that this will rise to about six to four by 1985 (Geriatric Focus Report, 1966b). Only one-third of American women sixty-five years of age and older live with their husbands in their own household. About half of the women sixty years of age are widows. It is probable that the percentage of men who are classified as widowed by age sixty is far less, because men who are widowed tend to remarry more frequently than do women (Geriatric Focus Report, 1966b). Most married women spend their last years living without a spouse. This presents problems for the aging woman in the culture. She may have to live on less money, move to less adequate quarters, or live with children or relatives. The probability is high that she does not want to do this.

Of the 8,364,000 males who were sixty-five years of age or older in 1970 (United States Bureau of the Census, 1971), 1,510,000 were widowed and 199,000 were divorced. There were 11,349,000 women in the sixty-five or over age group. Of these, 6,196,000 were widowed and 259,000 were divorced. The data also indicate that over 25 percent of our aged live alone in a household. It can be observed from these data that not only are there over a third more women than men in this age group, but there are about four times as many widowed women as there are men. The problems of loneliness are many.

Relatively few older people fully appreciate the problems that are produced by widowhood; even though the possibility of widowhood is recognized and some planning for it does take place, most have difficulty adjusting to being alone.

Loneliness can be considered a major problem of widowhood (Tanenbaum, 1967). Remarriage is one of the ways by which older people deal with the problem of loneliness in widowhood. Older women do not remarry as frequently as do older men. This is true because there are more elderly women than men, some women are reluctant to give up their pension rights, and older men tend to select women who are younger when they remarry. With relaxed standards about sexual matters, more of the elderly may decide to live together without marriage and thus preserve pension rights and maintain income.

Singleness

It is popularly believed, by those who are married, at least, that an old person who has never married and has no family will face an unhappy and lonely old age. This does not appear to be the case. People who live alone for years adjust to living without family. They develop interests and activities independent of family ties and companionship. They are probably better equipped to face old age than are people who have been married for the major part of adult life and then have to adjust to living without a spouse. There is no reason why a bachelor or spinster should not live happily and actively in old age (Lowenthal, 1964).

SOCIAL-PERSONAL LIVING

The aged are to be found living under the same variety of circumstances that are common to the culture in general. The aged belong to all educational and socio-economic levels of society. There are, however, special needs of the aged that should be met. Their need for convenient services, housing, and health and recreational services is most likely to be adequately met among the more affluent families. Income limitations may severely restrict the kinds of housing and services available to the aged.

Social life

Social theorists have indicated that one of the effects of industrialization on the family has been to produce social isolation, particularly for the aged, who have been described as isolated from kinship and community ties. This picture may be somewhat more gloomy than that which actually exists. A lengthy investigation of the aged in the United States, Britain, and Denmark (Shanus et al., 1968) presents a somewhat rosier picture of the aged than previously had been common. They depict a relatively large proportion of the aged in all three countries as maintaining reasonably active and culturally involved lives. The aged in these countries apparently continue to maintain kinship contacts and mingle with other older persons in the community as well as with the young. They are further depicted as making satisfactory personal adjustments to their role in society and to their declining physical status. This no doubt is true for large numbers of the aged. In focusing attention on the poor and dependent minorities of aged, it can easily be overlooked that many of the elderly do well in the culture.

A survey of the opinion of 317 white adults on generational differences in happiness uncovered interesting findings (Cameron, 1974). P. Cameron found that regardless of age or sex, his subjects believed that middle-aged persons (forty to fifty-five) are happiest, followed by young adults (eighteen to twenty-five), who were trailed by oldsters (sixty-five to seventy-nine). The only disagreement with this general finding was among the wealthier and better educated, who regarded old people as the happiest generation. Perhaps the latter years may indeed be pleasant, if one has the financial and physical resources to enjoy them. The sample of adults used in this study, however, do not personally support their prejudices about age and happiness. When asked to compare their own happiness to that of all other adults, all age groups believed they were above average in happiness.

It cannot and should not be ignored, however, that the aged are heavily and disproportionately represented in the ranks of the poor. Then, too, 4 to 6 percent of the aged are institutionalized. Many of these aged people are in essentially custodial institutions or in mental hospitals, not because of mental illness but because of the lack of appropriate community facilities (Mechanic, 1969). Ralph Nader has urged the elderly to form a retired people's liberation movement to resist "geriatric segregation" that forces many to exist in shabby nursing homes (UPI, 1970).

Housing   Many of the aged poor live in the central city in inadequate, unattractive, and relatively expensive housing (Birren, 1970a). Although the aged often appear to dislike their housing, they do not move as frequently as the young. A Los Angeles investigation revealed that 90 percent of individuals over fifty were dissatisfied with their living arrangements, but that only 13 percent actually moved during a one-year period (Birren, 1970a). The aged are less mobile than the young and many may be unable to move because of lack of funds. Urban redevelopment has failed to relieve the plight of the aged and in some cases has made matters worse for them. Frequently the aged are displaced by redevelopment programs that build housing and shopping facilities that are beyond the economic grasp of the aged poor. There are serious psychological consequences to the relocation of any group of people, and particularly the aged. People are often extremely unhappy about losing their homes and neighborhoods. This grief may turn into depression for older residents whose self-identity is maintained through stable physical surroundings and social relationships. What may look like deterioration and disorganization of a community to city planners may represent low rent, interaction with friends, and proximity to relatives to the aged. J. E. Birren (1970a) has argued convincingly that city structure should be dictated by function, not vice versa. Cities, he asserts, are primarily social organizations; only secondarily are they collections of concrete, steel, and wooden structures. An adequate environment should offer many options and opportunities for individual self-expression, development, and activity. This is true for the aged as well as for the young.

Birren (1970a) has urged that city planning take into account the needs of the aged. Older people may be overwhelmed by environmental obstacles that are really not obstacles at all for the young. Such things as high steps to climb into a bus or street car, busy streets, fast changing traffic lights, inadequate street signs and lighting, and poor labeling of buildings can present problems of such magnitude as to produce real discouragement. The aged may do without goods and services that they should have when they are too inconvenient or troublesome. Services of banks, medical doctors, dentists, shops, lawyers, repair persons and recreational facilities may be forgone because they are too inconvenient or require too much energy to obtain.

With advancing age there occurs a shrinking in one's "life-space." That is, objects and events that are near at hand and immediately available provide more and more of a person's psychological support. Thus, the immediate environment assumes great importance for the aged. This concept of life-space and its diminution with time should be employed in the design of personal and community facilities to accommodate the aged (Birren, 1970a).

The partial segregation of the aged provided by retirement communities and retirement homes may be advantageous for some, because older persons do enjoy the companionship of other older people just as the young enjoy the young. However, many elderly should live in communities designed to enhance the quality of living for all ages. Familiar people, familiar objects, and buildings designed to facilitate living are an advantage to the aged as well as to the rest of society. As the aged population increases, developers and contractors are just beginning to pay attention to their housing needs.

ADJUSTMENT AND BEHAVIORAL DISORDER

Behavioral disorders and adjustment of the aged have not been given the investigative attention that has been given these processes in the young. It is known that older people undergo psychological changes. The physical decline of aging poses adjustment problems, as do the changes that occur in the social life of the aged. The friends of the aged die, many of the aged will outlive their friends and many of their relatives, including some of their children. These events, occurring with passage of time, add to the problems of adjustment presented by the physical processes of aging that were described earlier in this chapter. It is possible that if more research attention were paid to adjustive problems of the aged, we would discover that their problems are of comparable magnitude with those of the young. Psychological changes tend to come about gradually and many of them do not interfere in the processes of effective living for the aged. Research findings (Wolk & Kurtz, 1975) indicate that the adjustive patterns of earlier life are likely to be characteristic of aging persons. E. Palmore and C. Luikart (1972), who employed the Internal-External Locus of Control (I–E) Scale (Rotter, 1966), reported that elderly persons with strong internal control were more satisfied with their lives. Internal locus of control has been found to correlate with positive coping styles among the elderly (Kuypers, 1971), whereas external locus of control seems to be related to some of the more extreme behavior present in severe forms of mental illness (Levenson, 1973). The American Psychological Association has emphasized the need for research on adjustment and aging and has provided guidelines for such research, as well (Eisdorfer & Lawton, 1973).

Behavioral disorders

Aged persons must respond to the stresses and strains of living and they probably become a bit less adaptable to stress with age. The aged person who was neurotic when he was younger may develop additional behavioral patterns of a neurotic nature in his old age as life stresses accumulate. Aged persons suffer from anxiety, exaggerated concern for health and well-being (hypochondriacal reactions), depressive reactions, and other neurotic behaviors. Severe depressions and feeling of persecution (paranoid reactions) are the most common disorders of the severely disorganized aged person (Straker, 1963).

The two major severe disorders of older people are those associated with physical deterioration. *Senile brain disease* (senile dementia) and *cerebral arteriosclerosis* account for about 80 percent of the behavioral disorders of the aged (Marks, 1961). The brain changes in senile dementia (cerebral atrophy and degeneration) and in cerebral arteriosclerosis (blocking or rupture of cerebral arteries) are held to be directly causative of the behavior disorganization and aberrations that occur. However, it is now recognized that there is little relationship between amount of neurological damage and the severity of the behavioral disorganizations.

Senile dementia   Typically it is gradual in onset and involves a general slowing up of physical and mental functioning. The symptoms vary from one patient to another. They appear to depend upon the personality organization of the patient, his life situation, and the nature and extent of cerebral degeneration. There is usually a gradual personal-social withdrawal, a narrowing of interest and activity, a loss of alertness and a general resistance to innovation and changes in routine. Periods of confusion and loss of memory for recent events are common. Insomnia is common, as is a preoccupation with bodily processes and well-being. As the condition becomes advanced there is a lack of interest in appearance, depression that is severe, reduced comprehension, confusion, and disorientation.

Senile psychoses account for about 18 percent of first admissions to mental hospitals. Average age of first admission is about seventy-five for both men and women. Average age of onset is no doubt considerably less than this because of care in the home before the decision to hospitalize.

Senile dementia typically is classified into several types, depending upon the predominant symptoms. If the clinical picture is much like that described above (an exaggeration of normal changes in aging), it is called simple deterioration. If a dominant feature is that of delusions of persecution, it is classified as paranoid reaction. The *presbyophrenic* type is characterized by a marked impairment in memory. The patient is amiable, talks a great deal, and fabricates events to fill in his loss of memory. Many senile dementia patients are extremely confused and subject to spells of delirium. These are the *delirious and confused*. The patient who is severely depressed and excessively and morbidly hypochondriacal is designated as *depressed and agitated*.

Although there may be some remission of symptoms in some patients, the prognosis for those classified as senile dementia is one of continued deline in psychological and physiological function until death. The decline may occur over a period of months or years.

Cerebral arteriosclerosis   Behavior disorders associated with cerebral arteriosclerosis do not differ greatly from those of senile dementia. Cerebral arteriosclerosis involves a hardening of the arteries of the brain. Senile plaques (deposits of fatty and calcified substance) in the inside layers of the blood vessels produce a gradual closing of the artery and its consequent impairment of circulation. The arteries can become blocked by a blood clot or by blocking from a piece of fatty or calcified material. The vessel may then rupture and bleeding will occur.

If there is a sudden blockage, or if a small blood vessel ruptures, this is termed a small stroke. The behavioral symptom will be dependent upon the severity and location of the resultant damage. A major stroke (one in which there is a generalized impairment of brain function) results from massive damage. Generally, arteriosclerotic brain diseased patients do not show the profound deterioration found in senile patients.

In over half of the cases the noticeable effects of cerebral arteriosclerosis are sudden (a stroke). The patient is confused, disoriented as to time and place, incoherent, and suffering from some paralysis. This acute confusional state may last for several days or even months before there is a remission of symptoms. There are varying amounts of brain damage resulting in impairment of functioning. Rehabilitative measures can be instituted and some of the physical and mental handicaps can be improved or compensated for by the patient.

When the onset of the disorder is gradual, there may be a slowing of activity and involvement in living. The person may complain of being chronically tired, of being dizzy, or of having a headache. Frequently there are periods of depression, confusion, and loss of memory. By the time the person is eventually hospitalized the symptoms are much the same as for senile dementia.

About 15 percent of all first admissions to mental hospitals are classified as psychoses associated with cerebral arteriosclerosis. Average age of first admission is about seventy-four years.

Treatment and care facilities for the aged with adjustive problems are grossly inadequate. The number of persons needing assistance is very great, the number of individuals trained to assist is inadequate, and the physical facilities are extremely limited. The section on the clinical psychology of old age of the *Psychology of Adult Development and Aging* (Eisdorfer & Lawton, 1973) contains data supporting considerably increased services for the aged.

SUCCESSFUL AGING

One of two conditions is inevitable for all people. Either one dies before he becomes classifiable as being old, or he lives to be so classified and experiences some aspects of aged living before death. Attention can be focused on the life and living of the aged, but the life and living of the aged cannot be divorced from the processes of life and living that have preceded being aged. Adequate living as an elderly person is a function of adequate preparation for life as an older person. Education and planning for aging, retirement, old age, and eventual death can probably enhance the quality of life for all when they grow older.

It is difficult if not impossible to describe, identify, or define successful aging. The goals, the purposes, and the functions of aged living are probably not different in principle from those for any other group. However, special problems that exist for the aged are unlike those of most other people. Old age is the period of decline. It is the period preceding life's termination. It is a period when physical and mental powers are declining. It is a period when family life changes and many who have lived life as married persons must now live alone. Loneliness may be a problem. Financial uncertainty or inadequacy may be severely limiting as an inflationary economy continues. Most social benefits to the aged are not currently designed to be other than "assists" in the lives of the aged. Social Security was not designed as a complete supportive system but as a supplementary or auxiliary part of retirement. Most pensions are considerably less than they should be, either because of inflation or because they too were designed to be supplemental. Supplemental services are fine if there is something to supplement, but large numbers of the aged have little in the way of savings or other assets. Financial inadequacy and loneliness are two problems that many of the aged must contend with that many do not plan to have to contend with in their latter years.

M. E. P. Seligman (1974) makes an excellent case for "helplessness" being a strong contributive factor to the earlier than expected deaths of those aged who felt they had little or no control of their destiny. Indeed, many older citizens probably accurately assess their situations, and may feel helpless because they are not in a position to have viable alternatives among which to decide.

Successful aging involves the personal element of self-satisfaction. If the person is reasonably satisfied and content with his life and regards himself positively, his *personal* aging can be regarded as successful. In addition to the personal element of successful aging there is a *social* aspect that is interactive with it. If society is reasonably satisfied with the individual's fulfillment of his social roles and cultural obligations, the individual can be said to be aging successfully in a social sense. These two aspects to successful aging are of necessity mutually supportive, but they are not completely interdependent.

Successful aging results in successful living as an old person. Throughout life motivational changes occur, goals change, and personality changes. Each portion of life offers aspects that can result in feelings of fulfillment, adequate self-regard, social acceptance, and dignity. Living for the aged should be as filled with these qualities as their earlier lives and their culture can provide.

SUMMARY

Aging can be considered biologically, sociologically, and psychologically as well as chronologically. Age sixty-five has come to be fairly well accepted as the beginning of the period of old age. This is an arbitrary designation that coincides with a frequent age for compulsory retirement and for eligibility for the receipt of certain social benefits. There are about 20 million people over sixty-five in the United States. A greater proportion of the population lives to old age than even before. People are not living to be older, but more are living long enough to reach old age.

The aged do not fare well economically in our culture. Thirty to 40 percent of the aged readily can be classified as poor. The aged are to be found in all economic strata, however, just as they are to be found among all intellectual levels and social classes.

Many of the research investigations of the aged have been conducted using institutionalized elderly people as subjects. The generalizability of such findings to the aged population as a whole is highly questionable. Only about 5 percent of the aged reside in institutions and nursing homes, and they cannot be said to be representative of the aged as a group. The aged are a very heterogeneous group of people on most variables except chronological age.

The aged suffer a loss of physical status, a diminution of certain sensory functions, and a general slowing down of various intellectual functions. They become more vulnerable to injury and disease and they are less mobile than younger individuals.

As people age they tend to become a bit more self-centered and have an enhanced concern for health and general well-being. Retirement, widowhood, and loneliness are serious problems for the aged. The aged have difficulty functioning in an environment that is not too kind to them. The aged are heavily and disproportionately represented among the ranks of the poor. Urban housing costs are high and the housing tends to be inadequate. The aged are subject to the stresses of living the same as are other groups in the culture. The adjustment of the aged has received less investigative attention than has the adjustment of the young. The aged are subject to the additional stresses of physical deterioration and do suffer from some disorders that tend to produce adjustment problems and behavior disorders. Even with these handicaps, most of the aged apparently adjust rather well to their personal-social situation.

REFERENCES

ASSOCIATED PRESS, "Elderly Poor Ranks Grow," *San Jose Mercury,* 18 January 1971, p. 8.

BADER, I. M., & D. M. HOFFMAN, "Research in Aging," *Journal of Home Economics,* 1966, *58,* 9–14.

BALTES, P. B., & G. V. LABOUVIE, "Adult Development of Intellectual Performance: Description, Explanation and Modification," in C. Eisdorfer & M. P. Lawton, *The Psychology of Adult Development and Aging* (Washington, D.C.: American Psychological Association, 1973).

BAYLEY, N., "Research in Child Development: A Longitudinal Perspective," *Merrill-Palmer Quarterly,* 1965, *11,* 183–208.

BAYLEY, N., & M. H. ODEN, "The Maintenance of Intellectual Ability in Gifted Adults," *Journal of Gerontology,* 1955, *10,* 91–107.

BERKOWITZ, B., & R. F. GREEN, "Changes in Intellect with Age: V. Differential Changes as Functions of Time Interval and Original Score," *Journal of Genetic Psychology,* 1965, 179–92.

BIERMAN, E. L., & W. R. HAZZARD, "Old Age, Including Death and Dying," in D. W. Smith & E. L. Bierman, eds., *The Biologic Ages of Man from Conception through Old Age* (Philadelphia: W. B. Saunders, 1973).

BIRREN, J. E., "Research on the Psychology of Aging: Concepts and Findings," in P. H. Hock & J. Zubin, eds., *Psychopathology of Aging* (New York: Grune & Stratton, 1961).

BIRREN, J. E., "The Abuse of the Urban Aged," *Psychology Today*, 1970a, *3* (10), 36–38, 76.

BIRREN, J. E., W. R. ALLEN, & H. G. LANDAU, "The Relation of Problem Length in Simple Addition to Time Required, Probability of Success, and Age," *Journal of Gerontology*, 1954, *9*, 150–61.

BIRREN, J. E., M. W. BICK, & M. YIENGST, "The Relation of Structural Changes of the Eye and Vitamin A to Elevation of the Light Threshold in Later Life," *Journal of Experimental Psychology*, 1950, *40*, 260–66.

BIRREN, J. E., E. A. JEROME, & S. M. CHOWN, "Aging and Psychological Adjustment: Problem Solving and Motivation," *Review of Educational Research*, 1961, *31*, 487–99.

BIRREN, J. E., K. F. RIEGEL, & D. F. MORRISON, "Age Differences in Response Speed as a Function of Controlled Variations of Stimulus Condition: Evidence of a General Speed Factor," *Gerontologia*, 1962, *6*, 1–18.

BONDAREFF, W., "Morphology of the Aging Nervous System," in J. E. Birren, ed., *Handbook of Aging and the Individual* (Chicago: University of Chicago Press, 1959).

BOTTWINICK, J., "Research Problems and Concepts in the Study of Aging," *Gerontologist*, 1964, *4*, 121–29.

BOTTWINICK, J., "Cautiousness in Advanced Age," *Journal of Gerontology*, 1966, *21*, 347–53.

BOTTWINICK, J., *Cognitive Processes in Maturity and Old Age* (New York: Springer, 1967).

BOTTWINICK, J., "Disinclination to Venture Response Versus Cautiousness in Responding: Age Differences," *Journal of Genetic Psychology*, 1969, *115*, 55–62.

BRODY, J., "Organization of the Cerebral Cortex: III. A Study of Aging in the Human Cerebral Cortex," *Journal of Comparative Neurology*, 1955, *102*, 511–56.

BURGER, R. E., "Who Cares for the Aged?" *Saturday Review*, January 25, 1969, 14–17.

BUSSE, E. W., "Studies in the Process of Aging: The Strengths and Weaknesses of Psychic Functioning in the Aged," *American Journal of Psychiatry*, 1955, *116*, 896–901.

CAMERON, P., "Social Stereotypes: Three Faces of Happiness," *Psychology Today*, 1974, *8* (3), 62–64.

CHOWN, S. M., & A. HERON, "Psychological Aspects of Aging in Man," *Annual Review of Psychology*, 1965, *16*, 417–50.

CHRISTENSON, C. V., & J. H. GAGNON, "Sexual Behavior in a Group of Older Women," *Journal of Gerontology*, 1965, *20*, 351–56.

CLAQUE, E., "The Working Life Span of American Workers," *Journal of Gerontology*, 1949, *4*, 285–89.

COOPER, R. M., I. BILASH, & J. P. ZUBECK, "The Effect of Age on Taste Sensitivity," *Journal of Gerontology*, 1959, *14*, 56–58.

CORSO, J. F., "Sensory Processes and Age Effects in Normal Adults," *Journal of Gerontology*, 1971, *26*, 90–105.

COVALT, N. K., "The Meaning of Religion to Older People," in C. B. Wedder & A. S. Lefkowitz, eds., *Problems of the Aged* (Springfield, Ill: Charles C Thomas, 1965).

DENNIS, W., & E. GIRDEN, "Current Scientific Activities of Psychologists as a Function of Age," *Journal of Gerontology*, 1954, *9*, 175–78.

DENNY, N. W., & D. R. DENNY, "Modeling Effects on the Questioning Strategies of the Elderly," *Developmental Psychology*, 1974, *10*, 458.

EISDORFER, C., & M. P. LAWTON, eds., *The Psychology of Adult Development and Aging* (Washington, D.C.: American Psychological Association, 1973).

EISDORFER, C., J. NOWLIN, & F. WILKIE, "Improvement of Learning in the Aged by Modification of Autonomic Nervous System Activity," *Science*, 1970, *170*, 1327–29.

FOX, C., & J. E. BIRREN, "The Differential Decline of Wechsler Subtest Scores in 60–69-Year-old Individuals," *American Psychologist*, 1950, *5*, 467.

FREEMAN, J. T., "Sexual Capacities in the Aging Male," *Geriatrics*, 1961, *16*, 37–43.

FRIEDMAN, H., "Memory Organization in the Aged," *Journal of Genetic Psychology*, 1966, *109*, 3–8.

GERIATRIC FOCUS REPORT, "Menopause Not End of Sex," *Geriatric Focus*, 1966a, *5* (5), 1, 6.

GERIATRIC FOCUS REPORT, "Widowhood in Old Age," *Geriatric Focus*, 1966b, *5* (9), 1–5.

HAVIGHURST, R. J., & R. ALBRECHT, *Older People* (New York: Longmans, 1953).

HENRY, W. E., & E. CUMMINGS, "Personality Development in Adulthood and Old Age," *Journal of Projective Techniques*, 1959, *23*, 383–90.

HORN, P., "Rx Sex for Senior Citizens," *Psychology Today*, 1974, *8* (1), 18, 20.

HURLOCK, E. B., *Developmental Psychology* (New York: McGraw-Hill, 1968).

JARVIK, L. F., & D. COHEN, "A Biobehavioral Approach to Intellectual Changes with Aging," in C. Eisdorfer & M. P. Lawton, eds, *The Psychology of Adult Development and Aging* (Washington, D.C.: American Psychological Association, 1973).

JARVIK, L. F., C. EISDORFER, & J. E. BLUM, eds., *Intellectual Functioning in Adults: Some Psychological and Biological Influences* (New York: Springer, 1974).

JOHNSON, D. E., "A Depressive Retirement Syndrome," *Geriatrics*, 1958, *12*, 314–19.

KALLMAN, E. J., & L. F. JARVIK, "Individual Differences in Constitution and Genetic Background," in J. E. Birren, ed., *Handbook of Aging and the Individual* (Chicago: University of Chicago Press, 1959).

KENT, D. P., "Social and Cultural Factors Influencing the Mental Health of the Aged," *American Journal of Orthopsychology*, 1966, *36*, 680–85.

KINSEY, A. C., W. B. POMEROY, & C. E. MARTIN, *Sexual Behavior in the Human Male* (Philadelphia: W. B. Saunders, 1948).

KINSEY, A. C.; W. B. POMEROY; C. E. MARTIN; & P. H. GEBHARD, *Sexual Behavior in the Human Female* (Philadelphia: W. B. Saunders, 1953).

KLEEMEIR, R. W., "The Relationship Between Orthorator Tests of Acuity and Color Vision in an Aged Population," *Journal of Gerontology*, 1951, *6*, 372–79.

KUYPERS, J. A., "Internal-external Locus of Control and Ego-Functioning Correlates in the Elderly," *Gerontologist*, 1971, *11*, 39 (Abstract).

LEHMAN, H. C., *Age and Achievement* (Princeton, N.J.: Princeton University Press, 1953).

LEVENSON, H., "Multidimensional Locus of Control in Psychiatric Patients," *Journal of Consulting and Clinical Psychology*, 1973, *11*, 397–404.

LOWENTHAL, M. F., "Social Isolation and Mental Illness in Old Age," *American Sociological Review*, 1964, *29*, 54–70.

MARKS, H. H., "Characteristics and Trends of Cerebral Vascular Disease," in P. H. Hoch & J. Zubin, eds., *Psychopathology of Aging* (New York: Grune & Stratton, 1961).

MASTER, A. M., & R. P. LASSER, "Blood Pressure After Age 65," *Geriatrics*, 1964, *19*, 41–46.

MECHANIC, D., "The Social Condition of the Aged," *Science*, 1969, *163*, 1049–50.

ORBACH, H. L., "Aging and Religion," *Geriatrics*, 1961, *16*, 530–40.

OWENS, W. A., "Age and Mental Abilities: A Second Adult Follow-up," *Journal of Educational Psychology*, 1966, *57*, 311–25.

PALMORE, E., & C. LUIKART, "Health and Social Factors Related to Life Satisfaction," *Journal of Health and Social Behavior*, 1972, *13*, 68–80.

Report of President's Council on Aging (Washington, D.C., 1963).

ROFFWARG, H. P., J. N. MUZIO, & W. C. DEMENT, "Ontogenetic Development of the Human Sleep-dream Cycle," *Science*, 1966, *152*, 604–19.

ROSE, A. M., "Class Differences Among the Elderly: A Research Report," *Journal of Social Research*, 1966, *50*, 356–60.

ROSENBLATT, A., "Interests of Older Persons in Volunteer Activities," *Social Work*, 1966, *11* (3), 87–94.

ROTTER, J. B., "Generalized Expectancies for Internal Versus External Control of Reinforcement," *Psychological Monographs*, 1966, *80* (1, Whole no. 609).

RYAN, M. S., *Clothing: A Study in Human Behavior* (New York: Holt, Rinehart and Winston, 1966).

SCHAIE, K. W., P. BATES, & C. R. STROTHER, "A Study of Auditory Sensitivity in Advanced Age," *Journal of Gerontology*, 1964, *19*, 453–57.

SCHAIE, K. W., & K. GRIBBIN, "Adult Development and Aging," in M. R. Rosenzweig & L. W. Porter, eds., *Annual Review of Psychology*, vol. 26 (Palo Alto, Ca.: Annual Reviews, 1975).

SCHONFIELD, D., & B. A. ROBERTSON, "Memory Storage and Age," *Canadian Journal of Psychology*, 1966, *20*, 228–36.

SCHULDERMAN, E., & J. P. ZUBEK, "Effect of Age on Pain Sensitivity," *Perceptual and Motor Skills*, 1962, *14*, 295–301.

SELIGMAN, M. E. P., "Submissive Death: Giving Up on Life," *Psychology Today*, 1974, 7 (12), 80–85.

SHANAS, E.; P. TOWNSEND; D. WEDDERBURN; H. FRIIS; P. MILHOJ; & J. STEHOUWER, *Old People in Three Industrial Societies* (New York: Atherton Press, 1968).

SMITH, A. D., "Response Interference with Organized Recall in the Aged," *Developmental Psychology,* 1974, *10,* 867–70.

STEPHEN, B., "Are Senior Citizens Really Having Sex?" *San Francisco Chronicle,* June 22 1975, 18.

STRAKER, M., "Prognosis for Psychiatric Illness in the Aged," *American Journal of Psychiatry,* 1963, *119,* 1069–75.

STRUMPEL, B., "The Aged in an Affluent Economy," in C. Eisdorfer & M. P. Powell, eds., *The Psychology of Adult Development and Aging* (Washington, D.C.: American Psychological Association, 1973).

SWARTZ, D., "The Urologist's Viewpoint," *Geriatric Focus,* 1966, *5* (5), 1, 5.

TANENBAUM, D. E., "Loneliness in the Aged," *Mental Hygiene,* 1967, *51,* 91–99.

TAUB, H. A., "Effects of Coding Cues upon Short-term Memory of Aged Subjects," *Developmental Psychology,* 1975, *11,* 254.

TERMAN, L. M., & M. H. ODEN, *The Gifted Group at Mid-life* (Stanford, Ca.: Stanford University Press, 1959).

THOMPSON, W. E., G. F. STREIF, & J. KOSA, "The Effect of Retirement on Personal Adjustment: A Panel Analysis," *Journal of Gerontology,* 1960, *15,* 165–69.

TURNER, A. N., "The Older Worker: New Light on Employment and Retirement," *Personnel,* 1955, *32,* 246–57.

UNITED PRESS INTERNATIONAL, "Nader Blisters Elders' Neglect," *San Jose Mercury,* 18 December 1970, 4.

UNITED STATES BUREAU OF THE CENSUS, *Current Population Reports* (Series P–25, no. 448) (Washington, D.C., 1970).

UNITED STATES BUREAU OF THE CENSUS, *Current Population Reports* (Series P–20, no. 212) (Washington, D.C., 1971).

White House Conference on Aging (Washington, D.C., 1972).

WOLK, S., & J. KURTZ, "Positive Adjustment and Involvement During Aging and Expectancy for Internal Control," *Journal of Consulting and Clinical Psychology,* 1975, *43,* 173–78.

ZUBIN, J., "Foundations of Gerontology: History, Training, and Methodology," in C. Eisdorfer & M. P. Lawton, eds., *The Psychology of Adult Development and Aging* (Washington, D.C.: American Psychological Association, 1973).

Name index

Aase, B. H., 101, 124
Abelson, R. P., 49, 65
Abraham, W., 166, 168, 187
Adams, C., 237, 269
Adams, J., 443, 451
Adams, M. R., 466, 478
Adams, R. I., 250, 269
Adelson, E., 377, 392
Adinolfi, A. A., 30, 65
Ajax, E. T., 307, 331, 470, 478
Albrecht, R., 498, 514
Alexander, F. G., 92, 93, 123
Allen, H., 84, 88
Allen, R. M., 237, 238, 269, 275
Allen, W. R., 496, 513
Alvy, K. T., 348, 349, 355
American Foundation for the Blind, 363, 392
American Medical Association, 400, 404
American Speech and Hearing Association, 456, 457, 476, 478
Anastasi, A., 178, 187
Anastasiow, N. J., 7, 23, 282, 301, 473, 479
Anderson, E. M., 283, 292, 301
Anderson, K. A., 144, 158
Anderson, S., 238, 269
Anderson, V. M., 417, 431
Andreoli, V. A., 81, 89
Andrews, G., 466, 479
Angle, C. A., 270, 273, 274, 276
Anttonen, R. G., 45, 64
Apgar, V., 258, 269
Apthorpe, J. S., 154, 158
Arasteh, J. D., 194, 223
Arkans, J. R., 96, 125
Arkowitz, H., 38, 64
Armstrong, J., 374, 392
Arnhoff, F. N., 98, 123
Aronson, E., 30, 65
Arvey, R. D., 350, 355
Asch, S., 68, 87
Ashcroft, S. C., 379, 396
Asher, P., 445, 451
Ashurst, D. I., 240, 269
Associated Press, 489, 513
Astin, H. S., 178, 187
Astrup, C., 54, 62
Axelrod, S., 377, 379, 392
Ayers, D., 51, 64

Azrin, N. H., 298, 301

Babcock, R., 423, 431
Babeghian, G., 404, 434
Babegian, H., 54, 63
Backus, O. L., 476, 479
Bader, I. M., 491, 512
Bahr, H. M., 71, 87
Bailey, C. J., 292, 301
Baker, C., 265, 275
Baker, H. J., 446, 451
Baldwin, A. I., 7, 8, 23, 87
Baldwin, C. P., 7, 8, 23, 87
Balia, D. A., 97, 123
Balken, E. R., 261, 269
Balow, B., 112, 125, 329, 332
Baltes, P. B., 495, 512
Balthazar, E. F., 237, 269
Banham, K. M., 237, 269
Barbe, W. B., 175, 187
Barker, R. G., 80, 87
Barnes, B., 263, 269
Barnes, E. J., 350, 355
Barnett, C. D., 327, 331
Barnett, M. R., 385, 392
Barnette, W. L., 173, 181, 187
Barocas, R., 31, 62
Baron, P. H., 82, 87
Barraga, N. C., 365, 386, 392
Barron, F., 193, 202, 203, 207, 210, 223
Barry, H., 471, 479
Barsch, R. H., 313, 320, 331
Bartel, N. R., 7, 23, 69, 89, 282, 301
Bateman, B., 311, 331, 472, 479
Bates, P., 494, 513
Bauman, M. K., 361, 376, 380, 392
Bayley, N., 85, 86, 88, 495, 512
Beagley, H. A., 405, 431
Beasley, J., 476, 479
Beattie, M. S., 468, 479
Becker, L. D., 327, 333
Begab, M. J., 257, 269
Behrens, K. L., 127, 158
Belden, K. H., 288, 304
Bell, W., 178, 190
Benda, C. E., 251, 269, 446, 451
Bender, L., 309, 331
Benjamin, J. M., Jr., 374
Bennett, J. M., 135, 143, 158

517

Subject index